Fundamental Concepts of Educational Leadership and Management

Taher A. Razik
State University of New York—Buffalo

Austin D. Swanson
State University of New York—Buffalo

Merrill, *an imprint of*
Prentice Hall
Englewood Cliffs, New Jersey   Columbus, Ohio

Library of Congress Cataloging-in-Publication Data

Razik, Taher A.
      Fundamental concepts of educational leadership and management / Taher A. Razik, Austin D. Swanson.—1st ed.
                p. cm.
      Includes bibliographical references and indexes.
      ISBN 0-02-398732-4
      1. School management and organization—United States. 2. Educational leadership—United States.   I. Swanson, Austin D. II. Title.
  LB2805.R29   1995
  371.2'00973—dc20   94-3598
                                                 CIP

Editor: Debra A. Stollenwerk
Production Editors: Laura Messerly and Louise N. Sette
Text and Cover Designer: Jill E. Bonar
Production Buyer: Deidra M. Schwartz
Electronic Text Management: Marilyn Wilson Phelps, Matthew Williams, Jane Lopez, Karen L. Bretz
Illustrations: Maryland CartoGraphics

This book was set in Swiss 721 and Garamond ITC by Prentice Hall and was printed and bound by R.R. Donnelley & Sons Company. The cover was printed by Phoenix Color Corp.

 © 1995 by Prentice-Hall, Inc.
A Simon & Schuster Company
Englewood Cliffs, New Jersey 07632

Printed in the United States of America

10 9 8 7 6 5 4 3 2 1

ISBN: 0-02-398732-4

Prentice-Hall International (UK) Limited, *London*
Prentice-Hall of Australia Pty. Limited, *Sydney*
Prentice-Hall of Canada, Inc., *Toronto*
Prentice-Hall Hispanoamericana, S. A., *Mexico*
Prentice-Hall of India Private Limited, *New Delhi*
Prentice-Hall of Japan, Inc., *Tokyo*
Simon & Schuster Asia Pte. Ltd., *Singapore*
Editora Prentice-Hall do Brasil, Ltda., *Rio de Janeiro*

Introduction

We hold our leaders and managers responsible when solutions are not forthcoming (Schön, 1983).

Grant (1988) writes about the disturbing evolution of Hamilton High School during the last half of the twentieth century from an elite public high school, through deconstruction, to a student rights movement, and into a second transformation. Starting as a relatively affluent school in the 1950s, Hamilton traverses the period reacting to the major societal events occurring in the nation: through periods of varied economic stability, the civil rights movement, the Vietnam era, Watergate, the Reagan era, and other significant events. As we closely investigate the school environment, we see that at Hamilton these societal changes had dramatic effects. In the same period we find student rioting, teacher apathy, common curriculum giving way to liberalized curriculum to a back-to-basics movement, and role conflicts among leadership. Although the story of Hamilton High School ends, educators today are cognizant of further concerns.

In our schools today, pupils "graduate" who cannot read. Students must pass through metal detectors upon entering school buildings, and security guards patrol the halls. Upon completing schooling, late adolescents find the prospects of attaining meaningful employment bleak. Business people claim that the schools' curricula are irrelevant to the business world and that educational standards are unacceptably low. In each case, leadership and/or management in the schools is cited as a leading cause of decline.

In an effort to understand these broad and complex issues and promote a return to stability, we frequently resort to narrow-minded solutions. To curb confusion, we view problems conventionally through a single lens in search of linear solutions. Various disciplinary approaches are taken from shelves, brushed off, and offered up to combat deficiencies. Organizational leaders are retrained in the latest rendition of short-term, minimalist fixes that suffice until the next round of crises. The sum of our efforts is too often a series of superficial, symptomatic solutions, rarely providing fundamental resolution which can be obtained only from holistic reflection and action (Senge, 1990). Across disciplines and professions, we find ourselves falling short of our original set of long-term broadly defined goals; education is no exception.

This book is about those problematic culprits, leaders and managers, and most particularly leadership and management in education. Educational institutions today are in crisis. But is the offender the individual leader or manager? Too often our principals, superintendents, and teachers are scapegoats. Very often the performance of these individuals is labeled inadequate without thorough review of the educational system and its subsystems—not its processes, not its activities, not its membership, nor the larger suprasystem. How does leadership or management occur in the educational environment? Do we have a firm grasp of the meaning of leadership and management? Can our definitions remain adaptable in a post-industrial paradigm, in a society where leaders and managers help to remodel or redesign our vital institutions, including education?

As the twenty-first century dawns, we find that leadership and management have been studied extensively. While the study of leader/manager traits and behaviors has resulted in more detailed understanding of roles, no consensus on leadership theory has yet emerged. Leadership and management are different; but we have not fully investigated the reasons why nor arrived at plausible interpretations that explain the divergence. At best, Yukl (1989) postulated an expanded conceptual framework that brings together much of the existing leadership knowledge. But, at the same time, he stated, "The terms leader and manager are used interchangeably in this book" (p. 5). Undoubtedly, he might also use leadership and management interchangeably. So what is leadership? What is management? Are leaders and managers really different? Do the definitions coincide? Does it matter? Apparently, to educational reformers, the difference does matter. The assignment of the title *leaders* to administrators and reas-

signment of management tasks to staff members suggests that there is more of a difference in the roles than mere semantics.

It is common to elevate *leadership* and to denigrate *management.* This is a mistake. While it may be possible to be an effective manager without strong leadership skills, it is not possible to be an effective leader without good management skills. When administrators "minister" to the needs of the schools, what appears superficially to be managerial can be transformed into leadership by communicating meaning and purpose in the context of the mundane.

This book addresses general principles underlying the knowledge base of leadership and management as specifically applied to educational institutions. We intend to stir learners' thoughts in introductory/preparatory educational administration programs. The review of current scholarship in a wide range of areas will compel potential administrators to critically consider theoretical underpinnings of current educational administration. Being aware of issues and problems and devising short-term remedies is no longer enough. As we incorporate technological developments and as social, political, and economic complexity multiply exponentially, there is need for both systematic and systemic understanding within, and, more important, *across* content areas. Analysis, synthesis, flexibility, and adaptability must cross a variety of venues before evolving into action. Leadership must evolve *with* societal change and empower all our teachers and administrators.

In this text, leadership will take on four exploratory dimensions: inquiry, communication and human interaction, analysis and planning, and decisionmaking and change. Specific concepts are developed within each dimension, as illustrated in Figure I–1. These concepts are discussed in separate chapters and are interrelated to the broader dimensions. Case studies and activities are included to relate theory to practice. A final chapter discusses the role of the leaders within the context of contemporary expectations of and conditions surrounding educational institutions. The text concludes with an author index and a subject index. An annotated bibliography of primary references and a reference list are placed at the end of each chapter to assist readers with future in-depth study.

The organization of this text is illustrated by Figure I–1. In Part 1 we build theoretical and contextual foundations for the study of educational leadership. An updated version of systems theory is used to unify the many concepts of educational leadership that are discussed subsequently. This theory is presented in Chapter 1 and is represented by the outer ring in the figure. Chapter 2 provides a syn-

thesizing discussion of leadership in general; leadership theory is represented by the second ring. The third ring refers to the context in which educational leadership takes place— the social, political, legal, and economic environments of educational enterprises, which are described in Chapter 3. The fourth ring represents the bulk of this volume and addresses specific concepts of educational leadership: inquiry, communication and human interaction, analysis and planning, decisionmaking and change. Each dimension is organized as a separate part of the text (Parts II–V), with three or more chapters discussing specific concepts related to the dimension. The inner circle, educational leadership, is the ultimate object of our interest

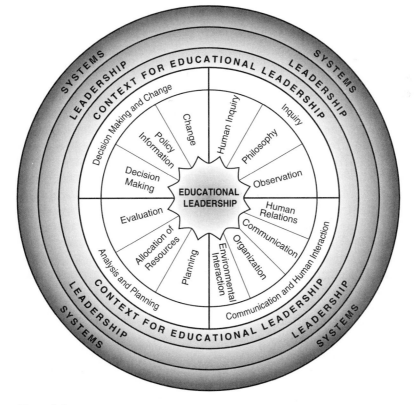

Figure I–1
Conceptualization of Fundamental Concepts of Educational Leadership and Management

and is the subject of Chapter 17, the only chapter in Part VI.

The careful reader will quickly detect that the authors do not subscribe wholly to any particular philosophy of science. We attempt to report the best of what has been produced by researchers regardless of their paradigm and orientation. We view the study of leadership and management as a multiple-perspective activity. Theories of management and leadership should not be viewed as competing with one another in the quest for the "one best view" (Sergiovanni, 1984). Each approach, each theory, has inherent strengths and weaknesses. Each theory is better able to illuminate and explain *certain aspects* of each concept. Taken together, a more complete understanding of the concept is possible through the power of triangulation and perspective.

Chapter Descriptions

PART I: LEADERSHIP IN A PERIOD OF DYNAMIC CHANGE

Chapter 1: Systems Theory and Educational Administration: Rediscovering the Power of Systems Thinking Chapter 1 briefly traces the history of the systems theory. Systems frameworks and properties of systems are studied generically. Further discussion looks into the organizational implications associated with system thinking through early theorists, various management roles and contexts, organizational stages, intervention, and feedback. The chapter closes with an examination of the requirements of the post-industrial paradigm in its current state of unrest, complexity, and variety, and finally applies the theory to educational systems.

Chapter 2: Leadership This chapter discusses multiple dimensions of leadership. We define *leadership* as influencing others' actions in order to achieve desirable ends. Leaders are people who *shape* goals, motivations, and the actions of others. The chapter elaborates on the conceptual and theoretical examination of transformative/collaborative leadership and asserts the importance of leader and followers in such a relationship. In addition, their conceptualized view of leadership is more context-oriented than person- or role-specific. Leadership practiced within a cultural context may be capable of enhancing the abilities of social organizations to realize visions and achieve goals.

Chapter 3: The Context for Leadership Chapter 3 recounts the societal, political, legal, and economic concepts and issues within which educational leadership is *currently* exercised. The chapter discusses the structure of pre-collegiate education from the classroom to the Department of Education and a brief history of how this structure evolved. We report the current criticisms of public education and the proposed solutions.

PART II: INQUIRY

Chapter 4: Impact of Universal Principles, Social Expectations, and Personal Values on Leadership Human beings are constellations of value potentials. Schooling is intended, at least in part, to shape those potentials. Educational leaders must understand their own value systems (or philosophy of life), the process of value development, and the influence of value positions on human motivation and activity. Chapter 4 explores the impact of value perceptions on the roles of educational leaders and describes a number of frameworks for examining values.

Chapter 5: The Process of Inquiry Chapter 5 discusses the nature of human inquiry, common errors made in human inquiry, safeguards provided by systematic inquiry against those errors, and fundamental issues that distinguish social science from other methods of studying social phenomena. Theory-based quantitative approaches to research are contrasted with naturalistic approaches.

Chapter 6: Observation and Reflection

A great deal of our success as educational leaders depends upon the power and clarity of our observational skills—our ability to see and hear what is going on in the classroom, the school, and the community—and our competence in accurately comprehending what we have observed. In this chapter, we discuss the need for keen observational skills on the part of educational leaders. The chapter describes skills required in effective observations and methods for honing those skills. A discussion linking observations and reflective practice closes the chapter.

PART III: COMMUNICATION AND HUMAN INTERACTION

Chapter 7: Schools as Organizational Systems

In Chapter 7, readers venture into the realm of organization theory through approaches ranging from classical to modern. Depending on one's views, organizational effectiveness may be linked to goal attainment. At another extreme, effectiveness may be measured by how well an organization maintains its internal and external integration. The chapter reveals the disparity that exists in this sphere of thought.

Chapter 8: Communication: The Breath of Organizational Life

Across many disciplinary domains, communication is regarded as a primary building block. From the classroom to bodies that govern educational systems, communication demands understanding. The pervasiveness of communications issues is investigated within the whole educational environment and from a social systems viewpoint. Chapter 8 explores a key mechanism in understanding educational leadership.

Chapter 9: Human Relations: The Revolving Base for Educational Leadership

Chapter 9 focuses on human factors and their characteristics and behaviors in the organization. The chapter explains how well a person understands and is able to work within the human enterprise system affects organizational effectiveness.

Chapter 10: Educational Environments

The qualities of a child's environment, to a large extent, determine his or her ability to succeed in school. Educational leaders must understand the relationships between environment and achievement in order to design school programs and settings that facilitate learning. This examination in Chapter 10 extends beyond cultural and physical aspects of the school to external environments.

PART IV: ANALYSIS AND PLANNING

Chapter 11: Strategic Planning

Chapter 11 discusses strategic and tactical or operational planning. Strategic planning is a visioning process, or doing the right thing, and is generally a top-down process. Within the context of the strategic plan, tactical planning is a bottom-up process, or doing things right. Special consideration is given to planning in a devolved system. Budgeting and information systems are discussed as well.

Chapter 12: Allocation of Resources in Education

The pattern of allocation of resources is one of the clearest indicators of values and priorities of an educational organization. Educational leaders must understand the significance of relationships, as well as the political and economic processes by which resources are allocated. Chapter 12 explores the implications of various allocation strategies for the efficient realization of common educational objectives.

Chapter 13: Evaluation in Education: Theories, Models, and Processes

Theories and methodologies of evaluation and the expertise of professional evaluators are among the most valued resources of educational leaders. Chapter 13 focuses on explaining ways in which such resources may be mobilized to help school leaders improve their decisionmaking processes.

PART V: DECISIONMAKING AND CHANGE

Chapter 14: Policy Formulation Chapter 14 defines public policy as whatever governments choose to do or not to do. It addresses policy analysis from perspectives of economics and political science and describes several conceptual models that are useful in examining public policy. Aspects of the political economy of education are addressed, along with the relationships between the distribution of power in society and educational structures and the identification and formulation of solutions to educational issues.

Chapter 15: Decisionmaking The analysis of decisionmaking involves an examination of three basic strategies: the classical model, an optimizing strategy; the administrative model, a satisficing strategy; and the incremental model, strategy of successive limited comparisons. In Chapter 15, decisionmaking is seen as a major responsibility of all administrators. It is a process by which decisions are not only surveyed but also implemented. Until decisionmaking is converted into action, it is only good intention. An understanding of decisionmaking is a *sine qua non* for all school leaders.

Chapter 16: Change Chapter 16 considers some basic issues surrounding the analysis of educational change. Three types of change—enforced, expedient, and essential—are defined. The chapter discusses our separate approaches to educational change: problem solving, social interaction, research-development-diffusion-utilization, and linkage models. Implementation of change is shown to interact dynamically and continuously with leadership and decisionmaking. The chapter concludes with several examples of how educational leaders serve as effective change agents.

PART VI: CONCLUSION

Chapter 17: Educational Leadership in Practice Being a leader involves the ability to have a vision of the future, to see into the intentions of others, and to take effective action. Chapter 17 discusses the role of the leader within the context of contemporary expectations for and conditions surrounding educational institutions.

Acknowledgments

We would like to express our appreciation to the reviewers of this book: Frank Brown, University of North Carolina at Chapel Hill; James A. Burchyett, Miami University; Glen I. Earthman, Virginia Polytechnic Institute State University; Karen Gallagher, University of Cincinnati; Leonard L. Gregory, University of Nebraska at Kearney; Daniel B. Keck, The Ohio State University; Thomas W. Mize, Northeast Louisiana University; Van D. Mueller, University of Minnesota; Cynthia J. Norris, University of Houston; Richard A. Rossmiller, University of Wisconsin–Madison; Joseph Rost, University of San Diego; Caryl Cook Schunk, Educational Consultant, Durham County Schools, North Carolina; Walter E. Sistruck, Mississippi State University; and Carl R. Steinhoff, University of Nevada, Las Vegas.

References

Grant, G. (1988). *The world we created at Hamilton High*. Cambridge, MA: Harvard University Press.

Schön, D. (1983). *The reflective practitioner: How professionals think in action*. New York: Basic Books.

Senge, P. (1990). *The fifth discipline*. New York: Doubleday.

Sergiovanni, T. J. (1984). Cultural and competing perspectives in administrative theory and practice. In T. J. Sergiovanni & J. E. Corbally (Eds.), *Leadership and organizational culture* (pp. 1–17). Urbana, IL: University of Illinois Press.

Yukl, G. (1989). *Leadership in organizations*. Englewood Cliffs, NJ: Prentice-Hall.

Taher A. Razik
Austin D. Swanson

Contents

PART III
Communication and Human Interaction   *193*

Chapter 7

Schools as Organizational Systems   195

Chapter 8

Communication: The Breath of Organizational Life   231

Chapter 9

Human Relations: The Revolving Base for Educational Leadership   269

Part I

Leadership in a Period of Dynamic Change

Education in the United States is going through a period of reform and restructuring. Many of the old certainties have been shaken by the multiplicity of new demands placed upon schools, while new certainties have not yet formed. One thing that is clear is that the educational structure of the twentieth century will not meet the needs of twenty-first century America.

To effectively guide human organizations, leaders must possess an understanding of the context in which leadership is exercised. Educational institutions, like all other human organizations, function in and are shaped by a web of external and internal expectations. It is in the context of complexity and change that the leaders of educational enterprises will have to function now and in the future. Complex systems, embedded in the complexities of the social structure, require leadership that can maneuver skillfully within such complexity. The potential impact of decisions on the broad scale and on the specific problem at hand must be clearly understood. Traditional linear, cause-and-effect thinking is no longer adequate for the task of leadership.

Educational leaders have to facilitate the development of a vision of the organization's mission, and communicate that vision effectively so that it is shared by all members. Leaders must also act strategically to bring that vision to fruition, shaping new schools and institutions from an amalgam of the useful old and the desirable new. To succeed, they must provide direction for the future while managing within the context of the present systems, ensuring smooth day-to-day operations.

Such leadership springs from understanding the realities of the world as a suprasystem, what it means to be a leader, and when the exercise of leadership is required. In Part I of this volume, we build a theoretical foundation for the study of educational leadership. In Chapter 1, we present a modified version of systems theory as a lens for perceiving the many facets of leadership and as a framework for understanding the interrelationships of those facets. In Chapter 2, the theories about leadership itself are discussed. Chapter 3 recounts the societal, political, legal, and economic contexts within which educational leadership is currently exercised. The structure of precollegiate education in the United States is presented and many of the problems that must be corrected are described.

Chapter 1
Systems Theory and Educational Administration: Rediscovering the Power of Systems Thinking

The current reform efforts in the American school system offer a rich setting for the use of systems theory. Schools are inherently composed of critical subsystems such as administration, instruction, finance, and transportation. As administrators seek methods to implement multifaceted school improvement programs, the systems perspective can empower an administrator to emerge as vision setter instead of task manager. Educational administrators, like managers in the private sector, have been using systems analytic administrative methods for more than twenty years. A clearer understanding of systems theory, however, can occur as the practitioner is exposed to the interactiveness, interdependence, and integrativeness of critical school subsystems.

Systems thinking in educational administration has proven to be particularly helpful in identifying variables and organizing processes associated with schooling. Understanding the educational environment from a systems point of view enables systems thinkers to more thoroughly capture its holism. Still, it may be time to reflect upon which aspects of the systems paradigm are being enriched through practice and which are being ignored. Definitions of systems are currently growing more visible in popular literature. However, as definitions multiply, clarity is lost. General System Theory (GST) terms have been misconstrued in academic literature as well. As a result, the popularized versions of "systems thinking" has had less of an impact. This review will more clearly characterize GST and enable educators to gain a greater understanding of how powerful a tool systems thinking can be in both the maintenance and reform of school organizations.

Systems thinking in the last two decades may have been too constrained as it coexisted with the industrial age. Applications of systems thinking in schools may be currently too dependent upon management science, instructional theories, and systematic applications. As a result, educators may be unaware of the role GST can play in providing conceptual knowledge of school organization processes. Current research on systems concepts (Ashmos & Huber, 1987; Salisbury, 1990) indicated that relatively few systems concepts have been researched and put into operation. These findings may indicate both an untapped potential in the general system paradigm and a lack of risk in the application of general system concepts.

Despite evidence that the ore of systems thinking has hardly begun to be mined, systems terms and approaches have proliferated across disciplinary boundaries and slipped quietly past one national boundary after another. The use of systems ideas is now worldwide, attracting large numbers of scientists, theorists, artists, and philosophers. It has caught the interest and imagination of practitioners in nearly every field as the globalization of knowledge and practice proceeds on many fronts. Global ecological-environmental cooperation owes much to General System Theory.

Understanding how any theory and practice interrelate is crucial to an administrator's attempts to lead a school organization. Offhand practice, sometimes demanded by the constant pressures within a school organization, may seem more practical than reflection on a theory that will provide a basis for one's actions. However, without a sufficient base of knowledge from which to act an administrator may be doomed to making immediate decisions that may damage the well-being of the organization. Theorist Jaques (1989) said: "If you dislike theory and seek only 'practical action,' that is unfortunate. Anything you do is founded upon a theory of some sort, and eschewing theory merely means that your decisions are being misdirected by some bad theory which you do not know about" (p. 3). Systems theory has evolved a wide range of concepts to enable the knowledgeable administrator to take appropriate short- and long-term action to promote the overall growth of all elements of the school organization. A thorough understanding of systems theory can empower an administrator to develop as a leader, by helping him or her identify and

define all components comprising organizational life. To avoid misunderstood theory, then, an administrator must become reacquainted with the original sources and the evolution of the systems movement.

By looking at the development and history of systems theory, administrators can see systems theory and analysis applied to human organizations in general and school systems in particular. We need to develop systems thinking in relation to the schooling enterprise, i.e., *to redesign the future of education more systemically*. Systems thinking must become commonplace. A thread that must run steadily throughout these explorations is the thread of critical reflection, for to accept ideas uncritically is surely to model "uneducated" behavior. The administrator using GST is asked to be a scholar-practitioner in the discipline. The following explanation of systems theory invites an administrator to consider the value of the theory in light of his or her practice.

Conceptualizing Systems

DEVELOPMENT OF SYSTEMS THINKING

Up until the 1920s and 1930s, the physical sciences dominated scientific endeavor. Scientific minds were engaged almost exclusively in the effort to establish "a predictive system of laws" (Bertalanffy, 1968b, p. 12). On the other hand, other disciplines were uncovering problems that were unsolvable by classical scientific methods. Many of these were problems posed by organized complexity— that is, the whole entity under study could not be broken into discrete elements without losing its organization and, in fact, its essential character. Bertalanffy, a theoretical biologist, and others called for the development of new conceptual models to facilitate the study of complex biological and social phenomena.

Bertalanffy began incorporating concepts from physical chemistry, kinetics, and thermo-dynamics into his own work. From this point he says, "I could not stop on the way once taken and so I was led to a still further gener-alization which I called 'General System The-ory'" (1968b, p. 13). He expressed the germ of this theory as early as 1937. As the theory developed, he viewed it as having the charac-ter of a basic science. Its correlate as an applied science is now known as systems sci-ence. Systems science has since emerged as operations research, systems engineering, cybernetics, organizational theory, and other sciences that use systems theory, concepts, and methodologies.

At a 1954 meeting of the American Associa-tion for the Advancement of Science, Berta-lanffy and three colleagues—economist Ken-neth Boulding, biomathematician Anatol Rapoport, and physiologist R. W. Gerard— agreed to collaborate as founders of a society for general systems thinking and research. Their goals were to encourage the develop-ment of adequate theoretical models, to mini-mize the duplication of theoretical effort across disciplines, to promote the unity of sci-ence through communication, and to investi-gate correspondence of concepts, models, and laws in various fields.

What Bertalanffy and other systems thinkers accomplished was the creation of a theoretical bridge across scientific disciplines, diminishing the fragmentation that once so severely limited cross-disciplinary exchanges and contributions (Emery, 1970). Their devel-opment of a systemic metalanguage was sig-nificant in conducting these exchanges. Another contribution of GST was its emphasis on the study of wholes over microanalysis of parts. This shift applied pressure on scientists and practitioners alike to design new inves-tigative strategies. However, in systems think-ing the analytical study of parts, insofar as they are accessible, is not abandoned. Such analysis is pressed into the service of the study of whole entities and the relationships and processes within and among these wholes.

SYSTEMS DEFINITIONS

Some critics say that the very idea of a "sys-tem" loses force because anything and every-thing can be viewed as a system. While it is true that proponents of General Systems The-ory find systems existing in all "shapes and flavors," this view is also exclusionary. An *aggregate* of units does not constitute a sys-tem. An often-cited example is an unorga-nized and inactive pile of marbles. Another example might be an aggregate of severely impaired mental patients who are oblivious to each other and their surroundings. An out-side organizing agent is needed to act upon either aggregate to create and understand sys-tem interactivity.

This differentiation between aggregates and systems is important since systems are sometimes treated as if they were aggregates. An exclusively top-down model of organiza-tional communications, for example, assumes that each unit or person is insulated from interaction with any other unit or person inside or outside of the organization. In other words, top authorities presume there are no other systems (whether intrapersonal, organi-zational, family, or community) to prevent an employee or student from obeying every order instantly.

Corporate mergers, acquisitions, or divesti-tures also exemplify aggregate rather than sys-tems thinking. If managers perceive people as noninteracting aggregates, then they will also assume that pushing people into, around, or out of an organization will have no substan-tial negative effect on the organization as a whole. In a similar light the dictatorial relocation of teachers from one school to another, or hair-trigger decisions to expel troublesome students regardless of their home situations, are examples of aggregate thinking. The aggregate mentality is additive. It assumes that aggregate units can be added or subtracted at will without damage to the larger aggregate called "the company," "the school," or "the office." Politically, the aggregate mentality may even encourage the aggression of large nations against small nations, with nearby additions of territory, people, and resources not presumed to have much effect on the world. In truth, disturbance in one part of a system creates ripple effects that are unsettling for the whole system, often for extraordinarily long periods of time. Systems thinkers can anticipate this, knowing that multisystem interactions are inevitable.

Aggregate nonsystems are also closely associated with the idea of system closure. In a *closed system* all energy is drawn from within the system, all events occur within the system, and all products are used by the system. Nothing is imported or exported. This is a recipe for system deterioration and demise, since the closed system exhausts itself in repeated cycles of self-consumption.

The closed system is largely a theoretical construct. It may be impossible to find a real-world example of a totally closed system. Theorists more commonly speak of relative closure or openness. The relatively closed system is most susceptible to *entropy,* which in the physical law of thermodynamics is a condition of running down, becoming chaotic and disorganized, and falling into a state of unbalance or disequilibrium that endangers a system's survival. Relatively closed systems need new energy as input. Input is the system justification for medical or spiritual intervention in the case of human illness or, in the case of organizational disorder, the justification for hiring a consultant or new executive. All such interventions are aimed at overcoming entropy.

Similarly, the completely open system is a conceptual convenience, for if such a system actually existed it would have no boundaries and probably no separate identity. When systems theorists speak of *open systems,* they are actually referencing degrees of openness. The relatively open system remains open to many interventions, some of which are deliberately sought and others which are simply unpreventable. An open system may also reach beyond its boundaries to exert external influence. The notion of permeable boundaries is important in studying relatively open systems. The extent to which any system allows communication and other exchanges in both incoming and outgoing directions determines its degree of boundary permeability. This same principle applies to subunits within each system.

Relative closure of systems appears to be psychologically comforting to many people. In a closed system, unwanted intrusions are guarded against and people rarely have to cope with anything new or different. On the other hand, excitement and benefit can be enjoyed in relatively open systems. In open systems, *self-regulatory* devices are established to monitor boundary exchanges and the effects these exchanges have on parts of the system, the whole system, and the environment. The process is somewhat like the regulation of water release from dams: the structure accommodates downstream users and recreational users of the lakes above the dams, prevents floods, prevents droughts, eases pressure on the dam structure, and adjusts to catastrophic weather conditions. The decision to build a dam in the first place is a multisystem consideration, requiring permeable boundaries in political, economic, cultural, agrarian, industrial, and other domains.

For a school administrator, maintaining a relatively open system involves commensurate tasks, such as regulating school enrollment, making schooling enjoyable for all concerned, monitoring downstream entry of students into work life, anticipating growth in school populations, etc. Administrators cannot simply turn switches, oblivious to the potential variety and potential value conflicts in the environment. The role of the administrator steeped in an understanding of systems theory, therefore, is one of leadership, not mere management.

Once it is clear that systems are not aggregates and are relatively closed or open, other system characteristics must be understood. Every definition of system denotes a connection between parts and wholes. Rapoport (1968), for example, explains, "A whole which functions as a whole by virtue of the interdependence of its parts is called a system" (p. xvii). Although they expanded this definition in several ways, Hall and Fagen (1968) define a system quite simply as "a set of objects together with the relationships between the objects and their attributes" (p. 81). Ackoff's (1974) definition is more complex: "A system is a set of two or more interrelated elements of any kind; for example, concepts (as in the number system), objects (as in a telephone system or human body), or people (as in a social system)" (p. 13). Even from the beginning of General System Theory, *interrelationship, interaction,* and *interdependence* have defined the characteristic elements of systems (Bertalanffy, 1968b).

Onlookers or *observers* are also by their simple act of observation part of the systems that they observe. It is imperative in complex human systems that individual perceptions be considered as part of the system. These onlookers or observers for a school or school district might include various stakeholders such as the public, industry, political groups, boards, and legislators.

Many of the definitions of systems refer to *organization* as a condition that enables parts to work together on behalf of the whole. Thus, the ideas of interrelationship and interdependency migrate into the broader concepts of *organized complexity* and *holism* (Hodge & Anthony, 1988; Kast & Rosenzweig, 1972). As mentioned earlier, understanding a school must involve more than the comprehension of its internal functioning. Internally, schools may be viewed as being composed of administration and instruction. These may even comprise our primary definition. But schools equally must be understood in combination with their external environment—beyond building boundaries to include the school district and state and federal governments. Attempting to understand the school in the absence of these larger arenas is ineffective. Each external group is important and adds complexity.

SYSTEMS FRAMEWORKS

Systems literature treats the general characteristics of systems in several ways. Authors may first discuss the elements of a system and then describe the functions of these elements. They may undertake system model-building that seeks to incorporate all pertinent variables and processes, or they may begin with taxonomies that categorize systems and their variables in thought-provoking ways. This variety of approaches can serve as a model for a school administrator when attempting to use systems theory to study a school situation. Given the relative youth of the theory and the range and scope of ideas and components system analysis considers, this variety of approaches is not only understandable but also appropriate. Most theorists conceptualize a vertical dimension to systems that allows them to speak of hierarchies *of* systems, hierarchies *within* systems, or hierarchical levels of abstraction to be used in thinking *about* systems. A horizontal dimension extends across disciplines as well as across systems which might at first glance appear to have nothing in common. These dimensions allow researchers to envision the graphing of a system with "x" and "y" coordinates, i.e., intersections of horizontal and vertical dimensions varying according to different assigned values. Yet vertical or horizontal references do not represent all the dimensions inherent in systems. Systems thinking may require a third "z" axis, or, more likely, may be multidimensional.

Banathy (1972) offered one useful set of ideas with "a map of systems education." On a continuum of abstraction from low to high, he speaks of learning about "systems tools" (a technician level of understanding) that are instrumental to "systems approaches" (a tactical level of understanding). These "approaches" are derived from "field (systems) models." Banathy is speaking here about systems models in education, business, and health care, and the need to learn how models are profitably applied at a strategic level. Finally, he lists "general systems models" that provide frameworks for understanding the constructs and laws of General System Theory at a level that allows synthesis.

By arranging theoretical systems and systems constructs in an ascending order of complexity, Boulding (1968) created what he called "levels of discourse," or a system for talking about systems. While he viewed this arrangement as more systematic than systems actually are, it yields rich insights about organized complexity. The lowest level of system constructs includes static structures and relationships which he calls "frameworks." As his examples illustrate, frameworks are the skeletal level of systems—patterns of electrons, genetic material, the solar system, etc. It is the "thing" level of systems discourse and free of system dynamics. Boulding calls the second level "clockworks"; this level provides a category for simple, dynamic systems with preset, necessary motions. At the third or "cybernetic" level, regulatory mechanisms adjust system activity at a set-point of equilibrium. Furnaces controlled by thermostats are a classic example of cybernetic (clockworks) systems. These first three levels are subsequently grouped together as *physical/mechanical* because they represent concrete entities.

The fourth level of system constructs is the "open system," a dimension that enables differentiation and provides for system maintenance. Boulding spoke of this as the "cell" level at which life becomes differentiated from nonlife. At this level of discourse, to speak of "organizational life" is to speak of the organization as a living, self-reproducing entity. Boulding's fifth level, the "genetic-societal" level, is indicative of a unitary division of labor. Roots, leaves, and stems of plants are examples of growth systems typical of this level. At the sixth or "animal" level, the system gains mobility, purposeful behavior, and information-organizer abilities. Here, other system differentiations also occur. The fourth, fifth, and sixth levels are clustered as *biologically based* systems in keeping with correlate levels of biological growth and development in the physical world.

The seventh level is the human level, where "symbol processing systems" emerge. This is a level marked by self-consciousness, valuation, language use, and complex concept formation. From the human level it is a short step up to the eighth level, "social organizations." At this level the entity has the ability to take concerted action. The final, ninth level is the "transcendental" level and includes systems about which little is known and for which there are no answers. The complexity of these transcendental systems makes them indescribable by currently available scientific means.

The human, social organization, and transcendental levels lie in the realms of social science, the arts, humanities, and religions. These levels are the new frontiers for the application of systems theory. Education is embedded as a practice within and across each of these levels. While it is certainly possible to take issue with any point in Boulding's formulation, it serves well as an invitation to rethink systems. He proposed that its value might lie in pointing out the gaps in both theoretical models and empirical knowledge, more noticeable at some levels than at others.

Another way of framing systems thinking is to identify broad categories and then develop functional classifications. For example, *abstract* systems are composed of interrelated symbols, ideas, concepts, principles, and so on. *Concrete* systems are composed of interrelated physical and material resources. *Real* systems are observable, i.e., they are "visual-tactile" systems falling within the compass of human sensory experience. *Human* systems add interrelated organic and psychological dimensions, and embody elements of abstract, concrete, and real systems. *Cybernetic* systems steer organizations through turbulence toward stability. Organizations include all these systems, and each must be accorded its own importance and value.

The functional behavior of these systems can be classified as (1) state-maintaining, (2) goal-seeking, (3) multigoal-seeking, and (4) purposeful (Hodge & Anthony, 1988). A state-maintaining system wants to continue in a customary pattern. A goal-seeking system moves toward a different but highly specified outcome. A multigoal-seeking system pursues several outcomes which are not mutually exclusive. A purposeful system has a clear sense of mission, in a broad, value-laden sense. School organizations, from the district to the individual classroom units, exhibit qualities of all four system behaviors.

Simon (1970), as well as Boulding (1968), spoke of a "system of systems" in hierarchical arrangement. Furthermore, some scientists have decided that there are also systems of systems theory. According to Immegart and Pilecki (1973), there are five theoretical approaches to understanding these metasystems: (1) comprehensive system theories of wholes and components, (2) subsystem or

process theories, with microscopic analysis of input processing, (3) feedback and system control theories, with cybernetics as a prominent contender, (4) theories of system properties that help to formulate longitudinal, evolutionary systems analyses, and (5) output theories and output analysis, i.e., results of system activity. Operations research is a primary example of the latter. Immegart and Pilecki claim that there is value in multiple approaches to system evaluation and reconsideration. The rate of organizational change in the mid-twentieth century warrants the use of multiple approaches.

Because systems are viewed as wholes, their structures and functions are also studied as a dynamic and ongoing process, rather than as subsets of analytical interest. For those scientists who either cling to the hope that all system science can be made linear and predictable or who reject the scientific method on the basis that no such chaining of predictability can be achieved, the dynamism and change within systems make it difficult to believe that the realities of systems at and above the human level will ever yield to holistic scientific description. Critics who ground their opinions in a positivistic view of the world, by what Simon (1957) called "bounded rationality," may impose valuation systems belonging to one world view upon another—a vastly different world view afforded by general system thinking. A world view founded in holism is not compatible with a reductionist's world view. What is more legitimate is to measure the success of systems science on its own terms. For scientists who have escaped the rigid cause-and-effect line of thought, other criteria of science are not only possible but actually hold more promise. Naturalistic inquiry, for example, has enormous potential for translating observations of systems at work into scientific probabilities and challenging bodies of knowledge. The qualitative research that has resulted and been applied in numerous academic areas has demonstrated new part-whole variables that may prove more valuable.

To many, systems thinking is a confusing mix of positivistic and naturalistic, or nomothetic and idiographic, points of view (Getzels, 1958; Kimbrough & Nunnery, 1988). For the systems scientist, this is as it should be. By definition, General System Theory organizes and subsumes widely divergent scientific views and methodologies. Systems thinking requires a synthesizing, "both-and" perspective, rather than the piecemeal exercise of serial "either-or" judgments.

Systems approaches relying heavily on either all-analytical or all-conceptual modeling are not able to express all of the existing relationships among systems. Presumed causes cannot always account for observed effects in complex systems, and neither quantitative nor qualitative studies provide all the answers everyone would like. Consequently, whatever approach is used contains the danger of oversimplifying organizational relationships. Using multiple points of view to study organizations may initially yield overwhelming amounts of data, some of which may conflict with other data, but from this muddle new and testable hypotheses arise. It takes complex science to study complex systems.

PROPERTIES OF SYSTEMS

The simple input-throughput-output model for system activity has been the source of theory-building and the metaphoric bane of systems thinkers. It represents an oversimplified version of systems inquiry that can lead to the very rigidity and scaling down of ideas that systems thinking seeks to avoid. Graphically, the model overemphasizes analytical, procedural, and directional properties of systems, casting them in a "systematic" stepwise mold. When this mold is all that is visible, the *systematic approach* is taken for the whole of

Figure 1.1
Input-Throughput-Output Model

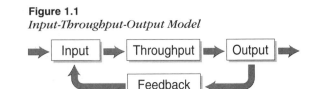

General System Theory. This belies the system's actual, "lived" dynamism and diversity. The input-throughput-output model robs the system of its energy, interactivity, and interdependence.

Paradoxically, this otherwise regrettable simplicity helps GST newcomers identify important system elements from which more *systemic* ideas and models are constructed. For example, management and instructional design models are often more systematic and procedural than systemic and functional. These models should be understood to be limited accordingly in their explanatory power. In simplest graphic form, this is the systematic (procedural) model. (See Figure 1.1.)

Only by placing an environment around such a model and by making the boundaries between the system and the environment permeable is this systematic system saved from its circular, repetitive tilt toward entropy. (See Figure 1.2.)

Schools provide an excellent example of the environment requirement of a system model. The social, economic, and political milieu in which schools exist often determines their survival. To ignore the milieu is to ignore the environment that constantly interacts with a system. By incorporating the environment into the system model, one begins to see the new energy, information, material resources, and people from the environment moving into the system as inputs, providing new "raw materials" for system activity. Other sources of new input activity may include: (1) feedback about the input the system has consumed and (2) feedback about the outputs the system has produced. For example, a

Figure 1.2
Simplified System Model

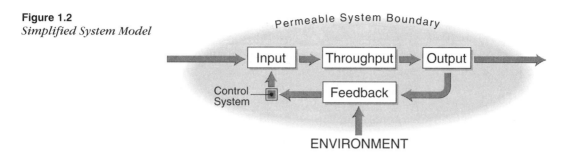

more specific input activity could be family impact on the student, community job availability, state and federal mandates, or local or regional economic conditions. Schools obviously rely heavily on all these forms of input, although there is often a conviction that human resource inputs are the most critical. The basis for this is the belief that the proper input mix of skills, knowledge, and ability is neither purchasable nor expendable. However, proper mix cannot just happen; there are regulatory, "control" processes that shape the "mix." Controls in a school setting may range from contractual agreements to state regulations.

Installing a cybernetic control device in the feedback loop to show regulation and self-correction of the system completes the basic model. At this point, the organized complexity of systems may be present but can scarcely be inferred from the diagram. However, as the mix of inputs ensues, and the transformation process takes place, input-throughput-output inputs become outputs. Considerable variation is apparent here as the system becomes dynamic. Even in an "assembly-line" transformation, inputs and processes can vary from one "batch" to another. Even in modern organizations the application of more and more standardization cannot cope with the vast complexity that arises as input continues to vary and grow exponentially. This is particularly evident today in the information age, when system complexity is fueled by more available information.

Outputs may be products, services, energy, damages, or any combination of these. For example, a systems solution to environmental damage might be to capture toxic emissions or substances (outputs) and reuse (input) them in some ecologically sound way. In school systems, capturing dropouts and carefully "recycling" their energies is an appropriate systems solution to educational waste. Outputs can thus become new inputs for the same system as well as inputs for other systems.

Environment generally refers to the collections of systems which lie outside the system under study. Environments are not controllable by the system, but can be selectively responsive to the system's behavior. Environments may be stable, dynamic, or even chaotic. Churchman (1979) suggested that analysis of a system ought to determine whether influences on the system are environmental, systemic, or neither—for such influences are potential growth and survival factors. Strategically, the organization must know of the existence of resources, employ managerial talent to import and organize their use, and then call upon organizational intelligence to make sure that the whole system, including its environments, is well-served.

Synergy, or the presence of synergism, is an important concept in systems thinking. Synergy is a process-equivalent of *structural holism,* wherein structural components (e.g., bricks and mortar, classrooms, libraries, offices, gyms) become more than the sum of the parts. Together, these concepts aptly describe part-whole relationships in General System Theory: the whole is structurally, functionally, and synergistically greater than (and other than) the sum of its parts.

Functionalism in systems designates how a particular system or subsystem functions. Parsons (1960), an early supporter of the pattern-and-function view of systems, urged a systemic examination of structures, processes, and functions. Just as the openness of a system is perceived to lie somewhere on a continuum between open and closed, so too, the functionality of a system lies on a continuum between optimal functioning and complete dysfunction. The system that functions well has dynamic properties; the system that becomes dysfunctional or "neurotic" suffers from static processes and relationships (Kets de Vries & Miller, 1989; Hodge & Anthony, 1988). Obviously, static and dynamic components may coexist in any system at any given point in time. Consider individual student differences, for example; the need for standardized control mechanisms coexists with a particular teacher's need for more flexibility in the classroom. These dichotomies exist everywhere, but are balanced more often by our control.

This raises the issue of *leading parts* (Hall & Fagen, 1968). Which parts of a system act as its leading parts: the static components or the dynamic ones? Administrators may "switch the line-up" or change the dysfunctional components from static to dynamic. In small group behavior, leading parts may be individuals who emerge when needed or when prepared to do so. Larger organizations display this same flexibility and potential for emergence of unexpected leading parts. The school band may unite pride throughout the school, the adoption of a dramatic and new teaching method may raise achievement, or shared decisionmaking may allow teachers and administrators to more effectively balance

standardization and flexibility. This may be the very pulse of innovation, and systems thinking invites this perception. Leading parts and *emergence* are interdependent concepts; both are situational rather than positional. School administrators are defined by their positions as leaders, but this neither guarantees that they are leading parts nor excludes them from that status. There may be other leading parts which, at critical times, may emerge to help a school become more functional—for example, an energetic new teacher, lead teacher, student opinion leader, or someone from the external environment. Perhaps the leading part is a new computer system or a new building. System thinkers ought not to assume that the authority figure is, or ought to be, the leading part of the organization.

Cybernetically, leading parts help "steer" the organization toward *dynamic homeostasis* (relative equilibrium), a condition that allows the organization to grow and change in a stable way. Thinking of the organization in this systemic way helps to keep system dynamics in perspective. The organization is viewed by more than its positional or status dimensions, in essence, more than a management system and/or instructional system. Systems need the fresh inputs of leading parts, as well as the information-communication regulatory systems to magnify helpful forces and minimize destructive ones wherever these leading, regulating components may be found. A system may have structures that are *isomorphic* (show correspondence) to structures in another system. This means that, structurally, the parts correspond one-to-one to each other. Obviously, what is learned about one structure (even if it is an abstract structure like a concept) is applicable to its isomorph. Therefore, looking for isomorphism is a way to infer knowledge from one organization that may hold true in a second organization. One caution is needed: while all isomorphisms are analogies, not all analogies are isomorphisms. The difference is that analogies do not have to meet the condition of one-to-one correspondence (Schoderbek, Schoderbek, & Kefalas, 1990).

Differentiation and specialization in a system refer to a single process of internal elaboration of subsystems and their relationships. This can account for system *symbiosis,* a situation in which one subsystem becomes so differentiated that it cannot perform certain functions for itself and thus must "live off" another subsystem. If one of the symbiotic pairs is self-sufficient, the relationship is unipolar; if each has something vital to offer the other, the relationship is bipolar. Another type of differentiation occurs in redundant subsystems where design and functioning is duplicated as a back-up in case processes in another subsystem are interrupted. An example is central database duplication and access at more than one location of a company. Hodge and Anthony (1988) identified still another kind of subsystem—a *decomposable* one. This is a "short-run independent" system that has many internal sustaining interactions. A project group might exemplify the decomposable subsystem.

Bertalanffy (1968a) also postulated a principle of *progressive mechanization*. This principle implies that control functions can be decentralized when subsystem routines proceed to the point that regulation is more easily managed at that level. *Progressive inclusion* and *progressive centralization* indicate system tendencies to centralize and become more and more integrated and complex. These properties of systems may cyclically emerge and recede, depending on how system variety is managed (Willis, 1977). *Progressive segregation* refers to the subdivision of systems parts into recognizable, separate subsystems.

According to Bertalanffy, one cannot talk about organisms, behavior, and society without taking into account the concepts of goals and adaptation toward those goals. Conse-

quently, the property of *teleology* has a critical role in systems thinking. All systems, living and nonliving, may have directedness or *purposiveness,* but human systems clearly have purposes, i.e., desired "end states" or teleologies. For example, businesses create profit, schools educate, and students learn. Identifying this property leads naturally to the idea of *equifinality,* where a system may reach equal-final goals by means of different paths and strategies. Clearly, businesses achieve profit in varying ways, and different schools educate using a variety of different but successful methods.

Katz and Kahn (1966) reported another property of open systems, *negentropy* (negative entropy), the systems defense against decline. Negentropic inputs (feedback) keep a system healthy. The system's dilemma is to determine which of many possible inputs will be most beneficial. Feedback is the mechanism that allows the system to self correct. Vocal parents demand change, teachers evaluate performance, and administrators review resource utilization. Each of these self-correcting mechanisms change the system in fundamental ways.

The properties of organized complexity, holism, teleology, emergence, synergy, isomorphism, and leading part activity are often given short shrift when predictive or quasi-predictive systems analysis methods are used. When more qualitative approaches are taken, these properties become vital to the analysis. The *cybernetic* (Weiner, 1968) and *adaptive* aspects of systems receive much attention from scientists, although some recent writers have suggested that organizational inertia vitiates the notion of adaptability (e.g., Carroll, 1988).

This review of systems theory approaches and concepts serves as a foundation for an administrator's possible use of systems theory as both a means of understanding the life of a school organization and a means of promoting that life by leadership initiatives.

Organization Implications of Systems Thinking

GROUND-BREAKING: EARLY ORGANIZATIONAL THEORIES

Organizational theory has not totally ignored the impact of system theory. Educational institutions that prepare school administrators cannot sensibly ignore the impact of systems thinking on other disciplines nor have they done so. Taking a systems view frees administrators from single-cause analysis, narrow interpretations of what systems are and do, and misunderstandings about the meaning of isolated events. Systems thinking can also add a more thorough cultural perspective to institutional history, to present concerns, and to projections of the future. There are unprecedented opportunities for building new models when the whole system is the material for modeling. This, in turn, leads to hypothesis generation and research with rich heuristic and scientific value. Chin, Bennis, and Benne (1961) reported that systems approaches were becoming a major operating framework for physical as well as social sciences. Bertalanffy's (1968) experimental approach to interdisciplinary "parallelism" became everyday reality. Cities now depend on systems thinking to plan urban renewal and transportation; NASA launches space ships replete with systemic environments; and global economies are understood to be interdependent and synergistic. In place of single-cause thinking of an organization, the systems view promotes: (1) multiple perspectives on interdependent phenomena, (2) recognition that the first system interventions are usually made between human and structural subsystems, (3) recognition that change is related to technology and that socio-technical systems have emerged, (4) understanding that techniques for change need to be selected for appropriateness and feasibility, and (5) realization that continuous diagnosis is needed to protect system viability and growth.

While some historians of the systems movement reported that early organization analysts did not recognize the importance of environment in relation to the systems being studied, Ashmos and Huber (1987) believe that only the constraint of identifying enormous numbers of environmental variables kept them confined to "closed system" modeling. In the following paragraphs, an overview of the research demonstrates the depth and breadth of the systems movement. Barnard (1938) and Simon (1964) were among the first organization theorists to adopt systems thinking in their work. Both recognized that organizational activity could not be modelled in linear forms only.

Homans (1950), an interactionist, believed that *activities, interactions, and sentiments* were at the very core of social organization. He used systems methods in his study of social groups. Parsons (1960) referred extensively to structures or subsystems in managerial systems. The *technical/production* system is concerned with task performance, research and development, production control, marketing research, etc., according to his taxonomy. The *organizational/managerial* system coordinates task performance, using materials, information, and energy for its accomplishment. The *institutional/community* system relates the activities of the organization to its surrounding environment. The managerial system as a whole spans the entire organization and directs technology, people resource utilization, and communication. More simply, these elements are identified as technical, intra-organization interactions, and interorganization relationships. These early works with systems show relationships overlapping, functions interacting, and interdependence within organizations. The elements present a more realistic model for understanding how organizations actually function.

They set the stage for exploring new roles for administrators/managers.

With new theory, managers can realign system components, reduce uncertainty and ambiguity in the system to tolerable levels, act decisively, and maintain flexibility, all in the service of an organizational balancing act among systems, subsystems, suprasystems, and environments. Managers may be classified as technical, organizational, or institutional, another more systemic view.

Katz and Kahn (1966) felt that using physical models to represent psycho-social phenomena causes problems. Physical models overlook the "loose coupling" of variables and ignore dynamic system maintenance activities. Systems are influenced by multiple goals and objectives, and change in any subsystem engenders change in others. *Role* is defined by Huse and Bowditch (1973) as, first, a psychological link to the organization, and second, as a complex set of expectations of others in the system. These two components of role sometimes produce role conflict, ambiguity, personal dissatisfaction, and organizational stress. Katz and Kahn gave simultaneous attention to structural design, work flow, and human factors that operate in organizations.

Lewin's (1951) concern for human and organizational equilibrium produced *force-field analysis,* a conceptual device for assessing the relative strength of various organizational "vectors" for or against change. Changing the force of the vectors in either direction results in "unfreezing" the system. This results in a period of change or "moving;" then the new state of the system "refreezes" and becomes institutionalized. Lippitt, Watson, and Westley (1958) added two steps to Lewin's model: the development of changing relationships and the achievement of a change-process-ending relationship.

Dynamic homeostasis is another consideration in systems. Perfect equilibrium needs to be overcome if the system is to grow, change, and, then, restabilize. System growth relies heavily on the type and quality of human, technological, and organizational inputs as well as on the social structures and norms that prevail in the system. Huse (1975) mentioned cost-control and value-adding as strategies for organizational change, human resource accounting propositions, the need for human resource departments to separate into human resource management and human resource development systems, and a topology of personal, interpersonal, and multi-group systems.

In describing the elements of a thriving system, Kimbrough and Nunnery (1988) listed organizational imperatives: (1) the achievement of objectives, (2) internal maintenance, and (3) adaptation to the environment. Individuals in organizations move from immaturity toward maturity, from passive to active, dependent to independent, "now"-oriented to future-oriented, from external to internal locus of control, and from a limited to a profound sense of commitment.

As this brief review illustrates, these organizational theories reflect systems thinking and support systems thinkers' belief that understanding the wholeness of an organization may enable administrators to work more effectively.

CHANGES IN MANAGEMENT ROLES AND CONTEXTS

Boundaries of systems are continually redefined by events in the system or the environment. A case in point is the series of school district reform/restructuring efforts that parlay bureaucratic systems against site-based management systems. An emerging function of management, in addition to combatting entropy, is to manage these boundary shifts successfully.

In Miles' 1975 classification of management philosophies (Hodge & Anthony, 1988), approaches to management that either support or impede system activity are discussed. *Traditional* philosophy demands hierarchical layers, extreme specialization, and formalized policies and procedures. The *human relations* school of thought, however, gives attention to environmental and system linkages and carefully designed, long-term measures of organizational effectiveness. *Human resources* philosophers hope to create a network of effective environmental sensors and design system interface activities that ensure optimal use of resources. They assert that all human resource activity is linked to the achievement of organizational goals. This may mean that some subsystems are marked for inclusion, and some are targeted for elimination.

Hodge and Johnson (1971) argued that consideration of micro, intermediate, and macro environments is a helpful strategy in understanding major approaches to management. The *micro environment* includes: (1) the goal and work system, which outlines the organizational mission, specific objectives to be attained, and the work needed to accomplish these; (2) the power, authority, structure, and communication system, charged with organizational decisionmaking and linkage; and (3) the human factors system, concerned with informal, formal, and interpersonal exchanges, role perceptions, leadership, and motivation. *Intermediate environment* links the organization to its macro environment, facilitates resource acquisition and product or service distribution, and considers the use of outside agencies, consultants or internal specialists such as recruiters, attorneys, or advertising designers to reach its goals.

The *macro environment* consists of seven major systems: (1) cultural, (2) political, (3) economic, (4) field of competition, (5) technological, (6) human resource skill/educational mix (dependent on the available labor pool) and (7) customer/client groups. If environments are disregarded, organizations become ineffective, inflexible, unable to satisfy needs and cease to exist. Hodge and Johnson see these environments as the basis for all organization. Therefore, systems analysis models must take the environments into account. The above analysis concludes with a taxonomy of six analytical management models: (1) mechanistic/bureaucratic, (2) human relations, (3) individual behavior, (4) technological, (5) economic, and (6) power. The first, or mechanistic/bureaucratic model of management, depends on stimulus-response, programmability, and predictability of outcomes for its success. Management in this context is seen as efficiency and control based. The second, or *human relations* analysis model, is Lewinian and interpersonal and places little emphasis on formal organization. Management in this context is seen from a more humanistic perspective. The third, the *individual behavior* model in the Herzberg and Maslow traditions (cited in Immegart & Pilecki, 1973) is useful for exploring individual perceptions, motivations, and work life satisfaction. The fourth model is the *technological* model, and investigates the way an organization internalizes parts of the macro environment. In the fifth, *economic,* model all decisions are assumed to be both economically and rationally motivated. The sixth and last model, the *power* model, presumes that organizational life is a series of power struggles through which individuals and organizations attempt to achieve deliberate objectives. These six models invite analysts to explore new strategies for understanding organizational processes.

These models proceed from several other assumptions: (1) the organization exists to satisfy environmental needs; (2) the organization's work system mobilizes to meet objectives that will in turn meet environmental needs; (3) the organization structures itself to facilitate the work system activity; (4) the design of power/authority relationships, system differentiation, and delegation are all dedicated to work facilitation; and (5) renewal and change processes are mandatory for survival and effectiveness. Hodge and Johnson (1971) further suggested that mapping input-throughput-output models onto the micro, intermediate, and macro models might be productive. These analytical models are significant in that they explicitly seek to investigate organizational management from a systemic point of view. The models explore the management of organizations in light of their reality: as open and dynamic systems and subsystems, as interrelated across functional boundaries, as interactive combinations, and as integrative processes. The models specifically demonstrate the necessity for interdependence; one system or subsystem cannot and does not act individually, but always acts in concert with other systems or subsystems. Management, for example then, cannot simply justify singular problem solving confined in individual micro, intermediate, or macro arenas. Analysis must become holistic.

While literature on the organization of schools borrows from all the above theories, there is no specific body of literature that links systems theory to school organizations. Nevertheless, systems concepts are continually applied in analyses of schools. Current literature on school administrators casts them in the gray area of roles existing between that of managers and leaders. Systems theory requires both managers who handle operations to promote homeostasis and leaders whose vision enables them to act in concert with members to promote the growth of an organization. In this regard the theory plus elements from other organizational theories can help an administrator design his or her situational roles. Systems theory validates situational leadership as an implied practice for school administrators (Yukl, 1989). A look at

the subsequent information on organizational stages may further illustrate this possible link among systems theory, organizational life, and the role of the administrator.

ORGANIZATIONAL STAGES

To assess organizations, Greiner (1972) identified five organizational dimensions: organizational age, size, stage of evolution, stage of revolution, and growth rate of the industry. Viewing organizations across growth stages enables the practicing manager to understand related, systemic organizational needs as development continues. At times during a cycle of growth, organizations can be seen as evolutionary, progressive, or striving to change. At other times in the cycle problematic issues arise as the organization confronts internal crisis and strives to continue its existence. These periods are revolutionary. With organization growth, differing managerial styles are needed. Five different management stages and their attributes are explained below.

1. *Evolutionary creativity leading to a leadership crisis.* At this stage technical and entrepreneurial competence become insufficient. Managers have to be created or imported.

2. *Directed evolutionary growth leading to an autonomy crisis.* Here, communication is often lacking as people become frustrated and alienated. Management begins to share decision making.

3. *Growth through delegation leading to a control crisis.* Subsystems appear to be too independent. Situations develop that trigger centralization. Other problems emerge as a result.

4. *Growth through coordination leading to a crisis in bureaucracy.* The organization

becomes rigid, inflexible, rule-bound, and inefficient.

5. *Collaboration leading to a crisis of unknown origin*. At this organizational stage, the organization has presumably matured enough to be able to assess its risks and act accordingly.

Contingency theory appropriately links with the model above, since structural forms and managerial characteristics are contingent on the stage the organization is apparently undergoing. Each successive growth stage corresponds to a managerial style. Other aspects of contingency theory are long-range structural adaptation within the system (Darwinian) and within the environment (Singerian). Prerequisite to change is familiarity with the environment, willingness and ability to change, and information acquisition and feedback response (Schoderbek, Schoderbek, & Kefalas, 1990). Contingency theory also builds on the concept of systems equifinality; there is no one best way to reach systems goals. Initial inputs do not determine the extent of goal achievement, and outputs may vary even when the inputs are consistent (Kimbrough & Nunnery, 1988). This latter feature may be one reason why systems thinking has been overlooked in circles that espouse scientific management models. Yet the concept of equifinality strengthens since it provides answers to problems in organizations. The nonlinear approach can promote a manager's ability to cultivate an environment for creative problem-solving. Problem-solving, therefore, takes the shape of multi-faceted intervention.

SYSTEMIC INTERVENTIONS

Young (1964) proposed a four-way quadrant analysis of systems concepts to guide how we classify and use systemic intervention. The first category is *systemic and descriptive*. This permits discrimination between systems,

organizes and analyzes large quantities of data, and helps to conceptualize the fundamental nature of different systems. For example, a state curriculum might begin by describing the totality of the curriculum system to capture all of its essential elements. The second class of concepts, *regulation and maintenance*, provides information on the status of components, the state of feedback systems, negentropic interventions, and communication. In this quadrant numerous processes may be explored. The third category, *dynamics and change*, allows examination of teleology, growth, dynamism, and adaptation. An example could be the development of strategy. The last class, *decline and breakdown*, identifies stress, disturbance, overload, increased entropy, and decay. Problem solving would be an example here. This model allows zeroing in on one quadrant at a time and then moving to other quadrants as necessary. In school systems, for example, budget votes, critiques of instructional systems, constituent demands, teacher/student demands, or technology may all impose regulatory effects on the system and thus signal the need for attention from the regulation and maintenance quadrant.

Marney and Smith (1964) provided another intervention model and cited four major determinants of system change: feedback, organizational memory-learning (refined and developed over time), change capacity, and system/environmental relations. For example, a system can choose to change or not. If the decision is to change, then resources and energies must be marshalled accordingly. Change is costly, however, and the system needs to balance its immediate fiscal position against long-range survival needs. In other words, the system must utilize its feedback mechanisms. In another example, Selye, in his classic work on stress (1957), showed the effects of stress on individuals and organizations. Although researchers such as Brown (1967) see positive motivation possibilities in stress, others such as Lasell (1969) report quite the opposite effect. Stress needs monitoring at both individual and organizational levels; individuals experience stress differently and demonstrate varying degrees of success in coping with it. Coping mechanisms provide for maintenance of individuals and organizations and operate on the basis of specific input, output, and feedback structures. Change, therefore, requires continuous feedback, a capacity to learn from feedback, and knowledge of how to design mechanisms that allow change to occur. In each case the system must be cognizant of its relations with the environment.

FEEDBACK REQUIREMENTS

Like their counterparts in business and industry, educational administrators need to sense organizational signs of decline and assess the cost of system disruptions. Defenses against decline should be applied in the least costly manner. Rusche (1968) showed that schools receive more negative feedback than positive. It is a challenge to turn perceptions around and alleviate the demoralizing and stressful effects of criticism. A built-in and ongoing feedback system can act against system decline by identifying regulatory and maintenance necessities.

The importance of feedback from within as well as from outside the organization can scarcely be overemphasized. Feedback is an information exchange, often solicited and seldom random or disorderly. Feedback feeds the self-regulatory processes, allows the system to valuate its viability and contributions, and detects needed changes in the communication system. Purposeful feedback reviews past events, enables present adjustments, and encourages future planning. System functionality and goal achievement depend on feedback. Systems require specific mechanisms, both formal and informal, for receiving, manipulating, and using the data gained from feedback.

In his review of a feedback classification system developed by Carlson and others, Hearn (1958) outlined the various types of feedback. *Continuous feedback* allows a controlled amount of feedback to be monitored regularly. Mechanized continuous feedback, nonlabor-intensive, can provide continuous, valuable self-correction. Security systems are an example. *Intermittent feedback* arrives at specified intervals or, on some occasions, unexpectedly. Open-door office hours, regular meetings, or regular classroom observations are examples of intermittent feedback mechanisms. *Proportional feedback* designates feedback that is controlled by the amount and type of information the system needs. For example, if an administrator is out of touch with faculty, students, staff, or constituents, or unaware of how others perceive him or her, then feedback needs tend to be higher. Proportional feedback can also be targeted feedback as it is capable of prioritizing informational needs. *Relay feedback* refers to an "on" or "off" flow of information: feedback is relayed only if and when it is requested. Continuous and intermittent feedback usually incur high costs. Relay feedback loses data or promotes other inefficiencies. Proportional feedback has the most value, but it is time-consuming and time-bound. A combination of relay and proportional feedback allows timeliness to become less of an issue. In the "informated" organization, however, feedback may be quickly generated via electronic mail and quickly analyzed by computer programs designed for that purpose.

Looking Toward the Future

UNREST IN ORGANIZATIONS

Systems thinkers have sought and continue to seek the "law of laws," the "system of systems," and the "order of orders," as parallel cognitive processing occurs across disciplines. Systems theory does not purport to fill the gaps. General System Theory does insist on inclusiveness rather than exclusiveness, more breadth and depth, and the fullest range of methodologies that can be brought to bear on the study of systems phenomena. GST promotes far more than a problem-solving methodology, and it is at its core far more significant than the innumerable "approaches" derived from it. It simultaneously provides a unified concept of the system and a means for detailed analysis. Those who disclaim the legitimacy of General System Theory because they doubt it can generate testable hypotheses proceed from the assumptions of quantifiable science and quasi-experimental designs. For those researchers within positivistic practice and theory, adopting systems thinking may appear risky or revolutionary. Kuhn (1962) articulated how normal science can amount to paradigm paralysis.

There are many new directions and applications of systems theory to organizational theory and practice. Some of these new applications have their roots in earlier work; some seem to be radically new departures from what has been previously done. For systems thinkers this is an exciting time, marked by a convergence of naturalistic inquiry, General System Theory, and any number of auxiliary paradigms. The little research that management systems scientists have offered is now being recognized as only a preview of what systems science can do. Bertalanffy's (1968) interdisciplinary energy is being reinfused to encourage businessmen, educators, and scientists to read widely outside their own disciplines. A part of this new energy is being generated by common recognition that old ways of thinking about and doing things simply are not responsive to all that is happening in system environments. This new state of affairs in organizations has often been described in terms like "chaos," "turbulence," and "permanent white water." Harmon (1989) asserted

that executives all over the world are experimenting to find a new standard of organization. Before any such new design can emerge, three dynamic trends must be integrated: (1) technological revolutions in communications; (2) the demand by employees for more complete and meaningful work; and (3) the rising pressure for efficiency, fueled by fast-paced and increasingly global competition. Traditional organizations everywhere suffer acute stress or even psychological breakdown. The underlying cause is the struggle to fit these trends into an organizational design created for a disappearing world. Engdahl (1989) also speaks wistfully of the need for an improved organization theory net with which to "catch the world."

Toffler (1990) thinks that the "survival of the fastest" will be the hallmark of the twenty-first century. The "fastest" are those with the ability to shorten development times, to move products and services faster and closer to consumers, and to use information almost instantaneously. Toffler envisions a new and accelerated role of knowledge in the creation of wealth. Imagination, values, images, and motivation will be components of this knowledge. Toffler made an interesting system observation when he suggested that there will be "new economic significance of free expression," as governments that were closed begin to "open the valves of public discussion."

Schein (1989) concurred that this may be the beginning of a major organizational revolution and mentioned new system forms being considered: holographic, multi-goal, heterarchical, coordinational, informated, systems designed for controlled diversity or for harmonies of dissimilar elements. Organizations need covenantal relationships according to DePree (1989), who views contractual relationships as stifling and having nothing to do with reaching human potential of any kind. In his view, the advantages of covenantal relationships are that they (1) induce freedom, not paralysis, (2) rest on shared commitments, (3) fill deep needs and make work meaningful, (4) reflect unity and poise, (5) enable organizations to be hospitable to the unusual person and unusual ideas, and (6) tolerate risk and forgive errors.

Six themes of recent organizational research have been identified by Weick (1985): (1) rationality is less prevalent; (2) organizations are more segmented than monolithic; (3) organizational segments are small and stable; (4) connections among segments are variable; (5) organizations have a high degree of ambiguity; and (6) the basic task of management is to reduce that ambiguity. Weick notes that ambiguity implies the presence of unregulated variety in the organization. Variety, or lack of it, is a theme that surfaces over and over in contemporary systems and organizational theory.

One way to approach organizational change is to be consciously involved in futuring, Weisbord (1989) believes. Futuring focuses attention away from interpersonal relationships and toward the experiences and values that affect everyone. He considers futuring a purposeful action taken to design a preferred future. Mohr (1989) also prefers conscious, socio-technical organizational design, a process he says will create high performance organizations.

At the international level, Ohmae (1990) described an economic system that "follows its own logic and develops its own webs of interest, which rarely duplicate the historical borders between nations" (p. 183). In a borderless world, any small movement in any economy affects all economies. Pluralism is a fact of life, not a generous concession to other nations. Another economist (Carroll, 1988) believes that whole organizations will be selected or replaced in the future, as some organizational forms become obsolete and others become more viable. He views adaptation as severely constrained by the existing forms. Carroll insists that organizational ecology demands that organizations and environ-

ments move toward isomorphism. There should be an empirical correspondence between environmental change and patterns of organizational founding and mortality.

Change occurs daily in contemporary organizations. Without theory to organize means of coping with change, breakdown can occur within organizations and in their environments. Systems thinking may provide that needed theory.

REGULATING VARIETY IN ORGANIZATIONS

Conflict emerges in organizations when the need for variety is unappeased. As Ackoff (1974) suggested, "few have tried to redesign education in broad interactive terms. To do so requires recognizing that the current system is a Machine Age product of reductionist, analytic, and mechanistic thinking. We need a system that is the product of expansionist, synthetic, and teleological thinking" (p. 74). How much formal educational systems have learned since then about adaptation and reconfiguration is still to be determined. Ackoff speaks about Wilma Dykeman, who believes that students experience enough control and too little commitment; students do not dislike discipline, they dislike our inadequate commitment to our own self-discipline. In systems terms, this implies that the regulation of system variety is occurring in the wrong subsystem. In practical terms this suggests that the "products" of our mechanistic schools are not highly adaptable or able to meet the educational needs of our society. A cursory glance at current political and business claims about the ineffectiveness of our schools reflects this same implication.

In circles concerned with performance technology, Nickols (1990) sounded a similar note: "The era of compliance has ended, and with it the dream of engineering individual human performance. The era of individual contribution has just begun, and we do not even have a vocabulary suitable for discussing the issue, let alone formulating decisions and then carrying them out" (p. 196). He saw this as a paradigm problem; "unengineered" variety that organizations face today freezes paradigms.

Beer (1974) felt that variety engineering is performed in the wrong place with scientifically calculated goals and norms. The system is robbed of the crucial reference point without which it cannot learn, cannot adapt, cannot evolve. Variety regulation is performed at the local level, not at the top of the organization. Referring to Ashby's *law of requisite variety,* Beer asserted that there are only two ways to provide the requisite variety to keep organizations alive: (1) reduce the variety generated by the system in order to match the available regulatory variety (variety attenuation) or (2) amplify the variety of the system's regulatory part (variety amplification).

While this may sound complicated, Beer simply means that if administrative variety is insufficient to handle the amount of variety existing in the system, then the administrator lessens the variety and everyone follows the rules. That is one way of regulating. The other way is to increase the variety in the regulatory systems. This can be done by deciding how to deal with more information from the system, and/or by passing on regulatory responsibility to the lowest levels. The law of requisite variety, an organizing rule for systems, has important implications for educational administrators. Human need for autonomy and internal locus of control is a psychological equivalent of self-regulation in system theory.

Gleick (1987) saw evolution as chaos with feedback. Chaotic variety becomes organized when feedback is available, pertinent, and psychologically usable by the receiver. Feedback, so often depicted as linear, in reality is optimally multidirectional. Those in charge generally have the most intimate knowledge of how decisions made elsewhere affect the rest of the organization. Leaders should be encouraged to organize their feedback for use throughout the organization. The rank-and-file enjoy requisite variety when, acting as feedback senders, they self-select the most important data to be diffused.

METAPHOR AND SYSTEM MODELING IN EDUCATIONAL ADMINISTRATION

Metaphors are in vogue primarily in natural and social sciences as a means of describing complex phenomenon to the lay student. Poets have used metaphors for years as a means of capturing and sharing multi-dimensional human experiences which are simultaneously unique and universal.

Clancy (1989) stated that in a world of "endemic complexity" metaphors help to sort out and classify phenomena, helping humankind to understand and express one phenomenon in terms of another. While metaphor is not the thing-in-itself and does not enable users to grasp the whole implied experience, as Clancy argued, a metaphor can shape views of experience. "It is important to recognize that metaphor is an integral part of our thought process. We use metaphor much as we breathe; we cannot avoid its use or its consequences." If this is true, then surely the power of metaphor is its ability "to suggest a reality beyond ordinary, discursive thought" (p. 13).

Pre-modern metaphors have furnished business with its self-perceptions. Since schooling predates business as it is today, it is useful to ask why schooling has not furnished the metaphors for business. The answer is that schooling has, but until recently the competing metaphors of games, wars, machines, and heroic journeys have been dominant. The metaphor of "the learning organization," i.e., the organization that learns (Kiechel, 1990), has not received much credence even in educational institutions. The difference is that organizations are not *for* learners, but *of* and *about* learners. Yet no organizational member should be exempt from universal, system-wide continuous learning.

Three metaphors in the pre-modern era which apply here are the *journey, game,* and *war.* The journey elicits images of ships, captains, even ships of fools. The *game* metaphor is associated with players, playing fields, and winning or losing. The metaphor of *war* engenders visions of "pinstriped soldiers," receiving and giving marching orders. These are not particularly systemic metaphors; instead, they call up visions of heroic life and heroic death. Educators have always resisted these as images for schooling, even as they adopted some of the philosophical underpinnings.

Another set of metaphors is closer to Boulding's terms (1964): the machine, the organism, and society. The spirit of the *machine* metaphor remains in organizations in the form of Taylorism, the term for unreconstructed "scientific management." The mechanical metaphor implies systems which are ultimately predictable, rational, and deterministic. People are cogs in the machinery and the leader is an omniscient machine operator. The *organism* metaphor retains traces of determinism—there is a "genetic" fate in the evolution of the system, which must grow and adapt even in the face of complexity and ambiguity. The *society* metaphor, which educational administration theories have often embraced, is built upon and may overemphasize culture, stakeholders, rituals-myths-symbols, shared values, and meaningful leadership.

Systems thinkers can accept part or all of the organism and society metaphors but still find them insufficient for the future. The metaphors of journey, game, and war can be associated with three paradigms that may have failed: journey, wealth, and the institution. Much of the organizational literature has been concerned with wealth and institutionalization. A new eclectic paradigm needs to be merged with all three metaphors in order to

see the problematic future. The paradigm of the moment seems to be the prototype of the "market fair," a medieval convenience that allowed craftsmen, sellers, and clients to conduct their affairs anywhere. The watchword of this paradigm is extreme flexibility; the most important role is that of the "shape-changer," a leader whose role and work constantly shifts according to need.

Hopefully, a new paradigm of "invisible powers" will emerge involving a sense of infinite playing out of the unending human spirit. Organizational coactivation must be idiographic (person-oriented) and transactional rather than normative and nomothetic (conformist, controlled). Systems theorists think in terms of the interrelatedness of subsystems rather than "taking sides."

Self-assessment in school organizations typically begins with an analysis of symptoms, but symptoms of what? The answer is typically symptoms of problems as defined by feedback. But feedback is a double-sided coin. The term *negative feedback* is typically used in conjunction with problem solving. In problem identification we typically search for negative feedback, i.e., what went wrong. On the other hand, positive feedback is usually associated with variety. System variety is rarely explored. Systems analysts set out to describe organizational elements, assess environmental demands, discover how congruent the organization is with those demands, predict problem causes, formulate plans, and evaluate plans. This process is certainly embedded in a metaphor more nomothetic than idiographic. The serious question for the new administrator is whether the balance in planning can be shifted at all toward the idiographic, transactional, empowering side.

Benne (1990) believes that "Power is to social dynamics what energy is to physicochemical dynamics. One cannot understand or change a human system without taking the uses and distribution of power into account. We desperately need to understand the oper-

ation of power if we are to plan democratically" (p. 11). According to him, humans fail
to understand that power is not a fixed sum,
to be distributed or withheld at will up to
some imagined limit. Power is self-amplifying
in the positive sense. The empowerment of
subsystems is the empowerment of the
whole; this is a mutual relationship.

Benne also claimed that students often
view the power of school systems over them
as naked, illegitimate power, not authority.
School resources generally are not perceived
as oriented to meeting students' needs for
free and responsible learning and growth, but
rather to meeting teachers' needs or oriented
to meeting the manpower needs of one or
another established bureaucracy. Therefore,
to the student, power appears to lie everywhere except within himself or herself. Similarly, Benne also noted that organizations
everywhere are being forced to bring temporary organizations into being: task forces,
advisory groups, project groups. Crossing
departmental boundaries and even the
boundaries of the system itself can be
detected.

Frame (1987) has identified some forms
that these project teams take. One is the *isomorphic team,* which is configured to match
the structure of the "deliverable" product or
service. If the product is a report, then different chapters may be allocated to different
team members. Another form is the *specialty
team,* where specialists are asked to provide
input on two or more of the team's efforts.
Using the report example, one specialist
might be working on several different chapters without being solely responsible for
them. The *egoless team* structure is highly
interactive; everyone is working on everything, and responsibility for the final product
is shared as work flow demands. In the *surgi-
cal team* structure, Frame said that it is the
"surgeon" who defines effectiveness. For
report-writing, this would mean that the chief
report writer has the final word and the inte-

grating responsibility. Since this "surgeon"
bears the conceptual and skill weight, administrative tasks are carried out by others.

Developing new metaphors and models in
any field can be risky since the new forms
may elicit commitments to new roles, policies, and an organizational life that continually change.

SYSTEMS THINKING AS A WAVE OF THE FUTURE IN EDUCATION

Throughout this discussion, references have
been made to the unrealized potential of systems thinking in all fields, with educational
administration being no exception. But what
can a systems-literate administrator plunged
into the district, the school, or the principal's
office achieve in practical terms?

He or she can think differently and
approach organizational issues, positive or
negative, differently. The practice of conceptual modeling should become second nature,
allowing the administrator to devise maps
and diagrams that help to organize data,
enable system members to choose alternatives, and enact them. Every case of variety-
out-of-control needs this decisive thought:
Can this variety-producer contain the means
of self-regulation or must regulation be
imposed from outside? This mandates an
administrator's clear understanding of energy
sources and drains in a school system.

Literature on school administration over
the past several decades reveals a marked
influence of nomothetic biases. Nevertheless,
idiographic themes have persisted and seem
to be coming into their own in the present
state of organizational turmoil. After all,
nomothetic planning and evaluation has not
yielded what educators or businessmen and
women seek—the sense of productive, quality, enjoyable work. The place to begin to
change the systems of the world is in the
minds of the new thinkers in that world. But

to change others, the minds of educators need to change. All that may be required is a return to ancient metaphors of what it is to learn. Ironically, these are systems metaphors.

One example of an ancient metaphor in new dress is provided by Engleberg's (1991) discussion of integrative study. He insisted that acute social and political problems cannot be solved by specialists, because resolution of these problems lies at the integrative level. Integrative study takes place in the here and now, among those we live with, and exerts a benign influence on the community in which it takes place. There could hardly be a more cogent belief statement in support of lowering walls between schools and the communities they serve. Engleberg adds that everyone is capable of some level of integrative study. Integration implies participation in schooling by teachers, parents, students, and all other stakeholders. It is intrinsically democratic.

Bredeson (1985), however, found that in only one out of five schools studied were parents highly involved in a formal sense. "In fact, one principal indicated that there were problems in having parents in the schools because they often do not understand many things that are occurring. Therefore, parent involvement was more often viewed as supportive and tangential as opposed to a rich source of expertise and knowledge" (p. 44). Structures for parental involvement were bounded by predetermined roles much like the roles of all other school stakeholders.

Aside from the implications for less "bounded" schools, the notions of integrative study deserve closer inspection for their systemic version of curriculum. Engleberg believes that since living systems can be understood only by reference to their transformations over time, the objects of integrative study are narratives (histories, case histories, works of literature, etc.). Specialists can function only as long as there is an integrative matrix in which they can find a place. The

occupants of the realm of wholes create and maintain these matrices. Engleberg calls for educators to "face away" from their specializations, which have been so powerfully developed and researched by the "realm of parts." He suggests that educators fear facing "nothingness" when they turn away from the disciplines, but instead they will find themselves *facing life*. The challenge then becomes the difficulty of sharing wisdom without imposing dogma that accentuates fragmentation. This implies a new vision of teachers and administrators as facilitators of learning, not mere sharers of facts.

Engleberg assumed that language exists to facilitate integrative study, carrying learners forward through an integration of differences in which differences are maintained and preserved. While integrative study sessions require a moderator and rules of discourse, their object should be works of art, dense in information, rich in meaning. "Framework statements" (i.e., "a cumulative repository of insights") are the specified outcomes. Correlative outcomes are personal and social integrations. Extending Engleberg's thesis logically, competency-based (specialist) education may be no more than part-sensitive, able to function only if whole-sensitive integrative studies provide the matrices on which the carefully honed parts can hang without fragmentation.

The old metaphors invoked may be "liberal arts," "great books," story-telling, or even myth-making. Speaking of the qualitative uses of myth-making in organizational development, Boje, Fedor, and Rowland (1982) identify the development of myths with the development of specific organizational situations. When a myth is successfully guiding decision-making and strategy, it is a *developing myth*. When the myth and the organization have become completely intertwined, it is a *solid myth*. Myth split occurs when some groups in an organization begin to develop competing myths in order to encourage renewal or survival. *Myth shift* occurs when reformulation and perhaps new leadership of the organization is imminent. While this is reminiscent of Kuhn's (1962) discussion of paradigm shifts, it is obvious that new metaphors and myths appear with every "scientific revolution" and that sometimes older metaphors and myths are reinstated in contemporary, more acceptable forms.

Bredeson (1985) referred to the influence of studies in general semantics, studies that called attention to the importance of metaphors as a mediator of reality. Bredeson said that the very words or analogies used may limit one's view of phenomena and the world. Aristotelian logic is seen as having drawn researchers in the Western world into a habit of "two-valued" thinking, accompanied by broad sets of fundamental and pervasive silent assumptions and premises. Thus, thought is governed by perceptions of "either-or" rather than "both-and," or even more sensibly, "many and all." On this basis, educators imagine ultravariability in systems with difficulty, if at all. Unchanged semantic traditions may prevent administrators from handling diversity and welcoming the "chaos" of accommodating many simultaneous "truths" and interpretations.

Bredeson cited a number of authors and their uses of prevailing metaphors about the nature or the role of school administrators: the *principalship* as a "constellation of positions" (Knezevich, 1975) and the *principal* as consummate manager, organizational change agent, educational/curricular leader, applied philosopher, school manager, behavioral scientist, politician, gamesman, broker, facilitator, missionary, and gardener (Kmetz & Willower, 1982; Martin & Willower, 1981; Roe & Drake, 1974; Small, 1974; Wayson, 1971; Miklos, 1983; Blumberg & Greenfield, 1980; Lipham & Hoeh, 1974; Sergiovanni et al., 1980; Getzels, 1958). Bredeson believed that such topologies are inadequate to represent any school leader and that, instead, a *compos-*

ite imagery is needed. Further, he suggested that *metaphors of purpose* might be more instructive. If the perceived purpose is to behave like a chief executive officer (CEO), then command center behavior will follow and the principal will rarely leave the office. If the perceived purpose is student control (disciplinarian), that will be the principal's modus operandi. If the perceived purpose is to ensure that a school survives in a tight economy, that will engender another set of behaviors. These prevailing metaphors result, systemically, in a maintenance function that occupies more than three-fourths of an administrator's time and energy, overriding any vision or holistic view of the present an administrator might otherwise have. Bredeson suspects that the expectations of education administration students skew their preparation toward specific skills development that will help them survive immediately in new administrative appointments. This, he says, may help create, foster, and maintain a culturally standardized image of the school principalship that reinforces metaphoric themes and old myths, all of which can stand in the way of change. The obvious solution is to teach skills *and* theory, with coursework geared toward reflective, theory-based, systemic considerations. Two-valued thinking will not suffice in twenty-first century schools.

Conway (1985), for example, called for a rediscovery of values in schools that would parallel current efforts to rediscover values in business organizations. He felt that society asks schools to restructure themselves and their culture, to go through an organizational learning of the most difficult type. Efforts to control time spent on tasks or to extend the school year represent a linear, unitary approach to change that Conway associates with *single-loop learning*. In contrast, Argyris and Schon (1978), Bateson (1972), and Friedlander (1983) have all envisioned a more complex approach called, respectively, *double-loop learning, deutero-learning,* and *reconstructive learning*. Conway noted that culture change will not take root without appropriate reconstructive learning. The way beliefs are ordered and linked in a psychological framework can be an analogy of the way organizations believe or disbelieve. In the world map of the organization, what are the *structural connections?* He asked whether new information can enter to reorganize beliefs, revise ideology, and repattern paradigms. How, also, does the organization view time? If there is a fixation on a given time period, for example, the system tends toward closure. The closure is effected through a "narrowing" process which may include denigration of the past, dissolution of future-oriented functions like planning, or institutionalizing of a "now" attitude to the exclusion of other time frames. The excluded frames then represent disbelief regions. Conway reported that, in his own experience, certain indicators of structural closed-openness conditions have surfaced: knowledge disavowal (it can't be true), belief avoidance (silence), and the relative time perspective that can either expand or truncate organizational memory.

Hoy and Ferguson (1985) attempted to create a model for assessing school effectiveness across such variables as innovation, student achievement, cohesiveness, and organizational commitment. They borrow Steers' (1977) argument that the *goal model* of school effectiveness and the *systems model* are complementary. This supports the synthesis of the two models that resulted in the dimensions or variables used in Hoy and Ferguson's study. The researchers chose these dimensions specifically because they addressed Parson's (1960) imperative for social organizations: adaptation, goal attainment, integration, and latency (creation and maintenance of motivational and value patterns). They sought to draw on the perceptions of different groups in the schools they assessed. Notable for its absence was any effort to sample student perceptions. While

their empirical analysis was considered reasonably successful, the researchers believed an expanded model could be developed to allow more focused comparative study of schools on both rational systems and subjective dimensions. This would imply the use of various methodologies.

LIBERATING SYSTEMS THEORY: THE CRITICAL STANCE

Earlier in the chapter, the systems paradigm was described as being merely surface-minded and transported far from its origins. Flood (1990) produced a detailed, reasoned argument for a complementarist theoretical position that is open and conciliatory, overcoming the theoretical fortress mentality that has developed in the various streams of systems thinking. Subservience of any of these streams to another, he states, is a distortion of what systems thinking represents. Certainly such subservience has kept systems thinking from realizing its full potential. Flood felt that those who seriously consider the *systems epistemological ideal* cannot help but conclude that beyond the positivistic (objectivist) and the interpretivistic (hermeneutic) ideals of science, the emancipatory force of critical self-reflection is necessary. He is concerned that managers tend to hide behind the facade of common interests, claiming to have surveyed opinion and reached consensus when, in fact, only a narrow band of interests are being served. The critical approach has the potential to destroy the facades of rationality and objectivity that allow decision makers to defend their own interests on grounds of rationality.

Further, while much of management and systems literature applauds *convergence* and *universality,* Flood argues for *divergence* and *multiple truths,* reminding us that it is anti-critical to expect that we can work toward a view we all feel comfortable with. In the interests of social conservatism, Flood notes, ideological positions are ignored and objectivist research is preferred. However, in the critical inquiry framework, debates over soft versus hard systems research are irrelevant, since the choice is not between non-reflective positivistic and non-reflective interpretivistic research positions, but between non-reflection and critical self-reflection. It is conceptual reflexivity, those self-confirming and self-perpetuating aspects of systems science, that has constrained system thinking, according to Flood. He says that this has ensured that the abstract, paradigmatic richness of the word system is hidden under an avalanche of desolate labels for things like "hair-replacement systems," "school systems," and "information systems," which have no metatheoretical connection. What Flood demands is antiprovincialism, a thinking-between-paradigms, a mapping of the intellectual world of systems thinking, in order to embark in new directions. It appears that Boulding's (1968) levels of systems discourse have hit a glass ceiling imposed between biologically based systems and human social systems. Nothing learned or seen above that ceiling can be valued by systems scientists unless it has yielded both positivistic and predictive systems knowledge, because that is the current map of "flat-world" systems thinking. As Columbus had need for a globe, so, too, the adventurers of the future need to be steered by more than positivistic, predictive science.

Greatly oversimplified, Flood's map includes positivistic, interpretivistic, and critical-reflective (complementarist) regions of system theory. He places Herbert Simon squarely in the positivistic region, with Ackoff (1979), Churchman (1977), and Checkland (1981) belonging to the interpretivistic region. Jackson and Keys (1984) occupy the complementarist region along with Ulrich (1991) and Flood. The first two regions are isolated by their methodologies, while those oriented to critical-reflection view all theories and methodologies as complementary. What the complementarists see as necessary is a way to break through the "colonized" territory ruled by traditional management and operations research scientists, and also through the paradigmatic isolation of competing world views, into the openness and "emancipation" of critical systems theory.

This pioneering would allow researchers to deal with issues like employee empowerment, workplace diversity, cultural anomalies, coercion, ideologies, and ownership of values in a deliberately normative way. Subjective inquiry would be openly acknowledged, not as antithetical to systems science but as part of its legitimate discourse.

Postulating a role for critical systems theory immediately removes most of the "two-value" constraints that have plagued systems literature on educational administration. "Machine" images as metaphors for social systems, those associated with management by objectives, management information systems, accountability, control, efficiency, competencies, and performance objectives (Sergiovanni et al., 1980), can be complemented by contextual analysis and "getting the drama right" (Bolman & Deal, 1991). Surely in an era that speaks incessantly about the need for liberation and empowerment, control must be imagined differently.

Choosing whatever analogue inspires, a school's administrator may motivate the school's inhabitants toward that analogue, that inspiration. Images are unlimited and may be used to liberate thought and practice.

Orton and Weick (1990) argued that researchers (and practitioners) must continue to transform methodology to serve theory, and not the other way around. DeGreene (1990) also admitted that the theory and practice of management must change with the dynamic reconfiguration in the environment. Also, the approaches and tools that appeared to be well adapted to more "linear" times may be counterproductive during today's epoch of massive structural change. Robb (1990) noted that "getting a better tailor" to alter organizations will not work, for it is necessary to enter into states of disorder from which new orders can emerge. The future is unknowable. Surprise is the order of the day; strategic imagery and forward planning have no meaning in the traditional systems science sense.

Tomorrow's school administrator need not abandon systems thinking. On the contrary, systems thinking is needed now more than ever, beyond the ceiling positivistic science has constructed. Analogues and models are also needed more than ever. Hawes (1975) stated that developing analogues should lie at the heart of the social scientist's activity.

Beer (1990) believes that a polyhedron might well be the organizational metaphor of the future. He quotes Buckminster Fuller, creator of the architectural marvel known as the geodesic dome, as having said that all systems are polyhedra. Beer imagines that a management team could be represented, together with its connection to other teams, at one of the nodes of a regular polyhedron. Such a polyhedron is held together by "tensile integrity," for struts between the faces of the geometric figure intensify its structural cohesion. Beer's idea is that an organization might be characterized as a 20-sided, 30-edged icosahedron, gathered together by 12 nodes, each connecting five edges, with each edge representing a person. Each of 30 people would belong to two teams and no two people would belong to the same two teams. Beer calls this "complete democracy" in an "organizational globe" which is "absolutely and regularly cohesive," having only nodal hierarchy. It might be interesting to arrange an imaginary classroom this way.

In a positivistic framework the polyhedron is an image not easily understood as a metaphor for organization. But the school administrator of the future, leaving the cocoon of two-value (either-or) thinking, may embark on even more imaginative journeys in

the century ahead. It is not that the nomothetic (i.e., real) world must be left behind but that the idiographic (i.e., subjective) world is ever more insistent and more complex.

If schooling is to flower in the future, if integration is to democratize institutions and nations, then systems thinking is indeed a wave of the future. The old systems science will be applicable to limited classes of problems, but the leading edge of systems thinking will be made transparent in new metaphors of humanity, its social systems, and the way they organize and act.

The study of systems thinking in this chapter carries implications for the reader's reflection on both organizational life and the research that examines that life. Both avenues for reflection lead to new questions and, furthermore, to a questioning of the conventional established two-dimensional focus of schooling and positivistic research. At no other time in the history of American education has such questioning been more needed than it is today. Perhaps the following questions will stir the reader's understanding of the promise of systems thinking as a theory for the development of effective twenty-first century schools.

■ **CASE STUDY**

Systems: The Case of Karen Avery

Introduction

Too often classrooms are relatively closed systems. Guided by regulatory bodies, students achieve outcomes that have too little applicability to current need and practice. Likewise, our schools and school districts suffer from this paralysis and tend to be relatively closed.

Consider in the case that follows how we have widened or narrowed the purview of the classroom, the school, and school district and created a relatively closed or open system. Look for interactions, interdependencies, and interrelationships in the organized complexity of this hypothetical assimilation. The case as developed is derived in part from Reigeluth's (1987) third-wave educational system description.

Convulsions and Vertigo

For many years now, Karen Avery has increasingly been losing the excitement she felt when she first began teaching. Now a department chair, she feels she has even less impact on teaching and governance and over the individual learning of students. She often considered what further limits she would encounter with her next promotion. Her classroom exchanges with students provided fewer insightful moments. Meetings with colleagues were devoted to symptomatic problem solving: discipline, absenteeism, scarcity of time, and relations with school and district administration centered largely on the necessity of meeting growing demands with limited resources.

During the past year Karen participated in a task force created to devise a new strategic agenda for the school district. The national mood to discredit schools, educational practices, and school administration had settled abruptly in her community 14 months ago as a result of national media coverage of a lengthy student-led strike. High visibility at this national level demanded unequivocal action. A variety of subgroups to the task force had met over the last year to study and recommend rigorous improvements, actions, and changes. Each subgroup drew from the latest research, simulations, and actual prac-

tices in industry in its efforts to devise solutions to the multitude of student problems. In particular, one subgroup of the task force recommended adoption of total quality management (TQM) to access outcomes on a continuous basis and act on the findings. Another subgroup recommended a service management-based program to include better strategic planning, decentralization of control, more flexibility, and consistency; all designed to release the intrinsic motivation in administrators, teachers, and students alike. A third subgroup recommended "a return to basics," stronger discipline, greater expectations, more definitive rules, and structure. Karen's subgroup was locked in controversy and had not provided its own singular solutions. Other subgroups acted similarly and without much effect. Now, a year later, students again grew restless.

As Karen reflected on the year's events, she realized the limitations of the task force in response to student unrest. Overall the task force accomplished little to foster an understanding of the variety of circumstances existing in their district. It had only offered piecemeal solutions to problems that appeared unmanageable. The multidimensional problems certainly needed methodology beyond that which existed within the task force. Questions raced through her thoughts. "How can we integrate our expertise and our reflections to address the complexity of the tasks we face? Do inquiry methods move squarely to solutions? Do other organizations face similar circumstances? Can we learn from them? Are our problems mutually exclusive? Do our own comfort levels inhibit individual, group, or organizational action?"

Tomorrow Today

During the summer break Karen attended a series of seminars at a national education convention held in her community. By accident she elected to attend several seminars dealing with systems theory and another seminar that sketched a preliminary model for a new school system. During the remaining summer months Karen contemplated the new philosophy and reviewed the model of the new school system over and over. "How can we better understand the systemic nature of our district when all we produce is independent judgments and solutions? Where do we start looking for these so-called interactions, interdependencies, and integration mechanisms? Does the essence of our organizational model really control us at the expense of individuality and concerted action? Are student reactions just a symptomatic expression of more fundamental problems? Has our task force and its subgroups achieved anything of value or consequence? And how do we proceed?"

Early in the fall at the first meeting of the subgroup Karen explained the rudiments of systems thinking and the new school model to her subgroup. Her thoughts had begun to crystalize and she began the process of swaying other group members' paradigmatic stances. Although still somewhat conceptually oriented, her group's progress report is revealed below.

Their model attempts to capture one of the classical meanings of learning, an environment whereby learners achieve their own capacity to act. As devised, the system specifically proposes an integrative framework that exposes the learner to an everchanging variety of learning methods, learning environments, and outcomes. The learner, the teacher, and the learning system are the research cornerstones. As an individual, each learner brings a variety of abilities, skills, and values to the learning environment. The task of education is to outfit learners with an amalgam of abilities, skills, and values to use and align uniquely with the expectations of the sociocultural environment. At a subgroup

meeting one member, quite by accident, coined the phrase, "to earn a living and live a life." The metaphor stayed with the group.

Karen's group first proposed a new structure. In their system teachers would become guides, advisors, motivators, and managers versus content disseminators and disciplinarians. New resources including interactive computers, video discs, peer tutors, projects, and learning laboratories would be employed to transfer knowledge to the student. A guide would advise, motivate, and manage students and also coordinate the efforts of other new elements in the system such as inexpensive assistants, apprentice guides, senior citizens, parents and peer tutors, well-designed projects, discussion groups, learning laboratories, and resource people. Parents, in particular, would help decide instructional goals in conjunction with their guide and the individual student. A student's development in the physical, social, moral, psychological, and intellectual domains would each be considerations. The classroom environment as we know it would disappear. A guide and student or small groups of students would work together to attain agreed-upon developmental goals. A guide would be responsible for a student through one of the four developmental stages within K–12, about four years per student per development stage. Each student's educational goals would be matched to uniquely suited educational resources orchestrated by a guide and other assistants.

A guide would not work independently, but would be integrated into a cluster of three to six guides. The guides would participate in decision making and exert control over a particular cluster. In each cluster all guides would be responsible for cluster success. Clusters themselves would create and meet goals. A master guide would also serve in the cluster as an instructional leader. Success of a cluster would depend on parent and student satisfaction. As clusters succeeded in meeting the specified developmental goals, more satisfied parents would elect the very best clusters. Effective clusters survive as a result of incentive/reward and financial support from the school district based on parental choice.

As goal achievement occurs and students pass through developmental stages, new student goals would become more specific. Learning laboratories would provide specialized expertise in traditional, discipline-oriented, and cross-disciplinary areas. Students' progress in their clusters would earn them the privilege of attending a variety of learning labs. These labs would operate independently of the clusters, but also cooperatively.

It is at this point in the case that we join Karen's group. Each of you have undoubtedly raised questions. Your questions and others outlined below, plus several small vignettes, should inspire further discussion.

■   ■   ■

Questions

1. From a systems perspective, what factors do you believe contributed to the marginal results obtained by the various subgroups within the task force?

2. In the case, identify and discuss instances of an aggregate mentality at work.

3. Would Karen today describe her school or school system as relatively open or relatively closed? Why? Classify the new model as open or closed. Why?

4. Discuss the feedback mechanisms that exist in the new school model.

5. Does the new school model appear to invite chaos or amplify variety? Discuss why.

6. In the case, glimpses of several management philosophies or taxonomies may be apparent to you. Although some tenets within these philosophies may overlap, can you identify and substantiate which actor or group of actors fit the categories below?

Traditionalist View

Human Relations View

Situational View

Systems View

From the case, as proposed by various subgroups, identify the situations that you view as systematic or systemic.

The TQM Model

The Service Management Model

The Back to Basics Model

The New School System

At the same time use some of the following systems properties to defend your viewpoint.

Input-Throughput-Output

Synergy

Leading Part and Emergence

Dynamic Homeostasis

Equifinality

Negentropy

Annotated Bibliography

Bailey, K. D. (1990). *Social entropy theory*. Albany, NY: State University of New York Press.

Social entropy theory as Bailey argues is based on the premise that understanding of society as a whole is the central task of sociology. The author uses systems theory as a means to return to classi-

cal concerns of sociology and criticizes functionalism.

Buckley, W. (Ed.). (1968). *Modern systems research for the behavioral scientist.* Chicago: Aldine Publishing Co.

An overview of General Systems research, discussing fundamental concepts such as parts, wholes, levels of integration, information, communication, and meaning. There is an emphasis on systems organization and logical relations. Entropy, order, and disorder are discussed at length, as are social control and organizational goalseeking. Behavior and meaning are discussed in terms of information theory, cybernetics, and homeostasis. Self-regulation and self-direction are considered in terms of psychological and sociocultural systems. Many of the contributors to this anthology are founders of the General Systems movement.

Hanken, A. F. G., & Rever, H. A. (1981). *Social systems and learning systems.* Boston: Martinus Nijhoff.

This general framework allows a classification of a number of more specific structures, including autocratic and democratic systems, systems with collective and individual decisionmaking, and systems with and without coalitions. In the second part of the book, various psychological schools are cited as specific instances of a departure for a taxonomy of learning systems.

Vickers, G. (1983). *Human systems are different.* London: Harper and Row.

This book applies systems thinking to human history in an effort to understand the present predicament of Britain, and more generally, of other Western industrial countries. It is both a historical and an ethical study. The author stresses the systemic nature of human history and argues that the standards that organize and define human societies develop through a process that is not wholly beyond human understanding or control.

Wilson, B. (1990). *Systems: concepts, methodologies, applications* (2nd ed.). New York: John Wiley & Sons.

This text explains the research that led to the development of the author's systems ideas and comments on the nature of problems in the organizations in which they reside. It also surveys the kind of modeling languages appropriate to various problems and categories in terms of human, management control, and organizational systems, emphasizing problem solving as the basis of discussion.

References

Ackoff, R. L. (1974). *Redesigning the future.* New York: John Wiley & Sons.

Ackoff, R. L. (1976). Towards a system of system concepts. In J. Beishon & G. Peters (Eds.), *Systems behavior.* New York: Harper and Row.

Ackoff, R. L. (1979). The future of operational research is past. *Journal of the Operational Research Society, 30*(2), 189-199.

Argyris, C. (1957). *Personality and organizations.* New York: Harper and Row.

Argyris, C., & Schon, D. A. (1978). *Organizational learning.* Reading, MA: Addison-Wesley.

Ashmos, D. P., & Huber, G. P. (1987). The systems paradigm in organization theory: Correcting the record and suggesting the future. *Academy of Management Review, 12*(4), 607–621.

Banathy, B. H. (1972). A systems analysis of systems education. *Educational technology, 12*(2), 73–75.

Barnard, C. I. (1938). *Functions of an executive.* Cambridge, MA: Harvard University Press.

Bateson, G. (1972). *Steps to an ecology of mind.* New York: Ballantine.

Beer, S. (1974). *Designing freedom.* New York: John Wiley & Sons.

Beer, S. (1990). On suicidal rabbits: A relativity of systems. *Systems Practice, 3*(2), 115-124.

Beishon, J., & Peters, G. (Eds.). (1976). *Systems behavior.* New York: Harper and Row.

Benne, K. D. (1990). *The task of post-contemporary education.* New York: Teachers College Press, Columbia University.

Bertalanffy, L. von. (1968a). *General system theory.* New York: George Braziller Publishing.

Bertalanffy, L. von. (1968b). General system theory—A critical review. In W. Buckley (Ed.), *Modern systems research for the behavioral scientist*. Chicago: Aldine.

Block, P. (1987). *The empowered manager: Positive political skills at work*. San Francisco: Jossey-Bass.

Blumberg, A., & Greenfield, W. (1980). *The effective principal: Perspectives of school leadership*. Boston: Allyn and Bacon.

Boje, D. M., Fedor, D. B., & Rowland, K. M. (1982). Myth-making: A qualitative step in O. D. interventions. *Journal of Applied Behavioral Science, 18*(1), 17-28.

Bolman, L. G., & Deal, T. E. (1991). *Reframing organizations*. San Francisco: Jossey-Bass.

Boulding, K. E. (1964). *The meaning of the 20th century: The great frustration*. New York: Harper and Row.

Boulding, K. E. (1968). General systems theory—The skeleton of science. In W. Buckley (Ed.), *Modern systems research for the behavioral scientist*. Chicago: Aldine.

Bredeson, P. V. (1985, Winter). An analysis of the metaphorical perspectives of school principals. *Educational Administration Quarterly, 21*(1), 29-50.

Brown, A. F. (1967, March). Conflict and stress in administrative relationships. *Administrator's Notebook, 10*.

Carroll, G. R. (Ed.). (1988). *Ecological models of organizations*. Cambridge, MA: Ballinger Publishing.

Checkland, P. B. (1981). *Systems thinking, systems practice*. Chichester, UK: John Wiley & Sons.

Chin, R., Bennis, W. G., & Benne, K. D. (1961). *The planning of change*. New York: Holt, Rinehart and Winston.

Churchman, C. W. (1977). A philosophy for complexity. In H. A. Linstone & W. H. Simmonds (Eds.), *Managing complexity*. Reading, MA: Addison-Wesley.

Churchman, C. W. (1979). *The systems approach*. New York: Dell Publishing.

Clancy, J. J. (1989). *The invisible powers: The language of business*. Lexington, MA: D. C. Heath and Company.

Conway, J. A. (1985, Fall). A perspective on organizational cultures and organizational belief structure. *Educational Administration Quarterly, 21*(4), 7-25.

DeGreene, K. B. (1990). Nonlinear management in technologically induced fields. *Systems Research, 7*(3), 159-168.

DePree, M. (1989). *Leadership is an art*. New York: Doubleday.

Dinsmore, P. C. (1990). *Human factors in project management* (rev. ed.). New York: American Management Association.

Drake, T. L., & Roe, W. H. (1994). *The principalship* (4th ed.). New York: Macmillan.

Emery, F. E. (Ed.). (1970). *Systems thinking*. Middlesex, England: Penguin Books.

Emery, F. E., Trist, E. L., & Rice, A. K. (1963). *The enterprise and its environment*. London: Tavistock Publications.

Engdahl, R. A. (1989, Spring). Thoughts on need for an improved organization theory net with which to "catch the world." *Organization Development Journal, F*(1), 42-50.

Engleberg, J. (1991). On integrative study. *Systems Research, 9*(1), 5-17.

Flood, R. L. (1990). *Liberating systems theory*. New York: Plenum Press.

Frame, J. D. (1987). *Managing projects in organizations*. San Francisco: Jossey-Bass.

Friedlander, F. (1983). Patterns of individual and organizational learning. In S. Srivasta & Associates (Eds.), *The executive mind*. San Francisco: Jossey-Bass.

Getzels, J. W. (1958). Administration as a social process. In Andrew Halpin (Ed.), *Administrative theory in education*. Chicago: Midwest Administration Center, The University of Chicago.

Gleick, J. (1987) *Chaos: Making a new science*. New York: Penguin.

Grenier, L. E. (1972, July-August). Evolution and revolution as organization grows. *Harvard Business Review*, 37–46.

Hall, A. D., & Fagen, R. E. (1968). Definition of system. In W. Buckley (Ed.), *Modern systems research for the behavioral scientist*. Chicago: Aldine.

Harmon, F. G. (1989). *The executive odyssey*. New York: John Wiley & Sons.

Hawes, L. C. (1975). *Pragmatics of analogying: Theory and model construction in communication*. Reading, MA: Addison-Wesley.

Hearn, G. (1958). *Theory building in social work*. Toronto: University of Toronto Press.

Helgesen, S. (1990). *The female advantage: Women's ways of leadership*. New York: Doubleday/Currency.

Herzberg, F., Mausner, B., & Snyderman, B. (1959). *The motivation to work*. New York: John Wiley & Sons.

Hodge, B. J., & Anthony, W. P. (1988). *Organization theory*. Boston: Allyn and Bacon.

Hodge, B. J., & Johnson, H. J. (1988). Management and organizational behavior. In B. J. Hodge & W. P. Anthony, *Organization theory* (3rd ed.). Boston: Allyn and Bacon.

Homans, G. C. (1950). *The human group*. New York: Harcourt Brace & World.

Hoy, W. K., & Ferguson, J. (1985, Spring). A theoretical framework and exploration of organizational effectiveness of schools. *Educational Administration Quarterly, 21*(2), 117-134.

Huse, E., & Bowditch, J. (1973). *Behavior in organization: A system approach to managing*. Reading, MA: Addison-Wesley.

Immegart, G. L., & Pilecki, F. J. (1973). *An introduction to systems for the educational administrator*. Reading, MA: Addison-Wesley.

Jackson, M. C., & Keys, P. (1984). Toward a system of system methodologies. *Journal of the Operational Research Society, 35*, 473-486.

Jaques, E. (1989). *Requisite organization: The CEO's guide to creative structure and leadership*. London: Cason Hall & Company.

Kast, F. E., & Rosenzweig, J. E. (1972). The modern view: A systems approach. In J. Beishon & G. Peters (Eds.), *Systems behavior* (pp. 11–28). New York: Harper and Row.

Katz, D., & Kahn, R. L. (1966). *The social psychology of organizations*. New York: John Wiley & Sons.

Kets de Vries, M. F. R., & Miller, D. (1989). *The neurotic organization*. San Francisco: Jossey-Bass.

Kiechel, W., III. The organization that learns. *Fortune*, (1990, March 12), *121*(6), 133-136.

Kimbrough, R. B., & Nunnery, M. Y. (1988). *Educational administration: An introduction* (3rd ed.). New York: Macmillan.

Kmetz, J. T., & Willower, D. J. (1982). Elementary school principals' work behavior. *Educational Administration Quarterly, 18*(4), 62-78.

Knezevich, S. J. (1975). *Administration of public education*. New York: Harper and Row.

Korzybsk, A. (1933). *Science and sanity*. Lancaster, PA: Science Press.

Kouzes, J. M., & Posner, B. Z. (1987). *The leadership challenge*. San Francisco: Jossey-Bass.

Kuhn, T. S. (1962). *The structure of scientific revolutions*. Chicago: University of Chicago Press.

Lasell, W. (1969). *An examination of the interrelationships of stress, dogmatism, and the performance of a stressful task*. Unpublished Ed.D. dissertation, University of Rochester.

Lewin, K. (1975). Field theory in social sciences. In E. F. Huse, *Organization development and change*. Boston: West Publishing.

Lipham, J. M., & Hoeh, J. A., Jr. (1974). *The principalship: Foundations and functions*. New York: Harper and Row.

Lippitt, G. L. (1982). *Organizational renewal: A holistic approach to organizational development*. Englewood Cliffs, NJ: Prentice-Hall.

Lippitt, R., Watson, J., & Westley, B. (1975). The dynamics of planned change. In E. F. Huse, *Organization development and change*. Boston: West Publishing.

Marney, M. C., & Smith, N. M. (1964). The domain of adaptive systems: A rudimentary taxonomy. *General Systems, 9*, 113.

Martin, W. J., & Willower, D. J. (1981). The managerial behavior of high school principals. *Educational Administration Quarterly, 17*(1), 69-90.

Miklos, E. (1983). Alternative images of the administrator. *The Canadian Administrator, 27*(7).

Miller, J. G. (1955, July). Toward a general theory for the behavioral sciences. *American Psychologist, 10*(3), 529.

Miller, J. G. (1978). *Living systems*. New York: McGraw-Hill.

Mohr, B. J. (1989). Theory, method, and process: Key dynamics in designing high-performing organizations from an open sociotechnical systems perspective. In W. Sikes, A. B. Drexler, & J. Gant (Eds.), *The emerging practice of organization development*. Alexandria, VA: NTL Institute for Applied Behavioral Science.

Monahan, W. (1973). *Introduction to the systems approach*. Englewood Cliffs, NJ: Educational Technology Publications.

Muniz, P., & Chasnoff, R. The cultural awareness hierarchy: A model in OD interventions in cross-cultural settings. In W. Sykes, A. B. Drexler, & J. Gant (Eds.), *The emerging practice of organization development*. Alexandria VA: NTL Institute for Applied Behavioral Science.

Nickols, F. W. (1990, Summer). Human performance technology: The end of an era. *Human Resource Development Quarterly, 1*(2), 187-197.

Ohmae, K. (1990). *The borderless world: Power and strategy in the interlinked economy*. New York: HarperCollins.

Orton, J. D., & Weick, K. E. (1990). Loosely coupled systems: A reconceptualization. *Academy of Management Review, 15*(2), 203–223.

Parsons, T. (1960). *Structure and process in modern societies*. New York: Free Press.

Rapoport, A. (1968). Foreword. In W. Buckley (Ed.), *Modern systems research for the behavioral scientist*. Chicago: Aldine.

Reigeluth, C. (1987). The search for meaningful reform: A third-wave educational system. *Journal of Instructional Management, 10*(4), 3–14.

Robb, F. F. (1990). Morphostasis and morphogenesis: Contexts of design inquiry. *Systems Research, 7*(3), 135-146.

Rokeach, M. (1954). *The open and closed mind*. New York: Basic Books.

Rubin, B. D., & Kim, J. Y. (Eds.). (1972). *General systems theory and human communication*. Rochelle Park, NY: Hayden Books.

Rusche, P. J. (1968). *A study of selected aspects of the communication flow between a school and a community*. Unpublished doctoral dissertation, University of Rochester.

Salisbury, D. F. (1990, February). General systems theory and instructional system design. *Performance and Instruction, 29*(2), 1-10.

Schein, E. (1989, May). Corporate teams and totems. Across the board, *26,* 12-17. (Reprinted from *Sloan Management Review,* Winter, 1989)

Schoderbek, P. P., Schoderbek, C. G., & Kefalas, A. G. (1990). *Management systems: Conceptual considerations*. Boston: BPI/Irwin Publishing.

Selye, H. (1957). *The stress of life*. New York: Longmans Green.

Sergiovanni, J. J., Burlingame, M., Coombs, F. D., & Thurston, P. W. (1980). *Educational governance and administration*. Englewood Cliffs, NJ: Prentice-Hall.

Simon, H. A. (1988). Models of man: Social and rational. In B. J. Hodge & W. P. Anthony, *Organization theory* (3rd ed.). Boston: Allyn and Bacon.

Simon, H. A. (1960). *The new science of management decision*. New York: Harper and Row.

Simon, H. A. (1964). On the concept of organizational goals. *Administrative Science Quarterly, 9*(9).

Simon, H. A. (1970). *The science of the artificial*. Cambridge, MA: MIT Press.

Small, J. F. (1974). Initiating and responding to social change. In J. A. Culbertson, C. Henson, & R. Morrison (Eds.), *Performance objectives for school principals: Concepts and instruments*. Berkeley, CA: McCutchan Publishing.

Steers, R. M. (1977). *Organizational effectiveness: A behavioral view*. Santa Monica, CA: Goodyear.

Toffler, A. (1990, November). Toffler's next shock. *World Monitor, 3*(11), 34-44.

Ulrich, W. (1991). Toward emancipatory systems practice. In R. L. Flood & M. C. Jackson (Eds.), *Creative problem solving: Total systems intervention*. Chichester, England: John Wiley & Sons.

Wayson, W. W. (1971). A new kind of principal. *The National Elementary Principal, 50*(4), 9-19.

Weick, K. C. (1985). "Source of order in underlying organizational systems: Themes in recent organizational theory." In Lincoln, Y. E. (Ed.), *Organizational theory and inquiry: The paradigm revolution*. Beverly Hills: Sage Publishing Co. In Kimbrough, R. B., & Nunnery, M. Y. (1987). *Educational administration: An introduction* (3rd ed.). New York: Macmillan.

Weiner, N. (1968). Cybernetics in history. In W. Buckley (Ed.), *Modern systems research for the behavioral scientist*. Chicago: Aldine.

Weisbord, M. (1987). *Productive workplaces*. San Francisco: Jossey-Bass.

Weisbord, M. R. (1989). Future search: Toward strategic integration. In W. Sikes, A. B. Dresler, & J. Gant (Eds.), *The emerging practice of organization development*. Alexandria, VA: NTL Institute for Applied Behavioral Science.

Willis, V. J. (1977). *Emergent-devolvent synchrony in general systems: Creativity as a special case*. Unpublished doctoral dissertation, State University of New York at Buffalo.

Young, O. R. (1964). A survey of general systems theory. *General systems, 9.*

Yukl, G. A. (1989). *Leadership in organizations* (2nd ed.). Englewood Cliffs, NJ: Prentice-Hall.

Chapter 2
Leadership

In the 1980s, leadership, or the lack of it, became the named excuse for myriad national problems. According to Rost (1991), leadership in the United States was at fault for our decline in the global economy while at the same time being the vehicle needed to restore our lost power and prestige. Bennis and Nanus (1985) asserted that "a chronic crisis of governance—that is, the pervasive incapacity of organizations to cope with the expectations of their constituents—is now an overwhelming factor worldwide" (p. 2). Burns (1978) maintained that "the crisis of leadership today is the mediocrity or irresponsibility of so many men and women in power" (p. 1). Bennis and Nanus claimed that leadership is necessary to develop visions that can move organizations to change from what they are to what they can be. Insightful leadership could help the United States deal with its loss of stature in the world and teach the significance of excellence.

Scholarly attempts to analyze leadership have resulted in many diverse definitions, theories, models, and applications; however, there is no general consensus of what consti-
tutes leadership or effective leadership within organizations. Apparently, most scholars would agree with Burns' (1978) conclusion that "leadership is one of the most observed and least understood phenomena on earth" (p. 2). Rost (1991) contended that a conceptual framework for leadership cannot be constructed until "a clear, concise, easily understandable, researchable, practical, and persuasive definition of leadership" (p. 8) is formulated. However, most definitions and theories of leadership have served the temporal needs of researchers, organizations, and societies.

In terms of academic and practical efficacy, definitions of leadership endure for about twenty years. When research uncovers deficiencies in the theories new perspectives for studying leadership are identified. The complexity of modern organizations, perhaps best microcosmically pictured in the changing socioeconomic configurations of the family, suggests that leadership paradigms may change rapidly as we begin the twenty-first century. This condition raises several questions for students who will assume leadership positions in the future. How will leadership paradigms need to change as leaders and followers are observed in new roles and contexts? An examination of leadership reflects one conclusion—leadership is not definitive but elusive and constantly changing, reflecting an ever-changing society and world. How do present organizational contexts impact on current theories of leadership and/or lead to new conceptual frameworks concerning leadership?

Leadership or Management

This book examines leaders and managers and the problems they face, and, most particularly, leadership and management in education. Educational institutions today are in crisis. But is the offender the individual leader or manager? Too often our principals, superintendents, and teachers are the scapegoats for larger institutional problems. Very often the performance of these individuals is labeled inadequate before there is a thorough review of the educational systems and their subsystems. Educators, however, can only perform within that system, within its processes, activities, and membership.

How does leadership or management occur within this educational environment? Do we have a firm grasp of the meaning of leadership and management? Are leadership and management the same? Can our definitions enhance our understanding of leadership, and, at the same time, remain adaptable in a postindustrial paradigm, in a society where leaders and managers help to remodel or redesign our vital institutions including education?

As the twentieth century closes, we find that leadership and management have been studied extensively. While the study of leader/manager traits and behaviors has pro-

vided greater understanding for practitioners, and while theories and models of leadership and management have enlightened us, there is no scholarly consensus on what distinguishes leadership from management or what defines each. Leadership and management are different. But the reasons for that difference have not been fully investigated, nor have we arrived at plausible interpretations to explain those differences. Could our beliefs simply be founded in our desire to make them different? At best, Yukl (1989) postulated an expanded conceptual framework of leadership that brings together much of the existing knowledge on leadership. But, at the same time, he states, "The terms leader and manager are used interchangeably in this book" (p. 5). Undoubtedly, he might also use leadership and management interchangeably. So what is leadership? Management? Are leaders and managers really different? Do the definitions coincide? Does it matter?

This book and this chapter intend to stir learners' thoughts in introductory/preparatory educational administration programs. Its more specific intent is to broaden the scope of our outlook, create greater understanding, and greater subsequent reflective action. Being aware of issues and problems and devising remedies to understanding effective leadership is no longer enough. As we incorporate technological developments and as complexity multiplies exponentially, the need arises for both systematic and systemic understanding within content areas, and, more importantly, across those same areas. Analysis, synthesis, flexibility, and adaptability must cross a variety of venues before evolving into action. Our beliefs about leadership must evolve *with* societal change as we empower all our teachers and administrators to new action environments.

This chapter examines the following theories and/or major research approaches to leadership: (a) trait studies that attempt to identify personality traits and intelligence of leaders and the identification of relationships of these to specific skills, (b) behavioral studies that explore activity patterns and content to identify behavior patterns, (c) power-influence relationships that investigate how leaders obtain and use power to influence others, (d) contingency/situational studies that explore how varying situations may influence the relationship of leader behavior to leadership effectiveness, (e) transformative/transactional leadership beliefs that develop mutual relationships between leaders and followers, and (f) cultural relationships, leader behavior in relation to building an organization's culture. While many studies narrowly focus on one of the approaches above without examining the possibility of integrating the findings of multiple approaches (Yukl, 1989), our hope is to acquaint the reader with the many dimensions of leadership, and further, to explore each in a more systematic and systemic manner.

LEADERSHIP TRAIT THEORIES

Early studies on leadership were based on the assumption that individuals possessed certain physical characteristics, personality traits, and intellectual abilities that made them natural leaders (Yukl, 1989). Using correlational statistics these studies compared successful leaders with unsuccessful leaders to see if the possession of specified traits might be a prerequisite for effective leadership. On the other hand, organizational theorist Stogdill (Bass, 1981) contended that leadership cannot be explained only in terms of the individual or group but must take into account the interaction of leader traits with situational variables (p. 38). The belief that people possessing leadership traits can be effective regardless of the situation therefore is no longer supportable (Gardner, 1990). Additionally, Smith and Peterson's (1989) review of trait research criticized trait studies that

provide too little uniformity in design. Bennis and Nanus (1985) discounted the Great Man theory of leadership that attributes power to character and limits the number of potential leaders to birthright. Their research also refutes the idea that great events can transform ordinary people into great leaders.

BEHAVIORAL THEORY

Behavior theorists attempt to determine what effective leaders do by identifying both the behavior of leaders and the effects leader behavior has on subordinate productivity and work satisfaction. Studies of leader behavior at the University of Iowa (White & Lippitt, 1990) examined the effect on subordinate attitudes and productivity as leadership style is varied. Leaders were trained to demonstrate three leadership styles—democratic, authoritarian, and laissez-faire. Individual leaders demonstrated behavior attributes consistent with each leadership style. Authoritarian leaders determined all policies and work partners dictated tasks and task procedures in disjointed segments, and gave praise or criticism within a personal context. Democratic leaders utilized group decisionmaking in policy determination, provided discussion of work tasks and alternative procedures for goal achievement, allowed subordinates to choose work partners, and gave objective and guiding suggestions when offering praise and criticism. Laissez-faire leaders gave groups complete freedom to make decisions, provided information only when it was sought, refrained from participating in work tasks, and provided little or no praise, criticism, evaluation, or regulation of work efforts.

White and Lippitt's study (1990) determined that the democratic leadership style was preferred by workers and there was more group-mindedness, friendliness, and efficiency in democratic situations. In sum, workers preferred laissez-faire style over authoritarian style. In other cases, subordinates demonstrated aggressive or apathetic behavior in response to authoritarian leaders. Productivity was also slightly higher with an authoritarian leader than with a democratic leader and subordinates exhibited more dependence and less individuality with authoritarian leaders. Although the Iowa studies were highly criticized, they still are considered a classic research effort on the effects of leadership styles on subordinates' attitudes and productivity (Lunenburg & Ornstein, 1991).

A similar group of leadership studies was done at The Ohio State University identifying two dimensions of leadership: consideration and the ability to initiate structure (Stogdill & Coons, 1957). Consideration was defined as the leader's expression of trust, respect, warmth, support, and concern for subordinates' welfare. Researchers defined the capacity to develop initiating structure as the leader's attention to organizational goals, the organization and assignment of tasks, the delineation of superior-subordinate relationships, and the evaluation of task performance (Lunenburg & Ornstein, 1991). The Ohio State leadership studies formulated a two-dimensional leadership model (see Figure

2.1) identifying four leadership behaviors: low structure, high consideration; high structure, low consideration; low structure, low consideration; and high structure, high consideration. Correlations were established between two items, initiating structures and consideration, and subordinate work satisfaction and performance/productivity as demonstrated by the leaders' behavior. However, causality between leader behavior and subordinate performance could not be substantiated (Yukl, 1989). This behavioral approach to leadership analysis proved that leader behaviors may be quantifiable and observable. The Ohio State studies indicate that subordinate satisfaction and productivity may be improved by leaders who demonstrate high initiating and high consideration behaviors (Lunenburg & Ornstein, 1991).

Leadership studies done at the University of Michigan attempted to identify the relationships between leader behavior, group processes, and group performance. These studies showed three leadership styles: (a) task-oriented behavior similar to initiating structure, (b) relationship-oriented behavior similar to consideration, and (c) participative leadership (Likert, 1961). Preliminary research indicated that productive work

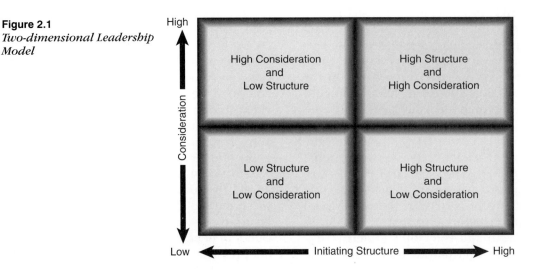

Figure 2.1
Two-dimensional Leadership Model

groups have leaders who are relationship-oriented rather than task-oriented. Inconsistency in research findings, however, later led researchers to conclude that effective leaders are both task- and relationship-oriented. These findings are echoed by Bowers and Seashore (1966) who contended that group effectiveness is determined by the quality of the leadership present in the group rather than task differentiation. The University of Michigan continues to study leader behavior.

Likert's (1961) four leadership styles (see Figure 2.2) are exploitative authoritative, benevolent authoritative, consultative, and participative (democratic). Likert demonstrated that, in situations where leaders used consultative or participative leadership, there was evidence of trust, collaborative goal setting, bottom-up communication, and supportive leader behavior. In organizational situations where exploitative authoritative or benevolent authoritative leadership was utilized, organizations were characterized by threats, fear, punishment, top-down communication, and centralized decisionmaking and control. These characteristics were used to elicit subordinate conformity to organizational goals and productivity standards. Likert also suggested that leaders who utilize participative decision procedures are more effective. Likert's continuum is still referred to frequently by leadership analysts because it provides systematic understanding of concepts that can often be applied to cross-organizational studies.

In an attempt to identify one leadership style that is optimal in all circumstances, various research on theories of universal leadership (Blake & Mouton, 1981; Likert, 1967; Likert, 1961) concluded that effective leaders are supportive and task-oriented. In these cases the value orientation, rather than the behavior pattern of the leader, becomes the salient theoretical concept.

For example, Mazzarella (Mazzarella & Grundy, 1989) made an attempt to integrate leadership trait research with behavior research. Mazzarella contended that leader traits and qualities influence leader behavior. These traits, in turn, enable leaders to interact effectively with their subordinates, peers, and superiors in both human relationships (e.g., the ability to communicate with others) and task-oriented situations (as in their intellectual ability to define and structure tasks). The leader's behavior may be influenced by a group of qualities correlated with effective leadership: inherited traits (IQ, birth order, socioeconomic status), attitudes (social participation, communication skills, and listening skills), characteristic leadership qualities (goal setting, goal clarification, vision, security, proactivity). Although these traits and qualities can be grouped and identified, studies reveal that effective leaders usually do not exhibit all of these traits (Immegart, 1988, 1991). This suggests that leadership as viewed by trait theorists may not have identified the full compliment of traits and further demonstrates the problematic nature of trait theories.

Current research emphasizes a behavioral approach and seeks to identify the behaviors and skills that could be taught to potential leaders. Ensuing research efforts have attempted to identify elements of leadership,

Figure 2.2
Likert's Four Leadership Styles

System 1	System 2	System 3	System 4
Exploitative Authoritative	Benevolent Authoritative	Consultative	Participative (Democratic)

Low ◄─────────────────────────► High
Degree of Trust

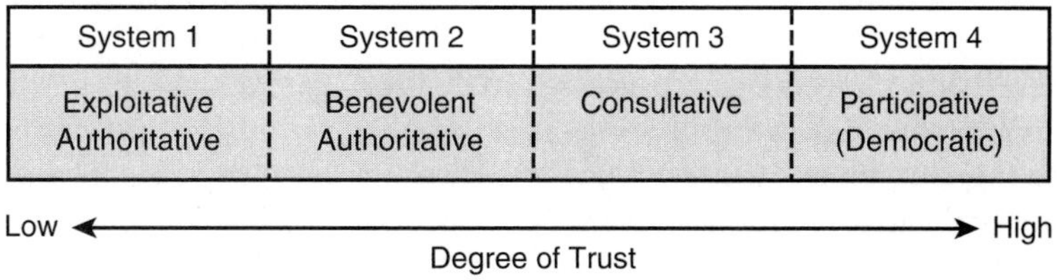

Table 2.1
Five Bases of Power

Bases of Power	Types of Influence
Reward	1. The leader is capable of providing the reward. 2. The follower finds the reward desirable. 3. The follower perceives the leader's offering rewards as legitimate.
Coercive	1. The follower perceives that the leader is capable of administering punishment for nonconformity to influence attempts.
Legitimate	1. It arises from internalized values or norms in the follower that legitimize the leader's right to influence the follower and obligate the follower to accept this influence. 2. It can be derived from cultural values, acceptance of social structure, and designation by a legitimate agent.
Referent	1. The follower perceives the oneness and identification with leader.
Expert	1. The follower believes that the leader has some superior knowledge or expertise in a specific area and that this power is limited to this area of expertise.

based on social and task behaviors, and to rate them on a continuum to determine leadership effectiveness. Behavior research, however, does not take into consideration the situational factors (i.e., task differentiation, group composition, environmental variables) that influence leadership behavior (Lunenburg & Ornstein, 1991). Behavioral variables cannot be treated but must be examined as interrelating factors (Smith & Peterson, 1989). These studies were criticized for their leadership research but later resulted in further efforts to explain leadership from a more systemic view.

POWER-INFLUENCE

Other studies attempt to understand leader behavior from a power-influence perspective. Defining power as "a force that determines behavioral outcomes in an intended direction in a situation involving human interaction,"

Abbott and Caracheo (1988, p. 241) limited their treatment of power to an organizational context and argued that there are only two bases of power—authority and prestige. Power based on authority is derived from the leader's established position within a social institution's hierarchy and is delegated by the institution. Prestige power is based on the leader's possession of natural (honesty) or acquired (expertise) personal characteristics that are valued by others. This power must be earned by the leader through demonstration of these characteristics. The exercise of "institutional power, the potential to elicit intended behaviors from others . . . takes the form of either coercion or persuasion" (Abbott & Caracheo, 1988, p. 243). They argued that reward and coercive power are not the bases of power, as French and Raven (1968) purported, but ways in which power is exercised in an institutional environment based on either authority or prestige or both. Abbott and Caracheo (1988) also stated that legitimate power, derived from followers' conceding legitimacy to those who rule, is based upon authority in institutional environments. They view referent and expert power as two of the elements that may comprise prestige power in an institutional setting.

By redefining reward and coercive power as means of exercising power rather than forms of power, and by maintaining that referent and expert power are elements of prestige power, their studies help us understand that authority is also legitimate power. Abbott and Caracheo (1988) postulated that there are only two bases for power. This is clearly more than a semantic finding since it can result in the closer identification of leadership behaviors (see Table 2.1).

Yukl (1989) defined power as an agent's capacity to influence one or more persons. To "influence" here means to have an effect on the target's attitudes, perceptions, and/or behavior. The power to influence, which can be exerted downward, laterally, or upward, stems from three sources—position, personal, and political (Yukl, 1989) (see Figure 2.3).

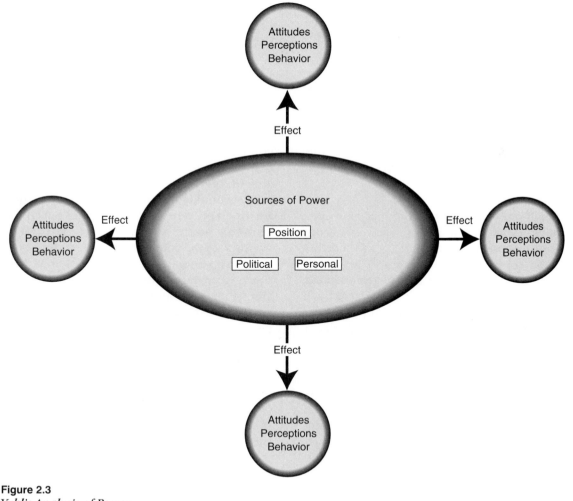

Figure 2.3
Yukl's Analysis of Power

Position (or legitimate) power is derived from the organizational hierarchical structure. In this model followers are motivated to comply with and perceive the legitimacy of the leader (selection process). Followers recognize the leader's scope of authority and control over resources, rewards, punishments, information, the physical environment, and organizational subsystems.

Personal power is categorized as expert, referent, or charismatic power. Expert power depends upon followers' recognizing and requiring the expertise of a leader who possesses rare skills that cannot be easily replicated and who uses logic and evidence to prove his unique abilities. Charismatic power depends on the leader's ability to identify the followers' needs and values and to motivate commitment within followers. Unlike charismatic power that is intense and quickly formed, referent power is developed slowly through symbolic actions that demonstrate the leader's consideration of followers and their reciprocity through task compliance and the formation of similar attitudes toward the organization.

A leader's power base may be increased through political power or the means of controlling decisionmaking processes, coalescing parties to obtain desired results, and increasing the commitment of others to decisions through participation in the decisionmaking process (cooptation).

An alternative way to view power is to define relationships using a power spectrum within which social power is distributed to accomplish a task. From this perspective, Blake and Mouton (1961) identified three areas—competition, collaboration, and powerlessness—and build a power continuum that can be applied to decisionmaking. Competition describes a situation in which each participant attempts to achieve or retain complete decisionmaking ability. Powerlessness describes a situation in which participants have no power to influence others or to

obtain decisions that permit needed actions. Collaboration describes a situation that allows followers varying degrees of power ranging from one with little or no power where the leader has complete power in decisionmaking (1/0 relationship), to one in which the two participants have equal power (.5/.5 relationship), and one in which the subordinate has total power (0/1 relationship). Blake and Mouton concluded that as a power relationship becomes balanced (.5/.5 relationship), work satisfaction and feelings of responsibility become optimal. Thus, mutual sharing of decisionmaking responsibilities may lead to the highest balance of satisfaction and responsibility between superiors and subordinates (see Table 2.2).

The strategic contingencies theory of Hickson, Hinings, Lee, Schneck, and Pennings (1971) proposes that the use of problem-solving skills in critical situations necessitating unique expertise will lead to increased subunit power and authority over strategic decisionmaking. Hickson et al. (1971) asserted that power is contingent upon specific variables (ability to cope with important problems, centrality of function within the organization, and degree to which expertise is unique). As these variables are altered by changes in the internal and/or external environment, once critical subunits may lose power to subunits that have newly acquired ability, responsibility, and power to perform critical functions. However, the theory proposed by Hickson et al. does not explain how organizational subunits no longer in critical positions in some instances do maintain their power (Yukl, 1989). The contingency theory *does* conclude, however, that constant change, growth, and deterioration determines in a near-Darwinian manner the efficacy of certain leadership behaviors.

In another strategic contingency model of power, Salancik and Pfeffer (1977) clarified and proposed that the political power of non-critical subunits is used to protect and main-

Table 2.2
Power-Influence Studies of Leadership

Representatives	Study Concerns		
J. French & B. Raven (1968)	Reward power Coercive power Legitimate power Referent power Expert power		
M. Abbott & F. Caracheo (1988)	Authority power Prestige power		
G. A. Yukl (1989)	Directions	Downward, Lateral, Upward	
	Sources	Position, Personal, Political	
R. Blake & J. Mouton (1961)	Power situations	Competition, Collaboration, Powerless	
E. Hollander (1979)	Power processes	Gain and loss	
D. Hickson, C. Hinings, C. Lee, R. Schneck, & J. Pennings (1971)	Contingent variables	Ability to cope with problems Centrality of function Degree of uniqueness	
G. Salancik & J. Pfeffer (1977)	Utilization	Shared power	
	Variables	Scarcity, Criticality, Uncertainty	
Y. Shetty (1978)	Situational variables	Managerial Subordinate Organizational	
W. Bennis (1986)	Transformative power		
R. House (1984)	Charismatic, Authority, Expertise, Political		
P. B. Smith & M. F. Peterson (1989) J. W. Gardner (1990)	Social and culture-based power		

tain the subunits' position even though their expertise is no longer required. They maintained that power is shared in organizations not because of a belief in organizational development or participatory democracy but because no one person can control all the critical activities (p. 7). Three variables that affect the use of political power are scarcity, criticality, and uncertainty. When resources are scarce or critical to the subunit's survival and when there is disagreement over the organizational goals or methods of achieving objectives, those subunits that are critical to the organization assert power to influence resource allocation and enhance their survival. When critical contingencies change, the power held by individuals and subunits (the bases of power), usually change. However, these individuals and subunits will use their power to influence organizational decisions that ensure their survival. Thus, power becomes institutionalized and protected by the power holder's ability to establish permanent structures and policies that ensure the power holder's position and influence.

Shetty (1978) contended that three situational variables may affect the type of power leaders choose to employ. The variables affecting approaches to power are characteristics of the manager (authoritarian, self-confident, and training); the subordinate's characteristics (professionalism, need, cultural background, and training); and the organizational characteristics (task definition, visibility of task performance, organizational structure, and environmental conditions). These variables determine which characteristics of power may be appropriate in specific situations. Although most managers revert to authority or legitimate power when problems occur, Shetty states that managers might better "broaden their power bases in order to effectively respond to different demands" (p. 185).

According to Bennis (1986), leadership involves managing internal and external relations. As organizations find themselves in an environment where stakeholders, public and organizational, desire a voice in decisionmaking concerning problems that have an impact on diverse, sometimes conflicting, societal groups, decisionmaking becomes more complex and ill-defined. Power is diffused over a broad base creating a new power relationship. Bennis contends that transformative power requires leadership that "knows what it wants, communicates those intentions successfully, empowers others, and knows when and how to stay on course and when to change" (p. 66).

Transformative power is not based on organizational structures or management func-

tions. Its source of power is the leader's ability to raise consciousness, build meanings, and inspire human intent. Vision, purposes, and beliefs embedded in the organization's culture empower participants to excel as meaning is found in routine actions uniting individuals and the organization in a symbiotic relationship (Bennis, 1986, p. 71).

While the above views of power in organizations are instructive, Smith and Peterson (1989) asserted that there is an "implicit assumption that leaders are valued and constructive members of their organizations" (p. 126). They challenged French and Raven's (1968) five bases of power by stating that only one type of power can be operant at one time. Similarly, they criticized House's (1984, 1988) four typologies of power (charismatic, expertise, authority, political) as arbitrary. Smith and Peterson contended that in both classifications of power, some of the bases of power (such as referent, legitimate, expertise) can be exercised only when leaders and followers have a shared perception of the meanings of the actions in which they participate. They stated that a "leader's exercise of power resides in the ability to transmit influence by way of a network of meanings which constitutes the organization's culture" (p. 130), not in qualitative descriptions of power bases.

Power is the "capacity to bring about certain intended consequences in the behaviors of others," Gardner observed in a 1990 study. He proposed that only the power to accomplish specific objectives, and not a generalized power, functions in a pluralistic society such as the United States. Sources of power can be varied widely (property, position, personality, expertise, persuasiveness, motivational abilities). Possession of one source may provide accessibility to other sources. Within human systems (organizations and institutions), organizational power is given to those possessing key positions; these positions constitute the most common source of power in the modern world. Although a belief system firmly embedded in cultures may significantly legitimize leaders and validate their acts, any belief system usually places constraints on those trying to uphold the belief system. Eventually, this diminishes the leader's power.

All of the aforementioned studies of power serve to illustrate important concepts and further our understanding of leadership and leader styles. Leadership style is the pattern of behaviors of a person who assumes or is designated to a position of influence in an organization.

LEADERSHIP STYLES

The ways that leaders perceive workers and interpret their actions affect the leader's behavior toward the workers (Hall, 1990). Establishing relationships with subordinates is a critical factor in their work as leaders. People react to what they think they see in others. The degree of accuracy of perception determines the appropriateness of those actions taken. This is a mutual leader-follower behavior.

McGregor (1990) presented two perspectives that leaders use in dealing with workers, Theory X and Theory Y. Theory X is based on three assumptions: (a) Humans inherently dislike work and try to avoid it. Management must counteract this natural tendency. (b) People must be coerced, controlled, directed, and threatened in order to achieve organizational goals. Rewards will not lead to achievement; only external coercion, control, and threats will. (c) Humans are irresponsible, want to be controlled, are lazy, and are searching for security.

Theory Y is based on quite different assumptions: (a) People voluntarily work when conditions are appropriate. (b) Workers will achieve organizational goals to which they are committed. (c) Commitment to organizational goals is based on the rewards of

goal achievement. (d) Workers will seek responsibility when conditions are appropriate. (e) Many workers possess the ability to solve organizational problems. (f) Human intellectual potential is not fully utilized in organizations.

Theory Y, allegedly founded in human growth, development and selective adaptation rather than direct control, implies that leaders may create constraints that impede workers from achieving their potential in the organizational setting. Thus, Theory Y challenges many of the routine actions and beliefs of leaders that operate from Theory X assumptions.

The central principle of Theory X, the scalar principle, is based on the belief that followers need direction and control through the exercise of authority (McGregor, 1990, p. 21). The integration principle, Theory Y's central principle, is based on the belief that workers can achieve their goals best by working toward organizational success. Some pervasive characteristics of many organizations are so firmly ingrained in Theory X that it is difficult for members to adopt a Theory Y viewpoint. One of these beliefs is that organizational requirements supersede individual needs. The basis of employment contracts is that workers will accept external control in exchange for wages. However, the principle of integration proposes that organizations can be successful only if they adjust to workers' needs and goals. In this way, the needs of both the organization and the individual are recognized.

Although integration means working together for the success of the organization, "management's implicit assumption is that working together means adjusting to the requirements of the organization as management perceives them" (McGregor, 1990, p. 24). Integration, however, requires that individuals be encouraged to develop and utilize their capabilities in ways that lead to the success of the organization and the fulfillment of individual needs. Theory Y is based on the assumption that workers will achieve organizational goals they are committed to through self-control and self-direction. McGregor believes that the degree of commitment is influenced by managerial (leadership) policies. Therefore, integration, not authority, is a viable means for obtaining commitment to organizational objectives. However, he also contends that even in Theory Y organizations external control may be an appropriate leadership strategy when genuine commitment cannot be achieved.

Assumptions have a tendency to limit our views and perceptions rather than widen them. The assumptions that inform Theory X and Theory Y define the way human effort is organized and directed. These theories place limits on the strategies and procedures that leaders choose to direct, plan, control, and organize in the work situation.

A third theory combining elements of Theory X and Theory Y has been developed that advocates claim offers ways to improve relationships between workers and leaders. Ouchi's (1981) Theory Z provides different strategies and perspectives for organizing human effort focusing on consensual decisionmaking and a team approach to organizational processes and change. Unlike Theory X and Theory Y, which define the leadership style of a superior or leader, Theory Z defines the leader's style according to his ability to create an organizational culture where open communication, trust, and commitment to organizational goals is fostered. Consensual decisionmaking "provides for the broad dissemination of information and of values within the organization, and it also serves the symbolic role of signaling in an unmistakable way the cooperative intent of the firm" (p. 66).

Theory Z views the organization as the development of informal relationships between persons. The development emphasizes the individual person over a narrow role

distinction. Theory Z perceptions of organizational members eliminates the dehumanization, authoritarianism, and class distinctiveness found in Theory X and Theory Y organizations that eventually alienate leaders and subordinates. To overcome this alienation, Theory Z advocates maintain that shared goal development undertaken by workers and management can contribute to the development of a consistent organization culture. This process forms a type of insurance for the leader who hopes that his workers' efforts are closely and constantly aligned with organizational goals and objectives.

Long before Ouchi's Theory Z, in 1961, Likert developed four management systems. These four systems resemble some of the conceptual frameworks that have subsequently emerged in Theories X, Y and Z. Likert proposed that his four-system management model of participative management approaches an ideal state. Three key factors of this system were supportive relationships, group decisionmaking, and high managerial performance goals. Likert believes that workers perform best when they function as members of effective work groups, not as individuals. The significance of Likert's system is that it acknowledges the important factor of worker behavior as a leadership goal and as a factor in modifying leadership behaviors.

McGregor's Theories X and Y, Ouchi's Theory Z, and Likert's four management systems illustrate that the perspective, or lens, through which leaders view workers' characteristics and the subjective validity system developed for those characteristics determines what leadership style, strategies, and procedures will be employed. Leaders must be able to evaluate objectively and challenge the approaches that they use to be certain they are viewing their workers through a lens that does not distort their image of workers. Theory Z challenges the traditional assumptions of Theories X and Y and specifically prescribes a new lens through which to view workers as well as leadership structures and policies. Theory Z sees the organization as a living system demanding constant adaptation on the part of the leader. This adaptation may alter organizational goals and climate due to the leader's response to internal and external forces.

CONTINGENCY AND SITUATIONAL THEORIES/MODELS

Contingency theories of leadership effectiveness focus on the leader's immediate work environment. Early contingency models focused on leader emergence by studying how the group's tasks and norms (situation) determine the leadership skills and values that would be effective in the group and acceptable to the subordinates (see Table 2.3).

Fiedler's (1967) research represents the first attempt to study leadership by examining the situation, its people, tasks, and organization. Fiedler (Lunenburg & Ornstein, 1991; Smith & Peterson, 1989; Yukl, 1989; Rost, 1991) hypothesized that leaders can improve

Table 2.3
Contingency and Situational Theories and Models

Theories	Situational Variables	Leadership Styles
Fiedler's Contingency Theory	The quality of leader-subordinates relations The leader's position power The degree of task structure	Task-oriented Relationship-oriented
House's Path-Goal Theory	The subordinates The environment	Directive Supportive Participative Achievement
Hersey and Blanchard's Situational Leadership Theory	Subordinate maturity	Task Relationship
Blake and Mouton's Managerial Grid	All situations	Participative
Kerr and Jamier's Substitute Theory	Substitutes Neutralizers	
Vroom and Yetton's Decision Model	Decision quality importance Leaders' possession of relevant information Degree of structure contained in problem Importance of subordinates' acceptance of the decision Probability that subordinates will accept the leader's decision The importance of shared purpose and goals The amount of conflict among subordinates	Autocratic Consultative Group

their effectiveness by modifying situations to fit their leadership styles. Fiedler identified three situational factors that influence leader effectiveness: (a) the quality of leader-subordinate relations, (b) the leader's position power, and (c) the degree of task structure (Smith & Peterson, 1989, p. 17).

As a result of Fiedler's (1967) work, leadership styles are no longer rated good or bad. Styles are rather defined according to their effectiveness in specific situations. Fiedler's research recognized that leadership results from the interaction between leadership style and situational variables. This view opened the door to subsequent research that describes leadership behaviors holistically.

During the 1970s, leadership theories reflected this more descriptive flair. For example, House's (House, 1971; House & Dessler,

1974) path-goal theory of leadership is based upon the expectancy theory of motivation. House focuses on the leader's ability to analyze the task environment and choose behaviors that maximize subordinates' ability and desire to achieve organizational goals. To accomplish this analysis leaders examine situational variables such as (a) the subordinates (personal qualities and skills, locus of control, and needs and motives), and (b) the environment (work group, authority system, and task structure) and then select one of four leadership styles (directive, supportive, participative, and achievement-oriented) to apply in the specified situation (see Figure 2.4).

This analysis should result in a clear picture or set of premises that a leader may use to initiate and adapt policies and procedures to organizational goals. Various strategies are,

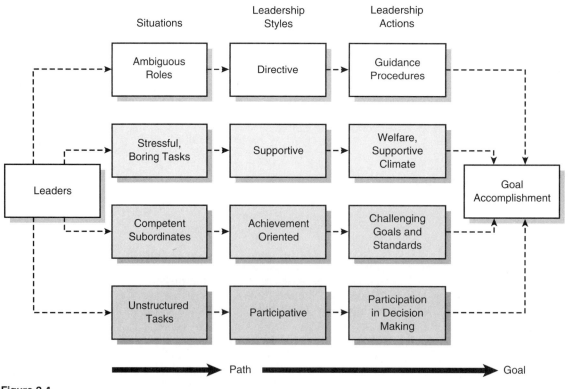

Figure 2.4
House's Path-Goal Theory

therefore, more appropriately selected by a leader hoping to maximize worker commitment. By increasing the probability of goal achievement and attainment of rewards, leaders can influence subordinates' motivation, satisfaction, and goal accomplishment. The subordinate and environment variables determine the type of influence leadership style will have on motivation, satisfaction, and goal accomplishment. The analysis results in a best-fit scenario between the organization's needs and the leader's style.

Directive leadership, by providing guidance, procedures, and coordination, may increase subordinate motivation and satisfaction in situations containing role ambiguity. Supportive leadership, by providing consideration for subordinates' welfare and a supportive work atmosphere, may increase subordinate motivation and satisfaction in situations where tasks are stressful, boring, or tedious. Achievement-oriented leadership may increase goal achievement by setting challenging goals and standards while maintaining the leader's confidence in subordinates' abilities to accomplish the stated goals. Participative leadership, by providing subordinates with the opportunity to participate in decision-making about task-related matters (goals, procedures), may increase subordinate motivation in situations where tasks are unstructured. Overall job satisfaction may also increase if the subordinates desire the opportunity to participate in decisionmaking and planning organizational goals.

Descriptive leadership theories that emerged in the 1980s served to illuminate a range of variables. Hersey and Blanchard's (1982, 1988) situational leadership theory asserted that leader behavior is based upon two dimensions of leadership, task behavior and relationship behavior. These dimensions are influenced by one environmental variable, subordinate maturity (Blanchard, Zigarmi, & Zigarmi, 1987; Rost, 1991; Smith & Peterson, 1989; Yukl, 1989). As subordinates develop

confidence and ability, leaders vary their behavior by adjusting the amount of task direction and psychological support they give them.

Behavior variables in leaders (directive/ supportive) interact with behavior variables in group members (high/low commitment and high/low competence). As the group members pass through different stages of commitment and competence, the leader varies the amount of direction and support given. The leader plays various roles of directing, coaching, supporting, and delegating as the group matures and becomes able to perform group activities. Group maturity is dependent on individual maturity.

Examining the validity of Hersey and Blanchard's (1982, 1988) theory, Hambleton and Gumpert (1982) concluded that there is a definite, significant relationship between leadership style in specific situations and a manager's perceptions of subordinate job performance. Their study also suggests that in situations where situational leadership was applied correctly, subordinate job performance was increased.

Hersey and Blanchard's (1982, 1988) situational leadership theory has not been adequately tested. It contains some broad, ambiguous terms and omits some obvious situational variables. Nevertheless, it does emphasize the effectiveness of a flexible, adaptive leadership style that varies treatment of subordinates according to maturity levels in the same work environment and in varied work situations (Yukl, 1989).

Blake and Mouton (1978, 1981, 1982a, 1982b, 1990) reexamined leadership theory using a two-factor framework, in which concern for production and concern for people are interdependent but uncorrelated (see Figure 2.5). They believe there is one best leadership style. Their managerial grid provides "a schematic behavioral science framework for comparing nine theories of interaction between production and human relation-

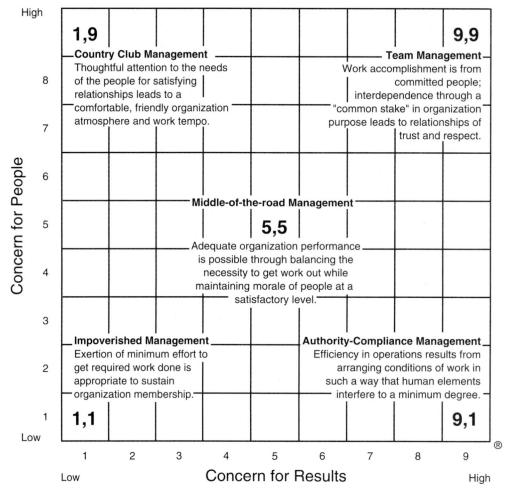

Figure 2.5
The Leadership Grid

SOURCE: The Leadership Grid® Figure for Leadership Dilemmas-Grid Solutions, by Robert R. Blake and Anne Adams McCanse. (Formerly the Managerial Grid figure by Robert R. Blake and Jane S. Mouton) Houston: Gulf Publishing Company, Page 29. Copyright 1991 by Scientific Methods, Inc. Reproduced by Permission of the owners.

ships" (Blake & Mouton, 1978). Each variable is delineated on a nine-point scale where one represents minimum concern and nine represents maximum concern. The model develops five management styles and nine theories of how production and people can be integrated to accomplish organizational goals. Based on the belief that concerns for production and relationship are conflictual,

Blake and Mouton (1978) posit that three theories evolve: (a) task management (9,1) where the focus is on attainment of production goals and where humans are viewed as machines; (b) country club management (1,9) where the focus on relationships dominates to the extent of compromising production goals; and (c) impoverished management (1,1) where the focus is on avoidance of conflicts between production and relationships by ignoring or withdrawing from such situations.

The theories of Blake and Mouton (1978, 1981, 1982a, 1982b, 1990) represent a situational approach toward leadership. Researchers assume that concerns for production and relationship building will conflict and, therefore, must be viewed more systemically or risk being compromised. In practice, the systemic nature of this model is accomplished by alternating styles that focus on each concern (1,9 and 9,1), by providing for both concerns through separate organizational structures (management-production, personnel-relationships), or by perceiving each factor as a separate concern that can be dealt with exclusively. Because production and relationship concerns are evident in all management situations, Blake and Mouton contend that the team management theory is the only style that can effectively integrate both production and relationship concerns. All members of the team plan for production and deal with conflict openly.

Vroom and Yetton's (1973) earlier model examines how the decisionmaking process is affected by the leader, subordinates, and situation to enhance decision quality, decision commitment, and decision satisfaction. The model analyzes decision situations and prescribes feasible decision procedures. Vroom and Yetton evaluate seven questions dealing with power sharing and participation in the decisionmaking process and their impact on the leadership style or amount of participation prescribed for each decision situation.

Using a decision tree, Vroom and Yetton (1973) analyze problems using seven questions to assess the following: (a) decision quality importance, (b) leader's possession of relevant information, (c) degree of structure contained in the problem, (d) importance of subordinates' acceptance of the decision, (e) probability that subordinates will accept the leader's decision, (f) the importance of shared purposes and goals in decisionmaking, and (g) the amount of conflict among subordinates that may result from the decision. After the leader moves through the decision tree and answers the seven questions, he or she can identify either one or several feasible alternative ways of dealing with the problem. These alternatives are classified in five leadership styles: two autocratic, two consultative, and one group.

Although its complexity (five leadership styles and seven environmental contingencies) may require computer assistance for data analysis, Vroom and Yetton's (1973) model does provide information that can lead to precise, reliable, and effective decisionmaking procedures (Smith & Peterson, 1989). Further studies of Vroom and Yetton's model have substantiated its validity and reliability. Its focus on specific behaviors and meaningful intervening variables lends credence to its use as a situational leadership model.

However, Vroom and Yetton's narrow focus on only one situational leadership behavior, decisionmaking, and their assumption that leaders possess the necessary skills and ability to use this skill and diagnose situations weakens the model. As a theory-to-practice model, the Vroom-Yetton (1973) model also has some deficiencies. The model indicates only what a leader should not do instead of what a leader should do, it gives no guidance for choosing alternatives when the process results in multiple alternatives, and it assumes that all seven factors can be delineated by clear "yes" or "no" responses. The model also fails to address such situational variables as the amount of information needed by subordinates in decisionmaking, time constraints for reaching decisions, and the ability of all necessary participants to be physically present at decision time. Like many models for leadership, the strengths and weaknesses of the Vroom-Yetton model illustrate the complexity of modern organizations and the consequent intensified complexity of the leadership role.

Vroom and Jago (1988) revised the Vroom-Yetton model to address its deficiencies. In addition to the original five decision processes for group problems, two new processes (one group and one delegative) were added to address individual problems of decisionmaking. To evaluate problems and decision processes according to decision quality, decision commitment, time, and subordinate development, equations were developed to determine decision effectiveness. These equations also accounted for the trade-offs incurred when the size of a decisionmaking group varied. Because of the use of mathematical equations and the employment of computers, the Vroom-Jago model is capable of weighing answers to the situational factors (that now include time, geographical, and motivational constraints—expanded from seven to twelve) along a five-point continuum instead of using simple "yes" and "no" answers. The new model's use of continuous rather than dichotomous responses, the use of mathematical functions, and expanded situational factor consideration, may result in greater validity of the decision-process decisions reached with the model's use. However, until the Vroom-Jago model is adequately tested, its validity is tenuous.

SITUATIONAL DETERMINANTS THEORIES/MODELS

Situational determinants theory defines leader behavior as determined by situational characteristics (role expectation, group mission and tasks, and flexible role definition) and leader traits and qualities. Leaders' personalities and values may bias their perceptions of their roles, causing role conflict. The theory suggests that leaders' expectations of behavioral outcomes influence their behavior choice (Nebecker & Mitchell, 1974). Osborn

and Hunt's (1975) multiple influence model attempts to explain the complex interactions of macrovariables, namely, organization structure and external environment, and microvariables, namely, task characteristics, and subordinate characteristics and the influence of each in determining leader behavior. The simultaneous interrelationship of multiple variables in leadership and management situations provides a picture of the complexity of the situation. Often variables cannot be separated into categories of dependent or independent variables that might be validated for causality and/or correlations.

The study of leadership remains complex as seemingly different situations tax theorists' analysis capabilities. Leadership theorists have attempted to integrate theories for many decades under the crush of increasingly complex situations for analysis. Koestenbaum's (1991) leadership model is one attempt to integrate leadership research strategies—traits, behaviors, contingencies, and situational determinants—into one model. The theory looks beyond the individual or traits and immediate work environment or behavior and contingency and examines the interactions of leader traits and behavior with the macro internal and external environment. Leadership is viewed as a mindset and a pattern of behaviors. Koestenbaum contends that leadership can be learned and taught; therefore, leaders should empower and support subordinates to develop their own leadership potential. He also believes that a majority of a leader's time and energy should be used to facilitate skill development in frontline people in the complex organizational system and in interactions with the external environment. Koestenbaum equates leadership with greatness, however, perpetuating the mistaken belief that leaders are superhuman. Effective leaders are people who understand their roles in organizations, can analyze and diagnose task- and human-oriented variables in the environment, can prescribe actions, and can provide vision for goal achievement. Koestenbaum's theory suggests a born-again leader orientation that emphasizes an individual's emotional appeal as a qualification for leadership.

TRANSFORMATIONAL/TRANSACTIONAL LEADERSHIP

Burns (1978) examined leadership in a political context by studying distinctions among power, leadership, transactional leadership, and transformative leadership. Burns believed

that "power over other persons is exercised when potential power wielders, motivated to achieve certain goals of their own, marshal in their power base resources (economic, military, institutional, or skill) that enable them to influence the behavior of respondents by activating motives of respondents relevant to those resources and to those goals" (p. 18). The purpose of such a power wielder is to achieve goals whether or not the followers share in those goals. However, Burns defines leadership as "the reciprocal process of mobilizing, by persons with certain motives and

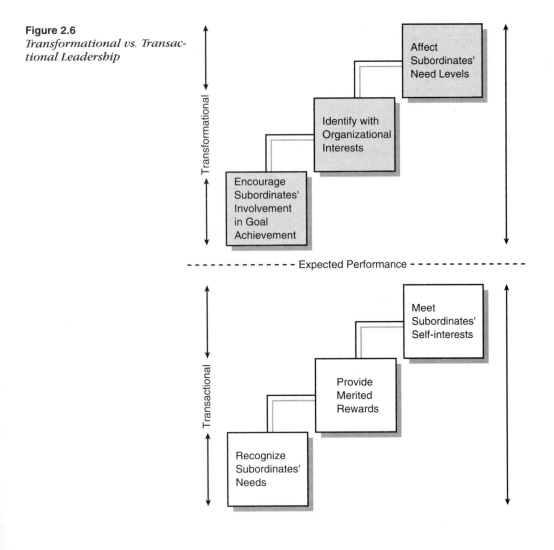

Figure 2.6
Transformational vs. Transactional Leadership

Transformational

Affect Subordinates' Need Levels

Identify with Organizational Interests

Encourage Subordinates' Involvement in Goal Achievement

- - - - - - - - - - - Expected Performance - - - - - - - - - - -

Transactional

Meet Subordinates' Self-interests

Provide Merited Rewards

Recognize Subordinates' Needs

values, various economic, political, and other resources, in a context of competition or conflict, in order to realize goals independently or mutually held by both leaders and followers" (p. 425) (see Figure 2.6).

Burns (1978) further differentiated between transactional and transformative leadership. He argued that in transactional leadership, persons engage in a relationship for the purpose of exchanging valued things. They are conscious of each other's power, usually pursue their own purposes and goals, and form temporary relationships. In transformative leadership, "one or more persons engage with others in such a way that leaders and followers raise one another to higher levels of motivation and morality" (p. 20). In such a relationship purposes are fused, power bases are linked, and leadership becomes moral as leaders and followers unite to achieve higher goals. Burns bases his general theory of leadership on a hierarchy of human needs, structure of values, and stages of moral development (p. 428). The role of the leader is to help followers transcend the levels of need and stages of moral development to achieve mutually held higher purposes.

Burns (1978) further contended that "political leadership, however, can be defined only in terms of purposeful, substantive change in the conditions of people's lives. The ultimate test of practical leadership is the realization of intended, real change that meets people's needs" (p. 461). For Burns, the test of a leader is the ability to achieve significant change that represents the mutual interests of followers and leaders. Burns believes that transformative leadership, with its ability to raise people to higher moral purposes, is the basis for a general theory of leadership that may be applied in all contexts, not just a political context.

As a criticism of Burns' (1978) unilateral leadership theory, Bass (1985) stated that "the

first order of change—changes of degree—can be handled adequately by the current emphasis on leadership as an exchange process, a transactional relationship in which followers' needs can be met if their performance measures up to their contracts with their leader" (p. 4). Bass further stated that second order changes require a change in individual attitudes, beliefs, and values, and a different paradigm for leadership—transformational leadership.

Based upon Maslow's hierarchy of needs, Burns' (1978) interpretation of transformative leadership proposes that by raising followers' maturity level of needs (concerns for recognition, achievement, and self-actualization), leaders are able to improve goal achievement. Unlike Burns' theory of transformative leadership, which is based upon Maslow's higher level needs of satisfaction and is presented in a political context, Bass (1985) differentiated between transactional and transformational leadership within an organizational context. For Bass, transactional leadership involves three key elements: (a) recognizing what subordinates seek from work and attempting to provide the rewards sought, (b) providing those rewards when merited, and (c) responding to subordinates' self-interests when they have a positive impact on organizational goal achievement (p. 11). Transactional leadership results in motivating subordinates to attain the desired performance outcomes of the organization.

Transactional leadership seeks to motivate subordinates to perform beyond the expectations of the organization, thus causing an observable change in subordinates' behavior. The exercise of transformational leadership might be accomplished through any of the following methods: (a) raising subordinates' awareness of the importance and value of achieving specified outcomes and the means of goal achievement; (b) persuading subordinates to replace self-interest with team or organizational interests; or (c) altering subordinates' need levels (Maslow) or broadening subordinates' needs and wants (Bass, 1985, p. 20).

Bass's (1985) conceptualization of leadership differs from Burns' (1978) in three areas: (a) Bass includes both the idea of expanding subordinates' array of needs and wants in addition to Burns' emphasis of raising subordinates' need levels; (b) Bass eliminates the moral implication of transformational leadership that Burns believes is a requirement (Burns considers all transformative leaders to be good, not evil); (c) although Burns views transactional and transformative leadership as opposite ends of a continuum, Bass argues that leaders exhibit both types of leadership depending upon the situation.

Bass (1985) contended that transactional leaders work within the organizational culture, the shared values and meanings of organizational members, whereas transformational leaders work to change subordinates' values and beliefs in order to change the organizational culture (p. 24). Thus, for Bass "the transactional leader induces performance among followers by negotiating an exchange relationship with them of reward for compliance. Transformational leadership arouses transcendental interests in followers and/or elevates their need and aspiration levels" (p. 32).

Bennis and Nanus (1985) argued that transformative leadership is the ability of leaders to shape and elevate followers' motives and goals to achieve significant change through common interests and collective energies (p. 217). Leaders define a vision that is congruent with followers' key values and construct a social architecture, or an organizational culture, that provides shared meanings where followers can pursue tasks and strive for success. To accomplish this, leaders must be able to create a vision, communicate the vision through symbolic actions and shared meanings, exercise integrity through persistent pursuit of that vision, recognize their own strengths and weaknesses, evaluate ability in relation to job requirements, and focus on positive goals.

A key ingredient of transformative leadership for Bennis and Nanus (1985) is empowerment. Empowerment is the ability of leaders through an active and creative exchange of power to encourage followers to achieve a vision and realize goals. Leaders empower followers by bringing significance, competence, community, and enjoyment to leader-follower work relationships where extraordinary efforts are perceived as the means to realizing vision and achieving goals. Bennis and Nanus focus their interpretation of transformational leadership on the behavior and skills of the leader. Although a key point of Burns' (1978) definition of transformation refers to the ability of leaders and followers to raise each other to higher levels of motivation and morality, Bennis and Nanus's beliefs appear unidirectional with no reference to the moral implications of the participants' motives and actions.

LEADERSHIP WITHIN A CULTURE CONTEXT

As shown by the previous discussion, theories about leadership are multidimensional. No one theory has embraced all the necessary variables to satisfactorily define the complexity of the leadership role or to predict best-case leadership scenarios. Some researchers suggest a total reconceptualization of the leadership problem/phenomenon. Among these are Sergiovanni and Corbally (1986) who argued that to change we must move "from a conception of leadership where effectiveness is defined as accomplishing objectives to one of building identity, increasing understanding, and making the work of others more meaningful" (p. 14).

Sergiovanni (1986) defined quality leadership as a balance between tactical leadership (achieving objectives effectively and efficiently) and strategic leadership (obtaining support for policies and purposes and devising long-range plans). Tactical leadership, in which evaluation is quick and success is based on short-term accomplishments, has been the focus of Western societies. Sergiovanni contended that in a cultural perspective of leadership "cultural aspects of organization are being offered as better able to account for the artificial purposive, and practical aspects of organizational life" (p. 106). Organizations are viewed not as systems but as cultural entities, where meanings derived from actions are more important than the specific actions. "Leadership as cultural expression seeks to build unity and order within an organization by giving attention to purposes, historical and philosophical tradition, and ideals and norms which define the way of life within the organization and which provide the bases for socializing members and obtaining their compliance" (p. 107). Sergiovanni's discussion of Western philosophy highlights the hollowness of some Western theories directed toward assessing effective leadership solely by a measurement of productivity. The inability of theorists to integrate the concerns of culture and productivity surfaces here philosophically just as it surfaces in Theory X and Theory Y practices discussed earlier in this chapter.

As discussed by Sergiovanni (1986), leadership as cultural expression relies on the analysis of the complex interplay of tactical leadership skills (management skills) and strategic antecedents and meanings within a framework of ten principles that form a cognitive map for quality leadership. To achieve leadership excellence, antecedents and meanings are needed to provide a basis for and direction to leadership skills. Antecedents are defined as perspective, principle, platform (operational framework), and politics (influence others to achieve desired goal) required

to guide the leader's decisions, actions, and behavior. Meaning develops in a belief system through purposive reflection (giving meaning to ordinary activities), planning (articulating purpose), persisting (creating climate through attention to issues, goals, or outcomes), and matching people to organizational goals and objectives. From the interaction of these components, Sergiovanni writes that a culture emerges that defines what is important and governs behavior. Organizational patriotism, commitment, and loyalty to a shared set of common beliefs and governing behavior create a strong bond among organizational members and give the organization unique meaning. These actions require leadership behavior (see Figure 2.7).

Sergiovanni's (1986) model appears to represent his interpretation of Burns' (1978) transactional and transformational leadership in one model where quality leadership is achieved by the leader's ability to move beyond the tactical skills component (transactional leadership) to the integration of antecedents and meanings (transformational leadership) achieving a quality leadership model. The leader here oscillates between the roles of transactional and transformational leader as the situation changes. In this respect, Sergiovanni's perception of leadership is closer to that of Bass rather than Burns.

Smith and Peterson (1989) contended that leadership as an aspect of organizational behavior can be best studied in a social context, not as an influence relationship within the leader-follower dyad. From a global perspective, organizational leadership is seen as comprising two aspects—task and relationship—within a team structure. Assignment of meanings to leadership acts derives from the cultural context of the group or organization. In assimilated cultures, attribution of meaning may be more consensually shared than in western individualistic, pluralistic societies. Rather than searching for one best type of

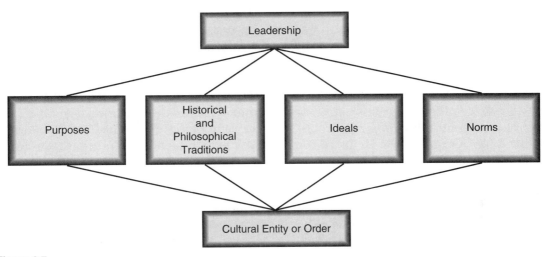

Figure 2.7
Leadership as Cultural Expression

leadership, this theory implies that there may be one best organizational culture that can be created through a hierarchical structure. The hierarchy can develop shared meanings for organizational activities and events and, thus, foster shared visions and strategies for achieving organizational goals, a cultural form of control. Smith and Peterson state "a leader's exercise of power resides in the ability to transmit influence by way of the network of meanings which constitute the organization's culture. . . . Such meanings are deeply rooted and amenable only to gradual change" (p. 130). However, within a participative management structure, group members must be able to define participatory mechanisms and purposes through a cultural context. The leader here is a network monitor, creator and nurturer.

Schein (1985) said that creating, managing, and sometimes restructuring organizational culture may be one of the most decisive functions of leadership (p. 2). Viewing culture as the element that most strongly affects how members of human systems think, feel, and act, Schein refuted the assumption of some leadership theorists that culture can be

changed to suit one's purposes. Schein (1985) defined culture as "a pattern of basic assumptions—invented, discovered, or developed by a given group as it learns to cope with its problems of external adaptation and internal integration—that has worked well enough to be considered valid, and therefore, to be taught to new members as the correct way to perceive, think, and feel in relation to those problems" (p. 8).

Because environmental conditions are constantly changing, leadership must be able to manipulate the organizational culture to ensure the system's ability to adapt to and survive in the environment through the evolution of new cultural assumptions. Leadership in practice verbalizes its assumptions and "embeds them gradually and consistently in the mission, goals, structures, and working procedures of the group" (Schein, 1985, p. 317). Leaders need to know how an organization's culture can help or hinder a mission's accomplishment. Leaders need to provide the impetus to implement the intervention strategies necessary to adapt the culture for organizational survival. Although leaders are responsible for replacing or redefining discarded assumptions, organizational members should be involved in the change process to ensure their renewed insight and motivation to achieve the new organizational mission.

Each of the above theories sheds some light on the patterns in leadership research since World War II. The uniqueness and complexity of mid-twentieth century organizations has both increased the demand for effective theories and confounded the researchers working at developing those theories. Recently, researchers have quietly begun to abandon tenets of organizational thought which suggest that leadership may be analyzed or predicted in a linear fashion. New theories are emerging that may shape a new paradigm for thinking about leadership as we move into the twenty-first century.

Women in Authority

Additional differences in leadership and management styles can be discerned when reviewing the literature on women in positions of authority. While currently there are relatively few women in top leadership positions, those numbers have increased to the point that it is possible to detect some distinctive ways that men and women differ in leadership roles.

Fitzpatrick (1983) described a competent communicator as one who can accurately perceive the environment and create and understand messages based on subsequent interpretation. His goals for communication are: (1) getting the job done, (2) avoiding damage to the relationship between sender and receiver of the message, and (3) projecting the desired image while communicating. According to Fitzpatrick, males generally operate from a problem solving, aggressive, and focused routine and suppress strong emotion. On the other hand, females tend to give and expect to receive rewarding responses and are inclined to emphasize relational goals in interactions.

From this base comparison, Fitzpatrick (1983) conceptualized three models of organizational communicators. The first, or "masculine" model, focuses on task goals and impression management to the exclusion of relational goals. The second, or "feminine," model, emphasizes relational goals to the exclusion of task goals. The third, or androgynous model, blends the previous two styles. Androgynous communicators can be assertive and dominant as is typical of task behaviors, or they can be warm and nurturing, reflecting relational behaviors.

While Gabler (1987) argued that successful women do not necessarily lead differently than successful men, others such as Carroll (1989) have found that women have a more sharing style of leadership than men, and claim that women tend to give more recognition and create an "empowering" team atmosphere. In replicating a study by men in leadership roles (Mintzberg, 1973), Helgeson (1990) found distinct differences in leadership style. The women in her study worked at the same pace and under similar conditions as the men in Mintzberg's study, but they were less likely to feel controlled by the work schedule, thereby reducing job stress. More time was spent with people, and there was emphasis on sustaining good working relationships. By maintaining a more complex network of relationships both on and off the job, the women were less likely to feel isolated. In Helgeson's view, female leaders were more likely to feel themselves at the center of things instead of viewing themselves "at the top," as the men in the study did.

In another context, decisionmaking for men and women also shows distinctiveness. Putnam (1983) identified differences in ways that the two groups deal with conflict. Males are apt to arrive at a settlement using bargaining techniques, logical arguments, and anger in an effort to resolve the conflict. Women tend to work to understand others' feelings, handling conflict by smoothing over and playing down differences and emphasizing similarities. The male focus on independence, competitiveness, and autonomy often creates a win/lose scenario, where the female focus on interdependence produces a win/win scenario where possible.

Shakeshaft (1987) argued that research finding no distinctions between men and women in managing schools is faulty in that it is conceptually based on the white male model. Under these circumstances, successful women match successful men. However, when the additional motives and approaches of women are factored in, they can be seen to perform not only as well, but differently. She argues that the work of female leaders in schools has five major elements: (1) relationships with others are central to all actions of women administrators, (2) teaching and learning are the major foci of women administrators, (3) building community is an essential part of the female administrator's style, (4) women administrators are constantly made aware of their marginality or status, and (5) the line separating the public and private lives of women administrators is blurred far more than for men.

A New Paradigm for Leadership

In criticizing previous leadership studies' emphasis on peripheral aspects (personality, trait, goal attainment) and content (knowledge-possessed leader), Rost (1991) contended that these studies do not address the essential nature of leadership and the process by which leaders and followers relate to each other to achieve purposes. He believed that leadership has not been defined "with precision, accuracy, and conciseness so that people can label it correctly when they see it happening or when they engage in it" (p. 6). He further proposed that most theories of leadership reflect an industrial paradigm that is no longer acceptable or applicable to leadership needs for the twenty-first century. According

to Rost, a paradigm shift is necessary so that leadership theory and practice can relate to the needs of a postindustrial world.

Leadership as defined by Rost (1991) is "an influence relationship among leaders and followers who intend real changes that reflect their mutual purposes" (p. 102). This is in contrast to management, which he defined as an authority relationship. He maintained that four elements must be present for a relationship to be considered a leadership relationship: (a) a relationship based on influence; (b) leaders and followers who are participants in the relationship; (c) both parties intending that real changes are to take place; and (d) both parties developing mutual purposes. Rost reinterprets transformation as the involvement of "active people, engaging in influence relationships based on persuasion, intending real changes to happen, and insisting that those changes reflect their mutual purposes" (p. 213). Therefore, leadership is seen as a relationship involving multiple followers and multiple leaders who engage in shared or collaborative leadership. The roles of leaders and followers are not etched in stone but can shift.

Management for Rost (1991), in contrast, is an authority relationship between at least one manager and one subordinate who coordinate their activities to produce and sell particular goods and/or services. In addition, Zaleznik (1977) argued that there are distinct differences between the potential manager personality and the potential leader personality. Managers tend toward rationality and control. They adopt impersonal attitudes toward goals. They view work as an enabling process and strive to coordinate and balance the diverse interests of many so that a compromise allowing for problem solving can be developed. They tend to take low-risk positions, seeing themselves as effective when they have been able to perpetuate and strengthen existing institutions.

Leaders, on the other hand, are able to look beyond the rational and controlled perspective to draw on a vision of what the organization can be and should be. They are active instead of reactive, shaping new ideas instead of responding to the ideas of others. They take active personal possession of goals and objectives. Instead of controlling options to develop consensus as managers do, they seek new approaches and expand options as a technique for problem solving. They take high-risk positions.

Leaders are often talented persons who become highly involved in their own internal development, more so than those persons who develop into managers, and possess attitudes that lead to self-reliance and expectations of high achievement. Potential managers form moderate and widely distributed attachments. Potential leaders, on the other hand, establish and break off intensive one-to-one relationships.

Considering these differences between manager and leader, Zaleznik (1977) argued that the key to developing leaders rather than managers is the focus on the impact of one-on-one mentoring relationships. Whether it be formalized in an internship or apprentice relationship or in the informal links between a talented young person and a nurturing supervisor, he believes this approach stands the best chance of drawing out the leadership qualities of a person with that potential.

This chapter presented a brief compilation of the important leadership research that has been accomplished to date. It attempts to build a framework that can serve as a guide to further reflection about educational and organizational leadership in the future. It is also evident that leadership research has not stood the tests of time well. Numerous authors have commented about leadership theory deficiencies. Theory ought to inform practice and as will be evident throughout the remainder of this book. While progress is always evident, too little of value has occurred in leadership arenas. We sorely need combinations across disciplines and dimensions of intellectual

thought before we can begin to be comfortable with leadership today.

CASE STUDY

Leadership: The Case of the Invisible Principal

John Alvarez was a superior teacher who was known throughout the school district for his intellectual ability, stimulating classes, popularity with students, colleagues, and administrators, and problem-solving techniques. No one was surprised when John was appointed principal of one of the district's secondary schools. What was astounding were the complaints coming from the chairpeople, faculty, building personnel, and students that nothing was really being accomplished. Department chairs were particularly vocal about John's insistence on knowing every detail of their decisions before permitting them to move forward. They also complained about their inability to arrange meetings with John and his lack of communication. Days would pass without any word from him about decisions. Teachers, building personnel, and students also found it difficult to arrange for personal communication with their principal.

While acknowledging John's superior teaching ability, successful student management, and creative problem solving, several of the department chairs, faculty, and building personnel questioned whether John would ever be a leader or even would understand the difference between classroom responsibilities and those of leadership. John responded that his classroom abilities were the type of leadership that the school needed. He believed that if intelligent people were doing their jobs they did not need close personal contacts with their leaders. John viewed leadership as an extension of his classroom abilities and was amazed that some of his faculty, building personnel, and students were doubtful of his contribution. He could hardly believe that they labeled him their "Invisible Leader."

■　　■　　■

Questions

1. Is John's perception about leadership appropriate?

2. Are classroom academics and successful student management evidence of the type of leadership that a school principal really needs to provide?

3. Is it possible that both John and the faculty, building personnel, and students are right?

4. How can we define leadership responsibility particular to this situation?

5. Can the definitions that we develop be universally applied? Why or why not?

Annotated Bibliography

Bennis, W. (1993). *An invented life: Reflections on leadership and change.* Reading, MA: Addison-Wesley.

Most of the essays in this book deal with facilitating leadership and managing change. However, a significant minority deal with the ethics of organizational life. The author says that effective leadership is not enough as it is essential that leadership in corporate and public life remember their societal obligations as well as their organizational ones. Every organization tempts its leaders to become preoccupied with the priorities of the moment at the cost of ignoring the far-reaching questions that determine the quality of our lives. This book looks at some of the ethical dilemmas inherent in modern organizational life.

Greene, M. F. (1988). *Leaders for a new era: Strategies for higher education.* New York: Macmillan.

Conventional wisdom on the nature of leadership in higher education is challenged in this collection of 12 essays. They are divided into three sections: (1) The Context, (2) New Leaders and New Models, and (3) Strategies and Resources. Chapters highlighted are: "Leaders and Their Development," "Toward a New Leadership Model," "Department Chairs: Leadership in the Trenches," "In Support of Faculty Leadership: An Administrator's Perspective," and "Developing Faculty Leadership: A Faculty Perspective." Each chapter contains references. An action agenda is presented in the concluding chapter.

Haas, H. (1991). *The leader within: An empowering path of self-discovery.* New York: HarperCollins.

This book is a look at how today's tough-minded executives operate in the new corporate world they are helping to shape. Simplicity and speed are vital elements in keeping modern corporations keenly competitive, and this book contains the reflections and experiences shared by the CEOs of some of the most respected companies in the United States. At the essence of this text are ideas and thoughts distilled from exclusive interviews conducted over the past three years with more than 150 of the nation's top business leaders. The author is both a teacher and a practitioner, and has crafted his book as a personal odyssey, inviting insight, focusing on creativity, risk taking, and flexibility.

Hodgkinson, C. (1991). *Educational leadership: The moral art.* Albany, NY: State University of New York Press.

This book is about values and the art of administration. It is also about philosophy, human nature, and the quality of life in organizations—especially educational organizations. The reader is introduced to a paradigmatic theory of values, which has been developed over the last twenty years and is sufficiently established in the literature to constitute a robust model that can be used for analytical purposes in the daily life of administration. The book proceeds through three parts (education, leadership, morality) which, though logically contingent on each other, call for different treatments both conceptually and linguistically.

Hunt, J. G. (1991). *Leadership: A new synthesis.* Newbury Park, CA: Sage Publications.

The author advocates a pragmatic perspective concerning leadership knowledge orientation and argues that without such pragmatism we can't fully realize the potential of the multilevel model. The focus of the book is an emphasis on a new synthesis and an expanded view of leadership based on an open-minded approach to leadership knowledge content and leadership knowledge orientation. This work is largely consistent with conceptual and empirical work done by the author over many years, which is intended to broaden the knowledge orientation of how the reader understands and explores the reality we call leadership.

Sergiovanni, T. J. (1992). *Moral leadership: Getting to the heart of school improvement.* San Francisco: Jossey-Bass.

In this book, the author seeks to build a theory of school leadership practice based on moral authority, but to establish such practice requires the value structure of an authority basis for school leadership to be expanded. He critiques traditional views of leadership and discusses the reasons why they have not worked well in the past; examines what motivates and inspires teachers and principals to work in extraordinary ways; discusses substitutes for leadership; and discusses the importance of collegiality in building a morally responsive school community.

References

Abbott, M., & Caracheo, F. (1988). Power, authority and bureaucracy. In N. J. Boyan (Ed.), *Handbook of research on educational administration* (pp. 239–257). New York: Longman.

Argyris, C. (1957). *Personality and organization.* New York: Harper and Row.

Argyris, C. (1964). *Integrating the individual and the organization.* New York: John Wiley & Sons.

Bass, B. M. (Ed.). (1981). *Stogdill's handbook of leadership.* New York: The Free Press.

Bass, B. M. (1985). *Leadership and performance beyond expectations.* New York: The Free Press.

Bennis, W. (1986). Transformative power and leadership. In T. J. Sergiovanni & J. E. Corbally (Eds.), *Leadership and organizational culture* (pp. 64–71). Urbana, IL: University of Illinois Press.

Bennis W., & Nanus, B. (1985). *Leaders: The strategies for taking charge.* New York: Harper and Row.

Blake, R. R., & Mouton, J. S. (1961). How power affects human behavior. In J. Hall (Ed.), *Models for management: The structure of competence* (2nd ed.) (pp. 113–120). The Woodlands, TX: Woodstead Press.

Blake, R. R., & Mouton, J. S. (1978). *The new managerial grid.* Houston: Gulf Publishing.

Blake, R. R., & Mouton, J. S. (1981). Management by grid principles or situationalism: Which? *Group & Organization Studies,* 6(4), 439–455.

Blake, R. R., & Mouton, J. S. (1982a). How to choose a leadership style. *Training and Development Journal, 36,* 38–47.

Blake, R. R., & Mouton, J. S. (1982b). Theory and research for developing a science of leadership. *The Journal of Applied Behavioral Science, 18*(3), 275–291.

Blake, R. R., & Mouton, J. S. (1990). The developing revolution in management practices. In J. Hall (Ed.), *Models for management: The structure of competence* (2nd ed.) (pp. 422–444). The Woodlands, TX: Woodstead Press.

Blanchard, K., Zigarmi, D., & Zigarmi, P. (1987). Situational leadership: Different strokes for different folks. *Principal, 66,* 12–16.

Bowers, D., & Seashore, S. (1966). Predicting organizational effectiveness with a four-factor theory of leadership. *Administrative Science Quarterly, 11,* 238–263.

Burns, J. M. (1978). *Leadership.* New York: Harper and Row.

Carroll, S. (1989, February). Cited in strategies for women in academe. *Academic Leadership, 5*(2).

Fiedler, F. E. (1967). *A theory of leadership effectiveness.* New York: McGraw-Hill.

Fitzpatrick, M. A. (1983). Effective interpersonal communication for women of the corporation.

In J. Pilotta (Ed.), J. *Women in organizations.* Prospect Heights, IL: Waveland Press.

French, J., & Raven, B. (1968). The bases of social power. In D. Cartwright & A. Zander (Eds.), *Group dynamics: Research and theory* (pp. 259–269). New York: Harper and Row.

Gabler, J. E. (1987). Leadership: A woman's view. In L. T. Shieve & M. B. Schoenheit, (Eds.), *Leadership: Examining the elusive.* Association for Supervision and Curriculum Development.

Gardner, J. W. (1990). *On leadership.* New York: The Free Press.

Hall, J. (1990). *Models for management: The structure of competence* (2nd ed.). The Woodlands, TX: Woodstead Press.

Hambleton, R. K., & Gumpert, R. (1982). The validity of Hersey and Blanchard's theory of leader effectiveness. *Group & Organization Studies, 7*(2), 225–242.

Helgesen, S. (1990). *The female advantage: Women's ways of leadership.* New York: Doubleday Currency.

Hersey, P., & Blanchard, K. H. (1982). Leadership style: Attitudes and behaviors. *Training and Development, 36,* 50–52.

Hersey, P., & Blanchard, K. H. (1988). *Management of organizational behavior* (5th ed.). Englewood Cliffs, NJ: Prentice-Hall.

Hickson, D., Hinings, C., Lee, C., Schneck, R., & Pennings, J. (1971). A strategic contingencies theory of intra-organizational power. *Administrative Science Quarterly, 16,* 216–229.

Hollander, E. (1979). Leadership and social exchange processes. In K. Gergen, M. Greenberg, & R. Willis (Eds.), *Social exchange: Advances in theory and research.* New York: Winston-Wiley.

House, R. J. (1971). A path-goal theory of leader effectiveness. *Administrative Science Quarterly, 16,* 321–339.

House, R. J. (1984). *Power in organizations: A social psychological perspective.* Unpublished paper, University of Toronto, Faculty of Management, Toronto.

House, R. J. (1988). Power and personality in complex organizations. In B. M. Staw (Ed.), *Research in Organizational Behavior* (Vol. 10), (pp. 305–357). Greenwich, CT: JAI Press.

House, R. J., & Dessler, G. (1974). The path-goal theory of leadership: Some post hoc and a pri-

ori tests. In J. Hunt & L. Larson (Eds.), *Contingency approaches to leadership* (pp. 29–55). Carbondale, IL: Southern Illinois University Press.

Immegart, G. L. (1988). Leadership and leader behavior. In N. J. Boyan (Ed.), *Handbook of research on educational administration* (pp. 259–278). New York: Longman.

Immegart, G. L. (1991). Leadership. In M. C. Alkin (Ed.), *Encyclopedia of educational research* (6th ed.) (pp. 717–724). New York: Macmillan.

Kay, B. (1959). Factors in effective foreman behavior. *Personnel, 36,* 25–31.

Kerr, S., & Jermier, J. (1978). Substitutes for leadership: Their meaning and measurement. *Organizational Behavior and Human Performance, 22,* 375–403.

Koestenbaum, P. (1991). *Leadership: The inner side of greatness.* San Francisco: Jossey-Bass.

Likert, R. (1961). *New patterns of management.* New York: McGraw-Hill.

Likert, R. (1967). *The human organization: Its management and value.* New York: McGraw-Hill.

Lunenburg, F. C., & Ornstein, A. C. (1991). *Educational administration: Concepts and practices.* Belmont, CA: Wadsworth.

Mazzarella, J., & Grundy, T. (1989). Portrait of a leader. In S. Smith & J. Piele (Eds.), *School leadership: Handbook for excellence* (pp. 9–27). Eugene, OR: ERIC Clearinghouse on Educational Management, University of Oregon.

McGregor, D. (1990a). Theory X: The traditional view of direction and control. In J. Hall (Ed.), *Models for management: The structure of competence* (2nd ed.) (pp. 11–18). The Woodlands, TX: Woodstead Press.

McGregor, D. (1990b). Theory Y: The integration of individual and organizational goals. In J. Hall (Ed.), *Models of management: The structure of competence* (2nd ed.) (pp. 19–27). The Woodlands, TX: Woodstead Press.

Mintzberg, J. (1973). *The nature of managerial work.* New York: Harper and Row.

Nebecker, D., & Mitchell, T. (1974). Leader behavior: An expectancy theory approach. *Organizational Behavior and Human Performance, 11,* 355–367.

Osborn, R., & Hunt, J. (1975). An adaptive-reactive theory of leadership: The role of macro variables in leadership research. In J. Hunt & L. Larson (Eds.), *Leadership frontiers*. Kent, OH: Kent State University Press.

Ouchi, W. (1981). *Theory Z: How American business can meet the Japanese challenge*. New York: Avon Books.

Putnam, L. L. (1983). Lady, you're trapped: Breaking out of conflict cycles. In J. J. Oiletta (Ed.), *Women in organizations*. Prospect Heights, IL: Waveland Press.

Rost, J. C. (1991). *Leadership for the twenty-first century*. New York: Praeger Publishers.

Salancik, G. & Pfeffer, J. (1977). Who gets power—and how they hold on to it: A strategic contingency model of power. *Organizational Dynamics, 5,* 3–21.

Schein, E. H. (1985). *Organizational culture and leadership: A dynamic view*. San Francisco: Jossey-Bass.

Sergiovanni, T. J. (1986). Leadership as cultural expression. In T. J. Sergiovanni & J. E. Corbally (Eds.), *Leadership and organizational culture* (pp. 105–114). Urbana, IL: University of Illinois Press.

Sergiovanni, T. J., & Corbally, J. E. (Eds.). (1986). *Leadership and organizational culture*. Urbana, IL: University of Illinois Press.

Shakeshaft, C. (1987). *Women in educational administration*. Newbury Park, CA: Sage Publications.

Shetty, Y. (1978). Managerial power and organizational effectiveness: A contingency analysis. *The Journal of Management Studies, 15,* 176–186.

Smith, P. B., & Peterson, M. F. (1989). *Leadership, organizations and culture: An event management model*. London: Sage Publications.

Stogdill, R., & Coons, A. (Eds.). (1957). *Leader behavior: Its description and measurement*. Columbus, OH: Bureau of Business Research, Ohio State University.

Tannebaum, R., & Schmidt, W. (1973). How to choose a leadership pattern. *Harvard Business Review, 51,* 162–180.

Vroom, V., & Jago, A. (1988). *The new leadership: Managing participation in organizations*. Englewood Cliffs, NJ: Prentice-Hall.

Vroom, V., & Yetton, P. (1973). *Leadership and decision making*. Pittsburgh: University of Pittsburgh Press.

White, R., & Lippitt, R. (1990). Leader behavior and member reaction in three "social climates." In J. Hall (Ed.), *Models for management: The structure of competence* (2nd ed.) (pp. 146–172). The Woodlands, TX: Woodstead Press.

Yukl, G. A. (1989). *Leadership in organizations*. Englewood Cliffs, NJ: Prentice-Hall.

Zaleznik, A. (1977). Managers and leaders: Are they different? *Harvard Business Review, 55,* 67–78.

Chapter 3
The Context for Leadership

I f there were ever a time when educational institutions required effective leadership, it is now. This is the first time in history that the quality of the education of citizens has been recognized politically as being strategically important to national success and survival. As a result, educational institutions around the world have come under the very close scrutiny of politicians and social critics—and have been found wanting; consequently, "educational reform" has become epidemic.

The forces leading to educational reform are not unique to education; rather, they reflect worldwide changes in social, economic, political, and technological relationships. Alvin Toffler (1980) dubbed the forces "the third wave" and John Naisbitt (1982, 1990) identified them as "megatrends." Drucker (1989) has referred to their amalgam as "the post industrial society," "the post business society," and "the information age." Whatever it is called, the age we have entered is quite different from that which preceded it. The magnitude of the shift has been likened to the shift from feudalism to capitalism or from an agriculturally based economy to

industrialization. All social institutions must make appropriate adjustments; educational institutions are no exception.

This is a time of shifting paradigms (Kuhn, 1970). Social and economic structures are in a state of flux. Many of the world's totalitarian governments have fallen and, in several instances, have been replaced with more democratic institutions. In others, near anarchy prevails. We see a very real possibility of peace among the superpowers and, simultaneously, growing conflict among ethnic groups and violent regional rivalries.

There is both optimism and concern as we approach the new millennium. Naisbitt and Aburdene (1990), optimists, building on Naisbitt's (1982) successful predictions of a decade earlier, see the triumph of the individual and the demise of the collective. With new found freedom, they predict a global economic boom in the 1990s, a Renaissance in the arts, and a growing interest in things spiritual. According to them, a new free-market socialism will become the dominant socioeconomic structure and the welfare state will be privatized. Women increasingly will assume leadership roles and global lifestyles and cultural nationalism will emerge. Biology will dominate the sciences and Pacific rim nations will dominate economic relationships.

Not everyone is as optimistic about the future, however, as are Naisbitt and Aburdene. Galbraith (1992), for example, saw a growing disparity between the haves and the have nots in the United States and that eventually the have nots will rise in rebellion. The disparity is growing according to Galbraith because, for the first time in American history, "the contented" constitute the majority of the population and are in complete control of government. "The contented" do not support social legislation that redistributes wealth through higher taxes on the rich and greater services for the poor. He argues that it was the social legislation engineered by Lloyd George in the early twentieth century that saved British capitalism during the years between the two world wars and, likewise, it was the social legislation of Franklin Roosevelt that saved capitalism in the United States during the Great Depression. In each instance, the legislation was opposed by the contented, who lost. Now that the contented are firmly in the majority, there is little hope of government enacting legislation to bridge the gap between the haves and the have nots. Galbraith predicts social breakdown as a consequence.

For better or for worse, this is, indeed, a dynamic and exciting period in human history. Because of the fluidity of the situation, it is a period of unparalleled opportunity and potential danger. To capitalize on the opportunities and to minimize the dangers demands extraordinarily wise leadership in all sectors and in all enterprises including education.

In short, our reality is pervasive social change. While these changes affect persons in all walks of life, there is bound to be greater impact upon those in positions of greater social visibility and concern such as persons holding administrative and supervisory responsibility for educational systems. Society has a right to expect competent performance in those positions. Under these circumstances, competent leadership cannot be a matter of copying conventional behavior. To advance education, there is a clear need for educational leaders to have the ability to comprehend the dynamics of human affairs as a basis for relevant action under novel conditions, the need for better understanding of issues and processes in educational institutions, and the need for greater originality and collaboration in designing strategic policies. Their approach to the opportunities and problems confronting them needs to remain hypothetical and open-ended so that more may be learned by what is done.

Among other things, leadership is a function of context. In this chapter we summarize some of the causes for concern over public education as reported by many evaluative reports and books published during the past decade. Special attention is given to the reported decline in achievement by American students and their relative international standing. Statistics are presented showing that the conditions under which many schools operate are becoming more difficult because the populations they serve are increasing in ethnic diversity, in variation of family structures, and in the proportion of children coming from impoverished homes. We then briefly examine the political and professional responses to the criticisms and step back to look for historical roots of the current dilemmas. The evolution of the tradition of local control of school governance and contemporary challenges to the tradition are summarized. Evidence of the increasing politicization of educational issues is presented. The chapter closes with a capsulated description of the current organization of school governance and selected statistics to illustrate the magnitude of the educational enterprise in terms of people served and employed, and in terms of resources consumed.

The context for educational leadership today is different from any other time in history. It is essential that contemporary issues and processes be understood if leadership is to result in relevant action.

Causes for Concern

"A NATION AT RISK"

Even if the most optimistic of futurist scenarios prove to be true globally, there is much concern among thoughtful Americans as to how well the United States is equipped to compete in this new world. With respect to education, the alarm was first sounded in our current round of reform[1] by the National Commission on Excellence in Education (1983) in its report, *A Nation at Risk*. It claimed that a rising tide of mediocrity had engulfed the schools threatening the economic competitiveness of the country and, indeed, its very survival. The theme was repeated with growing urgency in dozens of reports throughout the 1980s.

The Commission on the Skills of the American Workforce (1990) focused on the integral relationship between education and economic growth in its report, *America's Choice: High Skills or Low Wages*. The Commission admitted its discomfort with emerging trends. Japan has replaced the United States as the world's economic juggernaut and Germany, with only a quarter of the United States' population, almost equalled the United States in exports. At the same time that the United States was becoming the world's biggest borrower, Singapore, Taiwan, and Korea grew

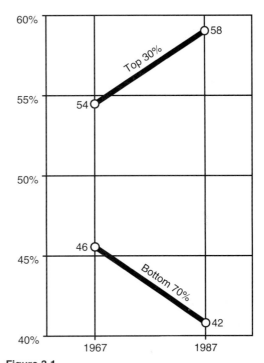

Figure 3.1
Distribution of income in the United States: 1967–1987
SOURCE: Commission on the Skills of the American Workforce (1990).

from third world outposts to premier world exporters. The Commission pointed out that American growth in productivity has slowed to a crawl and its standard of living has, at best, stagnated, while its competitors are growing in both productivity and in standards of living.

The cost of the loss of ability to compete economically is, for many Americans, a lower standard of living than what at one time was taken for granted. The purchasing power of average weekly earnings for American workers has actually dropped by 12% since 1969. But the hardship has not been borne equally by all Americans. The top 30 percent of American families with highest earnings have increased their share of national income from 54 percent in 1967 to 58 percent in 1987 while the bottom 70 percent lost ground (see Figure 3.1). The top 30 percent are made up

---

[1] This is not the first time education has been in a state of perceived crisis. After the Russians launched the first earth satellite in 1957, American education came under close scrutiny. Best-seller lists included books with such provocative titles as *Why Johnny Can't Read, What Ivan Knows That Johnny Doesn't,* and *Death at an Early Age*.

primarily of professional/technical workers, usually graduates of four-year colleges, who are prospering. However, front-line workers have seen their wages shrink year after year. From 1972 to 1987, the relative wage of craft workers dropped from 98 percent of that earned by professional and technical workers to 73 percent; for laborers, the drop was from 70 percent to 51 percent (see Figure 3.2).

The United States is facing the real possibility of developing a structural underclass and many believe that the nature of the public school system is a primary cause. These fears have been supported by findings of the 1990 U.S. Census. More people are living in poverty than in 1980 and the middle class is shrinking while the number of rich is growing. The percentage of households living on less than the equivalent of $25,000 per year in current dollars has risen to 42 percent from 31 percent a decade earlier. In 1979, three-quarters of Americans were enjoying middle incomes compared with two-thirds in 1989. At the same time, the percentage of Americans classified as having high incomes grew from 11 percent to 15 percent of the

Figure 3.2
Change in wages for selected occupations relative to each other

SOURCE: Commission on the Skills of the American Workforce (1990).

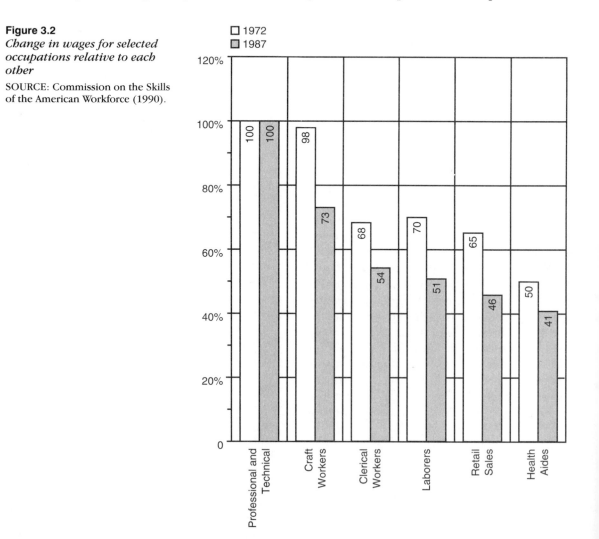

total population. Reform of education is seen by many as central to overcoming the United States' economic and social shortcomings.

The Commission on the Skills of the American Workforce believes that, if the United States is to reverse its economic decline, it will have to transform its work organizations by reducing bureaucracy and giving front-line workers the responsibility to use judgement and make decisions. To do this, the Commission asserts, requires the mobilization of "our most vital asset, the skills of our people—not just the 30% who will graduate from college, but the front-line workers, the people who serve as bank tellers, farm workers, truck drivers, retail clerks, data entry operators and factory workers" (p. 14). An essential element in the Commission's strategy for accomplishing this mobilization is the improvement of the education received by front-line workers in elementary and secondary schools, increased on-the-job training, and mechanisms for smoothing the school-to-work transition. Redesigning elementary and secondary schools to meet these ends is a responsibility of educational leadership working together with their counterparts in the community-at-large and in business.

The W. T. Grant Foundation (1988) also focused in on the plight of the "Forgotten Half," the 50 percent of American youth who do not go on to college. Their study dramatically documents the shrinking opportunities for "a job with a future" for the noncollege-bound, extraordinarily high unemployment rates, and a steep decline in real income. The Foundation faults the schools for having become distracted from their main mission. "Educators have become so preoccupied with those who go on to college that they have lost sight of those who do not. And more and more of the non-college bound now fall between the cracks when they are in school, drop out, or graduate inadequately prepared for the requirements of the society and the workplace" (p. 3).

The disparity between what Americans do for the college-bound and the noncollege-bound is great. Those in college receive social subsidies that average $5,000 per year while those not going to college are frequently viewed as failures and receive little, if any, public support. The Foundation calls for the development of an integrated approach to the education, training, and service needs of all youth. Further, it recommends stronger linkages between youth, adults, and their communities; access to a full array of developmental, preventative, and remedial services; and public support to ease the financial burden of raising children and adolescents.

Kozol (1992) focused on schools themselves—especially inner-city schools. He graphically describes the conditions in which many of the underclass are being educated.

> [T]hese urban schools were, by and large, extraordinarily unhappy places. With few exceptions, they reminded me of "garrisons" or "outposts" in a foreign nation. Housing projects, bleak and tall, surrounded by perimeter walls lined with barbed wire, often stood adjacent to the schools I visited. The schools were surrounded frequently by signs that indicated DRUG-FREE ZONE. Their doors were guarded. Police sometimes patrolled the halls. The windows of the schools were often covered with steel grates. Taxi drivers flatly refused to take me to some of these schools and would deposit me a dozen blocks away, in border areas beyond which they refused to go. . . . In Boston, the press referred to areas like these as "death zones"—a specific reference to the rate of infant death in ghetto neighborhoods—but the feeling of the "death zone" often seemed to permeate the schools themselves (p. 5).

OUTCOMES AND DEMOGRAPHIC CONSIDERATIONS

Frequently, critics document the decline in the quality of schooling with statistics of falling Scholastic Aptitude Test (SAT) scores, comparisons with the achievement of children in other countries, high drop-out rates, violence in the schools, and low achievement of minority children compared with majority children.

SAT scores did decline steadily from an average total score of 980 in 1963 to 890 in 1981 (National Center for Education Statistics (NCES), 1991b, p. 152). Scores declined for both verbal and mathematics subtests although they dropped more dramatically for verbal tests. Since 1981, the total average score and the mathematics subscores have increased modestly while the verbal subscores have stabilized. The average total score stood at 900 in 1990. The Sandia study (Huelskamp, 1993), however, concludes that "the much-publicized 'decline' in average SAT scores misrepresents the true story of SAT performance." The reason for the decline is attributed to the fact that more students in the bottom halves of their classes are taking the SAT today than in years past. In fact, every minority ethnic group is performing better today than 15 years ago (Huelskamp, 1993). Berliner (1993) also challenges the common interpretation of declining SAT scores by pointing out that, of the group of current students who match the characteristics of those who took the SATs in 1975, there has been a 30 point increase, more than ten percentile ranks.

Composite scores on the American College Testing (ACT) have also declined, but averages on the subscores show a different pattern than the SAT statistics show. The ACT subscores for English have remained relatively stable since 1970 while subscores for mathematics and social studies have declined sharply and subscores for natural sciences have shown a modest increase (NCES, 1991b, p. 153).

The National Assessment of Educational Progress (NAEP) has not detected a decline in educational achievement over the past 20 years, although its findings do present cause for concern about the low level of average proficiency of American youth. Over the years, about 40 percent of 17-year-olds have been classified as performing at the "Adept" level in reading which is described, "Can find, understand, summarize, and explain relatively complicated information" (NCES, 1993a, p. 202). Eighty-four percent of 17-year-olds perform at the "Intermediate" level or better. Performance at this level is described, "Can search for specific information, interrelate ideas, and make generalizations." The percentage performing at the "Advanced" level has increased since 1971 from six percent to seven percent in 1990. Advanced performance is described, "Can synthesize and learn from specialized material."

While average performance of minority groups on NAEP tests had shown improvement, it remained well below that of majority students. Over half of majority students examined in 1988 understood basic historical terms and relationships and specific government structures and functions compared to about a quarter of African-American and Hispanic students (NCES, 1991b, p. 142).

Of even greater concern to some analysts is the performance of American students in comparison with students in other countries. The results of a twenty-nation study published in 1992 found that American 13-year-olds outperformed only those from Jordan, Portugal, Brazil, and Mozambique in mathematics, and only students from those countries and Ireland in science (Rothman, 1992a). Nine-year-olds in the United States were among the highest performing of 14 nations in science, but near the bottom in mathematics. The results are summarized in Table 3.1. On the other hand, students in the United States outperformed those from nearly every other country in a 32-nation study of reading literacy (Rothman, 1992b).

There are those who think that the criticisms of public schools in the United States are overblown and unwarranted. "Contrary to

Table 3.1

Average Percentage of Questions Answered Correctly by Students in the Second International Assessment of Educational Progress

Countries	Participation Age →	Math		Science	
		9	13	9	13
Brazil	Cities of Fortaleza and Sao Paulo, in-school population, restricted grades Fortaleza Sao Paulo	— —	32 37	— —	46 53
Canada	Four provinces at age 9 and nine provinces at age 13 out of a total of 10	60	62	63	69
China	20 of 29 provinces & independent cities, restricted grades, in-school population	—	80	—	67
England	Representative of all students, low participation at both 9 and 13	59	61	63	69
France	Representative of all students	—	64	—	69
Hungary	Representative of all students	68	68	63	73
Ireland	Representative of all students	60	61	57	63
Israel	Hebrew-speaking schools	64	63	61	70
Italy	Province of Emilia-Romagna, low participation at age 9	68	64	67	70
Jordan	Representative of all students	—	40	—	57
Korea	Representative of all students	75	73	68	78
Mozambique	Cities of Maputo and Beira, in-school population, low participation	—	28	—	—
Portugal	Restricted grades, in-school population at age 13	55	48	55	63
Scotland	Representative of all students, low participation at age 9	66	61	62	68
Slovenia	Representative of all students	56	57	58	70
Former Soviet Union	14 out of 15 republics, Russian-speaking schools	66	70	62	71
Spain	All regions except Cataluna, Spanish-speaking schools	62	55	62	71
Switzerland	15 out of 26 cantons	—	71	—	74
Taiwan	Representative of all students	68	73	67	76
U.S.A.	Representative of all students	58	55	65	67
	IAEP Averages:	63	58	62	67

SOURCE: *Education Week,* February 12, 1992, p. 13.

the prevailing opinion, the American public schools are remarkably good whenever and wherever they are provided with the human and economic resources to succeed" (Berliner, 1993, p. 36). Berliner pointed out, for example, that today's students actually average 14 IQ points higher than their grand-parents and seven points higher than their parents. The number of students scoring in the gifted range today is seven times greater than the generation now retiring from leader-ship. Hodgkinson (1993a) concludes that the top 20 percent of our high school graduates are world class and getting better. The next 40 percent are mostly capable of completing college. There is widespread agreement that our higher education system is one of our great strengths (Kirst, 1993) and the envy of the world. In spite of falling average SAT scores, scores on the Graduate Record Exami-nation (GRE) have risen 16 points (verbal), 36 points (quantitative), and 30 points (analyti-cal) since 1981 even though the number of test-takers has increased by 16 percent (Hodgkinson, 1993a). Further, 40 percent of all research articles are written by American scholars; no other nation produces more than 7 percent.

The failure of many American students to complete high school and the linkage between dropping-out and unemployment and crime are also of concern to many policy analysts. Nearly 87 percent of white 19-year-olds have completed high school compared with 75 percent of African-American students and 59 percent of Hispanic students (NCES, 1991b, p. 28). From an international perspec-tive, however, it should be noted that only Belgium and Finland exceed the United States in the percentage of 17-year-olds enrolled in school (Huelskamp, 1993).

Only about one-quarter of minority high school dropouts find employment shortly after leaving school compared with half of white dropouts. Even the high school gradu-ate has difficulty in finding employment; 75 percent of majority students are successful in finding employment shortly after graduation compared with barely half of minority stu-dents. Some 82 percent of persons in prisons are high school dropouts; it costs about $24,000 per year to support a person in prison (Hodgkinson, 1993b).

The linkage between education level and employment and income is very strong. Of 25–34 year olds, 76 percent of high school dropouts are employed compared with 87 percent of high school graduates and 93 per-cent of college graduates. Earnings of white male dropouts are only 73 percent that of white high school graduates and about half that of college graduates. The relative earn-ings disadvantage of the dropout has been growing over the past two decades. Relation-ships are similar for females and minority groups (NCES, 1991b, p. 44), reinforcing the concerns previously cited of the Commission on the Skills of the American Workforce over an emerging permanent underclass.

While the statistics may suggest that schools are not doing their job as well as in the past, it is also true that their job may be more difficult now than it was in the past. During the 1980s the characteristics of Ameri-can families continued to move away from the traditional two-parent, two-children configu-ration; by 1990, barely one-quarter of house-holds were of that variety (Hodgkinson, 1991), fewer in actual number than they were a decade earlier—the only classification of families to show a decline (see Table 3.2). Sin-gle female head households increased by 36 percent, male heads by 29 percent, and mar-ried couples without children by 17 percent. Sixty percent of all households have no chil-dren at all—a fact that makes funding of pub-lic schools by locally levied property taxes exceedingly difficult where such levies require voter approval. Almost 50 percent of America's young people will spend some years before they reach 18 being raised by a single parent. The 15 million children being raised by single mothers will have about one-third as much family spending on their needs as children being raised by two parents (Hodgkinson, 1991). One-quarter of American children are living in households below the poverty level and 59 percent of all children in poverty belong to households headed by females (NCES, 1991b, p. 200).

The proportion of public school enrollment represented by minority groups (those most likely to be ravaged by poverty) is on the rise. In 1976, minorities represented 24 percent of elementary and secondary enrollment. Projections suggest that this proportion will rise to 46 percent by the year 2020 (NCES, 1991b). The growth in numbers and proportions of the minority population is due only in part to their higher fertility rates as compared with the majority. Another important factor is an upsurge in immigration of persons from Asia and Latin America. It is estimated that approximately five million children of immigrant parents will enroll in elementary and secondary schools during the 1990s, representing more than 150 languages (Huelskamp, 1993).

In addition to being three times as likely to be impoverished, minority children are more likely to encounter other "risk" factors such as coming from a single-parent household, having limited English proficiency, and having a parent or sibling (or both) who has dropped out of school. Minority children are 3.5 times as likely to have two or more of these risk factors as white children. The effect is also intergenerational; 62 percent of children under age six who are below the poverty level have parents who did not complete high school. If one parent completed high school, the rate drops to 26 percent, and to 7 percent if one parent had some schooling beyond high school ("Poverty and Education," 1992).

While the top 20 percent of American elementary and secondary students are well served by the current educational system and the next 40 percent are served acceptably well, the bottom 40 percent are poorly served and this is the focus of most concern (Hodgkinson, 1993a; Kirst, 1993). Some analysts, however, place the blame not so much on the schools, but on the problems the bottom 40 percent bring to the school door, particularly poverty, physical and emotional handicaps, lack of health care, difficult family conditions and violent neighborhoods. Solving our "educational" crisis will require coordination of schools' efforts with those of other community agencies including health

Table 3.2

Numbers of U.S. Households by Characteristics, 1980 and 1990

SOURCE: Hodgkinson (1991, September). *Phi Delta Kappan*, p. 11.

	1980	1990	Percent Change
All households	80,467,000	93,920,000	+16.7
Family households	59,190,000	66,652,000	+12.4
Married couples	48,990,000	52,837,000	+ 7.9
Married without children	24,210,000	28,315,000	+17.0
Married with children	24,780,000	24,522,000	− 1.0
Single female head	8,205,000	11,130,000	+35.6
Single male head	1,995,000	2,575,000	+29.1
People living alone	18,202,000	22,879,000	+25.7
Living with nonrelatives	3,075,000	4,500,000	+46.3

care, housing, transportation, and social welfare (Hodgkinson, 1993a; W. T. Grant Foundation, 1988).

Thus, past assumptions used by educators
in designing school curricula no longer hold
across the board. Children are less likely to
come from majority backgrounds. They are
more likely to be members of nontraditional
families, and they are more likely to be poor.
Education through high school and beyond is
essential if graduates are to be employed in
other than menial jobs and to enjoy comfortable standards of living. Well-paying employment opportunities increasingly require
sophisticated intellectual skills. Educational
leadership is being challenged to design new
curricula that recognize the multicultural
nature of students, provide institutional support for those at risk, and link schooling and
employment.

The Education Reform Movement

WAVES OF EDUCATIONAL REFORM

Response to the current situation confronting
public education has been portrayed as coming in three waves. The first wave focused on
student performance and teacher quality.
Between 1980 and 1986, nearly all states
increased their standards for high school
graduation through such means as requiring
more courses, expanding their distribution
requirements among subject areas, and
achieving minimum test scores. One-third of
the states require students to pass a competency test to graduate from high school
(Council of Chief State School Officers, 1990).

Certification standards for teachers were
also raised. By 1987, two-thirds of the states
prescribed standardized tests for people seeking teacher certification and permanent certification for teachers was ended in many states

while others tied certification renewal to further education or satisfactory performance
(Farrar, 1990).

But legislating higher standards did not
necessarily produce higher outcomes (Iannaccone, 1985), and state governors, among others, were quick to notice. The National Governors' Association (1986) issued a report
entitled, *Time for Results,* which acknowledged that structural reform was also needed
in addition to raising standards, thus initiating the second wave of reform. The report
indicated that the governors were ready for
some "old fashioned horse-trading." They
committed the states to regulate less if
schools and school districts would produce
better results.

> *The kind of horse-trading we are talking
> about will dramatically change the way most
> schools work. First, the governors want to help
> establish clear goals and better report cards—
> ways to measure what students know and
> can do. Then we're ready to give up a lot of
> state regulatory control—even to fight for
> changes in the law to make that happen—if
> schools and school districts will be account-
> able for results. These changes will require
> more rewards for successes and consequences
> for failure for teachers, school leaders, schools
> and school districts. They will mean giving
> parents more choice in the public schools
> their children attend as one way of insuring
> higher quality without heavy-handed state
> control (National Governors' Association
> (1986), p. 4).*

In addition to the series of national commission reports and privately funded studies
that appeared in the early part of the eighties,
Farrar (1990) identified two other important
changes in the environment of national education policy in that decade that spurred on
the educational reform movement. The first
was President Ronald Reagan's education
agenda; it sought to reduce the federal role in
education which had been steadily growing
since President Lyndon Johnson's Great Soci-

ety and War on Poverty initiatives of the mid-1960s. The reduced federal role induced by the Reagan policies created a vacuum in educational leadership at the federal level and simultaneously urged state governments and private enterprise to fill the void. The second change was the willingness of state leaders and business executives to take an active role in educational reform.

Petrie (1990) suggests that the restructuring of the teaching profession initiated by the second wave of reform has profound implications for our concept of educational leadership.

> *It seems clear that if teachers are to be viewed as reflective practitioners exercising professional judgement, educational leaders will not tell such professionals what to do. There will not be detailed syllabi imposed. Bureaucratic rules and regulations will be kept to a minimum. Structures will be developed that allow a broad range of discretion and influence, not merely in how to teach the syllabus once the classroom door has been closed, but in the very construction of those syllabi. The leadership will be associated with groups of semiautonomous professionals rather than the leadership associated with hired help. Relationships will probably look more like the collegial models of higher education or of the associations of professionals in accounting or architectural firms, or like health maintenance organizations rather than like the industrial labor-management arrangements (Petrie, 1990, p. 22).*

Petrie's views are compatible with those of Cuban (1988) who laments that teaching and administering are no longer viewed as one career even though they are anchored in a common history sharing common roles. Cuban views teaching as central to thoughtful administration. According to him, two images dominate teaching and administering schools—the technical and the moral—and they share three common roles: instructional, managerial, and political. While the images

and roles are played out in different settings, teaching and administration are inexorably entangled. The instructional role is central to teaching, but there are elements of the political and the managerial. The political role dominates the superintendency and principalships are likely to experience all three roles in relatively equal proportions.

Cuban also saw the current design of schools and school systems as standing in the way of providing the quality of education we all desire for our children. In differentiating between leaders and managers, he sees leaders as people who shape the goals, motivations, and actions of others while managers maintain current organizational arrangements efficiently and effectively. Leaders frequently initiate change to reach existing and new goals; the overall direction of management is toward maintenance. He argues that:

> *schools as they are presently organized press teachers, principals, and superintendents toward managing rather than leading, toward maintaining what is rather than moving to what can be. The structures of schooling and the incentives buried within them produce a managerial imperative (Cuban, 1988, p. xxi).*

Cuban sees autonomy as the necessary condition for leadership to arise.

Jacobson and Conway (1990) anticipate that the redefinition of educational leadership will result in a third wave of reform. *Leaders for America's School*, the report of the National Commission on Excellence in Educational Administration (1988), was the precursor of this most recent reform effort. This Commission's report, sponsored by the University Council for Educational Administration, addresses what schools must become, how they will be led, and policy changes needed with respect to preparing and supporting school leadership. Its recommendations strive to alter the structure of schools including the relationships between teachers and administrators, the preparation of educational administrators, and their licensure and work. Ten major deficiencies in current educational leadership were identified:

1. lack of definition of good educational leadership,
2. lack of leader recruitment programs in the schools,
3. lack of collaboration between school districts and universities,
4. lack of minorities and women in the field,
5. lack of systematic professional development for school administrators,
6. lack of quality candidates for preparation programs,
7. lack of preparation programs relevant to the job demands of school administrators,
8. lack of sequence, modern content, and clinical experience in preparation programs,
9. lack of licensure system to promote excellence,
10. lack of a national sense of cooperation in preparing school administrators.

Fuhrman, Elmore, and Massell (1993) have also seen evidence that the reform movement is moving into a third phase which they refer to as "systemic reform." They identify two themes that characterize this phase: (1) comprehensive change that focuses on many aspects of the system, and (2) policy integration and coordination around a clear set of outcomes. Greater professional discretion is being allowed at the school site under the umbrella of centralized coordination.

School leaders of the future will not only be working with a student body markedly different from that of the past, but the organizational structures and professional and political relationships are also likely to be quite different. The relationships between teachers and administrators are likely to be collegial rather than authoritarian. Principals and teachers are likely to have greater professional discretion as many decisions formally made at the district, state and federal levels are left to schools. Local, state and federal authorities will continue to set certain parameters, however. Parents and community representatives are likely to have greater influence on the organization and operation of the schools through membership on school councils or through parental choice of schooling. As a result, acceptable leadership styles and strategies will be quite different in the future from what they have been in the past.

IMPLEMENTING REFORM

To bring focus to the educational reform movement, the state governors joined with President George Bush in 1989 and articulated six national goals for public education to be realized by the year 2000. The six goals, originally known as "America 2000" and now labeled "Goals 2000" by the Clinton administration, are reported in Table 3.3. Although there has been a change of presidents since 1989, there has been little change in the overall strategy. It should be recognized that this has been a bipartisan effort and that the current incumbent in the White House was Chair of the National Governors' Association at the time the America 2000 initiative was promulgated and was influential in shaping its design.

The National Education Goals Panel was appointed to monitor progress being made toward those goals and to coordinate efforts of state and national organizations. Panel membership is politically balanced allowing two members to the national administration, eight governors (only three of whom may be from the President's own party), and four members of Congress appointed by the

Table 3.3
Goals 2000: Six* National Goals for Public Education
SOURCE: National Education Goals Panel (1993).

Goal 1. By the year 2000, all children in America will start school ready to learn.

Goal 2. By the year 2000, the high school graduation rate will increase to at least 90%.

Goal 3. By the year 2000, American students will leave grades 4, 8, and 12 having demonstrated competency in challenging subject matter, including English, mathematics, science, history, and geography; and every school in America will ensure that all students learn to use their minds well, so that they may be prepared for responsible citizenship, further learning, and productive employment in our modern economy.

Goal 4. By the year 2000, U. S. students will be the first in the world in mathematics and science achievement.

Goal 5. By the year 2000, every adult American will be literate and will possess the skills necessary to compete in a global economy and to exercise the rights and responsibilities of citizenship.

Goal 6. By the year 2000, every school in America will be free of drugs and violence and will offer a disciplined environment conducive to learning.

* Two new goals were added by the 1994 Educate America Act concerning teacher education and professional development and parental participation.

---

majority and minority leaders of the House and Senate. All members have voting privileges.

In 1991, the Goals Panel cooperated in the creation of the National Council on Education Standards and Testing and endorsed the Council's recommendations for national standards and related systems of student assessment. The Goals Panel is committed to five principles to guide standards-based reform:

1. *The development of nationwide standards must be highly inclusive, blending expert classroom knowledge with that of researchers, policymakers, and the general public.*

2. *The standards must not be considered a uniform national curriculum.*

3. *The standards must be deliberately set at high levels.*

4. *The standards must be viewed as dynamic, subject to periodic review and change.*

5. *The importance of nationwide standards must be clearly and effectively communicated to the American people (The National Education Goals Panel, 1993, p. xiv).*

The "Goals 2000: Educate America Act," enacted in 1994, established a National Education Standards and Improvement Council to develop criteria and a process for reviewing and approving nationwide standards. Three broad themes characterize this nationwide approach to reform: education reform must be *systemic;* the nation's commitment to education reform must be *long-term;* and, to achieve the goals, state, local, and federal governments must form an education *part-*

nership. In all of this, the federal role is seen as "a leader, partner, and catalyst for systemic reform by leveraging scarce resources toward state and local initiatives with broad impact and long-term benefit" (The National Education Goals Panel, 1993, p. 186). States and school districts will be required to set standards for curriculum content and student performance as well as opportunity-to-learn standards to qualify for federal Chapter 1 funds.

While the reform movement is experiencing an unusual amount of voluntary coordination at the national level, most of the action is taking place at the state, school district, and school levels. The best example of systemic change is in the state of Kentucky where all elements of the education system have been modified including its governance and finance. The Chicago school system is undergoing a radical form of decentralization placing policymaking authority in the hands of lay-controlled boards attached to individual schools. Michigan has eliminated the local property tax as the primary source of financial support of schools. Charter schools have been legalized in at least five states and a number of states are experimenting with limited voucher schemes. Site-based management is the order of the day, and increasingly, states and school districts are allowing family choice of schooling.

There is also increasing involvement of the private sector in the running and support of public schools. The New American Schools Development Corporation was formed by American business leaders in July of 1991 at the request of President Bush. The purpose of the corporation is to underwrite the design and implementation of a new generation of "break the mold" schools. It has pledged to raise $150 million from private sources between 1991 and 1996 to finance the effort of which $103 million had been raised by January 1994. In response to its call for proposals, 686 design teams responded from which

11 were selected to be supported for further development over a five-year period. The overriding criteria for selection was the likelihood that a design would enable all students to reach the national education goals and attain "world-class" standards (Olson, 1992).

Members of the private sector are also working in other ways to promote and to profit from school reform. Their efforts range from school-business partnerships to creating foundations and trusts to outright entrepreneurial initiatives. The largest of the latter has been launched by Tennessee businessman and media magnate, Chris Whittle. His Edison Project is moving ahead with the design of a chain of for-profit private schools to operate in urban areas across the country. The $60 million for the design phase is coming from Whittle Communications, L. P., and its major owners Time-Warner, Inc., Dutch-based Phillips Electronics, N. V., and British-based Associated Newspapers Holdings Ltd. Benno C. Schmidt, Jr., president of Yale University, resigned his position at Yale to lead the effort.

Other ventures into public education by private for-profit companies include the operation under contract of nine Baltimore schools and Chapter 1 tutoring programs. The Minneapolis school board has hired a private firm to run the school system in place of a traditional superintendent. In Chelsea, Massachusetts, the school board has turned over the reins to Boston University under contract.

Obviously, there is much concern over the quality of our educational system and the implications it has for our societal well-being. The concern has generated much debate and experimentation. The issue of national goals, for example, raises myriad additional controversial issues such as national standards, a national curriculum, national assessment, and national teacher certification. There are also issues of balance—among federal, state, and local governments, between political and professional authorities, and between public and private sectors. Structural changes will emerge from the current turmoil, but it is too early to predict just what those may be. The related issues strike at the heart of American social beliefs and traditions. Persons now preparing to assume leadership roles in education are likely to spend their entire careers addressing those issues.

Having looked at the symptoms of malaise and early efforts made to address them, we need to examine the nature of the educational system which produced the malaise because this is the system within which new leaders must begin their careers. We will start by briefly examining the historical origins of the current structure of school governance.

The Scope and Structure of School Governance

HISTORICAL DEVELOPMENT OF PUBLIC EDUCATION

In a critical analysis of public education in the United States in 1943, Morrison (1943) referred to its structure disdainfully as "late New England colonial" (p. 258) and described the school district as "a little republic at every crossroads" (p. 75). Morrison was focusing on a characteristic of the system of American public education which makes it unique among the school systems of the world—its extreme decentralization. Herein lay both its strengths and weaknesses.

Decentralized systems seem to be more adept than are highly centralized and bureaucratic ones at mobilizing the energies of their constituents and adapting curricula and instructional systems to the diversity of their constituents. Yet decentralized systems have a tendency to become inequitable, providing uneven quality of services. The good schools in a decentralized system tend to be very, very

good; but such a system also generates—and tolerates—very poor schools. To bring about a greater degree of equity and set minimally acceptable social standards requires intervention of higher levels of government, i.e., state and/or federal. This has been happening with increasing frequency over the fifty years since Morrison made his analysis.

Collective concern over formal education of the young dates to the beginning of European settlement of the continental United States. Massachusetts was particularly influential in setting the pattern for public education. It was the Massachusetts Colony that first required parents to train their children in reading and writing, first required towns to establish schools, first appropriated colonial funds to encourage the establishment of schools, and first permitted towns to use revenue from property taxation to support schooling. All of this was accomplished before 1650. These events, however, must be interpreted in light of the interrelationships between the government of the Massachusetts Colony and the Congregational (Puritan) Church. Suffrage and office holding were limited to male church members, a minority of the total population. The property tax that supported the school also supported the church and its clergy. The "meeting house" served as the school as well as the church and the town hall (Johnson, 1904). This early pattern of community control of schools in Massachusetts left its imprint upon the organization of public education in the United States today although the connection between church and state has been severed.

Several of the authors of the United States Constitution in 1787 had firm beliefs about the importance of an educated citizenry to the success of the new republic. But the Constitution, itself, is silent on the subject of education; and the Tenth Amendment to the Bill of Rights assured that the powers not specifically delegated to the federal government were "reserved to the States respectively, or to the people." Founders, such as Thomas Jefferson, pursued the provision of public education at the state level. In his *Notes on the State of Virginia,* written in 1781–1782, Jefferson (1968) argued:

> *Every government degenerates when trusted to the rulers of the people alone. The people themselves therefore are its only safe depositories. And to render even them safe, their minds must be improved. . . (p. 390).*

In seeking additional funds for education from the New York State Legislature, Governor DeWitt Clinton (1909) noted the importance of state sponsorship of education in a democracy:

> *The first duty of government, and the surest evidence of good government, is the encouragement of education. A general diffusion of knowledge is the precursor and protector of republican institutions; and in it we must confide as the conservative power that will watch over our liberties, and guard against fraud, intrigue, corruption and violence (p. 114).*

In a desperate bid in 1834 to save Pennsylvania's newly enacted common school legislation from the repeal of tax cutters, Thaddeus Stevens (1900), fully aware of the externalities of public education, stated plainly the common benefit to be realized from those tax dollars.

> *Many complain of this tax, not so much on account of its amount, as because it is for the benefit of others and not themselves. This is a great mistake; it is for their own benefit, inasmuch as it perpetuates the government and insures the due administration of the laws under which they live, and by which their lives and property are protected (p. 520).*

Stevens went on to draw the connection between education and the prevention of crime and argued that it is wiser, less expensive and more humane to aid "that which

goes to support his fellow-being from becoming a criminal, and to obviate the necessity of those humiliating [penal] institutions." This is a theme which is commonly repeated even today.

Thus, from the country's beginning, the social importance of education was recognized by some of its most influential citizens and its provision was made deliberately a function of the states, not the federal government. Centralized control at state or federal levels was not feasible in the eighteenth and nineteenth centuries because of the dispersion of the population, the primitive means of communication, and the general lack of resources. The school district was invented to create and oversee schools under these conditions. Cubberley (1947) commented on the spread of the school district concept nationwide.

> *As an administrative and taxing unit it was well suited to the primitive needs and conditions of our early national life. Among a sparse and hard-working rural population, between whom intercourse was limited and intercommunication difficult, and with whom the support of schools was as yet an unsettled question, local control answered a very real need. The simplicity and democracy of the system was one of its chief merits. Communities or neighborhoods which wanted schools and were willing to pay for them could easily meet and organize a school district, vote to levy a school tax on their own property, employ a teacher, and organize and maintain a school. . . . On the other hand, communities which did not desire schools or were unwilling to tax themselves for them could do without them, and let the free-school idea alone (pp. 212–213).*

Cubberley's description points to one of the difficulties of the district system once universal education became the policy of a state. The district system worked well for the willing and able, but for those who were unwilling, there was not the leadership to organize a district, and for those who were not able, there were not the resources. Inequities within the district system became apparent even during the colonial period, but with the increasing concentration of capital wealth through industrialization and urbanization, inequities became much more severe in the nineteenth and twentieth centuries.

Attempts to address these inequities began in the nineteenth century through greater state oversight, the beginning of state aid to school districts, and the encouragement of school district consolidation. Districts that voluntarily came into existence, however, quickly attached loyalty to their achievements and took great pride in them with the result that they were not responsive to criticism of their endeavors from the state and resented any and all constraints placed upon them. Those areas that chose not to operate a common school were equally resistant to external pressure to do so, especially when it involved compulsory taxation.

In an effort to establish order out of chaos, state boards of education were formed and provided with an executive officer. The first state to take such action was New York in 1812. As testimony to the sensitive nature of the position, New York's first Superintendent of Instruction served only until 1821 when the office was eliminated. A similar office was not created in New York until 1854. Horace Mann, the first Secretary to the Board of Education of Massachusetts, ran into similar difficulty; however, attempts to dissolve his office and the board were unsuccessful.

The first school districts to go through the process of consolidation were in cities. While New England cities were coterminous with their school districts from the beginning, this was not typically true of more western cities. Buffalo, the first city to employ a superintendent of schools, serves as a good illustration. Although it had private schools prior, the first school supported by taxes was established in 1818. By 1837, the city had 15,000 inhabi-

tants and seven one-teacher school districts. That year, a superintendent of schools was appointed to supervise and to coordinate those seven schools, to establish schools in wards of the city which were without schools, and to provide for a central high school. Detroit, Chicago, and Cleveland followed similar patterns. A few cities in the far west continue the practice of multiple school districts within the city limits.

Today, the tradition of local control remains strong, but the inequities inherent in such a policy are a primary cause of the system's malaise (Kozol, 1991). Satisfying national educational concerns while accommodating unique local needs and priorities remains a dilemma.

CURRENT ORGANIZATION OF SCHOOL GOVERNANCE

Governance patterns constitute a network of educational resources available to highly diverse communities with highly diverse sets of interests. While the particulars vary from state to state, the dominant pattern of educational governance which has evolved provides five levels of influence: the federal government, the state, intermediate districts, school districts, and schools. The authority for making policy is concentrated at two of these levels: the state and the school district.

The primary level of authority is the state, as represented by the legislature, governor, state board of education and superintendent, state education department, and state courts. This level is responsible for establishing basic policy for the system, including its financing, and overseeing and coordinating its components. Structural and financial considerations are usually attended to through formal legislation involving the governor and the legislature.

Oversight of the education law within allowed discretion is delegated to the state board of education and state superintendent of schools. State boards of education are most commonly appointed by the governors, although some are popularly elected. In New York and South Carolina they are elected by the state legislatures and in Washington, they are elected by local school board members. The chief state school officer (CSSO) serves as head of the state education department and in most cases is the chief executive of the state school board. The CSSO is most commonly a professional educator appointed by the state board of education, although in some states he or she is appointed by the governor and popularly elected in others. State education departments are the administrative agencies that implement the education laws of the states and policies of the state school boards.

States exercise their authority over public education through general statements in their constitutions that give state legislatures authority to establish a system of public schools. For example, the New Jersey Constitution provides that the state legislature shall provide a "thorough and efficient" system of education. For the most part, the detail of school governance, i.e., procedures for establishing, financing, and governing school districts, teacher certification, etc., is established by statutes enacted by state legislatures or regulations established by state boards of education. This permits states a great deal of flexibility in reforming school governance structures without going through the cumbersome process of constitutional amendment.

The second level of authority is the local school district which is charged with implementing state policy. School districts are governed by boards of education that focus on the delivery of educational services. Most school boards are fiscally independent, i.e., have taxing authority, although some are fiscally dependent on another unit of local government such as the city or county. School board members are typically elected in non-

partisan elections, although some board members are appointed, especially in larger cities. One of the board's most important responsibilities is to appoint a superintendent of schools to serve as chief executive officer of the school district and to supervise its professional and support personnel.

The school is the basic operating unit; but this third level, until recently, is usually permitted little discretion, as it is constrained by policies formulated at higher levels. The range of discretion at the school level is likely to increase in the future as school-site management and governance reforms are implemented. This discretion may not always be placed in professional hands, however. As already noted, in Chicago, policymaking has been entrusted to school-level boards that have professional representation, but are controlled by lay persons.

The intermediate unit or district is the middle echelon in a state system, serving as an arm of the state while performing services for affiliated school districts of a region. Its organization and governance varies markedly from state to state and some state systems do not include any intermediate unit. It typically has no direct or operational authority over local school districts, but may facilitate state regulatory functions. It provides certain administrative and supervisory functions as well as supplementary educational programs and services where substantial economies of scale can be realized as with occupational education, education of the severely handicapped, staff development, and maintaining information networks and systems.

The fifth level of governance is the federal government. While the United States Constitution is silent about education, leaving responsibility for it to the states, from time to time Congress does pass legislation under its authority to provide for "the general Welfare," national defense, and the protection of civil rights. The Office of Education, more recently upgraded to the Department of Education, was created in the Executive Branch to administer federal laws and to keep statistics. The Secretary of Education, who heads the Department of Education, is appointed by the president with congressional approval. The secretary is a member of the president's cabinet.

Federal courts are arbitrators of the United States Constitution. Litigation concerning school desegregation and school finance inequities have invoked provisions of the Fifth and Fourteenth Amendments to the Constitution. The Fifth Amendment restrains the federal government from depriving any person of "life, liberty or property without due process of law." In the wake of the Civil War, the Fourteenth Amendment was adopted to extend this restraint to the states. The amendment also restrains states and their agents, including school officials, from denying any person "the equal protection of the laws."

Unlike many countries in the world, religiously affiliated elementary and secondary schools are not permitted to receive public monies in the United States, although children attending such schools may have access to publicly provided services—especially transportation and some compensatory services. The basis for exclusion of public funds for religiously oriented schools is a narrow interpretation by the courts of the First Amendment which states that "Congress shall make no law respecting an establishment of religion, or prohibiting the free exercise thereof." This provision was made applicable to the states by the Fourteenth Amendment; but many state constitutions have provisions of their own which are less ambiguous, clearly stating the prohibition of the use of public funds or credit in support of any activity, including operation of schools, sponsored by religious groups.

The variation in the organization of school governance among states and within states is even greater than the above discussion would

suggest. Hawaii is the only state to function as a single unit and, with 165,000 students, it is smaller than a number of large city districts. Texas leads the states in numbers of school districts with 1,087. Of these, 1,061 are fiscally independent. Another twenty-six are fiscally dependent in that another unit of local government provides for their financial support. California has 1,028 school districts including 271 which are unified (provide for pupils in all grades K–12), 645 which operate elementary schools only, and 112 which operate high schools only (Salmon, Dawson, Lawton, & Johns, 1988, p. 44). Over half of California's school districts enroll fewer than 500 pupils.

Small school districts are not only a phenomenon of remote rural areas; there are literally hundreds in the metropolitan counties surrounding major cities. In fragmenting metropolitan communities, great diversity is found among school districts and municipalities in their ethnic and racial composition and in their ability to support public services. Table 3.4 illustrates this for selected units among the subdivisions of Los Angeles County, California (U.S. Department of Commerce, Bureau of the Census, 1992). These municipalities are not necessarily coterminous with school districts, but a similar disparity exists among school districts.

Median family income ranged from $22,279 in Cudahy to $101,320 in Palo Verdes Estates. The population of Cudahy had a median age of 23.5 years; 30 percent were white, 1 percent African-American and 69 percent of other racial and ethnic groups. Sixty-eight percent (68%) of the adult population and 45 percent of the school age population spoke English poorly or not at all. Only 31 percent were high school graduates. Median value of owner-occupied housing was $153,500 and the median contract rent was $599 per month in 1990.

In contrast, the median age of those living in Palo Verdes Estates was 44.5 and 85 percent were white. Only 1 percent were African-American and 14 percent represented other minority groups. Thirty-four percent (34%) of the school-age population and 38 percent of the adult population spoke English poorly or not at all. Nearly all of the adult population had graduated from secondary school. Median value of owner-occupied housing was over $500,000 and the median contract rent was over $1,000 per month in 1990.

In examining the table further, other examples of socio-economic and ethnic segregation are easily found. Hawthorn shows the best balance among ethnic groups. On the other hand, while 11 percent of the county population are African-American, less than 3 percent of the population in Agoura Hills, Artesia, Beverly Hills, Palo Verdes Estates, Cudahy, and Baldwin Park are African-American. While 59 percent of the county population are classified white, over 90 percent of the population in Agoura Hills and Beverly Hills are white. Thirty-two percent (32%) of the county population are classified as "other," but the percentage reaches nearly 70 percent in Cudahy. With the public schools of the county divided in a similar fashion, the ideal of common or integrated schooling is difficult to realize.

A much different policy of school district organization than California's, but less common, is illustrated by Maryland. Maryland's school districts are organized by county and the City of Baltimore. It has 24 school districts, all of which are fiscally dependent. The county organization prevails in the southeast region of the country; Florida, for example, has 67 fiscally independent school districts and Alabama has 129 fiscally dependent school districts. Some western states also follow a regional pattern of school district organization. Nevada has 17 fiscally independent school districts, and Wyoming has 49 districts of which 10 are fiscally independent (Salmon et al., 1988). There is much less inequality among school districts as far as financial and

other provisions in states whose districts are organized along county lines than in state's whose districts are organized into subcounty units.

THE SCOPE OF ELEMENTARY AND SECONDARY SCHOOLING

Education today represents major economic, social, and cultural commitments in the United States. Annual spending on public elementary and secondary schools is about a quarter of a trillion dollars, making expenditures for education the largest single budgetary component of state and local governments (NCES, 1989). Four and three-tenths percent (4.3%) of the Gross Domestic Product (GDP) is spent on preprimary, elementary, and secondary schooling in the private and public sectors combined (3.6 percent in the public sector alone) compared with 2.6 percent in Japan and Germany, 3.3 percent in the United Kingdom, 3.5 percent in France, and 3.8 percent in Canada (NCES, 1993c, p. 140). Schools enroll 47,600,000 pupils (NCES, 1993a, p. 37) and employ nearly 4.5 million professional educators and support personnel (NCES, 1991a, p. 11). In 1985, school districts employed 26.5 percent of all public workers—more than either state or federal governments. Including enrolled pupils, about one in every five persons in the United States is involved directly in formal elementary and secondary education.

Figure 3.3 shows the national trends in revenue sources for public elementary and secondary education for the period 1890 to 1990. In 1890, 79 percent of revenues for public schools were derived from local sources, primarily the property tax. The states provided the balance. By 1988, 47 percent of public school revenues were provided by states, 47 percent came from local sources, and 6 percent from the federal government. The peak years for federal participation in the

Table 3.4
Demographic Statistics for Selected Municipalities in Los Angeles County, California, 1989

	Los Angeles (County)	Los Angeles	Agoura Hills	Artesia	Baldwin Park	Beverly Hills	Cudahy	Culver	Hawthorn	Palo Verdes Estates
Population*	8,863,164	3,485,398	20,390	15,464	69,330	31,971	22,817	38,793	71,349	13,512
Male**	49.9%	50.2%	49.3%	50.0%	50.5%	44.5%	50.7%	47.8%	49.5%	49.4%
Female**	50.1%	49.8%	50.7%	50.0%	49.5%	55.5%	49.3%	52.2%	50.5%	50.6%
White**	56.8%	52.8%	90.1%	56.0%	55.6%	91.3%	30.4%	69.2%	42.3%	84.6%
Black**	11.2%	14.0%	1.2%	2.7%	2.4%	1.7%	1.1%	10.4%	28.3%	1.2%
Other**	32.0%	33.2%	8.7%	41.4%	42.0%	7.0%	68.5%	20.4%	29.4%	14.2%
Percent Foreign Born	32.7	38.4	14.0	38.0	43.0	34.8	55.2	23.5	29.3	16.5
Percent Who Do Not Speak English "Very Well" (5–17)	43.2	46.6	11.3	37.2	38.6	16.8	44.9	33.5	38.2	34.2
Percent Who Do Not Speak English "Very Well" (18+)	58.9	62.8	34.0	57.5	58.2	35.4	67.8	45.0	58.1	37.8
Percent High School Grad+	70.0	67.0	92.9	56.5	50.5	89.4	31.3	84.1	73.9	96.0
Percent Unemployed	7.4	8.4	3.6	6.6	8.5	3.8	10.2	4.1	6.9	3.6
Percent Below Poverty Level	15.1	18.9	3.5	9.3	15.7	6.6	27.5	6.7	13.9	2.3
Median Age*	30.7	30.7	32.8	30.7	25.6	42.2	23.5	36.3	29.3	44.5
Per Capita Income	16,149	16,188	27,539	12,724	8,858	55,463	5,935	21,471	13,880	50,273
Median Household Income	34,965	30,925	70,919	36,383	32,684	54,348	22,279	42,971	30,967	101,320
Median Owner Occupied Housing Value*	226,400	224,500	368,400	205,800	151,100	500,000+	153,500	328,900	226,100	500,000+
Median Gross Rent*	626	600	962	700	648	925	599	788	629	1,000+

*U.S. Department of Commerce, Bureau of the Census. (1991) *1990 Census of Population and Housing: Summary Population and Housing Characteristics* (California) CPH–1–6. Washington, DC: U.S. Government Printing Office.
**Percentages calculated from source data.

SOURCE: U.S. Department of Commerce, Bureau of the Census (1992). *1990 Census of Population and Housing: Summary Social, Economic, and Housing Characteristics* (California) CPH-5-6. Washington, DC: U.S. Government Printing Office.

financing of public schools were 1979 and 1980 when it provided 9.8 percent of their revenue (NCES, 1993b, p. 32).

Figure 3.4 shows the trends in operating expenditures per pupil for public schools since 1971 in current and in constant dollars expressed in terms of 1992–93 purchasing power. In current dollars, per-pupil expenditures have increased over sixteen-fold from $320 in 1971 to $5,149 in 1993. Taking into account the effects of inflation, expenditures have increased over five times from $960 to $5,149 (NCES, 1993a, p. 46). Expenditure increases between 1950 and the late 1970s enabled educational spending to keep pace with inflation and to allow for significant pro-

gram expansions and improvements. The slight decline in constant dollars in the early 1980s (see Figure 3.4) indicates lower spending for schools relative to increases in the cost of living; expenditure growth for public education once again has exceeded inflation since.

Data on public and private school enrollments are displayed in Figure 3.5 for the period 1970–1989 with projections to 2001. Public school enrollments at the elementary level (K–8) were at their peak in 1970 with nearly 33 million pupils; secondary level (9–12) enrollments peaked in 1976 at 14.3 million. The subsequent decline in elementary enrollments reversed in 1985, and has

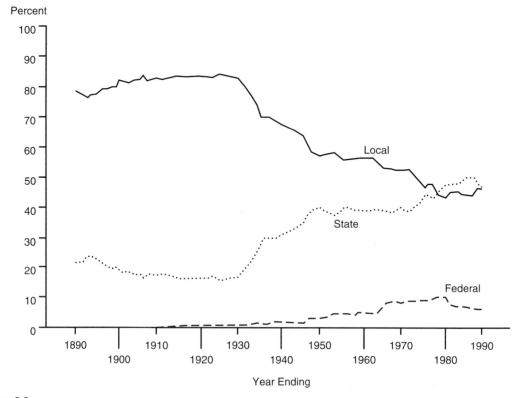

Figure 3.3
Trends in revenue sources for public education: 1890–1990
SOURCE: NCES, 1993b, p. 32.

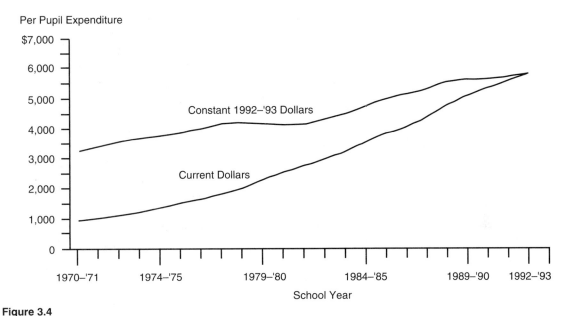

Figure 3.4
Trends in current expenditure per pupil in average daily attendance in current and constant dollars in public schools: 1970–1993
SOURCE: NCES, 1993a, p. 46.

been increasing since. Secondary enrollments began to increase again in 1991 (NCES, 1993c, p. 321).

Enrollment in the elementary grades peaked in 1964 for private schools at 4.5 million; they are currently at about 4.3 million and are projected to rise again to 4.5 million by the end of the century. Enrollment at the secondary level rose to 1.4 million during the period 1981–1984, but has since declined to 1.2 million. Secondary private school enrollments are projected to reach 1.4 million again early in the new millennium. The percentage of pupils enrolled in private schools has remained between 10 and 12 percent for the period 1970–1990 (NCES, 1993c, p. 321).

Although many fear an exodus of students from public to private schools, there is no current evidence that this is happening. The perception of private school growth may be caused by the shifting composition of private school enrollments. In 1966, 87.5 percent of the 6,369,807 pupils in private schools were enrolled in Catholic schools; by 1983, only 57.1 percent of the 5,305,041 private school pupils were in such schools (Cooper, 1988). Enrollment in Catholic schools has dropped 46 percent while increasing 186 percent in non-Catholic schools. Enrollment in evangelical schools approached one million in 1983, an increase since 1966 of 627 percent. Over half of the private schools and 28 percent of their enrollments were related to Protestant churches in 1983.

To serve the 45 million pupils in public schools, local school districts employ the full-time equivalent (FTE) of 4.4 million persons of which 2.3 million are classroom teachers. There are 477,000 instructional support personnel including aides, guidance counselors, and librarians and 200,000 administrators and supervisors. Secretarial and clerical, media personnel, bus drivers, security officers, cafeteria workers, etc. number nearly 1.4 million.

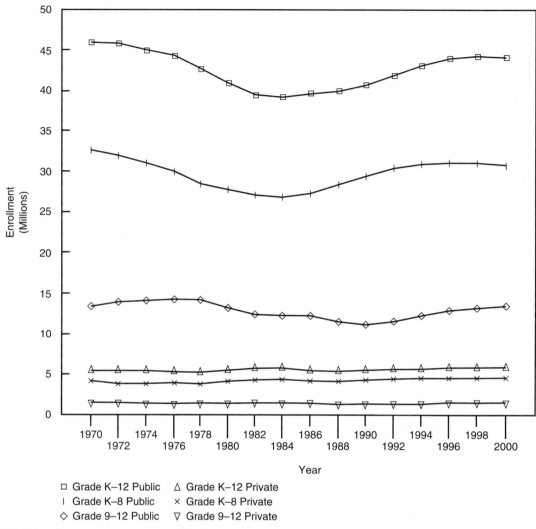

Figure 3.5
Enrollment in grades K–8 and grades 9–12 of public and private schools, with projections: Fall 1970 to Fall 2001.
SOURCE: NCES, 1991b, pp. 198–199.

The percentage of total staff who are classroom teachers dropped from 70 percent in 1950 to 53 percent in 1989. The proportion of administrators in 1989 was 4.5 percent; professional support staff was just under 11 percent and other support staff, 32 percent. The proportion of professional employees, teachers, and administrators has decreased over the years while the proportion of noncertified support personnel has increased from 23 percent in 1950 (NCES, 1990, p. 88).

Despite declining enrollments in public schools since 1971, the total number of professional educators has actually increased. This has produced a continual decline in pupil/professional ratios from 25.6 to one in

Table 3.5
Trends in Pupil-Teacher Ratios and Median Class Size in Public Elementary and Secondary Schools for Selected Years

SOURCE: Data in Column 1: U.S. Department of Education (1991a), *Digest of Education Statistics,* 1988. Washington, DC: Department of Education. Data in column 2 from National Center for Education Statistics (1988b), *The Condition of Education* (Vol. 1). Washington, DC: U.S. Government Printing Office, p. 103; National Education Association (1987). *Status of the American Public School Teacher 1985–1986.*

Year	(1) Pupil-Teacher Ratio	(2) Median Class Size	
		Elementary	Secondary
1961	25.6	30	27
1966	24.1	29	27
1971	22.3	27	26
1976	20.4	26	25
1981	18.8	25	24
1986	17.9	24	22
1990	17.2	NA	NA

1961 to 17.2 to one in 1990. There was a corresponding lowering of the median class size (NCES, 1988a, pp. 102–103). These statistics are reported in Table 3.5.

Declining pupil enrollments ushered in a period of teacher surplus and weakening support for growth in teacher salaries. The trends in teachers' salaries, 1960–1992, are shown in Figure 3.6. While average teacher salaries continued to rise from $10,174 in 1973 during peak enrollments to $34,934 in 1992, their purchasing power did not keep pace with inflation for much of the period. Stated in terms of the purchasing power of the dollar in 1992, the 1973 salary was equivalent to $33,345. From that high point, the purchasing power of the average teacher's salary declined to a low of $28,577 in 1981 when the trend was reversed (NCES, 1993a, p. 419). Salaries paid in 1992 represented a new high in teacher purchasing power. Even though all teachers within a school district are normally paid according to a single salary schedule, secondary teachers average about $1400 more than elementary teachers in salaries reflecting their greater formal education and experience. The average beginning salary in 1992 was $23,054, exceeding the purchasing

power of any previous period. With increasing enrollments and with increasing numbers of retirements of teachers in service, the demand for new teachers is likely to continue to be strong for the rest of the century and teacher salaries should continue to increase at an above-average rate.

Diversity among political subdivisions at the local level and its impact upon equity in the provision of educational opportunities for children have been discussed above. The inequities are compounded by a similar pattern among states. This is illustrated by 1992 statistics reported in Table 3.6 for the fifty states. Variation is on every dimension: size, wealth, expenditure, and effort. Enrollments in state school systems range from over 5,700,000 in California to 105,000 in Vermont and Wyoming. Per capita personal income, a measure of wealth or ability to support public services, ranges from $26,677 in Connecticut to $13,740 in Mississippi. The state with the lowest per pupil revenue is Mississippi at $3,007; Arkansas is only slightly better at $3,095. Excluding Alaska, whose figures are distorted by an unusually high cost of living, the highest spending state is New Jersey at $7,887—nearly $5,000 per pupil more than

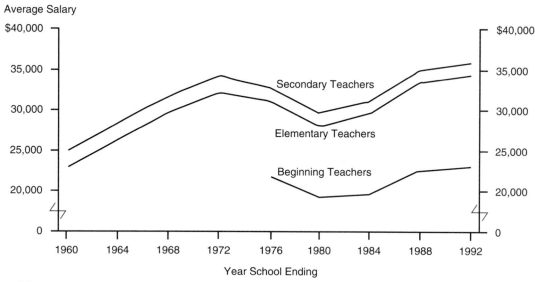

Figure 3.6
Trends in average annual salary of public school teachers and average beginning salary for teachers (in constant 1992 dollars): 1960–1992

SOURCE: National Education Association, Estimates of School Statistics, 1992; American Federation of Teachers, *Survey and Analysis of Salary Trends,* 1992; cited in NCES, 1993c, p. 151.

Mississippi and Arkansas. Again excluding Alaska, average teachers' salaries range from $48,229 in Connecticut to $23,644 in South Dakota. The pupil/teacher ratio is most favorable in New Jersey and Vermont at 13.8 to one; the least favorable is in Utah at 24.9 to one followed by California at 22.8 to one.

The National Center for Education Statistics (NCES, 1993c, p. 397) measures state effort to support public education by the ratio of public school revenues per pupil in relation to per capita income. This ratio, called the Index of Public School Revenues, is presented in the right-hand column of Table 3.6. It reflects what is spent on the average public school student relative to the typical taxpayer's ability to pay (p. 138). According to the index, Alaska puts forth the greatest effort at 38.2 followed by Vermont at 34.9 and Wyoming at 34.5. Tennessee makes the least effort at 20.0. The ratios reported for Wyoming and Alaska may be inflated by a high proportion of oil-producing property, the

taxes on which are exported to oil consumers in other states and do not reflect taxes actually paid by residents of Wyoming and Alaska. From 1930 through 1972, the national index increased by 11.7 points, more than doubling. From 1972 to 1985, the index remained relatively stable, ranging between 21 and 23. Since then, the index has increased 3.0 points or about 13.5 percent.

In this section, we have described the structural context of education in which today's leaders must function. The prevailing pattern of school governance outside of our major cities is one of small, self-governing school districts which function within general parameters set by state and federal governments. The economic, ethnic and social characteristics of school district populations tend to be relatively homogeneous within their boundaries, but very diverse across boundaries. Despite decades of judicial and legislative efforts to desegregate the schools and make the distribution of resources more equi-

Table 3.6
Selected Public School Statistics Related to Enrollment, Wealth, Expenditure, Staffing and Effort of State Systems, 1991–92

State	(1) Enrollment (thousands)	(2) Per Capita Personal Income*	(3) Per Pupil Education Revenues	(4) Average Salary Instructional Staff	(5) Pupil-Teacher Ratio	(6) Index of Effort
U.S.A.	47,197	19,683	5,010	34,934	17.3	25.1
Alabama	793	16,028	3,394	27,326	17.8	21.2
Alaska	125	22,606	8,639	44,463	16.7	38.2
Arizona	701	16,902	4,446	31,668	19.3	26.3
Arkansas	467	15,190	3,095	27,579	17.0	20.4
California	5,708	21,582	4,719	41,037	22.8	21.9
Colorado	638	20,017	4,834	33,573	17.9	24.2
Connecticut	554	26,677	6,931	48,229	14.0	26.0
Delaware	124	20,960	5,020	35,071	16.8	24.0
District of Columbia	97	25,315	5,461	40,274	13.2	21.6
Florida	2,172	19,463	5,087	31,540	17.6	26.1
Georgia	1,280	17,886	4,622	29,986	18.5	25.8
Hawaii	211	21,904	4,727	35,010	18.5	21.6
Idaho	237	15,854	3,489	26,744	19.4	22.0
Illinois	2,181	21,455	4,678	37,081	16.8	21.8
Indiana	1,064	17,734	5,468	34,765	17.5	30.8
Iowa	543	18,033	4,273	29,638	15.7	23.7
Kansas	487	19,065	4,834	29,541	15.2	25.4
Kentucky	716	16,008	4,124	31,347	17.2	25.8
Louisiana	918	15,590	3,656	26,811	16.6	23.5
Maine	230	17,836	5,728	30,553	14.0	32.1
Maryland	859	22,749	5,512	39,664	16.9	24.2
Massachusetts	981	23,587	5,847	37,820	15.1	24.8
Michigan	1,800	19,216	5,256	41,316	19.2	27.4
Minnesota	864	19,684	5,196	34,210	17.2	26.4
Mississippi	561	13,740	3,007	24,737	17.9	21.9

*The figures shown are for calendar year 1991.

SOURCE: Data in column 5: NCES (1993a), *Digest of Educational Statistics*, p. 76; data in column 4: NCES (1993c), *The Condition of Education, 1993*, p. 420.; other columns: NCES (1993c), *The Condition of Education, 1993*, p. 397.

table, this local control tradition has perpetuated the *status quo*. Correcting the inequitable flow of resources while maintaining the vitality and flexibility of decentralized governance is one of the major challenges facing today's educational leadership.

Activities for Discussion

1. Collect statistics on the achievement of students in a nearby school or school district. Compare them with those of

Table 3.6, *continued*
Selected Public School Statistics Related to Enrollment, Wealth, Expenditure, Staffing and Effort of State Systems, 1991–92

State	(1) Enrollment (thousands)	(2) Per Capita Personal Income*	(3) Per Pupil Education Revenues	(4) Average Salary Instructional Staff	(5) Pupil- Teacher Ratio	(6) Index of Effort
Missouri	961	18,381	4,053	29,361	15.8	22.0
Montana	166	16,515	5,015	28,008	15.8	30.4
Nebraska	318	18,385	4,346	27,643	14.7	23.6
Nevada	223	19,765	5,191	37,549	18.6	26.3
New Hampshire	197	21,596	6,294	33,672	15.5	29.1
New Jersey	1,328	26,161	7,887	41,648	13.8	30.1
New Mexico	330	15,278	4,409	26,641	17.6	28.9
New York	3,175	23,135	6,973	43,991	15.4	30.1
North Carolina	1,166	17,145	4,941	29,778	16.8	28.8
North Dakota	126	16,561	4,414	24,866	15.3	26.7
Ohio	2,058	18,452	4,690	33,701	17.3	25.4
Oklahoma	625	16,302	3,745	26,915	15.6	23.0
Oregon	539	18,121	5,033	34,617	18.6	27.8
Pennsylvania	2,063	19,708	5,772	38,753	16.8	29.3
Rhode Island	167	19,394	5,395	39,993	14.6	27.8
South Carolina	681	15,882	4,300	28,636	16.9	27.1
South Dakota	142	16,869	4,010	23,644	14.8	23.8
Tennessee	908	16,816	3,365	29,054	19.4	20.0
Texas	3,688	17,827	4,470	30,169	15.8	25.1
Utah	470	14,968	3,281	26,925	24.9	21.9
Vermont	105	18,269	6,384	33,703	13.8	34.9
Virginia	1,105	20,596	5,095	32,731	15.7	24.7
Washington	943	20,050	5,546	35,408	20.2	27.7
West Virginia	336	14,584	5,001	27,780	15.3	34.3
Wisconsin	963	18,586	5,235	35,760	15.7	28.2
Wyoming	98	17,615	6,073	30,886	15.6	34.5

*The figures shown are for calendar year 1991.

SOURCE: Data in column 5: NCES (1993a), *Digest of Educational Statistics,* p. 76; data in column 4: NCES (1993c), *The Condition of Education, 1993,* p. 420.; other columns: NCES (1993c), *The Condition of Education, 1993,* p. 397.

regional, state and national norms. What are the implications of your findings for school, district, state, and national policy?

2. Collect statistics for a nearby school district that correspond to those reported for states in the United States in Table 3.6. How does your district compare with your state's averages? How does your state compare with other states? What are the implications of your findings for school district, state, and national policy?

3. Select one of the school reform proposals listed below; study its pros and cons and make a recommendation concerning its

acceptance or rejection and under what circumstances:

a. school site-management
b. parental choice of schools
c. raising high school graduation standards
d. year-round schooling and/or longer school day/week
e. national assessment
f. national teacher certification
g. national curriculum.

4. Discuss the "Goals 2000" listed in Table 3.3. Do you believe that they represent the most important challenges to public schools in the United States today? Are they achievable by the year 2000? What changes will have to be made in the elementary and secondary schools of the United States if these goals (or goals which you think are more important) are to be realized?

Annotated Bibliography

Commission on the Skills of the American Workforce. (1990). *America's choice: High skills or low wages!* Rochester, NY: National Center on Education and the Economy.

America's Choice is a product of The National Center on Education and the Economy, a not-for-profit organization created to develop proposals for building an education and training system sufficient to support a national economy that is highly competitive internationally. This report focuses on increasing the productivity of American businesses and industries, thereby protecting the standards of living of American citizens. The Commission observes that no nation has ever produced a highly qualified workforce without first providing its workers with a strong general education. Two factors are identified as standing in the way of producing a highly educated workforce:

lack of a clear standard of achievement and few students motivated to work hard in school. The report documents the seriousness of the condition in which the United States finds itself today and makes recommendations for the establishment of educational performance standards at the national level and means for accomplishing those standards.

Education Week. (Weekly).

Education Week is "American education's newspaper of record." It chronicles the major events that affect elementary and secondary education throughout the United States at all levels of government. This is a vital reference source for educational practitioners and students who wish to keep abreast of the educational scene. In-depth analyses and opinion editorials are included in its weekly coverage.

Elam, S. (Ed.). (1993). *The state of the nation's public schools: A conference report.* Bloomington, IN: Phi Delta Kappa.

The book contains sixteen papers on the state of America's public schools commissioned by Phi Delta Kappa, the professional education fraternity. Both school critics and defenders are represented. Contributors include Michael Kirst—a policy analyst, Harold Hodgkinson—a demographer, Denis Doyle—a futurist with the Hudson Institute, David Berliner—a professor of education, Nathan Glazer—a sociologist, and Albert Shanker—President of the American Federation of Teachers. In addition to the papers, the book records the discussion of the issues addressed and the conclusions arrived at.

Jacobson, S. L., & Berne, R. (Eds.). (1993). *Reforming education: The emerging systemic approach.* Thousand Oaks, CA: Corwin Press.

The editors have assembled an international set of educators, researchers, and thinkers to examine the present and future of educational reform, worldwide. The original pieces are organized into three parts. Part I looks at school reform in the United States. This section reviews the effectiveness of cooperative performance incentives, professional development programs for teachers, decentralization, school-based management, community control of schools, and educa-

tional choice for constituents. Part II focuses on reform initiatives abroad. They include: efforts in England to decentralize decisionmaking power while maintaining national curriculum and assessment systems; Canadian efforts to produce "schools with heart" through volunteerism; and efforts in a unified Germany to reform education in order to keep pace with radical political and social transformations. Part III considers the future of school reform in light of changing realities. The authors discuss the extent to which educational policy and practice will be increasingly politicized, and the likely practical impact of the changes on schools and educators.

National Center for Education Statistics. (Annually). *The condition of education* (Vol. 1). Washington, DC: U.S. Government Printing Office.

The Condition of Education reports annually key data that measure the health of education, monitor important developments, and show trends in major aspects of education. These reports are divided into six areas: (1) access, participation, and progress; (2) achievement, attainment, and curriculum; (3) economic and other outcomes of education; (4) size, growth, and output of educational institutions; (5) climate, classrooms, and diversity in educational institutions; and (6) human and financial resources of educational institutions. Within each section, indicators on issues in elementary and secondary education are integrated with those on issues in post-secondary education to reflect the continuity of educational experiences. Each report includes the text, tables, and charts for each indicator plus technical supporting data, supplemental information, and data sources. These reports are intended to provide federal, state, and local policymakers with the information they need to develop, implement, and monitor policies intended to improve education. They are also a valuable resource for the student of educational leadership.

National Center for Education Statistics. (Annually). *Digest of educational statistics*. Washington, DC: U.S. Government Printing Office.

The Digest of Educational Statistics has been published since 1962. Its primary purpose is to provide a compilation of statistical information covering the broad field of American education

from kindergarten through graduate school. The Digest includes a selection of data from many sources, both government and private, and draws especially on the results of surveys and activities carried out by the National Center for Education Statistics. It is divided into seven chapters: All Levels of Education, Elementary and Secondary Education, Post-Secondary Education, Federal Programs for Education and Related Activities, Outcomes of Education, International Education, and Learning Resources and Technology. To qualify for inclusion, material must be nationwide in scope and of current interest and value. The Digest contains information useful for education researchers and administrators, government officials, the media, the business community, and the general public.*

National Education Goals Panel. (Annually). *National education goals report*. Washington, DC: U.S. Government Printing Office.

Since its creation in July 1990, the National Education Goals Panel has built a cumulative record of the nation's progress toward meeting the goals set at the Charlottesville Education Summit in 1989. At that summit, the nation's governors and President George Bush agreed on six national goals in education to be achieved by the year 2000. Each year at the anniversary of the Charlottesville Summit, the Panel issues a comprehensive report to the nation on the progress being made in achieving each of the goals. The purpose of these reports is to reinforce commitment to the goals process by revealing where progress has been made and where more progress needs to be made. Each annual report consists of two volumes: The National Report and State Reports. Volume One reports progress for the nation as a whole and Volume Two contains a separate section for each state.

U.S. Department of Commerce, Bureau of the Census. (1991). *1990 census of population and housing*. Washington, DC: U.S. Government Printing Office.

Each decade a thorough census is conducted by the U.S. Department of Commerce of the characteristics of the nation's population, including the conditions in which the people live. The data collected are reported in separate volumes at varying levels of aggregation and in varying amounts of detail. At the very least, separate volumes are available for each state and for each major metropolitan area. Within each volume information is provided for subdivisions of the unit. Census information provides public administrators, including school administrators, with information about their communities which is vital for making informed policy decisions. For the researcher, census data are available on magnetic tape for computer analysis in much greater detail than in published format.

W. T. Grant Foundation Commission on Work, Family and Citizenship. (1988). *The forgotten half: Pathways to success for America's youth and young families.* Washington, DC: Author.

Recognizing the needs of older adolescents in a changing society, the W. T. Grant Foundation established the Commission on Work, Family and Citizenship in 1986. After a two-year study, its final report was published based on numerous contracted subanalyses, many of which were also published by the Commission. The Commission did not engage in new research, but sought to evaluate current knowledge, stimulate new ideas, and increase communication among researcher, practitioners, and policy makers. The focus of the Commission's concern is on the 50 percent of American youth who do not go on to college. The Commission concludes that there are far too many young Americans who flounder and ultimately fail in their efforts to navigate the passage from youth to adulthood. "Half of our youth are in danger of being caught in a massive bind that can deny them full participation in our society and the full benefit of their own talents" (p. 1). The report provides documentation supporting that statement and recommendations of policy designed to remove the bind.

References

Berliner, R. F. (1993). Mythology and the American system of education. In S. Elam (Ed.), *The state of the nation's public schools: A conference report* (pp. 36–54). Bloomington, IN: Phi Delta Kappa.

Clinton, D. (1909). Annual message to the legislature. In C. Z. Lincoln (Ed.), *State of New York—Messages from the governors* (Vol. III) (p. 114). Albany, NY: Lyon Co.

Commission on the Skills of the American Workforce. (1990). *America's choice: High skills or low wages!* Rochester, NY: National Center on Education and the Economy.

Cooper, B. S. (1988). The changing universe of U.S. private schools. In T. James & H. M. Levin (Eds.), *Comparing public and private schools* (Vol. 1). Philadelphia: Falmer Press.

Council of Chief State School Officers (CCSSO). (1990). *State education indicators: 1990.* Washington, DC: CCSSO.

Cuban, L. (1988). *The managerial imperative and the practice of leadership in schools.* Albany, NY: State University of New York Press.

Cubberley, E. P. (1947). *Public education in the United States.* Cambridge, MA: Riverside Press.

Drucker, P. F. (1989). *The new realities: In government and politics, in economics and business, in society and world view.* New York: Harper and Row.

Farrar, E. (1990). Reflections on the first wave of reform: Reordering America's educational priorities. In S. L. Jacobson & J. A. Conway (Eds.), *Educational leadership in an age of reform* (pp. 3–13). White Plains, NY: Longman.

Fuhrman, S. H., Elmore, R. F., & Massell, D. (1993). School reform in the United States: Putting it into context. In S. L. Jacobson & R. Berne (Eds.), *Reforming education: The emerging systemic approach* (3–27). Thousand Oaks, CA: Corwin Press.

Galbraith, J. K. (1992). *The culture of contentment.* Boston: Houghton Mifflin.

Hodgkinson, H. (1991). Reform versus reality. *Phi Delta Kappan, 73,* 9–16.

Hodgkinson, H. (1993a). American education: The good, the bad, and the task. In S. Elam (Ed.), *The state of the nation's public schools: A conference report* (pp. 13–23). Bloomington, IN: Phi Delta Kappa.

Hodgkinson, H. (1993b). Keynote address. In S. Elam (Ed.), *The state of the nation's public schools: A conference report* (pp. 194–208). Bloomington, IN: Phi Delta Kappa.

Huelskamp, R. M. (1993). Perspectives on education in America. *Phi Delta Kappan, 74,* 718–721.

Iannaccone, L. (1985). Excellence: An emergent educational issue. *Politics of Education Bulletin, 12*(1), 3–8.

Jacobson, S. L., & Conway, J. A. (Eds.). (1990). *Educational leadership in an age of reform.* White Plains, NY: Longman.

Jefferson, T. (1968). Notes on the State of Virginia. In *The annals of America,* Vol. 2 (pp. 563–573). Chicago: Encyclopedia Britannica, Inc.

Johnson, C. (1904). *Old-time schools and school books.* New York: Macmillan.

Kirst, M. W. (1993). Strengths and weaknesses of American education. In S. Elam (Ed.), *The state of the nation's public schools: A conference report* (pp. 3–12). Bloomington, IN: Phi Delta Kappa.

Kozol, J. (1991). *Savage inequalities: Children in America's schools.* New York: Crown.

Kuhn, T. S. (1970). *The structure of scientific revolutions* (2nd ed.). Chicago: University of Chicago Press.

Morrison, H. C. (1943). *American schools: A critical study of our school system.* Chicago: The University of Chicago Press.

Naisbitt, J. (1982). *Megatrends: Ten new directions transforming our lives.* New York: Warner Books.

Naisbitt, J., & Aburdene, P. (1990). *Megatrends 2000: Ten new directions for the 1990s.* New York: William Morrow.

National Center for Education Statistics (NCES). (1988a, 1989a, 1991a, 1993a). *Digest of educational statistics.* Washington, DC: U.S. Government Printing Office.

National Center for Education Statistics (NCES). (1993b). *120 years of American education: A statistical portrait.* Washington, DC: U.S. Government Printing Office.

National Center for Education Statistics (NCES). (1988b, 1989b, 1990, 1991b, 1993c). *The condition of education* (Vol. 1). Washington, DC: U.S. Government Printing Office.

National Commission on Excellence in Education. (1983). *A nation at risk: The imperative for educational reform.* Washington, DC: U.S. Government Printing Office.

National Commission on Excellence in Educational Administration. (1988). *Leaders for America's schools.* Berkeley, CA: McCutchan.

National Education Goals Panel. (1993). *National education goals report, Volume One: The national report.* Washington, DC: U.S. Government Printing Office.

National Governors' Association. (1986). *Time for results: The governors' 1991 report on education.* Washington, DC: Author.

Olson, L. (1992). 11 design teams are tapped to pursue their visions of "break the mold" schools. *Education Week, 11*(40), 1, 47.

Petrie, H. G. (1990). Reflections on the second wave of reform: Restructuring the teaching profession. In S. L. Jacobson & J. A. Conway (Eds.), *Educational leadership in an age of reform* (pp. 14–29). White Plains, NY: Longman.

Poverty and education. (1992). *Education Week, 11*(16), 5.

Rothman, R. (1992a). 20-nation study shows U.S. lags in math, science. *Education Week, 11*(21), 1, 13.

Rothman, R. (1992b). U.S. ranks high on international study of reading. *Education Week, 12,* 1, 14–15.

Salmon, R., Dawson, C., Lawton, S., & Johns, T. (Eds.). (1988). *Public school finance programs of the United States and Canada, 1986–87.* Blacksburg, VA: American Education Finance Association.

Stevens, T. (1900). Speech on the common school law repeal to the Pennsylvania House of Representatives, 1834. In *Reports of the Department of the Interior for the fiscal year ended June 30, 1899* (Vol. I) (p. 520). Washington, DC: U.S. Government Printing Office.

Toffler, A. (1980). *The third wave.* New York: Bantam Books.

U.S. Department of Commerce, Bureau of the Census. (1991). *1990 census of population and housing: Summary population and housing characteristics* (California) CPH-1-6. Washington, DC: U.S. Government Printing Office.

U.S. Department of Commerce, Bureau of the Census. (1992). *1990 census of population and housing: Summary social, economic, and housing characteristics* (California) CPH-5-6. Washington, DC: U.S. Government Printing Office.

W. T. Grant Foundation Commission on Work, Family and Citizenship. (1988). *The forgotten half: Pathways to success for America's youth and young families*. Washington, DC: Author.

Part II

Inquiry

Inquiry is the close examination of a phenomenon in the quest for information and understanding. It is the process of knowing, of solving puzzles, and of finding truth. For all of the twentieth century, and most of the nineteenth century, inquiry has been dominated by a positivist paradigm. An optimistic attitude that answers to our problems can be discovered through the study of the world as we experience it pervades this paradigm. Positivism requires an empirical verification for all knowledge through use of the scientific method, i.e., hypotheses are stated in advance and subjected to empirical tests under carefully controlled conditions. In the latter part of the twentieth century, the relevance of the positivist paradigm for inquiry into social issues has been seriously challenged by critical theory and other interpretivistic paradigms.

Inquiry into any subject is shaped by one's view of reality, which is a philosophical issue. Part II begins with a discussion of the philosophy of administration and related issues of values, ethics, and morality. Chapter 4 surveys various philosophical points of views and then turns to social science perspectives on values. A person's philosophy determines how one interprets what is experienced. Everyone has a philosophy of life whether or not it has been thought out thoroughly and definitely phrased. To be an effective tool of administrative behavior, however, it is preferable for this philosophy to be understood and intellectualized.

Chapter 5 addresses the process of inquiry directly, lamenting the fact that research in the social sciences has been inconclusive and barren. It suggests that this condition may be a function of the positivist paradigm that has dominated social inquiry. Other paradigms are explored and their strengths and weaknesses examined. The conclusion is drawn that different systems of inquiry will yield different results, even in investigating the same issue; each system of inquiry has its own unique set of strengths and weaknesses. We are beyond the point of once again trying to establish hegemony of one paradigm over all others. Rather, it is time to realize that no one paradigm can fulfill all the needs of social inquiry and that, in our search for truth and understanding, we need to draw upon the insights that each provides.

The last chapter of Part II discusses the act which is fundamental to all inquiry, observation. We tend to see (and hear) in varying degrees of completeness. A great deal of our success as educational leaders depends upon the power and clarity of our observational skills. Chapter 6 suggests ways in which our observational skills can be improved through training and reflection.

Chapter 4
Impact of Universal Principles, Social Expectations, and Personal Values on Leadership

Philosophy, in its broadest meaning, is a systematic attempt to make sense out of our individual and collective human experience (De George, 1982). The philosopher's primary intellectual tool is reason. Ethics is that part of philosophy concerned with morality, a complex of ideals showing how individuals should relate to one another in particular situations, to principles of conduct guiding those relationships, and to the kind of reasoning one engages in when thinking about such ideals and principles (L.M. Smith, 1990).

Practically all of our activities occur within the context of decisions made about good and bad, right and wrong, or better and worse. Behavior, therefore, is a constant reflection of beliefs about how the world is structured and decisions are made, and how actions taken are based, implicitly or explicitly, on those philosophical considerations (Foster, 1986). Everyone has a philosophical view of life even though it may not have been thoroughly thought through and articulated (Nyberg, 1974). To be an effective guide to administrative behavior, however, it is best if

this philosophy is understood and intellectualized. Such an understanding permits a leader to act consistently on pertinent issues and to reflect critically upon those actions. For this reason, it is important that persons in leadership roles learn "to do" philosophy for themselves rather than leave it to be done by others by default.

According to Hodgkinson (1983), the essence of the art of administration is the manipulation of people by people about goals. He sees the most persuasive reason for doing philosophy in the field of executive action as being derived from the fact that administrators possess power; they make decisions that affect other people. "If morality is interpreted as a concern for others then it follows that administration is a peculiarly moral activity" (p. 29).

The field of executive action and the administrative endeavor which embraces it make philosophical demands. It is the highest function of the executive to develop a deep understanding of himself and his fellows, a knowledge of human nature which includes motivation but reaches beyond into the domain of value possibilities. . . . At its lowest level, organizational life is sort of a daily combat. Even here, however, the deadliest weapons in the administrative armory are philosophical: the skills of logical and critical analysis, conceptual synthesis, value analysis and commitment, rhetoric and most fundamentally, the depth understanding of human nature. So in the end philosophy becomes intrinsically practical. (Hodgkinson, 1983, p. 53)

Preparation programs for school administrators have been roundly criticized for emphasizing organizational, behavioral, and managerial theories while neglecting contextual considerations of culture, politics, morals, and ethics (Foster, 1986). Cambron-McCabe (1993) saw in the current school debate a challenge to the technocratic perspective that has traditionally characterized administrative preparation programs. She pointed out that traditional programs taught administrators that organizations are rational, mechanistic structures that operate in a bureaucratic fashion. The programs focused on operational tasks, training administrators as management functionaries; consideration of moral, ethical, and values dimensions of leadership were largely absent. She observed that "[o]ne of the stances of the current reform effort is to make visible that leadership involves moral choices, not simply an adherence to technicism" (p. 157).

Sergiovanni (1992) holds a similar position. He charged that the dominating emphasis in contemporary programs on rationality, logic, objectivity, the importance of self-interest, explicitness, individuality, and detachment causes us to neglect the importance of group membership, sense and meaning, morality, self-sacrifice, duty, and obligation as additional values. "[W]e have come to view leadership as behavior rather than action, as something psychological rather than spiritual, as having to do with persons rather than

ideas" (p. 3). To overcome this bias, he believes that it is necessary to give more attention in the preparatory curriculum to concepts of professional and moral authority.

The National Policy Board for Educational Administration (1989) has recommended that the curriculum preparing school administrators be designed to provide frameworks and tools to assist students in assessing the moral and ethical implications of the decisions they make. According to the Board, students of school administration must come to understand the concept of public trust and to realize how values affect behaviors and outcomes.

The board also recommended that students need to be encouraged to examine their own belief systems, their reasons for wanting to be administrators, and their images of the mission of schooling as a social process. Daresh (1988) referred to such understandings as "professional formation" which is defined as an effort to enable an individual to become aware of his or her own personal values and assumptions regarding the formal role of a school administrator (Daresh & Playko, 1992, p. 54). Professional formation addresses personal growth and development in the training of school administrators. It includes mentoring or coaching by experienced administrators and university faculty, the identification of one's personal administrative style, development of an ability to reflect in action, and commitment to constant self-preparation and taking moral and ethical stances.

In a similar vein, Sergiovanni (1984b) used the term "platform" as the articulation of one's principles into an operational framework. The platform governs a person's outlook and behavior in that it represents a set of criteria and an implicit standard from which decisions are made.

In studying trends in the reform of school administrator preparation programs, Murphy (1993) concluded that there is a new and general concern for including ethics in the curriculum. He hypothesizes that underlying this concern is a shared understanding among program staff that sound professional judgement and conduct are contingent on sound ethical judgement and conduct and that, in on-the-job contexts, routine practical decisions and ethical decisions are often indistinguishable. More specifically, these reformed programs acknowledge the fact that administrators are representatives of values and that the responsibility of principals to their students, teachers, and communities is to provide leadership based on an informed ethical reflection about education and public life. Murphy believes that, unless leaders develop a moral and ethical conscience, they will find it difficult to make decisions and will lose a sense of purpose.

In this chapter, we look at the importance of ethical considerations in the practice of educational leadership. We begin by describing selected philosophical views of the world and how they might influence executive behavior. Then, drawing also from social science perspectives, we focus on values and value hierarchies as they are found in individuals and organizations. How leaders analyze the world in the context of value systems is described. In the final section, we show how values in the form of metavalues shape the perception of reality in organizations and challenge administrative leaders to accept those value parameters or transform them to direct change.

Philosophical Guides to Leadership

To be effective, administrative behavior must rest on certain philosophical assumptions about such fundamental considerations as human nature, the nature of reality, conditions of knowledge, and the nature of value. Further, such behavior must be in harmony with great cultural movements and the ideas that impel them—ideas that are inevitably philosophical in character (Graff et al., 1966). Today's leaders must develop a holistic perspective that enables them to comprehend the myriad forces and conditions affecting important social, economic, scientific, and governmental institutions.

School administrators today are faced with pressures from all sides. Bewildering expectations are placed on the schools and the people who staff them. There is bitter conflict over what the purposes of education should be and how educational services should be delivered. The function of administration in relation to educational leadership is not clearly understood. School administrators desiring to provide effective leadership need a philosophical reference point from which to evaluate and base their actions. Without such a reference point, the administrator drifts like a rudderless ship on a stormy sea. This section provides a brief overview of some of the major philosophical systems that have been, or are, particularly influential in shaping our culture and the lives of individuals: idealism, liberalism, positivism and postpositivism, pragmatism, existentialism, critical theory, and constructivism. One system is not necessarily better than another, but the orientation to life and the behavior of a person subscribing to one system will be different from that of a person subscribing to another. Personal philosophies tend to be eclectic, having elements of several of the basic systems.

The roots of idealism can be traced back to ancient Greek scholars who conceptualized the idea that there exists a system of perfect ideas that should serve to guide human decisions and behavior. Being highly compatible with the Judeo-Christian tradition enhanced idealism's influence on Western culture. Liberalism, which emphasizes individual freedom, began to emerge along with rationalism, scientific inquiry, free market capitalism, and a growing middle class in the seventeenth and eighteenth centuries. It subscribes to universal natural laws and provided the intellectual basis for several political revolutions during the eighteenth and nineteenth centuries, including the American Revolution. It is largely the philosophy of liberalism that is expressed in the American Declaration of Independence and the United States Constitution.

Positivism and postpositivism have dominated intellectual thought from the late nineteenth century until today. Both stem from the philosophy of science and subscribe to a reality which is independent of the human observer, but discoverable through science. The hegemony of postpositivism seems to be waning at the close of the twentieth century as is discussed at the end of this section. The claim to objectivity by the postpositivists (i.e., the separation of fact and value) is being challenged currently by critical theorists and constructivists. Critical theorists continue to hold along with postpositivists a belief in a reality independent of human experience; however, critical theorists reject the idea of the objectivity of science and claim that all inquiry is mediated by value considerations. Constructivists also reject the objectivity of science and, further, they reject the concept of any reality beyond that of individual human experience.

Pragmatism and existentialism are included as examples of two highly influential philosophies of the twentieth century. Pragmatism has much in common with postpositivism, but emphasizes the importance of utility or consequences in determining what is truth—or reality. John Dewey was a prominent pragmatist and, through him, pragmatism has had a strong influence on thinking about education—the progressive education movement in particular. Existentialism reached its zenith of influence beginning with World War I and continuing for several years following World War II. It has much in common with constructivism, accepting no reality other than individual human experience. It urges individuals to assume full responsibility for their own actions.

Table 4.1 has been developed as a summary and guide for the reader through the discussion on philosophies that follows. The table presents abbreviated statements for each philosophy considered on how it tends to view the nature of reality (ontology), the relationship between the knower and the known (epistemology), conceptions of the desirable (values), and the nature of the schooling experience likely to be preferred.

IDEALISM

Idealism dominated learned thought until late in the nineteenth century. It is still deeply ingrained in the thinking and institutions of Western civilization. There are many variations of idealistic thought, often identified with their originators such as Plato, Kant, and Hegel.

The philosophy of idealism conceives the universe as being dualistic in nature. It assumes that the ultimate reality consists of a system of great ideas that transcend everyday experiences and are universal, enduring, and absolute. The world of everyday experience which is open to empirical or sensory exploration is not believed to be the real world, but a reflection of it. The ultimate reality is a system of perfect ideas. The world of everyday experiences is considered to be a world of illusions and the *real* world can only be reached through pure reason, intuition, or through revelation, in the case of religion. Similarly, idealists assume a dualistic nature of humankind, the body and the mind (or soul), the latter being the more important.

The elevation of universal truths over experience differentiates idealism from all other schools of philosophy. The idealist believes that absolute knowledge is obtained through the exercise of pure reason uncontaminated by empirical data. Thus, deductive logic

Table 4.1

Summary of the Beliefs of Selected Philosophies on Fundamental Philosophical Questions and the Type of Schooling Most Compatible with Those Beliefs

Philosophies	Questions			
	Ontology: What is the nature of the knowable "reality?"	Epistemology: What is the nature of the relationship between the knower and the known?	Values: Conceptions of the desirable	Schooling Preference
Idealism	Universal, enduring, and absolute ideas which transcend everyday experience	Experienced world is a reflection of reality; humankind is dualistic in nature, i.e., the spiritual and the physical; understanding is gained from deductive logic removed from everyday experience	That which is identical with universal truths; coherence; stability; great minds	Training of the mind, i.e., the classical tradition, emphasizing Socratic Method; imitation; dialectics
Liberalism	Universal laws rooted in nature; natural rights discoverable through science	Human and physical actions operate according to natural law; understanding is gained through rational inquiry	Liberty; freedom; reason/rationality/ scholarship; goodness; tolerance; human perfectability	Liberal education to sharpen the tools of reason and to further the development of individuals; objective, experimental and observational techniques
Realism, Postpositivism and Logical Positivism	Reality is in and of this world—governed by universal law which can be discovered through empirical research	Objectivist: value is separate from fact; human and physical interactions operate according to universal law; understanding is gained through empirical verification/ scientific method	That which is harmony with discoverable universal law/theory; objectivity; empiricism; reason/rationality/ scholarship	Clinical/laboratory/experiential learning; basic skills

Table 4.1, continued
Summary of the Beliefs of Selected Philosophies on Fundamental Philosophical Questions and the Type of Schooling Most Compatible with Those Beliefs

Philosophies	Questions			
Pragmatism	Truth is known through its practical consequences; it is a product of social practices	Knowledge is constructed in the minds of humankind through their collective experience; understanding is gained through rational inquiry/scientific method	Utility; experience; new ideas and newly discovered facts; reason/rationality/scholarship	Clinical/laboratory; problem solving experiential learning; Progressive Education
Existentialism	The world as it is experienced and interpreted by each individual; there are no universal laws or principles of importance to humankind	Meaning and purpose are defined by each individual through free choice; understanding is gained through introspection to find guidance and direction	Autonomy; authenticity; personal freedom and responsibility; human will; introspection	Arts and humanities; concern with emotions and feeling; personal relationship between teacher and student; enhance individuality
Critical Theory	There is a reality independent of human existence, but may never be fully understood	Subjectivist: values mediate inquiry; paradigms are of human construction; understanding is gained through dialogic and transformative processes	Autonomy; responsibility; emancipation; commitment; reason/rationality/scholarship	The elimination of false consciousness and facilitating transformation
Constructivism	Socially and experientially based mental constructions by the person who holds them	Subjectivist: values mediate inquiry; understanding is gained through dialogical process between the self-understanding person and that which is encountered	Relativism; social consensus; personal experience; solidarity	Experiential, multicultural, self-reflection, relativistic, continuing

becomes the primary intellectual tool in the search for truth. Since truth is not seen to exist in the world of experience, studying phenomena of this world is not a necessary source of knowledge. The idealist holds that the validity of truth is tested through one or more rigorous systems of logic (Graff et al., 1966), i.e., does it stand the test of logic by the great minds of the ages? The application of idealism to education is best illustrated by the "classical tradition" which gives priority to the "training of the mind."

The idealist assumes that there are ultimate and absolute values. The values of greatest worth are those that are identical to "Truth." (Knowledge is virtue; virtue is happiness; happiness is living in accord with Truth.) These true values are not to be questioned, but accepted as guides for living. Idealism seeks the maintenance of the status quo; in the face of great social, economic, political and technological changes, it looks to the past for solutions. Idealism resists change.

LIBERALISM

The central idea of liberalism is liberty; but the liberal's view of liberty is not absolute. Liberalism strives for a society that freely acts together to ensure the welfare of the many using methods that fortify the freedoms of individuals, enabling them to fulfill their potentials as each sees fit. Freedom is sought as a method and a policy of government, as an organizing principle in society, and as a way of life for the individual.

The golden age of liberalism dates roughly between the era of the French philosophers (c. 1750) and the start of World War I. Many of the founders of the United States (e.g., Thomas Jefferson and Benjamin Franklin) were committed to liberalism and the Declaration of Independence and the United States Constitution are political expressions of liberalism. The emphasis of liberalism on liberty

and freedom aligns naturally with economic concepts of free market capitalism; thus, it has had a particularly strong appeal to the middle class and to business interests. Liberalism experienced a relative decline in popularity and influence after World War I. With the recent failure of the monolith totalitarian and communist states, liberalism has gained new credibility and vitality. Among the European scholars contributing to liberal thought are Voltaire, Locke, Rousseau, Hume, Kant, A. Smith, and J. S. Mill.

In addition to holding liberty as a central value, liberalism perceives humans as being equipped with reason and goodness and endowed with certain natural rights, presented in the American Declaration of Independence as "life, liberty and the pursuit of happiness." It is mankind's meddling with the natural order which, according to liberals, accounts for social disorder; it is the social structures of customs, traditions, and institutions that corrupt individuals. Therefore, the best course of action, for the most part, is to leave things alone.

Other central concepts of liberalism include the creation of social conditions that allow individuals to maximize their freedom to think, to believe, to discuss, to act, to organize, to work, to carry on commerce, to choose their rulers and their form of government—and to change both rulers and government by revolution, if necessary. Liberalism stresses the importance of self-interest as a motivational force, reason as the instrument of science, and individual effort leading to self-realization (Lerner, 1972).

Liberalism does recognize, however, that while humankind is basically good, attributes like ambition, desire for power, and political passions in excess can cause difficulty for others, and a majority gone awry can be as tyrannical as any other despot. Thus, the liberal view supports building safeguards into governmental structures to protect minority interests such as the Bill of Rights and the doctrine of separation of powers as found in the Constitution.

Liberalism dilutes the certitude of revealed religious dogma and emphasizes tolerance toward all religious and other philosophical expression. It encourages free thought and scholarship and endorses rationalism and science. The focus is on human perfectibility—what mankind can achieve for itself to enhance the happiness of all. Removal of governmental, religious, and other traditional/structural restrictions provide humankind with the freedom to function; but an educated populous is necessary to provide the tools by which reason can function and through which human perfectibility may be furthered. Thus, universal education is fundamental to the realization of liberal ideals.

REALISM, LOGICAL POSITIVISM, AND POSTPOSITIVISM

Unlike idealism, the central tenet of the philosophy of logical positivism, or just positivism, is that reality is in and of this world. (See the related discussion of positivism and postpositivism in Chapter 5.) Realist truths are not figments of the mind; they are discovered in everyday experiences. There is confidence that answers to our problems can be discovered through studying experience. This philosophy gained influence with the rise of science, and some positivist philosophers view science as a substitute for philosophy. It has been the dominant philosophy during the mid- to late-twentieth century although it is now being seriously challenged—at least in the social sciences—by critical theory and other interpretivistic paradigms. Positivism requires an empirical verification for all knowledge through use of the scientific method, i.e., hypotheses are stated in advance and subjected to empirical tests under carefully controlled conditions.

Positivists do not believe in a mind separate from the body as idealists do. The great truths of the universe are believed to be bound up in matter and can be discovered by using the methods of science whether studying natural, social, or human phenomena. The positivist assumes that human interactions operate according to universal law as does the physical world and can be discovered through research. The happiness and well-being of humankind depend upon how well members of society keep in tune with those laws governing conduct, social relationships, and economic endeavors.

The positivist practices an objectivist epistemology, i.e., value is separated from fact. This is done using a manipulative methodology that controls for the inquirer's bias on the one hand and nature's propensity to confound on the other, and empirical methods that place the point of decision with nature rather than with the inquirer (Guba, 1990).

The positivist and the idealist assume the same rigidity regarding truth. Their difference is the process by which truth is discovered. In both philosophies, it is assumed that truth has a universal quality (Graff et al., 1966).

Postpositivism is a modified version of positivism that moves away from what is now seen as a "naive" realist posture and toward a posture called "critical realism" (Guba, 1990). The essence of this position is that, given their imperfect sensory and intellectual mechanisms, it is impossible for humans to perceive perfectly the real world driven by real natural causes. Postpositivists, nevertheless, maintain that there are universal truths, although no one can be sure that those ultimate truths have been discovered. Reality is driven by natural laws that can be only partially understood.

For postpositivists, objectivity remains a governing ideal, but with a recognition that it can only be approximated. They seek a modified objectivity that comes reasonably close to the ideal by striving to make their research designs as value-neutral as possible. This is accomplished by revealing one's own predispositions (biases), by requiring reports of any inquiry to be consistent with the existing scholarly tradition of the field, and by subjecting the results of every inquiry to the judgement of peers in the "critical community," i.e., editors and referees of journals as well as their readers (Guba, 1990).

Positivism and postpositivism deal only with what is, not what ought to be. Aims and value judgments cannot be made through analysis of purely empirical propositions. "Ought" issues remain within the realm of philosophy.

PRAGMATISM

Pragmatism developed out of traditional positivism. It holds that the real essence of ideas is to be found in their utilization as guides to action and behavior, i.e., truth can be known only through its practical consequences. Pragmatists have a basic distrust of the reliability of human ideas until they are tested by experience. Graff et al. (1966) refer to pragmatism as the "American philosophy."

According to Graff et al. (1966), pragmatism makes the following assumptions: (1) it is impossible for humans to gain knowledge of ultimate reality; (2) the universe is in a constant state of change and motion; (3) the world of ideas as we know it is incorporated in systems of symbols, letters, words, and mathematical formulae which have no reality in themselves but refer to items of practice and ways of doing things; (4) the scientific method is the most valid way of testing ideas; and (5) the social aspects of living are extremely important to the individual.

Pragmatism accepts the world of sense impressions and scientific study and rejects idealism's supernatural notions of an outside world of true and perfect ideas as the ultimate reality. In an evolving universe, the pragmatist finds it meaningless to speculate about the nature of reality. Instead, the pragmatist believes that, to know reality, one must immerse oneself into all aspects of the world, experiencing it to the fullest. Thus, the pragmatist is always open to new ideas and newly discovered facts.

Pragmatists hold that all social institutions are servants and not masters of humankind and that educational institutions are among the most important. People are viewed as products of both heredity and environment (social and natural); they are neither "good" nor "bad" at birth, but may develop in either direction depending upon their experiences with other people and social institutions. This concept of humans as pliable entities places a heavy responsibility on schools and demands of them the best possible service (Graff et al., 1966).

EXISTENTIALISM

Existentialism is a philosophical tendency or attitude rather than a philosophical school; thus there are few doctrines common to all of its exponents. It grew out of the aftermath of World War I, the Great Depression, and World War II and concerns itself with the darker and more foreboding aspects of human life. It is a protest against views of the world and policies of action in which individual human beings are regarded as helpless creatures whose destinies are shaped wholly by historical forces or natural processes. Existentialism urges humankind to rid itself of the palliatives that have been devised to cushion the despair of human existence and to face up to the realities of a meaningless world full of anguish, loneliness and death. Its fundamental tenets are autonomy, authenticity, and the complete freedom of the individual to choose a way to live. Reality is considered to be the world of the existing as it is experienced and interpreted by each individual (Graff et al., 1966).

Existentialist writers seek to justify the freedom and importance of human personality. They emphasize the place of human will in contrast with reason. Each individual is considered unique and inexplicable in terms of any metaphysical or scientific system. Because the individual is totally free in making choices, his or her future is not wholly predictable and the burden of free choice generates personal suffering.

Existentialists believe that individuals must look within themselves to find guidance and direction through today's crises. It is believed that such direction cannot be derived from universal laws and principles, the lessons of history, government, other human beings, God, or modern science. They consider it a grievous error to view the world as possessing order and purpose that can or should determine the course of life. Such course is the creation of the individual living it.

Existentialists place the final responsibility on the individual for deciding who and what he or she is and, thereby, defining his or her own reality. They implore individuals to reject the escapism of social conformity and orthodox values and to face the stark reality of what it means to exist as a free individual and the pain and suffering that such freedom entails.

Existentialists see education as a process of unfolding from within and are concerned with emotions, feelings and matters that deal with the real existence of humankind. They tend to place greater emphasis on liberal education than on vocational and professional preparation. They emphasize a personal relationship between the teacher and student whereby the teacher reaches to the heart and mind of students, creating inner conflict, and challenging and stimulating students' thinking (Graff et al., 1966). Existentialists warn against overemphasis on socialization and

group togetherness in education. Believing in the preeminence of individuality, they look with disfavor on any educational arrangement that might impinge on the completely free development of the individual.

CRITICAL THEORY

Like the postpositivist, the critical theorist believes that there is a reality that exists independent of human experience, but that this reality may never be fully understood. Both share the assumption that theory possesses the power to affect progress positively and to transform human life. Here the similarities between the two philosophies end, however. The critical theorist is subjectivistic in epistemology, rejecting objectivity and claiming that values mediate inquiry. Because paradigms are human creations, critical theorists assert that paradigms inevitably reflect the values of those who created them. Nature cannot be seen as it "really is" except through a values window that distorts that reality.

The task of critical theory is to raise the consciousness of people (the oppressed) to the true nature of their condition and to the forces causing it. Appreciating how oppressed they are and why, individuals can act to transform their world (Guba, 1990). Knowledge enlightens people by revealing the structural conditions of their existence, how these conditions came about, and the distortions and injustices they create. Such knowledge brings with it the power to stimulate action seeking greater autonomy, responsibility, and emancipation (Greene, 1990). Thus, the governing ideal for critical theory is the uniting of reason and commitment, i.e., the integration of knowledge and purposeful action. It seeks to make transparent the causes of distorted communication and understanding (House, 1990).

Critical theory focuses on the conceptualization of education as part of the social, political, cultural, and economic patterns by which schooling is formed. It gives reference to schooling as a socially constructed enterprise that contains continuing contradictions (Popkewitz, 1990). (See the related discussion of critical theory in Chapter 5.)

CONSTRUCTIVISM

The constructivist does not believe in a universal reality, but rather, in multiple social- and experience-based mental constructions that depend upon the person holding them for form and content. These constructions are local and specific. As with critical theory, the epistemology of constructivism is subjectivist. The observer and the observed are fused into a single entity; observations are literally the creation of the process of interaction between the two. Constructivism does not pretend to predict and control the "real" world nor to transform it but, rather, to reconstruct the world at the only point at which it is believed to exist: in the minds of the constructors. It is the mind that is to be transformed, not the "real" world (Guba, 1990). "Reality," as a social construction, can only be seen through windows of theory and values derived from human interactions. Theories and values are aimed at constructing meaning through social consensus among participants in a given context (Greene, 1990).

No unequivocal explanation is ever possible according to constructivists. There can be many constructions but, for constructivists, there is no foundational way to choose among them. Unlike critical theory, constructivistic inquiry is not directly concerned with judging, evaluating or condemning existing forms of social and political reality, or with changing the world; rather, it is concerned with describing and understanding their essence. Common goals of constructivistic inquiry are to enlarge and enrich human discourse by bringing experiences of strangers together with our own understandings and our own experiences (Greene, 1990). Since the constructivist rejects the concept of universal laws and principles, each person must determine for himself or herself the relevance of others' experiences to one's own experience.

Knowledge, as a human construction, is never certifiable as ultimately true according to constructivists; knowledge is problematic and ever changing. Knowledge is the result of a dialogical process between the self-understanding person and that which is encountered—whether a text, a work of art, or the meaningful expressions of another person (J. K. Smith, 1990). Constructivist knowledge is grounded in experience and resembles context-specific working hypotheses more than generalizable propositions that warrant certainty or even probability (Greene, 1990). It constitutes holistic pattern theories or webs that reflect an intertwinement of part and whole and a view of knowledge that is more "circular" than hierarchic (Lincoln, 1990).

At the core of constructivism is the governing ideal of solidarity rather than objectivity. Thus, the constructivist position takes on many aspects of relativism. Relativism is seen as a key to openness and the search for more informed and sophisticated constructions (Guba, 1990).

The relativistic characteristics of constructivism has led to charges from idealists, postpositivists, and progressives that, in rejecting foundational standards, constructivism takes on a form of irrationalism. Constructivists respond that if there is no foundation, there is no structure against which other positions can be "objectively" judged (Lather, 1990). According to Lather, relativism appears as a problem only for dominating groups at the point where the hegemony of their views is being challenged. "In sum, fears of relativism and its seeming attendant nihilism or Nietzschean anger seem to me an implosion of Western, White male, class-privileged arrogance—if we cannot know everything, then we can know nothing" (p. 321).

Nyberg (1993) also tends to discount the danger of runaway relativism because he saw that "even as values clash, there is a great deal of agreement within the moral universe about right and wrong, good and bad, which the majority of humankind assumes" (p. 208). There is much more that unites us than divides us.

TWO VIEWS OF THE WORLD

The hegemony of postpositivist thinking directly affected the study of educational administration in the mid-1950s with the application of social science constructs and methodologies (in turn derived from the natural sciences). In embracing a postpositivist perspective, attention to the qualitative dimensions of educational administration was sorely neglected according to many critics of its "science" and practice (Greenfield, 1984; Hodgkinson, 1983; Sergiovanni, 1984a, 1992; Lather, 1990; Foster, 1984). The emphasis placed by the scientific method on quantitative measurement and value objectivity focused research and discussion on "what is" and the search for relationships among observable phenomena rather than on "what should be." Interest in the roles that values, emotions, meaning, and morality play in the practice of school administration has been largely absent until the relatively recent challenge to postpositivist thinking made by critical theorists and constructivists.

Greenfield (1978) was among the first educational administration theorists of the critical theory persuasion to attack the postpositivist hegemony although others (e.g., Graff et al., 1966) had earlier pointed to the postpositivist insistence on the empirical verification of knowledge as a most serious error. Greenfield challenged the perceptions of organizations as manifestations of natural order that are subject to universal and impersonal scientific laws (Greenfield, 1984). Rather, he argued, organizations are manmade, arbitrary, ephemeral, and not universal; in other words,

they are "nonnatural." Greenfield saw organizations as cultural artifacts and what goes on within them as products of individual action, intention, and will rather than of universal natural laws of social action. This view characterizes organizations as human creations which provide contexts for the negotiation and construction of meaning, moral order, and power (Bates, 1984).

Bates (1984, p. 260) is highly critical of mainstream theorists of educational administration for continuing to declare the incommensurability of fact and value and their pursuit of positivistic attempts to develop generalizable laws and principles to explain the structure and dynamics of organizations. He bases his criticisms on the contemporary positions of philosophers and social scientists. Philosophers, he points out, acknowledge the impossibility of eliminating evaluative judgments from the interpretive frameworks within which facts are both sought and understood and social theorists have largely abandoned the value-free science of society.

Foster (1984) pointed out that the "objectivity" of postpositivism is not objective at all; by removing reflective and dialectical thought from the province of meaningful expression, postpositivism is biased in perpetuating the existent social order unchallenged. In focusing on reflective and dialectical thought, however, Foster does not demean the relevance of an administrative science by saying, "it does a disservice to critical theory to suggest that such reflection must remain limited to subjectivistic impressions: empirical verification is required; data are necessary" (p. 249). Elsewhere, Foster (1986) proposed a three-tier model for the study of administration. The first tier involves the empirical study of organization and administration through descriptions of perceived reality and economic and political structures. The second tier consists of the development of individual constructions and interpretations of reality. The third tier is critical inquiry, a reflective process that includes dialogue intended to achieve true democratic participation by all members of the community.

Sergiovanni (1984a) joined Foster in calling for a multiple-perspective approach to the analysis of administration and organizations:

Theories of administration, therefore, should not be viewed as competing, with the thought that one best view might emerge. Instead, the alternative and overlapping metaphor is offered. When viewed this way, each theory of administration is better able to illuminate and explain certain aspects of the problems administrators face but not others. Increased understanding depends upon the use of several theories, preferably in an integrated fashion. (p. 1)

Nyberg (1993) divided philosophers (and other people) into two broad orientations toward formulating moral judgments. The "moral-principle" orientation favors "ideas that are extensive, inclusive, universal and elegant in their simplicity" (p. 206). These would tend to include idealists and positivists. The "personal-value" orientation prefers to see "individuals with perfect clarity, in all their literal, particular, factual fullness. . . no matter how fragmented the world may then seem" (p. 206). These would include existentialists and constructivists. The moral-principal orientation tends to view rationality as the striving for economy of means of thought by holding allegiance to a single conception or idea that can be applied broadly. The personal-value orientation's view of rationality is that "people can think and act in ways they themselves can understand and alter, that individuals are not merely victims of structural causes, and that justifications and explanations of human conduct must be in terms of personal, subjective motives and reasons, however idiosyncratic they may seem" (p. 198).

To close this section, we refer to an article by Gage (1989) entitled "The Paradigm Wars and Their Aftermath." In it, he addresses the current conflict among educational researchers who adhere to one of the competing philosophies of postpositivism, constructivism, critical theory, and antinaturalism. He issues an appeal to our educational intellectual leaders—philosophers, scientists, scholars, research workers—not to become bogged down in an intellectual no man's land and reminds us that "even as we debate whether any objectivity at all is possible, whether 'technical' research is merely trivial, whether your paradigm or mine should get more money, I feel that I should remember that the payoff inheres in what happens to the children, the students. This is our end concern" (p. 10). Our tasks carry with them moral obligations.

Thus, there seems to be a great divide between those who view the world in terms of a single paradigm and those who accept none as absolute, but are willing to be guided by insights provided by many. The authors of this book fall into the latter category. We recognize that educational administration is a moral pursuit and that the effective administrator must act with an understanding of the relevance of value structures to his or her executive actions. This chapter focuses on such aspects of administration. We also appreciate, however, the contributions of the social sciences to the enlightenment of the practice of educational leadership, and these "scientific" aspects are highlighted in the next section of this chapter and elsewhere in this book.

Values and Value Systems

In this section, our discussion is expanded to include insights gained from social scientists as well as philosophers.

VALUES DEFINED

Values are conceptions of the desirable (Parsons, 1951; Hodgkinson, 1983; Hoy & Miskel,

1991). A value is an enduring belief that a specific mode of conduct or state of existence is personally or socially preferable to an opposite or converse mode of conduct or state of existence. Values are synonymous with personal beliefs about the "good," the "just," and the "beautiful;" they propel us to a particular kind of behavior and lifestyle (Lewis, 1990). Values reflect the world view (philosophy) of an individual or organization (Hall et al., 1990). They are consciously or unconsciously held priorities that are expressed in all human activity. A value system is an enduring organization of values along a continuum of relative importance (Rokeach, 1973).

Values are subjective because they are concepts and they deal with the phenomenology of desire. We value things or states because we choose to attribute worth to them, not because of any innate worth. In so doing, we superimpose onto a thing a subjective element to indicate its level of importance for us (Beare, 1989). To be collectively functional, others must assign similar degrees of value to the same thing or state. "The essential point to grasp in thinking about value is that values do not exist in the real world. They are utterly phenomenological, subjective facts of the inner and personal experience. . . ." (Hodgkinson, 1983, p. 31).

Rokeach made five assumptions about the nature of human values: (1) the total number of values that a person possesses is relatively small; (2) all people possess the same values to different degrees; (3) values are organized into value systems; (4) the antecedents of human values can be traced to culture, society and its institutions, and personality; and (5) the consequences of values will be manifested in virtually all phenomena that social scientists might consider worth investigating and understanding. An individual holds countless beliefs that are organized into thousands of attitudes, several dozens of hierarchically arranged instrumental values and several

hierarchically arranged terminal values. Taken together, they form a belief system in which terminal values are more central than instrumental values and instrumental values are more central than attitudes. Terminal values refer to desired end-states of existence; they can be either self-centered or society-centered. Instrumental values refer to morality (having an interpersonal focus) and competence (having a personal focus without interpersonal implications) aspects of modes of conduct. Terminal values are motivational in that they represent super goals beyond immediate, biologically urgent goals. Since the total belief system is functionally interconnected, a change in any part of it should affect other parts and should ultimately affect behavior. To make a lasting change on human perception and behavior, the most central part of the system—terminal values—must be changed according to Rokeach (1973).

Hodgkinson (1983) takes a different approach to differentiating among values by placing them into a hierarchy according to the approach implied in determining what is good or right. His four grounds or justifications for valuing are principles (Type I), consequences (Type IIA), consensus (Type IIB), and preference (Type III). The hierarchy is illustrated in Figure 4.1.

Type I values are transrational; they go beyond reason, implying an act of faith or will as it is manifested in the acceptance of a principle. "Though such principles may often be defended by rational discourse they are essentially metaphysical in origin or location" (Hodgkinson, 1983, p. 39). Their philosophical orientations are found in religion and intuition. They are the universal ideas of the idealists and the natural law of liberalism.

Type III, preference, justifies a value on the grounds that the object or action is liked or preferred by the subject; these values may be innate or learned. All animals possess such values and such values are self-justifying. Type III values originate from affect, emotion and

Figure 4.1
The value paradigm
SOURCE: Hodgkinson (1983), *The Philosophy of Leadership*, 38.

Value Type	Grounds of Value	Psychological Faculty	Philosophical Orientations	Value Level	
I	Principles	Conation Willing	Religion Existentialism Intuition	I	**Right** ↑
II A	Consequence (A)	Cognition Reason	Utilitarianism Pragmatism Humanism Democratic Liberalism	II	
II B	Consensus (B)	Thinking			
III	Preference	Affect Emotion Feeling	Behaviorism Positivism Hedonism	III	↓ **Good**

feeling. Their philosophical orientations are found in behaviorism, positivism, and hedonism.

Type II values of both subsets A and B are justified on the ground of rationality. This can appear first as consensus (IIB). At the next higher level of rational process, the value is established upon an analysis of the consequences (IIB) of holding it. The philosophical orientations of Type II values lie in utilitarianism, pragmatism, humanism, democracy, and liberalism.

Type II values represent a middle ground between the commitments of ideology (Type I) and the turbulence of affectivity (Type III). At one extreme is immediate experience (Type III) and at the other, ideology (Type I); in between is the realm of pragmatics and common sense.

> *This is fortunate for human nerve and tissue. Even at best the demands of ideology are rooted in abstraction and men do not live in intellectual abstractions, however much they may subscribe to them or be governed by them. As for affect, men cannot constantly be engaged in the internecine warfare of the ego. Between Type III realities and the Type I blueprints there lies the vast region of normality—the everyday, workaday world of organizational life. A banal world perhaps, but one in*

> *which man is at relative ease: habituated, conditioned, programmed, modest and content. (Hodgkinson, 1983, p. 121)*

If values were completely stable, individual and social change would be impossible. If values were completely unstable, continuity of human personality and society would be impossible. The hierarchical conception of values enables us to define change as a reordering of priorities and, simultaneously, to see the total value system as relatively stable over time. Consensus is easier where Type III values are involved and most difficult where Type I values are present; indeed, in the latter case, conflicting Type I commitments may be irreconcilable. Because of this, the practical person seeks to avoid engagement on matters of principles and searches instead for the politically possible (Hodgkinson, 1983; Lindblom, 1959). "Pragmatics will take us through the day but will not take us where we want to go" (Hodgkinson, 1983, p. 135).

Hall et al. (1990) take a different approach in developing a hierarchy of values. They hold that value development is a growth process that goes through eight stages to reach full maturity, a point that few reach. In the first four stages, authority is perceived by the individual as originating outside the self while in the last four stages, authority is perceived as originating within the individual. The values associated with each stage from lowest to highest are: self-preservation, security, self-worth, self-competence, independence, new order, independence, and rights/world order. At the lower stages, the individual is self-centered, seeking security in a world over which the individual perceives no control. The ego stages grow into a recognition of a social world that must be accommodated; an external "they" is perceived as being in control and the individual seeks acceptance, affirmation, approval and achievement within the parameters set by "they." In the next stages, the individual begins to assume control over his or her own life and seeks to create his or her own identity. At the highest levels, the individual assumes responsibility for others as well as himself or herself. In these upper stages, the individual joins ranks with others seeking global harmony.

Value analysis neither implies nor entails any demands for logical closure where values are in contention. According to Hodgkinson (1983), true value conflict is always intrapersonal; the essential subjectivity of values dictates that any conflicts between values must occur within the individual consciousness. Hodgkinson views what is usually thought of as intervalue conflict as really a conflict of interests; ultimately, it is in fact a power struggle between value actors. Overt value actions of value actors tell us nothing of the value conflict within the individual actors. For example, does the loser of a war or a civil suit thereby change his or her conception of the desirable?

Nyberg (1993) holds a somewhat different position from Hodgkinson on the clash of values. While both agree on the intrapersonal conflict of values, Nyberg also sees interpersonal and intergroup value conflicts that are not merely conflicts of interests. Nyberg con-

tends that the pluralism of competing values is as much a part of society as it is of each individual consciousness because it is human nature to see things differently. "This collision of values is the moral core of what it is to be human" (Nyberg, 1993, p. 198).

ARCHETYPES OF LEADERSHIP

Hodgkinson (1983) used several archetypes to describe leaders as they act within his value hierarchy previously presented (Figure 4.1). The lowest archetype from the standpoint of moral or ethical regard is that of "careerist" which is characterized by the values of the ego, self-interest, primary affect and motivation. Self-preservation and enhancement, self-centeredness and self-concern are the dominant value traits. The careerist functions at the Type I level in the values hierarchy. The basal form of the careerist archetype is predator and the higher form is opportunist. Such persons may subscribe to the philosophical orientations of behaviorism or hedonism.

The second level of the value paradigm is the modal level for administration. Most administrators[1] tend either to the "politician" (Type IIB) or "technician" (Type IIA) archetype. Hodgkinson (1983, p. 141) refers to politics as "administration by another name." The politician archetype is associated with the administrator whose interests have extended beyond those of self to the point where they embrace a collectivity or group. This group, typically the organization for which he or she is responsible, is then allowed to have some degree of influence over the establishment of organizational values to the point of affecting the leader's own value structure and behavior. It thus refers to a value complex that

---

[1]It should be noted that Hodgkinson does not differentiate between "leaders" and "administrators."

takes into account the values of others, individually and corporately.

The politician is both moral and rational. The archetype is moral because his or her concern goes beyond that of self. The basic claim to rationality is that group preferences, if actualized, will advance the potential for individual realization of preference more than if laissez-faire pursuit of private desires are permitted. In all this, the politician has a relatively short-term orientation; it is the immediate problem that is pressing. "True politicians practicing the true art of the possible make the organizational world work. . . . But one can go beyond it" (Hodgkinson, 1983, p. 167). The politician, at worst, is a demagogue and, at best, a democrat. The politician's philosophical orientation tends toward that of liberalism, humanism, or pragmatism.

The technician archetype is primarily rational-cognitive and rational-legal. The values of Weberian bureaucracy, including dispassion, impartiality, logical analysis and problem solving, efficiency, effectiveness, goal accomplishment, planning, and maximization of the good, fit with this archetype. In contrast to the politician, the technician stresses institutional concerns over individual concerns. Utilitarian doctrines best reflect the philosophical orientation of the technician.

The technician "represents the highest of the archetypes that it is ordinarily possible for the administrator to aspire to and attain. This sets the safe limit to the moral ambitions and aspirations of administration" (Hodgkinson, 1983, p. 177). The technician can degenerate to the disengaged bureaucrat but also can aspire to the guardian-technocrat as described below.

Hodgkinson (1983) called the archetype carrying Type I values "The Poet." "The poet 'carries the fire,' makes things and men grow warm, extends the reach of language (and hence thought, concept and rationality), steals fire from the gods, even—in the limit—

reconciles the instant God and Man" (p. 178). Hodgkinson likens the poet to Plato's Guardian or philosopher-king whose moral base extended into the transrational domain of faith-activated will. The poet's *will* is the justification of right and the determinant of good. As a result, leadership of a poet may result in nirvana or in total destruction. At best, the poet is Guardian, but at worst, megalomaniac. Or, in the words of Nyberg (1993), "Always to choose principles, or worse, The One Right Principle, over individual values and needs in resolving specific moral situations may sometimes be the road to martyrdom and sainthood, but it is also the road to inhumanity, which ironically is paved with illusions of perfection" (p. 205).

Hall et al. (1990) have also developed a leadership hierarchy that bears some resemblance to Hodgkinson's (1983), especially at the lower level. In their hierarchy, Hall et al. recognize the reciprocal relationship between leadership and followership. Their seven leadership cycles are reported in Column II of Table 4.2. Each cycle is placed between two operative values for the cycle which are reported in Column I. Since value development is seen as a growth process, the leader experiences a tension between the two values as he or she shifts priority from the lower to the higher. The leadership mode is reported in Column III of the Table. Leadership and followership characteristics are summarized in Columns IV and V respectively.

The lowest level of leadership in Hall's et al. (1990) hierarchy, *Primal,* operates from values of self-preservation and security. Such a leader functions in an autocratic mode, controlling the organization closely and making all major decisions. The primal leader maintains a discrete distance from subordinates and demands loyalty to himself or herself and to the organization. Followers respond with passivity and docility, exhibiting immature behavior. They view the leader as being unap-

Table 4.2
Summary of Hall, Kalven, Rosen, and Taylor's Cycles and Educational Leadership.

I Value Stage	II Leadership Cycle	III Leadership Mode	IV Leadership Characteristics	V Follower Characteristics
Self-Preservation Security	Primal	Autocratic	Makes all major decisions; seeks absolute control; demands loyalty; maintains distance from followers	Docility, blind obedience, passivity; infantile; views leaders as distant and infallible
Self-Worth	Familial	Benevolent Authority	Listens, but makes all major decisions; demands loyalty; seeks adherence to rules	Feeling cared for; dependency views leaders as approachable, but in control
Self-Competence	Institutional	Bureaucratic	Management by objectives; stresses order, clear policies, goals and rules; demands loyalty to institution; delegates only to highly skilled and loyal employees	Exercises delegated authority; views leader as approachable and good listener
Independence	Intrapersonal	Enabling	Attempts to reconcile institutional demands and personal values; acts as listener/clarifier uncertain in making decisions	Confusion; willingness to express feelings; needs good interpersonal skills

I Value Stage	II Leadership Cycle	III Leadership Mode	IV Leadership Characteristics	V Follower Characteristics
New Order	Collaborative	Charismatic	Democratic; clear vision about how to make institutions humane; modifies rules to personal conscience	Small group interactions; participation as peers in some decision making; group dynamic skills; conflict resolution skills
Interdependence	Mystical or Integrative	Servant	Concern over impact on society and productivity; maximizes individual development; seeks agreement on values	Willing to assume responsibility; works at high levels of trust and intimacy; well developed imaginal skills
Rights/World Order	Prophetic	Interdependent	Leadership and Followership are merged; collaborative efforts to improve balance between material and personal needs; seeks reconciliation among conflicting groups and the humane use of technology	

SOURCE: Adapted from: Hall, B. P., Kalven, J., Rosen, L. S., and Taylor, B. (1990). *Developing human values*. Fond du Lac, WI, International Values Institute of Marian College.

proachable and as having an aura of infallibility. This type of leadership is preferred only at times of imminent danger.

In the *Familial* cycle, the leader is a benevolent despot, assuming a parent/child relationship with subordinates. Such a leader operates from values of security and self-worth. While listening to subordinates, the familial leader still reserves all decisions to himself or herself. A personal loyalty to superiors and compliance with the rules of the organization are demanded. Followers develop a feeling of dependency. They view the leader as approachable, but recognize that he or she is clearly in charge. Leadership of this type is most appropriate when the leader is highly skilled and the followers are not. Relationships are based on fairness and mutual respect.

Managerial efficiency becomes a primary concern in the *Institutional* cycle of leadership. This type of leader works from values of self-worth and self-competence. The institutional leader functions in a bureaucratic mode, managing by objectives and stressing the need for order and clear policies. Loyalty to the institution is demanded. There is some delegation of authority, but only to the skilled and to the loyal. Interpersonal, social and technical skills are required at this level. This type of leader is likely to be rigid and resistant to change. Followers adhere to the clearly stated policies. They accept the delegation of authority and view the leader as being approachable and a good listener.

The *Intrapersonal* cycle of leadership represents a transition from a self-oriented to a socially oriented philosophy. As a result, it is characterized by confusion and inconsistency in decisionmaking and by conflict between values of organizational efficiency and human needs. The leader acts as a listener and clarifier and operates from the values of self-competence and independence. Followers exhibit confusion derived from the mixed signals given by the leadership. There is a general willingness to express feelings and there is a need among followers to display good interpersonal skills.

The *Communal or Collaborative* cycle works from the values of independence and new order. Its mode is charismatic. Hall et al. (1990) view this as being the ideal level of leadership for educational institutions, especially for secondary and postsecondary schools. "Individuals have passed successfully through the often paralyzing laissez-faire period and now have a new sense of personal creative energy and renewed vision of an institution that can be efficient, as well as dignifying, for its members" (p. 61). Leaders operating at this level are democratic in their style and able to modify rules according to their personal conscience. Followers are characterized by small group interactions; they need well-developed skills in group dynamics and conflict resolution. Followers regularly participate as peers in some decisionmaking. This level bears some resemblance to Hodgkinson's (1983) "Technician."

At the *Mystical or Integrative* cycle, values of new order and interdependence predominate. Leadership is interactive and collaborative with the leader functioning as servant. In addition to organizational productivity, there is concern for the quality of organizational interactions and the organization's impact on society. Group decisionmaking is the norm with mutual responsibility and collegiality assumed by all members of the organization. Followers are willing to assume responsibility and they have well-developed inventive skills. All members work at high levels of trust and intimacy. The values of new order and interdependence are dominant.

While both are rarely found, Hall's et al. (1990) highest level of leadership, *Prophetic*, is not nearly as doctrinaire as Hodgkinson's (1983) "Poet." At this level in Hall's et al. hierarchy, the concepts of leadership and followership are merged. The mode of operation is interdependent or transformational. All persons are engaged in the task of improving the balance between material goods and human needs and dedicated to reconciling conflicts among groups and using technology in creative and humane ways. The values of interdependence and rights/world order dominate at this level.

VALUES AS PART OF ORGANIZATIONAL CULTURES

Values are motivating determinants of behaviors (Spindler, 1955). Persons joined together by a similar set of values, beliefs, priorities, experiences, and traditions are said to form a common culture, whether it be in a small organization such as a school, a large nation such as the United States, or a group of nations such as "the West" or "the Western world."

Shared values define the basic character of an organization and give it meaning (Hoy & Miskel, 1991). Ouchi (1981) argued that successful corporations in both Japan and the United States are energized by distinctive corporate cultures that are internally consistent and characterized by shared values of intimacy, trust, cooperation, teamwork, and equalitarianism. Similar observations have been made by Deal and Kennedy (1982), Peters and Waterman (1982), and Peters (1988).

Bates (1984) saw cultures, also, as providing the framework within which individuals establish meaning for themselves. He noted that part of culture is factual, but most is mythical. The latter part is concerned with meaning, i.e., the interpretive and prescriptive rules that provide the basis for understanding and action.

Getzels and Thelen (1960) portrayed the classroom as a social system and clearly demonstrated the function of values within the system. Their model is reproduced in Figure 4.2. The model represents the interplay among individuals, groups (e.g., classrooms), and institutions (e.g., schools). Schools as institutions are imbedded within a culture holding certain mores and values that influence institutional, group, and individual goals, roles, and social behavior. These are a function of continuing negotiations between individuals and their group, groups and their

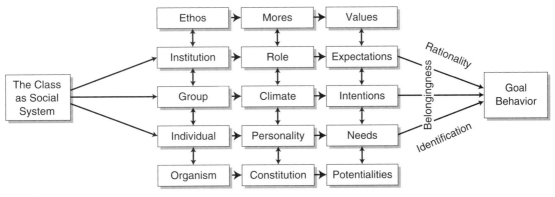

Figure 4.2
The Getzels-Thelen model of the classroom as a social system

SOURCE: "The classroom group as a social system" (p. 80) by J. W. Getzels and H. A. Thelen in N. B. Henry, Ed., *The Dynamics of Institutional Groups,* 1960, 59th Yearbook of the National Society for the Study of Education. Used with the permission of the National Society for the Study of Education.

institution, etc. Thus, value conflicts may develop within groups and institutions and between groups and institutions and institutions and the larger social culture. A primary function of leadership is to monitor these conflicts and to guide them in organizationally and socially positive directions.

Of primary concern to the administrator is the institutional or nomothetic dimension of the model which seeks to link the organization with its goals by way of formally creating roles and role-expectations (or jobs and job-expectations). On the other hand, nonadministrative organization members are primarily concerned with the individual or ideographic dimension. The institutional dimension, for nonadministrative members, is viewed as constraints which limit their satisfactions while providing the rational-legal foundation for their contracts with the organization. The task of the executive is one of reconciliation: reconciliation of the organization to society and of organization members towards organizational goals.

Sergiovanni (1973) observed that school executives too often avoid value confrontation by attempting to deal with conflict at the lowest level of abstraction possible—at the interpersonal level on a one-to-one basis. He believes, however, that the major problems concerning value differences that face most school executives are at the organizational level and are expressed in the form of competing organizational cultures. Such competition needs to be dealt with at the organizational level. According to Sergiovanni, administrative effectiveness requires the continuous examination of internalized value assumptions including comparing and testing value structures for goodness of fit and for overlap with those held by other educational workers, students, and society at large. In the words of Hodgkinson (1991, p. 90), "An organization is, strictly speaking, an arrangement for conflict management through the device of superordinant or overriding goals."

Hodgkinson (1983) developed a model (Figure 4.3) that reconciles personal values with institutional elements such as those included in the Getzels and Thelen model (Figure 4.2). Level V_1 in the Hodgkinson model represents the value structure of the individual within the organization or the ideographic dimension; Level V_2 represents the shared value structures of groups within the organization that modulate individual belief structures; Level V_3 is the organizational or nomothetic dimension; V_4 represents the value structure of the subculture(s) that influence the organization's operations; and, V_5 represents the overarching societal ethos.

The individual organization member (V_1) meets with the nomothetic dimension of the organization (V_3), not directly, but through workday encounters with formal and informal groups (V_2). These groups intervene between the member and the executive suite (V_3) and modulate the consciousness and experience of the member. In other words, the member's organizational perspective (V_1) is quite different from that of the administrator (V_3).

In a similar way, the prevailing ethos (V_5) does not impinge directly upon the organization (V_3) but is modulated through intervening subcultures (V_4) such as professional organizations and local political groups. These levels overlap, intertwine and interact in dynamic and contingent relationships (Hodgkinson, 1983).

Getzels (1957, 1980) differentiated values into only two levels: sacred and secular. National core or "sacred" values are relatively stable. These would correspond to Hodgkinson's ethos (V_5). "Secular" values are transient, subject to change and wide interpretation at the operational level. Examples of secular values are the work-success ethic, future orientation, independence and Puritan morality. Such values govern one's everyday behavior with regard to work, time, relation to others, and personal morality. "[T]he fact that values do shift at least in emphasis and

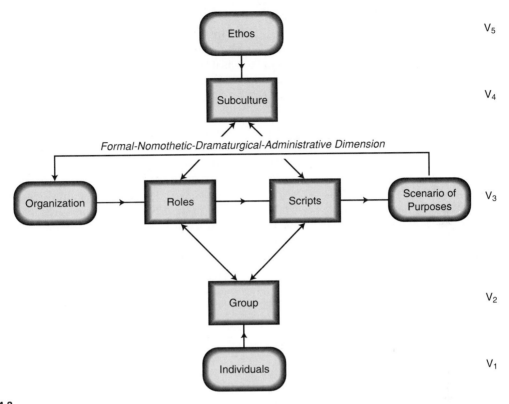

Figure 4.3
The total field of action
SOURCE: Hodgkinson (1983), *The Philosophy of Leadership*, 24.

that individuals and groups do differ in the expression of the values may make for strains between generations and between school and community, with consequent problems and implications for the educational administrator" (Lipham, 1988, p. 177).

ORGANIZATIONAL LEADERSHIP: VALUES AND VISION

Greenfield (1984) postulated that "[o]rganizations are built on the unification of people around values. The business of being a leader is therefore the business of being an entrepreneur for values" (p. 166). Greenfield referred to organizations as cultural artifacts that are founded in meanings, in human intentions, actions and experience. They are systems of meaning that can only be understood through the interpretation of meaning. The task of leaders is to act as interpreters, creating a moral order that binds them and the people around them.

Of the five leadership forces identified by Sergiovanni (1984c)—technical (management), human, educational, symbolic, and cultural—the last two are the most relevant in studying values. "The object of symbolic leadership is the setting of human consciousness, the articulation of key cultural strands that identify the substance of a school, and the linking of persons involved in the school's activities to them" (pp. 7–8). The symbolic leader signals to others what is of importance in the organization. In so doing, the leader gives to the organization purpose and direction. Vision becomes the substance of what is communicated through symbolic aspects of leadership. It provides a source of clarity, consensus, and commitment for students and teachers alike (Vaill, 1984).

The cultural leader seeks to define, strengthen, and articulate those enduring values, beliefs, and cultural strands that give a school its unique identity.

> *The net effect of the cultural force of leadership is to bond together students, teachers, and others as believers in the work of the school. Indeed, the school and its purposes are somewhat revered as if they resembled an ideological system dedicated to a sacred mission. As persons become members of this strong and binding culture, they are provided with opportunities for enjoying a special sense of personal importance. (Sergiovanni, 1984a, p. 9)*

Sergiovanni (1992, p. 102) noted that two important things happen when purpose, social contract and school autonomy provide the foundation upon which to build the structure of schooling. The school is transformed from a mere organization to a covenantal community, and the basis of authority changes from an emphasis on bureaucratic and psychological authority to moral authority. In other words, the school changes from a secular to a sacred organization—changing from an instrument designed to achieve specific ends to a virtuous enterprise.

The mission of the cultural leader is to focus sharply the minds of the membership of a school organization on collectively held values, symbols, and beliefs. The more that these are understood and accepted, the better able the school is to move in concert toward the ideals it holds and the goals it wishes to pursue. A strong culture is characteristic of excellent schools. A tight value structure permits an otherwise loosely structured organization to allow wide discretion among the professionals working within the organization. Shared values and beliefs become the glue holding the organization together, not close managerial supervision.

Organizations need leaders who can provide a persuasive and durable sense of purpose and direction, rooted deeply in human values and spirit. Leaders need to be deeply reflective, actively thoughtful, and dramatically explicit about their core values and beliefs. The best managers and leaders create and sustain a tension-filled balance between core values and elastic strategies. They know what they stand for and what they want, and they clearly and forcefully communicate that vision. They also know that they must understand and respond to the complex array of forces that push and pull organizations in many different directions (Bolman et al., 1991).

Bennis (1984) aptly summarized the function of leadership within the context of organizational culture.

> *In sum, the transformative power of leadership stems less from ingeniously crafted organizational structures, carefully constructed management designs and controls, elegantly rationalized planning formats, or skillfully articulated leadership tactics. Rather, it is the ability of the leader to reach the souls of others in a fashion which raises human consciousness, builds meanings, and inspires human intent that is the source of power. Within transformative leadership, therefore, it is vision, purposes, beliefs, and other aspects of organizational culture that are of prime importance. (p. 70)*

VALUES, DEMOCRACY, AND FOLLOWERSHIP

Maxcy (1991) proposed a pragmatic theory of value that stresses the importance of democratic cultural consensus in arriving at plans and policies that affect the school community.

She argued that the quality of life is enhanced and pedagogical responsibility is fulfilled when the deliberative process is enlarged to include all those involved in or affected by schooling. She observed that leadership is always truncated and narrow when power is invested in the few.

With democratic cultural consensus, leadership needs the capacity to interact with self or others in terms of moving a discourse/practice toward an end based upon criteria that are at once rational and moral. "Leading is not so much telling others what is true or false, but rather helping them to come to know for themselves the merits and demerits of a case" (Maxcy, 1991, p. 195). Maxcy called for a reconstruction and reconceptualization of leadership as enlightened, critical, and pragmatic action—a notion of leadership that looks to everyone who participates in the teaching/learning process for the kinds of thought and effort that will result in a reformed education.

In a similar vein, Cambron-McCabe (1993) argued that moral principles guiding groups or organizations are not a matter of personal preference or intuition but must be subjected to a democratic deliberative process. She asserted that values must be determined in a democratic context for democratic ends.

Sergiovanni (1992) pointed out that leadership and followership are reciprocal in an empowered organization. He believes that, in many ways, professionalism and leadership are antithetical insofar as, beyond a certain point, the more professionalism is emphasized, the less leadership is needed. Professionalism has a way of encouraging principals to be self-managers. Conversely, providing too much leadership, at least of the traditional type, discourages professionalism. Self-management and professionalism are complementary concepts. "If self-management is our goal, then leadership will have to be reinvented in a fashion that places 'followership' first" (p. 68).

Subordinates need external motivation. They do what they are supposed to do, but little else; they want to know exactly what is expected of them—they work to the rule. Followers, on the other hand, are self-motivated and work well without close supervision, assessing what needs to be done, when and how, and taking effective action on their own.

Followers are people committed to purposes, a cause, a vision of what the school is and can become, beliefs about teaching and learning, values and standards to which they adhere, and convictions. . . . When followership and leadership are joined, the traditional hierarchy of the school is upset. It changes from a fixed form, with superintendents and principals at the top and teachers and students at the bottom, to one that is in flux. The only constant is that neither superintendents and principals nor teachers and students are at the apex; that position is reserved for ideas, values, and commitments at the heart of followership. Further, a transformation takes place, and emphasis shifts from bureaucratic, psychological, and technical rational authority to professional and moral authority. As a result, hierarchial position and personality are not enough to earn one the mantle of leader. Instead, it comes through one's demonstrated devotion and success as a follower. The true leader is the one who follows first. (Sergiovanni, 1992, pp. 71–72)

The interaction between leadership and followership was previously noted in the presentation of the work of Hall et al. (1990) on developing human values (see Table 4.2). In their leadership hierarchy, the highest level was placed at the point where the concept of leadership and followership merge and the distinctions between them become meaningless.

Greenleaf (1977) wrote of the servant-leader. He referred to two polar types of leadership: that provided by persons naturally inclined to lead first, and that provided by persons naturally inclined to serve first but through service are endowed with leadership authority. Between the poles are many shadings. Leadership is bestowed upon the servant-leader; it is sought by the leader-leader. Greenleaf noted a reassessment of the issues of power and authority whereby people are learning to relate to one another in less coercive and more creatively supporting ways. "A new moral principle is emerging which holds that the only authority deserving one's allegiance is that which is freely and knowingly granted by the led to the leader in response to, and in proportion to, the clearly evident servant stature of the leader" (p. 10). Servant leaders differ from other persons of goodwill because they act on what they believe. Greenleaf stressed the importance to the functioning leader of listening carefully and understanding. He expressed a strong bias that only a true natural servant automatically responds to any problem by listening first. Greenleaf saw the only viable institutions of the future being predominantly servant-led.

These concepts of leadership, democracy, and followership were first developed by Burns (1978) and were summarized in the discussion of "Transformational Leadership" in Chapter 2 of this text. His foundational thoughts on leadership, particularly the moral implications of transforming leadership, are fundamental to this discussion. They place the reciprocal nature of transforming leadership in perspective as regards followers transforming leaders.

VALUES ANALYSIS

Hodgkinson (1983) asserted that a leader has a philosophical obligation to conduct a value analysis of significant problems being faced. In making such an analysis, the leader must separate personal interests and values from those of the organization and the interest of others must be placed above his/her own. To exercise such control requires the leader to

know the task, the situation, the group, and oneself. The following are among the questions to be answered in a value analysis according to Hodgkinson (1983, p. 207):

- What are the values in conflict and can they be named?
- What fields of values are most affected?
- Who are the value actors?
- How is the conflict distributed, interpersonally or intrapersonally?
- Is the conflict inter-hierarchial or intra-hierarchial?
- What strategies for conflict resolution are most fitted to the case?
- What are the metavalues involved in the case?
- Is there a principle (Type I value) raised or avoided?
- Can the tension of non-resolution be accommodated?
- What rational and pragmatic consequences attach to the possible and probable scenarios?
- What bodies of value consensus and political interest, if relevant, are affected within and without the organization?
- To what extent does the leader have control over the informative and affective media in the case (press, radio, television, lines of communication, informal organization, etc.)?
- What is the extent of affect control among the parties in the case?
- What is the extent of commitment among the parties in the case to their respective positions?

Hall et al. (1990) saw the collection of reliable data about the values expressed implicitly or explicitly by an institution as critical to the process of organizational development. Comparisons and discrepancies can then be analyzed and compared using a consistent methodology. In their analytical scheme, organizational diagnosis consists of three parts: document analysis, personal values inventories, and group values analysis.

Documents examined include mission statements and statements of philosophy that express the intent and purpose of the organization, and policies and procedures focusing on stated behavioral expectations and sanctions. Using content analysis and looking for value clusters, a value profile of the organization can be developed. Values being reinforced, intentionally or unintentionally, can be identified through this process, enabling a school to develop strategies to help it become more consistent and more focused in what it does and says.

A number of instruments are available for assessing personal values such as the Hall-Tonna Inventory (Hall et al., 1990). Such instruments generate personal values profiles that are useful for self-analysis and therapy or for aggregation by unit or organization permitting group analysis. Aggregated profiles can be compared with the intended values of the organization as revealed by the document analysis. Inconsistencies may reveal a need to restate the organizational values, to bring personal values in line with intended organizational values through staff development programs, or a combination of the two.

Taken altogether, document analysis, individual and group analyses can provide insight into a number of critical aspects of the school's organizational culture. The information collected will reveal the possible stress areas between teachers and administrators as well as between administrators and board members. It will identify and measure current priority issues and values which can then be examined in an objective manner. The process will reveal operative leadership styles among teachers, administrators and school board members. It will identify, describe and analyze underlying value patterns in mis-

sion, philosophy and procedures, and will suggest ways in which these value patterns impact on a school's day-to-day culture. Finally, the data generated will indicate needed skills training for individuals and groups of teachers, administrators, or board members. (Hall et al., 1990, pp. 64–65)

Metavalues

Hodgkinson (1983) defined the term *metavalue* as "a concept of the desirable so vested and entrenched that it seems to be beyond dispute or contention—one that usually enters the ordinary value calculus of individual and collective life in the form of an unexpressed or unexamined assumption" (p. 43). In administration and organizational life, he identified the dominant metavalues as efficiency and effectiveness.

Nyberg (1993, p. 196) contended that "[t]he moral universe is the same for everyone in that it is based on concern for human dignity, decency, voluntary relations that are not oppressive, and some kind of spiritual fulfillment." The specifics differ from person to person, group to group, place to place, and time to time; but the basis of concern remains consistent. We are all similar, but each is unique.

Rokeach (1973) sought to identify ideals or values that are singled out for special consideration by all political ideologies. He hypothesized that the major variations in political ideology are fundamentally reducible to opposing value orientations concerning the political desirability or undesirability of freedom and equality in all their ramifications.

Getzels (1957, 1978) referred to national core values as "sacred." He identified four sacred values as being at the core of the American ethos: democracy, individualism, equality, and human perfectibility.

The literature on educational policy makes frequent explicit or implicit reference to these and similar values. Guthrie, Garms, and Pierce (1988) referred to equality, efficiency, and liberty as values of particular societal concern. Wirt (1987) referred to general agreement among nations that the major values in education are quality (excellence or human perfectibility), equity, efficiency, and choice (liberty or freedom). Boyd (1984) focused on liberty, equality, and efficiency as "three competing values" in educational policy and school governance in Western democracies (p. 4). Swanson (1989) identified five values that have been historically prominent in shaping Western societies and that are also particularly relevant to provision and consumption of educational services: liberty, equality, fraternity, efficiency, and economic growth. There is a good deal of overlap among the various lists with freedom and equality appearing on most.

The name of a metavalue may continue to be the same, but definitions may vary from place to place and over time. Nyberg (1981, Part II), for example, cautioned that "freedom" (or liberty) derives its meaning at least in part from the times in which it is used. He pointed out that the United States saw a transformation between 1787 and 1947, as "freedom as natural rights (rights *against* the government, rights of independence)" became "civil rights (rights to *participate* in civil government)" and later became "human freedoms (rights to the *help* of government in achieving protection from fear and want)" (pp. 97–98).

Parallel transformations took place in the meaning of equality (or equity). Initially, equality consisted only of rights and not conditions, that is, people were to be treated the same by law, custom, and tradition with equality the instrument for guaranteeing liberty as originally defined. In recent times, the operational definition of equality has expanded to include factors of condition. For example, some persons are handicapped in enjoying liberty because of circumstances beyond their control such as minority status, gender, poverty, and physical and psychological impediments. While liberty and equality complemented one another as defined in 1787, the broader contemporary definition of equality brings it into direct conflict with the value of liberty (as originally defined) because the policies of remediation involve not only the disadvantaged person, but all others. Liberty requires an opportunity for expression through individual freedom, whereas equality of condition requires the curbing of individual freedom.

Because of the conceptual inconsistencies among values, it is not possible to emphasize all of them at the same time in public policy—or in individual lives—desirable though each may be. Individuals and societies must establish priorities. This is a dynamic process. Priorities of individuals change with circumstances, and where there has been a sufficient change among individuals, shifts in public priorities follow (Ravitch, 1985, p. 5). Agreement upon priorities is not necessary for private- or market-sector decisions beyond the family level. In the public sector, however, a singular decision is required involving negotiations and compromises among interested partisans (subcultures and groups), generating significant social stress in the process. The higher the level of aggregation, the more difficult agreement becomes because of the greater amount of heterogeneity introduced.

Spindler (1955) explained the attacks on public education in the 1950s by citing major societal value shifts following World War II. (Reference to Spindler's analysis reminds us that this is not the first generation of educators to be the recipients of hostile public criticism.) Spindler saw the criticism of that day as products of an American culture that was experiencing a real shift in values. Populations going through cultural transition are characterized by conflict, and in its most severe form, demoralization and disorganization. The conflict goes beyond groups and institutions because individuals in a transformational society are likely to hold elements of both the dominant and the emerging value systems concomitantly. Such situations are not only confused by groups battling each other, but also by individuals fighting themselves.

Spindler (1955) described traditional values as Puritan morality, work-success ethic, individualism, achievement orientation, and future orientation. These values were being threatened by emergent values: sociability, relativistic moral attitudes, consideration for others, Hedonistic present-time orientation, and conformity to the group. He concluded that there is a staunchness and a virility in the traditional value set that many viewed with nostalgia. But, in his view, rugged individualism (in its expedient, ego-centered form), and rigid moralism (with its capacity for displaced hate) had become nonfunctional in a society where people are rubbing shoulders in polyglot masses and playing with technology that may destroy, or save, with the push of buttons.

More recently, Nyberg (1993) similarly concluded that a moral-principle or positivist orientation (described earlier) thrives in a supportive environment, but finds it difficult to adapt to new conditions when the environment changes. On the other hand, the personal-value or constructivist orientation (also described earlier) has a better chance of long-term survival in this moral world of constant changes because of its flexible adaptiveness and its willingness to live with uncertainty.

The shifting of values identified by Spindler and referred to by Nyberg is likely to continue into the foreseeable future. In addition, the geo-political situation in the world has become fluid during the past decade. These, coupled with unparalleled technological advancements, seem to have actually accelerated the rate of major shifts in value priorities and in expressed dissatisfaction with the status quo. As a ripple effect, demands for educational reform have materialized. The old paradigms don't seem to fit anymore.

Major contemporary issues revolve around the competing social objectives of equality, personal liberty, and productive efficiency among others. The question of whether or not each can be furthered jointly through public policy is being hotly debated. The most likely scenario is that one or two values will be given priority, as in the past, to the jeopardy of the others. The ferment that we are experiencing today is a function of the dynamic political struggle to achieve the best balance among legitimate interests. The best balance has varied, and will continue to vary, from society to society and over time within a society as contexts and value definitions and priorities change (Wirt, 1986).

■ **CASE STUDY**[2]

Teen Pregnancy and AIDS Prevention

According to a National Survey of Family Growth done eight years ago, 19 percent of girls under the age of 15 were sexually experienced; today that rate is nearly 30 percent. Seven out of ten 18-year-olds are sexually experienced (Freeman, 1990).

The State Education Department has mandated AIDS Education to be implemented in every school district. Acquired Immune Deficiency Syndrome (AIDS) is a fatal viral disease that attacks the body's immune system, leaving patients vulnerable to numerous infections, and is considered to be "the gravest

---

[2]Developed by Anne Burnicki, James Higgins and Cheryl Hogg, graduate students in the Educational Administration Program, State University of New York at Buffalo.

public health threat of the century." The Center for Health Statistics predicts that AIDS will be one of the ten leading causes of death in the 1990s and that it will be the leading cause of death for people aged 25 to 44 (United Way, 1988).

Local hospitals report an increasing number of infants born to women diagnosed as HIV-positive or with AIDS. A number of school districts, especially those in large cities, are beginning to distribute condoms to the student population in an attempt to curtail the teenage pregnancy rate and as an AIDS prevention measure.

The problem of teenage pregnancy was viewed by the U.S. House of Representatives Select Committee on Children, Youth and Families in 1987 as "unacceptable," "devastating," and "chilling" (Keough, 1988). In addition, local census data indicate that the occurrence of teenage pregnancy has increased significantly.

Principals, health teachers, nurses, social workers, and counselors in your school district have reported observational information that supports the perception that there is an increase in the number of pregnancies within the student population. Although a number of students are opting for termination of pregnancy through abortion, the trend is that an increasing number of students are opting to keep their babies. The majority of pregnant teens are in eleventh and twelfth grades although more and more incidents are being reported from grades seven through ten. Teachers have reported that students seemingly want to be pregnant. Social service agencies concur that the girls see a value in being pregnant as it allows them a special status. There is some concern that a number of girls may have been raised in dysfunctional families, experienced child abuse or neglect and that being single moms will tend to continue the cycle.

Given the circumstances, the Board of Education has requested recommendations from the superintendent in order to determine Board policy on these issues of AIDS education and teen pregnancy. You are a member of a committee to study the issues and to make recommendations based upon the role you have been assigned. The decision will be based on consensus. The committee is composed of: a parent, health teacher, board of education member, student, school principal, and observer/recorder.

Minimally, the policy must address the issues of AIDS education and student pregnancy. There are suggested policies and resource materials (Brodinsky & Keough, 1989) to assist your committee in the formulation of the new district policy recommendation. It is suggested that after becoming familiar with the possible policies, the committee brainstorm and list the values that are implicit in the analysis. You may also wish to list group members' feelings about the topic.

The task of your committee is only to recommend; however it is likely that the superintendent will follow the advice of the committee and forward its recommended policy to the Board of Education. Therefore, you and other members of the committee will list alternatives, provide a consequential analysis for recommended and rejected policies. Arguments will be discussed that could be used to justify actions based upon values analysis.

The final recommendation must be consensual, that is, a decision that everyone in the group can accept. Among the policies suggested for consideration are:

- *Policy A:* Pregnant girls will be placed on home instruction upon their request. Girls will be encouraged to pursue a high school equivalency diploma if they are 16 years or older. Younger girls will return to school following the delivery of their babies and continue in the traditional program.
- *Policy B:* Students will be encouraged to leave school as soon as it becomes

evident that they are pregnant as a deterrent for other students. Students will be assigned to home instruction or can enroll in alternative social service program schools. Providing a nurturing environment for pregnant students sends a message to other students that it is acceptable and special to be pregnant.

- *Policy C:* Schools will allow students to continue mainstreaming in regular programs and treat the time away from school as illness.
- *Policy D:* Schools will develop special alternative programs for pregnant students and teen mothers. It is recognized that these students have special needs.

Pregnant students will be actively encouraged to enroll in this type of program.

- *Policy E:* Schools will provide day care for infants and toddlers in order for teen moms to stay in school.
- *Policy F:* Pregnant students and teen moms will be required to enroll in vocational and technical education courses as they will be responsible for supporting themselves and their child.
- *Policy G:* Schools will subcontract with day-care providers in the school's proximity for services for students who have children and are financially disadvantaged.

Values Considered

Teen Pregnancy/Parenting Policy

Values Considered: Feelings:

AIDS Education Policy

Values Considered: Feelings:

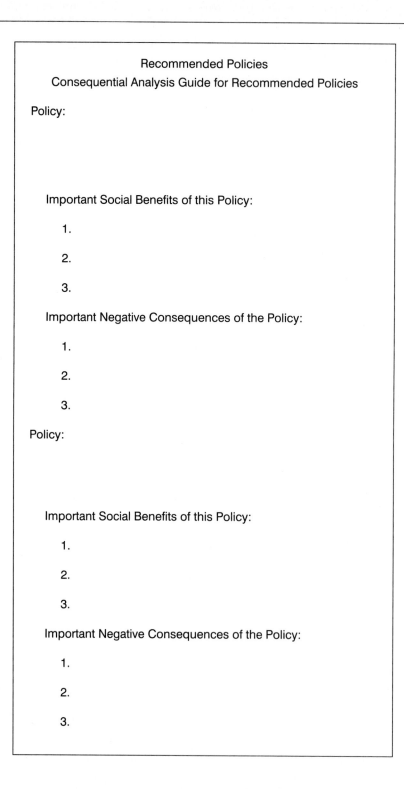

Recommended Policies
Consequential Analysis Guide for Recommended Policies

Policy:

Important Social Benefits of this Policy:

1.

2.

3.

Important Negative Consequences of the Policy:

1.

2.

3.

Policy:

Important Social Benefits of this Policy:

1.

2.

3.

Important Negative Consequences of the Policy:

1.

2.

3.

Rejected Policies

Consequential Analysis Guide for Rejected Policies

Policy:

    Important Social Benefits of this Policy:

       1.

       2.

       3.

    Important Negative Consequences of the Policy:

       1.

       2.

       3.

Policy:

    Important Social Benefits of this Policy:

       1.

       2.

       3.

    Important Negative Consequences of the Policy:

       1.

       2.

       3.

- *Policy H:* Even though other districts may have a problem with teen pregnancy, this district does not; therefore, we don't need a policy.
- *Policy I:* As a practical and educational approach to birth control and a deterrent to contracting AIDS, instruction on the use of condoms will be provided and condoms will be made available to all students throughout the school.
- *Policy J:* Sex education will not be taught in schools; it is the responsibility of parents.
- *Policy K:* A curriculum will be developed to include education concerning human sexuality and values. Self-esteem will be recognized as critical in fostering a positive learning environment as well as a deterrent to teen pregnancy.
- *Policy L:* AIDS education will be provided through subcontracting with medical personnel to provide assemblies and classroom presentations; other than this there is little need for education as this is not a problem in this district.
- *Policy M:* AIDS education will be infused into the K–12 curriculum.

Criteria considered for decisionmaking may include the following metavalues which affect social policy (Swanson, 1989):

- *Liberty:* the right of the individual to choose as one wishes, not subject to control or undue constraint.
- *Equity:* the treatment of the individual is the same by law, custom, and tradition as well as condition; education seeks to reduce liabilities that may handicap an individual in society.
- *Fraternity:* a recognition of a common bond which builds a sense of community, unity, and nationality.
- *Efficiency:* concerns which are expressed in terms of accountability and high standards.

Activities for Discussion

1. Everyone has a philosophical view of life even though it may not have been thoroughly articulated.

   a. Reflect on your philosophical view of life and summarize it in a few paragraphs.
   b. Is your philosophical view similar to any of those described in this chapter? Which one?
   c. How does your philosophy of life affect your professional behavior?

2. Develop for yourself a "professional platform" that can serve as an operational framework for decisionmaking. Include:

   a. a description of your own system of beliefs
   b. a statement of your opinion as to the mission of schooling as a social process
   c. a statement as to the reasons you want to be a school administrator
   d. a statement of your views on the role of administrators in schools, their ideal relationships with other members of the school and system, and how they should implement their role.

3. Numerous proposals have been presented for reforming education. Identify the macro-values associated with each of the proposed reforms listed below and show how each marks a departure from macro-values inherent in the status quo.

   a. family choice of public schools
   b. unconstrained educational vouchers
   c. tax credits for private school tuition
   d. school-based decisionmaking
   e. full state funding of schooling
   f. mandated state curriculum

Annotated Bibliography

Foster, W. P. (1986). *Paradigms and promises: New approaches to educational administration*. Buffalo, NY: Prometheus.

The book presents educational administration as a moral science informed by critical social theory. The author argues that the traditional presentation of the field neglects its cultural, political, moral, and ethical dimensions. A prime concern of the text is to present a critical analysis of educational administration premised on an understanding of the relationship of theory to practice. The definition given to the term "theory"—"a way of seeing, a perspective on the world, a means of putting together the disparate events of our life in a meaningful fashion" (p. 12)—is similar to the use of "philosophy" in this chapter. The text is divided into two parts. The first part develops the foundation for a critical approach by examining the strengths and weaknesses of orthodox theory and providing an alternative conception based in critical social theory. The second part provides a conventional and a critical review of the literature on organizations, leadership, and change. Strategies are proposed for implementing the concepts presented.

Graff, O. B., Street, C. M., Kimbrough, R. B., & Dykes, A. R. (1966). *Philosophic theory and practice in educational administration*. Belmont, CA: Wadsworth.

Written in 1966, this is one of the first books to specifically address educational administration from the perspective of philosophy. While the phraseology is obviously from another period, the concepts presented in the book are highly relevant to today's administrator and scholar. The term "theory" is used synonymously with "philosophy," but a careful distinction is made between philosophical theory and scientific theory. The thesis of the book is that an educational administrator needs a philosophy of life—a world view; the purpose of the book is to help school administrators develop and improve their abilities to theorize about their jobs on the philosophic level. It describes several systems of philosophical thought: idealism, logical positivism or scientific empiricism, pragmatism, and existentialism. The implications of each for education are presented.

Guba, E. G. (Ed.). (1990). *The paradigm dialog*. Newbury Park, CA: Sage.

The book explores three basic belief systems that have emerged as successors to conventional positivism and that strongly influence inquiry into education today: postpositivism, critical theory, and constructivism. The book reports the proceedings of an "Alternative Paradigms Conference" sponsored by Phi Delta Kappa. The chapters are papers commissioned for the conference. Editor Guba has done a remarkable job in giving unity to the work. The purpose of the book is to clarify the rival alternative orientations. In addition to thoroughly presenting the basic tenets of the three philosophies, the book addresses issues of accommodation, ethics, goodness criteria, implementation, knowledge accumulation, methodology, training, and values.

Hall, B. P., Kalven, J., Rosen, L. S., & Taylor, B. (1990). *Developing human values*. Fond du Lac, WI: International Values Institute of Marian College.

The authors take the position that the process of value development is not an automatic one. The process can be fostered by a number of teaching strategies including the techniques of self-discovery, the provision of learning environments that encourage growth, and the practice of specific skills. The monograph provides a theoretical basis for an understanding of value development together with practical materials for applying the theory in the lives of individuals and institutions. A model, the Four Phases of Consciousness, was designed to chart the progress of moral and intellectual growth in terms of what individuals value in life. The model projects a series of four phases through which all humans pass on their journey toward the fullest possible development.

Hodgkinson, C. (1983). *The philosophy of leadership*. Oxford, England: Basil Blackwell.

The basic canon of this book is that administration is philosophy in action. The book seeks to answer the questions: what does it mean to be an administrator, a person of action? what can it mean? what ought it mean? (The author treats the words "leader" and "administrator" synonymously.) The book is intended to relate the practical application of administration to philosophical orientation. Some topics addressed are: the need to philosophize, administration and values, realities, ideologies, pragmatics, and leadership archetypes. It concludes with a philosophy of leadership. A useful value paradigm is presented that suggests four levels of values ranging from higher order to lower order: principles, consequence, consensus, and preference. Leadership archetypes are described for each level. Another useful model, "the total field of action," incorporates Getzels' and Thelen's nomothetic and ideographic organizational dimensions into a values hierarchy that emphasizes the differences in values orientation among individuals, groups, executives, and society. Hodgkinson has written a more recent book (1991), Educational Leadership: The Moral Art, *but the 1983 book presents a more thorough look at his basic theory.*

Rokeach, M. (1973). *The nature of human values.* New York: The Free Press.

The book presents the Rokeach Value Survey instrument and summarizes and synthesizes the research completed with it up to the time of publication. Being the work of a social psychologist, it very carefully establishes a basis of quantitatively measuring philosophical concepts such as values. The author develops a two-value model (grid) of political ideology in which, using equality (brotherhood, equal opportunity for all) and freedom (independence, free choice), he claims that all political ideology can be classified. He also examines values held by persons according to socioeconomic class and race. He concludes that many of his findings are consistent with Maslow's hierarchical theory of human motivation in that members of lower socioeconomic groups place greater importance on values concerning material comfort, conventional forms of religion, and conformity, while higher socioeconomic groups place more importance on values concerning love, competence, and self-actualization. The value structure of African-Americans was found to be very similar to that of "poor whites" except that

African-Americans place a much greater importance on equality.

Sergiovanni, T. J. (1992). *Moral leadership: Getting to the heart of school improvement.* San Francisco: Jossey-Bass.

The author espouses a need for an expanded theoretical and operational foundation for leadership practice that will give balance to the full range of values and bases of authority. He argues that the management values now considered legitimate are biased toward rationality, logic, objectivity, the importance of self-interest, explicitness, individuality, and detachment. Emphasizing these values causes us to neglect equally important considerations of: emotions, the importance of group membership, sense and meaning, morality, self-sacrifice, duty, and obligation. Two sources of authority on which to base leadership practice stressed by the author are professional authority (seasoned craft knowledge and personal expertise) and moral authority (obligations and duties derived from widely shared values, ideas, and ideals). A case is built for the superiority of moral leadership based on compelling ideas. The author develops the concept of the school as a covenantal community in which the basis of authority changes from any emphasis on bureaucratic control and psychological authority to moral authority. In such a school, leadership and followership are joined and the traditional hierarchy of the school is upset.

References

Bates, R. J. (1984). Toward a critical practice of educational administration. In T. J. Sergiovanni & J. E. Corbally (Eds.), *Leadership and organizational culture* (pp. 64–71). Urbana, IL: University of Illinois Press.

Beare, H., Caldwell, B. J., & Millikan, R. H. (1989). *Creating an excellent school: Some new management techniques.* London: Routledge.

Bennis, W. (1984). Transformative power and leadership. In T. J. Sergiovanni & J. E. Corbally (Eds.), *Leadership and organizational culture* (pp. 64–71). Urbana, IL: University of Illinois Press.

Bolman, L. G., & Deal, T. E. (1991). *Reframing organizations: Artistry, choice, and leadership*. San Francisco: Jossey-Bass.

Boyd, W. L. (1984). Competing values in educational policy and governance: Australian and American developments. *Educational Administration Review, 2*(2), 4–24.

Brodinsky, B., & Keough, K. (1989). Students at risk: Problems and solutions (AASA Critical Issues Report No. 021-00213). Arlington, VA: American Association of School Administrators.

Burns, J. M. (1978). *Leadership*. New York: Harper and Row.

Cambron-McCabe, N. H. (1993). Leadership for democratic authority. In J. Murphy (Ed.), *Preparing tomorrow's school leaders: Alternative designs*. University Park, PA: University Council for Educational Administration.

Daresh, J. C. (1988). *The preservice preparation of American educational administrators: Retrospect and prospect*. Cardiff, Wales: British Educational Management and Administration Society, pp. 1–47 (ERIC Document number ED 294308).

Daresh, J. C., & Playko, M. A. (1992). *The professional development of school administrators: Preservice, induction, and inservice applications*. Boston, MA: Allyn & Bacon.

De George, R. T. (1990). *Business ethics* (3rd ed.). New York: Macmillan.

Deal, T. E., & Kennedy, A. A. (1982). *Corporate cultures: The rites and rituals of corporate life*. Reading, MA: Addison-Wesley.

Foster, W. P. (1984). Toward a critical theory of educational administration. In T. J. Sergiovanni & J. E. Corbally (Eds.), *Leadership and organizational culture* (pp. 240–259). Urbana, IL: University of Illinois Press.

Foster, W. P. (1986). *Paradigms and promises: New approaches to educational administration*. Buffalo, NY: Prometheus.

Freeman, P. (1990, November). Risky business. *People Weekly, 34*(18), 52.

Gage, N. L. (1989). The paradigm wars and their aftermath: A "historical" sketch of research on teaching since 1989. *Educational Researcher, 18*(7), 4–10.

Getzels, J. W. (1957). Changing values challenge the schools. *School Review, 65*, 91–102.

Getzels, J. W. (1978). The school and the acquisition of values. In R. W. Tyler (Ed.), *From youth to constructive adult life: The role of the school* (pp. 43–66). Berkeley, CA: McCutchan.

Getzels, J. W., & Thelen, H. A. (1960). The classroom group as a unique social system. In N. B. Henry (Ed.), *The dynamics of instructional groups: The 59th yearbook of the National Society for the Study of Education* (pp. 53–82). Chicago: University of Chicago Press.

Graff, O. B., Street, C. M., Kimbrough, R. B., & Dykes, A. R. (1966). *Philosophic theory and practice in educational administration*. Belmont, CA: Wadsworth.

Greene, J. C. (1990). Three views on the nature and roles of knowledge in social science. In E. G. Guba (Ed.), *The paradigm dialog* (pp. 227–245). Newbury Park, CA: Sage.

Greenfield, T. B. (1978). Reflection on organization theory and the truth of irreconcilable realities. *Educational Administration Quarterly, 14*(2), 1–23.

Greenfield, T. B. (1984). Leaders and schools: Willfulness and nonnatural order in organizations. In T. J. Sergiovanni & J. E. Corbally (Eds.), *Leadership and organizational culture* (pp. 142–169). Urbana, IL: University of Illinois Press.

Greenleaf, R. K. (1977). *Servant leadership: A journey into the nature of legitimate power and greatness*. New York: Paulist.

Guba, E. G. (1990). The alternative paradigm dialog. In E. G. Guba (Ed.), *The paradigm dialog* (pp. 17–27). Newbury Park, CA: Sage.

Guthrie, J. W., Garms, W. I., & Pierce, L. C. (1988). *School finance and education policy: Enhancing educational efficiency, equality and choice*. Englewood Cliffs, NJ: Prentice-Hall.

Hall, B. P., Kalven, J. Rosen, L. S., & Taylor, B. (1990). *Developing human values*. Fond du Lac, WI: International Values Institute of Marian College.

Hodgkinson, C. (1983). *The philosophy of leadership*. Oxford, England: Basil Blackwell.

Hodgkinson, C. (1991). *Educational leadership: The moral art*. Albany, NY: State University of New York Press.

House, E. R. (1990). An ethics of qualitative field studies. In E. G. Guba (Ed.), *The paradigm dialog* (pp. 17–27). Newbury Park, CA: Sage.

Hoy, W. K., & Miskel, C. G. (1991). *Educational administration: Theory, research and practice* (4th ed.). New York: McGraw-Hill.

Keough, K. (1988). At risk students: The challenge (Slide/Tape AASA No. 021-00217). Arlington, VA: American Association of School Administrators.

Lather, P. A. (1990). Reinscribing otherwise: The play of values in the practices of the human sciences. In E. G. Guba (Ed.), *The paradigm dialog* (pp. 315–332). Newbury Park, CA: Sage.

Lerner, M. (1972). Liberalism. *Encyclopedia Britannica* (Vol. 13) (pp. 1017-1020). Chicago: Benton.

Lewis, H. (1990). *A question of values: Six ways we make the personal choices that shape our lives*. New York: Harper and Row.

Lincoln, Y. S. (1990). The making of a constructivist: A remembrance of transformations past. In E. G. Guba (Ed.), *The paradigm dialog* (pp. 67–87). Newbury Park, CA: Sage.

Lindblom, C. E. (1959). The science of muddling through. *Public Administration Review, 19,* 79–88.

Lipham, J. M. (1988). Getzels' models in educational administration. In N. J. Boyan (Ed.), *Handbook on research on educational administration*. New York: Longman.

Maxcy, S. J. (1991). *Educational leadership: A critical pragmatic perspective*. New York: Bergin & Garvey.

Murphy, J. (Ed.). (1993). *Preparing tomorrow's school leaders: Alternative designs*. University Park, PA: University Council for Educational Administration.

National Policy Board for Educational Administration. (1989). *Improving the preparation of school administrators: The reform agenda*. Charlottesville, VA: The Board.

Nyberg, D. (1974). The inevitability of holding philosophical beliefs. *Metaphilosophy, 5*(1), 59–68.

Nyberg, D. (1981). *Power over power: What power means in ordinary life, how it is related to acting freely, and what it can contribute to a renovated ethics of education*. Ithaca, NY: Cornell University Press.

Nyberg, D. (1993). *The varnished truth: Truth telling and deceiving in ordinary life*. Chicago: The University of Chicago Press.

Ouchi, W. G. (1981). *Theory Z: How American business can meet the Japanese challenge*. Reading, MA: Addison-Wesley.

Parsons, T. (1951). *The social system*. New York: The Free Press.

Peters, T. J. (1988). *Thriving on chaos: Handbook for a management revolution*. New York: Alfred A. Knopf.

Peters, T. J., & Waterman, Jr., R. H. (1982). *In search of excellence: Lessons from America's best-run companies*. New York: Warner Books.

Popkewitz, T. S. (1990). Whose future? Whose past? Notes on critical theory and methodology. In E. G. Guba (Ed.), *The paradigm dialog* (pp. 46–66). Newbury Park, CA: Sage.

Ravitch, D. *The schools we deserve: Reflections on the educational crises of our times*. New York: Basic Books.

Rokeach, M. (1973). *The nature of human values*. New York: The Free Press.

Sergiovanni, T. J. (1984a). Cultural and competing perspectives in administrative theory and practice. In T. J. Sergiovanni & J. E. Corbally (Eds.), *Leadership and organizational culture* (pp. 1–17). Urbana, IL: University of Illinois Press.

Sergiovanni, T. J. (1984b). Leadership as cultural expression. In T. J. Sergiovanni & J. E. Corbally (Eds.), *Leadership and organizational culture* (pp. 105–114). Urbana, IL: University of Illinois Press.

Sergiovanni, T. J. (1984c). Leadership and excellence in schooling. *Educational Leadership, 41*(5), 4–13.

Sergiovanni, T. J. (1992). *Moral leadership: Getting to the heart of school improvement*. San Francisco: Jossey-Bass.

Sergiovanni, T. J., & Carver, F. D. (1973). Applied science and the role of value judgement. In T. J. Sergiovanni & F. D. Carver, *The new school executive: A theory of administration*. New York: Dodd Mead.

Smith, J. K. (1990). Alternative research paradigms and the problem of criteria. In E. G. Guba (Ed.), *The paradigm dialog* (pp. 167–187). Newbury Park, CA: Sage.

Smith, L. M. (1990). Ethics, field studies, and the paradigm crisis. In E. G. Guba (Ed.), *The paradigm dialog* (pp. 139–157). Newbury Park, CA: Sage.

Spindler, G. D. (1955). Education in a transforming American culture. *Harvard Education Review, 25*(3), 145–156.

Swanson, A. (1989). Restructuring educational governance: A challenge of the 1990s. *Educational Administration Quarterly, 25*(3), 268–293.

United Way of America. (1988). *The Future World of Work.* Alexandria, VA: United Way of America.

Vaill, P. B. (1984). The purposing of high-performance systems. In T. J. Sergiovanni & J. E. Corbally (Eds.), *Leadership and organizational culture* (pp. 85–104). Urbana, IL: University of Illinois Press.

Wirt, F. M. (1986). *Multiple paths for understanding the role of values in state policy.* Paper presented at the Annual Meeting of the American Educational Research Association, San Francisco, CA (ERIC Document Reproduction Service No. ED278086).

Wirt, F. M. (1987). National Australia-United States education: A commentary. In W. L. Boyd & D. Smart (Eds.), *Educational policy in Australia and America: Comparative perspectives* (pp. 129–137). New York: Falmer.

Chapter 5
The Process of Inquiry

Inquiry's Prelude

Educational research has been labeled in the recent past as "at best, inconclusive, at worst, barren" (Tom, 1984, p. 2). In classroom research, for example, Barrow (1984) contends that we know little of importance that would make us feel more secure. The scientific method as espoused by educational proponents like Thorndike, Barr, and Ryan, while rigorous and seemingly thorough, may have met the same fate as the Weberian bureaucratic system. Correlational studies in educational research investigating limited variables, some even combined with observational studies, are in large part not persuasive.

As we embark on the study of educational inquiry, cognizant of increased complexity and ambiguity in education today, many may have already arrived at the commonsense conclusion that scientific methods will never realize the truths they claim to discover. We might ask the question, aren't teaching and learning intimately tied to the intentions, goals, and purposes of education—from which meaning is derived? How can we claim that a one best way exists or that causal links exist everywhere, knowing that in reality we perceive and act differently? Or perhaps we can only approach research in this manner because our scholarly forbearers conditioned us to this methodology through the process of normal science (Kuhn, 1970).

Further, aren't we beginning to see many questioning the efficacy of the most recent renditions of the structure of knowledge brought to bear by so-called interpretivistic and critical theory paradigms? Despite some scholars' attempts, others may sense only modest progress from previous eras as scholars try to replace the problematic features of past inquiry paradigms with newer models. Melding old and new paradigms provides incremental/adaptive movement as a next step. But, at the same time, others are demanding that new tenets replace the old and outmoded. Interpretivists, for example, reject the underlying assumptions about a uniformity in nature and reject linear-causal sequencing. Interpretivists instead seek to understand behavior from a phenomenological perspective as a result of a social construction process (Erickson, 1985). From this perspective people's actions create the world that exists, not the reverse. In the interpretivistic paradigm, causation is determined from interpreted symbols which then provide meaningful understanding.

Another example is the critical theorist movement. Displeased with the technical, rational, efficient, and objective oriented approaches of the past, this paradigm supports methods that investigate relationships: for instance, relationships between schools and teaching and society and its political and economic foundations. Unwittingly, educational scholars may be simply reproducing the inequities prevalent in the most observed social class structures. Educational researchers must instead raise our awareness of these inequities and not replicate them. Educational research should seek to move society or the educational environment toward greater social justice, not simply mirror the current status. A transformation of the entire structure of schooling should be the intent of effective research (Gage, 1989).

Gage's (1989) article pinpoints the problems we face in the future. The questions below and others construct the context for this chapter on inquiry. How does a theory of knowledge interact with inquiry? What are the paradigms of inquiry, their nature, their relationship with the knower, and the methodology that informs them? What critiques exist of each of these paradigms? Strengths and weaknesses? Is there a necessity behind the paradigm wars, or is this just more of the same, intellectuals arguing about those same philosophical questions that they have for ages? Will older paradigms live on with newer ones?

Which will survive? Or will the debate just continue? Perhaps you'll recognize your own inquiry paradigm in the discussion that follows.

Inquiry Unraveled

EARLY BEGINNINGS

Inquiry has been described as the process of knowing, of solving puzzles, of probing, and finding truth (Guba, 1990; Kuhn, 1970; Eisner, 1981). With varying degrees of success scholars have attempted to characterize the nature of inquiry, to answer the question, "what is going on here?" Dewey defined inquiry as "the controlled or directed transformation of an indeterminate situation into one that is so determinate in its constituent distinctions and relations as to convert the elements of the original situation into a unified whole" (Dewey, 1938, p. 104). Kuhn (1970) referred to normal science as puzzle solving. Bebe (1989) opted for another less complex view and defines inquiry as a search for regularity. More recently, Guba and Lincoln (1989) and others asserted that inquiry is embraced in and reflected through the belief system of the inquirer.

Littlejohn (1992) believes inquiry is the "systematic, disciplined ordering of experience that leads to the development of understanding and knowledge" (p. 8). In this regard, inquiry is a focused and planned means, process, or method to arrive at an outcome. In a cyclical process of questioning, observation, and generalization scholars stage the continued development of knowledge creation and discovery. The process is structured and ordered by a community of scholars who ensure that scientific experience is "true" or adequate to meet the demands of a culture, time, or person. Thus, the normative force of logic is applied by the community of scholars in an ever unfolding process termed *inquiry* (Dewey, 1938). Inquiry then, as defined by the community of scholars, can only be understood within the context of a culture. Dewey also maintains that the logic of theory is subservient to the metaphysical and epistemological preconceptions of the inquirer. The process of inquiry, therefore, arises from a historical and cultural environment. While the creation of knowledge in and of itself may seem like a mundane task, scholars see the development of knowledge from differing circumstances. What is knowable and how knowledge arises is not as apparent as a cursory view may indicate.

Although many inquiry paradigms exist, knowledge creation is generally thought to evolve from the three distinctive approaches identified earlier. Littlejohn (1992) labeled them knowledge of discovery, knowledge of interpretation, and knowledge of criticism. In Littlejohn's view, the discovery approach seeks to achieve objective observations which, when refined, produce instances of structural reality. In contrast, the interpretive approach seeks to construct a picture of reality through the eyes of both the participant and observer. Knowledge is then reconstructed as the next instance(s) of reality. The critical approach seeks to define knowledge through critical judgments which then lead to social improvement and change.

From another vantage point, Eisner (1991) clarified building and defining the origins of inquiry further. Objectivity is surely among the world's most cherished beliefs. Objectivity seeks to see things the way they are. To see is to know. Within this context then, the aim of inquiry is to achieve truth and certain knowledge. In addition, understanding is derived from the community of believers. What inquirers say, therefore, is of equal importance. Just as important is the understanding that knowledge is used and developed via cer-

tain methodology. In part, knowledge is freed from personal judgment as a result of choice of method.

Representation, too, is problematic. Any account that furthers knowledge is offered via a symbol system (Eisner, 1991). Representations of knowledge are revealing and at the same time concealing, depending on the constraints of the symbol system. In this respect, we can begin to sense how the subjective view gains its stature. Subjective knowledge becomes an important distinctive view. But similarly, as we have developed the objective view above, so too can we erode the premier stations which comprise subjectivity. Eisner (1991) summarized the disparities herein as he explained that ontological subjectivity is possible if we accept the idea that truth exceeds belief. That is a belief in itself. Active minds in commerce with the world are the product of an active mind. To seek more than what ultimately is referenced in our own beliefs after using appropriate criteria for holding them is to retreat to a higher authority or to seek a dominant view that bypasses the mind's observation of nature (p. 51).

Eisner concluded that a different belief structure is needed to avoid the dichotomy between objectivity and subjectivity. What may be needed is a process by which we can enlist the strength of objectivity and subjectivity from their separate consequences and move to a unification of understanding and principle. Since what we know of the world is a product of the arbitration of our subjective life and an axiomatic objective world, life and worlds cannot be separated. To separate them would require that we engage the mind, and since the mind would need to be employed to make the separation, anything separated as a result of its use would reflect mind as well as what was separated from it (Eisner, 1991, p. 52). Inquiry in the absence of reality is simply a picture. We can already sense that inquiry has become a difficult and controversial subject. How were these developments shaped from the past and how are they exhibited today?

Historical Development

Today's version of inquiry can be traced back to Greek times. The Greek culture viewed the world in wholes. Inquiry, as a developing science, involved "maneuvering to get a better view" of something already there (Dewey, 1938, p. 88). All knowledge was seen as part of the whole, a larger good. Anything quantifiable was subject to change and, therefore, not worthy of sustained study. The Greeks looked for order and structure in the universe, based on philosophical and religious foundations, a teleological view. The aim of science in this regard was to differentiate knowledge from belief. Whatever we know is true. If it were not true, we didn't know it (Eisner, 1981). Scientists, therefore, were the discoverers of laws that rule the universe. Scientific practice was to uncover the facts.

During the Middle Ages, changes to empiricism included the teleological view of the Greeks. The "new scientist" replaced the philosopher and cleric. Descartes and the Cartesian philosophy of certainty have since dominated the search for knowledge. Newton, Bacon, Galileo, and others stressed the need to discover the order within nature through experimental confirmation (Polkinghorne, 1983). To discover the order in the universe, measurement and quantification became essential. Positivism and the development of the scientific method as a way to discover unchanging truths ushered in the physical sciences and the technological advances of the nineteenth century.

In the 1800s a parallel development to positivism as it applied to human behavior occurred. Compte, writing between 1830 and 1850, proposed that the study of human

beings conform to methods used in the study of natural science (in Polkinghorne, 1983). John Stuart Mill's *System of Logic* (1843) supports the positivistic approach in his study of human behavior, stating that the "backward state of moral sciences can only be remedied by applying to them the methods of physical science, duly extended and generalized" (in Polkinghorne, 1983). Dewey supported this positivistic stance, stating that the inability of social sciences and natural sciences to "act in accord with logical conditions which have been pointed out [positivism] throws light on its retarded state" (1938, p. 487). This positivistic approach proposes that human problems would finally be solved using the one correct approach to inquiry, positivism.

The view that social sciences should adopt the methodology of the physical sciences developed throughout the twentieth century. Polkinghorne (1983) identified five phases of the current "received view" of science (postpositivism). The first phase proposes that science should describe only the observable. The second phase expands this theory to include nonobservable entities and searches for axioms based on universal statements. The third phase consists of the critique of positivism which allows the inclusion of alternate systems of science based on the history of science in the fourth phase. The fifth phase is based on pragmatic reason and inclusion of the contextual considerations of inquiry.

The current positivist approach has broadened its methodologies and its definition of truth. However, science is still viewed as the search for ever closer approximations of truth through the stringent application of scientific methods. Although frequently denied by the current positivists, science still aspires to the Cartesian ideal of certainty; however, positivists might relate, "I'm relatively sure" rather than "I'm certain." Methodologically, this view generates more latitude.

At the same time that Mill proposed the use of the positivistic methods for the study of behavior, the antipositivist movement arose. It argued that individuals are part of a complex structure made up of historical and social reality. It was believed that life could be ordered into laws or broken into analyzable parts. The term *life* denotes what is to everyone the most familiar and intimate, and at the same time, darkest, even most unthinkable. One can delineate its peculiar and characteristic traits. One can even inquire about its tone, rhythm, and melody. But one cannot totally analyze it into all its factors, for it is not totally resolvable in this manner. It cannot be verbalized in a simple formula or explanation. Thought is an expression of life, but it does not supersede life. Polkinghorne's (1983) writings contain the seeds for interpretivistic inquiry. They discuss a holistic approach to inquiry, viewing the individual as part of the whole of culture in a search for meaning. All are basic to naturalism, but were largely ignored until recently.

Weber, while generally supportive of the above views, did not accept the differences others created between the physical and social sciences (Smith & Hesusius, 1986). Weber believes that the two sciences needed to think in terms of integration (Aron, 1967; Benton, 1977; Outhwaite, 1975; Simey, 1969; Smith & Hesusius, 1986). Weber further believes that explanation and understanding are two essential parts of social research. Both are essential to understanding the two strata of man, the animal and mechanistic level, and the level of rational evaluation of subjective meanings. Although he realizes that the science of humans was vulnerable to bias, he believes that the two approaches can be synthesized.

PARADIGMS?

Currently, methods of scientific inquiry can be described as suffering an identity crisis. Each of the three methods described earlier have

avid disciples and equally avid critics. The general patterns of inquiry, more recently called paradigms, have received special attention over the past thirty years. Kuhn, in the *Structure of Scientific Revolutions* (1970), challenged the traditional view of science as developing knowledge by accumulation or the knowledge of piecemeal facts. He suggested that the growth of knowledge also occurs through scientific revolution, and enables thinkers to move from current assumptions to new paradigms of understanding. Normal science, according to Kuhn, was the building of existing knowledge in a developmental fashion. The growth of knowledge, he surmised, is bounded, restricted by the world view of scholars and educators in the community. Within a paradigm then, science accumulates knowledge related to that particular world view, using its own paradigm symbols, tools, and values learned from its own narrow existing scientific community. However, in order for progress to occur, science must undergo a revolution. Science, in Kuhn's view, proceeds from anomaly in a current map, to preparadigm struggles, to crisis, and finally to revolution. During the crisis period, existing paradigm symbols, tools, and values are discarded in exchange for new ones. The revolution frees the community from the restrictiveness of the old paradigm to allow new questions to be asked.

So inquiry paradigms form the basis of how we as theorists and practitioners see the world. As we internalize our paradigms they take on great power and determine how we interact with the world. Educational inquiry, like inquiry in general, revolves around numerous paradigms. Our inquiry paradigms become so powerful that more concern is given to methods of inquiry than to determining what has really happened. Practitioners of the positivistic paradigm often refer to it as scientific, experimental, or behavioral, or, too loosely, as simply quantitative. The second mode of inquiry, interpretivistic, is dominated by ethnographic research, and is often termed *qualitative* or *constructivistic inquiry*. Lastly, the critical theorist inquiry paradigm, sometimes termed *conflict theory*, explores power, dominance, and conflict in society.

One of the difficulties in defining inquiry is the paradigm community's reliance on the means-ends argument to substantiate its various viewpoints. While the scientific model of inquiry is highly valid in the proper context, inquiry in this model is more than an outcome driven by a series or set of means. Inquiry as a process implies a system of inquiry with component parts, outcomes, methods to change, and a philosophical base around which the process itself is built. To enable further discussion and thought about this identity crisis, each of the three, often considered competing, paradigms will be described and clarified further.

Positivistic and Postpositivistic Theory

Since Descartes, inquiry has been firmly entrenched in the positivistic and postpositivistic paradigms. Both are foundational paradigms and rooted in a realist ontology, a belief system that a reality exists out there. The true nature of science is to discover truth, and thereby, enable prediction and control. As a consequence of this ontology, the realist research practices are objective. As inquirers, the realists separate their values from reality. Only then can experimentation or manipulation result in an independence necessary for nature to truly expose itself. Such scientific inquiry seeks to uncover natural laws which are then summarized in the form of generalizations or cause and effect laws (Guba, 1990).

Postpositivism evolved as a result of the problematic tenets of positivism. Criticism of positivism has, therefore, forced positivistic theorists to revamp and soften their ontological stance. Although a real world exists, it is

impossible for the realist to truly perceive it outside one's own values and judgments. As a result the postpositivist is a critical realist, recognizing that objectivity on the part of the observer can never truly be achieved. In this more critical tradition, postpositivistic inquiry must be more consistent as determined by scholarly tradition within a research paradigm. All inquiry is subjected to the community's critical review. Methodologically, the postpositivist also moves away from previous objectivity requirements and posits development of findings that have been exposed to as many methodological sources as possible. Inquiry in this research arena then attempts to isolate objective knowledge and apply the new knowledge to practice or policy. Emphasis is placed on creating knowledge that allows further prediction and control of educational processes and products (Soltis, 1992). Methodology is statistical and experimental and relies on creating validity through objective testing, mathematical rigor, and reliable observation instruments.

Postpositivistic science has maneuvered, some would say migrated, far from many of the original positivistic precepts. Although critics have been relentless, postpositivists have worked diligently to address imbalances that prevailed from their new postures surrounding objectivity. Guba (1990) cited four imbalances: those between rigor and relevance, precision and richness, elegance and applicability, and discovery and verification. For example, a shift can be noted to more naturalistic inquiry in regard to rigor and relevance differences. As rigor is relaxed to gain greater external validity, generalizability increases; relevance is assumed to increase at the expense of internal validity.

In the most recent developments, positivism has become untenable and postpositivism more thorough about its own tenets. In mid-century, Hempel (1966) and other theorists acknowledged that operational science must begin to remove itself from notions that concepts can each be reducible to a string of observation statements. More appropriately, the concepts of science are like the bindings in a network of systematic interrelationships: the more inclusive the convergence of bindings, or that issue from a conceptual binding, the stronger the orderliness of the system (Hempel, p. 94).

Instances of changing views of theorists as demonstrated above cause some to distance themselves from positivistic research. While some researchers may never depart from the older views, others view the newest directions of postpositivistic science as illustrative of its resilience. Firestone (1990) confirmed the views of Phillips (1990) and contended that scientists, like any workers, are in the business of providing reasonable justifications for their assertions. Dewey (1938) attempted to explain this same principle in his preference for the term *warranted assertibility* in lieu of truth. A warrant is not forever and thus assertions aren't ever safe from criticism and may even be proven false. In this sense, objectivity only comes closest to the firmest warrants. Adequacy is judged through an internal competitive process that rules out error. In total, postpositivism is no longer held up as a "queen science" (Firestone, 1990), but firmly entrenched and still possibly useful in practice. In fact, most would claim that disparities between these paradigms erode as we move farther from philosophical debate forums. As will be noted in later discussions, accommodation between paradigms is more prevalent than some would acknowledge.

Critical Theory

Critical theory developed in the middle of the nineteenth century. More recently, it has been formulated by the Frankfurt School (Marcuse, Adorno, Horkheimer, and others) and most recently revived by Habermas (1970, 1987). Critical theory focuses on educational prob-

lems and their role in relation to social, political, cultural, and economic patterns that result. In this regard, critical theory is the systematic inquiry into contradictions that exist in educational practice. Agger (1991) contended, however, that critical theory must today be rejuvenated for it to remain adaptable. Critical theory may have lost much of its power to analyze the social problems of modernity and postmodernity in society and, in particular, in the educational realm. Critical theory may need to be fortified with additional currency, from a poststructural, postmodern, and feminist perspective.

Critical theory has demonstrated convoluted beginnings as authors' translations and applications need further clarification due to their extreme variability (Agger, 1991). As developed by the Frankfurt School, early critical theories attempt to explain the failure of Marx's socialist revolution. In their revisitation, the theorists attempt to link economic, cultural, and ideological analyses to explain the revolution's failure. In these early versions of critical theory, the Frankfurt School believes that Marxism failed to recognize the ability of the capitalist economic system to exploit the working class. Capitalism, it is postulated, deepens the false consciousness of the working class by developing its own coping mechanisms that forestall social revolution. This is termed *domination* by the Frankfurt School. Workers adopt new shared values and beliefs that are seemingly rational; at the same time the capitalistic system exploits sociopolitical and economic liberties in exchange for freedom of consumer choice. Positivism, they argue, is just another coping mechanism. Positivism, a descendant of the Age of Enlightenment, also becomes the shared problem-solving methodology. People are taught and assume the "world as it is" is the prominent reality. The positivistic system, therefore, perpetuates itself. With these convictions, one experiences the world as rational and necessary and thus sees little that needs to or can be done to change it.

Critical theory, however, breaks from the rational-reality viewpoints (positivism) and develops into a mode of consciousness and thinking that views social facts as history that can be changed (Jay, 1973). Critical theory looks beyond the appearance of social fact finding, and seeks ways to achieve new social understanding. More precisely, critical theory attunes researchers to their own underlying empirical beliefs through rigorous self-reflection and self-criticism (Horkheimer & Adorno, 1972).

Guba (1990) briefly outlines the basic beliefs of critical theory. Although the label *critical theory* seemingly narrows the philosophical landscape comprising this expansive view, all beliefs about critical theory converge in light of a rejection of "value freedom." Our values are inevitably reflected in numerous ways: in selecting the problem to study, in the choice of tools for analysis, and in the interpretations, conclusions, and recommendations created. Given these possible value premises, inquiry becomes a political act as participants are either empowered or disempowered through the inquirer's choice of a value system. The burden of inquiry is, by definition, to raise oppressed people to a level of true consciousness (Guba, 1990). Once they acknowledge how oppressed they are, they can act to revolutionize the world (Guba, 1990, p. 24.). This transformation extends beyond the typically manipulative-interventionist methodology, as critical theorists seek to establish a commonness through a dialogic/hermeneutic approach. Features of the real world are scrutinized and judgments created which then alter reality and energize and facilitate future action. So critical theory has also evolved.

In recent times critical theory can be seen to exist under differing banners. Poststructuralism is a theory of textuality and knowledge. Within this framework, Derrida (1981, in Culler, 1982) posited a process termed *deconstruction*; text conceals conflicts

between differing voices (text and subtext). What appears to be said must be understood in conjunction with references that are concealed; meaning is more than it appears to be on the surface. People often make important assumptions about this concealed meaning and their assumptions are suppressed or even become tacit. This diverts a reader's/listener's attention, making text undecipherable. Derrida termed this *deference*, the ability to produce meaning only with reference to other meaning. Thus, to the poststructuralist, meaning is held in the constitutive practices of language. Deconstruction demystifies by revealing suppressed values and interests. The poststructuralists believe that, ". . . every rhetorical gesture of text contributes to its overall meaning" (Agger, 1991, p. 30). How we arrange a plan, title a section of a paper, describe a decision process, and more, contribute to the sense that exists in the text.

Postmodernism, another translation of critical theory, requires the investigation of society, culture, and history. In this tradition, the social world is examined from the multiple perspectives of class, race, gender, and other affiliations. Additionally, the postmodernists rely on heterogeneous "subject positions" to explain social phenomena (Agger, 1991). As a result, ". . . knowledge is traced through discourse/practices that frame the knowledge formulated from within them" (Foucault, 1976, 1980, in Agger, 1991, p. 32). From "subject positions" the experiences of the world are framed against its own perspective. In this realm, social science becomes an accounting of multiple perspectives rather than a universal truth. Social science in the educational realm becomes a discourse, suggesting that by "reading" a school, we can "do" social science (Agger, 1991).

In educational practice, critical science involves finding the conditions that produce selectivity in the process of teaching and the organization of schooling (Popkewitz, 1990). In this regard, Popkewitz attached critical science to inquiry of the commonplace and socially accepted contradictions that may result in various struggles in the educational environment. Exploration of the constraints produced in school affairs occurs through understanding how boundaries and structures limit our active potential. Debates about the constructions of schooling give rise to differing structural representations, around such issues as ethnicity, class, and gender, for example. Thus, deference creates sensitivity to potentially new concepts and builds a relationship between knowledge and identity.

Popkewitz (1990) further argued that a commitment to critical methods requires greater responsibility on the part of researchers to reflect on proper rules and standards of the work of science. A critical stance reconstructs education by providing relevance to history as it relates to methodology and accommodates the influence of questioning, conceptual development, and strategies to social values, struggles, and interests. He further asserted that six themes should frame any discussion of practices of a critical science of education.

1. Institutional practices support the contention that educational inquiry is comprised fully in procedural practice. In actual practice we may be inappropriately separating social movements, historical issues, or political interests from the strategies of research. As a philosophy of science, intellectual traditions *and* institutional conditions are of equal import. Rules of inquiry are bounded in both traditions. Methodology is in constant flux as it is reworked through its relationship with questions, concepts, and procedures directed at empirical phenomena. Methodology emerges from inquiry in this sense, not the other way around.

2. Popkewitz (1990) also claimed, despite conventional beliefs about logic as a process of continued clarification, that the logic of sci-

ence must also be a problem of social epistemology. The concepts, rules, or procedures of inquiry are not inevitable, but made real within institutions and through social construction. Critical science deals with questions that are a part of a field of science including its ontology and epistemology, what is known and the means of knowing.

3. On another theme, Popkewitz (1990) admonished us and our willingness to simplify the context of inquiry in a objective and subjective dichotomy. "Objectivity has nothing to do with external laws or a 'nature' to be discovered or verified" (p. 56). Objectivity rules when it is unquestioned, but most important, detracts when it fails to recognize dynamic and changing patterns. Paralleling this, subjectivity directs our focus into the minds of people. By themselves neither can confront the complexity that exists in social relations but, in combination, they may be able to provide the inquirer with greater ability to confront interrelations of objective and subjective conditions. Inquiry must not relegate itself to individual schema formed by unforeseen or unacknowledged rules acting as a horizon for individual reason (Popkewitz, p. 57).

4. The above rejection of a singular prescription with which to evaluate the products of science is accompanied by the belief that the scientist is a disinterested observer. In its most profound form, disinterest can imply relativity, but Popkewitz contends not without paradigmatic boundaries formulated in the practice or beliefs of one's own paradigm. But this cannot mean that ". . . a lack of commitment or ideas that have no social location or consequence. . ." exists (p. 59). Today, our educational research must investigate more than teaching, learning, or organization, and seek more than an understanding of the conflict of values across these considerations.

5. The multiplicity of values must be seen as multiples of knowledge. Knowledge creation and value creation are ideological. When we separate the creation of knowledge from its value contexts we create poverty in understanding. Methodologically, when values are separated to control or identify bias we lose the interactiveness within all of science. In this view, then, critical theory posits an added systemic panorama.

6. Finally, Popkewitz contrasted the ability of science in its present form as a method for understanding boundaries that exist or have existed with the generalizability of science to enable a future condition. While science can predict and control by sensitizing us to issues, critical theory more appropriately recognizes that science is an ongoing construction that challenges us to find our relation to it.

Critical theory makes a sociological contribution in two differing manners: methodologically in the ways researchers write and read, and substantively in the contributions to the studies of state, ideology, culture, discourse, and social movements (Agger, 1991). Agger's implications are (1) critical theory forces interrogation of the unquestioned reliance on value freedom, (2) critical theory establishes a new science capable of recognizing its own grounded interests, (3) poststructuralism can deconstruct most rhetoric by examining hidden meanings, (4) poststructuralism reveals how language can constitute reality, and (5) postmodernism rejects a one best way. Substantively, Agger contends that critical theory may suggest new ways of theorizing about the role of the state and culture, offer valuable contributions through the study of discourses, suggest empirical studies of the ways discourses are structured by gender themes, and offer new social movements theories displaying insights that explain historical meaning and display impact.

Critical theory posits a view that is antifoundational, reflective, and recognizes the perspective of the knower. In this sense, inquiry can be recast between the object of study and a conditioned observer. In another sense, this establishes critical inquiry as engagement. Its main emphasis may be more thorough than we hoped as we realize that knowledge is born from being open to multiple dimensions of reality. The task for the future may be to move beyond these strict distinctions contained within paradigmatic definitions through discourse and to reunite schooling with democracy and justice (Skrtic, 1990).

Interpretivistic Theory

Most interpretivistic theorists believe the positivistic and critical theorist viewpoints are flawed. For example, Guba (1990) contended that: (1) Reality exists only as a mental framework for thinking about reality. In this view, the major premise of the interpretivistic approach can be noted. Reality is constructed on a moment-by-moment basis, not a cultural or historical basis as the realists or critical realists surmise. (2) There are no unequivocal explanations for one best way, nor is there, as so often quoted, one best way to pursue inquiry and discover truth. In this view, the interpretivistic framework posits a multitude of possible theories that could each possibly provide a reasonable explanation of fact. Reality then, becomes the window of theory—seen only as it occurs. (3) As many differing constructions of theory are possible, it also follows that inquiry must be value laden—tied to the values of the researcher. (4) And lastly, since theory is value laden, inquiry is shaped by the interaction of the inquirer and those issues of study. Even today, the physical sciences have disproved their own stance on objectivity.

With these critiques in mind, the full panorama of the interpretivistic framework can be completed. The interpretivistic approach is antifoundational and relativistic. Reality is found in multiple constructions of, and entails the continued search for, more informed reconstructions of peoples' own reality. Equally, the interpretivistic position relies on the social constructions of the researcher and referent agent(s). In this regard, the interpretivistic epistemology is subjective, as social interaction cannot be possible without the inquirer/inquired dyad. Lastly, the interpretivist seeks to understand by identifying the variety of possible constructions of knowledge. This variety is investigated with the sole purpose of bringing consensus to understanding. Methodologically, hermeneutic reasoning of the interpretivist seeks to depict individual constructions as accurately as possible while ongoing dialectic compares and contrasts individual constructions to enable the inquirer and the client to come to grips with their constructions. More informed choice results as the methodological process enables continuously deeper communication to ensue. In this sense, the interpretivist seeks to derive more thorough understanding via an ongoing reconstruction process (Guba, 1990).

Interpretivistic inquiry, like critical theory, has had a complex history. Often termed *naturalistic inquiry*, the interpretivist position lies in direct contrast to the realist posture found in the positivistic or postpositivistic inquiry framework. While the axioms of positivism are generated in value-free "environments," the axioms of the interpretivistic framework are created and shaped in the social processes of interacting minds. Reality is, therefore, the product of the collective cognition of value-laden inquiry (Levine, 1985, 1992). Research cannot be thorough without due consideration to the values, beliefs, and preconceptions of inquiry's set of actors. This interpretive process, termed *versteben,*

acknowledges and utilizes the constant flux inherent in human activity and thereby incorporates behavior in its natural settings.

The naturalistic research paradigm is new to educational circles and, more importantly, is still at odds with the existing positivistic paradigm ingrained through time. Many educational researchers are still largely tied to their old paradigms. For example, Babbie (1989) offered a full text on sociological research largely based on realist methodology. Borg and Gall (1989) offered scant explanations of the most current sociological research methods. Clearly, those interested in developing, adapting, or changing their inquiry beliefs and methodology can not fully internalize an interpretivistic epistemology. Their basic beliefs are still largely informed by earlier value traditions, research methodologies, and theories (Smith & Hesusius, 1986). Many prefer to remain adamant about and continue to operate within their earlier paradigms. They also continue to critique the research methods of the interpretivist position with fervor. Their critique would include a lack of parallel validity and reliability constructs (Guba, 1978; Miles & Huberman, 1984), a lack of tools to provide ethnographic description and comparison, codification of the role of the researcher, role management within the research context, observational strategies, and more. But progress has been accomplished as those adopting newer views struggle with a generation of newer methods. More generally today, researchers are clarifying field techniques, outlining participants-observer-agent traditions, enhancing mechanisms that derail outsider-insider constraints, developing better criteria about what to observe versus what to infer, and becoming more attuned to the inherent flux in the social interaction process.

Early authors and philosophers have become disconcerted by measurement research methodology that relies on measurement and quantification perspectives in which ". . . the indices of a phenomenon seemingly were more important than the phenomenon itself" (Giorgi, 1970, p. 291). In their earliest works, Guba and Lincoln (1981, 1982, 1985) grappled with conventional assumptions associated with older paradigms. More precisely, Guba and Lincoln (1989) outlined problematic features of the positivistic paradigm. In their terms, the Standards for Evaluation Practice (Rossi, 1982), as developed by the Evaluation Research Society, are unacceptable from the standpoint of a new generation of evaluators. Speaking strictly about evaluative practice, Guba and Lincoln critiqued the Society's views and outlined the rationale behind their inability to accept its compatibility stance. Their positions include the following.

1.   They disagree about the interactive role of the evaluator in relation to the client. While traditional methodology postulates a formulation and negotiation role, researchers today see research activities as a cyclic and iterative process.

2.   Equally important, Guba and Lincoln do not see the standards for practice enlightening the methodological tenets of the interpretivistic approach, as the standards do not directly identify or specify criteria appropriate to constructivist evaluation efforts. Most often, treatments relating to quantitative methodology are prevalent, embodied in terms like *sampling, reliability, generalizability,* and more. Lacking are interpretivistic terms Guba and Lincoln (1989) see as equal or more applicable—terms like *authenticity, trustworthiness, credibility,* and so forth.

3.   Like interpretivistic philosophy since its inception, the older positivistic standards still rely almost exclusively on the cause and effect relationship that Guba and Lincoln contend blinds evaluators and clients from discerning more powerful social forces operat-

ing in individual situations. In their view, social construction is at least equally as important as possible cause and effect relationships.

4.   Guba and Lincoln (1989) additionally cite the constant unfolding of ethical dilemmas, as client and researcher in the traditional model of inquiry typically leave information availability, decisionmaking, and power relationships in the hands of the client. But newer models of inquiry necessitate removing this leverage from the client-sponsor to more fully enable a broad spectrum of decisionmaking to arise from more readily available information and subsequent interaction with other stakeholders.

5.   Lastly, Guba and Lincoln (1989) make a plea in defense of the mounting body of evidence that posits a value-bound approach to evaluation. "In retrospect, the possibility of acting to 'value' a project (program, curriculum, and so on) while acting as though values were unimportant or corrupting to the valuing (evaluation) effort should have struck us long ago as bizarre, if not contradictory, behavior" (p. 233).

In light of these numerous problematic features, Guba and Lincoln (1989) and Lincoln and Guba (1986) continued in their quest to create criteria for judging the adequacy of evaluation and more suitable to the interpretivistic paradigm.

A brief review of their thinking in this regard can be helpful. Their beliefs can be summarized into three broad categories: trustworthiness criteria, the nature of the hermeneutic process, and authenticity criteria.

Trustworthiness.   Trustworthiness criteria are intended to parallel the standards for rigorous research within the positivistic framework (i.e., validity, reliability, and objectivity). While each of these is grounded firmly in positivistic frameworks and are very familiar, there are no direct translations of these criteria to the interpretivistic realm. A realist ontology cannot pretend that there is a concurrence between findings and a real world nor can findings within the interpretivistic tradition then be generalizable. Too many other possible constructions are possible. Lincoln and Guba (1986) posit that establishing credibility, transferability, dependability, and confirmability are more appropriate criteria to the interpretivistic framework.

They submit that establishing a parallel concept of credibility establishes a more appropriate likeness, matching constructed realities of respondents to the reality of the evaluator. Techniques that enhance the possibility of greater credibility are more prolonged engagement enabling greater rapport, persistent observation allowing greater scope, peer debriefing as a disinterested quality control, negative case testing assuring subjective confidence, progressive subjectivity to capture the privileged view of other contributing others, and member checks to enlist the construction of stakeholders.

Equally critical, transferability is foundational to the interpretivistic paradigm. It parallels generalizability criteria of the positivistic paradigm. Generalizability in the positivistic framework stems from adherence to random sampling techniques. The burden of proof lies with the inquirer. But this cannot be the case with the interpretivistic approach, as the burden of proof lies with the agent and client(s), and, therefore, is always relative. The consequences of transferability are not considered relevant to confidence limitations prevalent in a positivistic sense. Rather, degrees of transferability are established by providing as complete a data base as possible (thick descriptions) to facilitate traversing to other contexts.

Another criterion of the interpretivistic paradigm is reliability, or the stability of data over time. Design alterations and shifts in hypothe-

ses would render research studies unstable in the traditional research paradigm, but are considered normative in the interpretivistic framework. This ability to change or redesign purpose is commonplace considering the emergent characteristic that defines naturalism. In deference to the importance of reliability, interpretivists need to guarantee a sense of tractability. This method of inquiry needs to be continuously scrutinized as others attempt to recreate for their edification the decisions and interpretations of the inquirer. For example, can others track the inquirer's logic of process?

Lastly, Lincoln and Guba (1986) submit that inquiry must maintain a sense of objectivity to assure that data, interpretations, and products of the inquiry are affixed in contexts and persons different and separable from the inquirers. But unlike objectivity from previous traditions, interpretivistic inquiry relies on confirmability of the data itself. In this sense, integrity is maintained by assuring that data can be tracked to various sources and that coherent interpretations are both distinctive and implied.

The Hermeneutic Process. Within the hermeneutic/dialectic process, data input are immediately available for feedback, elaboration, correction, revision, or expansion. As such, inputs are another form of assuring quality in the inquiry process. As data originate and are revisited, they immediately become accessible to emergent and joint reconstruction efforts. This alliance of information and elaboration mechanisms allows data to be continuously challenged by a variety of clients which in turn sustains credibility in outcomes. This partitioning of inspection requirements prevents impoverishment of information.

Authenticity Criteria. While the above approaches to the maintenance of "health" in the interpretive process are worthwhile, they also typically originate from and parallel positivist methodological assumptions about goodness. Interpretivistic inquiry needs its own explicit set of criteria based on constructivist assumptions (Lincoln & Guba, 1986). These authenticity criteria would need to include: fairness, ontological authenticity, educative authenticity, catalytic authenticity, and tactical authenticity. Fairness arises from the requirement to provide equal "voice" and balance to the value pluralism that arises from varying constructions. In this sense, the inquirer's role is one of mediation, as conflicting constructions must each have their "day in court." Fairness also requires that the inquirer conduct what Lincoln and Guba term an *appellate mechanism*, whereby stakeholders can arbitrate process procedures and policy. The remaining derivatives of authenticity build the power of this process. Any inquiry process must be able to be improved upon and matured. Ontological authenticity seeks to continuously enhance the sophistication of both stakeholders and inquirers. Educative authenticity requires that inquirers fulfill their moral responsibility to stakeholders by assuring that a variety in design viewpoints is present. Catalytic authenticity demands that the inquiry process not rest solely as a experiential exercise, but that the process agitates decisionmaking and action outcomes. Theory must evolve through praxis (commitment and understanding) to practice. Lastly, tactical authenticity requires the competition of a complete process that additionally includes granting stakeholders the power to act.

Inquiry and Educational Administration

After having explored the three major paradigms in depth, a more thorough look at inquiry in educational practice is appropriate.

Evers and Lakomski (1991) provide a vehicle for us to relate the philosophical underpinnings described above to educational practice. The three major areas addressed by Evers and Lakomski correspond to those previously discussed: the theory movement, the paradigm approach, and coherence. The theory movement in educational administration flourished in the 1980s. During these years educational researchers looked to the "hypothetical-deductive structure with laws at the top and facts at the bottom" (Evers & Lakomski, 1991, p. 3). The purpose of research was to provide educational administrators with findings that would allow them to more accurately predict events and to better control those events. Organizational elements were identified, operationalized, and measured in an attempt to increase efficiency and effectiveness within the educational environment.

In this classical paradigm, educational organizations were viewed as simple, hierarchical, and mechanical. Predictions of events were considered and research faithfully followed foundational scientific practice. Inquiry's goal was unchanged: break down the object of inquiry into discrete parts, examine them, and arrive at generalizations to extend to other domains. In keeping with changing practices in other organizational arenas, however, educational administration also began a shift. Literature is replete with examples of ongoing attempts to change the way organizations function and create new knowledge. Certainly the extreme tenets of the positivistic paradigm in organizational inquiry is no longer an acceptable archetype (Howe & Eisenhart, 1990; Cziko, 1989). But while postpositivism was more palatable to youthful research participants, the old empiricism remained entrenched (Howe & Eisenhart, 1990).

Guba and Lincoln (1989) provide other illustrations of inquiry's coming of age in educational administration. While each generation concentrated on its own particular methods to accomplish inquiry and their research represented an advance, pervasive problems remained. Collection of data for measurement was fundamental. For example, in educational circles, the measurement of the attributes of school children was primary. The purpose of schooling was to teach what was known to be true of the basics and to assure that students were then able to demonstrate their knowledge on standardized tests. As the humanistic movement became more prominent, findings that individual differences in reaction times were typical of human subjects and led to suggestions that measurement was indeed a proper new inquiry trail. Business and industry also contributed to the era of measurement as researchers prospected for efficiency and effectiveness criteria. While this first generation of educational administration researchers provided valuable data, the limited scope of the findings has garnered calls for greater breadth.

In a second generation, researchers began to utilize other methods to increase the influence of their scholarly activity. Descriptions of programs, material, teaching strategies, and organizational patterns attempted to broaden the scope of inquiry results, but also retained much of the measurement era's almost religious reliance on quantification. This research almost certainly resulted in beneficial change as more broad-based curriculum resulted, deeper understanding of students occurred, and testing revealed whether students learned what teachers had intended. However, more change was needed. Value determination became the area of study for the next generation of inquirers.

In this new period, researchers became seasoned adjudicators of differing research methods in addition to masters of measurement and description. In this arena, not only was performance a matter of concern to the inquirer, but goals and objectives became the subject of inquiry. Researchers now were required to deal with merit, both inside and outside the school educational research perspective. Researchers, although not competent in this venue, suddenly entered the "political realm." In the section that follows we address the problematic features of this area of research more fully.

Quandaries of Inquiry

Earlier in this chapter we discussed the emergence of various inquiry paradigms. Now it is necessary to also discuss a line of practical problems that emerge in research approaches. Eisner (1981), Agger (1991), and Guba and Lincoln (1989) each provide thoughtful discussions of the failings of research in general and more specifically educational research.

Eisner (1981) postulated several points of concern. Given the reliance on interpretivistic inquiry found today, exploitations of the inquirer's own unique strengths are paramount. While some see this as a singular political problem, others point to broader ethical concerns. Researchers in classrooms or schools or from universities each must address the privilege of both the agent and the client. In this light, thoroughness of research training, individual researcher's attributes, and contractual arrangements each reflect a necessary concern that inquiry be more thorough. Another consideration involves the timeliness of research outcomes. Thorough research in the interpretivistic frame is often kin to the "action science" orientation of Argyris (1985), taking weeks, months, even years before closure in a study is available, if ever. Thus research often gravitates to procedural preoccupations which disempowers—the effect of inquiry becomes too short term and loses its applicability over time. To maintain the inherent flexibility of interpretive methods, the complete realm of the inquiry, from aims to findings, must be available for adjustment. In light of the above, Eisner submits that qualitative research is frequently viewed as less deterministic and final than previous methodologies. Clients may become discouraged as results cannot generate immediate and effective change as assumed in the positivistic eras.

Guba and Lincoln (1989) contended that three major defects have dominated administrative inquiry in education: a tendency toward managerialism, the failure to accommodate value pluralism, and overcommitment to scientific inquiry (p. 32). In the first case, Lincoln argues that managerialism yields a number of faults, in effect, disempowering the participant stakeholders, disenfranchising evaluators' findings, and lacking the ability to assert accountability. In aggregate, managerialism combines several distasteful features that can compromise a whole research scenario. Also important is the realization that value pluralism is paramount in all research efforts. Research that disregards value tenets sets aside differing heritages of students in schools, differing learning rates, and disassociates researcher bias possibly due to monetary necessities, among other problems. Lastly, as Guba and Lincoln contended, educational inquiry is still largely committed to the scientific approach. From textbook issues brought to light earlier to graduate programs that still resonate with methodological courses that are largely quantitatively focused, the scientific method is firmly entrenched. In education administration and across management science, the scientific method is viewed as the right way to do things. This reliance often strips evaluations from their context and renders research results of questionable value. Only recently has the scientific method been questioned. Guba and Lincoln (1985) argued for responsive constructivism, beyond

the initial views of the constructivistic approach.

Agger (1991), a critical theorist, contended that applications of postmodernism and critical theory that we see today are resolved by commodifying popular culture. While it may be important to transform society's structures, this cannot be accomplished by simply remembering the collective experience of events. It must develop by identifying the meaning and identity of events—both their text and texture. Concentration on the events of popular experience creates the possibility that as events become more the norm, they will become idealized and become the norm of behavior. Our investigation in a sense stops and does not further critically examine those events except from superficial points of view. Postmodernism, replacing substance with style, can be seen in numerous instances; in quick-fix adjustments like empowerment, school choice, or school-based management. Everyone seems intent on gaining access to the bandwagon to define their own unique versions of needed change.

Guba and Lincoln (1985) outlined the parallel movement of inquiry paradigms as a result of ongoing change in organizations. Seven contrasting concepts provide the basis for an in-depth exploration of the impact of ongoing change in the way we construct knowledge. Understanding this parallelism can further substantively help to counteract some of the previously cited problem areas.

Simple to Complex. This change implies and is largely a result of an organization's inability to change and its tendency to continue to view the world simplistically. In previous eras our ability to identify, comprehend, and quantify the entirety of a problem was assumed. For example, it is unlikely that we would fully comprehend the impact of high dropout rates by only surveying those who left, or further by including a sequence of other variables in search of correspondence.

A more complex question demands a more complex approach to science, one that includes, in this case, a systemic panorama of the school, the family, the teaching environment, and more. Even more important, this situation demands an exploration of the relationships between other variables identified above. Most important may be the realization that there may be no objectivity in the above example. Identifying poor teaching as causal or any other single or multiple cause excludes relationships and conceals more appropriate findings.

In educational research, strong reminders of simplistic accommodation to problems exist everywhere. Rationality as demanded by the realists postures *is* still problematic. Even today we find university teaching institutions focused on older, possibly largely irrelevant research practices that have lived past their time. Complexity necessitates dramatic change. In the future, those who teach research methods must acknowledge that meaningful inquiry must account for "history and detail rather than permanence and generality" (Guba & Lincoln, 1985, p. 89). Huff explains that in order to " . . .understand the complex . . .aspects of the world, one must have complex sources of information" (Huff, 1985, p. 165).

Hierarchical to Heterarchical.

If we look at organizations today, we find many examples of unusual organizational structures. Clusters, networks, upside down pyramids, interlocking links, and more are representations of changes in organizational structure necessitated by other forces. Similarly, in educational circles, further revision of organizational structure has emerged in examples like school-based management, and more decision-making interaction between learner and teacher. Even schools without principals are not hard to find. Pluralism or multiplism is replacing "pecking order" organizations that have constrained knowledge

creation. In the new world view, any set of factors can become a controlling phenomenon, depending on the context.

In the traditional view, educational systems were organized top down, from the federal level all the way to the teacher. Hoy and Miskel (1987) described administrative theory as "a set of interrelated concepts, assumptions, and generalizations that systematically describe and explain regularities in behavior in educational organizations" (1987, p. 2). Literature is laden with organizational charts reflecting a top-down organization, full of sequential-linear-systematic curriculum development charts, and saturated with stepwise models of instructional practice. Inquiry in times past validated the hierarchical nature of school organizations and schooling.

The newer paradigm views educational organizations as heterarchical, oriented to pluralism and a heteracity of guiding principles (Guba & Lincoln, 1985). For example, the realization that language is descriptive, or that visual arts depict, opens new knowledge creating venues that cannot be subsumed as singular, as top down, or stepwise. Latitude must be available to researchers who insist on newer interactional research methods, latitude that allows a variety of approaches to reconstitute our understanding.

Mechanical to Holographic.

In chapters to come, school organization will be described as an "iron cage" or as machine-like. Metaphors connect mental images with reality. Schools are machine-like: classes are 45–50 minutes long, five or six classes per day is common, the school year is 180-plus days long, and it takes twelve years to complete schooling; unless, of course, your standardized tests reflect greater ability and you plan to apply to college, at which time you can then increase the number of years of schooling to sixteen. Even teachers are like robots. The agenda of inquiry in this environment is no different. Are there not enough studies of class length in journals already? Need we say more?

Holograms are dimensional images from reflected light, but more important they possess unique properties. Conceptualizing the school organization as a hologram is difficult and attempts to visualize a holographic school often result in chaos and confusion. In a hologram, every part contains enough information to reconstitute the whole. "The part is in the whole and the whole is in the part . . . parts have access to the whole" (Wilbur, 1985, p. 2). When light is shown on the holographic image, the image can be reconstituted from any portion or part. Consider the holographic school organization, an organization where compartmentalization is absent, where teachers share information broadly, or where students are colleagues. Learning is the issue in this school as the whole school is built to facilitate learning. In the holographic sense, as you walk into a school can you sense the learning going on, or did you sense those iron cages? Similarly, educational inquiry has just begun to consider the relevance of organizing features that inspire holistic knowledge creation.

Determinacy to Indeterminacy.   Is it possible to predict and control? Or is everything relative? These disparate views evolve from distinctly different organizational theory and inquiry paradigms and have far-reaching implications. If, as the traditionalists believe, there is one right way to organize and administer education, than hypothetico-deductive inquiry will result in a body of knowledge about that "right way." Weber thought that the bureaucratic system was "superior in precision, in stability, in the stringency of its discipline, and its reliability" (Parson, 1947, p. 337). Time studies and efficiency models also serve to validate a determinate approach to administration.

The emerging research paradigm, however, provides a critique of logical empiricism and assumes an indeterminate universe where

prediction is not possible. The goal of organizational inquiry would have to be to "realize an interpretive understanding of the meanings people give to their own situations and their interactions with others" (Smith & Blase, 1991, p. 11). Law-like generalizations are not possible because the social world is not determinate. Therefore, the best that an inquirer can hope for is to describe the complexity of organizations in the context of their history, people, and environment. Matters of human significance will render interpretive understanding possible (Smith & Blase, 1991).

Linear Causality to Mutual Causality.   Instances of singular cause and effect scenarios in real life, if we reflect, are hard to imagine. But traditional research establishes just such causality as foundational. Assuredly, if our purpose is to reduce the origin of events to finite causal variables we may find them, even find proper ones. But generalizing from these finite circumstances back then to issues more complex must be done with extreme care. If-then relationships are established in normative inquiry and represent a specific set of variables for the relationship to hold true. Stepping outside the confidence of the relationship leads to error.

Naturalistic inquiry, on the other hand, assumes mutual causality, nonlinear, and growth-oriented relationships between variables. As an inquiry methodology, case studies are built purposely as a historical-cultural sketch of, for example, a school or classroom environment. In this sense, the case study is a living example from which actions are connected to their total environment. Once actions are understood to occur within, an interpretive discourse can reconstitute the school or classroom environment, but from the view of the inquirer. A deeper understanding of the total environment can result.

Assembly to Morphogenesis.   In the inquiry paradigms, assembly implies construction from simple to complex. In the reductionist view, wholes are separated into smaller and smaller segments as a method to control/manipulate experimental parameters and arrive at truth. Experimental findings then generalized are attached to larger and larger wholes. An aggregate of findings must not, however, substitute for license to apply across greater and greater range. Poor mathematics scores in New York inner city schools may not be related to poor mathematics scores in Los Angeles or anywhere else. Generalizations can only transfer when we can confidently relate across those environments.

Morphogenesis is a mutual change that occurs across parts and the whole of a structure. It can be considered the combined use of objectivity and subjectivity, a balance of rigor and relevance, or other paradoxical features of inquiry. While a rigorous school-based experiment may serve to address a local issue, relevance of broader issues to the whole issue is then lacking. Proper balance of these two validity concerns creates a different whole. Thus, disparate measures combine to recreate a greater whole. Similarly, school organization was long thought to revolve around building the proper functions into the environment and operationalizing them— adding functions, operationalizing, adding-operating. In this sense the school was never able to truly adapt itself and create those new organizing relationships necessary as a result of growth or any other measure. Without this process-relationship orientation the large school becomes cumbersome, inflexible, procedural, and bureaucratic. If our previous decisionmaking and problem solving had related concern for form and function, perhaps flexibility mechanisms could have co-developed, or procedures could have adapted to encompass newer relationships. In this sense, schooling could become self-organizing and self-renewing.

Objective to Perspectival. As a corollary to the change discussed above, newer inquiry paradigms seek to expose multiple perspectives through inquiry and enable multiple findings. If we continually reduce the variety of issues that can impact a research effort, we also reduce the ability of the inquirer to pursue the most informed effort. Inquiry needs requisite variety to function effectively.

These axioms as Guba and Lincoln (1985) describe them develop a new view of knowledge creation in educational organizations— as an ongoing process. Traditional methodologies continue to have a strong impact on administrative inquiry (Smith & Blase, 1991). However, there has been a steadily growing body of research based on the interpretivistic perspective and the above "new" axioms as described by Schwartz and Olgivy (1979) and Guba and Lincoln (1985). We must be familiar with both the traditional and the newer views of organizational inquiry. As Gage (1989) pointed out, we may still be in the midst of a battle for paradigm supremacy or, alternately, cooperation. Educators in the future must heed these multiple approaches to educational administrative research.

Inquiry Processes and the Paradigm Debates

The process of inquiry is not merely philosophical debate, but, instead, is intended to answer specific questions and thereby result in specific knowledge. To illustrate the process of inquiry several examples are developed in an effort to observe inquiry processes in action.

Salomon (1991) analyzed several sets of studies in his thought-provoking argument for analytic and systemic inquiry. In his first study, a controlled experiment, he and his colleagues tested the hypothesis that interaction with an interactive computer tool, the *Writing Partner,* would improve writing ability. Students were required to test a variety of variables: internalization, expenditure of effort, quality of writing, and transfer after subsequent use of the writing tool. Essay writing pre- and post-tests were developed. Students were randomly assigned to two groups. The results supported their hypothesis. A new era of computer usage was born. In another separate test, in experiments using a similar design, reading skills were also enhanced. Finally, a third study in geography using a computer data base yielded similar results. Inspired by all the above results, a fourth test introduced the data base format to studying the United States Constitution. It became apparent that the limited scope of the experimental model would not suffice for a project of this magnitude. Instead, a new series of social science classroom activities would need to be developed: team events, a Constitutional Convention, and more. As the project progressed, new events demanded other on-the-spot changes. With this plethora of differing activities came the need for the use of different tools of measurement: interviews, self-reports, questionnaires, and other unobtrusive measures. Teachers' roles changed, too, as they hovered around students, directing them, guiding them, and suggesting and advising new avenues of exploration. Clearly normative inquiry parameters were not useful. This obviously suggests the utilization of differing inquiry paradigms. But, before we specifically explore these differences here, a few additional anecdotes are needed to fully grasp the nature of the inquiry process.

For decades the study of leadership has unfolded in two different research domains: the empirical and the hermeneutic (Smith & Blase, 1991). In the empirical tradition, the educational leader is seen as a decisionmaker, a controller, and a manager of resources. Instructional leaders accomplish similar tasks that revolve around instructional demands. These views of leadership as technical expertise are equated with effectiveness and seen

to be efficiency oriented. In these scenarios, leaders seek to rationally choose between competing options. The leader seeks to study properly organized organizations and learning processes in order to arrive at law-like generalizations, theory, and so forth. The laws, generalizable then, allow them to predict further alternate programs and policy. Others, however, contest this approach as they cite multiple instances where generalization is not possible. What is missing is the discovery of enduring causal connections between and among events and processes. In this new paradigm, there is no law-like, bottom-line world out there. Hence, the set of rational choices cannot be available to the educational leader.

In contrast, the hermeneutic view describes leadership in terms of the leader acting in various situations. In the previous representation, leadership emphasizes the calculation of means and ends, while a significance view seeks interpretive understanding of matters of human significance. Leadership then, is an openness to issues of human significance. Decisions about what and how to teach are not a matter of technical development but are grounded in reasoned discourse, sharing of personal experience, and taking into account the experience of others. Leadership is not a controlled phenomenon, an ordering, or orderliness, but tied to who we are and how we lead our lives. Leadership in the dialogic tradition seeks deeper understanding so that we can live our educational lives more fruitfully. What is to be done, and why we must do it, takes on added significance in this discourse. These two views, seemingly at odds with each other, have a dramatic effect on inquiry.

In one last narrative, a further audit of how inquiry processes unfold is explained. Stevenson (1993) addressed the problem of educating administrative and teaching professionals and develops for the reader the more typical approaches to administrator development. In the craft orientation (a metaphor), prospective professionals are treated like novices and participate in a kind of apprenticeship. In a traditional scientific approach, the developing professional is seen to be an agent outside the curriculum development process whose only responsibility is empirically tested knowledge assigned by an appropriately research-oriented teaching staff: Lastly, Stevenson outlined a reflective approach whereby budding professionals develop the ability to make informed, reflective, and self-critical judgements about their practice. Even more importantly these professionals are readily exposed to other systemic means of analysis as they interact with real life cultural and structural conditions in schools. It is in this last tradition that a preparation program becomes critically reflective. Preparation takes on an action orientation as professionals' critical reflection includes the "articulation and reasoned justification of educational intentions (to create more defensible reasons for action) and the examination of the relationship between those intentions and the consequence of one's actions" (Stevenson, 1993, p. 107). This newer convention demands that professional preparation programs, while properly maintaining a strong research tradition, must also begin to develop the means for new professionals to engage knowledge as part of their instructional program. Some would require total commitment to only this venue. Stevenson (1993) suggested that colleges and universities need to learn to do both collaboratively.

The previous anecdotes suggest the multitude of methods through which people address inquiry problems. As Stevenson (1993) implied, theory and practice are both of concern. Perhaps we can also shed some valuable light on the paradigm debate issues at the same time. Although the issues addressed in the anecdotes above were com-

plex ones, complexity had little to do with researchers' decisions on how to proceed. Salomon (1991) and his colleagues were not particularly interested in selecting a process of inquiry. Process selection seemingly results from their traditional mode of researching problems—as defined by a series of questions that the researcher sought to answer. While these researchers were presumably familiar with a multitude of research methodologies, they were most adept at scientific research.

In each case discussed above, however, researchers moved beyond the paradigm problems within scientific inquiry to consider the applicability of their research approach to a community. Debating philosophical points of view may be worthwhile, but at the practical level debate must end as researchers and stakeholders need to address questions of importance to a community in need of action outcomes. Our anecdotes demonstrate important constructs which if explored have immediate relevance to professionals and students alike. Debates aside, an outcome orientation subsumes from acceptance of a "logic in use" (Firestone, 1987) and its own necessary localness. And, as Goodman (1978) implied, the world in its multiplicity has as many ways to describe it. Salomon (1991) contended that this encourages a multiplicity of methods. We would add, a multiplicity of venues too.

Methodological practice often concerns itself with validity concerns. In specific cases this may range from extreme concern for validity to little concern. Even qualitative approaches need to portray some sense of validity, some adherence to validity, or as Guba and Lincoln (1989) labeled it, *authenticity*. In the use of the scientific method, validity was a "planned for" event. Discrete events lend themselves to traditional measures and the results seemed highly appropriate. But, in other cases, we begin to sense the real necessity for authenticity measures as systemic events and contexts must utilize a more ecological approach to believability. Correspondingly, how do we also assure trustworthiness or transferability of findings? While standards are a concern and necessary consideration, they are not as important as the generation of reflective and critical outcomes of value as judged by the community of users. Authenticity and trustworthiness and other measures are not created for a community of scholarly auditors, but are more valid criteria for qualitative research when applications of research derive satisfactory outcomes for stakeholders.

If we listen to many proponents of soft educational science, we might hear them implying that research should only be used to describe, appreciate, interpret, or explain socially constructed phenomenon. In other instances, positivists proclaim that universality is foundational. Cziko (1989) apparently takes both sides of the issue as he suggests an interpretive stance, followed by a desire to see research "lead to the implementation and dissemination of innovative educational practices" (p. 23). Proponents of no accommodation argue that both are not possible together, but a review of dissimilar research projects shows the semblance of both. There are attempts to arrive at an accommodation of differing paradigms within a larger framework of complementarity. In the larger sense, as inquiry occurs from a larger ecological viewpoint, it can only provide usefulness and applicability. In the discrete sense, combinations of variables can be shown to have broader usefulness and hence possibly generalizability.

Proceeding to more process-oriented concerns also helps us to further understand. While we've already critiqued validity concerns prevalent to basic and applied research, and the experimental versus natural distinctions, some other important considerations must be at work in our application of inquiry. Bertalanffy (1968) long ago argued that bio-

logical systems presumed a formidably different approach to discovery. The rational-reductionist heritage does have applicability, but, as Bertalanffy would assert today, not before we have investigated the dynamics of the whole. In the computer examples above, Salomon (1991) and his colleagues found as they extended their research model to a larger experimental project, their proclivity for seeking discrete variables in the material studied could not be sustained. In Stevenson's discussion of professional education requirements, developing formidable structure or investigating individual processes cannot alone support a critically reflective inquiry program. It is not that these studies pose problematic variables (statistical methods have aspired to overcome this), but that, as our earlier discussion of holography suggests, form and function studied in their separateness lose vital interactiveness, their essence in conjunction with the operation of the whole. Mechanical separation for the convenience of methodological concerns is only effective when we fully consider and understand the effects of form and function. Our inquiry may be more appropriately termed *systemic* in these ecological cases.

In considering the above further, we see the consequences of Bartlett's (1932, in Iran-Nejad et al., 1990) simplification by isolation versus simplification by integration (see also Bertalanffy, 1968). For example, in leadership studies, authors today are only beginning to realize the necessity for studying leadership from a systemic perspective in its multiple contexts and roles (Smith & Blase, 1991; see also Hunt, 1991; Rost, 1991; Senge, 1991). To help the researcher pursue systemic inquiry Salomon (1991) suggests a mapping process, Senge (1991) develops archetypes, and others develop similar mapping models. Working with these differing "maps," one soon realizes that, while inquiry can be contrived, it is also human-made, full of variety, and still applicable in its own localness.

As Salomon (1991) contended, four considerations are important when selecting a process of inquiry: the paradigmatic assumptions one adopts, the perceived nature of the phenomenon studied, the question analyzed, and the research methodology employed. Each differing selection, regardless of where one starts the process, yields separate kinds of knowledge. Epistemologically the system chosen justifies the "terms" of the whole process. In this light, differing inquiry systems are expected to yield different results with their own unique set of methodological requirements. As Lakatos (1978) also said, each separate inquiry system builds on the other. Theoretically based inquiry leads to empirical progress through testing of hypotheses, and theory evolves from a more systemic approach. Shulman (1985) suggests a sort of metasystem for teaching research, starting with the qualitative paradigm and progressing to controlled experimentation.

For researchers and those who study inquiry, it may be time to realize that no one paradigm can fulfill all the needs of sociological research. But to arrive at this conclusion by assuming various forms of inquiry are then fragmentary is ill-advised. Inquiry is not just hit or miss. This type of belief structure leads to the same limited view posited throughout the history of positivism.

What may be clear from the preceding discussion is the necessity for theorists to stop debating and begin a valid search for the form and function of inquiry. We have seen examples of many who would choose to remain strapped in their own expertise, and others who have begun to shake off their paradigm paralysis in hopes of riding the crest of those newest successful developing paradigms. Perhaps as philosophers we need to look to many of those practitioners who live in the real world and adapt to the future. "The systemic study of complex learning environments cannot be fruitful, and certainly cannot yield any generalizable [applicable] findings and conclusions in the absence of carefully controlled analytic studies of selected aspects in which internal validity is maximized" (Salomon, 1991, p. 16). As Salomon also contends, if we do not look to the real world more often, we may end up researching the least educational significant aspects of that reality.

■ CASE STUDY

Inquiry: How Do You Know?

In the fall of 1985, then-Secretary of Education William Bennett visited a high school near Washington, D. C. to teach a lesson on James Madison's Federalist Papers. While his original intent was to show a Secretary of Education coming into contact with the U.S. education system, Bennett also saw his visit as a demonstration of how substantive teaching can be valuable to America's youth. Eisner (1991) was one of four educational analysts asked to study Bennett's performance. He provides a unique look into the Secretary of Education through a narrative analysis of the proceedings. Eisner's analysis has been adapted for this study. After reading the adaptation, consider the exercise provided at the end of his study.

Adaptation of Eisner's "A Secretary in the Classroom"

Secretary Bennett prepares to deliver a lesson on the Federalist Papers to a class of high school students. The secretary, at one time a professor of philosophy, enters the classroom at the beginning of the new school year to teach a class of multiracial students. No secretary has ever taught like this in the past. How will he do? Can this man teach adolescents? How will teachers in the school react?

From the start, one gets a sense of Bennett's purpose and intensity. Adjusting the electronic equipment provided to nationally televise and record the event, Bennett opens by acknowledging sarcastically, "This is no typical day here," and then tells the class, "If you want to, turn around and say hi." "Hi mom!" he says, and the class of students do likewise. As an icebreaker, this works and helps to release the tension that has developed.

"All right, let's get to work. I'm putting my name on the board so you can write me if I make any mistakes."

Neither Bennett nor the students laugh. With the preliminaries over, Bennett hangs his coat on the chair next to the desk, and rolls up his sleeves, as he begins pacing back and forth in the front of the room. "Why read the Federalist 10—Why bother? Why not catch the Georgia-Alabama game?" He leaves no doubt that this is a serious encounter. "Let's get to work." Today's lesson will be no once-over-lightly, no open-ended superficial discussion of anything on anyone's mind, but a serious examination of ideas about which the secretary cares deeply.

The task the secretary has set for the students is to read and understand the Federalist Papers, specifically, paper number 10. The aim of the lesson is twofold. He wishes to convey to the students the idea that assumptions about government are built upon a conception of human nature, in particular, Madison's view of human nature and his beliefs about how government should be formed. Secondly, Bennett is interested in developing the students' analytic and critical thinking abilities. He has planned teaching tactics that are typically a teaching strategy employed in teaching the humanities. He is interested in sharing his ideas about the nature of a just government and the joy of helping the young slowly discover what he has already learned. Bennett is no stranger to the material as he has taught the Federalist Papers many times before. The book he uses, he tells the class, is "properly dog-eared." "What is a faction?" he asks, "and

why is it a problem in a society like ours? Why does liberty cause the problem of factions?" Liberty, faction, and self-interest were problems in Madison's time and still exist now.

"Liberty provides the opportunity to hold different opinions," one student responds. "If you get liberty and give it to people, people will have different views about liberty. There will be factions."

"How do we solve the problem of faction?" Bennett asks. "Remove liberty," he responds and then quickly follows with a question, "Why not remove liberty?"

This problem of faction has at least two solutions. The first is to remove liberty. But do that and our country as we know it disappears. That cure, to quote Madison, is worse than the disease. Secondly, give everybody the same opinion. But that is not probable either. How then does one keep a self-interested majority from exploiting the interest of a minority while maintaining liberty that all wish to have?

The pattern of repartee on these issues is predictable. Bennett asks an open-ended question, one that requires recollection of material read and an interpretive understanding of it. Students respond by asking for elaboration and clarification. After a period of bantering, Bennett expands upon the students' elaboration in a context that none of the students are able to comprehend.

Bennett's responses are usually about ten times longer than his students' responses. Bennett uses two pedagogical moves that are often acknowledged but seldom employed. He summarizes main points the class has discussed at various intervals and he teaches for explanation. His intensity is fierce, he paces, sometimes clenches his fists, his eyes dart from side to side. He is on camera, but one senses that this is more than just a show for the camera. Bennett seems to truly care about what he is teaching. The ideas he expresses are part of him, his earnestness takes the whole affair beyond the media event; he is intent on helping the students understand just how important this subject is.

"I get so frustrated when I hear people talk about special interest groups as though they were a new thing. Madison had to deal with them in his own time. Pick up your newspaper—you read the newspaper every day don't you?" he jibes the class, implying that they should be reading it. "Pick up any newspaper and you'll find special interests groups pleading their case." He demonstrates his point with a newspaper he brought to class for that purpose. He illustrates his point about the self-interested nature of human beings by describing a situation in which a crowd of 150 people are trying to buy 25 tickets to a Bruce Springsteen concert. He illustrates complex and abstract notions from the Federalist Papers with an example from today that these youths can understand.

Not only does Bennett try to link the past to the present, but he also relates the problem of self-interest and violence to his own college days. He brings credibility to himself and at the same time shows his own humanness. Bennett also uses the makeup of the class to his advantage, as he fine tunes examples to particular students. "Was the Union saved?" he asks. He talks about Lincoln's desire to save the Union and the tension between two goods, the liberty of the slaves and the maintenance of the Union. At least five times during his lesson such connections are made. "Madison was intent on observing that the latent causes of faction are sown in the nature of man." Human nature, therefore, breeds potential conflict and violence. Government is a means through which self-interest can be reconciled to the public good. Bennett addresses government and the virtues of our view of people and government. Bennett has a mission and a message and shares them both readily with the students. He relishes the fight, cultivates questions, probes, and challenges the students continuously. Questions are asked intensely and each makes a point,

designed to lead the students through the main ideas and to a deeper understanding of the material.

■ ■ ■

Questions

1. What is your inquiry paradigm?

2. Based on your paradigm, how would you analyze the teaching environment described above?

3. What are the major tenets of your inquiry paradigm that would help us to teach more effectively?

4. As a result of the research you would accomplish under your inquiry paradigm, what are some further generalizations we could make?

5. Could you make any generalizations after viewing the original tapes of this event? What is your hypothesis?

Annotated Bibliography

Connelly, M., & Clandinin, J. (1990, June–July). Stories of experience and narrative inquiry. *Educational Researcher, 19*(5), 2–14.

Connelly and Clandinin provide an overview of narrative inquiry and propose possibilities for narrative inquiry in education. Narrative inquiry is the study of ways in which people construct and reconstruct personal and social stories. In education the story tellers are the researchers, teachers, and students. The goal of narrative inquiry is to describe the depth and breadth of the human experience through a description of life narratives. Methods in narrative inquiry can include field notes, biographical writing, and other qualitative methods. The authors believe that the bene-

fit of such research is the enhancement of the researcher/practitioner relationship to produce useful information based on mutual experiences.

Cziko, G. A. Unpredictability and indeterminism in human behavior: Arguments and implications for educational research. *Educational Researcher, 18*(3), 17–25.

Cziko presents arguments for discontinuing the use of quantitative research methods in education. He discusses the view that human behavior is unpredictable and, therefore, positivistic research that searches for prediction and control is not possible. He argues that human behavior is unpredictable based on (1) individual differences and the complexity of human beings, (2) chaos theory or anti-Newtonian physics, (3) the evolutionary nature of learning and development, (4) the existence of free will and consciousness and (5) the developments in quantum mechanics which demonstrate that "identical physical situations give rise to different outcomes." For these reasons, Cziko calls for research in education that is primarily a descriptive process that will not predict student outcomes or prescribe teaching practices. The primary goal of educational research is the reporting of educational findings to other researchers, educators, administrators and policymakers.

Evers, C., & Lakomski, G. (1991). *Knowing educational administration.* Oxford: Pergamon Press.

Evers and Lakomski's book is an overview of the development of organizational theory as it has followed three paradigm shifts. The authors trace organizational theory through three major paradigmatic developments: logical empiricism (positivism), the paradigms approach (constructivism), and, finally, the coherence epistemology (a combination of paradigms). The authors describe a fourth development in their own proposal for a "coherentist epistemology." This view provides criteria applicable to both paradigms and functions as a "touchstone" for developing theory. The "touchstone" approach permits the use of either paradigm or both, depending on the nature of the inquiry. The authors believe that by focusing on coherence criteria rather than foundational pluralism the growth of knowledge in educational administration will be facilitated.

Gage, N. L. (1989). The paradigm wars and their aftermath: A "historical" sketch of research on teaching since 1989. *Educational Researcher, 18*(7), 4–10.

Educators' dissatisfaction with the search for a scientific basis for the art of teaching led to the search for a new way to validate effective teaching. This search resulted in the paradigm wars of the eighties. Gage describes the paradigm wars as having occurred between the positivists, the anti-naturalists, the interpretivists and critical theorists. He projects the results of the battle and a view of education from each perspective. The three versions of history that Gage proposes are that, first, positivism dies along with all quantitative research, second, the three approaches "live peacefully together" and engage in productive discussion, and third, the wars continue. Gage places a moral obligation on educators to put aside paradigm wars and engage in "productive rapprochement between the paradigms" toward a better future for education.

Howe, K., & Eisenhart, M. (1990, May). Standards for qualitative (and quantitative) research: A prolegomenon. *Educational Researcher, 19*(14).

Howe and Eisenhart propose a nonpositivistic view of inquiry that delineates standards that are applicable to all educational research. The authors view education as a field of study that draws on many disciplines and inquiry perspectives. In order to be useful, educational inquiry must bring the other disciplines to bear on an educational question; therefore, more inclusive standards are necessary. The authors propose five broad standards: (1) there must be a fit between research questions and data collection and analysis techniques, (2) data collection and analysis techniques must be competently applied, (3) studies must be judged against a background of existent knowledge, (4) studies must exhibit overall warrant, and (5) studies must meet external and internal value constraints. The standards, as stated, are applicable to both qualitative and quantitative inquiry. Since all scientific investigation is theory laden, these standards will provide some method of deciding the worth of a study.

Kaplan, A. (1964). *The conduct of inquiry—methodology for the behavioral sciences.* San Francisco, CA: Chandler Publishing Co.

Kaplan's text is a foundational work on post-positivistic inquiry in the behavioral sciences. He states that the behavioral sciences are the same as other sciences except in subject matter. According to Kaplan, the behavioral scientist searches for "constancies, invarients . . . for the control or appreciation of a future event." He views the outcome of successful inquiry as either a fact or a law that can be generalized to other situations with relative certainty (positivism). However, Kaplan stresses the value inherent in the investigation, as well as the context of action and meaning in the study of human behavior, a departure from a purely positivistic perspective. His text, then, demonstrates in detail the application of the hypothetical-deductive model to the behavioral sciences which are value laden and explore acts and actions of human beings.

References

Agger, B. (1991). *A critical theory of public life: Knowledge, discourse, and politics in an age of decline*. New York: Falmer Press.

Argyris, C. (1985). *Action science*. San Francisco: Jossey-Bass.

Aron, R. (1967). *Main currents in sociological thought* (R. Howard & H. Weaver, trans.). New York: Penguin.

Babbie, E. (1989). *The practice of social research* (5th ed.). Belmont, CA: Wadsworth Publications.

Barrow, R. (1984). *Giving teaching back to teachers: A critical introduction to curriculum theory*. Totowa, NJ: Barnes and Noble.

Bartlett, F. C. (1932). *Remembering: A study in experimental and social psychology*. Cambridge, England: Cambridge University Press.

Bebe, E. (1989). *The practice of social research*. Belmont, CA: Wadsworth Publications.

Benton, T. (1977). *Philosophical foundations of the three sociologies*. London: Routledge & Kegan Paul.

Bertalanffy, L. von. (1968). *General systems theory: Foundations, development, applications*. New York: Braziller.

Borg, W. R., & Gall, M. D. (1989). *Educational research: An introduction* (5th ed.). New York: Longman.

Culler, J. (1982). *On deconstruction: Theory and criticism after structuralism*. Ithaca, NY: Cornell University Press.

Cziko, G. (1989). Unpredictability and indeterminism in human behavior: Arguments and implications for educational research. *Educational Researcher, 18*(3), 17–25.

Dewey, J. (1938). *Logic: The theory of inquiry*. New York: Holt, Rinehart & Winston.

Derrida, J. (1981). *On grammatology*. Baltimore, MD: Johns Hopkins University.

Eisner, E. W. (1981, April). On the differences between scientific and artistic approaches to qualitative research. *Educational Researcher,* 5–9.

Eisner, E. W. (1991). *The enlightened eye: Qualitative inquiry and the enhancement of educational practice*. New York: Macmillan.

Erickson, F. (1985). Qualitative methods in research on teaching. In M. C. Wittrock (Ed.), *Handbook of research on teaching* (3rd ed.) (119–161). New York: Macmillan.

Evers, C. W., & Lakomski, G. (1991). *Knowing educational administration: Contemporary methodological controversies in educational administration research*. Oxford: Pergamon.

Firestone, W. A. (1987). Meaning and method: The rhetoric of quantitative and qualitative research. *Educational Researcher, 16*(7), 16–21.

Firestone, W. A. (1990). Accommodation: Toward a paradigm-praxis dialectic. In E. Guba (Ed.), *The paradigm dialog*. (105–124). Newbury Park, CA: Sage.

Foucault, M. (1976). *The archaeology of knowledge*. New York: Harper and Row.

Foucault, M. (1980). *Power/knowledge*. New York: Pantheon.

Gage, N. L. (1989, October). The paradigm wars and their aftermath: A historical sketch of the research on teaching since 1989. *Educational Researcher, 18*(7), 4–10.

Giorgi, A. (1970). *Psychology as a human science: A phenomenologically based approach*. New York: Harper and Row.

Goodman, N. (1978). *Ways of worldmaking*. Indianapolis: Hackett.

Guba, E. G. (1978). *Toward a methodology of naturalistic inquiry in educational evaluation*.

Los Angeles: University of California, Center for Studies of Evaluation.

Guba, E. G., (1990). *The paradigm dialog*. Newbury Park, CA: Sage.

Guba, E. G., & Lincoln, Y. S. (1981). *Effective evaluation*. San Francisco: Jossey-Bass.

Guba, E. G., & Lincoln, Y. S. (1982). Epistemological and methodological bases of naturalistic inquiry. *Educational Communication Journal, 30*, 233–252.

Guba, E. G., & Lincoln, Y. S. (1985). *Types of inquiry*. Unpublished paper, Indiana University, Bloomington.

Guba, E. G., & Lincoln, Y. S. (1989). *Fourth generation evaluation*. Newbury Park, CA: Sage.

Habermas, J. (1970). Technology and science as ideology. In J. Habermas, *Toward a rational society*. Boston: Beacon Press.

Habermas, J. (1987). *The philosophical discourse of modernity*. Cambridge, MA: MIT Press.

Hempel, C. (1966). *Philosophy of natural science*. Englewood Cliffs, NJ: Prentice-Hall.

Horkheimer, M., & Adorno, T. W. (1972). *Dialectic of enlightenment*. New York: Herder & Herder.

Howe, K., & Eisenhart, M. (1990). Standards for qualitative (and quantitative) research: A prolegomenon. *Educational Researcher, 16*(1), 5–13.

Hoy, W., & Miskel, C. (1987). *Educational administration: Theory, research, and practice*. New York: Random House.

Huff, A. S. (1985). Managerial implications of the emerging paradigm. In Y. S. Lincoln (Ed.), *Organizational theory and inquiry: The paradigm revolution* (pp. 161–184). Newbury Park, CA: Sage.

Hunt, J. G. (1991). *Leadership: A new synthesis*. Newbury Park, CA: Sage.

Iran-Nejad, A., McKeachie, W., & Berliner, D. (1990). The multisource nature of learning. *Review of Educational Research, 60*, 509–515.

Jay, M. (1973). *The dialectical imagination*. Boston: Little, Brown.

Kuhn, T. S. (1970). *The structure of scientific revolutions* (2nd ed., enlarged). Chicago: University of Chicago Press.

Lakatos, I. (1978). *The methodology of scientific research programs*. Cambridge, MA: Cambridge University Press.

Levine, H. G. (1985). Scientists and culture heroes in the classroom. *Reviews in Anthropology, 12*, 338–345.

Levine, H. G. (1992). Types of naturalistic inquiry. *Encyclopedia of educational research* (6th ed.), *2*, 889–892.

Lincoln, Y. S. (Ed.). (1985). *Organizational theory and inquiry: The paradigm revolution*. Newbury Park, CA: Sage.

Lincoln, Y. S. (1990). The making of a constructivist: A remembrance of transformation past. In E. Guba (Ed.), *The paradigm dialog* (pp. 67–87). Newbury Park, CA: Sage.

Lincoln, Y. S. & Guba, E. G. (1986). But is it rigorous? Trustworthiness and authenticity in naturalistic evaluation. In D. Williams (Ed.), *Naturalistic evaluation (New directions for program evaluation)* (Vol. 30)(73–84). San Francisco: Jossey-Bass.

Littlejohn, S. W. (1992). *Theories of human communication* (4th ed.). Belmont, CA: Wadsworth Publications.

Miles, J. K., & Huberman, A. M. (1984). *Qualitative data analysis: A sourcebook of new methods*. Beverly Hills, CA: Sage.

Outhwaite, W. (1983). *Concept formation in social science*. London: Routledge & Kegan Paul.

Parson, T. (Ed.). (1947). *Max Weber: The theory of social and economic organization* (A. Henderson & T. Parsons, trans.). New York: The Free Press.

Phillips, D. C. (1990). Postpositivistic science: Myths and realities. In E. Guba (Ed.), *The paradigm dialog* (pp. 31–45). Newbury Park, CA: Sage.

Popkewitz, T. S. (1990). Whose future? Whose past? Notes on critical theory and methodology. In E. Guba (Ed.), *The paradigm dialog* (pp. 46–66). Newbury Park, CA: Sage.

Polkinghorne, D. (1983). *Methodology for the human sciences: Systems of inquiry*. Albany, NY: State University of New York Press.

Rossi, P. H. (1982). Standards for evaluation practice. *(New directions for program evaluation)*, (Vol. 15). San Francisco: Jossey-Bass.

Rost, J. (1991). *Leadership for the twenty-first century*. New York: Praeger.

Salomon, G. (1991, August–September). Transcending the qualitative-quantitative debate:

The analytic and systemic approaches to educational research. *Educational Researcher, 20*(6), 10–18.

Schwartz, P., & Olgivy, J. (1979). *Emergent paradigm: Changing patterns of thought and beliefs* (Analytical Report: Values and Lifestyles Program). Menlo Park, CA: SRI International.

Senge, P. (1991). *The fifth discipline: The art and practice of the learning organization.* New York: Doubleday.

Simey, T. (1969). *Social science and social purpose* (E. Shils & H. Finch, Eds. and trans.). Glencoe, IL: Free Press.

Shulman, L. (1986). Paradigms and research programs in the study of teaching: A contemporary perspective. In M. C. Wittrock (Ed.), *Handbook of research on teaching* (3rd Ed.) (pp. 3–36). New York: Macmillan.

Smith, J., & Hesusius, L. (1986, January). Closing down the conversation: The end of the qualitative-quantitative debate among educational inquirers. *Educational Researcher,* 5–10.

Smith, J. K., & Blase, J. (1991). From empiricism to hermeneutics: Educational leadership as a practical and moral activity. *Journal of Educational Administration, 29*(1), 6–21.

Skrtic, T. M. (1990). Social accommodation: Toward a dialogical discourse in educational inquiry. In E. Guba (Ed.), *The paradigm dialog* (pp. 125–135). Newbury Park, CA: Sage.

Soltis, J. (1984, December). On the nature of educational research. *Educational Researcher,* 55–10.

Stevenson, R. B. (1993, March). Critically reflective inquiry and administrator preparation: Problems and possibilities. *Educational Policy, 7*(1), 96–113.

Tom, A. (1984). *Teaching as a moral craft.* New York: Longman.

Wilbur, K. (1985). *The holographic paradigm and other paradoxes.* Boulder, CO: Shambala Press.

Chapter 6
Observation and Reflection

We are continually observing the world around us. We see; yet we don't see all, and we don't necessarily understand what we do see. At the same time and at the same place, different people see different things and attribute different meanings to the same event. Individuals react differently to similar incidents occurring at different times in their lives, depending upon changes in mood, interest (focus), and intervening experiences. In other words, we tend to see (and hear) with varying degrees of completeness and often alter our interpretation of those things we do see and hear from time to time. A great deal of our success as educational leaders depends upon the power and clarity of our observational skills—our ability to *see and hear* what is going on in the classroom, the school, and the community, and our competence in accurately comprehending what we have observed. Our skills in hearing and seeing are ones whose accuracy and comprehensiveness can be improved through training and reflection.

In their book *In Search of Excellence,* Peters and Waterman (1982) used the term *management by wandering around* to describe the type of administrative behavior they recommended—getting out of the office at least 50 percent of the time to confer (systematically and unsystematically) with employees at all levels, observing what is going on, and receiving information directly rather than relying solely on information filtered through a chain of command. Expanding on that theme, Peters (1988) wrote, "If talking and giving orders was the administrative model of the last fifty years, listening (to lots of people near the action), is the model of the 1980s and beyond" (p. 434).

Schön (1983), in studying the way professionals think, coined the term, *reflective practitioner.* A reflective practitioner is a keen observer of events. He or she carries on "conversations" with situations, observing, comparing notes from previous experiences, taking experimental action, observing the results, and continuing until the situation takes on the desired shape.

In this chapter, we discuss the need for keen observational skills on the part of educational leaders. Skills required in effective observation are described and methods for honing those skills are presented. The chapter closes with a discussion linking observation and reflective practice.

Observation as a Function of Administration

It may seem ironic that, with the availability of sophisticated, electronic information systems, we stress the importance for every administrator to maintain a substantial degree of independence from these formal systems by continuing close personal contact with other members of the organization. The typical information system contains primarily quantitative data—measures of inputs and outputs. When the school administrator gets out of the office and relates to students, teachers, support staff, parents, and other members of the community, access is gained to qualitative information that may have importance for improving school processes and calling attention to misdirected or neglected goals.

Each of us carries around a crippling disadvantage—we know, and probably cherish, what we are attempting to do and the procedures we have developed for doing it. As a result, we, and those closest to us in the organization—including the information systems we have designed—develop effective filters for accepting only information that supports our biases. If we are open to the kind of random, multisources of information we obtain through wandering, we can significantly reduce such blindness.

It is also important for leaders to create environments where listening is valued by all members of the organization and where opportunities and expectations for observing and listening are built into the system. All managers need to listen to the people under their supervision; teammates need to listen to each other; everyone needs to listen to the school's clients, i.e., students, parents, and the community. Members of the school organization also need to pay attention to those in support functions and in other schools, eliminating time-honored barriers that cut us off from valuable insights gained from criticism and comparison. At a time when empowerment of everyone is paramount, listening is the single best tool for empowering large numbers of others (Peters, 1988).

Peters (1988) stressed the importance of motivating everyone in the organization to keep in touch with its clients through unfiltered involvement. In the case of schools, that means students, parents, and community. Noting that 90 percent of the information systematically collected by an organization is internal in emphasis, he calls for turning organizations inside out, making them fully aware of the exploding world of the client. "Too few people, at too few levels, in too few functions, listen too little and too late—and ignore what they hear too often, and act too late" (p. 156). Peters' suggestions for turning the organization inside out are geared to the private sector, but many apply also to public schools such as home visits by teachers and administrators, publishing home and school telephone numbers of teachers and administrators, and making schools easily accessible to parents and members of the community.

Members of the school community have pluralistic sets of values that may from time to time cause conflict. In order to manage, the educational leader needs to understand what those sets of values are and at which points they are likely to come into conflict. (See the discussion of values conflict in Chapter 4.) Differences should be viewed as legitimate, and the leader should seek descriptions and explanations of the multiple realities, truths, and perceptions held by members of the organization, individually and in groups (LeCompte & Preissle, 1993). To accomplish this, the leader needs to observe the varied value systems within the context in which they are expressed. "Those multiple realities are contained in the unique, the singular, the idiosyncratic, the deviant, the exceptional, the unusual, the divergent perceptions of individuals, as they live or lived the experience" (Guba & Lincoln, 1981, p. 157). Such values are not found in information systems, but only experienced through direct observation.

Thus, a manager's task is to make certain that conflicts are neither suppressed nor circumvented; rather, they need to be "worked out." Working out conflicts is an iterative process that involves developing an understanding of the multiple cultures creating and confronting the organization, seeking common ground among those cultures, generating trial proposals, analyzing the reactions, generating new proposals, etc., until the conflicts are resolved (Schön, 1983). It is a type of circular decisionmaking discussed in Chapter 15.

Direct experience seems to be the most widely used test of reality. The vernacular is rich with sayings testifying to the importance that we as a society place on direct experience. For example, "Seeing is believing," or, "Experience is the best teacher." Management by wandering enhances the administrator's ability to understand complex situations through directly observing behavior and events as they occur, building on both formal and tacit knowledge.

The basic methodological arguments for observation, then, may be summarized as these: observation (particularly participant observation) maximizes the inquirer's ability to grasp motives, beliefs, concerns, interests, unconscious behaviors, customs, and the like; observation (particularly participant observation) allows the inquirer to see the world as his subjects see it, to live in their time frames, to capture the phenomenon in and on its own terms, and to grasp the culture in its own natural, ongoing environment; observation (particularly participant observation) provides

the inquirer with access to the emotional reactions of the group introspectively—that is, in a real sense it permits the observer to use himself as a data source; and observation (particularly participant observation) allows the observer to build on tacit knowledge, both his own and that of members of the group. (Guba & Lincoln, 1981, p. 193)

Observation Techniques

In the above quotation, Guba and Lincoln are describing the value gained from participant observation in the formal ethnographic sense; yet there are strong parallels between the participant observer and the effective wandering administrator. The wandering administrator can greatly improve his or her observations and the ensuing analyses through embracing ethnographic techniques. Using the terminology of the ethnographist, the administrator is an "instrument of evaluation." At one and the same time, he or she is instrument, administrator, data collector, data analyst, and data interpreter. In situations where motives, attitudes, beliefs, and values direct much if not most of human activity, the most sophisticated instrumentation we possess is still the careful observer—the human being who can watch, see, listen, question, probe, and finally analyze and organize his or her direct experience (Guba & Lincoln, 1981).

As an instrument, the administrator is responsive to an environment and to the persons who occupy and create that environment. The administrator responds to clues—foreseen and unforeseen—but also provides clues to others in the forms of questions, comments, and bodily expressions, and is alert to the responses of those being observed to the clues given. One of the great advantages of humans as instruments (rather than a paper and pencil survey, for example) is that they are highly adaptable as data-gathering devices, being able to assess any number of things at once such as artistic orientation and intellectual interests. Further, they can adapt their data collecting approach as circumstances and contexts warrant.

Humans (administrators) as data collecting instruments are holistic in their approach rather than segmented and can develop a contextual sense of the situation including mood, climate, tone, pace, texture, and feelings. Thousands of bits of data are captured, filtered, and instantaneously put through a mental process that sorts the data and places them into patterns that make a complex, but meaningful, whole. In the process, the observer draws upon both tacit and formal knowledge. Immediately upon acquisition, hypotheses are generated and tested on the spot and, if necessary, the direction of the inquiry is changed. The ability to extend and amplify meanings that might have been lost through other forms of inquiry is unique to the human observer (Guba & Lincoln, 1983). The sensitive administrator can tell immediately if previous statements were unclear and in need of clarification. His or her understandings may be summarized orally and tested against the perceptions of those conversed with or observed. This provides a valuable reliability check and allows for those being queried to point out key items that may have been missed or misunderstood.

> *The human instrument can duplicate virtually any other instrument people have devised, perhaps with a little less reliability or discriminatory power, but probably well enough for most purposes—and for many simultaneous purposes at that! . . . Moreover, the advantage of beginning with a fund not only of propositional knowledge but also of tacit knowledge and the ability to be infinitely adaptable make the human investigator ideal in situations in which the design is emergent; the human can sense out salient factors, think of ways to follow up on them, and make continuous changes, all while actively engaged in*

> *the inquiry itself. (Lincoln & Guba, 1985, p. 107)*

Without direct input from members of a group, it is virtually impossible to gain a complete understanding of the norms, expectations, attitudes and latent values and assumptions of that group. Informants can alert the administrator to potential social blunders that would alienate the group and describe events and situations to which the administrator is not privy. Informants can interpret events and behaviors that may have significance within a subculture unknown to the administrator. Such are not contained within information systems.

TACTICS OF AN EFFECTIVE OBSERVER

In wandering as a participant observer, the administrator plays two roles. First, he or she must attend to responsibilities outside the situation being observed. In addition, the administrator has a relationship with the person or group interacted with and has a stake in their activities and their outcomes.

Interactive modes can vary from semihostile, adversarial exchanges to emotionally neutral but cognitively intricate dialog; but most observers prefer to conduct interviews in the conversational style of everyday interaction (LeCompte & Preissle, 1993). The conversational style permits interviewers to respond neutrally without risking the loss of support. At the same time, it is most likely to elicit the trust necessary for producing valid information.

The conversation is the oldest and most respected way of exchanging information and collecting data. The effective manager who wanders should become highly skilled as a conversationalist/interviewer. A critical characteristic needed to carry out this function successfully is empathy (Guba & Lincoln, 1981). The administrator must find others intrinsically interesting and carefully attend to their social and behavioral signals. The effective conversationalist/interviewer also needs a clear sense of self and an inclination to talk and listen to as many different people as possible, including those disliked and mistrusted (and who dislike and mistrust him or her). In trying to understand those things that are unpleasant and, perhaps, personally uncomplimentary, it is not sufficient to talk only with the charming and the powerful. The humane administrator who maintains positive relationships with co-workers throughout the school organization is able to maintain open communications naturally, and through those communications be well informed about what is happening within the organization.

Attitude is vital in wandering; if you don't believe that there is much worth listening to out there, you won't hear much! The administrator needs to be at ease, but not overly casual, friendly but not too familiar, and chatty, curious, and investigative but not nosy or pushy. He or she should show sincere interest in and respect for the feelings and opinions of co-workers, empathizing without becoming involved. He or she should show curiosity and pleasure in listening without diverting attention to himself or herself or injecting his or her own feelings and opinions. The administrator should stay neutral and uninvolved in feelings, being self-confident but not opinionated, rigid, or moralistic. He or she should be self-aware, trying to see himself or herself as others do in the situation. The administrator should be able to take rebuffs without exploding into anger, and tolerate changing moods and divergent opinions while keeping reactions private (Tymitz & Wolf, 1977, pp. 39–40).

A reflective stance is best, where two reflecting persons try to figure out how things happen and what to do about it. The most important strategy is listening in such a fashion that the interviewer is able to immerse himself or herself in the respondent's frame of reference. "The ability to 'hear' accurately and clearly what another is saying, without overlays of values, attitudes, preconceptions, stereotypes, beliefs or prejudices is perhaps the hardest 'skill' for the inquirer to come by" (Guba & Lincoln, 1976, p. 176). Open-ended, naive questions that raise an issue but do not suggest any structure for the reply are best for eliciting responses; the respondent is, thereby, given the opportunity to answer in his or her own terms and from his or her own frame of reference.

The administrator generally operates in a discovery mode (rather than a verification mode), looking for nonstandard and/or unique information, the exception, the unusual interpretation. It is best if the conversation is free flowing. In these conversations, no matter the status of the partner, the administrator must assume that the partner has more expertise about the subject than the administrator does. The administrator becomes the eager learner.

> *Mostly, its the "dumb," elementary questions, followed by a dozen even more elementary questions, that yield the pay dirt. . . ."Experts" are those who don't need to bother with elementary questions anymore—thus, they fail to "bother" with the true sources of bottlenecks, buried deep in the habitual routines of the firm, labeled "we've always done it that way." (Peters, 1988, p. 438)*

Whenever a term or concept isn't clear, the astute administrator asks for clarification and is not afraid to display ignorance.

In wandering, and in conversing with people, the administrator should be as aware of nonverbal as well as verbal communication. Nonverbal communication is the exchange of information through nonlinguistic signs (Guba & Lincoln, 1981). Included are body movements, gestures, facial expressions, spacial relationships with respect to other persons and things, rhythmical relationship between sender and receiver, use of time (pacing, probing, pausing), voice characteristics (volume, quality, accent, inflections, etc.), touching, and implicit verbal indicators such as Freudian speech errors. Analysis of nonverbal communication should be used in tandem with some other technique; therefore, the first step in analyzing the significance of nonverbal cues is to test for dissonance between what the verbal language says and what the nonverbal language suggests.

Debriefing interviews can be another useful source of information for the administrator. Employees who are leaving the organization because of retirement or to take another job, know the organization well. Because they are severing their relationships with the organization and they no longer have vested interests in it, their opinions may be expressed frankly and with deep insight. Similarly, interviews with guests may also provide useful information, particular those guests who have spent some time in the school such as accrediting teams, consultants, etc.

ASSURING QUALITY OF DATA

The administrator does not establish the reliability and validity of data picked up while "wandering" in a formal sense; nevertheless, quality control of data should be a primary concern. A number of methods used in naturalistic inquiry are appropriate here. Guba and Lincoln (1981) suggest four: host verification, triangulation and corroboration, independent observer analysis, and phenomenon recognition.

Host verification involves checking selected facts drawn from the observations of the administrator against the experiences and understandings of the person with whom the conversation/interview was held or of members of the group observed. Independent observer analysis involves asking another dependable person or other persons to check the situation out and then compare observa-

tions. Phenomenon recognition involves checking the administrator's "structured reality" with those who live it and asking them to assess its accuracy as a portrayal of their common and shared experiences.

Triangulation and corroboration is the process of comparing and contrasting information drawn from different sources and/or determined by different methodologies. It requires testing the accuracy of observations with other knowledgeable persons—possibly in, or close to, the group—and seeking other readings of the situation through documents or data included in the management information system. "If a proposition can survive the onslaught of a series of imperfect measures, with all their relevant error, confidence should be placed in it" (Webb et al., 1966). Equally important, triangulation permits identification of multiple value perspectives in the same situation and allows for their presentation and explanation alongside one another. In other words, the facts may be verified, but the interpretations as to the significance of those facts may vary. The latter is as important as the former for the administrator to know.

Techniques used in investigative journalism can be useful to administrators in gathering information from reluctant informants; these include circling, shuffling, and filling (Smith, 1988). Circling is a process whereby data or information obtained from one source are referred to the administrator's circle of contacts for refutation or confirmation. Circling is appropriate when cooperative contacts are available.

Shuffling deals with situations where contacts may be non-cooperative or even hostile. In this procedure, stories from one source will be checked against the stories of others— probably in an iterative fashion, i.e., going back and forth among contacts as new information comes out, confronting inconsistencies in reporting, and trying to narrow the gap in perceptions. Shuffling not only verifies or disputes information, but is also a useful process for acquiring additional information (Williams, 1978).

Filling is also a useful technique for the wandering administrator when there is a specific concern that needs to be defined and its boundaries established. As information is gathered, gaps are noted and efforts are made to fill those gaps.

Discoveries made through wandering frequently need to be followed up on by consulting documents and records. Documents and records are invaluable resources for tracing transactions that may shed light on cases and situations under scrutiny. Documents have certain virtues that complement the virtues of direct observation. Documents and records tend to persist over time. While documents constitute a legally, unassailable base of authority, both are natural sources of information, readily available at little or no cost. They can be accessed unobtrusively and both are nonreactive. Documents and records provide supplementary and contextual data that may be useful in the "shuffling and circling" process. Records are used primarily for tracking events; documents are useful for making inferences about the values, sentiments, intentions, beliefs, or ideologies of the sources or authors of the documents (Guba & Lincoln, 1983; Smith, 1988).

MAXIMIZING THE VALUE OF OBSERVATION[1]

The wandering administrator should not attempt to keep all observations in memory alone. Details are quickly forgotten and one event becomes blurred and confused with another. To protect against this, records

should be discretely maintained. A variety of ways are available for going about this, but not all are appropriate for all situations.

Field notes are always appropriate. When and where notes are taken depend upon circumstances. Sometimes notes can be written on the spot. At other times, the conversation will have to be reconstructed later, but any record is better than no record at all (LeCompte & Preissle, 1993).

The administrator may not wish to take notes as conversations progress, although this is a way to show respect for the information giver and interest in the subject being discussed. When it is not appropriate to take notes during a conversation, they can be made as soon after as possible. Perhaps even better, if the administrator carries a portable recording device, observations can be quickly dictated to be transcribed, recorded in the journal, and analyzed later. No conversation should be recorded without the explicit consent of those participating in the conversation. Even with consent, it should be recognized that the presence of a recording device may inhibit the free flow of information. The usefulness of field notes is enhanced when they include information on the time and place of the incident, who was present, and under what circumstances the information was obtained. Such contextual information aids in the subsequent analysis (Fetterman, 1988).

Field notes address critical incidents that produce a positive or negative feeling and/or a positive, negative, or neutral perception. They may include events which take place in the administrator's office, e.g., a conversation over the telephone or with a drop-in visitor, as well as events encountered while wandering. For the most part, field notes record interactions between the administrator and other people in the organization and the administrator's subjective reactions to those interactions. They may also include verbal

---

[1]This section is adapted from J. Chimera. (1974). Appendix: The art of journal keeping. In *Developing observational skills*. Buffalo, NY: Department of Educational Administration, State University of New York at Buffalo.

quotes, notes about the physical environment, hypotheses about future events, critical and evaluative comments about others, attempts at theory building, and reality testing, etc.

A suggested recording format is displayed in Figure 6.1. Note that it contains only two columns; the first is for the recording of "facts" about a critical incident and the second is for reporting subjective reactions or evaluations of the critical incident. LeCompte and Preissle (1993) recommend making such distinctions in the recording process. The first column contains low-inference descriptors including verbatim accounts of what people say as well as descriptions of behavior and activity. They should be phrased as concretely and precisely as possible. High-inference interactive comments are recorded in the second column. These represent the recorder's

interpretation of what is perceived to be happening and its meaning and significance.

Field notes should subsequently be organized into a journal. Keeping a journal assists in preserving observations and is also a valuable tool for analyzing and making sense out of what has been seen and heard. The journal provides a record of occurrences that happened in the past and of changes or similarities in perception over time. The record also provides: food for thought; a vehicle for making connections between events that were not connected at the time; a vehicle for planning strategies or actions for the future based on events of the past; and a base from which progress can be measured in altering administrative behavior in a desired direction.

Journal keeping usually occurs on a daily basis and consists of a simple stream of consciousness of the day's events. Journal entries

Figure 6.1
Suggested format for field notes and journal page

Entry Number	Narrative (Facts)	Subjective Reaction or Evaluation (Questions and Comments)

can be constructed from field notes, putting them in more legible and organized form. The rerecording process forces reflection on the day's events and new insights may be gained from looking at the events as a whole. Information surfacing in the afternoon may shed new light on events of the morning; information gathered today may help clarify an event that happened yesterday—or even last week. Analysis and reanalysis should be a continuous and iterative process.

> *From the beginning of data collection, the qualitative analyst is beginning to decide what things mean, is noting regularities, patterns, explanations, possible configurations, causal flows, and propositions. The competent researcher holds these conclusions lightly, maintaining openness and skepticism, but the conclusions are still there, inchoate and vague at first, then increasingly explicit and grounded. . . . In this sense, qualitative data analysis is a continuous, iterative enterprise.* (Miles & Huberman, 1984, pp. 22–23)

To maximize the usefulness of journal keeping, a weekly review should be made. The journal keeper asks himself or herself some standard questions after reading past notes with particular attention being given to those of the past week. Questions to be answered in reflecting on the week's observations might include:

1. Did I accomplish what I planned?
2. How could I have accomplished what I did
   a. more effectively?
   b. more efficiently?
3. Is follow-up needed on any items?
   a. Immediately or later?
   b. What kind of follow-up is needed?
4. How can I improve my administrative behavior and responses?
5. How can I capitalize on events of the past week?

6. Can I foresee any negative consequences of any specific events?
   a. What are they?
   b. How can they be rectified?
7. Are there any significant linkages among events?
8. What are my predictions for future occurrences?
9. Have I broadened my scope of viewing? Do I consistently filter out certain kinds of data?

Reflecting on observations as guided by the above or similar questions will assist in gaining insight into past actions of others as well as into the impact and effectiveness of one's own actions. The analysis should also assist in evaluating old administrative strategies and in planning for new initiatives.

Other ways in which the journal can be used to enhance observation and listening skills and to improve administrative performance include:

1. rereading the journal periodically, reflecting on what is written;
2. checking your perceptions with others through direct questioning or, alternatively, asking a trusted colleague to read your journal and to critique it;
3. drawing a set of conclusions from a free-flowing nonstructured analysis rather than using a standard set of questions as suggested earlier;
4. using a checklist of behaviors in order to generate frequency counts or trends that might reveal personal patterns of behavior having positive or negative consequences;
5. analyzing the journal contents for assumptions or frames of reference, conclusions, inferences, biases, prejudices, objectivity, values, accuracy of predictions, etc.;
6. looking for changes in personal perceptions and/or sophistication over time.

In spite of the variety of techniques available to the journal keeper, there are a number of obstacles that might weaken the value of the final results. These include: (1) the process takes a great deal of time; (2) many separate threads of thoughts are produced without any unifying theme; (3) the information may be specific to the journal keeper or to a time and place, and not generalizable; and (4) no automatic insights are produced.

Journal keeping is basically a self-help technique and a number of possibilities exist that can be used to overcome these obstacles. Among them are: (1) constructing a more appropriate set of questions; (2) training the journal keeper to make more insightful analyses; and (3) the use of either a trained or naive outside reader to ask questions of the journal keeper. Whether critiquing the journal oneself or with the assistance of an outside reader, the following should be looked for: (1) variety and depth in the observations; (2) differentiation between objective and subjective observations; (3) the journal keeper's frame of reference or point of view, i.e., psychological, sociological, anthropological, educational, positivistic, critical, constructivistic, etc.; (4) growth or change in perceptions over time, i.e., expansion in the scope of analysis; (5) importance of the events recorded and the insights produced; and (6) unfinished situations that appear to need closure.

Journal keeping is time-consuming and at times it may produce frustration, but the payoff can be substantial if systematic procedures are followed conscientiously. It can lead to better understanding of one's self and co-workers. It can sharpen one's awareness of personal biases and weaknesses. It can provide insights into how one is accepted in the organizational structure. It can help sharpen one's listening and observational skills and it can help improve one's ability to predict future events from present and past events.

Time and patience with the process can produce great rewards.

Reflection in Practice

TECHNICIAN VS. CRAFTSMAN

The field of management is marked by two competing perceptions of management professionals. One perception views the manager as a technician whose practice consists of applying principles and methods derived from management science to the everyday problems of the organization. The other perception portrays the manager as a craftsman involved in the art of management that cannot be reduced to explicit rules and theories. In trying to reconcile these views, Schön (1983) developed the concept of the "reflective practitioner."

In describing how professionals think in action, Schön (1983) referred to two kinds of knowledge, scientific theory and technique (that which is associated with the technician) and tacit understanding (that associated with the craftsman). The former (scientific theory and technique) has dominated the curricula of preparation programs in all of the professions—an outcome of the hegemony of positivist philosophy (described previously in Chapters 4 and 5) and the natural sciences within universities—to the neglect of practical competence and professional artistry (development of tacit understandings). This has led to growing tension between practitioners, who claim that their professional preparation is largely irrelevant to the realities of practice, and university faculty who guided the professional preserve preparation programs. Professional practitioners of all varieties are becoming increasingly disturbed over the fact that they have not been prepared to account for processes they perceive as being central to professional competence such as making sense out of uncertainty, performing artistically, identifying problems, and choosing among competing professional paradigms.

To redress this imbalance, Schön (1983) calls for an epistemology of practice beginning with the assumption that competent practitioners usually know more than they can verbalize, i.e., they possess tacit understandings. Technical problem solving needs to be placed within a broader context of reflective inquiry and linked to the art of practice under uncertainty and unique conditions. Schön contends that when someone reflects in action, he or she becomes a researcher in the context of practice and that such research can be just as rigorous and demanding as that done in the scientific laboratory. Schön sees thinking and doing as complementary.

If we separate thinking from doing, seeing thought only as a preparation for action and action only as implementation of thought, then it is easy to believe that when we step into the separate domain of thought we will become lost in an infinite regress of thinking about thinking. . . . When a practitioner keeps inquiry moving, however, he does not abstain from action in order to sink into endless thought. Continuity of inquiry entails a continual interweaving of thinking and doing. (Schön, 1983, p. 280)

Professional preparation programs in universities tend to emphasize "thinking" and neglect "doing"; certainly there is little deliberate attempt to integrate the two.

Eisner (1988) approaches the tension between theory and practice through the concept of "educational connoisseurship." He sees teaching (and we would expand this to include administration) as an activity that requires artistry. "Theory plays a role in the cultivation of artistry, but its role is not prescriptive, it is diagnostic. Good theory in edu-

cation, as in art, helps us to see more; it helps us think about more of the qualities that constitute a set of phenomena" (p. 142). Theory provides a framework through which intelligence can be exercised to interpret perception and action.

Schein (1973) explained the gap between the professions and the academy by noting that the logic of basic and applied sciences—the ethos of the university—is convergent, whereas the experiences of practice are divergent. Ackoff (1979) is more graphic.

[M]anagers are not confronted with problems that are independent of each other, but with dynamic situations that consist of complex systems of changing problems that interact with each other. I call such situations messes. Problems are abstractions extracted from messes by analysis; they are to messes as atoms are to tables and charts. . . . Managers do not solve problems; they manage messes. (pp. 99-100)

These comments are especially significant coming from Ackoff who was one of the founders of operations research, a movement to apply scientific methods, mathematical models in particular, to operational problems. After two decades of applications, Ackoff (1979) concluded that "the future of operations research is past." The formal highly structured, highly quantified, highly mathematical approach to problem solving drawn from the tradition of positivism was ill suited to the messes faced by professional managers. More important to administrators than the analytical skills engendered by operations research (and university preparation) were the synthetic skills of designing new systems through "conversations with the situation" and the political skills of bringing them about (Schön, 1983).

From the perspective of scientific technical rationality, professional practice is a process of problem solving, using the means best suited for achieving established ends. But, in the real world of practice, problems do not present themselves as givens; they must be defined through an interactive process in which the practitioner specifies the things to be attended to and frames the context in which they will be managed. Thus, the practitioner must identify and define the problem within the context of the mess before it can be dealt with and a reasonable solution found. In the academic world, the mess is delimited into a problem and the optimal solution is determined; all outside the boundary of the problem is ignored. Practitioners do not have the luxury of doing this.

A further difference between the professional and the scientist is that, for the professional, each case is unique and cannot be solved by applying standard theories or techniques (Schön, 1983). The scientist, on the other hand, deals with samples and populations and looks for generalizations. This does not mean that the professional acts as though there were no prior relevant experience to draw upon. Quite to the contrary, the professional draws upon one element or another of his or her repertoire of experience used as an exemplar for the new situation. But seeing one situation as being similar to another is not the same as subsuming the new under a familiar category or rule. Rather, we see that the unfamiliar situation is, at the same time, similar to and different from the familiar situation without being able to say initially in what respects the situations are similar and different. The familiar situation serves as a precedent or a metaphor. This may be done consciously by comparing the two situations, or by describing the unfamiliar situation in light of a tacit reference to the familiar.

It is our capacity to see unfamiliar situations as familiar ones, and to do in the former as we have done in the latter, that enables us to bring our past experience to bear on the unique case. It is our capacity to see-as and do-as that allows us to have a feel for prob-

lems that do not fit existing rules. . . . Reflection-in-action in a unique case may be generalized to other cases, not by giving rise to general principles, but by contributing to the practitioner's repertoire of exemplary themes from which, in the subsequent cases of his practice, he may compose new variations. (Schön, 1983, p. 140)

Based on comparisons of the familiar and the unfamiliar, the practitioner formulates hypothetical solutions and tests them with experimental actions that also serve as moves to reshape the situation and as probes to promote better understanding of the situation. In observing the results generated by the experimental actions, the situation is reassessed, new hypotheses are formulated, etc. until the situation assumes a shape satisfactory to the practitioner. It is an iterative process. The practitioner's relation to the situation is transactional in that he or she shapes the situation, but in reflecting on it, his or her own models and appreciations are reshaped on the basis of feedback. Unlike the scientist, the professional needs not only to understand the situation but also to change it. The professional becomes a part of the situation, while the scientist remains "objectively" removed (Schön, 1983).

In Schön's (1983) words, the practitioner carries on a "reflective conversation with the situation" (p. 268). Inquiry begins with an effort to solve a problem as initially defined; but the inquirer remains open to the discovery of phenomena incongruent with the initial problem definition and, on discovering incongruency, reframes the problem. The situation "talks back," and, in reflecting on the feedback, new meanings are discovered and new initiatives are taken. "The process spirals through stages of appreciation, action, and reappreciation. The unique and uncertain situation comes to be understood through the attempt to change it, and changed through the attempt to understand it" (Schön, 1983, p. 132).

It is difficult to teach this kind of knowledge and to develop these kinds of skills, but it is possible to learn them (Schön, 1987). The technical, science-based knowledge of a profession is the essence of the professional school curriculum; it can be reduced to words and presented in books and lectures. Development of tacit knowledge is a different matter, however, and tends to be neglected in formal educational curricula. Tacit knowledge is learned through trial and error in experience. But professionals deal with such sensitive human issues that it would be immoral for a neophyte to experiment on an unsuspecting client primarily to further his or her professional education and understanding. To overcome this difficulty, many professions include in their preparation programs mentoring experiences such as internships and residencies. In these situations, the neophyte is permitted to practice, but under the close supervision of a seasoned professional who serves as a coach and mentor. Through this process, the neophyte builds up tacit knowledge to serve him or her in a lifetime of independent practice. The closest we come to this in education is a brief stint as student teacher or as a part-time administrative intern. There is a growing recognition that these field-based experiences are inadequate preparation for the beginning teacher or administrator (Murphy, 1993; National Policy Board for Educational Administration, 1989; Jacobson & Conway, 1990).

A New Client-Professional Relationship

Schön (1983) concluded that viewing the professional as a reflective practitioner rather than as a "technical rationalist," implies the need for a new client-professional relationship. The need for reform in relationships is as great between teachers and school administrators and their clients as it is for other professions. The new relationships could be characterized as symbiotic in which mutual information exchange is encouraged.

Schön (1983) described the client-professional relationship as a contract or a set of norms governing the behavior of each party to the interaction which enables both professional and client to know what they can expect from one another. In the traditional contract, the professional acts as though he or she has agreed to deliver services to the client to the limit of his or her special competence, to respect the confidences granted by the client, and not to misuse for the professional's own benefit the special powers given within the boundaries of the relationship. The client acts as though he or she has agreed to accept the professional's authority and knowledge, to submit to the professional's services, and to pay for the services rendered. Under the traditional contract, the professional's accountability is primarily to professional peers. This traditional professional-client relationship is a product of positivistic philosophy.

In the new (and preferred) relationship, the professional recognizes that his or her technical expertise is imbedded in a context of meaning and that the client must be involved in the process of discovering that meaning. Rather than a relationship of authority and submission, the relationship between the professional and the client becomes reciprocal and symbiotic.

He [the professional] attributes to his clients, as well as to himself, a capacity to mean, know, and plan. He recognizes that his actions may have different meanings for his client than he intends them to have, and he gives himself the task of discovering what these are. He recognizes an obligation to make his own understandings accessible to his client, which means that he needs often to reflect on what he knows. . . . Although the reflective practitioner should be credentialed and technically competent, his claim to authority is substantially based on his ability to manifest his special knowledge in his inter-actions with clients. He does not ask his client to have blind faith in a "black box," but to remain open to the evidence of the practitioner's competence as it emerges. (Schön, 1983, pp. 295-296)

In other words, the professional must be able to solicit from the client, through observation and conversation, information that is relevant to their mutual concern, to evaluate that information, and to use it in prescribing a treatment or service. Within the new contract, the professional is more directly accountable to the client than in the traditional contract. Rather than accept the practitioner's authority, the client agrees to join with the practitioner in a mutual inquiry into the situation for which the client seeks help. The alternative professional view reflects a constructivist philosophy.

Under the traditional contract, the professional is presumed to have complete technical knowledge of his or her field of expertise and claims to do so regardless of any uncertainty. A professional distance is maintained from the client while playing the role of the expert—perhaps conveying a sense of warmth as a "sweetener." The traditional professional emphasizes a status differential between himself or herself and the client. The reflective professional, on the other hand, openly acknowledges that he or she is not the only one to have relevant and important knowledge in the situation. The reflective professional views uncertainty as a potential source of learning for all involved and seeks to be connected with the client's thoughts and opinions. Respect for the professional is not assumed but is expected to grow out of the competence displayed by the professional in the handling of the situation. In not needing to maintain a professional facade, the reflective professional is free to develop an authentic relationship with the client which enhances the quality and quantity of informa-

tion available to diagnose the situation and the effect of trial solutions. (Schön, 1983).

Looking at it from the standpoint of the client, in the alternative client-professional relationship, the client assumes much greater responsibility for the treatment, cure, or service rendered, giving up the security based solely on faith in the professional's competence and joining with the professional in making sense out of his or her case. The client exercises some control over the situation and complies with the professional's advice only after being convinced that it is the most sensible course of action to take.

For the teacher, embracing this new professional contract means a recognition that no learning can take place without the cooperation of the student—and probably the family. Both are in possession of information—attitudes, understandings, background and history—that is critical to the success of the teaching mission and available to the teacher only in collaboration with the student and the family. Similarly, for the administrator, this new professional relationship implies the end of unilateral, authoritarian, top-down decisionmaking. It is an acknowledgement that all persons affected by a decision must be involved meaningfully in making the decision and that the success of the organization is a function of all involved. These requirements go well beyond the capacity of even the most sophisticated information system and imply that each educational leader should have finely tuned observational and listening skills and that the current pattern of school governance needs to be restructured into an inclusive system.

For this alternative relationship to function well in the public education sector, the aspect of compulsion must be reduced or eliminated. This suggests a reformed governance structure for education that permits, on the one hand, family choice of school and, on the other hand, site-based management. Site-based management provides educating professionals with the freedom necessary to exercise the pedagogy that they judge to be most appropriate and to design schools according to professional judgement and client demand. Family choice ensures that the professional-client relationship is a voluntary one.

The emerging style of educational leadership is one of parity with other members of the organization. It requires reflective professionals who have keen observational skills and the ability to interpret accurately the observations they make. Instead of talking and giving orders, the new leadership observes carefully, listens attentively, and skillfully interprets that which is seen and heard. Leadership is interactive and facilitating.

Activities for Discussion

For one week, keep a journal of your professional interactions. Record your field notes on a form similar to that in Figure 6.1. Enter your field notes into a journal using a similar format. Analyze your entries using questions similar to those suggested on p. 183. Exchange your journal and analysis with another member of the class, critiquing one another's work using criteria suggested on p. 183.

Questions

1. Give two reasons why having good observational skills is important to the school administrator. Explain each reason.

2. List and explain the way three of your biases might influence your observations.

3. List and explain three instances when an administrator might see things differently than a teacher.

Annotated Bibliography

Fetterman, D. M. (Ed.). (1988). *Qualitative approaches to evaluation in education: The silent scientific revolution.* New York: Praeger.

This book presents a number of qualitative approaches to educational evaluation which can be adapted to improving the observational skills of the "wandering" administrator. It stresses that the fundamental differences between scholarly orders is based on philosophical and epistemological differences and not on methodological grounds. Of particular interest to the administrator is E. W. Eisner's chapter on connoisseurship and criticism as a form of evaluation and N. L. Smith's chapter reviewing the relevance of practice in other fields for use in education.

Guba, E. G., & Lincoln, Y. S. (1983). *Effective evaluation.* San Francisco: Jossey-Bass.

The authors believe that the failure to use evaluation findings illustrates the poverty of traditional methods used in making evaluations. "[T]hey do not begin with the concerns and issues of their actual audiences and . . . they produce information that, while perhaps statistically significant, does not generate truly worthwhile knowledge" (p. ix). This book offers a new model of evaluation built on a constructivist paradigm. The model combines two streams of thought: "responsive" evaluation, and "naturalistic" inquiry, so called because the researcher is actively involved with the people, places, and events being studied. The book does an excellent job of contrasting the philosophy underlying naturalistic inquiry with those of other methodologies. It also has useful discussions of how to conduct such inquiry including interviewing and observational techniques, using records and documents, and implementing naturalistic, responsive evaluation.

LeCompte, M. D., & Preissle, J. (1993). *Ethnography and qualitative design in educational research* (2nd ed.). San Diego, CA: Academic Press.

This book is a treatise on how to do qualitative and ethnographic research. It addresses ways to collect data, methods for assuring the quality of data, the roles researchers enact in the course of their efforts, and techniques for organizing results, conclusions, and interpretations. It emphasizes the role that theory plays in the research process. Of particular relevance to the "wandering" administrator is the treatment of participant observation in Chapter Six.

Lincoln, Y. S., & Guba, E. G. (1985). *Naturalistic inquiry*. Beverly Hills, CA: Sage.

This book covers much of the same ground that is covered in Guba and Lincoln (1981), but with different emphases. Between the two books, the issues surrounding naturalistic inquiry are well covered. This book contains more complete discussions of such subjects as implementing naturalistic inquiry, establishing trustworthiness, obtaining data, case reporting, and establishing audit trails. The book helps one understand and, therefore, conduct naturalistic inquiry.

Miles, M. B., & Huberman, A. M. (1984). *Qualitative data analysis: A sourcebook of new methods*. Beverly Hills, CA: Sage.

This book addresses the issue of drawing valid meaning from qualitative data. It seeks methods of analysis that are practical, communicable, and "scientific." It is a useful sourcebook focusing on data reduction, data display, and analysis. Its contents include: focusing and bounding the collection of data, analyzing data during data collection, within-site analysis, cross-site analysis, matrix displays, and drawing and verifying conclusions. Strong emphasis is placed on types of data displays including graphs, charts, matrices, and networks.

Schön, D. A. (1983). *The reflective practitioner: How professionals think in action*. New York: Basic Books.

The book investigates how professionals go about problem solving and how such techniques are learned. In the process, Schön discovers the source of conflict between practicing professionals and their mentors in research universities. Practitioners rely more on their tacit knowledge and improvisation than they do on theories and formulas learned in graduate school. They carry on a "conversation with the situation" and "reflect in

action." Their approach to problem solving is interpretivist in philosophy in contrast with the positivist philosophy of most in the academic community. Schön urges that professional schools declare their independence from intellectual domination by the natural science disciplines and organize preservice programs that are relevant to practice.

References

Ackoff, R. (1979). The future of operational research is past. *Journal of Operational Research Society, 30* (2), 93–104.

Chimera, J. (1974). Appendix: The art of journal keeping. In J. Chimera, *Developing observational skills.* Buffalo, NY: Department of Educational Administration, State University of New York at Buffalo.

Eisner, E. W. (1988). Educational connoisseurship and criticism: Their form and functions in educational evaluation. In D. M. Fetterman (Ed.), *Qualitative approaches to evaluation in education: The silent scientific revolution.* New York: Praeger.

Fetterman, D. M. (1988). Ethnographic educational evaluation. In D. M. Fetterman (Ed.), *Qualitative approaches to evaluation in education: The silent scientific revolution.* New York: Praeger.

Guba, E. G., & Lincoln, Y. S. (1983). *Effective evaluation.* San Francisco: Jossey-Bass.

Jacobson, S. L., & Conway, J. A. (1990). *Educational leadership in an age of reform.* New York: Longman.

LeCompte, M. D., & Preissle, J. (1993). *Ethnography and qualitative design in educational research* (2nd ed.). San Diego, CA: Academic Press.

Lincoln, Y. S., & Guba, E. G. (1985). *Naturalistic inquiry.* Beverly Hills, CA: Sage.

Miles, M. B., & Huberman, A. M. (1984). *Qualitative data analysis: A sourcebook of new methods.* Beverly Hills, CA: Sage.

Murphy, J. (Ed.). (1993). *Preparing tomorrow's school leaders: Alternative designs.* University

Park, PA: University Council for Educational Administration.

National Policy Board for Educational Administration. (1989). *Improving the preparation of school administrators: The reform agenda*. Charlottesville, VA: Author.

Peters, T. (1988). *Thriving on chaos: Handbook for a management revolution*. New York: Alfred A. Knopf.

Peters, T. J., & Waterman, Jr., R. H. (1982). *In search of excellence: Lessons from America's best-run companies*. New York: Warner Books.

Schein, E. (1973). *Professional education*. New York: McGraw-Hill.

Schön, D. A. (1983). *The reflective practitioner: How professionals think in action*. New York: Basic Books.

Schön, D. A. (1987). *Educating the reflective practitioner*. San Francisco, CA: Jossey-Bass.

Smith, N. L. (1988). Mining metaphors for methods of practice. In D. M. Fetterman (Ed.), *Qualitative approaches to evaluation in education: The silent scientific revolution*. New York: Praeger.

Tymitz, B., & Wolf, R. L. (1977). *An introduction to judicial evaluation and natural inquiry*. Washington, DC: Nero and Associates.

Webb, E. J., et al. (1966). *Unobtrusive measures*. Chicago: Rand McNally.

Williams, P. N. (1978). *Investigative reporting and editing*. Englewood Cliffs, NJ: Prentice-Hall.

Part III

Communication and Human Interaction

C ommunication is the flow of ideas, information, and data through the systems of education. From the classroom to the national network, effective communication is a key to the functional life of educational enterprises. Leaders at all levels, from those who work with students through the maze of the daily tasks of learning to those who deal with the multilevel complexities of the local, regional, state, and national educational bureaucracies, have to develop the ability to *understand* and *to be understood*.

In Part III, the broad concept of communication is developed through a discussion of schools as organizational systems and the human interactions that take place within them. For today's educational leader, it is not enough to be skilled only as a writer or speaker. Memos sent down from the central office to those laboring in the classroom and the occasional public relations release to the community at large are not adequate to bind together individuals into a functioning, cohesive unity. Effective leadership requires the ability to create social environments that facilitate good communication through the establishment of mutual respect and trust among all upon whom the organization depends. Such an environment permits information to flow freely within the school system and messages from the outside to be interpreted accurately and acted upon appropriately and in a timely fashion.

Chapter 7 explores schools as organizational systems through the use of metaphor. Classical, humanistic, and systemic constructs are described as enduring parameters of schools. We encourage a more thorough understanding of the organic nature of education and educational administration and propose that both be released from dysfunctional, bureaucratic constraints.

Chapter 8 addresses the diversity in theories related to communication. All communication is seen as relating to and affecting the organizational body; metaphorically, communication is the breath of organizational life, enabling members to work in concert—hopefully with a sense of craftsmanship and joy— and to reach outside the organization in service.

Communication is only one aspect of human interaction. In Chapter 9, we address other aspects. Human relations is perceived as the integration of people into a situation that motivates them to work together productively and cooperatively with resulting economic, psychological, and social satisfactions. Good human relations are intended to motivate people in organizations, and to develop teamwork that effectively fulfills their personal needs while achieving organizational objectives.

Chapter 10 addresses social and cultural contexts within which human interaction takes place and which influence the educational process. Providing school leadership is a complex and pervasive human endeavor in which the executive role looks outward to the external environment and inward toward internal order. The essential administrative dilemma is that, on the one hand, administrators must reconcile personal goals of the members of the organization with organizational goals, and, on the other hand, all school activity must be reconciled with the constraining, competing, and conflicting pressures of its external environment. This chapter examines the impact that environments created by the family, the school, and the larger society have upon the educational process and upon children's ability to learn.

Chapter 7
Schools as Organizational Systems

"I am coming not to know what educational administration is and doubt that it ought to continue an existence as an independent field" (Culbertson, in Allen, 1992, p. 1). Culbertson's statement takes dramatic issue with schooling and education in the United States. Allen (1992) assessed national educational guidelines as inadequate. National control of schools is important, but it is significantly outdated and in need of drastic reconstruction. Speaking from other points of view, other authors report similar concerns.

Levine (1992) recounted how, as a researcher, he enrolled in high school classes. What he observed and reported was more desperate than anyone realized: schools then as today are facing the decline of the family, rising poverty, changing demographics, a drug explosion, and a lack of parental support. But problematic issues in the economy or the nation are only part of the problem. Hentschke (1992) explained that real school dilemmas are lost in a plethora of overused professional issues and problems: school-based management, shared decisionmaking, performance-based instruction, authentic assessment, accountability, and teacher-parent improvements.

Coombs (1991) cited four reasons for his dismal prognosis: (1) failure to understand fundamental assumptions about schooling, (2) failure to react to today's realizations spawned by rapid change in a modern world, (3) failure to adapt to new understanding about the nature of the human organism, and (4) failure to construct a system that values and facilitates innovation and true professionalism. Each of these occurs as a result of inadequate attention to our school systems. Lack of student centeredness, lack of adjustment to changing needs, discouragement of innovation, misunderstanding culture, poor motivational methods, lack of leadership and governance, insufficient funding, and lack of purpose all play their parts as well.

It takes little effort to uncover extensive literature about the endless list of problems evident in schools. The scope and scale of the problems seem unmanageable. Exploring the issues casually leads one to infer necessary changes needed in organizational climate, organizational development, organizational variance, and organizational adaptability. Quick fixes such as study of school structure, relations with the environment, management, decisionmaking, human behavior and others abound. While this list may appear incomplete, one can immediately sense the diversity of needs and the complexity of issues surrounding schools and school performance.

Schools suffer many of the same ills that we find occurring across society. Schools, in fact, may more closely mirror society than we prefer to acknowledge. Schools appear to be locked in extensive red tape, unable to react in a rapidly changing environment, wasting resources uncontrollably, and suffering from misdirected efforts, inadequate and poor performance, discontented employees, and inadequate and political leadership. Schools are also highly bureaucratic. But, as with many organizations, schools are in need of significant change. Our schools languish at the expense of society's most valuable resource, its young people. As shown already (Coombs, 1991; Sergiovanni & Moore, 1989; Solomon & Hughes, 1992; Levine, 1992) many believe that our schools as organizations are in need of revitalization, even complete renewal— changes across the many contexts of organization.

Organizational thinking has dramatic historical breadth. The complexity of organizational issues driven by the technological knowledge explosion and a variety of changes in societal values, beliefs, and expectations only compounds what must now be apparent. Change is the driving need, or perhaps, the demand felt by most. School systems based on the Weberian model, defined by control, efficiency, and routinization are not able to effectively deal with current needs (Weber, 1947). In a different sense, other organizational models and theories such as management science that develops a "science of work" perspective (Fayol, 1949; Taylor, 1947;

in Pugh & Hickson, 1989), a human sociological or psychological perspective (Mayo, 1945; McGregor, 1985; Herzberg, 1968; in Pugh & Hickson, 1989), or any number of other typologies for thinking about organizations may not have served us well. Contingency approaches to organization, while encompassing more variables, may be too narrowly focused as well.

In all this, however, the purpose of education has not changed significantly. Many view the purpose of schooling to include basic skills development, knowledge of a common heritage, good character development, and preparation for work and/or further study (Allen, 1992; Bennett, 1992; Hentschke, 1992; Hodgkinson, 1991; Levine, 1992; Solomon & Hughes, 1992). At the same time, educational practitioners have molded schools as mirror images of society and organizations in that society. The purposes of schools, as well as societies, include: an aesthetic purpose associated with the fulfillment and enjoyment of life; an economic purpose, making money; and an ideological purpose, a conveyor of society's cultural, idealistic, and humanistic traits (Hodgkinson, 1991). While these differences render education more diverse among occupations in society, all organizations exist to achieve similar purposes. But none carries with it the degree of totality and uniqueness of purpose found in schools. While the simple marketing slogan "this isn't your parents' Oldsmobile," implies for the year's quality shopper a desirable product and a narrowly defined purpose for General Motors, schooling's purpose is infinitely more complex and demonstrates greater scope and scale of action.

Schooling for most represents a substantial portion of one's lifetime, yet as shown briefly already, ambiguity present in thinking about schools is widespread. As organizations, our schools are not keeping pace with changes in society. Like many other private and public organizations, they are becoming "iron cages" that control and stifle action through rigid rules and bureaucracy (Clegg, 1990). Schools consume limited resources and too often house discontented, even apathetic, employees. Perhaps most profound and saddening, they often produce graduates not capable of assuming effective roles in our society. Schools should lead society into the future. As purposeful organizations using an equitable amount of resources, schools should prepare participants for a positive and lifelong adaptation and interaction with society. But schools frequently succumb to the same problems, the same inadequacies, and the same paradoxes found in other organizations. They mirror what exists in the larger environment.

This chapter explores the enduring parameters of schools as organizations today. Classical, humanistic, and systemic constructs are discussed and, additionally, the integrating elements that unite organizational thought are investigated. Using metaphor, we look at schools as organizations. In addition, current school issues are identified and related to metaphors discussed. A last section discusses schools for tomorrow as grounded in quantum science.

Traditional Ways of Thinking about Organizations

Organizations can be conceptualized in a variety of ways: through definition, through one's perception of reality, through theoretical constructs, even metaphorically as in such terms as turbulence or chaos. Weber (1947) devised the term *bureaucracy* to represent tightly controlled organizations. Organizations were understood to be well-oiled machines. Specialized parts of the machine were differentiated by function and combined through an authority-based, hierarchial structure. Rules, policy, and procedures enabled the special-

ized parts to achieve maximum effort. Woodward (1981), on the other hand, described organizations through their technology, a combination of processes or functions that were the result of technological operations. Individuals, in turn, are utilized and identified in relation to a technology component. Thus organizations are conceived through a convergence/divergence lens. The principal effect on specialized organizations is the differentiation of activities so as to integrate the organization with its common purpose(s). As this rational deterministic view maintains primacy, additional theorists began to question the relevance of this "things or events" focus. Authors today visualize organizations as being much more ubiquitous and complex (Mintzberg, 1983; Drucker, 1987; Ouchi, 1981; Peters, 1992; Barnard, 1938). Fayol and Taylor (in Pugh & Hickson, 1989) perceive organizations as instruments to maximize efficiency, a deterministic view that gives greater credence to the "science of work" and management, and their applicability to the human component.

Taylor's work concentrated on the area of scientific management. His five principles of work design advocate the following. (1) Shift work responsibility to management. Managers plan and design work while workers implement. (2) Use scientific analysis to devise precise worker actions. (3) Select the best workers for a given job. (4) Train workers effectively. (5) Monitor work and worker performance (Morgan, 1986). Both Frank and Lillian Gilbreth (Spreigel, 1953) tested Taylor's principal contributions studying human motion through work study analysis of performance. Fayol (1949) provides a comprehensive explanation of organizations in his discussion of management. The functions of management are planning, organizing, directing, coordinating, and controlling. By and large, Fayol's perspective is seen in most discussions of organization today. Although Taylor and Fayol are not viewed as human relations pioneers, their work lead to further studies of the human component in organizations. Their scientific analysis combined with Weberian classical structure has had a long and profound effect on organizations as they exist today.

Others viewed organizations additionally as systems of interdependent human activities, as humans were considered another essential resource required to achieve specific organizational purpose(s). Numerous authors and theorists viewed the human component as special in regard to the organization, not only as a resource for the organization to consume, but as an element whose behavior affects both the structure and function of the organization. To these writers, humans were the organization. For Mayo (1945), the major task of management was to organize the individuals in the organization and to secure the commitment of individuals to achieve ends for the organization. In tightly structured and controlled organizations, workers needed an outlet, an informal mechanism, to combat the ill-effects of bureaucracy, Mayo noted. Mayo's work, in addition, addresses the importance of communication to successful management as managers succeeded or failed based on their acceptance or disapproval by workers. McGregor (1985) postulated further that managers exhibit beliefs about human behavior in two broad categories of assumptions: Theory X, viewing employees as distrusting, lazy, and in need of careful controlling; or Theory Y, a more positive view of the employee. Similarly, Likert (1987) questioned why units in organizations with low efficiency ratings tended to have job-centered supervisors, while supervisors with the best performance records appeared employee-centered. Both Likert and McGregor consider building supportive relationships an ideal supervisory practice. Blake and Mouton (1988) support an analogous approach. "The manager's job is to foster attitudes and behavior which promote efficient performance, stimulate and use creativity, generate enthusiasm for experimen-

tation and innovation, and learn from interaction of others" (Pugh & Hickson, 1989, p. 183). Blake and Mouton's managerial grid identified behaviors they believe can be taught and learned. Other human behaviorists have examined a variety of aspects of human components in organizations. Herzberg (1968) found distinctively different factors associated with job satisfaction and job dissatisfaction. As a result, theorists who simply maintain being more supportive must further recognize that job enrichment brings about more effective utilization of people in organizations and increases job satisfaction.

In another view, Schein (1985) extended assumptions about the human aspects of organization beyond the rational, social, and needs-based models. His complex model recognizes that life events and development drive individual motives and that these motives vary across situations and time. Management, therefore, simply cannot be coordination and control, nor even largely supportive, but must also include a diagnostic component whereby managers learn and react to both individual employees and organizational expectations. This added level of understanding of people enables the organization to cope with internal and external realities, adapting to the external and integrating the internal.

Argyris et al. (1985) developed a strikingly similar diagnostic view. In organizations, people are often confronted with built-in contradictory elements. These contradictory elements cause people to adhere to stability-producing conformance mechanisms and, in the next instant, be penalized for lacking initiative, aggressiveness, or adaptability. Different norms are needed in organizations, norms that decree openness in communication, openness to action, and openness to learning.

To this point, organizations have been viewed as structure, as management, and as human relations. While each of these perspectives provides valuable data to use in understanding organizations, another approach to organizations is provided by systems theorists. Ultimately, in this view, organizations are organic entities or seen as sets of processes that interact with an environment. In the traditional rational/deterministic, scientific, and human relations perspectives, theorists attempt to constrain uncertainty in the organization. With the advent of systems theory, organization study addresses the uncertainty across various boundary conditions. The input-throughput-output-feedback model became the cornerstone of organizational inquiry.

In the earliest studies of organizations using systems methodology, environment, boundaries, variety, feedback, and other elements were treated as another set of scientific variables with which to contend. School systems' environments were thought to include the school, the school district, the state, and the federal government. Others added the community, parents, businesses, and various professional and educational associations. In the mechanistic organization, problems were resolved in various specialized departments. As change, innovation, and uncertainty continued to grow, the organization became incapable of handling the ensuing variety. In the short term, the organization's communications broke down from the maze of problems that were encountered.

Burns (1966) maintained that this breakdown is inevitable. Organizations function in differing social systems: an authority system, a cooperative system of people, and a political system. Organizational structure in Burns' view was the result of a process whereby the continuous development of these three social systems occurs within and adapts to an ever changing environment.

Lawrence and Lorsch (1986) maintain that the additional requirement of the organization to interact with its environment complicates organization thinking processes even further. By advocating a contingency approach, they address the issue of integration and differentiation in the organization's internal environment and externally within the organization's suprasystem. In the organization's attempt to integrate and differentiate effectively, conflict resolution founded in compromise and competence balances organizational functioning. Thompson (1967) termed this an alignment function, where structure, technology, and environment interact. Miles and Snow (1978) cited a similar alignment typology to help managers diagnose and pursue a more effective organizational strategy.

Other authors further expand systems thinking as applied to organizations. Understanding organizations in terms of biology and evolution, Hannan and Freeman (1988) proposed a population ecology perspective of organizations. They attempt to explain the replacement of outmoded forms of organization with newer forms. Some organizations prosper and survive while others die out. Emery and Trist (1969), in their work at the Travistock Institute, conceptualized organizations as "open socio-technical systems." In this view, the organization is viewed as being essentially dynamic and having a continual interchange across boundaries with its environment. The work of management is to manage boundary exchanges rather than internal regulation. No longer would traditional redundancy of parts, common in traditional views, suffice. In turn, a redundancy of function in individuals and units would be capable of coping with complexity and change across boundaries. Rather than rely on controls to contain variety, organizations must rely on new, self-regulating mechanisms to achieve effective functioning in a turbulent environment. The true dynamic nature of organizations is exhibited through this new understanding.

Silverman (1971) saw all organizational study as inadequate and conceptualized an "action" frame of reference. This approach views organizations as outcomes of the interaction of motivated people who are attempting to resolve their problems and pursue their needs.

The traditional organizational viewpoints focus principally on a series of impersonal elements to explain organizations' functions while the human relations viewpoint focuses too far into a relationship orientation. However, to understand organizations further, we need to construct thinking about organizations as they occur in reality. Hypothesizing about either the traditional or human relations focus only serves to limit our true understanding of the reality within and surrounding organizations.

Decisionmaking in Organizations

Another school of thought maintains that decisionmaking is the key to understanding organizational effectiveness. Organizational effectiveness is thought to reside principally in managerial actions. For decision theorists, all managerial action is decisionmaking. In older theories, rationality is thought to be a cornerstone to decisionmaking. The decisionmaker rationally determines a best course of action from a multitude of variables to maximize organizational functioning. Simon (1977) replaced the rational-economic person who maximizes decisions with the administrative person, one who merely "satisfices." "Satisficing" is defined as a situation where the manager does not take the time to seek the optimal resolution of a problem, but settles for one that is satisfactory, one that will do. Organizational action is based individually or organizationally on selection of satisfactory alternatives using a few comparatively relevant factors with which the individual is capable of dealing.

Organizations, in this viewpoint, should necessarily strive to create situations in which unprogrammed decision contexts become programmed. Using these unprogrammed contexts, such as habits, routines, standard procedures, structure, and culture, allows the decisionmaker and the organization to function effectively. Both March (1988) and Simon (1977) believe the decisionmaker capable of a "bounded rationality." The limits of one's knowledge or an organization's knowledge severely limits organizational capability. Cognitive constraints and a scarcity of attention connect with the political aspects of the organization and provide a multitude of action possibilities. Through negotiation and bargaining, the organization progresses to an organizational limit.

Organizations rarely completely resolve conflict because they avoid uncertainty by creating acceptable decisionmaking. Accepting this short-term view results in the need to search for more "satisficing" alternatives. Over a period of time this process leads to organizational learning based on a reactive stance. March (1988) contended any "garbage can" full of decision rules and action alternatives will suffice if the organization continues to persist in the short-term action environment. Mintzberg (1989) postulated that individuals as decisionmakers fall into four patterns: the entrepreneur, who leads and determines new purpose; the disturbance handler, who resolves others' problems; the resource allocator, who disperses financial resources; and the negotiator, who seeks compromises.

Lindbloom (1980) termed his version of the decisionmaking disjointed incrementalism or the "science of muddling through." It is nearly impossible, according to Lindbloom, to find a rational/deterministic model of decisionmaking in use in most organizations. At best, decisionmaking in organizations may suffer from too much reactiveness, too few long-term horizons, and little effective control.

Tannebaum (1968) challenged this view. While many believe that effective control in organizations is and should be primarily concerned with how managers use a particular decisionmaking model or process, Tannebaum in contrast argued that decisionmaking as a process should be shared with a wider variety of players. This provides a greater volume of realistic alternatives from which to "satisfice." In Tannebaum's studies, people in organizations aren't interested in exercising more control than others, but simply exercising more control themselves. Organizations would be wise to consider diminishing the slope of hierarchies to some degree and restrict their attention to who exercises power. In turn, the organization should institute processes or models that allow members of the organization to increase the volume of decisionmaking. This shared responsibility firmly moves organizational thinking away from its machine connotations to a shared decisionmaking perspective.

Power in Organizations

Thinking about organizational decisionmaking leads to discussions about power in organizations. Individual, unit, or organizational decisions are based on interests, an orientation to act in one manner or another. Power in organizations relates directly to how these interests are pursued and defined, and the variety of ways that individuals then position and perceive their interests. Various agendas collide as different players defend their interests. Power in organizations results as systems simultaneously compete and collaborate (Burns, 1966). Up and down the traditional organization, power is a mechanism by which the organization resolves conflict.

Sources of power in organizations are numerous (Morgan, 1986). In the Weberian tradition, power is derived from legitimate authority. The right to rule is a recognized tra-

dition in most organizations, as formal authority is typically associated with position or command structure. Organizations also gain additional sources of power from control of scarce resources. Dependance must be established for this source of power to provide control. Structure and policy or regulation also is a source of power and another form of control in organizations. Bureaucratic regulation, plans, promotion requirements, and other regulatory rules give power potential to various controllers. The ability to influence decisionmaking through these structural mechanisms is most often seen in the control of decisionmaking whether controlling decision agendas, actual decisionmaking, or organizational objectives. The control of knowledge and information and the determination of what receives attention is also of vital importance. Key actors often resort to information and knowledge control, whether weaving a pattern of dependency via structure, change, gatekeeping, or limiting information or knowledge capability. Boundary management also is a source of power. Control of integrating mechanisms can promote progress while isolation can limit progress. Other sources of power include networks, control of power relations, alliances, control of technology, coping with uncertainty, managing meaning, and gender management (Morgan, 1986).

Recognizing and understanding these sources of power enables the practitioner to cope with power's many political milieus. In a complex pluralistic society, power is viewed as inevitable. The questions become how to compete, how to collaborate, how to avoid, how to accommodate, or how to compromise (Thomas, 1977). While radical views pit factions against each other, or unitary views integrate interests, in the pluralistic view the nature of the traditional organization is checked by the free interplay of various interest groups that have a stake in the organization.

Culture in Organizations

If power in organizations is as ubiquitous as it seems, it certainly appears that its presence can also become ingrained. In a similar fashion, other elements of the organization can also become habitual. Organizational theorists, sociologists, anthropologists, even managers, have long recognized this trait in organizations. From an anthropologist's perspective, culture is a complex system that includes knowledge, beliefs, arts, morals, laws, customs, and other habits acquired by people in society (Sackmann, 1991). In this respect, a cultural study of organizations has become a means to study components of an organization. Whether uncovering mainstay principles, realizing hidden mental constructions, or identifying how members' personalities are determined or represented within the organization, cultural study in the organizational context has become the study of the conditions that create the ability of organizations to more effectively function and behave. The study of culture in organizations thus becomes a holistic integration mechanism whereby theorists and consultants study ways of thinking, feeling, and reacting that individuals and organization have acquired and that somehow have been stored and transmitted through some form of symbolism. As a product of action, a shared system of meaning that incorporates the way people live and work in the organization, culture becomes a method to codify, modify, and control the organization (Sackmann, 1991). Schein (1985) related that as the culture integrates the organization internally and adapts the organization externally, it defines the valid, correct way to inculcate new members. Phillips (1984) added that these products of action may become so typical that they become tacit.

Numerous authors argue about the value of understanding culture. Problems cited include accurate definition of culture, determining the appropriate dimensions of culture, homogeneity versus heterogeneity, and difficulties with measurement. In spite of all this, viewing organizations as culture has stood the tests of time and become part of the vocabulary of organizations (Meyerson, 1991). This view of organizations is promising in that it is neither an oversocialized nor an undersocialized view (Clegg, 1990). The study of organizational culture makes sense of organizations' experiences and behaviors, various norms of action can be compiled, and organizational understanding and new learning can result (Bolman & Deal, 1991). Culture is probably something an organization *has* and *is* despite rhetoric that argues otherwise.

Leadership in Organizations

In the modern age, theorists, authors, and practitioners alike have sought a connection between leadership and organization. Leadership is often confused with management in this regard. Some authors choose to emphasize similarities, others differences, while still others remain oblivious to these issues (Rost, 1991). Leadership and management are both processes and necessary elements of organizations. In the humanistic frame of reference, the behavior of the leader or manager also becomes a point of relevance. As processes and behaviors that have been discussed over time, however, neither is clearly understood. Mintzberg (in Rost, 1991)) lamented that he and his counterparts have yet to thoroughly understand leadership or to define it adequately. Similarly, most authors and theorists have not been able to succinctly confine leader or manager definitions (Rost, 1991).

However, much has been uncovered. We know a lot about what constitutes leadership and what it isn't. Leadership in the human context is behavioral and situational (Yukl, 1989; Bass & Stogdill, 1990). Common findings are identifiable. Leadership can also be viewed from a functional orientation: as a set of relationships, as influence, as change, as motivation, as communication, as conflict, or as growth and development (Knezevich, 1989). Likewise, leadership can also be a set of personality traits, a particular formal position, or status. In each regard, leadership has been recognized as an imprecise concept. It can be rooted in values, in action, in power. Above all, it is indeterminate and variable across numerous contexts.

As we continue to attempt to define leadership in this human context, we will undoubtably continue to find leaders who are "all of the above." In this regard, Rost's (1991) definition seems highly appropriate. "Leadership is an influence relationship among leaders and followers who intend real changes that reflect their mutual purposes" (p. 98). But as we look to larger issues in the organization, leadership takes on a greater focus. In this respect, leadership can better be seen from Davis and Davidson's (1991) perspective. "Leadership is defined in terms which relate a vision of the future to strategies for achieving it, which are capable of coopting support, compliance, and teamwork in its achievement and serve to motivate and sustain commitment to its purpose" (p. 201). Leadership tomorrow takes on an architectural focus (Beckett, 1971).

Communication in Organizations

A great portion of our communication takes place in organizations, and as Etzioni (1964) said, we spend a great deal of time in different kinds of organizations. Monge and Eisenhart (1987) cited three frames of reference

that enable us to conveniently view organizations and communication. In the traditional era, the positional frame of reference viewed communication up, down, and laterally through set positions in the bureaucratic hierarchy. In a more modern era, the relational frame sees communication as occurring naturally among relationships between participants. The organization is shaped and given meaning through these interactions. In another view, the cultural frame stresses the importance of stories, rituals, and work among its members and determines from these how the organization communicates. The real organization in this sense emerges from daily actions of members in their work.

Littlejohn (1989) used the network metaphor to outline how these three different frames of reference enable understanding about organizational communication. In combination with information theory, Littlejohn feels that theorists are able to understand how individual, dyadic, group, and organizational networks function. In the classical organization, management uses formal networks to achieve the purpose of the organization. Power, authority, and legitimacy govern communication in bureaucratic organizations. Informal communication networks flourish in classical organizations as members lower in the hierarchy attempt to gain their own status and power.

Likert's (1987) Four Systems organizational concept transcends both the positional and relational frames. In the Four Systems approach, an organization functions along four continuums: exploitative-authoritative, benevolent-authoritative, consultative, and participative. Likert treats communication in organizations as one of many variables. In essence, the more authoritative an organization, the less individual and group loyalty there is to management and the less motivation toward organizational purpose is realized. Conversely, the more participative the organization, the more individuals and groups provide loyalty, performance, and mutual support to the organization. Overall, exploitative systems seem to produce more negative consequences than participative systems. Tompkins and Cheney (1985) outlined a similar model in their theory of organizational identification. Organizations employ simple control, technological control, bureaucratic control, and concertive control to realize productivity and achieve organizational purpose.

Most recently, communication has been conceptualized through relational and cultural frames. The importance of lines of communication has been set aside as theorists study emergent patterns and interactions among organizational members and how persons really act in organizations. In the traditional perspective on organizations, these frames of reference are an inappropriate parameter with which to study, as the dynamics of ongoing behavior depends on how they are organized. In the social realm peoples' activities create organizations (Weick, 1969). Any act is communication. Interaction serves to develop common meaning among individuals and others in the organization. Uncertainty among members is thus reduced in both internal and external relations through enactment, selection, and retention. Continuous individual, group, or organizational behavior and choice cycles result (Weick, 1969). The theory of structuration (Poole & McPhee, 1983) is similar to Weick's theory of organizing. Organizational structure is created at centers of structuration, implemented into formal codes, and enacted (termed *reception*) in organizational decisions. Organizational climate, an intersubjective phenomenon, arises from the structuration process through member interaction and results in organizational outcomes.

In each theory discussed above, communication develops into organizational networks. The social, structural, and functional channels are the essence of communication in organizations.

Size, Structure, and Complexity in Organizations

The implications of size, structure, and complexity in organizations was best addressed by Mintzberg (1983, 1989). In his detailed analysis of design in organizations, Mintzberg identified five general structural configurations. The key differentiating feature in the design occurs as the result of some predominant part in each. In the simple structure the upper echelon predominates and pulls the organization to centralize utilizing direct supervision. In the machine bureaucracy the technostructure predominates and causes standardization of work processes. In the professional bureaucracy the "operating core" rules and causes the organization to professionalize through standardization of skills. In the divisionalized form the "middle line" dominates by coordinating and standardizing outputs. Finally, the adhocracy coordinates the "support staff" and causes mutual adjustment in the organization.

The structure of the entrepreneurial organization (a simple structure) is characterized by little or no staff, a loose division of labor, and a small hierarchy. As its size is small, complexity also tends to be negligible. As an organization, the entrepreneurial firm tends to be informal, flexible, responsive, and operates with a sense of distinct purpose. Activities generally revolve around the owner/chief executive. As simple organizations mature, they tend to work toward the machine bureaucracy or professional bureaucracy. In the machine bureaucracy, formal procedures, specialization, differentiation, and extreme hierarchy are common. A powerful support staff and middle management are needed for regulation control complexity through standardization of the work. The organization is stable, consistent, and efficient in relatively stable environments. In unstable environments it tends toward inflexibility and can then only change through long drawn-out planning processes. As the size of the organization increases, the machine bureaucracy tends to become more and more controlled to the point of redundancy. Decentralization usually occurs as the organization develops into a divisionalized form. Loosely coupled, autonomous divisions are subjected to performance controls in the form of standardized output, as directed from a central or corporate headquarters. This form is generally also the largest and most mature of the Mintzberg configurations.

The professional bureaucracy is a decentralized form of machine bureaucracy. The organization is characterized by autonomous and democratic professional work groups, typically subject to controls of a profession. A large support staff functions as an administrative arm for the professional core. Complexity becomes extreme in this organization because various autonomous individuals or groups share allegiances to the organization and to a professional external group. As size increases, the professional bureaucracy becomes more and more difficult to operate.

Finally, Mintzberg postulates an adhocracy, a fluid, organic, and selectively decentralized organization. As the organization is characterized by autonomy and democracy, it is also the most innovative of the Mintzberg structures. Experts in teams typically work in highly dynamic and complex environments to carry out demanding and rapidly changing requirements. The organization appears to thrive on complexity. Size is a detriment.

In the recent past, Mintzberg (1989) added a sixth structure, the missionary organization. The organization is characterized by a rich system of values and beliefs, and a strong sense of mission. This organization thrives due to standardization of norms, reinforced by selection, socialization, and indoctrination. These organizations are typically highly decentralized and complex as they enact complicated norms steeped in ideology.

In thinking about organization, authors and theorists have had to recapitulate regularly. For example, Blau (1977) defined structure as " . . . the distribution, along various lines, of people among social position that influence role relations among these people" (p. 12). In this example, structure implies a division of labor, position, rules, and behavior. Structure uses power to achieve results. These organizations attempt to maintain a status quo. But as authors and theorists begin thinking beyond Weberian and, more recently, Japanese examples, they note that change may be the essence of organizations today. Thus understanding how structure, size, and complexity affect organizations has been critical in the past, but today our focus must include how organizations change.

Change in Organizations

Over time organizations of all styles begin, mature, and decline. The life cycle of organizations is thus considered through various maturity-decline and change models. In general, organizations spend a great deal of time in periods of stability punctuated by brief transition periods. Ecologists term this phenomenon *punctuated equilibrium*. Others call it *metamorphosis* or *dynamic equilibrium* (Starbach, 1981; Schön, 1987). These life cycle models usually address formation, development, maturity, and decline. Miles and Snow (in Pugh & Hickson, 1989) see an entrepreneurial, administrative, and engineering problem. Hannan and Freeman (Pugh & Hickson, 1989) see a founding and disbanding sequence. Faced with crisis, organizations either tend to move to a next stage of development or develop renewal or revitalization mechanisms. Depending on internal and external environmental factors, organizations may choose strategies of renewal or revitalization. In other contexts, organizations may adopt a particular model of change based on a shift in strategic alignment.

Lewin's (1951) three-stage model of unfreezing, change, and refreezing helps to explain these shifts in vision. Unfreezing involves overcoming natural defense mechanisms or discontinuities by scanning the environment for available change parameters. Change then demands creating a willingness to step into a new environment, a shift of mindsets. Refreezing involves vigorous pursuit of the new vision. In this process, people shed old frameworks and understand and implement new ones. In small, simple firms, this can be a relatively easy task, but as organizational size increases the change process becomes exponentially more difficult to invoke and keep on track.

Empirically based change strategies are structured on a systems management perspective. Setting new goals, monitoring change, and holding individuals accountable reflect a typical methodology. From the organizational development perspective, empirically based change seeks to focus on individual motivations for change. From a power perspective, empirically based change seeks to reduce conflict, bargain, and negotiate preference. In contrast, theory-based change seeks to derive change in other ways. The innovation management model focuses on developing factors that improve the probability of successful implementation. The social or cultural model focuses change directly at values held in the organization's domain and seeks change through development of different value sets (Schein, 1985). The organizational learning model focuses change on learning how to learn. Dysfunction and defensiveness are replaced by creating new ways of thinking about future states (Argyris, Putnam, & Smith, 1985). Last, the constructionalist model emphasizes social meaning. Change involves creating and realizing new behaviors, symbols, and activities (Deal & Kennedy, 1982).

In any of these models, the various factors that affect the success of organizational change must be considered. Centrality (core competence) emphasizes change that is closely tied to organizational core activities and perceived as significant. Additionally, as the scope and complexity of change lengthens, consideration must be given to a greater period of unfreezing. Change programs must also consider where the change impetus originates from, as improper pressure from the wrong constituencies can have negative effects. Organizational culture also presents roadblocks to change programs. While some tension is conducive to thoroughness and quality, organizational culture often presents formidable negative pressure. The degree of structural change is also important as change could also be viewed as just piling on more with less available resources. Successful change also involves thinking externally. Very often, crisis creates more willingness to change, but also greater scope. Recognizing the variety of external stakeholders often establishes a more effective and positive change environment. Consideration of broader social values also can bring positive results. While there is no universal change model or mechanism, these considerations offer a more powerful chance for change mechanisms to work.

At this point premodern and modern examples of organizations have been shown across the industrial age and through the systems movement, cultural manifestations, and organizational development. In the following section, modern organizations will be inspected more thoroughly. Issues that are particularly problematic to education will be highlighted. Finally, several new conceptions of organizations will be developed and discussed. These new constructions will again be explored from an educational perspective.

Early in this chapter, organizations were investigated from traditional perspectives. In the following section, the reader will be asked to think about organizations metaphorically. This approach will require readers to remain open and flexible, reserve judgment, and eventually develop a more thorough appreciation and detailed comprehension. The use of metaphor calls for a different way of thinking and seeing organizations. Since organizations are complex and paradoxical, and no one viewpoint is absolutely relevant, metaphors can allow us to see differences not otherwise visible.

Images of Organizations

Morgan (1986) and others (Clegg, 1990; Bergquist, 1993) highlighted the use of metaphor to comprehend organizations and many of their assertions will be discussed. Whether an "iron cage," "machine," "brain," or "turbulence," organizations today are stylized in our thinking by metaphor.

THE MACHINE

Classical management theory emphasized broad-based planning, coordinating, controlling, directing, and organizing (Fayol, 1949; Weber, 1947). Organizations whose major features resemble descriptions from the classical era abound, from the moderately large manufacturing firms or service firms to nearly every educational institution. As the machine metaphor implies, these organizations largely resemble the machine: efficient, hierarchial, highly centralized, planning oriented, highly

regulated, highly organized, and tightly controlled (Mintzberg, 1983, 1989). Productivity is, to a large degree, the most vital measure of success and effectiveness. Also, these organizations are deterministic, as demonstrated by the development of simple schedules or plans to larger, more encompassing strategic plans (Mintzberg & Quinn, 1989). Machine organizations move slowly and deliberately.

Machine organizations are highly rational. Tasks are straightforward and precision is usually at a premium. These organizations create consistency and maintain stable environments. They are mass-production oriented. Differentiation of function and specialization of task are primal. There are few strong contemporary counterparts to the machine organization as they existed in times past. As these organizations continued to flourish, limitations both internally and externally began to detract from their functioning. Political conflict between functions occurred. Power was sought to control resources, and informal mechanism developed whereby those lower in the hierarchy or with less power could also share in the power. In the machine organization, communication was straightforward or top down. Communication also tended to be slow as levels of hierarchy needed to be traversed for decisionmaking and problem solving to occur. Most important, the machine organization positioned the human component at two very different extremes. Management controlled and subordinates were controlled.

Early management theorists had somehow managed to believe they had discovered "the one best way," *the* principle of organizations (Morgan, 1986). However, many, if not all, of these theorists' "machine" principles form the basis of organizational problems. Understanding organizations from a rational or technical point of view underscores the lack of attention to human components. It also creates organizations that adapt to changing environments slowly, are often mindless and unquestioning, and place organizational and other goals at a premium at the expense of human concerns. In many instances, the humans in the machine organization became complacent, unmotivated, and lost their commitment.

But even more important, a thorough understanding of the writings of classical theorists is also problematic. For example, Clegg (1990) believes that Weberian beliefs run counter to the "efficiency" developments common in most organizations today. A cornerstone of Weber's work (1947, 1961) is not efficiency, but inefficiency (Therborn, 1976; Albrow, 1970). This is readily evident in bureaucratic organizations as inefficiency has prevailed in organization today. Or consider Taylor's (1947) development of efficiency in organizational settings. In Taylor's four underlying principles of management, several elements are directed at the human component of organizations: high reward for completion of work established through scientific task analysis, selection and development of the worker, and the constant and intimate cooperation between worker and management (Pugh & Hickson, 1989). Emery and Trist (1969) substantiated each of these Taylorisms. Clearly, portions of the "machine" organization have not been followed as strictly as others. Whether market forces, cultural distinctions, or other variables are at work here, the "machine" isn't the exact "machine" many envisioned. As Morgan (1986) illustrated, perhaps instrumental rationality, "fitting people and jobs together in a fixed design" (p. 37) needs to allow for substantial rationality, allowing for more reflection and self-organizing. It is interesting to note here that the lack of reflection and self-organizing is negated by the careerism focus in the machine organization as individuals compete within a closed system. Political issues abound and results often are seen which do not look anything like the originally

intended organizational purpose. In the end the organization may work at divergent purposes, in direct opposition to its organizational goals.

THE ORGANISM

The study of organizations as open systems has brought new light to a variety of issues compounded during the "machine" age. Bertalanffy (1968), the lead theorist and researcher of the systems movement, felt that viewing parts of an organization does not allow us to gain a holistic understanding of that organization. Inquiry into separate functions of an organization cannot realize patterns of interactions, interdependence, or the integration that occurs in the whole of the organization. Organizational elements are not independent but interdependent as they interact within the organization and with various boundary environments. As with all other living things, constant interaction, interdependence, and integration occurs. General Systems Theory attempts to explore organizations and their environments to seek explanations that can enhance understanding of the organization.

This image of organization has led to discounting many, if not most, of the ill effects prevalent in the "machine" image. The movement has largely been maintained in the human resources and organizational development perspectives. In the systems movement manifestations, it has been labeled an "it depends" movement." Regardless of one's philosophical beliefs, however, key organic ingredients do provide a different way of thinking about organizations.

In the organic view, the interaction of subsystems in an organization takes on vital importance. This process largely explores "communication" links between and within these subsystems and the system environment. The input-throughput-output-feedback model provides the methodology. As a system, an organization is internally connected to its environment through the importation of resources. These resources can be from internal feedback mechanisms or from the larger suprasystem. Each external source, whether it be customers, clients, the community, or the government, has a dramatic bearing on the organization. As the organization realizes and utilizes its true input resources, fundamental change takes place within the organization. No longer can separate functional units act without external consideration as well.

Lawrence and Lorsch (1986) explained that new markets, new technology, and differing societal expectations all impact organizational functioning. Organizations in the "machine" tradition were conceived largely as closed systems. Eventually they would degenerate and die out. The population ecology and growth-maturity-decline models explore these closed systems.

Equally vital, organizations in response to their new openness must be able to adapt internally. Flexible structure, responsive distribution, self-renewal and revitalization, and cooperation and collaboration are key components of these newer forms. In this fashion, organizations are more likely to be able to respond to change. As a consequence of this internal and external responsiveness, the organization's outputs also change. Customers, clients, and community partners respond to new capabilities within the organization.

The organization also measures this output differently than before, not simply from the production line or through cost/revenue parameters, but through quality, effectiveness, and satisfaction measures. These new measures become part of the organization's feedback systems in the form of new internal inputs. Self-renewal becomes consistent and constant. So, in this new organic organization, the questions become what technology is being used, what kind of people are needed, what is the culture of the organization, and

how do management philosophies relate to this new configuration (Morgan, 1986). Answers to these questions are the strengths found in the organic organization: openness, a process orientation, needs satisfaction, interactiveness, and a wide range of options both internally and strategically.

A key limitation of this metaphor is its reliance on adaptation. Many organisms in real life can make choices, but this organic model of organizations tends to create a marginal view whereby organizations can only hope to adapt to the environment. This may undermine the ability of the organization to control or change its own destiny. Also, organizations have historically been incapable of promoting harmony within. While some organizations have created harmonious interaction, others still cannot manage the levels of interaction necessary. Many organizations are still too "tall." Organizational adaptation may thus not be a possibility for many as long as their change mechanisms remain incremental.

THE BRAIN

Another view of organizations is to see them as models of the brain. In actual practice there are few organizations that have the capacity to become systemic. In these organizations the requisite task is the organization's ability to foster self-renewal and self-organization (Morgan, 1986). These models stem from numerous authors (Argyris et al., 1985; Senge, 1990; Weick, 1969). In contrast to the "machine" and "organic" views, this image implies almost complete change in the conception of the organization. The organization increases variety through a redundancy of function instead of a redundancy of parts. In this new part-whole schema, the whole is greater than the sum of its parts. For example, as is true of the brain, each activity in the organization is created in a separate part. This reduces the direct need for redundancy of parts in the organization. Secondly, as opposed to the "machine," this new image through redundancy in function encourages all members of the organization to think in congruent terms. The "machine" organization restricts thinking in this regard as political systems develop to control. As a result, boundaries internally and externally become more difficult to navigate. The "brain" organization encourages decentralization in structure, and, at the same time increases levels of activity among various agents in a decentralized core. Boundaries between activities and between the organization and the environment become permeable. Thirdly, whereas the "machine" organization develops structure to maintain accountability, rewards the accountable, and punishes the unaccountable, the "brain" image of organizations reduces and manages defensive structures, and, as a result, approaches new activity from a learning to learn emphasis. The "brain" organization explores differences in individual and organizational theories of action and exposed theories (Argyris et al., 1985). As a result, the organization seeks to face uncertain conditions from a whole organization perspective. The organization self-renews and self-organizes. In the long term, problems and decisions are brought to the forefront of organizational analysis rather than hiding issues, or worse, being unaware of them.

Significant differences also occur between this "brain" image and the "organic" image. More accurately, the "brain" image more fully realizes implications of General Systems Theory. While the manifestations of the "organic" organization have gravitated toward systematic implementation in organizations (modelling), "brain" organizations are more systemic (fluid). The redundancy in function enables self-renewal and self-organization fed by requisite variety and enabled by minimal specification (Morgan, 1986). While the "organic" form adapts, this newer form learns to learn.

While the "organic" form encourages openness, this form encourages openness coupled with reflectivity. As the "organic" form maintains structural foundations iterated in the input-output model, this form creates its own organization in an "on the spot" fashion. The organization is configured to action. The organization utilizes the full realm of theory, praxis, and practice in recognition of its norms and values and at the same time questions these symbols to generate further learning (Hodgkinson, 1991). In this sense, the "brain" image encourages inquiry *and* criticism. A broader range of unit and strategic goals is explored, understood, and acted upon. From this systemic format new attitudes and values emerge: activeness over reactiveness, autonomy over dependence, flexibility over rigidity, collaboration over competition, openness or closeness, and democratic versus authoritative. The "brain" form of organization is extremely difficult to imagine in practice. The questions become how to create this form, and how can we penetrate those older-strategic paradigms? These are difficult questions to answer. More problematic than "how?" is the question "what's next?" This will be explored in the final chapter of this book.

Political Systems and Power

In our society numerous organizational forms, each unique, have emerged. Each form must exist in a plethora of pluralistic forces. In one instance, organizations represent the freedom of the individual, in the next equality, in another sense collaboration, or in another competition. Organizations are constantly pulled by these contending concepts, and typically yield in a singular direction. As our organizations adapt to a single purpose, power molds a new political system. New images of organization then form: organizations as good management, as quality or excellence, as service, or as information. These new images affect organizational action in various ways depending on the current political emphasis in the organization. In a structural sense, organization becomes autocracy: we do it the way we're supposed to; or bureaucracy, we do it this way; or technocracy, we do it the best way; or democracy, we do it the way *we* decide. Analyzing its interests, the organization senses and creates an image of itself and proceeds to enlarge and protect its environment. Thus, we can observe how various earlier organizational paradigms can come into existence: the economic focus, the human relations focus, or the organizational development focus. We can also see society viewing its own afflictions more clearly.

This metaphor demonstrates how conflict arises and how organizations as political systems deal with those conflicts. Sources of power are formed, used, and endowed status. In the work unit and functional divisions, these power sources create, sustain, and support values and interests. They become the latest agenda. As the organization adopts these agendas the organization transforms itself to this new value-interest system. Organizational hierarchy breeds formation of new agendas. As career-focused individuals become more specialized, the organization loses its ability to function as careerists override new interests in favor of their own developed specialties. The organization tends toward superficiality as it loses its ability to know real necessities. Various power sources continue to act out their own agendas in lieu of pursuing substantive work. Consensus development abounds as individual sources seek support and favor for their interests (Bergquist, 1993). In this light, political forces can become the ideology of organization. In the end, understanding the "political" image

of organizations allows us to understand the real limits that exist in the socio-political organization.

Organizations as Culture

While the "political" metaphor is readily observable in organizations, many have disdain for truly political organizations. The metaphor of organizations as "culture," on the other hand, offers an ideological view of the organization. As the organization's values and interests become the norm, they become symbols, rituals, meanings, and interpretations that openly or tacitly govern how the organization interacts internally and externally. No longer is the organization a collection of individuals or agendas but an interdependent collection of shared meanings and circumstances. For example, American culture is one of individualism and separateness while the Japanese traditional culture is embodied in self-respect through service to a larger system. In an individualist culture, organizations reward individuals for "being first." In Japanese culture, the organization seeks commitment and loyalty to the collective.

Perhaps the greatest reason for studying organizational culture is that such an approach allows us to observe the organization as it truly exists. The integration, fragmentation, and differentiation perspectives are all available to the researcher/observer. This approach offers us a crucial illustration of the organization's "ethos," its historical purpose, power shaping, motivations, beliefs, informal settings, symbolic expression, visual data, and more. Culture is a part of the organization, and it is the organization. It resides in various subcultures of the organization whether they be related by gender or occupation or by political, economic, or aesthetic interests. Culture occurs as the human component objectifies reality. These norms, rituals, or symbols are open to scrutiny using various methods of inquiry (Jermier, 1991).

Garfenckel (1967) supported the enactment scenario as an explanation of culture. The questions become what are the shared schemes, where do they come from, and how are they created, communicated, and sustained? Seeking answers to these questions becomes the central task of analysis for the organizational practitioner. The process involves identification of the array of mundane and vivid aspects of the reality construction process (Morgan, 1986). Organizational structure, rules, policies, goals, measures, and job descriptions identify the organizations' shared frames of reference. Upon inspection of the varied and total group of perspectives, practitioners see the "language" of the organization and its derived meanings. New relationships, processes, and functions emerge as the organization communicates with itself. This view is often surprising as too few organizations are really introspective in this fashion.

Organizations as Psychic Prisons

We have Kuhn (1970) to thank for creating broad acceptance of the metaphor "paradigm" and Barker (1992) to thank for stretching its usage. Morgan (1986) applied the metaphor to organizations. People, even organizations, may become caged by unconscious images, ideas, thoughts, and actions. Examples of this thinking are predominant. Our educational program is so sound that complacency sets in as we come to rely on success factor after success factor; school systems hire administrative specialists to create curriculum rather than face the uncertain probability that

those "closest to the action" may know best what and how to teach. Rather than take a risk we create slack, or we politely, unquestioningly nod our heads in agreement rather than state that we need to explore other venues. These unconscious cognitive traps, once realized, can help us observe and predict the ways we see (culture), but they can also create blindness and eliminate other views. How long has it taken organizational America to react to the expectations of consumers, or for that matter, quality, or the global organizational environment of today?

Understanding our psychic prisons, more importantly, allows us to examine how entrenched our thinking about organizations has become. Have we really explored the complications of regulation of the human component? Why do we continually adopt the belief that we are often inhuman by varying degrees, but then fail to identify action orientations that can produce understanding and change? Have we fully explored our rationale for planning? Doesn't planning, at the same time, set the future and settle it into a possibly inappropriate future? Once we define culture, both its known and hidden elements, what do we do with that knowledge? Are we so locked into "one way" that we cannot fathom diversity, gender difference, or the disabled? Must we constantly then rely on a "ruling class" to pronounce acceptable action, and then to react against those same authority figures again?

Instances of side effects of our prisons can be noted across all organizations' functioning. Jacques (1955) showed how in labor management relations we project negative images of those with whom we differ. Chatov (1981) discussed the same phenomenon in relations between government and business. Zalesznik (1970) demonstrated how leaders are inclined to divide and conquer as a result of their inability to build coalitions. As Bion (1959) suggested, organizations regress to previously learned patterns of behavior to protect themselves. That is, they retreat into their psychic prisons.

Determining how organizations and their members explore psychic prisons is a critical aspect of organizational self-renewal. Organizations that study these human patterns and relationships can realize the full extent of ethical behavior, the critical role that power relations play, the barriers to change, and the overrationalization of our actions. While exploring our psychic prisons may conjure up instances of "organization man," it is not just another approach to controlling organizational functioning. Bringing the "unconscious organization" to the surface can help us further understand our organizations and the limits they impose.

Mirrors of Organizations

Organizations today are combinations of elements developed in the past and new images. "In a typical contemporary organization, one will now find a variety of different (and often contradictory) processes and functions as well as diverse forms and structures of premodern, modern, and postmodern origins, some of which are temporary and others permanent" (Bergquist, 1993, p. 177). Over the past several decades, writers have attempted to describe this changing scene: Kanter's (1985) entry into the postentrepreneurial age, O'Toole's (1985) vanguard organization, Deming's (1986) quality revolution, Peters' (1992) liberated-disorganized organization, and Clegg's (1990) de-differentiated organization. Mintzberg (1989) labeled this a trip from convergence, to congruence, to configuration, to contradiction, and to creation. His "life cycle" like Bergquist's makes the voyage from pre- to postmodern. Organizational thinking dominated by the machine image, creating its rationality through its own irrationality, reduces human systems to imper-

sonal skills and manifests its destruction through its politicization. Clark and Astuto (1991) summarized Weick's (1985) earlier work by stating that, in organizations:

1. There is less rationality than meets the eye.
2. There is less simplicity than meets the eye.
3. There is less sequentiality and coupling than meets the eye.
4. There is less causality than meets the eye.
5. There is less orderliness than meets the eye.
6. There is less goal-directed individual behavior than meets the eye.
7. There is less preference-directed individual behavior than meets the eye.
8. There is less planned change and predictability than meets the eye.
9. There is less hierarchy than meets the eye. (In Clark & Astuto, 1991, p. 960)

As a consequence, organizational thought may need new life, a generation of broader theoretical perspectives, an acceptance of equifinality and variety, and new tools for inquiry. In this sense, Bergquist (1993) suggested that the future holds many new organizational hybrids.

Mirrors of Education as Organizations

Historically, schools as organizations have been nearly perfect portraits of larger organizations in industrialized society. The influence of scientific management is prevalent throughout all schools and school systems (Owen, 1987). Traces of Taylor, Fayol, Weber, and others are readily perceptible in school organizations. School districts mandate efficiency through standardization of work processes, audit school adherence with control and measurement mechanisms, and certify minimum proficiency of the products. After the 1980 decade of "commissions" that demonstrated repeated and widespread evidence of schools' inadequacies, much more reflection may be required before we fundamentally understand the problems in schools. In too many cases, repeated calls for renewal and revitalization were accomplished by patching the system. Similarly, as the human relations movement garnered attention for the development and use of more favorable human resource models, the revitalization too often became still another set of poorly conceived or enacted sets of one-dimensional spot solutions.

As school achievement and performance ratings continued to decline over the past three decades, there were continued calls for new criteria for excellence: schools need good management, leaders, not just administrators, and schools need to understand and confront their cultures. Some claim that schools need to create their own distinctiveness as they decouple from mainstream organizational thought and become organized anarchies (Cohen, March, & Olsen, 1972). In this context, schools' purposes and definitions become fleeting, fuzzy, even fluid. Or they become reconstituted elements of more highly refined leadership studies, strengthening their core competencies and devising better communication mechanisms. For others, schools are viewed as systems in an effort to capture elements of the systems movement. The administrator or the supervisor at the school level is understood to be an integrative element to upper management, the community, teachers, staff, and students. Getzel and Guba (1957) take the social behavioral view of education, proposing that the whole social system of education comprised of the school, roles and expectations of various members and various individual personalities and needs interacts with tools, techniques,

and curriculum in a socio-technical arrangement, not unlike what Emery and Trist (1969) posited at the Travistock Institute. During this period schools were seen as dynamic organisms existing within numerous contexts.

Intertwined with the evolution of education as organization are other integrating elements. Hodgkinson (1991) outlined the historical purpose of schools from Greek liberal educational foundations to the Roman tradition of administration and governance, to religious and moral reflections of the Protestant ethic. Additionally, he cited the effects of the agrarian and industrialized eras that gave rise to mass education as it generally exists today. Our democratic system of education exists largely to protect the democratic rights of its citizens. As the scientific era spawns productive efficiency, schools find themselves engaged in creating social efficiency (Kowalski & Reitzug, 1993). Schools as well as industries devise methods to control, coordinate, plan, direct, and organize themselves; hence, administration continues its development around scientific and human resource principles. The parade of leadership and management literature crossed boundaries easily as education mirrored industry.

Sergiovanni and Moore (1989) borrowed Burn's 1981 transactional and transformational leadership viewpoints. Leaders in a traditional sense manage the consequences of an exchange process and assure that behaviors of various subordinate actors remain within established norms. In contrast, the transformational leader manages more intrinsic, moral consequences, building shared commitment, distributing and facilitating power, building the capacity in other members, and instigating awareness of self in order to crystalize a more thorough commitment to responsibility and accountability.

In education, teaching professionals mediate conflicting demands across the whole school environment (Sergiovanni & Moore, 1989). While teachers aspire to maintain their own professional responsibilities, the school and school administration ask them to work in a factory environment. The professional role is difficult to maintain in this situation and gives rise to the "informal organization." The autonomous teacher now lives, on one hand, profoundly tied to practice and expertise taught in a profession, and, on the other hand, tied to the realities of a bureaucratic school environment. But success in this political environment is hard to guarantee and requires that leaders and professionals collaborate to tap the strengths evident in both the informal and formal environment.

In the transitional periods of the last several decades schools have functioned as rational-objective organizations. They examine their training methodologies, strategies for change, and financial controls, and model new curriculums. Structure and audit remain, but frontline teacher and student expectations are often voiced but not heard. Often empirical reviews present new personnel practices for consideration. But these reviews crumble when confronted with the realities of the school's political structure. Although these transitional periods tout change, new leadership, or revised culture, in practice, they do not have a broad, long-lasting impact. Even with the realization that schools are multicultural, followed by demand for appropriate organizational changes, schools still found themselves mired in the traditional rational-objective structure. School culture and climate are expressed as an environment of learning, but also as restricted, confining, objective-laden, and out of touch with current teacher, student, and societal needs. Educational improvement requires more than a change of pencils and papers, but direct change in patterns of human interdependencies, collaboration, and commitment (Schmuck & Runkel, 1985).

In the true transformational sense, schools need to be viewed as living and dynamic. Schools can be natural environments that

demonstrate all desirable traits; social justice, freedom, responsibility, and maturing. As the Rand Corporation finds, and as we've alluded to in previous sections, self-renewal may best be a process of enactment and alignment and more effectively accomplished at the local level (the school or school district). Learning to cope with crisis over the longer term results in a school or school system that shows steady progress and achievement. But those who continually manage crisis only address symptoms (Miles, 1967; Senge, 1990). Through organizational development formulas schools can change if they have direction, show progress, and all players become involved. Administration must learn to command and control less and facilitate and encourage participation more (Hoy & Miskel, 1987). Leadership is more than just management or administration. Leaders in schools today must possess a clear sense of the true and evolving purpose(s) of education and, equally evident, its ambiguities.

Portraits of Contemporary Schooling

Restructuring has become a common theme in American education. The term *restructuring* now emerges any time a discussion of school reform arises (Olsen, 1988). As a label for new strategies, the term has become overused to the extent that we no longer have a clear understanding of its relevance.

Tyack (1990) believes that the term has become synonymous with choice, teacher professionalization, empowerment, decentralization, school site management, parental involvement, national curriculum standards, and a host of other change mechanisms. Chubb and Moe (1990) think similarly. They equate restructuring to the dysfunction of bureaucracy and the value of autonomy. To perceive the truth, long-term trends must be distinguished from the trendy. What is the true story? Perhaps a brief historic review can help us understand the school as an organization in this discussion.

In earlier parts of the twentieth century, school organization in terms of leadership had become a politicized issue. During the rural and growing urban periods, schools were decentralized as fears of highly centralized government control were widespread. In rural communities trustees, parents, and teachers were deeply involved in a localized structure. In contrast, urban school systems were more highly centralized and controlled. They were the early counterparts of the extreme centralization seen today. A group of highly professional and trained administrators, then called "administrative progressives," advocated innovative mechanisms to derive greater efficiency, equity, accountability, and expertise from the schools (Tyack, 1990).

Reorganization took many forms: centralizing districts to include the rural areas, increasing size and scope of district administration, huge staff agencies, and decreasing teacher autonomy. Schools were being driven by a new set of scientific management and educational science principles, perhaps a new ideology. Consolidation occurred from the district through the state and to the federal government. Schools, school districts, and state agencies became models of structure and process. They collected enormous amounts of data to justify their purposes and rationale. Superintendents became power figures, enrollments grew, curriculum expanded, and attempts to reduce costs per individual received constant attention.

During the equality reform period in the mid-twentieth century, numerous societal pressures focused on schools and schooling practices. Reformers demanded greater equality for all segments of society. There were calls for more current and applicable curriculum, more teacher responsibility, more equitable funding, and more substantive evalua-

tion of product. In retrospect, Meyer (1980) labelled the era "fragmented centralization" as laissez-faire administrators faced contradictory requirements. More "calculative management" resulted as administration attitudes toward schools as school organizations fueled more rationalization.

Many recent reports have depicted a nationwide crisis in education. Back to basics school movements ensued. Accountability in teaching was measured in terms of testing results in comparisons across districts, states, nationally, and internationally. The top-down approach beginning at the state level ruled. Learning was measured by "scores." Local mandates produced even more centralization in school districts. Greater bureaucracy in the divisionalized organizational form intensified and schools refocused on criteria for excellence.

Schools and school districts are by and large mirrors of the classical "machine" style of organization and locked firmly in the "iron cage" (Morgan, 1986; Clegg, 1990). What exactly does society find wrong with schools today? As the 23rd Annual Gallup Poll/Phi Delta Kappan Poll (Elam, 1991) demonstrated, the variety of issues is extensive. Americans want more report cards from schools. They want accountability. They want more education as shown by longer school years. They want education to begin at an earlier age. They generally want more productivity. They want to choose productive schools for their children. They want higher quality and more decentralized control. They want equality and an equitable use of resources, and they want schools and school systems to get in touch with current realities. While this list may appear incomplete to some, one can infer that Americans are broadly dissatisfied with teachers, principals, administration, schools, school districts, and state and federal controls.

Today the educational "machines" grind on. Our educational system is in need of major overhaul. Problems endemic to the bureaucratic organization are reflected in our schools and school systems. The professional bureaucracy (a school), the machine bureaucracy (a larger school), and the divisionalized configuration (a school district) are all exact replicas of bureaucracy in existence across the country (Mintzberg, 1989). While it is possible to argue about distinctions between what schools do and how they do it in comparison to business bureaucracies, these issues are largely irrelevant. This distinction only looks at symptoms.

In contrast, the organization of schools and schooling today should be largely organic. But upon closer inspection, we find a mixture of organic and bureaucratic school forms. Magnet schools are a good example of this blending (*US News and World Report*, 1991). Conceived during the 1980s, these "elite public schools" have achieved dramatic results. As schools of excellence, they embody significant educational reforms. Magnet schools thrive on interactiveness and interdependence, and integrate much of the best that is known about educational practice. They are generally intimate learning environments emphasizing personal contact, teacher designed and controlled, interactive with numerous partners in the community, and regionally, small in size, and have clear purpose. However, they also can resemble the bureaucratic environment of the past and suffer from similar consequences already discussed. Public reaction has been illustrative of the dissent in the magnet environment raising questions about equity, selection issues, huge costs, and funding support.

Across some of the largest population centers, such as New York City, the standard "bureaucratic schools" exist next to the magnet schools. For the most part, the magnet schools mirror the realities of quality and excellence. While in the more traditional schools, superintendents and principals struggle with every societal problem, every organizational problem, and every educational practice problem known to man (Tyack, 1990). These traditional schools in New York City, Chicago, and Los Angeles stand in stark contrast to Minnesota's Choice schools or Jefferson High School for Science and Technology, Fairfax, County, Virginia (*US News and World Report*, 1991; Ayers, 1991; Tyack, 1990). Across most traditional measurement categories the differences are significant. But even more curious, these "preferred schools" feel different. The sense that education is ongoing is powerful. In response to the organizational differences between them, understanding the organic nature of education and educational administration could be highly useful. Understanding how an organic school organization works in practice can be very instructive. Organic thinking requires seeing beyond aggregates of inspection, development, and implementation to create useful knowledge. Excellence in education is more than a quality list of issues (Eisner, 1991), more than steps in a total quality focus (Glasser, 1990), more than relating trends and forecasts (Cetron & Gayle, 1990), and more than demonstration of how the best of the best perform (Gatto, 1990). Even the professionalization of schools requires more than better teacher preparation, better follow-up, inservice training, and certification. These are only another instance of laying more golden eggs (Sergiovanni, 1989). Still attached to our previous educational paradigms, we view needed variety as complexity, leadership as management, higher test score results and low costs as efficiency, newness as inappropriate change, and autonomy as loss of control. In actuality these elements are necessary paradoxical components of equifinality, differing ways to arrive at the same goals. Reform in the organic sense demands added variety, creation of more usable products, greater autonomy as a means of control, and structure that reverts to fluid forms. We haven't really *adopted* the organic view in our thinking and action, only *adapted* it as a response to the strength of various existing power and political forces, or learned paradigms.

Future Organizations and Schools of the Future

We must focus our thinking about organizations and schools for tomorrow. In this process, we must consider whether the Newtonian tools and techniques most familiar to us are appropriate or whether the body of developing knowledge centered in quantum science can affect our understanding of organization. Science in any discipline needs to be grounded in the science of the time. Schroedinger's illustration of the cat in the box can help us define the major distinctions between these two thinking styles (Zohar, 1990). The problem is as follows. Place a live cat in a box with solid walls. No one is able to see into the box. A triggering device at some point is set to release, with equal probability, either poison or food. At some point the cat meets its fate and the box is opened to determine what the cat's fate has been. In the Newtonian world, since our organizations are deterministic, we'll looks for facts, variables, and parts in an attempt to be objective, calculative, and find the truth. Our organizations are built on these same premises as we seek solidarity, identity, distinctiveness, singularity, and rational solutions to issues. We'll measure the box, the food, the poison, or seek environmental clues, and hypothesize about everything. As Davies and Brown (1988) said, we have a theory for everything. In the quantum world, however, the problem in the cat story isn't a problem. Before observation, the fate of the cat is only a set of probabilities, only to be decided when we physically open the box. What we see is what we get.

In this exercise the role of the observer is critical. In organizations we confine humans,

students, and others to Schroedinger boxes. Organizations daily make these attempts at objectivity. In the quantum science world, however, objectivity is constructed at the moment of observation. As observers, we may only really be participants in a set of potentials. Herein lies one of the keys to effective quantum thinking about organizations. As participants in today's organizations, we often restrict who gets to "have a say." A senior management official interprets and decides, followed by a reinterpretation by middle management, and then supervisors. But in reality, each member of the organization is part of the potential of the organization. As we restrict who has a say, we lose those potentially critical and important interpretations at the specific moment of observation. Instead, we use the plans, organization, and policy of others. An organization that builds the capacity to utilize all interpretations swims in a sea of rich data which then can be discussed, combined, and built upon. Becoming wiser in this sense and more participative also effects true ownership as the organization builds a capacity to be flexible and responsive to ideas and then promote further action. Participation, ownership, and subjective data enrich relationship construction and further cement ownership.

Exploring further, we find the quantum world in varying degrees all around us. Some continue to try and package these quantum perspectives into the objective world. Key organizational practitioners and theorists, however, are making startling changes across organizations. Leadership study today concentrates on new perspectives: followership, worker empowerment, leader accessibility, and understanding and developing self identity. Motivation studies explore intrinsic factors. Field theory proposes that we may be able to sense influences of employee behavior not as a future desirable state, but as a way of knowing and then building vision. Organizational studies today concentrate on learning as a self-renewal process. In these views we must constantly fight off our attempts at creating just another "cat in the box" scenario. Our preference for orderliness prescribes limits where disorder may be a key configuration device that drives stability.

Weick (1969) suggested an alternative approach to organizational analysis. While planning is important, it must be accompanied by action because it is only through action and implementation that we create the organizational environment. In our strategic planning today, we may be accomplishing the opposite. We may be planning as though we are responding to demands from the environment when we should be, as Weick says, creating an environment where strategy should be "just-in-time . . . supported by more investment in general knowledge, a large skill repertoire, the ability to do quick study, trust in intuitions, and sophistication in cutting losses" (pp. 223, 229). Each of these new thinking methods requires us to view organizational life in new ways: thinking holistically, reducing our reliance on cause and effect scenarios, linking with thinking partners and partnerships, and using intuition more and determinism less. In this sense, images of organization again help us.

Morgan (1986) cited three convincing studies to help us further understand organization. The three studies provide insight from biology to help understand how organizations become self-producing, how circular relations may suggest a new logic for change, and how dialectic relations may help to induce change.

Maturana and Varela (1980) argued that organizations may be like closed, autonomous biologic systems. This view is obviously in contrast to the "organic" view that sees living systems as open and in constant interaction with their environment. In describing organizations as closed and autonomous, the authors aim to illustrate why organizations always attempt to strive toward stability. In this closed system view, internal circular interactions are built, maintained, and renewed in the effort to maintain stability. Any change in the system changes the whole system. Maturana and Varela's view does not represent a closed system view as the organization still interacts with its environment, but does close itself in order to maintain and regulate its functioning. To study the organization, we need to study the nature of these patterns of circularity, how this circularity promotes growth for the system and balances the system. Senge (1990) termed these *circles of causality*. These circular systems usually change from within as well as a consequence of random internal disorder that leads to new patterns of order and change. Prigogine and Stengers (1984) termed this change *dissipative structure*. Some believe human ideas and practices may develop similarly, accomplishing change when "critical mass" is achieved. Thus organizational systems may shape their own futures through self-referential patterns.

This view of organization allows us to see that as individuals and organizations the interaction that takes place doesn't necessarily have to be flavored with competition or struggle. Organizations can thus become more aware as they self-discover and analyze themselves through understanding their own circles of causality (Maruyama, 1963; Senge, 1990). Organizational elements become more aware of their roles and significance to the whole. They learn and develop patterns of change that allow evolution in a larger system through organizational self-reference.

Circles of causality incorporate positive and negative feedback loops that possess the potential to reveal patterns of relations. These patterns of relations not only reveal relationships, but also can be used to leverage change. In the organizational context, we constantly see relationships that, if their patterns are studied, can reveal both the internal and external organizational "ways we do business." The whole dynamic of an organization can be mapped and provide a richer picture of the whole system.

The development of this reasoning style is in direct opposition to the linear, cause and effect manipulation we've grown accustomed to using. Circles of causality allow organizational practitioners to identify principle subsystems or "nests" that unite the whole and then modify existing relations through change. In turn, we learn to appreciate the innate complexity of the organization and likewise learn to change with change. With the additional realization of new societal influences and changes, we can be poised as detectors and avoid those defensive and destructive tendencies that often aren't noted until they are out of control. A frog will attempt to immediately leap from the hand that threatens a boiling inferno, but may not recognize the gradual temperature increase of the comfortable, cool, but increasingly warmer environment until it is too late.

As briefly mentioned earlier, this is not to imply that circles of causality are the only form of interpretation available to us. We have grown accustomed largely to a view of organization that seeks understanding by looking at opposites, through dialectical analysis. Growth and decline, wealth and poverty, and industrialization and unionization are all dialectic viewpoints that often cause us to take sides. By understanding these dialectic forces, we can learn their importance and determine which of the forces are primary causes versus which are superficial and secondary. By combining self-producing systems, circles of causality, and dialectic analysis, we can better understand the logic of change as it unfolds rather than deal with change in our normal piecemeal fashion.

Self-organizing organizations provide a new view. Instead of viewing the organization through its system structures, contemplation of its system dynamics, its form and function, becomes important. We often incorporate understanding the role of negative feedback

as a revitalizing source, but neglect the essence and the importance of positive feedback. Positive feedback can be disruptive if it is taken on blind faith, leading to disorganization and disequilibrium and compromising the integrity of the organization. When thoughtfully considered, positive feedback can be a source of organizational change as well. Positive feedback is merely the variety that already exists in the organization. Disturbance then is a consequence that the organization ultimately responds to, as added neglect builds until the system must respond. In the quantum world this disintegrity system can build a new vital system. Thus disorder creates a new order. Over time, if we view the entropic system long enough, we'd possibly capture its orderly striving to become something new.

Managing this disorder, as De Pree (1987) writes, is in one instance "roving leadership" and points to the emergent qualities of the organization, using its indispensable people who always seem to make a difference. These indispensable members create "fields of action" in the organization in response to necessities generated on the spot. You can sense this in many organizations, a feeling of good customer service pervades the organization, or a feeling that "learning is going on here."

Once educated to sense these fields, we then "manage" too often in the Newtonian sense, devising, controlling, and instructing organizational purpose. Wouldn't creating this vision or purpose based on sensing the fields be more advantageous? Prahalad and Hamel (1990) argued that these "conceptual controls" can be built around an organization's "core competencies," self-organizing and self-renewing systems built around flexibility and sensing change versus rigid structure. The organization in its internal disorganization becomes stable and more capable of interacting with its environment. Embedded within the system are actors with the freedom to act autonomously guided by self-referential, conceptual controls. Freedom and order in partnership achieves greater, near automatic catalytical action. Organizations built in this fashion need absolute availability of information. Control of information short circuits an organization's ability to create this desired state.

Philosophically, we have described a view of organizational thinking for the future. How does this translate to schools for the future? The forecasts, trends, and the historical record are in place, but enactment must begin (Weick, 1969). Virtual schools must be developed along conceptual versus structural lines. Many ideas are already in place and under consideration.

The virtual school is composed of a partnership among the teacher, student, and learning. As the importance of these new participative relationships is realized and the school organization settles into creating its future, the school can draw new and necessary fields of skills and knowledge needed. The ongoing administration of the school system would occur within and be self-regulating. Delivery systems could vary according to the needs and expectations created within the organization. Processes to deliver can expand and incorporate new delivery contexts. Partners outside the school, such as parents, the community, state and federal agencies, become supportive and facilitative.

The virtual description of a school environment postulated by Reigeluth (1987) is given here as an example. Note the highlighted areas that display future organizational contexts.

The new school organization takes on new *form and function*. In this new system, teachers become guides: advisors, sensors, and managers *(self-organization)* versus content disseminators and disciplinarians. New resources including interactive computers, video discs, peer tutors, projects, and learning laboratories are employed to help transfer knowledge to the student *(variety)*. Guides advise, sense, and manage students but addi-

tionally coordinate the efforts of other partners in education *(participation and emergence)*, including inexpensive assistants (apprentice guides, senior citizens, parents and peer tutors), well-designed projects, discussion groups, learning laboratories and resource people *(self-organization and renewal)*. Parents, in particular, help decide instructional goals in conjunction with their guide and the individual student *(participation)*. A student's development (physical, social, moral, psychological, and intellectual) is considered *(core competencies)*. The classroom environment as we know it disappears and a guide and student or small group of students work together to attain agreed upon developmental goals *(creating their own vision)*. A guide takes a student through one of four possible developmental stages (four within K–12), about four years per student per development stage. Developmental stages can be expanded or changed depending on the needs of local constituencies *(equifinality)*. Each student's educational goals are matched to uniquely suited educational resources *(equifinality and variety)* orchestrated by a guide and other assistants.

Guides do not work independently, but are built into a "cluster of guides," three to six guides per cluster *(form)*. The guides participate in decisionmaking and control over a particular cluster *(function)*. In each cluster, all guides are responsible for cluster success with comparable power to meet established goals. A master guide also serves in the cluster to provide instructional "architecture" for the cluster *(purpose)*. Success of a cluster depends on parent and student satisfaction in meeting goals. As clusters succeed, more satisfied parents and students select the particular cluster. Effective clusters survive as a result of financial support from the district based on parental choice *(positive and negative feedback)*.

As goal achievement occurs and students pass through developmental stages, new student goals may become more specific. Learning laboratories *(variety)* provide specialized expertise in traditional, discipline-oriented and cross-disciplinary areas. Students' progress in their clusters advances them to a variety of learning labs. These labs operate independently of clusters, but also cooperatively as the labs' support depends on students being allowed to participate as determined by a student's guide.

In the last analysis, the degree of change in schooling for tomorrow may become an ethical discussion for society itself to engage in *(variety)*, as the realities of new school concepts are far from familiar to the established paradigms that we hold and value today.

■ **CASE STUDY**

School as Organization: The Case of the Future of Education

As changes occur in the global environment, business and society may have to take more responsibility for preparing the future labor force by forming partnerships with educational institutions. Other equally important changes are occurring. For example, the growing numbers of single-parent families will look to schools for more services beginning in pre-kindergarten, and then throughout the reminder of their children's schooling demand even more. Consider some of these facts below:

1. Fewer than 4 percent of families will consist of one spouse working, one at home, and two children.

2. Legal redefinitions of the term *family* are now occurring.

3. By the year 2000, both partners in the family will be in the work force in upwards of 75 percent of families.

4. By the year 2000, nearly 75 percent of three-year-olds will attend day-care centers.

5. Single-parent families will continue to expand due to divorce and parents who choose not to marry.

6. Lifetime employment with the same job or company is becoming a thing of the past.

7. The number of manufacturing and agriculture industries will continue to decline.

8. The advent of the knowledge worker will fill an estimated 43 percent of jobs by the year 2000.

9. The number of people who work at home will increase as office automation becomes more powerful and portable.

10. Shortages in entry level jobs will continue followed by increases in those jobs that pay very near minimum wage.

11. The next decade will bring eight million new highly skilled jobs, mostly in executive, professional, and technical arenas.

12. Small businesses will employ a majority of workers by the year 2000.

13. Over-qualified, highly skilled workers unable to find employment will displace lower-skilled workers in some areas.

As these events transpire, so too must the shape and scope of education change. Many demand a major restructuring of school organizations. Major change trends today may not suffice. In the sections below, many of the trends facing education today are identified across several general areas: general trends, students, teachers, curriculum and instruction, higher education, school reform and restructuring, governance and leadership, school law, and school funding. After reading the section below, address the questions posed at the end of the case.

General Trends

Education has been and will remain a major public agenda item for much of the remainder of this century and the beginning of the next. Most will view education as a means to cure economic ills and promote growth. Continued technological advancement and more flexible work environments at home and work will allow for more productive schooling and working. The mismatch in competencies of graduates will continue. Literacy, technological competence, and creative or critical thinking will be at a premium.

Students

The declining enrollments of the 1980s will stop and begin to climb again. But even more problematic will be the large numbers of students who annually drop out of school. Rising social problems (drug abuse, teenage pregnancy, violence) and increased academic standards will only create further risks for students and probably higher dropout rates than forecast.

Teachers

The demand for qualified teachers will increase. Low pay, difficult working conditions, and too little genuine responsibility will add to shortages as output will lag behind necessities by upwards of 40 percent. In part, teacher shortages will be quelled by implementation of alternate certification routes. The lack of qualified minority teachers will still be viewed as an obstacle to thorough education as the population of minority students increases drastically. Universities and schools will combine talents in partnerships and propose new forms of schooling. Teachers' motivation will be explored as formulas for incentives are sought.

Curriculum and Instruction

Lifelong learning will become a principal feature in the development of curriculum and delivery systems. A core curriculum may emerge from the university, teacher, business, school, and parental partnerships that develop. Curriculum will by necessity become more global as more diverse and competent graduates are required by society and business. Vocational education will become paramount as technically literate graduates become more in demand by industry. School reforms will need to consider the demands of highly technical needs in conjunction with academic education.

Higher Education

Fewer college graduates will be required in the work force, but at the same time more postsecondary graduates will enter the picture. Colleges and universities will recognize this trend and curriculum changes will cater to students who need education but require less than four years of college. Community colleges will see a great influx of students fulfilling these education requirements and help communities realize their growth potential.

School Reform and Restructuring

A national policy to improve schools still will not have been achieved and piecemeal efforts will comprise the bulk of activity. No appreciable change to better education will occur. A demand for more learning time will become a norm and result in more flexibility for the school. School-based management may too often still be a top-down approach that creates further conflicts surrounding accountability. Generally, increased accountability will result but not without friction among local, state, and federal agencies.

Governance and Leadership

All stakeholders will demand more involvement in decisionmaking processes but too often with too little understanding of the real necessities important to reform or restructuring. Centralized overall control from the higher levels will remain but with more latitude available at local and classroom levels. A shortage of superintendents and principals will occur due to many retirements in the mid-nineties. As a result, new principals will become the major change agents of the new era. Bureaucracy in education will diminish in favor of a shared governance formula but not without fragmentation among the various partners that already erodes traditional schooling.

School Funding

An extreme variety of financial initiatives will be tried ranging from privatization to more centralization. But the real crux of change may involve finding new formulas for funding outside mainstream practice. These new initiatives would likely include using partnerships as discussed earlier. Regional disparities will undoubtedly increase during the change periods.

As a result of disparities, minority groups will challenge school curriculum, expenditures, methodology, and seek access to education for the less privileged. Equity issues will become major obstacles to growth and change. Both issues of access and expenditure will remain problematic.

■   ■   ■

Questions

With the limited list of issues and trends identified above, consider your own or your group's beliefs about the future of education.

1.   What educational issues are of greatest concern to you or your group?

2.   What role should local, state, or the federal government play in educational reform?

3.   What changes in the national/world economy dictate or influence the directions you view necessary for education today?

4.   What economic factors do you believe affect the future direction of education? Social factors? Other factors?

5.   Are there more social factors looming on the horizon in your view?

6.   Do you believe schooling is in trouble today? Defend your belief(s).

7.   How can we really know the perceptions of the stakeholder in education?

8.   Do these stakeholders really have any clout? Defend your belief(s).

Annotated Bibliography

Allison, D. J. (1983). Toward an improved understanding of the organizational nature of schools. *Educational Administration Quarterly, 19*(4), 7-34.

   Allison discusses the need to study schools as organizations unto themselves and not try to fit them into an existing organizational theory. He argues that schools differ from other organizations in the problematic and/or ambiguous nature of their goals, the lack of useful measures of effectiveness, and their "people-processing" nature. The point of the article is to outline the ambiguities of trying to make schools fit into existing organizational theory and to suggest areas for new creative research.

Burns, T. R., & Flam, H. (1987). *The shaping of social organization. Social rule system theory with applications.* Beverly Hills, CA: Sage.

The organization of human activity through social rule systems is the subject of this book. The authors take the position that a single theoretical/methodological framework—social rule system theory—can be used to describe and explain the formation and reformation of major types of social organization in contemporary society. The theory is used in the study of such organizations as government agencies and planning systems; interorganizational networks and institutions including markets, negotiation systems, and local government; and role relations including authority relationships between superiors and subordinates in work organizations.

Carroll, J. S. (Ed.). (1990). *Applied social psychology and organizational settings*. Hillsdale, NJ: Lawrence Erlbaum Associates.

Presenting work that bridges social psychology and organizations, this book's primary goal is understanding organizations by bringing to bear the concepts and methods of social psychology (along with other social sciences) and understanding and developing social psychology by analyzing it through the phenomena of actual organizational life.

Firestone, W. A., & Herriott, R. E. (1982). Two images of schools as organizations: An explication and empirical test. *Educational Administration Quarterly, 18*(2), 39-59.

Competing images of schools as rational bureaucracies and anarchic, or loosely coupled systems, developed mainly by March and then Weick are used to describe organizations with ambiguous goals, ineffective hierarchies of authority, vague technologies, and fluid participation. Because interdependence is minimal and people work in relative isolation, instructors make important decisions on their own. The autonomy of the instructor is virtually absolute. Policies and rules place little constraint on instruction. Thus the key members—the instructors—are loosely coupled to the educational organization.

Singh, J. V. (Ed.). (1990). *Organizational evolution: New directions*. Newbury Park, CA: Sage.

Various chapters in this book address issues of organizational evolution and present the latest thinking on approaches to organizational evolution by leading thinkers in the area. The book examines population change as it is constituted by rates of creation and death of organizational forms and organizations, and rates of change in organizational forms. The collection is also multidisciplinary in spirit, thus several sections address evolutionary economics, sociocultural evolution, and mathematical sociology.

Townsend, R. (1984). *Further up the organization: How to stop management from stifling people and strangling productivity*. New York: Alfred A. Knopf.

A successful corporate leader at Avis, Townsend attempted to put behavioral organization theory into practice in his company and has reputedly been very successful. The book is an encyclopedia of do's and don'ts for corporate executives. Townsend looks at how most companies are run and shows how to increase productivity. The book applies many of the management concepts of McGregor, Barnard, and others. Townsend embraces participatory management as the key to productivity and uses examples from his own experiences to show how well this strategy works.

References

Albrow, M. (1970). *Bureaucracy*. London: Pall Mall.

Allen, D. W. (1992). *Schools for a new century: A conservative approach to radical school reform*. New York: Praeger.

Argyris, C., Putnam, R., & Smith, D. M. (1985). *Action science: Concepts, methods, skills for research and intervention*. San Francisco: Jossey-Bass.

Argyris, C., & Schön, D. A. (1978). *Organizational learning: A theory of action perspective*. Reading, MA: Addison-Wesley.

Ayers, W. (1991, May). Perestroika in Chicago schools. *Educational Leadership, 48*(8), 69-71.

Barker, J. (1992). *Future edge: Discovering the new paradigms of success*. New York: Morrow.

Barnard, C. (1938). *The functions of the executive*. Boston, MA: Harvard University Press.

Bass, B. M. (1990). *Bass and Stogdill's handbook of leadership* (3rd ed.). New York: The Free Press.

Beckett, J. (1971). *Management dynamics: A new synthesis*. New York: McGraw-Hill.

Bennett, W. J. (1992). What do we want our graduate to be like. In L. C. Solomon & K. N. Hughes, (Eds.), *How do we get the graduate we want: A view from the firing lines* (pp. 17–26). New York: Praeger.

Bergquist, W. (1993). *The post modern organization: Mastering the art of irreversible change*. San Francisco: Jossey-Bass.

Bertalanffy, L. von. (1968). *General system theory*. New York: Braziller.

Bion, W. R. (1959). *Experience in groups*. New York: Basic Books.

Blake, R. R., & Mouton, J. S. (1988). *Executive achievement: Making it at the top*. New York: McGraw-Hill.

Blau, P. M. (1977). *Inequality and homogeneity*. New York: The Free Press.

Bolman, G., & Deal, T. (1991). *Reframing organizations: Artistry, choice, and leadership*. San Francisco: Jossey-Bass.

Briggs, J., & Peat, F. D. (1990). *Turbulent mirror: An illustrated guide to chaos theory and the science of wholeness*. New York: Harper and Row.

Burns, J. (1978). *Leadership*. New York: Harper and Row.

Burns, T. (1966). On plurality of social systems. In R. J. Lawrence (Ed.), *Operational research and social sciences*. London: Travistock.

Cetron, M. J., & Gayle, M. E. (1990, September–October). Educational renaissance: 43 Trends for U.S. schools. *Futurists, 33–40.*

Chatov, R. (1981). Cooperation between government and business. In P. C. Nystrom & W. H. Starbuck (Eds.), *Handbook on organizational design* (pp. 487–502). New York: Oxford University Press.

Chubb, J. E., & Moe, T. E. (1990, Summer). Choice is a panacea. *The Brookings Review, 4–12.*

Ciampa, D. (1992). *Total quality: A user's guide to implementation*. Reading, MA: Addison-Wesley.

Clark, D. L., & Astuto, T. A. (1991). Organizational theory. In M. C. Alkin (Ed.), *Encyclopedia of educational research* (6th ed.) (pp. 955–963). New York: Macmillan.

Clegg, S. R. (1990). *Modern organizations: Organization studies in the postmodern world*. Newbury Park: Sage.

Cohen, M., March, J., & Olsen, J. (1972). A garbage can model of organizational choice. *Administrative Science Quarterly, 17*(1), 1–19.

Coombs, A. W. (1991). *The schools we need: New assumptions for educational reform*. Lanham, MD: University Press of America.

Davies, P. C. W., & Brown, J. (1988). *Superstrings: A theory of everything?* Cambridge, UK: Cambridge University Press.

Davis, S. M., & Davidson, D. H. (1991). *20–20 Vision*. New York: Simon and Schuster.

Deal, T. E., & Kennedy, A. A. (1982). *Corporate culture: The rites and rituals of corporate life*. Reading, MA: Addison-Wesley.

Deming, W. E. (1986). *Out of crisis*. Cambridge, MA: MIT Center for the Advancement of Engineering Study.

De Pree, M. (1987). *Leadership is an art*. East Lansing, MI: Michigan State University Press.

Drucker, P. F. (1987). *The frontiers of management*. New York: Harper & Row.

Eisner, E. (1991, February). What really counts in schools? *Educational Leadership, 48*(5), 10–11, 14–17.

Elam, S. M., Rose, L. C., & Gallup, A. M. (1991, September). The 23rd annual Gallup poll of public's attitudes toward public schools. *Phi Delta Kappan, 41–56.*

Emery, F. F., & Trist, E. L. (1969). Socio-technical systems. In F. E. Emery (Ed.), *Systems thinking*. New York: Penguin.

Etzioni, A. (1964). *Modern organizations*. Englewood Cliffs, NJ: Prentice-Hall.

Fayol, H. (1949). *General and industrial management*. Paris: Pitman.

Frost, P. J., Moore, L. F., Louis, M. R., Lundberg, C. C., & Martin, J. (Eds.). (1991). *Reframing organizational culture*. Newbury Park, CA: Sage.

Gatto, J. (1990, September–October). Our children are dying in our schools. *New Age Journal, 62–64.*

Garfenckel, H. (1967). *Studies of ethnomethodology*. Englewood Cliffs, NJ: Prentice-Hall.

Getzels, J., & Guba, E. (1957). Social behavior and administrative process. *School Review, 65,* 423–441.

Glasser, W. (1990, February). The quality school. *Phi Delta Kappan, 424–435.*

Gleick, J. A. (1987). *Chaos: Making a new science*. New York: Penguin.

Guba, E. G. (1990). *The paradigm dialogue*. Newbury Park, CA: Sage.

Hannan, M.T., & Freeman, J. (1988). *Organizational ecology*. Boston: Harvard University Press.

Hentschke, G. C. (1992). How should our schools be structured? A view from the top of the bottom of the heap. In L. C. Solomon & K. N. Hughes (Eds.), *How do we get the graduate we want: A view from the firing lines* (pp. 91–98). New York: Praeger.

Herzberg, F. (1968, Nov.–Dec). One more time: How do you motivate employees? *Harvard Business Review, 46*(4), 53–62.

Hodgkinson, C. (1991). *Educational leadership: The moral act*. Albany: State University of New York Press.

Hoy, W., & Miskel, C. (1987). *Educational administration: Theory, research and practice* (3rd ed.). New York: Random House.

Jacques, E. (1955). Social systems as a defense against persecutory and depressive anxiety. In M. Klein (Ed.), *New directions in psychoanalysis* (p. 478–498). London: Travistock.

Jermier, J. M. (1991). Critical epistemology and the study of organizational culture: Reflections on street corner society. In P. J. Frost, L. F. Moore, M. R. Louis, C. C. Lundberg, & J. Martin (Eds.), *Reframing organizational culture* (pp. 223–233). Newbury Park, CA: Sage.

Kanter, R. (1985). *Changemasters: Corporate entrepreneurs at work*. New York: Touchstone.

Kanter, R. (1989, Nov.–Dec.). New managerial work. *Harvard Business Review, 89*(6), 85–92.

Kerr, S. (1984). Leadership and participation. In A. Brief (Ed.), *Productivity research in the behavioral and social sciences* (pp. 229–251). New York: Praeger.

Knezevich, S. J. (1989). *Administration of public education: A sourcebook for the leadership and management of educational institutions* (4th ed.). New York: Harper and Row.

Kowalski, T. J., & Reitzug, U. C. (1993). *Contemporary school administration: An introduction*. New York: Longman.

Kuhn, T. S. (1970). *The structure of scientific revolutions* (2nd ed., enlarged). Chicago: University of Chicago Press.

Lawrence, P. R., & Lorsch, J. W. (1986). *Organization and environment*. Boston: Harvard University Press.

Levine, A. (1992). The graduates we want: Who are they and how do we get them. In L. C. Solomon, & K. N. Hughes, (Eds.), *How do we get the graduate we want: A view from the firing lines* (pp. 7–16). New York: Praeger.

Lewin, K. (1935). *A dynamic theory of personality*. New York: McGraw-Hill.

Lewin, K. (1951). *Field theory in social science*. New York: Harper.

Lewis, K. S., (1991). Organizational change. In M. C. Alkin (Ed.), *Encyclopedia of educational research* (6th ed.) (pp. 941–952). New York: Macmillan.

Likert, R. (1987). *New patterns in management*. New York: Garland.

Lindbloom, C. E. (1980). *The policy-making process* (2nd ed.). Englewood Cliffs, NJ: Prentice-Hall.

Littlejohn, S. W. (1989). *Theories of human communication* (4th ed.). Belmont, CA: Wadsworth Publishing.

March, J. G. (1988). *Decisions and organizations*. New York: Blackwell.

Maslow, A. (1970). *Motivation and personality*. New York: Harper and Row.

Maruyama, M. (1963). The second cybernetics: Deviation amplifying mutual causal processes. *Academy of Management Review, 7*, 612–619.

Maturana, H., & Varela, F. (1980). *Autopoiesis and cognition: The realization of living*. London: Reidl.

Mayo, E. (1945). *The social problems of an industrial civilization*. New York: Ayer.

McGregor, D. (1985). *Human side of enterprise*. New York: McGraw-Hill.

Meyer, J. W. (1980). *The impact of centralization of educational funding and control of state and local educational governance*. Stanford University: Institute for Research on Educational Finance and Governance.

Meyerson, D. E. (1991). Acknowledging and uncovering the ambiguities in cultures. In P. J. Frost, L. F. Moore, M. R. Louis, C. C. Lundberg, & J. Martin (Eds.), *Reframing organizational culture* (pp. 254–270). Newbury Park, CA: Sage.

Miles, M. (1967). Some properties of schools as social systems. In G. Watson (Ed.), *Change in schools systems*. Washington DC: National Training Laboratories, NEA.

Miles, R. E., & Snow, L. L. (1978). *Organizational strategy, structure and process*. New York: McGraw-Hill.

Mintzberg, H. (1983). *Structure in fives: Designing effective organizations*. Englewood Cliffs, NJ: Prentice-Hall.

Mintzberg, H. (1989). *Mintzberg on management: Inside our strange world of management*. New York: The Free Press.

Mintzberg, H., & Quinn, J. B. (1988). *The strategy process: Concepts, contexts, cases*. Englewood Cliffs, NJ: Prentice-Hall.

Monge, P. R., & Eisenhart, E. M. (1987). Emergent communication networks. In F. M. Jablin et al. (Eds.), *Handbook of organizational communication: An interdisciplinary perspective* (pp. 304–342). Newbury Park, CA: Sage.

Morgan, G. (1986). *Images of organization*. Newbury Park, CA: Sage.

Morphet, R., Johns, R., & Reller, T. (1982). *Educational organization and administration: Concepts, practices, and issues* (4th ed.). Englewood Cliffs, NJ: Prentice-Hall.

Nonaki, I. (1991, Nov.–Dec.). The knowledge creating company. *Harvard Business Review, 91*(6), 96–104.

Olsen, L. (1988, Nov. 2). The restructuring puzzle: Ideas for revamping "egg crate" schools abound, but to what ends. *Education Week,* 7.

O'Toole, J. (1985). *Vanguard management*. New York: Berkley.

Ouchi, W. A. (1981). *Theory Z: How American business can meet the Japanese challenge*. Reading, MA: Addison-Wesley.

Owen, R. (1987). *Organizational behavior in education* (3rd ed.). Englewood Cliffs, NJ: Prentice-Hall.

Peters, T. J. (1987). *Thriving on chaos*. New York: Knopf.

Peters, T. J. (1992). *Liberation management: Necessary disorganization for the nanosecond nineties*. New York: Knopf.

Peters, T. J., & Waterman, R. H. (1982). *In search of excellence*. New York: Harper and Row.

Phillips, M. E. (1984). *Industry as a cultural grouping*. Unpublished doctoral dissertation. University of California, Graduate School of Management.

Poole, M. S., & McPhee, R. D. (1983). A structurational analysis of organization climate. In L. L. Putnam, & M. E. Pacanowsky (Eds.), *Communication and organizations: An integrative approach* (pp. 195–220). Beverly Hills, CA: Sage.

Prahalad, C. K., & Hamel, G. (1990, May–June). The core competence of the organization. *Harvard Business Review, 3,* 79–91.

Prigogine, I., & Stengers, I. (1984). *Order out of chaos*. New York: Random House.

Pugh, D. S., & Hickson, D. J. (Eds.). (1989). *Writers on organization*. Newbury Park, CA: Sage.

Razik, T. (1993). Working papers. Graduate School of Educational Administration, State University of New York at Buffalo.

Reese, W. J. (1991). Organizational structure and governance. In M. C. Alkin (Ed.), *Encyclopedia of educational research* (6th ed.) (pp. 953–955). New York: Macmillan.

Reigeluth, C. (1987). The search for meaningful reform: A third wave educational system. *Journal of Instructional Management, 10*(4), 3–14.

Rost, J. (1991). *Leadership for the twenty-first century*. New York: Praeger.

Sackmann, S. A. (1991). *Cultural knowledge in organizations: Exploring the collective mind*. Newbury Park, CA: Sage.

Schein, E. (1985). *Organizational culture and leadership*. San Francisco: Jossey-Bass.

Schmuck, R. A., & Runkel, P. J. (1985). *The handbook of organizational development in schools* (3rd ed.). Prospect Heights, IL: Waveland.

Schön, D. (1971). *Beyond the stable state*. New York: Norton.

Schön, D., (1987). *Educating the reflective practitioner: Toward a new design for teaching and learning in the profession*. San Francisco: Jossey-Bass.

Schools that work (1991, May 27). *US News and World Report,* pp. 58–66.

Senge, P. (1990). *The fifth discipline: The art and practice of the learning organization*. New York: Doubleday-Currency.

Sergiovanni, T. J. (1987). *The principalship: A reflective practice perspective*. Boston: Allyn and Bacon.

Sergiovanni, T. J. (1989). The leadership needed for quality schooling. In T. J. Sergiovanni & R. H. Moore (Eds.), *Schooling for tomorrow: Directing reform issues that count*. Boston: Allyn and Bacon.

Silverman, D. (1971). *The theory of organizations*. New York: Basic Books.

Simon, H. A. (1977). *The new science of management decision*. New York: Harper and Row.

Solomon, L. C., & Hughes, K. N. (Eds.). (1992). *How do we get the graduates we want: A view from the firing lines*. New York: Praeger.

Spreigel, W. R. (1953). *The writings of the Gilbreths*. Homewood, IL: Irwin.

Starbach, W. H. (1981). A trip to view elephants and rattlesnakes in the garden of Aston. In A. H. de Van & W. F. Joyce (Eds.), *Perspectives on organizational design and behavior* (pp. 167–197). New York: John Wiley and Sons.

Tannebaum, A. S. (1968). *Control in organizations*. New York: McGraw-Hill.

Taylor, F. W. (1947). *Scientific management*. New York: Harper and Row.

Therborn, G. (1976). *Science, class, and society*. London: New Left Books.

Thomas, K. W. (1977). Toward multi-dimensional values in teaching: The example of conflict behaviors. *Academy of Management Review, 12*, 484–490.

Thompson, J. D. (1967). *Organizations in action*. New York: McGraw-Hill.

Tompkins, P. K., & Cheney, P. K. (1985). Communications and unobtrusive control in contemporary organizations. In R. D. McPhee & P. K. Tompkins (Eds.), *Organizational communication: Traditional themes and new directions* (pp. 179–210). Beverly Hills, CA: Sage.

Tyack, D. (1990, Winter). "Restructuring" in historical perspective: Tinkering towards utopia. *Teachers College Board, 92*(2), 171–191.

Woodward, J. (1981). *Industrial organization: Theory and practice* (2nd ed.). UK: Oxford University Press.

Weber, M. (1947). *The theory of social and economic organization*. New York: The Free Press.

Weick, K. E. (1969). *The social psychology of organizing*. Reading, MA: Addison-Wesley.

Yukl, G. A. (1989). *Leadership in organizations* (2nd ed.). Englewood Cliffs, NJ: Prentice-Hall.

Zalesznik, A. (1970). Power and politics of organizational life. *Harvard Business Review, 48*, 47–60.

Zohar, D. (1990). *The quantum self: Human nature and consciousness defined by the new physics*. New York: Macmillan.

Chapter 8
Communication: The Breath of Organizational Life

E ducational administration, like management in other settings, stands at a critical juncture in theory and practice. Comprehension and application of various effective communication models is a crucial competency needed by educators during this critical period of educational change. The quality of a school's communication seriously affects the nature of its effectiveness. Systems theory offers educators a means of perceiving the communication processes. The systematic view of both the organization and communication is global, abstract, and less easily codified. The systemic view is much more representative of how organizational communication actually occurs. The traditional understanding of linear communication fails to model the actual webs of communication in which school administration, instruction, and leadership function. To view communication systemically is to see communication acts as relating to and affecting the organizational body. A systemic metaphor for this view is to refer to communication as the "breath of organizational life."

Conventional wisdom restricts the ways in which the terms *communication* and *information* are defined and used in organizations. Conventionally, communication is thought of as a process people are more or less skillfully engaged in. Information is something people do or do not have. Information storage, retrieval, and display have been successfully automated. And there is popular agreement that such automation has changed human life. Contrast this with the unconventional idea that, as data has been *automated*, people have been *informated* through access to data and electronic ways of manipulating it. It is "informating" rather than "automating" that will fuel social and organizational change in the future. Communication then, is interactive, interdependent, and integrating, not just a stepwise model or a process that seemingly becomes lifelike as people communicate.

In the "informated" organization (Schuck, 1985), information is universally accessible. Accessibility to useful information enables the organization to be more responsive as each actor in the school environment shares equal information access. Combined with shared decisionmaking or problem solving, the school system becomes more flexible as it acts effectively with uniform information. Access is neither controlled nor controllable by people at the top of an organizational hierarchy. The "informated" are not defined by chronological age or status; anyone can be informated. Given all the new information they have or can easily access, informated students, teachers, and administrators can hardly be expected to understand and enact their roles in organizations in traditional ways. This has vast implications for school thinkers and implementers of the future. In an educational setting of the future, the administrator's communications must logically be derived from the same basic information accessible to all persons in the organization.

Changes in how processes and problems are conceptualized signal not only a shift in paradigms, but also an imperative to rethink and re-create organizational values, processes, and structures. The nation's businesses claim that schools are not meeting market and labor needs, but futurists say that businesses are in many ways as ineffective as the schools they criticize. It may be time for educational public and private sector organizations to curtail their dependence upon traditions founded in principles of management science. It is now necessary to look in unaccustomed places for new insights about their missions and productivity.

For educational administrators, the challenge is to look beyond the fences of their school yards and to embrace wider contexts and disciplines as they conceptualize problems in their schools. In many contexts, the global village has already arrived. Diversity and multidisciplinary viewpoints are a fact of informated life. Innovative educational leadership requires a deeper, broader understanding of the future. For this reason, applying the content of this chapter to educational admin-

istration practice must be the responsibility of each thoughtful reader.

In this chapter the reader is asked to continue generating new energizing beliefs—in this case to curb the impulse to dismiss this new content as just theory. The reader must be prepared to continue developing more personal insights about what leading means in highly informated organizations, what effective communication requires, how data are gathered and used, and how to ensure that the whole organization is communicating systemically.

Systemic Metaphors of Communication

Communication is a complex, systemic phenomenon of such immense proportions that it defies the explanatory capacity of current communication theories in use. The act of communication is not limited to human beings. With new ecological and information processing awareness, humankind has begun to sense that "knowledge" has linear, accrual, and goal dimensions. Genetic transmissions in living organisms are communications; so are the information exchanges bussed from one "smart machine" to another. Soon transmission methods will change so drastically that it will be conceivable to stop thinking in terms of classrooms and instead begin to posit new learning environments with learning groups connected to a provider from a distant place. The occasions and mechanisms for communicating in the near term will proliferate with unprecedented speed and intensity. The old adage that knowledge is power will breed newer meanings as information increases in availability and accessibility. *Information will become power*. What human beings do or should do with such power is of more than philosophical interest. "Information" will be seen as nonlinear, instantaneous, and capable of an indeterminate number of interpretations and purposes.

Both living and nonliving entities exchange information. The premise that communication is basic and only conveys information must begin to be enlarged. Communication must be treated as a system with general systems properties. Raising communication to this level of universality sends the message that human organizations can no longer afford to think of themselves solely as independent, self-contained, people-to-people communities. Communication is much more universal, more holistic. Confining communication to a philosophical-cultural, cognitive-behavioral, or social-psychological paradigm inhibits our ability to fully understand communication. The traditional sender-receiver-feedback model in these paradigms cannot explain the necessities we sense in an informated environment. *General systems thinking has the theoretical capacity to incorporate all of the prevailing human communication paradigms, and to "wire in" all of the communication processes among nonliving systems as well.*

To argue for the greatest generality represented by systems thinking is not a specious scholastic exercise. For example, how school administrators perceive and enact communication is a result of the frames of reference used. How the boundaries, processes, and practices of communication evolve depends on individual points of view about human beings and human organizations. At root, communication beliefs and strategies depend upon the administrator's personal view of the world and his or her participation in that world view.

If an administrator's view of the world is narrow or static, bounded by narrow past experience and biases of a limited, old paradigm, one type of communication environment will emerge in the school system. This administrator will seek to design and control

and even inhibit the process of communication in the organization. If, on the other hand, an administrator's world view takes into account the diversity of evolving systems in the world and the evolution of schooling within those systems, a different communications environment will exist. This administrator will recognize that communication is embodied in a variety and dynamic set of system properties distributed across every part of the school and its environment. Control will be exhibited in every part of the system, not simply as defined by a bureaucratic structure, but in a holographic sense where every part is a whole. This administrator will also recognize the necessity to enlarge the communication arena as additional partners' views add further variability, energy, and variety.

The shift in emphasis from the administrator who values control of communication to the administrator who values the dynamics of communication is a shift from a fixed and proprietary perception of "knowledge" as something gained and owned to a dynamic and open perception of "knowing." Knowing becomes a requisite need for the whole system. It is the personal, intellectual, and behavioral growth imperative for all members of the organization. What schools need are actors who carry within themselves the requisite variety of information and skills to incubate such dynamic and "knowing" schools as have never existed before. Nothing less will stem the tide of public disillusionment. Clearly, the communication processes in such a dynamic environment will often have to be "made up" on the spot. There is no one communication formula that may be taught or unilaterally applied.

Thoughtful school administrators are very quickly disabused of the notion that they can walk into a school system and lay claim to being solely in charge. They learn that many other variables are "in charge" in an operational sense, including economic realities, student ennui or enthusiasm, degrees of teacher optimism, energy, and insight, and external "education consumer" perceptions. Much as school administrators would like it to be otherwise, they are not solely in charge of anything except their own thoughts, behaviors, and accountabilities to those they serve. This may be a disquieting picture for those who enjoy command, but it is an unprecedented opportunity for those who view educational administration as educational leadership which is a human service occupation without peer.

Diversity in Communication Theories: A Twenty-first Century Paradox

To insist that systemic (not systematic) epistemology can shed the most light on understanding communication in the twenty-first century is not to discard or disregard all preceding theory. The bases for studying human communication in organizations must be made explicit. If the base of reference is a hierarchical model of organization, then questions of top-down, grass-roots-up linear communication are of interest. If, on the other hand, one assumes a heterarchical or holographic (systemic) model of organization, then communications and other organizational characteristics change dramatically. Such nonhierarchical models are emerging, generated in part by the computer-informated society, and in part by the human longing to live and function at work as persons who are not merely cogs in organizational machinery. Schein (1989) speaks of organizations groping toward new organizational forms even though they are haunted by hierarchies and conditioned by the belief in the "divine rights" of managers. Stephens (1989) cites the creation of what Adler of the Institute of the

Future calls virtual companies that exist only by virtue of their computer connections. The creation of Apple's Applelink, a wide area network, IBM's Learning Initiatives Network, and Internet in schools may be harbingers of the creation of "virtual schools."

The excitement afoot over the creation of new organizational forms, however, also evokes significant new anxiety. How much do self-autonomous work groups need administrators as communicators? In an environment where everything is negotiable by everyone (Kanter, 1989), what role does a manager or administrator play? These are not moot questions. Such organizations already exist in various forms in highly technological, entrepreneurial environments. Considering the growing public demand for school choice and increased achievement/productivity of public schools, it is not too great a stretch for school administrators to imagine themselves in such entrepreneurial environments in the future.

Recognizing that rapid, complex societal changes create the need for new communication theory, past theory becomes a useful building block. Normally one begins the study of any phenomenon with a definition arrived at by consensus over time. Most researchers agree that communication involves senders, receivers, information transmissions between senders and receivers, and interferences or enablers acting on those transmissions. Nearly everything else about human communication is left to be defined in the situation-specific operational definition of a particular researcher. Dance (1970) found 95 different and sometimes contradictory definitions of communication in use.

Message meaning, provision of feedback, and implications for human action are also attached to most definitions of communication as evidence of the social nature and function of the process. It is generally understood that non-verbal as well as verbal information is "encoded" and "decoded" differently by different participants in the communication process. Some theorists and researchers include extrasensory information, intuition, and unconscious phenomena as part of the communication event. Others are more interested in the overlapping of discontinuous messages from different systems and how that overlap becomes congruent and integrated in the human mind. In educational administration, as in the business world, communication as influence is a pervasive theme in the research literature. The goal of the manager or school administrator is to communicate "vision" and goal imperatives and persuade others to follow the leader to organizational success.

Berlo (1960) reported that the meaning of any communication is in the minds of the communicators. Individual experience confirms that communications are often misunderstood. Messages may never mean to the receivers exactly what the sender intended it to mean. Why, then, do people continue to struggle so determinedly to share meanings, find common ground, and act in concert? The answer may be simply that humans are social beings. Recent research seems to show through discourse analysis that groups of people who eventually act in concert are not doing so on the basis of full agreement on motivations or rationale but rather because they have agreed on certain mechanisms of communication that allow them to retain their autonomous values and points of view (Donnellon, Gray, & Bougon, 1986). If what these researchers found can be generalized, then the goal of communication is not consensus about content or interpretation of the communication but rather consensus that an equifinal meaning can be reached by each individual no matter how idiosyncratic that meaning may be. Stated very simply, participants in an activity do not need to agree on their reasons for taking action or on their perceptions of how they will benefit. They do

need to agree on taking collective action. Thus, the use of metaphors, logical argument, affect modulation, and linguistic indirection are simply understood and imply organized action.

The wealth of knowledge and varied disciplinary approaches brought to the field of communication have produced a new profession and a new set of academic specialties. This eclectic field of research comprises components of rhetoric, social psychology, linguistics, mathematics, and many other fields of study. Although there is a need for a more integrative systemic theory, investigating earlier genres is also helpful to educators.

Theory Genres in Communication

Littlejohn (1989) described four basic genres of communication theory, each having characteristics that provide unique ways to understand communication. These are identified as (1) structuralist and functionalist, (2) cognitive and behavioral, (3) interactional and conventional, and (4) interpretive and critical. Each genre contains a broad spectrum of research methodologies and practical applications to the social sciences. Each is associated with certain assumptions that educational administrators may find either closely or loosely aligned with their own belief systems.

Structuralist/functionalist theories are identified by their emphasis on a series of communication exchanges that occur and function almost simultaneously rather than over time, a curiosity about unintended consequences of actions at least as often as about purposeful outcomes, a shared belief in independent and objective reality, and a dualist insistence on the separation of symbols and language from the objects and thoughts being symbolized in communication. The genre borrows from General System Theory as well as from structuralist and functionalist philosophies.

Cognitive/behavioral theories of communication arise from the disciplines of the psychological sciences, employing many of the same assumptions about human knowledge and behavior that one finds in the structuralist/functionalist genre. The difference is that in the cognitive/behavioral paradigm knowledge is generated through the discovery of psychological "mechanisms." Theories of the cognitive/behavioral nature address communication as a manifestation of individual behavior and thought processes, including the neural basis for these manifestations. According to this genre, major variables having an impact on one's cognitive functioning and its appearances in behavior, including language behavior, are outside of the individual's control. Still, there are interactional components of the individual's behavior that contribute to the particular psychological manifestations studied in this genre.

Interactional/conventional theories of communication are largely derived from sociology, anthropology, and the philosophy of language. The cornerstone concept in this theory is symbolic interaction. Social existence is viewed as a process of continuous interaction that establishes, maintains, and sometimes alters certain social conventions like language and symbols. It is interactions, then, that create rules and norms, establish traditions, and on occasion overturn these traditions. Communication is a process of creating social reality and its corresponding culture, norms, and values.

Interpretive/critical theories arise from a variety of investigative traditions, including interpretive sociology, phenomenology and hermeneutics, Marxism and the Frankfurt school, and various text analysis and literary traditions. Common characteristics of the interpretive/critical theories include a preeminence of subjectivity and a high value associated with individual experience. "Meaning" in

the constructs of the interpretive/critical genre has great significance. This genre also borrows concepts from General System Theory.

It should be obvious from the differing points of emphasis that each of the genres Littlejohn described tends to cluster around specific communication contexts. These clusters and contexts provide a hierarchy of research domains that are defined primarily by the size of the groups involved in the communication acts. From lowest population numbers to highest, these groups include interpersonal, group, organizational, and mass communication areas of research.

Interpersonal theories address communication between individuals, primarily attending to personal and discourse processes and relationships. Group communication theories focus on the interpersonal behaviors and influences that occur in small groups. Therefore, group communication researchers are interested in issues associated with group dynamics, interaction within the group, effectiveness, decisionmaking, and stages of change in both personal and group development. Organizational communication researchers are mindful of interpersonal and group theories, but their primary concern is the role of communication in the achievement of organizational goals (Shockley-Zalabak, 1988). Mass communication carries interpersonal, group, and organizational communication theories into the public realm, generally concerned about the impact of various media on public understanding and resulting public actions.

Although interpersonal, group, and mass communication are of interest to the school administrator, organizational communication constitutes the "breath" of educational organizational life. Without effective communication, an organization is forced to languish in a state of suspended animation, without the nutrients or energy to pursue its collective goals. Understanding what constitutes communication in the organizations we live in is of vital concern—most of our life is spent in or interacting with organizations (Etzioni, 1964).

Metaphors and Assumptions in Organizational Communication

The assumptions everyday communicators make about humans and human organizations inevitably create differences in the way organizational communication phenomena are conceptualized, researched, adjusted, and used. Explicit assumptions are associated with differing metaphors. For example, a theory essentially conceptualized as mechanistic in approach and terminology may be based on the metaphor of the organization-as-machine. But machines exist to produce wealth in an economic sense, while schools produce educated citizen-workers. In these theories the instrumentality of good communication for getting work done is a constant theme. Theories that emphasize growth and change in organizations may be fundamentally conceptualized in the notion of the organization-as-organism. Here organizational communication is viewed as a crucial element to the organization's survival, akin to a life-force that in part drives the whole organization. For the last several decades, the prevalent metaphor that represents the anthropological perspective is the metaphor of organization-as-culture. Communication from this perspective takes on cultural-historical characteristics. Other theorists think of the organization as a complex psychological entity. Organization-as-psychoentity uses metaphors of the mind or psyche to describe organizational communication.

Three emerging metaphors of considerable interest to organization specialists are (1) the metaphor of organization-as-art, implying a continual shaping and reshaping by inner and outer forces or personal agents (e.g., Schein, 1989; Peters, 1992); (2) the metaphor of organization-as-brain (Morgan, 1986; Marsick, 1990), envisioning the organization primarily as an intelligent information-processing center; and (3) the metaphor of the organization-as-learner (Argyris & Schön, 1978), suggesting that organizational learning flow may be as critical for success as cash flow or SAT scores, drop-out rates, and numbers of college-bound students. In these newer perspectives, the systemic properties of organizations and organizational communication are dynamic and qualitative. These systems properties require new research methodologies.

The first four of these ruling metaphors: organization-as-machine, organization-as-organism, organization-as-culture, and organization-as-psychoentity, roughly parallel Littlejohn's theory genres. However, the metaphors of organization-as-art, organization-as-brain, and organization-as-learner are not as clear-cut. These metaphors may be the forerunners of the search for more holistic views of, and metaphors for, organizational communication. Similarly, the literature about school management and supervision, human resource development (HRD), and organizational theory are filled with competing metaphors as writers search for new ways to represent and think about old problems in human organizations. Many attempt to utilize General Systems Theory (GST) as the foundational thinking system.

Watkins' (1989) discussion of alternative theories for human resource development based on five metaphors of practice serve as a prominent example. HRD professionals, including staff developers for educational institutions, are typically concerned with organizational communication. In some ways they may be seen as the "keepers of the metaphors" that characterize organizations. In HRD, skill-building workshops, new-rule communication events, and other instructional leadership efforts are not exempt from inquiry and often use metaphors for their explanatory power. As an example, Watkins names these alternative metaphors for the human resource development role: (1) organizational problem solver, (2) organizational change agent/interventionist or helper, (3) organizational designer, (4) organizational empowerer/meaning maker, and (5) developer of human capital. If school administrators are performing or guiding the performance of others in light of any one role or any combination of these roles, then they are engaged in metaphor-based activity. Watkins may be only associating General System Theory with organizational problem-solving. She links field and intervention theory with the metaphor of the HRD practitioner as organizational change agent, partly on the strength of Kurt Lewin's (1951) field theory contribution to organizational development (OD) principles and practices. Watkins found a variety of theories of work as well as theories of design underlying the metaphor of organizational design. In using these new metaphors for organizations, Watkins concomitantly developed new metaphors for leaders in organizations. The organizational empowerer is a metaphor for the believer in critical theory, and the developer of human capital uses human capital theory. The point of making these metaphors and their theoretical origins explicit, Watkins believes, is to enrich and enlarge the understanding of the field of practice.

Other images that educators may profitably reflect upon are Morgan's (1986) pictures of organizations as political systems, psychic prisons, flux and transformation, and/or instruments of domination. Hall (1991) preferred a "realistic" notion of organizations as actors, and Helgeson (1990) noted that women in charge of organizations often think of them as intricate webs of relationships. These recent examples do not exhaust the metaphoric possibilities. However, they do verify the fact that single-notioned models of organizations are prevalent and, at the same time, differ drastically from the current life of modern organizations. In the midst of this rich development of metaphors, it is a practical necessity for educators to examine whatever is said about organizational communication with a healthy skepticism and an eye to discovering what metaphors and theories are actually being used in each exchange. It is subsequently imperative to understand the power of metaphor as a means of conceptualizing the school organization as it functions and evolves over time under the stress of constant conflict. For example, although educators in school settings may prefer to think of themselves as the developers of human beings, they often find that role obscured by "control" functions that seem contradictory in purpose or emphasis. What views of the world and what theories are associated with "control," what views and theories are associated with "development," and what part does communication play as we continue investigating schooling through these metaphors? Such questions should guide school administrators' and teachers' critical reflection about goals, purposes, processes, outcomes, and shareholders in organizational communication.

Distinguishing Features of Organizational Communication

Communication occurs in differing contexts in organizations. Berelson and Steiner (1964) defined four properties of organizations that affect these contexts. First, a typical organization is characterized by formality. Specifically, it has goals, regulations, policies, and procedures that give rise to its form and determine how it will communicate officially. Second, organizations are structured in a hierarchical manner. This structure patterns multidirectional communications. Third, the size of organizations tends to prohibit the development of close personal relationships with all other members and limits the scope of informal organizational communications. Last, organizations most often exist beyond the time frame of a given member's life. Those who work in schools will surely recognize these features as pertaining to educational organizations. They may also recognize that Berelson and Steiner's formulation is several decades old and may represent organizational aspects now in flux. At the same time, the salience of Berelson and Steiner's theory and the current organizational structure of many schools in the United States suggest that schools facing the challenges of the twenty-first century may be out of sync and their old structures and contexts may not fit well with tomorrow's communications needs. Berelson and Steiner's theory serves well, however, as a template for understanding key elements of today's school organizations.

If the feature of organizational communication that separates it from other kinds of communication is its deliberate focus on the achievement of a common or collective goal, then the specific form of any organization can be expected to be mirrored in its forms of organizational communication. According to Berelson and Steiner's premise that form follows goals, communicating organizational goals becomes a "first cause" and shaper of all organizational communication. This is perhaps one impulse behind the first school assembly of each academic year and the traditional goal-setting that some school leaders undertake in that forum.

Goals are useless if they are not communicated in ways that enlist the cooperative effort of members of the organization. Without the intention to attain goals, organizations would also appear to have no purpose. It is not surprising that those who write about organization see goal attainment and communication so systemically intertwined (Hoy & Miskel, 1987). Like Simon (1957), they believe there can be no organization without communication. This places a clear responsibility on school leaders not only to establish and maintain communication but also to be sure that it is both effective and efficient for goal attainment.

Many studies support the importance of communication in organizational leadership. Hoy and Miskel (1987) stated that "superintendents and principals spend 70 percent or more of their time communicating" (p. 356). Sigband and Bell (1989) reported that chief executive officers in corporations spend 78 percent of their time in oral communication, with lower level managers spending over 80 percent of their time similarly. Murphy and Peck (1980) cited the ability to communicate as the critical factor in manager promotability. It would appear that competent communication is regarded more highly than such skills as motivating employees, decisionmaking, delegating, flexibility, and educational background. In educational institutions, Striplin (1987) found that the ability of school principals to perform effectively as instructional leaders is contingent on their degree of competence in communication.

Communication's potential contribution to organizational success is present in virtually all organizational activities, from envisioning, to planning, to problem-solving and decisionmaking, to coordinating, controlling, accomplishing, evaluating, and reporting of organizational results. It is tempting to conclude that effective organizational communication is, therefore, a panacea for all organizational stresses and difficulties. To the contrary, Hoy and Miskel (1987) pointed out that the diffusion of communication processes throughout the organization makes organizational communication difficult to examine as a separate process. Difficulties in organizational communication that are often reflected in other problems in the school are another construct. While communication can help resolve problems, it can also obscure other problems not directly under consideration. Lastly, communication evokes action even though the quality of the action is questionable, and there is no general commitment to the action. Poor leaders can unknowingly use communication to expedite inadequate or irrelevant plans.

To assure effectiveness the school leader must be fully aware of the intricacy of the school unit/district communication channels on both the formal and informal level. How the leader facilitates the transmission of a given message can result in a deliberately orchestrated change in staff or student behavior. Given the reality of the constraints that Hoy and Miskel note, the school leader needs to be aware of the power of all communication as a potential force for maintaining or destroying some aspects of the organizational life. Theoretically, this calls for the school administrator to borrow from Yukl's (1989) theory about the role of a "leader" versus that of a "manager" in a school. Yukl suggested that the effective administrator may know when to communicate as a manager and when to communicate as a leader. In the former case the administrator chooses to minimize noise by sending messages, developing channels, and monitoring feedback in settings that are clearly role-defined. For example, a school administrator might give his staff a written questionnaire regarding supply requisitions. The staff writes a written response which the administrator subsequently responds to in the format of existing policy.

On the other hand, as an administrator seeks staff support on an issue, he or she is best advised to use a variety of communication skills in an effort to gain commitment to an issue. This is a function of leadership and,

according to Yukl (1989), requires administrative understanding of communication and a varied repertoire of communication skills. In examining communication processes, the school administrator in a continuous process shifts from the role of manager to leader.

Factors Affecting Clarity, Credibility, and Directionality of Organizational Messages

Khandwalla (1987) stated that the primary objectives of communication are to gain attention and to gain understanding and acceptance of the message. Sigband and Bell (1989) contended that the purposes of communication are to be understood exactly as intended, to secure the desired response, and to maintain favorable relations with those with whom one communicates. Reitz (1987) believed that the primary functions of communication are to provide information that makes the organization adaptable to change, to command and instruct employees, and to influence and persuade the organization's members. The processes involved in accomplishing these purposes above are recognized as contributing to success or failure of a given end. A leader may subscribe to any of these communication objectives either as an expression of commitment to the organization and its goals or as an expression of a personal desire for power and self-aggrandizement. The communicator's world view and personal motivations, therefore, affect clarity, credibility, directionality, and even the process of communication itself. Modeling communication as a quasi-mechanical process, a means to an end, leaves out important psychological data. Nevertheless, the linear, mechanical model of information processing, sender-message channel-receiver-

Figure 8.1
Model of communication: input-throughput-output

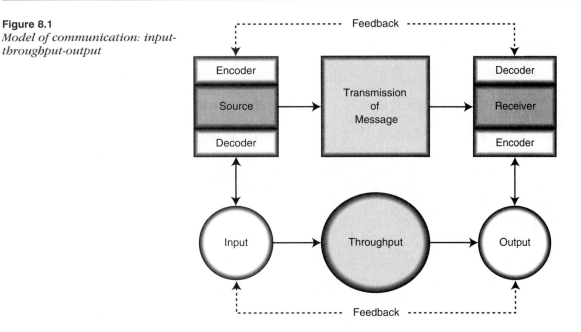

feedback, is the usual starting point for talking about communication (see Figure 8.1).

Using a quasi-mechanical model of communication allows the researcher to examine discrete elements of the communication process without the burden of holistic analysis. Thus, in speaking of the elements, sender and receiver, the linear model makes it possible to conceptualize communication as a sharing of messages, ideas, or attitudes that produce a degree of understanding between those elements. The idea of shared meaning permits the study of *how well* a particular meaning is shared. Shared meaning, however, can be problematic as the receiver's intention may differ from that imagined/meant by the sender.

The linear model provides a starting point not unlike the starting point of behavioral psychology. There is a sender or "source" of a stimulus somewhere in the environment that acts on and elicits a response from the receiver. Communication models insert a "channel" between sender and receiver so that response variations can be located and

accounted for. Recognition of intrapsychic processes within the senders and receivers helps to account for human barriers to communication and for discrepancies in message meaning. The feedback loop overcomes the essential linearity of the early models, looping to revisit any element in the process.

A basic assumption about organizational communication is that if messages are actually sent and if clarity, frequency, and completeness of those messages is increased, the probability that organization members will be working toward a common or shared goal is also increased. This leads organizational communication specialists to place considerable emphasis on message form and on "channels" that carry the messages. Their intention is to avoid channels that produce static or distortion, or, if those channels must be used, to reduce occurrence of "noise," static, or distortion within them. Channels include oral, written, and mediated routing of messages.

Sigband and Bell (1989) identified two communication channels, formal and informal. Formal channels of communication include the organizationally sanctioned flows of information such as electronic mail, scheduled meetings, and other functional necessities. The informal, "grapevine" channels provide access to information not normally obtained through formal channels. Khandwalla (1987) cited telephone and face-to-face conversations as the primary means for informal communication. Administrators can monitor the organizational climate by paying attention to messages in the grapevine. They may even intentionally "leak" off-the-record statements to informal channels to monitor communication flow. The advantage of using informal communication is that it transfers information very rapidly. The informal communication network prevents a communication vacuum. If the formal channels do not work, the informal ones will take over. The problem with informal channels is their potential inaccuracy. The lack of official sanction leaves informally conveyed messages at the mercy of unchecked distortions as they travel through the grapevine.

Sigband and Bell (1989) classified the major barriers to communication under two headings: nonverbal and verbal. Nonverbal barriers include differences in perception, lack of interest (particularly on the part of the receiver), lack of fundamental knowledge or specific cognitive basis for understanding a message, personal characteristics such as personality, emotions, prejudices, reactions to appearance of the communicator, distractions or actual interference, poor organization of the message, poor listening, and competition for attention. Common verbal barriers include language, which may result in "semantics problems," or inadequate vocabulary, both of which affect comprehension.

Another large category of barriers to communication results from cultural differences. This is particularly evident in the United States where educators constantly must address the cultural differences of diverse populations both in the student body and in the community. Hentges, Yaney, and Shields (1990) noted that because "no two groups ever experience the same cultural history, messages become more dissonant and ambiguous in a more heterogeneous population. To reduce the possibility of misunderstanding or dissonance potential, messages must be repeated many times" (pp. 39–40). Misunderstandings arise out of biases regarding accents and language, culturally defined signs and body language, acceptable degrees of physical proximity, the meanings of a handshake and eye contact, preferences for or against strong authority figures, and class systems brought from other countries. The diversity of cultural references to adversity or joy may seem inexplicable or bizarre to those outside that particular culture. A cultural or privation-induced orientation toward the "here and now" instead of toward the future may be misconstrued as lack of ambition or ability to plan. The roles and significance of particular minority family members may seem unusual to the dominant culture. An Asian student, for example, may not be able to answer a direct question until many older family members are consulted. Choices between being indirect or direct may be culturally determined, and symbolic messages are often unique to the country of origin. Surmounting these communication barriers calls for providing for shared experiences, regularly, often, and in great variety, with an emphasis on valuing rather than judging differences. The future American school administrators cannot ignore demographic information that mandates multicultural awareness.

The sender's credibility is always at stake in organizational communication. Khandwalla (1987) noted that the source of information must be perceived as knowledgeable to be credible. Thus, a memo about the financial status of a school district needs to come from the district's financial officer rather than the curriculum specialist if it is to carry maximum credibility. However, credibility does not hinge on position alone. Both advance reputation and ongoing experience with a communicator create a track record of credibility or noncredibility. Once credibility is lost, it is difficult, if not impossible, to regain within the organization where the loss occurred.

Message originators can assess the extent to which successful transmission has occurred by encouraging feedback from receivers. This is especially critical in school settings. The concept of feedback is often attributed to Wiener (1954) in his early discussions of cybernetics. In cybernetics, feedback refers to the ability of a person and of some machines to detect an error or deviation from what is desired in an operation. Feedback identifies deviation and communicates that deviation to a control mechanism that makes a subsequent correction. Expert systems may even suggest alternative new actions. In popular communication practice, feedback refers to the verbal or nonverbal response received from the individual or groups to whom the message is directed. Feedback implies at least a two-way communication. With feedback, the message originator can at least make a rough assessment of whether the message was received as intended (i.e., decoded to yield the same basic meaning as was encoded by the sender). Feedback helps to detect misunderstandings when it is accurate and timely. If delayed or distorted by interpersonal or organizational "noise," feedback may be useless. Feedback is most effective when it is obtained as close to the time of message transmission as possible (Sigband & Bell, 1989; Hellriegel, Slocum, & Woodman, 1986; Shockley-Zalabak, 1988).

Recognizing organizational features that affect the clarity, credibility, and directionality of messages is a function of the school administrator in the role of a leader. As the information above reveals, discovering barriers to effective communication requires the leader to examine an organization's channels through multidimensional lenses. This examination might occur through the school leader's reflection on critical incidents in the communication process. In each of these incidents, the school leader identifies situational variables which elicit a mix of communication approaches. A normative model of leadership is built on the situational exercise of various skills at various times. No one common variable/skill/approach works with the same degree of efficacy in every leadership situation. This model of leadership is best applied to the practice of communication. Just as clarity, credibility, and directionality are influenced by organizational changes, an administrator's clear perception of the organization and the power of communication as a shaping agent must constantly sharpen. No one set formula for monitoring the quality of communication exists for application in a complex school organization. In this context the school administrator bases communication processes upon the situational needs that create the communication event. As Smith and Piele (1989) believe, communication choices made by school leaders, like other aspects of their practice, must reflect three abilities: situational sensitivity that enables them to diagnose problems, style flexibility that allows them to match certain practices appropriately to situations, and situational management skills that enable them to alter aspects of a situation to fit work styles. Leadership in schools is context-bound. Nowhere is this more evident than in communication events where administrators must act upon a constantly changing climate and culture that influences the accuracy and diffusion of messages.

Types of Message Directionality

In hierarchical organizations, communications are directed downward, upward, and laterally. In most organizations (and certainly in most traditionally designed American schools), vertical top-down communication predominates (Khandwalla, 1987) and filters through successive layers of the organization until it reaches school children and non-supervisory personnel. Channels are typically of the formal variety. They direct, instruct, indoctrinate, inspire, or evaluate. Common forms of downward communication include policies and procedures, orders and memoranda, handbooks and reports for various stakeholders, and announcements considered to be of general public interest.

A problem with vertical, top-down communication is that it is premised on the "need to know." The stakeholders farthest away from the executive offices are presumed to need only that amount of information that enables them to perform the tasks assigned to them. Messages become ever more narrow as they move through the organization, often leaving those members of the lowest levels without a sense of connectedness to the organization and its purpose. School administrators, business managers, and supervisors decide how much to communicate in original form, how much to edit, add, interpret, or eliminate at each successive level. In one study, Reitz (1987) demonstrated that by the time a message from top management in business reaches individual workers 80 percent of the original message has been filtered out. In schools with overlapping formal and informal channels the filtering is even more prolific.

To overcome message erosion, school organizations need to formulate specific methods for communicating different messages. Planning should minimally address basic issues such as informing all concerned groups of ongoing activities and/or problems; announcing future plans, directions, and goals; encouraging two-way communication; ensuring timeliness of the messages; and allocating funds for communication purposes.

Sigband and Bell (1989) warned that administrative sponsorship of downward communication can forestall the fabrication in the grapevine of "facts." Establishing good communications from the onset is least costly.

Lateral or horizontal communication occurs between persons at the same authority level in the hierarchy. Organizational peers spend a significant amount of time communicating with each other, more time than they spend communicating with their superiors (Reitz, 1987). Sigband and Bell (1989) question the efficiency of lateral communication, considering how little pressure there is in organizations to use it productively. Problem-solving and coordination are clearly enhanced by lateral communication, and duplication of effort is often avoided by means of this fast, direct exchange of messages apart from the chain of command. However, potential disadvantages of lateral communication might include overuse, a burying of peers in inconsequential memos, or an increase in "activity" that carries with it a false impression of productivity. There may also be an unequal exchange, with some peers withholding information as an exercise of power. Since there is usually no system of accountability involved in lateral communication, the arbitrary bartering for power that occurs in these settings can be dangerous to the organization.

The efficacy and volume of upward communication depends on the degree of trust that lower-level stakeholders have in their superiors. Upward communication serves to alert upper levels of school management to the climate, activities, and performance declines or improvements that are of concern at the "grass roots" level of the organization. As is the case with downward communication, selective filtering occurs. Filtering occurs because lower-level employees often tell their superiors what they think those supervisors want to hear, thus introducing a "positive bias" toward themselves through the information they pass upward (Krivonos, 1982). Personnel at the bottom of the organizational pyramid rarely take the risk of initiating upward communication of their own accord. Mechanisms are often put into place just to encourage such communication. These mechanisms might include the use of employee suggestion boxes, creation of quality circles or employee (or student) councils, and the use of various employee and client/customer survey techniques. Anonymity is always an issue in data gathering at all levels of the organization.

Educational organizations are generally alert to the need to communicate with the community at large, as well as the need to enlist participation from that external environment. It is incumbent on school administrations to maintain "open system" perspectives, so that information coming in and going out is as useful to all concerned. Kefalas (1977) considered careful monitoring and response to incoming communication an identifying characteristic of the effective organization. Reitz (1987) underscored the importance of external communication by citing a study of small businesses that showed a direct positive relationship between time spent in outward communications and business financial success. Communication with the community at large requires a definite leadership role for the school administrator. The possibility for organizational noise increases as the size of the receiver group increases because of cultural and psychological interference. Schools increasingly must learn to rely on the support of local communities. The administrator can use communication to influence that support. In this sense the administrator, like his or her counterparts in other organizations, must project a vision and seek to implement that vision through partnerships with the community. However, vision is not enough. Schools must utilize the "human

agency," whether it be school board meetings, newsletters, or public appearances, to mobilize community members to share the values of the vision. This requires selective and direct communication. The creation of new communication channels can operationalize shared values with the community. The community and school become active partners in the larger system, society.

Communication networks are a special case of directionality, involving vertical, horizontal, and lateral communication. Much of the early research on communication networks was conducted in the laboratory setting and focused on the comparative effects of centralized and decentralized networks on the quality of communication. Although variations and elaborations exist, two basic patterns can be used to represent centralized and decentralized networks: the wheel and the circle. In the centralized network, or wheel pattern, persons at the periphery of the wheel send their communications to the hub person who has control over the distribution of information. The structure of this network imposes its own brand of hierarchy, with the hub person becoming the executive figure. In the decentralized network, or circle pattern, all members communicate with those on either side of them, and the network avoids the hierarchical structure. Helgeson's (1990) "web" image of organizations combines wheel and circle networks, with communication nodes at each intersection of the web. Miller (1978) also refers to the intersection of communication channels in "living systems" as nodes of a net.

Using success in problem solving as the criterion of efficiency, Hall (1991) contended that repeated investigations have found the wheel pattern to be superior to the circle pattern. Khandwalla (1987) qualified that position and suggested that the effectiveness of the differing patterns depends on the nature of the task. He found that centralized patterns are faster and more error-free for simple tasks, while decentralized networks perform better if the problems are complex and unexpected. Fisher (1978) noted that although the wheel can be an effective form of network, its effectiveness is largely contingent upon the encoding and decoding skills of the individual occupying the "hub" position.

Other Factors Affecting Organizational Communication

Reitz (1987) listed other major variables that affect direction, frequency, and participant satisfaction with communication. These include the availability of opportunities to interact, the degree of coherence of groups, the status of individuals or groups, and the two-direction communication flow. Each are of considerable importance in school environments.

Communication among individuals and groups can be fostered by arranging physical and psychological distance so that common facilities are shared and interaction is a natural occurrence. Campbell and Campbell (1988) showed in the study of physical environment and interaction that the location of lounges is a strong predictor of lounge use and that an effect on informal types of communication can, therefore, be inferred. A variety of business studies have shown that managers interact most often with subordinates who are located in offices closest to them. The resulting inequities in organizational communications are obvious. Altering spatial relationships can occur through the leadership of a school administrator. Modelling new spatial arrangements may improve communication and shape relationships.

Cohesiveness and communication are mutually reinforcing. As the level of one rises, so does the level of the other. Status affects both the frequency and the direction of communication because individuals tend to direct their communication to individuals of similar or higher status. Reitz (1987) attributed this to perceptions of common interests, to shared experiences, or to mutual reinforcement. The desired outcome of interaction with an individual of higher status may be to move closer to the person who controls the organizational reward structures.

The two-step communication flow refers to a process that depends on personal contacts with "opinion leaders" who in turn are influenced by mediated information from inside and outside of the organization. Information transmitted to the opinion leaders is disseminated to large numbers of people who turn to the opinion leaders for "news" and for "reality testing" of their own points of view. This is an important process for educational administrators who depend on such contacts for successful interface with the local community. Aside from effects that are triggered by status or distance, preference and perception also affect comprehension and overall effectiveness of a communication environment. Reitz (1988) reports that face-to-face communication tends to be more effective than written communication (i.e., if the verbal and nonverbal cues are compatible) but admits that written communication tends to yield greater comprehension. If the receiver typically relies on external guidance and is predisposed to act on information provided by others, the message will be more likely to have the desired effect. If, on the other hand, the receiver is independent, confident, and self-directed, the message may not have the same effect. In general, nonverbal cues can influence communication effectiveness either by corroborating or contradicting a given verbal message or by conveying a message that is independent of verbal material—for example, wearing a business suit or engaging in impatient pencil tapping.

A Sampling of Approaches to Organizational Communication

STRUCTURAL AND FUNCTIONAL APPROACHES

Productivity and task accomplishment are outputs (goals) of major concern to proponents of structural/functional approaches to communication. Shockley-Zalabak (1988) asserted that this results from adopting the principles of scientific management, following the lead of such writers as Max Weber, Henry Fayol, and Frederick Taylor. This approach stems from a bureaucratic management theoretical basis and results in communication style which is top-down, formal, of moderate load, and subject to minimal distortion.

This utilitarian model underpins most public schools in the United States today. Examining the structural/functional approach, along with the emerging concerns of General Systems theorists provides a clearer understanding of the organizational structure imbedded in our current school systems. By understanding these models, an administrator will more clearly recognize the differences in the roles of the administrator-as-manager and the administrator-as-leader. As persistent calls for school reform result in the restructuring of schools, it is natural for conflict of roles to occur. Variables affecting school climate and culture, the knowledge explosion, the advance of technology, the rapidly changing family, and the increase in national poverty and political pressures are forcing changes in school organizations. These changes will force changes in school administrators' roles. The emerging, successful administrators will undoubtedly be leaders who have a full understanding of organizational history and structure. Also, these leaders will be unrestrained in envisioning new models for both understanding and reshaping their school dis-

tricts for success through careful use of communication.

More recently, structural/functional theories of organizational communication have been dominated by the systems approach (Kefalas, 1977; Littlejohn, 1989; Shockley-Zalabak, 1988). These researchers view information processing as the primary function of organizational communication systems. The organization is defined as a system made up of interrelated units or subsystems. The system as a whole can be distinguished from other systems or organizations because it maintains organizational boundaries. If, however, the system is open, i.e., accepting and using environmental information and also communicating outward to the environment, its chances of success are greater than if it maintains closed boundaries and subsists only on internally generated, more bounded information. Because schools are so sensitive to their environments, the systems approach appeals to school administrators as a model for studying internal and external communication.

In the open communication system, incoming information is called *input*. The process by which input is transformed into a form usable by the system is known as *throughput*. Information transmitted from the system outward to its environment, whether intentionally or unintentionally, is referred to as *output*. Figure 8.1 demonstrates an input-output model of communication. Many General Systems theorists warn that the model is too simplistic; it lacks the ability to model the complex elements and dynamics of the actual communication process. System theorists find such a figure too linear and much more systematic than systemic, since the models obscure the richness and holistic orientation of the system paradigm.

Barnard (1938) is credited by many authors as a pioneer in the application of system concepts to the study of organizations and organizational communication. Farace, Monge, and Russell (1977) defined an organization as a system composed of members who are characteristically interdependent; who process input, throughput, and output; and who treat information as a critical resource for reducing uncertainty. Within this framework, communication depends on the use of common symbolic forms that have widely understood referents. Here information is subdivided into two types: absolute information that collectively refers to all of the information within the system, and distributed information that resides in different places throughout the system. Distributed information is often neglected by school administrators and other managers.

Farace et al. (1977) indicated that conceptualization promotes discussion of communication at three levels: the system level, the functional level, and the structural level. At the system level three hierarchical interchanges occur: individuals communicate in dyads; the dyads cluster into groups; and the interconnected groups form the organization or macro-network. At the functional level there is evidence of three organizational operations: production, innovation, and maintenance. At the structural level, communication elements of the frequency, regularity, and patterns of communication are plotted.

At the individual communication level, "load" is an important concept. Load refers to the quantity, volume, rate, and complexity of messages (Shockley-Zalabak, 1988). Major problems related to load include the extremes of underload, which is evident when the flow of messages falls below the individual's capacity for processing them; and overload, which represents a flow of messages that exceeds the individual's information-processing capacity. Technological advances enabling the transmission of vast quantities of messages at extremely high rates have been the source of chronic overload for many individuals, resulting in impaired deci-

sionmaking. *Chronic overload* is a term that resonates with teachers and administrators alike. It is imperative that an administrator understand technology and its impact on communication.

At the dyad level of organizational communication, the key concept is "rules." Rules are explicit and implicit norms or axioms for communications within the organization. Generally, rules are either thematic or tactical. Thematic rules are behavioral norms that reflect organizational values and beliefs, and tactical rules prescribe behaviors relevant to more general themes, such as referring analogically to the organization as a "family." An individual who is socialized into an organization and who learns to identify with it will generally comply with both thematic and tactical rules.

Littlejohn (1989) considered three structures within the group setting: the micro-network (the pattern of group interactions), the power structure, and the leadership structure (including interpersonal influence roles of group members). The various members and their links constitute the communication network. Links have five different properties: (1) symmetry (the extent to which linked members interact on an equal basis), (2) strength (frequency of interaction), (3) reciprocity (the extent to which individuals concur about the links), (4) the content of the interactions, and (5) mode (the vehicle that carries the interaction, e.g., verbal or written communication). Within the micro-network, individuals have distinct roles: acting as liaisons with other groups, becoming isolated and in essence "unlinked," or performing as gatekeepers who control information coming into or released by the group.

The systems approach to organizational communication is able to address large numbers of variables. Littlejohn (1989) contended, however, that such approaches do not adequately account for situational variables that are not systemlike.

No single approach may serve to explain or identify all the variables in the communication process, therefore, no single method of communication will suffice for *all* situations that a school administrator encounters. Again, the concern for situational leadership (Yukl, 1989) emerges. The more complex an organization is the more complex communication will be. The constant flow of communication in a school necessitates a constant practice of a variety of skills by the administrator who decides to get tasks done—to manage or to influence commitment to lead. In both these roles the administrator must have a clear knowledge of organizational structure in practice and in the ideal.

BEHAVIORAL APPROACHES

As management theories change to accommodate a more humanistic point of view, complementary changes occur in the way organizational communication is viewed. The Hawthorne effect demonstrates that giving management attention to human relations factors has a favorable impact on organizational success. This is an early example of many subsequent studies that reached the same conclusion. When communication theorists felt that the complexity of human behavior was misrepresented in the structuralist-functionalist approach as a handmaiden of scientific management, they sought other approaches.

Human relations theorists believe that messages should move in all directions, through both formal and informal networks. They emphasize oral over written channels and suggest a moderate communication load with predictable levels of distortion. One theoretical model representing this position is Likert's Four Systems. Likert (1967) suggests that organizations operate along a continuum of high-to-low-control leadership styles which have correlates in organizational communication styles.

The first style, "exploitative-authoritative," is associated with top-down management. This style rarely accommodates feedback and therefore limits both the directions and frequencies of communication. The second style, "benevolent-authoritative," is also identified with top-down management, but the communication patterns here tend to give at least the appearance of management sensitivity to employee needs. The third style, called "consultative," accommodates vertical communication interchanges both upward and downward in the organization. The fourth style, "participative management," accommodates the greatest amount of multidirectional communication, with employees expected to participate fully in organizational decision-making. Critics of Likert's model suspect that participative management is also constrained by hierarchical assumptions and suggest that there may be yet another, structurally different, power-sharing style (Schein, 1989). These styles were previously discussed in more detail in Chapter 2.

Human relations approaches are often criticized because of the implied notion that high morale leads, without exception, to high productivity. Other critics see a failure to address important structural and functional variables. In this regard the human relations perspective may be suffering from the same misapprehensions and "turf wars" that the system thinkers experience. Regardless of this academic criticism, in reality, organizations function on the basis of morale and missions of productivity at some echelons. How organizations are modeled for an understanding of the shaping/life-giving effects of communication may not be determined by solely viewing the organization through one of the less-structured approaches. Nevertheless, these approaches provide important elements for consideration by school administrators whose very job is to promote the delivery of a human service and enable teachers, students, and staff to achieve. The school administrator cannot ignore the inevitable "humanness" of the school's character, especially in attempting to understand communication needs and responses.

APPROACHES RELATED TO THE PROCESS OF ORGANIZING

Weick's (1969) theory of organizing appears systemic with an ethnographic or cultural accent. As characterized, it is considered to be one of the few "truly organizational communication theories" (Littlejohn, 1989). Weick believes that organizational environments do not preexist but are instead *enacted*. Organizational members continually enact and reenact the environment as attitudes, values, and experience warrant. Organizing is, therefore, evolutionary and contingent not only on enactment but also on information selection and retention processes. Enactment incorporates an acknowledgement of equivocality, but selection enables the group to admit certain relevant information and reject other data as irrelevant to the enactment. Retention entails decisions about which information should be saved for future use. In Weick's theory, assembly rules and interlocking behavior cycles are viewed as the root mechanisms for organizing. Assembly rules guide the choice of routines that are used for enactment, selection, and retention. Interlocking behavior cycles are sets of interrelated behaviors that enable the group to agree on which meanings should be included and which should be rejected. After retention occurs, organizational members must decide whether to reenact the environment in some manner or to modify their behavior to achieve consistency with the information they hold. The flexibility implied by these evolving decisions may be of particular interest to school administrators. This flexibility implies ways in which change can be orchestrated on the basis of understanding communication.

Poole and McPhee (1983) extended the principle of structuration (organizing) into the realm of organizational communication. Interactions create norms and rules relative to the achievement of organizational goals and markedly affect both structure and climate. Poole and McPhee believe that organizational structure is a representation and a product of organizational communication. Structure is also an indirect way of informing employees and others about the organization. Structure becomes a form of meta-communication by which an organization can address its needs and patterns.

Structuration can occur at three sites: (1) the site of conception, i.e., at any site where individual or group decisions are made about what will happen in the organization; (2) the site of implementation, i.e., the locations from which formal codification and dissemination of decisions about what will happen in the organization are proceeding; and (3) the site of reception, those points at which organizational members act in accordance with the decisions made. Although anyone in the organization can participate in communication at any of the three sites, structuration tends to be specialized. For example, administrators are primarily involved at the site of conception. At this site administrators have the most opportunities to serve as leaders by establishing the means to influence the commitment of staff and students. Through the deliberate creation of channels, i.e. committees, forums, jobs, etc., administrators may lead their organizations to build efficient communication systems. These systems can promote the general health of the organization. An administrator may be simply getting staff to commit to using channels. In this way the administrator has led them to follow an example of life-giving, multidirectional communication.

Equally important, Poole and McPhee (1983) defined the organizational members' collective attitude as climate, an attitude that is constantly affected by organizational interactions. Climate is viewed as both a medium and an outcome of interactions, influenced not only by the structure but also by such climate-modifying strategies as publication of newsletters or holding contests. Climate is also affected by the composite of individual attributes, such as the possession or lack of knowledge and skills.

In contrast to organizational climate, the term *organizational culture* commonly refers to the shared realities that are played out in "performances" displayed during interchanges (Pacanowsky & O'Donnell-Trujillo, 1982). These performances can be classified as (1) rituals—personal, task, or social in nature, performances that are regularly repeated; (2) passions, including storytelling or passionate repartee exchanged in dramatic and lively interactions; (3) sociality, including social performances dedicated to the creation of a group sense of identity, such as joking, talking shop, or sharing personal experiences; (4) organizational politics, creating and reinforcing notions of power and influence and perhaps involving activities such as bargaining; and (5) enculturation, including performances aimed at initiating new members into the accepted organizational culture. Most school-based educators easily accept the notion that schools are cultural entities.

As cultural entities, schools present myriad communication opportunities. The administrator must choose, in the context of a shared mission, how to emphasize positive school-cultural traits in each opportunity. In an increasingly multicultural context the role of the school administrator must be defined by communication that is reflective of school values and a school culture that is open to all stakeholders.

SOCIO-PSYCHOLOGICAL PERSPECTIVE ON INDIVIDUAL COMMUNICATION IN ORGANIZATIONS

Elements of other theories and approaches to organizational communication are incorporated in socio-psychological theories. Paramount in this genre of communications the-

ory are the effects on or created by individual communication acts. Here we revisit elements and processes associated with basic, quasi-mechanistic communication models in order to add psychological perspectives.

Psychological perspectives conceptualize organizational communication as a loop in which a sender initiates a message, a receiver obtains it, and then considers possible courses of action. If the receiver responds or provides feedback, the roles of sender and receiver reverse. This looping behavior occurs in an organization's "bureaucratic structure," which is subject to noise from the informal structure. It is this extraneous noise that often interferes with message understanding. The meaning of a message depends not only on the content but also on the organizational context. O'Reilly and Pondy (1979) utilized the formula *MEANING = INFORMATION + CONTEXT* to depict this process.

The message source may be a person or an intermediary medium, such as a newspaper, a memorandum, or a visual image. Credibility of the sender is critical in socio-psychological theory. Receivers may ignore noncredible messengers at will, regardless of message content. Not only are there psychological interpretations of the right of the sender to comment, but there are also psychological demands regarding a particular sender's choice of media. The encoding and decoding processes both allow "mental sets" to detract from or enhance message communication. According to psychological theorists, personality variables, values, gender or cultural differences, and personal interest ensure that a filtering process occurs at all points in the flow of communication.

Because the message form is often contingent on the channel or medium selected for message transmission, individual preferences can either override the communication system or be overridden by it. The channels or media selected determine, in large part, the routing pattern the message will follow, i.e., whether the message will be conveyed vertically or horizontally, formally or informally. Formatting the message also has psychological implications, because individuals do not perceive or process information in identical ways. Business executives are increasingly concerned that the medium selected may determine the richness and the impact of the information processed by receivers (Daft & Lengel, 1984; Lengel & Daft, 1988). Richness of medium is determined by the overall reception of a message. School administrators are also beginning to be selective about the medium they use. Face-to-face verbal communication is preferred while telephone communications and "written personal" are next in order. "Written formal" and "numeric formal" complete the low end of the richness continuum, with numeric formal completing the spectrum. Face-to-face, filmed or televised speech is considered "primary oral" communication, and all forms of written communication are considered "secondary verbal."

Communicators in educational settings place some reliance on the relationships between message chosen and medium selected. Message comprehension tends to be higher when it is in written form, but opinion change is greater when a face-to-face communication is employed. Media redundancy (i.e., a combination of written and oral) increases both message richness and accuracy of reception. Written communication tends to be effective when the message contains general information or requires future action. Oral communication tends to be effective in situations demanding immediate feedback. Examples of such situations are offering praise, giving procedural directions, settling disputes, issuing reprimands, and even saying "good morning" to other organizational members.

Nonverbal as well as verbal signals have meaning, and this meaning may conflict with or reinforce verbal message sending. Even nonword sound expressions, such as grunts or laughter, complicate the problem of message accuracy. Socio-psychological theorists

seem to believe that the best to hope for is that the message received will be functionally comparable to the message sent.

Because the range of message-sending options and the range of responses are both subject to individual differences, feedback itself becomes a psycho-social phenomenon. Feedback varies even in its degrees of purposefulness, especially in its nonverbal aspects. For example, an unintended yawn can convey entirely the wrong feedback message. The concept of feedback implies that constant adjustments in the communication process can and should be made on the basis of clues the communicators get from feedback. Feedback can improve task performance and positively influence organizational climate.

Feedback can, on the other hand, either reflect or actually create situational noise. If physical, social, or psychological barriers are in place, feedback can either strengthen or reduce those barriers. Telling a communication partner that a freight train is passing can help that partner understand your communication situation. Telling a partner that your boss is in the office helps the partner understand a reluctance to stay on the phone, and telling a partner that a particular phrase or mannerism is upsetting helps that person either adjust or decide not to adjust behavior according to his or her intent. Feedback is a powerful tool for educational administrators who can set the tone and examples for the whole school system. Feedback, therefore, can be verbal or nonverbal and, in any form, it must be situationally appropriate.

Nonverbal communication has been researched extensively in a variety of settings. For educators, two nonverbal modes are of particular interest: the impact of facial expressions and the use of spatial cues. Lipham and Francke (1966) studied nonverbal behavior of school principals as influencing promotability or nonpromotability. The variables they examined were (1) the structuring of self, i.e., self-maintenance, clothing, physical movement and posture; (2) the structuring of interaction, including interaction initiation, interaction distance, and interaction termination behaviors; and (3) structuring of environment, including such matters as office decor, spatial arrangements, neatness, and status symbols. The above researchers found significant differences in interaction and environmental structuring. Promotable principals tended to keep less distance in their interpersonal encounters. They also tended to use status symbols more casually, for example, using a desk nameplate as a paperweight versus using it as a kind of psychological fence.

Communication satisfaction suggests that a real or perceived lack of two-way communication is a critical variable in educational institutions. Situational noise also poses a considerable threat to the success of organizational communication. Interpersonal communication seems to be always more effective than organizational communication because face-to-face situations rule out many sources of distortion, permit immediate feedback, and encourage message reframing.

Bureaucratic models of organization, described by Barnard (1938), require that the channels of communication reach every organizational member, take the shortest and most direct route, remain available for constant use, and be authenticated by position power that tells receivers that the sender has the required authority to be a sender. The model assumes that such formality ensures message accuracy because it is "in writing," is from competent superiors, and is contextually the same for everyone. While context may change to coordinating activities, providing information, influencing or directing, or simply telling organizational stories, formality is prominent. School bureaucracies display the dimensions above to the extent that they are centralized, hierarchically shaped, and either more or less dependent on information technology.

Formal communication channels can carry both instrumental and expressive content, i.e., to help the organization reach its goals and to affect attitudes, norms, and values. Informal channels are complementary in the sense that they typically reflect the impact of content carried in the formal channels. Informal communication also serves to gratify social needs of busy people by helping them to express themselves personally and socially.

To understand formal and informal communication, researchers have used content analysis, sociometry, interaction analysis, participant observation, continuous observation, communication sampling, and general survey or network survey techniques. In educational institutions, general and network survey techniques are widely used. Surveys are designed to assess communication accuracy, openness, and frequency. Surveys provide useful pictures of informal communication patterns and structures and often identify attractions, resistance, or lack of opportunity to communicate. Communication problems identified sociometrically can be deliberately brought into the networks so that information and social meanings are not lost. Communications typically form along task-focused lines, so that members of some groups are not members of others and, therefore, communicate less often. This can prevent formal authority and social networks from overlapping, especially when school administrators wish to introduce new information or practices. In other cases, overlapping may be deliberately planned to increase the accuracy of message reception.

Pathways to the Future

Individuals in leadership positions spend the majority of their working days communicating, but at the same time communication skills are an acknowledged weakness of such leaders (Baeshen, 1987). In the United States, millions of dollars are spent every year on efforts to develop the leadership, communication, and interpersonal skills of business, industry, and government leaders (Carnevale & Gainer, 1989). Middle managers are especially targeted for such training, with close to one-fourth of Fortune 500 training and development budgets allocated for these purposes. School administrators do not have access to comparable developmental resources and, after professional education, are generally expected to attend to their own development.

Although school personnel may already be alert to interpersonal and organizational communication issues, business organizations more clearly understand the impact of communication processes on the organizational "bottom line," i.e., understanding how communication processes affect survivability. Schools do not have the same clear, generally agreed-upon standards of productivity, although the current efforts for national achievement standards and the high emphasis placed on test scores suggests that some stakeholders want more identifiable, unilateral outcomes. In the 1990s, more public pressure will undoubtedly plague schools. The public, especially political and business/industry leaders, see schools as factories that should be producing literate, law-abiding citizens who are well-prepared to enter the work force. At the same time, school-based administrators and staff struggle to maintain safe, effective, future-oriented environments. With varied perceptions of productivity and varied goals of stakeholders, communication becomes even more important as diverse actors seek to agree upon reform and restructuring efforts.

Employees' satisfaction is contingent upon the degree of autonomy they experience in doing their jobs; yet organizations are so oriented toward hierarchy that other social and work arrangements have not been considered. The challenge for school administrators

is to examine all organizational arrangements for their critical effect on communication processes and for their ultimate effect on school children, communities, and the future labor force. School administrators are called upon to imagine the unimaginable: new forms of schooling, new visions, new plans, procedures, and ways of measuring success.

Earlier in this chapter, historical roots of organizational communication theory were noted, and several authors were cited extensively for their comprehensive coverage of communication phenomena, theory, and research, especially in relation to school organizations. These are *retrospective* summaries, and while much of what is discussed is still operative in today's organizations, the future of organizational communication still can advance dramatically. Organizations and organizational leaders need to create that future consciously, not by tradition or default.

Educators are particularly interested in long-term goals and often view the short, hectic cycles of business planning, particularly in regard to demands for trained manpower with some alarm. At the same time, the positivistic, linear, cause-and-effect thinking of business organizations may be attractive to school administrators who must also find or create order in the midst of organizational chaos. Possibly neither private nor public sector paradigms and practices will suffice in the turbulent future. There is a growing discomfort in all sectors with "the way things are presently done." This discomfort may also refer to the way "things" are conceptualized. Nowhere is there a more important necessity than to fully understand how communication affects our organizations. Both internal and external communication helps to shape "realities." If school administrators wish to emphasize achievement scores at the cost of emphasizing an understanding of learning styles and paces, they may report achievement test scores to their staff as a motivation or evaluation measure. If school administrators focus on these scores in their district newsletter, they have communicated their emphasis externally. External feedback may commence to pressure and shape internal "realities": curriculum, scheduling, and methodology.

Able administrators need to analyze and interpret their personal frames of reference, their metaphors, beliefs, and biases about organizations and organizational communication. Are they finite, firmly bounded scientific management systems using finite control mechanisms? Are they open, dynamic, holographic, "reenacting" systems using multiple variety stimulation/regulation strategies? Whichever the case, administrators and teachers alike must be able to understand their own preferences and how their beliefs affect practice.

Synthesizing Known Principles of Organizational Communication

As discussed above, there is general agreement that communication is (1) purposive, (2) socio-psychological, (3) carried in both formal and informal channels, and (4) incomplete without feedback. There is still disagreement, however, about the importance of information theory in socio-psychological approaches. In essence, all of the approaches to organizational communication can make valid claims to definitions of communication because multiple perspectives and frames of reference are inevitable. By the same token, all of the described approaches can be challenged because they do not incorporate all possible perspectives or account for all possible communication variables. A more comprehensive understanding and use of General System Theory may help to integrate multiple perspectives and accommodate richer mixes of variables. This integrative theory-building seems to be a task for the future.

Message sending and receiving skills are so important (Haugland, 1987) that procedural models have been devised to help the communicator. Khandwalla's (1987) model suggests a front-end analysis to include (1) determining the objective of the message and (2) analyzing the situational variables, including available channels, best media, time constraints, and the nature of recipients. In this model, the communicator seeks to anticipate potential communication difficulties and devise strategies for overcoming them. At a minimum, words and phrases that are likely to be "emotional triggers" are avoided, and calls to action are crafted and understood as a collective enterprise rather than "military commands." The message sender thinks about potential miscommunication effects, even though there is no guarantee that negative effects will not occur. The school administrator will find that messages encouraging participation are generally well received, but that, by tradition, some organization members will expect and even welcome the "military command." Steering through the mine fields of individual differences is never easy and is always a situational "judgment call." From the perspective of a knowledgeable administrator whose primary communication goals are to maintain organizational status quo, the ever-active balancing of forces in an organization can prevent poor judgments from destroying positive organizational climate.

Employees and client groups want straight answers, straight information, and candid talk from their leaders (Ragan, 1990), even though there is often no agreement about what exactly ought to be communicated. Constituents reflect both a fear of communication and a fear of candor, but a fear of the unknown is far more unsettling (Wartenberg, 1990). The atmosphere of "waiting to find out" is an atmosphere of skepticism, insecurity and cynicism. This leads lower level stakeholders to engage in counterproductive speculations or self-preservation tactics. On such occasions, messages in informal communication channels can be organizationally destabilizing. The old adage that some news, however unpleasant, is better than no news remains true in organizational communication. Using "leaks," opinion leaders, and increased face-to-face communication can help educational administrators relieve the tension in such a situation. By openly accepting feedback from all parts of the organization, the administrator can build the unity and health of the organization.

Some of the imperatives for effective communication are stated in these guidelines:

The amount of redundancy and feedback along with the amount of face-to-face communication needed is situationally dependent. Giving short, concise messages or addressing problems of organizational climate are occasions for face-to-face communication, while delivering messages that require an understanding of background or context may be best accomplished in writing. There may be considerable value in communicating in both ways at the same time.

Personal skill and planning are essential for giving and receiving useful feedback. For positive effect, feedback should be helpful. It should be very specific and descriptive, accompanied by examples if possible. It should be given by someone who is perceived as trustworthy, should be timely, and should be presented in such a way that the receiver feels confident to do something about the situation. However, it should be noted that feedback is not automatic and often not voluntary; it may need to be pursued. Feedback consists of verbal and nonverbal messages that may or may not be congruent. It may even consist of misleading information that is meant to be tactful. Misleading information may also be used as a manipulative strategy by a person who fears for survival in a given organization.

The filtering of messages in all directions remains a serious problem in the communication process. If open and complete honesty is a threatening condition for either school leaders or followers, the filtering process can close down cooperation and yield erroneous messages. If open communication can prevail, subordinates can use it to get their work done with satisfaction, and leaders will have reliable sources of information to enable them to avert organizational problems. A positive organizational climate is the outcome of open communication. Miller (1978) cautioned, however, that even in the preferred channel-and-network arrangement of organizational communication, the relay nodes are also potential bottlenecks. He also notes the obvious: the longer the channels, the slower the flow of information.

Educational administrators serve organizational and personal interests well if they can devise a number of different ways to encourage upward and lateral communication. One successful method has been the use of "linchpin" or liaison structures, where an individual who communicates in two or more separate communication networks is deliberately charged with transferring information upward, downward, and laterally across groups. Such linch-pins can transcend a number of hierarchical levels. Another linking method is the formation of communications matrices where each educational staff member participates in at least two formal subsystems (e.g., instructional and school-wide). One should be warned, however, that these communication strategies are effective only as long as trusting relationships are maintained. Any serious breach of trust can take years to repair since many layers of the communication network are simultaneously damaged when trust is breached in one area of the network.

Boundary spanning roles, either formal or informal, can be established to help individuals or groups form communication links with their environments. The triangulation principle applies here: Multiple and independent sources of information provide data about matters that may not be researchable in any direct fashion. Creating overlapping and redundant information systems can be a means to overcome the possibility that some gatekeepers, liaisons, or isolates may misuse the power inherent in their position. In this connection even isolates have power, for either by their voluntary withdrawal or by their involuntary job demands they may block projects on which they are genuinely needed. Assigning isolates to task groups and altering job assignments to allow them to participate may enable the organization to draw on their skills and experience effectively. Leadership is a social act. Understanding the roles of groups and isolates and altering their roles

via selective communication modes is the responsibility of the school leader. Schools are social by nature and mission. Whether tasks need to be performed or commitment won, school leaders are necessarily bound to act on their awareness of the effects of social interaction.

Combining the Metaphors

Returning to the sets of metaphors and assumptions cited earlier in this chapter, it becomes clear that some metaphors are more helpful than others for exploring new forms of organization and new requirements for organizational communication. The machine metaphor has already been labelled problematic. Therefore, the heavy burden for produc-

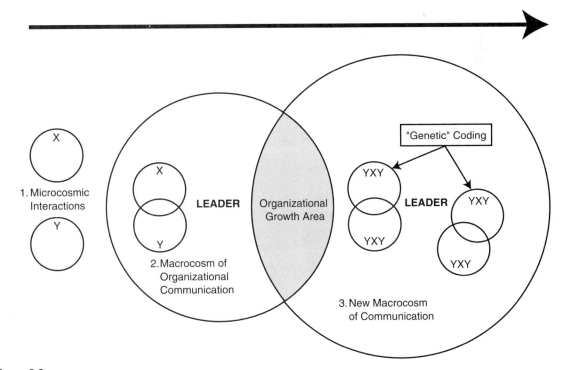

Figure 8.2
Organic migration and enlargement of microcosmic interactions in organizational communication

tivity also moves from the shoulders of humankind to the electronic data bases that support human thinking and information processing. The organization *possesses* machine-based components of organizational communication but *is not* itself a machine.

The organization-as-organism model is still a viable one, and supports the idea that humans and their interactions are microcosms of the organizations that they create around themselves. The holographic metaphor extends this idea. "Common cultural assumptions in an organization could be thought of as genetic codes that permit reconstruction of the whole from any part" (Schein, 1989, p. 12). The reference to genes as cellular reproductive microcosms of whole organizations is both biological in functioning and holographic in image. Organizational communication can be depicted similarly as shown in Figure 8.2.

The organic model overlaps with the cultural-anthropological model, but moves the focus from individual organism or organization to the organization as a culture embedded in a larger culture. The communication emphasis shifts accordingly with cultural transmission becoming its primary rationale. This perspective supports the mores of particular organizations and may even legitimize leaders as organizational gurus even though a culture may be expected to change over time (see Figure 8.3).

Psychological metaphors remind organizational communication specialists that no two human individuals send, receive, perceive, or interpret data—even sensory data—in exactly the same way. Human psychological uniqueness intrudes on every formulation of organizational communication. These claims cannot be denied and must be taken into account in modeling (see Figure 8.4).

The metaphor of the organization as brain permits analogies of computer-like information processing, much less dependent on structures and organizational layering for pro-

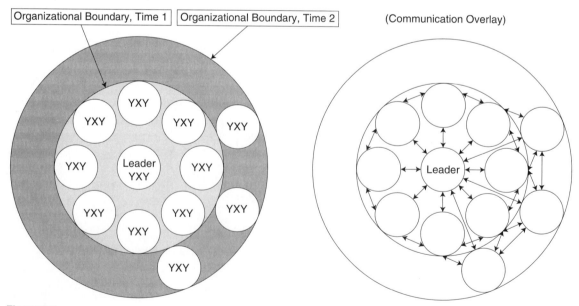

Figure 8.3
Culture-coded (YXY) organizational parts in systemic relationship, with organizational communication overlay

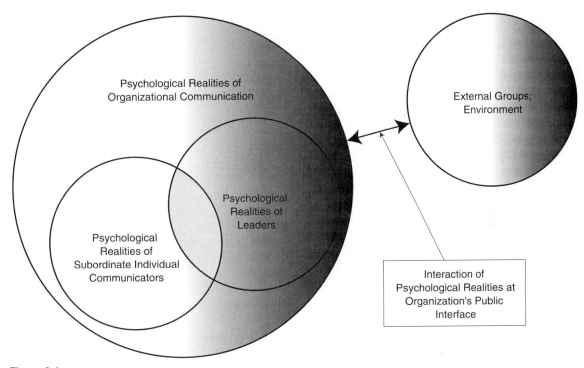

Figure 8.4
Psychological impacts of organizational communication

ductive activity. It also allows for continuous research, action, and research. The difficulty some have with this metaphor is that it is easily confused with leader as brain of the organization. No such idea is intended. Rather, the brain metaphor is meant to convey a broader, more holistic, more versatile picture of organizational thought and activity.

Organization as art easily allows the interpretation of organizational communication as a selective repertoire of plastic arts and media. Communication then becomes drama, painting and drawing, sculpting, prose or poetry, oration, conversation, or any other art form that conveys meaning throughout the organization. Art that is hung throughout corporate and other executive offices may be a minor acknowledgement of this point of view.

The metaphor of organization as learner shares many elements with the metaphor of organization as organism, brain, or art form.

This metaphor optimistically represents a human organization acting as a cooperative learning community that thinks, feels, performs, values, and adjudicates its own work and its relation to human life at every level of the organization. In many ways, it requires that informed systems erase the image of humans as production machines and insists on a restored image of humans as perpetually learning, growing, exchanging, and caring about those exchanges in both the personal and organizational sense. Communication modeling for such holographic, artistic, learning/growing models can be only rudimentary at this point in time (see Figure 8.5).

Individuals need to breathe to live. So do organizations, because they are composed of living human beings. Metaphorically, communication becomes the "breath" of the organization, enabling its electronic and human systems to work in concert, to reach outside the

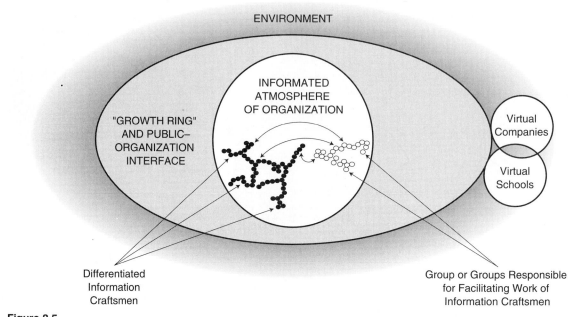

Figure 8.5
Informed atmosphere of organizational communication: the breath of organizational life

organization, and, perhaps, to work with a new sense of craftsmanship. In an ailing organization, an administrator with a clear understanding of the stakeholders' mission can provide the life-support system to sustain the breath of the organization. That life-support needs attentive monitoring, constant updating and the change of a vision. This life-support role may be the opportunity for an administrator to exercise a leadership role.

Moving Forward: Potential New Directions

Greenfield (1987) states that the top-down leadership style is characteristic of educational institutions. This style reduces distortion but also strangles organizational communication in the participative sense and drains creative energy away from the system. The limitations this style imposes on upward com-

munication are resented by self-confident, self-directed professionals, and, in school systems, even resented by students who receive the "most filtered" information of all. Fortunately, educational leadership styles appear to be shifting in the direction of greater openness with greater sharing of information and problem-solving occurring between levels.

Educational administrators have the opportunity to set a cooperative tone for the whole organization and can deliberately model the behaviors that they want to see in others. They can identify and correct chronic blocks and distortions in communication networks and, if pertinent, establish new channels and networks as well. As "open door" administrators, they can be willing to listen thoughtfully and be ready to go "the extra mile" to value others as persons and as senders/receivers of messages. Instructor involvement in the organization itself—and not just in the classrooms—is crucial to organizational success. The annals of educational administration are strewn with the wreckage caused by lack of such involvement. It should be acknowledged that it is a great deal to ask of both teachers and administrators to be involved organizationally in addition to their heavy work schedules; however, such involvement is an enabler for positive change and greater work satisfaction.

To be an instructional leader means to be concerned at least as much about teaching/learning as about organizational policies, rules, and regulations. If instructors do not see evidence of this concern, whatever else an administrator may say or do will be skeptically received. The administrator is immediately relegated to the role of a mundane manager. A powerful, and probably unintended, message has been communicated.

If it seems that the role of educational administrator is becoming too enormous to be embraced by a single individual, this may be because new roles are being adopted without eliminating older ones. Since many schools operate structurally as they did in the early 1900s, restructuring efforts that clarify the administrator's leadership role may diminish the conflict between roles. The current enormity of the school administrator's role is a result of administrators trying to manage and lead at the same time. In each role mixed messages are sent within and outside of the organization; it is no wonder that communication becomes muddled. "Informated" stakeholders may need translators for their twentieth-century counterparts who seek organizations the "way they were" at the turn of the century. Zuboff (1988) suggested, in a book resulting from ten years of intensive academic and field research, that leaders tend to rejustify their "right to rule" whenever sweeping social changes call previous justifications into question. In the "informated" society (Zuboff, 1988; Schuck, 1985), organizations cannot rely on twentieth-century justifications. They must not only respond effec-

tively to changes in their "image," or symbolic environment (Krippendorff & Eleey, 1986), but also alter their views about how information and work are distributed.

Those who interact with information on a "real-time" basis, e.g., those who are "in the trenches" of teaching or those who work with core data bases, use intellectual skills that are not different from those required elsewhere in the organization. It is the contexts that vary. In this model the justifications for hierarchy began to erode, and the emphasis shifts from "acting for" or "acting on" to "acting with." All members of the organization are engaged in data interpretation, since there are more data than can be gathered from or consigned to any one area or any one cadre of leaders. Therefore, it logically follows that communication becomes multidirectional. Some communication events are task-oriented and linear. Some are global/vision-oriented and definitely nonlinear.

Zuboff (1988) noted that organizational emphasis on wholeness causes leaders and many employees to feel initially disoriented. Changes in the distribution of authority are frightening. The level of involvement and commitment required of individuals in a new, flexible organization is daunting. There are implications for social integration that many fear are a precursor to the loss of individual rights. The fact is that while top-down regimes allow for little creativity, they also protect members from ambiguity. Different people have different thresholds for enjoying, tolerating, or breaking apart under conditions of ambiguity. This is not a slight concern to new organization planners.

New divisions of learning based on the premise that *learning is the new work of organizations* are at the heart of the post-hierarchical organization. In such organizations, the new leadership role that Zuboff (1988) described is facilitative, teacher-like, and very vulnerable. The new risk is needing constantly to admit that one does not have all the answers and that the answers where they exist at all may be found only by cooperative action. The new leaders in schools, as in other organizations, will need to be concerned about intellectual skill development, technology development, strategy formulation, and social system development. However, they cannot actually "control" any of these in the old sense of giving orders and being sure of specific action. The new leaders can only orchestrate opportunities to promote community and to develop communication skills throughout the organization.

Playing this different role imposes new communication imperatives. Optimal communication in the formal bureaucracies have been regarded as "two-way," but in an informated organization, two ways are not enough. In the informated organization an explosion of information is available to everyone. The communication questions become, how to share, interpret, and feed back information at specific points and times to specific places in the organization when it is needed. Communication in this sense becomes interdependent and fluid. At least some measure of skill homogeneity is implied. Another implication is that a higher baseline of entry level communication skills may be required of the leader. Communication in the informated organization changes the internal functioning of the organization itself and so changes the environmental expectations of the organization.

Educational administrators may personally either reject or accept the possibilities and challenges of inviting new forms of organization and new requirements for communication. The initial stages of new paradigms have always been ignored. Many are already thinking and writing seriously about such organizational changes and can scarcely be ignored. At present, school leaders are already trying to manage complexity, perhaps with old ideas

and tools, and quite possibly, with less than perfect success. Life has changed dramatically in the last few decades; schools have not. The lack of change has trapped administrators in structures that were designed to be successful in another age. The popular image of a successful "little red school house" is equally inadequate today considering emerging circumstances. Only risktakers who are willing to envision and create new school structures have a chance to develop a successful model appropriate for the future.

■ **CASE STUDY**

Communication: The Case of Communication Paralysis

After the previous evening's community and education forum, Superintendent John Shapiro immediately scheduled an emergency meeting with his most trusted staff. His ongoing promotion of a renewed school environment and pronouncement to the community was suddenly being derailed. His vision was collapsing. Community leaders were upset with the distinct lack of progress. Parents continued to be confrontational, complaining about calls for higher teacher pay and school district needs. Student achievement scores were, at best, barely average in the community. Lately, even his own teachers had begun to organize. They objected to the added expectations and responsibilities assigned to them and complained that they received too little allowance for autonomous action, too many unidirectional policy decisions, and little incentive to change.

At the staff meeting the next morning, Superintendent Shapiro spoke in a concerned tone. "Thank you for making room in your schedules for this meeting. This morning, I want to open new lines of dialogue. It appears we've reached an impasse. Last night's forum meeting was a disaster as everyone here can attest, and I'm not going to sit still and watch this happen." His voice become more distraught.

"I certainly don't understand the massively negative reactions to the reform effort. At last month's forum meeting, I thought we had made dramatic inroads and that the new third wave school program was really taking shape. Last night parents were relentless in their opposition to the new district budget. I also heard rumors that a small group of teachers are becoming vocal dissenters to the program. They'll probably raise union issues again. Worse than that, after the meeting, I was approached by the mayor." At this point his voice rose an octave. He even got up and began pacing as he spoke. "The mayor said that he was considering removing his support for the whole project until we get the teachers aligned. He was adamant! He said I'd better get our teachers on board now or the funding for the project would dry up permanently. For all I know, they've probably got the funds earmarked for his reelection campaign."

Superintendent Shapiro paused, returned to his seat, and spoke again more calmly. "I thought the project was really taking shape. We need to set a course and patch this up. I'm sure many of you felt some of this resistance too. Any thoughts?"

Assistant Superintendent Michelle Glazer said, "John, I didn't read last night's meeting like that at all." Michelle always brought a reassuring order to these meetings.

"Afterwards, I had some lengthy chats with several parents. They were all upbeat. Even Paul Tracy, the city controller, stopped by to talk. He and I had a long discussion about funding possibilities for the project. We discussed a couple of new and really promising avenues that he said he would call me about. He wanted to form a small discussion group to explore them more fully. In all, I found the whole agenda and reaction last evening very open and enlightening. Don't let the mayor or those more vocal teachers dampen your spirit. Listen to their reaction as a means to learn from them and move your program forward."

"Michelle, you're always right on target," said Superintendent Shapiro in a more composed state now. "I also spoke with Paul and he did have some interesting ideas about budgeting for the project. Charlie, how did you assess the meeting?"

Charlie Frantz, the Human Resource Director spoke. "I wasn't at all concerned, John," he said in a matter-of-fact tone. "As we all know, there are numerous variables that surround this project, and I didn't see that the meeting was any different from past meetings. We'll always be confronting issues like this and even more in the third wave system. I did hear a similar rumor. The mayor is running scared. How about you, Diane, did you read this any differently?"

Diane Hall, a training consultant working with the district, said to the superintendent in a conciliatory tone, "I think Charlie is on the right track, John. You all know that this project has been controversial from the start. Everyone has an opinion about this project and is operating from his or her own beliefs. Overcoming that diversity is difficult. Do you remember a month or so ago when I suggested we consider developing in-service training of our teachers? Perhaps this is an important opportunity for us. They're on the firing line constantly and, at the same time, they're the most important asset we've got. We need to communicate and share our beliefs about the program with them and improve our overall communication patterns. I've thought about this for some time now." Diane became more intent. "Perhaps we could develop some additional seminars for the upcoming district retreat in the fall. These seminars could improve our overall organizational communication. After all, how we communicate is our life's breath. What do you think? I could outline rough drafts of seminar work over the next month and pass around copies for each of you to look at."

The meeting went on for another hour. Diane obtained approval to develop the in-service training objectives more fully. Over the next several weeks while preparing drafts, she began thinking more critically about the aims of the seminars. She had done a fair amount of research in her doctoral studies about communication and knew the field of study was at an important evolutionary, even revolutionary, crossroad. She knew, for example, that the seminars would be explosive if the teachers perceived the new training to be just another group of quick fixes the school district had embarked upon over the last decades. She knew that the teachers needed an active voice and that their voice needed to be heard.

What could she include in the training seminars beyond the idea of communication as problem solving, as focused on change, or as empowerment? How could she release the potential of each individual teacher and construct new methodologies that might reshape and unite the group? How could new communication methods help to create a sense of oneness or collectivity of action in the teachers and effectively compensate for the variety evident in this diverse group—even more, with the availability of information prevalent today? What other internal and external strengths and constraints were important in the investigation, leadership, management, structure, and more?

Perplexed

Over a month had passed, and Diane found herself more confused. After an extensive literature review, she had not been able to address the important gaps that existed between theory and practice at the school dis-

trict. She knew more about organizational communication and had defined the district's needs. However, she still was not able to devise an in-service training program that would address the needs of the group and be adaptable enough to serve the school district well into the new third wave implementation. The two seemed diametrically opposed.

Diane's tentative objectives are listed below in the questions for this case. At this point, the reader and/or study group is invited to address the questions including discussion and formalization of the in-service training objectives. You may use the third wave school system as a general guide or any other current school system change project with which you are familiar.

■   ■   ■

Questions

1.   In the early narrative during the meeting you may have labeled the actors/individual mental models. These mental models often correspond to theory genre prevalent in communication research. These mental models also often elicit metaphors that describe particular theoretical approach. Are the mental models distinguishable? Discuss the theoretical approaches. How do the models and metaphors correlate with theory proclivities?

2.   Given the brief discussion among the actors, would you believe they are capable of understanding the following distinctions? Why or why not?

Systemic and systematic

Educated and informated

Knowledge and knowing

Communication and information

What distinctions do you make?

3.   Those participating in the meeting seem to be dealing with controversial issues from a retrospective viewpoint. How would

you suggest that they become more introspective?

Annotated Bibliography

Goldhaber, G. M. (1986). *Organizational communication* (4th ed.). Dubuque, IA: Wm. C. Brown Publishers.

In this revised edition, Goldhaber defines organizational communication and its effects on the organization itself. New research on communication, communication programs, and additions to the paradigm of organizational communication are presented. Research findings on leaders' styles and findings on the relationship between status and nonverbal indicators are also given.

Heiskanen, H., & Swanson, G. A. (1992). *Management observation and communication theory.* Westport, CT: Quorum.

Management theory, according to the authors, needs a global systemic conceptual framework that informs the development of organization-specific management theories. Organizations evolve by specialization and integration. Attempting to fit all organizations' workings into the same theory with slight variations ignores the latest evolutionary developments in particular organizations. The authors see such attempts as reactionary and not progressive.

Herndon, S. L., & Kreps, G. L. (Eds.). (1993). *Qualitative research applications in organizational communication.* Cresskill, NJ: Hampton Press.

Qualitative research in the field of communication has emerged since the 1970s as a legitimate and widely recognized phenomenon in two ways: it has produced a growing body of literature, and it has developed a significant number of methods by which to study the process of communication. The application of qualitative methods to the study of organizations has proven to be one of the most fertile areas of research in this field. The book attempts to identify and examine qualitative research methods that the authors and editors term interpretive, naturalistic, phenomenological, and ethnographic.

Pace, R. W. (1983). *Organizational communication: Foundations for human resource development.* Englewood Cliffs, NJ: Prentice-Hall.

This book represents an attempt to introduce the study of organizational communication as preparation for a career in human resource development. In addition, the book provides support for Barnard's observation that "the first function of the executive is to develop and maintain a system of communication." This text attempts to show how the study of organizational communication can contribute to more professional performance by executives, managers, supervisors, or other organizational communicators. Written and developed with simple models and basic ideas, the book is divided into three parts: systems, issues, and roles.

Reuss, C., & Silvis, D. (Eds.). (1985). *Inside organizational communication* (2nd ed.). New York: Longman.

The International Association of Business Communicators is responsible for most of the content of this text. They outline the pertinent aspects of organizational communication by focusing on assessing the need for communication and defining, analyzing, and selecting various vehicles of communication throughout the organization. Trends and issues are also discussed within.

Seiler, W. J., Baudhuin, E. S., & Schuelke, L. D. (1982). *Communication in business and professional organizations.* Reading, MA: Addison-Wesley.

The book discusses basic communication theories and skills that apply to business and professional organizations. The authors believe that an understanding of communication models and the ability to communicate effectively and successfully are essential to anyone in an organization. The writers provide examples about how effective communication occurs with corresponding theory, real scenarios, up-to-date research, and practical suggestions and applications in all areas essential to communication.

Shockley-Zalabak, P. (1991). *Fundamentals of organizational communication: Knowledge, sensitivity, skills, values* (2nd ed.). New York: Longman.

Effective communication in organizations is widely considered to be necessary both for the attainment of organizational goals and for individual productivity and satisfaction. This text explores the development of key communication competencies for the 1990s and beyond. It is organized to achieve interaction among theory, practice, and analysis through an emphasis on knowledge, sensitivity, skills, and values. The text's framework is comprehensive, with four basic components—process understanding, interpersonal sensitivity, communications skills, and ethical responsibility.

References

Argyris, C., & Schön, D. A. (1978). *Organizational learning: A theory of action perspective*. Reading, MA: Addison-Wesley.

Baeshen, N. (1987). *The effect of organizational communication on the middle and lower-level managers' participation in the decision-making process in Saudi Arabia*. Ph. D. Dissertation, The University of Arizona.

Barnard, C. (1938). *The function of the executive*. Cambridge, MA: Harvard University Press.

Berelson, B., & Steiner, G. (1964). *Human behavior: An inventory of scientific findings*. New York: Harcourt & Brace.

Berlo, D. K. (1960). *The process of communications*. New York: Holt, Rinehart & Winston.

Campbell, D. E., & Campbell, T. A. (1988, March). A new look at informal communication: The role of the physical environment. *Environment and Behavior, 20*(2), 211.

Carnevale, A. P., & Gainer, L. J. (1989). *The learning enterprise*. Alexandria, VA: American Society for Training and Development and U.S. Department of Labor.

Daft, R. L., & Lengel, R. H. (1984). Information richness: A new approach to managerial behavior and organizational design. *Research in Organizational Behavior, 6*, 195–198.

Dance, F. E. X. (1970). The "concept" of communication. *Journal of Communication, 20*, 201–210.

Donellon, A. G., Gray, B., & Bougon, M. G. (1986, March). Communication, meaning, and organized action. *Administrative Science Quarterly, 31*(1), 43–55.

Eblen, A. (1987, Fall–Winter). Communication, leadership, and organizational commitment. *Central States Speech Journal, 38,* (3-4), 181–195.

Etzioni, A. (1964). *Modern organizations*. Englewood Cliffs, NJ: Prentice-Hall.

Farace, R. V., Monge, P. R., & Russell, H. (1977). *Communicating and organizing*. Reading, MA: Addison-Wesley.

Fisher, A. (1978). *Perspectives of human communication*. New York: Macmillan Publishing

Greenfield, W. (1987). *Instructional leadership: Concepts, issues and controversies*. Newton, MA: Allyn and Bacon.

Hall, R. H. (1991). *Organizations: Structure, processes and outcomes* (5th ed.). Englewood Cliffs, NJ: Prentice-Hall.

Haugland, M. (1987, Fall). Professional competencies needed by school superintendents, as perceived by school board members in South Dakota. *Spectrum, 5*(4), 40–42.

Helgeson, S. (1990). *The female advantage: Women's ways of leadership*. New York: Doubleday/Currency.

Hellriegel, D., Slocum, J., & Woodman, R. (1986). Interpersonal communication. In *Organizational behavior* (4th ed.) New York: West Publishing.

Hentges, K., Yaney, J., & Shields, C. (1990). Training and motivating the new labor force: The impact of ethnicity. *Performance Improvement Quarterly, 3*(3), 36–44.

Hersey, P., & Blanchard, K. (1988). Communicating with rapport. In *Management and organizational behavior: Utilizing human resources* (5th ed.) (pp. 305–317). Englewood Cliffs, NJ: Prentice-Hall.

Hoy, W., & Miskel, C. (1987). Communication. In *Educational administration: Theory, research, and practice* (3rd ed.) (pp. 356–381). New York: Random House.

Kanter, R. M. (Nov.–Dec., 1989). The managerial work. *Harvard Business Review, reprint* 85–92.

Kefalas, A. (1977). Organizational communications: A systems viewpoint. In R. Huseman, C. Logue, & D. Freshley, *Readings in interpersonal & organizational communication* (3rd ed.) (pp. 25–43). Boston: Allyn and Bacon.

Khandwalla, P. (1987). Communication processes. In *The design of organizations*. New York: Harcourt Brace Jovanovich.

Knezevich, S. (1984). Leadership dimensions of educational administration: A review of human behavior, communication and conflict in organizations. In *Administrations of public education: A sourcebook for the leadership and management of educational institutions*. New York: Harper and Row.

Krippendorff, K., & Eleey, M. F. (1986, Spring). Monitoring a group's symbolic environment. *Public Relations Review, 12*(1), 13–36.

Krivonos, P. (1982). Distortion of subordinate to superior communication in organizational settings. *Central States Speech Journal, 33*(1), 335–352.

Lengel, R. H., & Daft, R. L. (1988, August). The selection of communication media as an executive skill. *Academy of Management Executive, 2*(3), 225–232.

Lewin, K. (1951). *Field theory in social science*. NY: Harper.

Likert, R. (1967). *The human organization*. New York: McGraw-Hill.

Lipham, J. M., & Francke, D. C. (1966). Nonverbal behavior of administrators. *Educational Administration Quarterly, 2*, 101–109.

Littlejohn, S. W. (1989). *Theories of human communication* (3rd ed.). Belmont, CA: Wadsworth Publishing Company.

Marsick, V. J. (1990, Spring). Altering the paradigm for theory building and research in human resource development. *Human Resource Development Quarterly, 1*(1), 5-23, 29–34.

Miller, J. G. (1978). *Living systems*. New York, McGraw-Hill.

Morgan, G. (1986). *Images of organization*. Beverly Hills, CA: Sage.

Murphy, H., & Peck, C. (1980). *Effective business communication*. New York: McGraw-Hill.

O'Reilly, C. A., & Pondy, L. R. (1979). Organizational communication. In S. Kerr (Ed.), *Organizational behavior*. Columbus, OH: Grid.

Pacanowsky, M., & O'Donnell-Trujillo. (1982). Organizational Communication as cultural performance. *Communication Monographs, 50*, 126–147.

Peters, T. (1992). *Liberation management: Necessary disorganization for the nanosecond nineties*. New York: Knopf.

Poole, M. S., & McPhee, R. D. (1983). A structurational theory of organizational climate. In L. Putnam, & M. Pacanowsky (Eds.), *Organizational communication: An interpretive approach*. Beverly Hills, CA: Sage.

Ragan, L. (1990, May–June). The great debate. *Communication World, 7*(6), 85–87.

Reitz, H. J. (1987). Communications. In *Behavior in organizations* (3rd ed.) (pp. 301–330). Homewood, IL: Irwin.

Schein, E. (1989, May). Corporate teams and totems. *Across the Board, 26*, 12–17. (Reprinted from *Sloan Management Review*, 1989, Winter).

Schuck, G. (1985, Autumn). Intelligent technology, intelligent workers: A new pedagogy for the high-tech workplace. *Organizational Dynamics, 14*(2), 66–79.

Shannon, C., & Weaver, W. (1949). *The mathematical theory of communication*. Urbana, IL: University of Illinois Press.

Shockley-Zalabak, P. (1988). *Fundamentals of organizational communication*. New York: Longman.

Sigband, N., & Bell, A. (1989). Communication in organizations. In *Communication for management and business* (5th ed.) (pp. 23–51). Glenview, IL: Scott, Foresman & Co.

Simon, H. A. (1957). *Administrative behavior* (2nd ed.). New York: Free Press.

Smith, S. C., & Piele P. K. (Eds). (1989). *School leadership: Handbook for excellence*. Eugene, OR: ERIC University of Oregon.

Stephens, M. (1989, March 27). Wired: How PC networks are changing the way we work. *Infoworld, 11*(13), 41–46.

Striplin, P. (1987). An exploratory study of teachers' opinions to important competencies needed by principals to perform effectively as instructional leaders (Doctoral dissertation, Florida State University, 1987). *Dissertation Abstracts International, 48,*12A.

Taylor, R. G. (1984, Spring). Assessing the strength of communication channels using sociographic techniques. *Education, 104*(3), 300–304.

Wartenberg, M. R. (1990, June). How to merge—and survive. *Management Review, 79*(6), 64.

Watkins, K. (1989). Five metaphors: Alternative theories for human resource development. In Deane Gradous (Ed.), *Systems theory applied to human resource development. [Theory to practice monograph]*. University of Minnesota Training and Development Research Center and American Society for Training and Development Research Committee.

Weick, K. (1969). *The social psychology of organizing*. Reading, MA: Addison-Wesley.

Wiener, N. (1954). *The human use of human beings: Cybernetics and society*. Garden City, NY: Doubleday Anchor.

Yukl, G. A. (1989). *Leadership in organizations* (2nd ed.). Englewood Cliffs, NJ: Prentice-Hall.

Zuboff, S. (1988). *In the age of the smart machine*. New York: Basic Books.

Chapter 9
Human Relations: The Revolving Base for Educational Leadership

Concerns about educational leadership have increased in recent years. This attention is, in part, related to the role principals and superintendents play in achieving excellence in education. In its 1987 report *Leaders for America's Schools,* the National Commission on Excellence in Educational Administration (Griffiths, Stout, & Forsyth, 1988) claimed that efforts to achieve excellence in education "cannot be successful without strong, well-reasoned leadership from principals and superintendents" (p. 6). Other recent reviews of school effectiveness reveal that principals and superintendents can and must help schools achieve excellence (Mangieri, 1985; Sergiovanni, 1991).

Calls for strong leadership in the search for educational excellence in public schools have been argued frequently (Berney & Ayers, 1990; Duignan & Macpherson, 1992; Guthrie & Reed, 1991; Kouzes & Posner, 1987; Maxcy, 1991; Reavis & Griffith, 1992; Schlechty, 1990; Sergiovanni & Moore, 1989). Schlechty states:

Educators and citizens who value the American system of education, and who believe, as

I do, that excellence in public education is directly linked to excellence in all other areas of social life in a democracy, have a special interest in ensuring that the leaders of American education, unlike the leaders of the railroad industry, get their business right before it is too late. (p. 151)

In addition, the search for strong educational leadership has been echoed simultaneously by public expectations for schools. With increasing global competition, our expectations of public schools are rising. Schools are perceived as places where human potential can be increased by raising levels of thought, knowledge, skills, and socialization. These expectations for schools require that educational leaders provide strong leadership to improve the quality of schooling and raise student achievement to new levels. Thus, as the 1980s and 1990s have become the era of reform, leadership correspondingly has been summoned to fulfill the new expectations, excellence.

This faith in the power of leadership and in its potential to make a difference in schools underlies much of the literature on leadership for educational excellence. The literature reveals that leaders in competent schools are skilled in managerial, instructional, and inter-personal tasks. In this era of excellence, more demands exist; school leaders must shape values, develop vision, create meanings, and develop unique culture based upon their moral values (Sergiovanni, 1984, 1991, 1992). Like other organizational domains, school leadership must not only "do the things right," but also "do the right things." In goal-driven organizations, complex human interactions necessitate that all educational constituencies, superintendents, principals, teachers, students, and community partners alike have a clear understanding of human nature and human behavior patterns. Hence, the necessity to understand human relations.

Excellence must also be matched by a broad social and technical appreciation of the educational environment. Individual leaders and followers interact across a wide variety of roles and activities. In this interactive and interdependent environment it is imperative that the study of human relations be investigated in a more open framework. As opposed to traditional inquiry, inquirers today must explore these larger contexts. Exploration of these larger contexts acknowledges the importance of reality and the variety in reality that leads to further understanding. Similarly, as other authors posit, the study of educational leadership should incorporate an action perspective in which sources of meaning for all members of the educational unit are viewed from a thinking-acting perspective and a theory-practice foundation (Argyris, 1985; Silverman, 1971).

Development of Human Relations Concepts

Although human relationships have existed since the beginning of time, the art and science of trying to deal with them in the work setting is relatively new. It was not until the second half of the nineteenth century that researchers turned their attention to worker's needs. The evolution of the main concepts of human relations occurred in six stages: (1) classical thinking, (2) systematic development, (3) teaching and practice, (4) refinement, (5) decline, and (6) revolving (Davis, 1967; Sanford, 1977).

The Stage of Classical Thinking (pre-1930s). This stage is characterized by classical economic theory and the scientific management movement. The proponents of the theory of economic man believe that human behavior is determined by economic needs and economic goals. Human relations is a matter of establishing an incentive that contributes to the necessities of life and the replenishment of the work force. The scientific management movement focuses on increasing efficiency and productivity while also drawing attention to the importance of people in the work situation. Taylor (1911), the father of scientific management, was one of the first to call attention to people in the work situation as an important factor in the quest for efficiency in production. In his view, human problems are what stand in the way of greater productivity. Taylor himself calls for the scientific selection and development of the worker.

Although some scholars (Dennison, 1931; Gantt, 1916; Frankel & Fleisher, 1920; Ure, 1835) emphasize individual human psychological and social needs, their ideas have been accepted slowly or not at all. In contrast, the dominant ideas of classical human relations research tend to view persons employed as a means or as specialized resources. Attempts were made to design bureaucratic structures to overcome the shortcomings of human factors. Practitioners and theorists recognized the importance of people in industries but did not include this more holistic view of humankind. Effective and efficient organizations were characterized as if they were machines. Workers were perceived from an efficiency perspective or as productivity resources.

The Stage of Systematic Development (1930–1950).

Most of the foundation of modern human relations theory and practice developed during this stage. As an early reaction to mechanistic interpretation of organization, Follett (1930) spoke out on the dignity and value of satisfied workers. The works of Mayo (1933) and Roethlisberger (1939) at the Hawthorne plant also sparked an early interest in human relations. Findings from the Hawthorne studies indicated that productivity had something to do with social and psychological interactions among human resources. Further studies showed that workers in continuous and close contact create informal social structures that may influence their productive behavior. Various iterations of the Hawthorne studies marked the beginning of the end of reliance on economic concepts as the primary explanation of work motivation and behavior. The study of organizations as social systems in which social needs are the most important motivator of workers became a focus.

To Taylor and his contemporaries, human problems stood in the way of production. However, little attention was paid to this viewpoint. In contrast to Mayo and his colleagues, human problems became a new field of study and an opportunity for progress. While Taylorism increased production by rationalizing it, Mayo and his colleagues sought to increase production by humanizing it.

Another proponent of human relations, Barnard (1938), viewed the organization as a system composed of human beings working cooperatively to reach goals rather than a formally structured impersonal mechanism. Barnard asserted that within every complex organization there are small operating groups interacting that often lead to the creation of informal working relationships and standards within the formal organization. Barnard was clearly ahead of his time, as many years passed before his concepts were taken seriously or practiced.

The Stage of Teaching and Practice (1950–1960).

After the conclusions of the Hawthorne research were disseminated, human relations concepts began to be applied on a significant scale. As a result of the Hawthorne studies, the focus of human relations practice shifted from an economic emphasis to a socio-psychological emphasis. Worker need satisfaction was seen to lead to greater productivity, and the social and psychological needs of the worker were seen as significant determinants of behavior. The expectation was that worker productivity would increase if human relations activity in the organization was attended to and manipulated. Workers would derive greater social and psychological satisfaction as a result.

It was also believed that social satisfaction demands freedom to socialize on the job. Psychological satisfaction could be fulfilled by allowing workers to participate in managerial decisions. This, in turn, would result in greater need satisfaction, resulting in increased performance and higher productivity. Morale, a related concept, also became an interesting research topic. All these concepts reflected an optimistic view of human nature.

Research and theory development in this stage continued. Tannebaum and Schmidt (1958), Blake and Mouton (1964), Fiedler (1967), Likert (1961), Herzberg et al. (1959), Maslow (1954), Argyris (1964), McGregor (1960), Porter and Lawler (1968), and Vroom (1964) were among the most important scholars. They elaborated on human aspects of organization as well as individual needs and motivation.

The Stage of Refinement (1960–1970).

Efforts continued in several arenas including the development of better theory and improvement in the practice resulting in a synthesis of human relations theories. Three major theory modifications include Miles' (1975) human resources model, Likert's (1967) supportive model, and Tosi and Hamner's (1974) contingency model.

Miles's human resource model assumes that work is not inherently distasteful and that people want to contribute to meaningful goals. For Miles, the most important matter in organizations is how to make use of untapped human resources. Likert's supportive model emphasizes the supportive climate of the organizational life. A supportive climate ensures that members in an organization will feel a sense of personal worth and importance in all their interactions and relationships with the organization.

Tosi and Hamner's contingency model requires that we explore the organization as a system or unit of behavior composed of subsystems or subunits that have identified boundaries within the system. The behavior of one unit is dependent on its environmental relationship to other subunits and has some control over the consequences desired by the subunit. Individual and group behavior are contingent on four related elements: psychological determinants, organizational determinants, internal organizational characteristics, and environmental characteristics.

The Stage of Decline (1970–1980). Research in human relations declined after the 1970s as researchers became interested in other factors. A majority of the theoretical studies in this period focused on leadership roles with reference to leaders rather than on the workers themselves. These studies explored functions, procedures, and the outcomes of human relations activities. A more detailed review of literature reveals that most of the studies and models developed in this period limited themselves to studies of various parts of the leadership process (e.g., communication, planning, decisionmaking, evalu-

ation). No significant attempts were made to construct an integrative framework of human relations.

The Stage of Revolving (1980–present). Today it seems apropos to study the phases of successful Japanese management performance and "revolve" through the various applications of Japanese human relations concepts. This period looks critically at the human side of organizations. Ouchi's (1981) Theory Z, which includes quality of work life, collective decisionmaking and responsibility, lifetime employment, implicit control, and quality circles, currently reflects the concepts being explored in the human relations paradigm (Kossen, 1987). Ouchi is credited with having drawn substantial attention during the 1980s to the differences between Japanese and North American styles of management. His models conceptualize organizations that maintain formal and explicit control mechanisms and believe in formal planning, management by objective, and sophisticated information and accounting systems. Quality circles, groups consisting of rank-and-file workers who exchange information for mutual improvement, began the revival of managerial concern back to workers.

Conceptualizing Human Relations Theories

While the stages above help us to trace the human relations movement, it is also important to understand the conceptual underpinnings of the movement. The human relations movement emphasizes the important roles of human factors in organizations. Researchers define human relations based upon the following concepts: optimistic assumptions of human nature, the clinical and ethical dimensions, human needs, human motivation and its roles in human performance, morale, and informal organizations.

DEFINITIONS OF HUMAN RELATIONS

Efforts have been made to conceptualize human relations from different perspectives. Saltonstall (1959) viewed human relations as the "study of people in action" (p. 3). Saltonstall also saw human relations as the study of people at work, "not only people as individuals but people as members of informal work groups, people as executives in management, people as union members, and people as members of organizations with economic goals" (p. 4).

From the management perspective, Scott (1962) defined human relations operationally as processes of effective motivation of individuals in a given situation to achieve a balanced objective that yields greater satisfaction and helps accomplish organization goals. Concern with human relations promises higher productivity, greater organizational effectiveness, and satisfied employees.

Like Scott, Halloran (1978) defined the term *human relations* as all the interactions that can occur among people whether they occur in conflict situations or cooperative behaviors. The study of human relations in organizations is the study of how people can work effectively in groups in order to satisfy both organizational goals and personal needs.

Realizing the complexity of human organizations, Davis (1977) gave a broad explanation of the concept of human relations. Davis explained that the term *human relations* applies broadly to the interaction of people in all types of endeavor, in business, government, social clubs, schools, and homes. Much of this interaction is in work organizations, where people have bonded together in some sort of formal structure to achieve an objec-

tive. The human interactions developed are called employee human relations or organizational human relations. Therefore, human relations is the study of human behavior at work and an effort to take action in operating situations in order to produce better results. Human relations is perceived as the integration of people into a work situation that motivates them to work together productively, cooperatively, and with economic, psychological, and social satisfactions. Human relations has the potential to motivate people in organizations and develop the teamwork that effectively fulfills their needs and achieves organizational objectives.

OPTIMISTIC ASSUMPTIONS OF HUMAN NATURE

The perceptions of basic human nature vary with the experiences of those addressing this controversial topic. Classical studies tends to adopt the pessimistic view of human nature. Humans are portrayed as rebellious, greedy, aggressive, and uncooperative. In contrast, human relations embraces an optimistic view. Proponents of this view believe that it is natural for human beings to be self-motivated and self-controlled, although behavioral reactions are influenced by the treatment received from others (Knezevich, 1984).

The optimistic view of human nature emphasizes four aspects: individual differences, the whole person, caused behavior, and human dignity (Davis, 1967, 1977). Davis and others hold that although people have much in common, each person in the world is also individually different. Individual differences requires that justice and rightness, therefore, be determined on a case by case basis and not statistically. Davis also maintains that a person's different traits may be separately studied, but in the final analysis, they are all part of one system making up a whole. Similarly, a person's emotional condition is not separate from one's physical condition. Each affects the other.

Psychological studies of human relations indicates that most human behavior is caused by a person's need structure. Behavior is influenced by motivating people to fulfill their needs as they see them. However, people are not motivated by what others think ought to motivate them, but by what they themselves want. More importantly, human relations emphasizes human dignity. The people in an organization deserve to be treated differently than the other aspects of production. An individual's humanness demands that he or she be treated with respect and dignity.

CLINICAL AND ETHICAL DIMENSIONS

The study of human relations can also be viewed from two other dimensions: a clinical dimension and an ethical dimension. From the clinical dimension, human relations uses tools and data to solve concrete human problems in situations where they occur. Human relations can also be studied from an ethical dimension, on a continuum from an individualistic to a sociological perspective. The former is a conglomeration of ideas pertaining to personal freedom and the preeminence of individual action. The latter is an affirmation of the value of human collaboration and solidarity (Scott, 1962).

THE IMPORTANCE OF HUMAN NEEDS

Human relations theory spotlights the needs of human beings. Human relationists maintain that all people have needs. As classical management study has determined, people cannot survive for long without the primary needs, such as food, drink, sleep, and air to breathe. Yet classical management thought also demonstrates that secondary needs are equally important, especially in daily organizational life. Therefore, we are eager to feel

secure, to be with other people, to be respected, and to fulfill our potential. Since these human needs arise from the biological and socio-psychological makeup of individuals, they are significant elements of human behavior. In practice, most human behaviors are influenced or motivated by human needs.

HUMAN MOTIVATION AND HUMAN BEHAVIOR

Motivation is a central concept used by human relations thinkers in the explanation of human behavior. They see the terms *motivation* and *behavior* as closely related because human behavior occurs as a result of motivation. However, they also recognize that motivation and behavior are not as synonymous as they may appear. Motivation is only one but probably the most important class of determinants of behavior.

Motivation and behavior are connected through needs and wants (desires) (see Figure 9.1). Needs create tensions that are modified by one's culture or situations to cause certain wants (desires). These wants are interpreted in terms of positive and negative incentives to produce a certain response or action. The action is directed toward the accomplishment or the satisfaction of the needs (Davis, 1967; Halloran 1978; Sanford, 1977).

Not all needs create tension and result in behavior. At any given point in time individuals have some needs that are relatively well-satisfied, or at least partially well-satisfied, as well as some unsatisfied needs. The satisfied needs do not motivate; the unsatisfied needs are the ones that create tension and motivate behavior.

THE ROLE OF MOTIVATION IN PERFORMANCE

In organizational life, the human relations school perceives motivation as one of two major factors an individual contributes to task performance. The other factor is the ability to

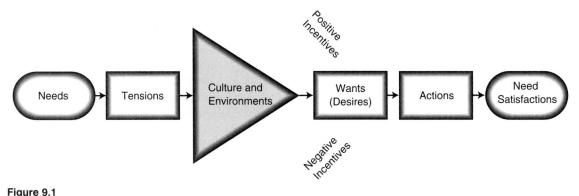

Figure 9.1
Motivation and behavior

perform the task. Ability includes the physical and mental skills and the knowledge and experience that an individual applies to a task. Motivation is the effort with which ability is applied to a task. Performance is viewed as a function of ability in interaction with motivation (Reitz, 1987):

$$Performance = f(Ability \times Motivation)$$

Generally speaking, when people of both low ability and high ability are unwilling to put effort into their performances, the differences in the performances will be minimized. Changes in level of effort make more of a difference in the performance of high ability people than in low ability people (Reitz, 1987). Motivation, therefore, is a vital constituent in terms of organizational behavior.

MORALE AND PRODUCTIVITY

Morale is one of the important concepts of the human relations school. Morale, a concept closely related to motivation and satisfaction, refers to the atmosphere created by the attitudes of the members of an organization (Reitz, 1987). The human relations school believes that there is a relationship between productivity and morale. Under conditions of poor morale, favorable output is difficult to sustain for long periods. However, good

morale does not necessarily cause high productivity. Although it may be an important factor, it is merely one influence on total productivity. For high morale to favorably affect productivity it must be accompanied by reasonable direction and control. Although morale is not a factor that can be bought or ordered, human relations theorists have warned against underestimating its power.

SIGNIFICANCE OF INFORMAL ORGANIZATIONS

One of the most significant and far-reaching conclusions of the Hawthorne studies relates the importance of the informal organization and its relation to the total work situation. The informal organization is a network of personal and social relations not established or required by formal authority but arising spontaneously as people associate with one another. In the formal organization, authority coincides with a position in the structure. Power in the informal organization resides with an individual. Since informal organizations exist within formal organizations, the behavior of individuals in organizations is influenced by the informal as well as formal organization.

Theorists also indicate that informal organizations sometimes create problems for organizations. They transmit false information through the grapevine, resist changes, cause excessive conformity to group norms, and even develop goals that conflict with those of the formal organization. The informal organization, however, also performs a variety of positive and useful functions. It provides most members with the opportunity to satisfy their psychological and social needs. Many of these needs go unsatisfied in the larger formal organization framework.

APPLICATION OF HUMAN RELATIONS CONCEPTS

It is worth noting that it is not true that dissatisfied workers will adversely effect productivity. Nor is it true that participation necessarily leads to job satisfaction and productivity.

Human relations management does not imply simply liking people. It is not a belief that workers adversely affect productivity, or that participation leads to job satisfaction and greater productivity. Its major emphasis should be on ways to make workers feel like contributors to worthwhile task accomplishment, and that they are doing something constructive and meaningful about working relationships within the organization. Human relations theorists are not a group of "do-gooders," but work to reduce discrepancies between individuals and their organizations, and to channel the remaining discrepancies into constructive results. Human relations does not simply focus on a specific group but all people within the organization (Argyris, 1957; Davis, 1967; Sanford, 1977).

Theoretical Perspectives of Human Relations

As seen above, research from various disciplines has contributed to the development of numerous usable human relations concepts. Nevertheless, most human relations concepts result from findings in industrial experiments and organizational psychology. Relevant

human relations studies and their relation to leadership are summarized into four categories and are examined in the following sections. The categories are human nature, human motivation, morale in organizations, and informal organizations. It should be noted that these studies use the terms management (managers) and leadership (leaders) interchangeably.

HUMAN NATURE

Theory X and Theory Y. Psychological studies indicate that our perception of others determines, for the most part, how we will treat others and respond to them. Our perception is the lens by which we judge and see others (Hall, 1980; Hammond, 1966). McGregor (1960) categorized two distinct lenses that managers use: Theory X and Theory Y. Actually, Theory X and Theory Y contrast the perceptions that classical managerial and human relations thinkers espouse.

Theory X, representing the traditional mechanistic view, assumes the following: (1) the average human being has an inherent dislike of work and will avoid it if he can; (2) because of this human characteristic, most people must be coerced, controlled, directed, and threatened with punishment to get them to put forth adequate effort to achieve organizational objectives; and (3) the average human being prefers to be directed, wishes to avoid responsibility, has relatively little ambition, and wants security above all. McGregor argued that although Theory X provides an explanation of some human behavior in organizations, there are many readily observable phenomena that are not consistent with this view of human nature.

Theory Y, representing the human relations view, provides a distinctly different assumption regarding human nature. It maintains the following: (1) The expenditure of physical and mental effort in work is as natural as play or rest. (2) External control and the threat of punishment are not the only means for bringing about effort toward organizational objectives. People will exercise self-direction and self-control in the service of objectives to which they are committed. (3) Commitment to objectives is a function of the rewards associated with their achievement. (4) The average person learns, under proper conditions, not only to accept but to seek responsibility. (5) The capacity to exercise a relatively high degree of imagination, ingenuity, and creativity in the solution of organizational problems is widely, not narrowly, distributed in the population. (6) Under the conditions of modern industrial life, the intellectual potential of the average person is only partially utilized.

Theory X offers a rationalization for ineffective organizational performance and the nature of the human resource. In contrast, Theory Y suggests that the ineffectiveness of organizational behavior lies in different organizational contexts and processes. The central principle of organization evident in Theory X is direction and control. The principle derived from Theory Y demands that the needs of both the organization and the individual be recognized. McGregor (1960) stated that since external control and direction are appropriate means under certain circum-

stances, assumptions in Theory Y do not deny the appropriateness of those of Theory X. Theory Y simply shows that Theory X does not apply in all cases.

Pygmalion Leadership. Research has shown that the selection of an appropriate style of management is a crucial task for managers. The perspective of a lens that filters our perceptions of reality and provides the basis for interpreting our own experiences exerts a powerful influence as workers may be caught in a self-fulfilling prophecy or Pygmalion effect (Berlew & Hall, 1966; Merton, 1948; Rosenthal, 1974; Rosenthal & Jacobson, 1968). Thus, when managers treat their subordinates as creative, committed, competent people, as in McGregor's Theory Y, and manage accordingly, both the manager and the subordinates will reap the rewards of the self-fulfilling prophecy. When managers vacillate and treat their subordinates as incapable people, subordinates are less likely to perform at their full potential (Eden, 1990a; Duchon, Green & Taber; 1986; Scandura, Graen, & Novak, 1986). In this scenario, the self-fulfilling prophecy has detrimental effects. Four factors that mediate the Pygmalion effect are:

Figure 9.2
The Pygmalion leadership

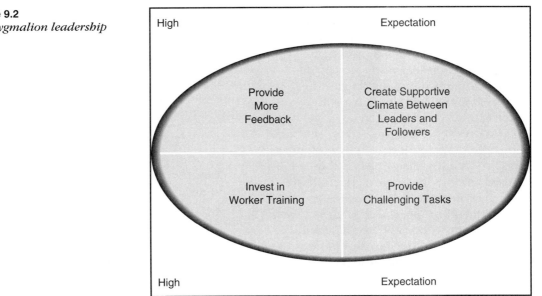

High   Expectation

Provide More Feedback

Create Supportive Climate Between Leaders and Followers

Invest in Worker Training

Provide Challenging Tasks

High   Expectation

socio-emotional climate, feedback, input, and output (Brophy, 1985; Rosenthal, 1981). These factors reveal that providing greater warmth, acceptance, and approval, as well as opportunities for challenge on the part of managers will result in better subordinate performance. This same "magic" is not to be expected, however, if subordinates are treated impersonally with less feedback and challenge.

Leadership plays an important role in mediating the effects of self-fulfilling prophecy in organizations. Pygmalion leadership is the consistent encouragement, support, and reinforcement of high expectations of followers (see Figure 9.2). Pygmalion leadership, according to Eden (1990b), is an approach leaders may adopt in order to lead their followers toward excellence. Pygmalion leadership can create a supportive climate between leaders and followers through such behaviors as looking the followers in the eye, nodding affirmatively and approvingly, smiling, voicing warmth, and speaking supportively. These behaviors are also the foundational factors of Likert's (1961) principle of supportive relations.

Pygmalion leadership can also provide more feedback. Evaluating followers' performances and letting them know where they stand are leadership acts that make followers aware that someone is observing and monitoring activities. The Pygmalion leader can use many opportunities in day-to-day interactions to comment on followers' performances, either as compliments or as corrections. Positive feedback maintains good work performances, while negative feedback encourages performance improvement (Komaki, 1986). Pygmalion leadership entails increased investment in workers. Training at every opportunity is thought to foster workers' growth and propel them to higher levels of achievement. Followers are provided with ample opportunity to tackle challenging assignments. Although this leadership style is risky, leaders must determine the real capabilities of their followers. Giving workers opportunities to show what they can do fosters high performance both by expressing high expectations and by allowing excellence to occur (Eden, 1990b).

Pygmalion leadership is effective only when it functions in all four interrelated dimensions, as shown in Figure 9.2. A leader providing continuous feedback to followers will guide them in the right direction with confidence. A leader showing enthusiasm in worker training will find that workers progress well. Thus, increases in expectations become possible. The result of a supportive climate in the organization will be mutual respect between leader and followers. This mutual respect enables the followers to put more effort into the job. A leader wishing to provide more challenging tasks can examine the potential of the workers, which are often not fully realized. Challenging tasks upgrade workers' performances and facilitate high expectations.

Human Motivation

Students of human behavior and human motivation have identified two basic types of theoretical models that deal with human motivation in organizations: process models and content models (Campbell & Pritchard, 1983). Process models explore how and why motivation generally works. Content models deal with what specifically motivates people.

PROCESS MODELS

Among the several different process models of motivation are the expectancy model, the behaviorist model, and the social learning model.

Expectancy Models. Expectancy models are principally derived from Tolman's (1932) cognitive theory and Lewin's (1938) field theory. Expectancy models suggest that the motivation to perform a task is a function of the individual's expectations or beliefs about effort, performance, and outcomes. Vroom's expectancy model and the Porter and Lawler model are two widely used expectancy models that explain human motivation.

Vroom (1964) contended that motivation is a function of three factors: (1) the strength or desirability of the goal, (2) the perceived ability to exhibit the required behavior, and (3) the perceived probability that the behavior will result in goal achievement (see Figure 9.3). Motivation is the product of how strongly one desires something and one's perception of the probability that certain strategies or instrumentalities are likely to fulfill those desires. Vroom called the intensity of the personal desire valence, and the achievement probability by pursuing a given strategy, expectancy.

Vroom's expectancy model has been replicated and refined numerous times (Dachler & Mobley, 1973; Feldman, Reitz, & Hiterman, 1976; Porter & Lawler, 1968). Porter and Lawler developed a more complete and complex expectancy model by investigating the relationship between satisfaction and productivity. They suggested that the effort an individual puts into work depends on (1) the value one places on the expected reward and (2) the likelihood that the reward actually will be received if the effort is made.

This process is completed in three steps (see Figure 9.4). First, the worker assigns some value to the possible reward for performing work. Based on this performance, the individual expects to receive a fair reward, and is then rewarded either intrinsically or extrinsically. Finally, this process is completed with two feedback loops. One results from the individual's perception of the likelihood that effort will actually yield the expected reward. The other feedback loop results from the individual's judgment as to the value of the rewards obtained. The Porter and Lawler model suggests that performance leads to satisfaction and that the level of satisfaction obtained shapes future effort to perform (Owens, 1987).

Path-goal theory is a leadership theory that utilizes the expectancy model. Path-goal theory, as developed, includes four differing

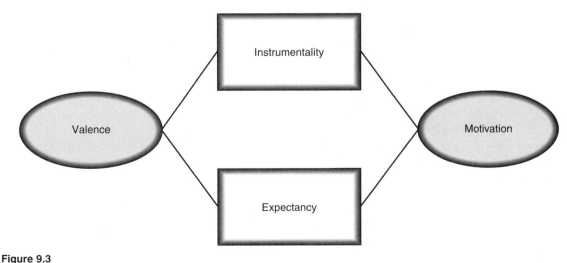

Figure 9.3
Vroom's expectancy model
SOURCE: Vroom, V. H. (1964). *Work and Motivation.* New York: John Wiley & Sons.

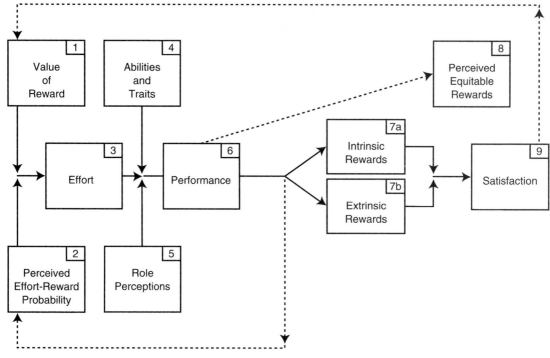

Figure 9.4
The Porter-Lawler model of motivation
SOURCE: Porter, L. W., & Lawler, E. E. (1968). *Managerial attitudes and performance* (p. 165). Copyright 1968 by Richard D. Irwin. Reprinted by permission.

behavioral styles to influence employee satisfaction, the employees' acceptance of the leader, and employee beliefs that effort can result in performance and that performance will result in deserved rewards (House & Mitchell, 1974).

The four styles of leadership derived from expectancy theory are directive, supportive, participative, and achievement-oriented. Path-goal theory assumes that leaders are capable of exhibiting more than one of those styles, depending upon the circumstances. In whatever situation, the exhibition of the leadership style should (1) recognize and arouse employee needs and attempt to increase the payoff to employees for successful performance when it occurs, (2) attempt to influence subordinates' expectancy beliefs by

assisting with the accomplishment of difficult tasks and clarifying vague task assignments, and (3) make the distribution of rewards contingent on the successful accomplishment of work.

Behaviorist Models. Origins of the behaviorist model can be traced back to 1910 and the behavioral approach advocated by Watson. Watson (1930) limited the behaviorist approach to acts that can be reliably observed, what a person says or does. The model, elaborated by Skinner (1953, 1971, 1974), in use today follows that tradition. The behaviorist model is based upon two simple assumptions. First, behavior is essentially determined by the environment through basic reinforcement processes: environmental stimuli, behavioral responses, and outcomes (S-R-O). Second, human behavior, like the behavior of physical and chemical elements, is subject to certain laws. Human behavior can be modified through reinforcement.

Behaviorist models question the concept of internal motivation that implies internal causal force that cannot by observed directly (Luthans & Ottemann, 1977). Instead, according to behaviorists, people are *motivated* by external events called reinforcers, and through positive and negative reinforcement processes (Skinner, 1974). Both positive and negative reinforcements strengthen the probability that a behavior is likely to occur. Positive reinforcement increases behavior frequency by the application of some circumstances, while negative reinforcement increases behavior frequency by the removal of some circumstances that were previously part of the environmental context. By definition, negative reinforcement is not punishment. It aims at decreasing, not increasing, behavior occurrence. Behaviorist models indicate that the timing of rewards is often more important than their magnitude. Immediate rewards can affect performance more effectively than larger delayed rewards, while variable reinforcement can more effectively maintain high levels of effort than mixed rewards (Reitz, 1987; Skinner, 1974).

The application of behaviorist models by management assumes that employees' desires for the rewards of positive reinforcement and recognition will, in large measure, motivate them to perform satisfactorily in anticipation of such rewards. Leadership then in this model requires the leader to (1) inform subordinates concerning which behaviors are desirable and are rewarded, and which behaviors are not rewarded, (2) provide continuous feedback to employees regarding the nature and quality of their work, (3) recognize employees for good work, (4) ensure that employees receive immediate, unscheduled reinforcement during or immediately after strong performance, and (5) reward differently depending upon the performance level (Hamner & Hamner, 1976).

Social Learning Models. A third process model of human behavior in organizations is called the social learning model. It was developed by Bandura (1968, 1976, 1977), Mischell (1973), Mahoney (1974), and Staats (1975) and combines features of both cognitive and reinforcement approaches to help explain human behavior. It places emphasis on learning from other people; i.e., social learning.

Social learning is based on the principles of behaviorism, and stresses the importance of reinforcement in explaining behavior. However, the social model maintains that the role of the environment shaping behavior is mediated by cognitive processes. These processes are depicted in social learning models by adding one element to the basic S-R-O reinforcement model: cognitive processes (C) mediate the effects of environmental stimuli (S) on behavioral responses (R), which then are followed by outcomes (O). The social learning model is then S-C-R-O. (Bandura, 1977).

Modeling and self-control are two types of behaviors that exemplify the social learning process. Modeling refers to the process by which the individual learns a behavior by imitating an observed model. Self-controlled behavior is exhibited by the individual's recognition of the external limits. Research of social learning reveals that people tend to reproduce the actions, attitudes, and emotional responses exhibited by models in modelling behavior (Bandura & Walters, 1963; Bandura, 1969; Flanders, 1968). Whether events or circumstances become reinforcing partly depends upon observing or modeling the reinforcing or punishing outcomes of other people's behavior. People are motivated not only by their direct experience of response outcomes but also by observing the consequences of other people's behavior. Social learning models also indicate that people are motivated not only by the external consequences of their behavior but by the consequences they create for themselves (Bandura, 1968; Kanfer & Karoly, 1974). When their own self-created consequences are not fulfilled, people are motivated to keep working until expected outcomes are accomplished.

One of the most important implications of social learning is that leaders need to be especially aware of their own behavior. Leaders who have one set of expectations for their followers but then behave differently themselves may be setting themselves up for disappointment. It may be true that most effective leaders lead by example. A second implication of social learning is also instructive. As illustrated earlier, both formal and informal organizational structures are of vital importance to leadership. While it is important for leaders to understand this informal agenda and monitor informal leaders' rhetoric, leaders may find that the best insights into greater understanding of the informal organization result from observing actions.

The behavioral and social learning models provide a means to further develop leadership skills. Leaders who are prepared to serve as mentors, or persons who wish to prepare themselves for future leadership opportunities can seek positive ways to achieve these opportunities. The efficacy of this approach has been directly demonstrated over the past few decades by women and minorities who have sought leadership roles. As more women and members of minority groups have ascended to leadership ranks, they have provided increasing opportunities for mentoring and role modeling. This has steadily increased access to leadership positions for these groups.

Motivation Approaches at Work.   Two concepts implied by process models deserve leadership consideration. These two concepts are (1) motivation to work harder versus motivation to work smarter and (2) positive motivation versus negative motivation. Motivating people to work harder means encouraging them to apply more physical energy to their work. Motivating people to work smarter means encouraging them to think and work creatively and to develop better ways of doing things. The first approach offers only limited increase in output and probably a decrease in satisfaction. The second approach is likely to offer greater reward without the necessity of harder work, because new and better ways of work can be developed to replace the old ones. In addition, leaders can use positive and negative reinforcement at their disposal. Positive motivation involves the cultivation of a cooperative attitude among followers so that organizational goals can be accepted and achieved. Stimulating action through fear is the foundation of negative motivation. Negative motivation forces the individual to select between undesirable alternatives. Most leaders use both. In light of the trend toward better employee education and greater independence, leaders need to reduce negative leadership and increase the positive. Followers need to cultivate working smarter.

CONTENT MODELS

Process models describe how motivation works in general terms. In application, managers need to know more about how models work and what specifically rewards or reinforces human behavior. Content models help to understand human behavior further. Content models of motivation can be classified into two schools based upon their research concerns. The first school focuses on common human needs while the second school concentrates on human motivation at work.

COMMON HUMAN NEEDS

Psychologists working on content models of motivation have identified scores of different rewards and reinforcers and have arranged them into categories to aid understanding. Cognitive psychologists and psychoanalysts have further refined these categories into classes of needs and motives.

Maslow's Need Hierarchy. The most widely known classification of needs was compiled by Maslow who described human motivation as arising from five categories of needs. Maslow (1954) conjectured that while different cultures satisfy these needs in different ways, the needs themselves remain the same. He identified five categories of needs.

1. *Physiological needs:* Needs basic to the survival of the human species, such as hunger, thirst, respiration, and sex.

2. *Safety needs:* Needs basic to the physical and psychological protection of the individual, such as shelter, orderliness, consistency, protection from threat and danger, and predictability in one's environment.

3. *Social needs:* Needs basic to one's association with and acceptance by other humans, such as needs for friendship, love, and affiliation.

4. *Esteem needs:* Needs related to respect, including two subsets: self-esteem and esteem from others. Need of self-esteem is the desire for achievement, for adequacy, for confidence, for independence, and freedom; need of esteem from others is the desire for reputation, prestige, recognition, attention, importance, or appreciation.

5. *Self-actualization:* The need to fulfill one's potential, to test one's limits, and to become whatever one can become.

According to Maslow (1954), these five categories of needs form a hierarchy. Each level of need has to be gratified to some extent before the next level in order assumes importance. Lower-order needs do not become unimportant, but higher-order needs achieve greater significance for the individual as basic needs become satisfied.

The first two levels of needs (lower-order needs) are primarily satisfied through economic behavior; the other three (higher-order needs) are primarily satisfied through symbolic behavior of psychic and social content. In light of these five basic needs, the classical economic-man concept can be considered incomplete in that it applies largely to lower-order needs. Self-actualization needs are the highest order of needs, and may rarely be satisfied by most individuals. An important feature of self-actualization needs is that they express themselves through different behaviors in different people. Moreover, unlike other levels of needs, the satisfaction of self-actualization needs tends to increase their importance rather than reduce it (Maslow, 1962).

In practice, behavior by any given individual during any given time probably is the result of more than one need or class of needs. Most acts are influenced by all five classes of needs with one of the levels having greater effect in the specific case.

Porter's Need Hierarchy. Porter (1961) reformulated Maslow's original needs hierarchy slightly. He assumed that *few* people are motivated by such basic physical needs as thirst and hunger, and instead, after self-esteem, have a need for autonomy. Autonomy refers to individuals' needs to participate in making decisions that affect them, to exert influence in controlling the work situation, to have a voice in setting job-related goals, and to have authority to make decisions and latitude to work independently.

Alderfer's Three Categories of Needs. In an attempt to reconcile Maslow's theory with research on human needs in work settings, Alderfer (1969, 1972) proposed three categories of needs: existence, relatedness, and growth. Alderfer argued that these three categories of needs are primary, and that they are innate to human nature rather than learned.

Existence refers to basic needs for survival, similar to Maslow's physiological and security needs. For Alderfer, Maslow's physiological and security needs are equal in importance to the existence of the individual. Typically, subordinates attempt to satisfy existence needs that are more concrete in nature. In addition, these needs often relate to scarce resources. More satisfaction for one person will tend to result in lower potential satisfaction for others. Pay and fringe benefits are two examples of existence needs in the work setting.

According to Alderfer, Maslow's concept of social needs, love, self-esteem, and belonging, are equally important. All people require interaction with others and the development of meaningful relationships with others. Alderfer refers to this category of needs as relatedness. Relatedness needs encompass social and interpersonal concerns, similar to Maslow's social and esteem-from-others needs. Unlike the zero-sum aspects of existence needs, satisfying relatedness needs for one person tends to be positively associated with the same satisfaction for others.

Growth needs suggest that people need to develop their own skills, abilities, and self-esteem. This is similar to Maslow's need for self-esteem and self-actualization. While Maslow saw self-actualization as consisting of the fulfillment of an innate potential, Alderfer's growth needs consist of desires to interact successfully with one's environment. As the person's environment changes, so will the expression of growth needs.

Although Alderfer's three categories cover roughly the same domains as Maslow's, he did not maintain that preceding needs have to be fulfilled before others can influence behavior. Instead, he proposed that cultural background or experience may make certain needs more important than others, and some needs may be insatiable.

McClelland's Social Motives. Another explanation and description of common human needs is provided by McClelland and Atkinson. Extending Murray's (1938) manifest need theory, McClelland and Atkinson (Atkinson, 1964; McClelland et al. 1953) maintained that only two needs are inherent: the need for pleasure and the need to avoid pain. All others are learned. However, since many of life's problem-solving experiences are almost universal, people tend to learn the same types of needs, called social motives, but in different degrees.

McClelland (1955, 1975) identified three important social motives. The motives are achievement, power, and affiliation. The achievement motive is the strongest common human need. Achievement refers to the desire of people to compete against a standard of excellence. The need for achievement is perceived as an important motive in organizations. For a worker with a high need for achievement, challenging work serves to cue the achievement motive. This, in turn, activates achievement-oriented behavior. When high-need achievers are placed in routine or non-challenging jobs, the achievement motive will probably not be activated (McClelland, 1961, 1987; Steers & Spencer, 1977). Realizing this characteristic, leaders can promote excellence.

A second strong common need is the need for power or dominance. Power motives represent a desire to influence others and to control one's environment. For leaders, power motives can take two forms: personalized power and socialized power. People who seek personalized power attempt to dominate others without regard to greater objectives. On the other hand, those who have a socialized need use their power to work with and through others to accomplish objectives. To them, power is important, but as a means to an end rather than as an end in itself.

Affiliation is the need for positive relationships with other people. A major aspect of the affiliation motive is the need for communication. People with a high need for affiliation tend to take jobs characterized by a high amount of interpersonal contact. They tend to perform better when given supportive feedback. In this regard, leadership attempts to create a cooperative, supportive work environment where positive feedback is tied to task performance.

According to McClelland (1975, 1976), those managers with a high need for socialized power are often excellent leaders. On the other hand, a high need for achievement can be detrimental. Similarly, a high need for affiliation leads to indecisiveness in decision-making. Instead, McClelland (1976) found that power-oriented managers, when truly concerned about the organization as a whole, provide the structure, drive, and support necessary to facilitate goal-oriented group behavior.

Ardrey's Territorial Theory. Another description of common human needs is derived from cultural anthropologists. According to Ardrey (1966), individuals have three types of basic needs: identity, security, and stimulation. Individuals strive for identity not anonymity; stimulation, not boredom; security, not anxiety. Ardrey believed that property or territory is one of the prime concepts that satisfies these needs; therefore, much individual behavior is directed toward acquiring property or defending territory. Property and territory refer to a range of things running from real property to a favorite and customary seat in the classroom.

Leadership Consideration. Although theorists propose a variety of need components or hierarchies, the question remains, is the hierarchy of needs plausible? There is evidence that different needs do exist, and that

they can be measured. There is also less empirical support that these needs vary so consistently in relative importance across differing individuals (Mitchell & Moudgill, 1976). To believe so seems to ignore substantial differences among people at various stages in their lives and careers (Katz, 1980; Pinder, 1984).

Despite the criticisms, some implications suggested by theories and models of common human needs are significant for leadership. Study of common human needs reveals that it is unrealistic for leaders to think that they can satisfy all needs through entitlement. This economic-man concept may apply only to individuals' lower-order needs. Individuals' higher-order needs are primarily satisfied through symbolic behavior of psychic, social, and cultural content. It is also necessary for leaders to recognize that normally gratified needs are no longer highly motivating. Employees are more enthusiastically motivated by their own achievements than by needs that normally would have been satisfied.

MOTIVATION AT WORK

There are almost as many theories of work motivation as there are writers on the subject of motivation. Their works commonly focus on the connection between motivation and work-related behavior. Two significant models are presented here; Herzberg's motivator-hygiene theory and Shamir's collectivistic motivation.

Studies in collectivistic motivation represent a new trend in work motivation. While the models described earlier help understand worker motivation to perform, their usefulness in everyday organizational contexts is limited. Leaders become confused when they try to apply these theories in practice to workers. If individuals all have changing needs, how can leaders or managers attempt to motivate an entire work force? What the practicing leader/manager needs is an answer to the question, "What will motivate most of the people most of the time?" Herzberg and Shamir sought to provide practical representations to answer the question.

Herzberg's Motivator-Hygiene Theory.

Herzberg's motivator-hygiene theory is one of the most recognized and most practical models. Herzberg and his associates aimed to determine what affects worker motivation and productivity in organizations (Herzberg, 1966, 1968; Herzberg, Mausner, & Snyderman, 1959). From their research, Herzberg and his colleagues developed the motivator-hygiene theory of work motivation. The theory assumes that employees are motivated to produce at high levels to the extent that they perceive satisfaction results. In his theory, Herzberg proposes that the opposite of satisfaction and motivation is not dissatisfaction, but simply no job satisfaction. The opposite of dissatisfaction, in turn, is not job satisfaction but simply the absence of dissatisfaction. The distinction between job satisfaction and dissatisfaction becomes clear when the two are related to levels of performance. There is a neutral point in performance levels where employees are not dissatisfied with their jobs, but neither are they experiencing job satisfaction. At this point, employees simply perform at the minimum acceptable level necessary to maintain their jobs and employment. Eliminating sources of dissatisfaction does not mean that the reduction is motivating to the worker or will lead to job satisfaction. Rather, job satisfaction and dissatisfaction are affected by different sets of factors and have different effects upon employee motivation and performance. One set of factors, hygiene, tends to affect dissatisfaction and performance below acceptable levels, while a second set of factors, motivator, tends to affect job satisfaction, motivation, and performance above acceptable levels.

Herzberg (1968, 1981) found that hygiene factors such as company policy, types of supervision, status, job security, salary, working conditions, and interpersonal relations keep employees from being dissatisfied although they do not necessarily motivate employees. Motivating factors such as achievement, recognition, the work itself, responsibility, growth, and advancement appear to motivate people and are associated with job satisfaction. Although Herzberg posited that motivation is composed of two separate, independent factors, the theory appears to be highly compatible with Maslow's and Porter's hierarchy models.

In order to motivate an employee, Herzberg claimed that those factors originally identified as motivators must be built into an employee's job. The content of the work, rather than the setting in which it is conducted, is the important factor. The work must be enriched in such a way that it allows the individual opportunities to feel achievement and recognition and provides for advancement and meaningful responsibility. When jobs are designed in this way motivation should be forthcoming. When these factors are missing, no dissatisfaction results. Satisfaction is simply not present (Herzberg, 1966). Enriching jobs to motivate workers has broad support among theorists and practitioners (Aldag, Barr, & Brief, 1981; Griffin, 1982; Hackman & Oldham, 1980). The two-factor aspect of the theory may not be a necessary element in the use of the theory for designing jobs. While the two factors may assist in clarifying and increasing understanding there is no need to assume that failure to provide these factors will not lead to job satisfaction, or that the provision of certain hygiene factors in the work place cannot also be motivating in the true sense of the word (Pinder, 1984).

Shamir's Collectivistic Work Motivation.

All models of motivation to this point are individually and rationally oriented due to their derivation from psychological and economic paradigms. These assumptions assume

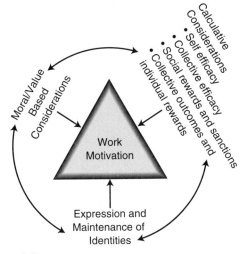

Figure 9.5
Shamir's collectivistic work motivation

that people are motivated to satisfy their own personal needs. Recent studies, however, have shown that not all human motivations can be explained on the basis of individualistic or hedonistic considerations (Shamir, 1990). This is particularly evident given the individual contributions to collective work efforts in most organizational life.

In his study, Shamir (1990) pointed out that many collective entities in such organizations as government agencies, schools, and hospitals, cannot be explained on purely individualistic and economic grounds, termed *calculative* by Etzioni (1961). Shamir maintained that "in order to understand individuals' contributions to such collective actions we have to consider both the calculative and the normal dimensions of the person's motivation simultaneously" (p. 314). Shamir proposed that understanding of individual contributions to collective work efforts should be approached from three aspects simultaneously: calculative considerations, moral or value-based considerations, and expression and maintenance of identities (see Figure 9.5).

An individual's motivation to contribute to collective efforts can be explained, in part, by

calculative considerations in terms of self-efficacy, collective efficacy, social rewards and sanctions, and social linkage between collective outcomes and individual rewards. Self-efficacy, i.e., expectancy, refers to the likelihood that an individual's contribution will increase group performance. Expectancy models have addressed how self-efficacy affects individuals' motivation to perform. In contrast, collective efficacy refers to the individual's subjective probability that collective efforts will result in collective accomplishment. Like self-efficacy, collective efficacy affects an individuals' effort to perform. In discussions of collective motivation, social rewards and sanctions are those employed to control the member's behavior. Obviously, social reward, such as social acceptance and social recognition or status, and social sanctions, such as pressure to conform, social rejection, and loss of status, influence an individual's effort at collectivistic work motivation.

The relationship between collective outcomes and individual rewards is twofold. On the one hand, collective outcomes can be translated into individual rewards in terms of profits consumed by individuals. On the other hand, many outcomes of collective work efforts constitute a common good, such as improved equipment or a better technology, which cannot be consumed individually. The two dimensions have equally important impacts on individuals' efforts at collective work motivation. Secondly, norms and values exert motivational influence through their association with expected social rewards and sanctions. When norms and values become internalized by the individual, the person may be motivated by the expected internal reactions to his or her actions. Finally, another element, other than norms and values, is the expression and maintenance of individuals' identities. Etzioni (1988) referred to this element as "a sense of affirmation." A person will seek out opportunities to maintain self-identity in a perceived social situation. People may be motivated to contribute to a collective effort, because by doing so they will maintain and affirm relevant identities. Shamir (1990) emphasized that the concept of identity is important in that it provides an obvious linkage between the individual and the collectivity. Japanese workers' strong tendency toward organizational identity is a typical example.

Shamir proposed (1990) that in order to increase collective cohesiveness (members' attraction to the collectivity and their identification with the collectivity), leaders should try to establish the symbolic environment in ways that emphasize the unique identity of the organization or sub-organization and increase organizational identity salience in members' self-concepts. Leaders need to instill norms of cooperation and contribution in an organization. Leaders also need to engage frequently in attempts to show organizational members the link between organizational actions and members' cherished values.

Morale in Organizations

Morale is an emotional attribute, providing energy, acceptance of leadership, and cooperation among members of an organization. Morale has been conceptualized from three perspectives: physiological, psychological, and social. From the physiological point of view, satisfaction of the basic human need of survival is the prime morale factor. From the psychological perspective, morale is determined by a continual satisfaction of higher-order needs. From the social approach, morale can be considered a social phenomenon caused by the strong desire of individuals to be associated with their peers.

In reality, morale is better described by the combination of the three perspectives. Morale is the atmosphere created by the attitudes of the members of an organization. Morale is more likely to be revealed by groups than by

individuals (Benge & Hickley, 1984). Morale is influenced by how employees perceive the organization and its goals in relation to themselves, in terms of their physical, psychological, social, and cultural background.

MAJOR MORALE FACTORS

The attitudes of employees are significantly influenced by the ways in which they perceive a number of important factors: the organization itself, their own activities, their self-concept, the nature of their work, their peers, the satisfaction of their needs, and leadership (Kossen, 1987). The organization significantly influences employees' attitudes toward their jobs. Higher employee morale results when an organization has a favorable reputation. An employee of a public agency encountering reduced public financial support might experience poor morale. Employees' personal lives may also affect their attitudes on the job. Relationships with families and friends, as part of their total environment, influence employees' morale in their working environment. Employees' self-concepts also tend to influence their attitudes toward organizational environments. Therefore, individuals who lack self-confidence or suffer from poor physical or mental health frequently develop morale problems. In addition, employees' current values and education have lead them to expect considerably more than just material prosperity from their work. However, many types of jobs seem to lead to boredom and obsessive thinking, such as uniform pacing, repetition, large impersonal organizational structures, and vague as well as unattainable goals. These characteristics are likely to lower employee morale without appropriate design.

The informal system and actions of leaders in an organization also affect morale significantly. As a member of a group, an employee's attitude toward a working condition could be swayed by the collective attitudes of his or her cohorts. High rates of turnover often indicate ineffective leadership.

How employees' personal needs are satisfied can influence their morale. Salary and employee benefits are two examples that help to satisfy personal needs. While increases in pay do not necessarily motivate employees to increase productivity, poor pay can be a source for poor morale, especially when compared to the pay of other employees doing similar work (Kossen, 1987; Reitz, 1987).

MORALE, JOB SATISFACTION, AND PRODUCTIVITY

Morale is closely connected with the satisfaction an individual hopes to derive from work. While work satisfaction is the result of various attitudes by an individual employee at a given time, morale is the result of the total satisfaction of the employees in an organization. As noted earlier, job satisfaction does not have to be immediately apparent, but it has to be anticipated by the individual. Low morale often accompanies high rates of absenteeism, tardiness, and high turnover.

Morale is also related to productivity. Some feel that there tends to be a direct relationship between high productivity and high morale. However, the nature of the relationship between morale and productivity is inconclusive. Others see an inverse relationship, circular, or even reciprocal relationship between productivity and morale. The morale/productivity relationship, therefore, can be perceived as situational.

APPROACHES TO STUDYING MORALE

At least three approaches have been developed to study employee morale. The first approach involves analyzing organizational records for changes in resignations, tardiness, absenteeism, productivity, and complaints. The second approach is to interview employees, using prepared questions or allowing employees to respond in an unstructured format. The third approach is to administer unsigned questionnaires and then report morale indices (Benge & Hickley, 1984). The three approaches are complementary and can be conducted simultaneously. To be effective, studies of morale should be conducted periodically, not just once.

QUALITY OF WORK LIFE

Regardless of the real relationship between productivity and morale, high morale remains an important organizational goal. However, morale frequently is not noticed unless it is poor. Far too often, leaders do not recognize how badly morale has deteriorated until they are faced with serious crises. Leaders must continually be alert to clues revealing the state of morale. Leaders need to be sensitive to the warning signs of low morale in their employees, such as absenteeism, tardiness, high turnover, strikes and sabotages, and lack of pride in work. They also need to secure actively all available information through statistical data (e.g., absenteeism and turnover records), employee counselors, observation and listening, or surveys. Studies on morale reveal that leaders should be concerned with the quality of employee work life. The more affluent and better educated work forces of today expect a higher quality of work life (O'Toole, 1981). To satisfy employees today, leadership is expected to improve the quality of work life.

Quality of work life (QWL) refers to how effectively the job environment meets the personal needs and values of employees. QWL consists of seven components: (1) adequate and fair compensation, (2) safe and healthy work conditions, (3) opportunity for continued growth and security, (4) a feeling of belonging, (5) employee rights, (6) work and total life span, and (7) social relevance of work life (Greenberg & Glaser, 1983; Walton, 1975).

Several recent methods have been developed to improve the quality of work life. They include job rotation, job enlargement, job enrichment, and socio-technical systems (Aldag & Brief, 1979; Champagne & McAfee, 1989; Hackman, 1983; Hellriegel & Slocum, 1976; Lawler, 1992; Pinder, 1984; Plous, 1987; Reitz, 1987).

Job rotation is the practice of training a worker in several different tasks and rotating that worker through those tasks in a given time period. Job rotation attempts to reduce the boredom and fatigue from endless repetitions of a task and increase job satisfaction, primarily by increasing task variety. Workers can also acquire a broader set of skills and knowledge, which increases efficiency during periods of absenteeism.

Job enlargement, like job rotation, increases the scope of a job. It intends to reduce boredom and fatigue and increase satisfaction by increasing the number of tasks a worker performs within a given job. It emphasizes the performance of a greater number and variety of skills. It also allows for more decisionmaking about work methods and more responsibility.

Job enrichment is an attempt to involve the worker in more than just the performance of the task. In job enrichment, employees are provided with greater work content that requires advanced skills and new knowledge. The worker is more autonomous and responsible for planning, organizing, and evaluating the work as well as carrying it out. This autonomy and responsibility provides the opportunity for personal growth and meaningful work experience.

It is important to note that job enlargement and job enrichment do not call for merely adding more low-level tasks to the worker's job. This may be demotivating. There are four criteria in deciding whether or not a job can be enlarged or enriched. Any addition to the job should (1) increase responsibility, (2) increase worker autonomy,

(3) permit the worker to do the complete task, and (4) provide feedback to the worker.

Socio-technical systems design jobs around groups of workers rather than individuals. In this approach, the leader defines a complete unit of work and assigns responsibility for that unit to a group. The workers in the group share responsibility for determining what each of them will do, for deciding how they will accomplish it, and for scheduling and completing the work. The group itself assumes the responsibility for supervising its work.

Informal Organizations

Informal worker networks emerge spontaneously in organizations from the needs of the worker. They are not planned but occur as individual social interactions within the formal organization. These informal networks have their own leaders, unwritten policy, hidden agendas, communication channels, and even their own goals. Informal networks can play a significant part in organizational life. Informal organizations arise and persist as a means of compensating for the inadequacy of formal organizations in providing individual need satisfactions and/or as a means of adding to the need satisfaction provided by membership in formal organizations (Bales, 1953, Davis, 1977; Kossen, 1987; Roethlisberger & Dickson, 1939). Workers enter into organizations with individually shaped expectations, and bring with them differing values, interests, and abilities. Informal activities emerge when some particular need is not being fulfilled by the formal organization. Informal organizations help members of formal organizations satisfy needs by performing three important functions: social interaction, social control, and communication.

One of the most important functions provided by informal organizations is the provision of social interaction. Individuals have social needs that they attempt to satisfy at work in formal organizations; however, the social satisfaction provided by the formal organizations is limited. Informal organizations arise to help individuals satisfy these social needs, thus giving an individual recognition, status, and further opportunity to relate to others.

The second major function provided by informal organizations is social control. This function helps preserve and maintain the existence, identity, and values of the informal organizations. Social control is maintained and enforced over informal organization membership through norms and standards of behavior. Norms are enforced through social pressure. Informal organizations also attempt to exert control over people outside their group but within the formal organization, e.g., by influencing the leadership or staff personnel. Much of this external control is exerted indirectly by regulating the behavior of members of the informal organizations.

A third informal organization function is communication. To keep its members informed of what is taking place and how it may affect them, the informal organization develops a system of communication to supplement the information provided by the formal organization. This communication system, as discussed in chapter 7, is known as the grapevine. Grapevines are inevitable as it is practically impossible for formal organizations to keep all individuals well-informed. It is worthwhile to examine informal organizations because they have a tremendous capacity for carrying and disseminating important information quickly.

INFORMAL LEADERS

The leaders of informal organizations arise for various reasons and under slightly different circumstances. There are typically several informal leaders of varying importance in an informal organization, but usually one primary leader who has the most influence. The general role of informal leaders is to help the informal organization achieve its goals and to maintain and enhance informal organizational life. In return for their services, informal leaders usually enjoy certain rewards and privileges, such as esteem and power (Davis, 1977; Wolman, 1956). As a result, these individuals' informal roles may take on more importance than their formal work roles. The informal organization may be a desirable source of potential leaders for the formal organization. However, caution is necessary here as the agendas of informal leaders often may not coincide with organizational agendas. The dynamics of informal organizations and their informal leaders can be studied using sociometric techniques (Moreno, 1947) and interaction-process analysis techniques (Bales, 1950).

EFFECTS OF INFORMAL ORGANIZATIONS

The existence of informal organizations always affects the operation of formal organizations. In most cases, informal organizations have both detrimental and beneficial effects (Davis, 1977; Kossen, 1987; Ruben, 1988; Sanford, 1977; Scott, 1981). Four potential disadvantages exist in informal organizations. They may transmit false information, resist changes, cause excessive conformity to group norms, and develop goals that conflict with formal organizational goals. Transmitting false information is one of the most troublesome problems attributed to the communications systems of informal organization. Rumors are efficiently and effectively transmitted through the grapevine. Since rumors often are inaccurate, they create problems in organizations. It should be noted that informal organizations do not necessarily cause rumors; however, they do transmit rumors. In trying to preserve and maintain their values and status, informal organizations tend to resist change, especially changes that will have detrimental effects on the organization. They resist changes through members' conformity enforced by social control. The quest for social satisfaction in informal organizations may lead their members away from organizational goals. What is good for the workers is not always good for the organization. Role conflicts occur and often lead to limited productivity.

The existence of informal organizations can also benefit the formal organization. Informal organizations satisfy employees' social needs, provide a useful employee communication network, provide employees with emotional escape valves, and complement the formal organization. A significant benefit of informal organizations is that they provide satisfaction and stability to employees and the formal organization. The existence of informal organizations provides employees a sense of belonging, acceptance, and security. The satisfaction provided by informal organizations compensates for some of the inevitable undesirable aspects associated with formal organizational membership. Thus, informal organizations help the formal organization reduce turnover, and may increase employee motivation. An additional benefit of informal organizations is that they provide a means for people to keep in touch, to learn more about their work, and to understand what is happening in their environment. Informal organizations serve as safety valves for employee frustrations and even other emotional problems. They provide an escape valve where negative feelings caused by the formal organization can be aired.

Overall, the existence of informal organizations tends to facilitate the functioning of the formal organization in certain important respects. They fill gaps in the formal organization's management, can promote more efficiency in the formal system, often supplement authority and responsibility mechanisms within the formal organization,

and provide additional channels of communication.

INEVITABILITY OF INFORMAL ORGANIZATIONS

Informal organizations are inevitable for at least two reasons. First, they supplement need satisfaction provided by formal organizations. Secondly, membership in formal organizations tends to stimulate people's needs for more information than formal organizations can provide. Informal organizations, therefore, always will be present and cannot be eliminated.

Realizing the inevitability of the informal organization, leaders must consider the possible effects their actions have on informal systems in order to integrate as far as possible the interests of informal organizations with those of the formal organizations, and to keep formal activities from unnecessarily threatening informal organizations in general. The most desirable informal/formal organization relationship seems to be one in which the two systems maintain unity toward goals. Leaders of the formal organization would be wise to consider the value of the informal organization and work to maintain and enhance overall group cohesiveness and teamwork through it (Davis, 1977; Scott, 1981).

Human Relations Theory in Educational Administration

The human relations view of educational administration incorporates two distinctive bodies of thought. The first school is democratic administration, a philosophy of administration originating shortly after 1900 in John Dewey's work. The second arose after 1945, when notions about democratizing school organizations combined with humanistic studies drawn from behavioral science and the industrial studies discussed earlier. The fusion of these two bodies of thought in the 1940s was described first as democratic human relations and later as simply the human relations approach to educational administration (Campbell, Fleming, Newell, & Bennion, 1987).

DEMOCRATIC EDUCATIONAL ADMINISTRATION

Unlike the human relations approach that originated in industrial and social science research, the democratic view of educational administration first evolved among educators in the early years of the twentieth century in response to several factors. These included new social changes in the character of school organizations and reactions on the part of some to autocratic and authoritarian supervisory practices in schools. One of the earliest promoters of democratic administration in education, John Dewey (1916), argued against the increasing popularity of scientific management techniques among school leaders and emphasized the need for educational managers to secure the consent of those they governed. Scientific management's preoccupation with efficiency did little to foster what he described as a well-balanced social interest. Dewey argued this as contrary to the proper ends of education. Giving teachers opportunities for greater participation changes both the character of the school organization and the quality and kind of relationships between teachers and administrators. For the educational leader, a cooperative approach to school management would necessitate that leadership provide intellectual stimulation and direction through give and take with others. A cooperative approach would not produce an aloof, official, imposing, or authoritarian environment. Others who supported democratic leadership

include educational scholars, social reconstructionists, and social and philosophical scholars.

According to its supporters there are three significant bases of democratic administration:

1. A widely shared belief that if teachers were treated in an autocratic manner by principals and superintendents, they would treat pupils accordingly.

2. The enormous growth in size and specialization of schools demanded that structural changes occur. Structural changes within school systems compel superintendents and other administrators to rely on the expertise of teachers and other staff members.

3. Democratic leadership promises to help school administrators secure the cooperation of their staffs by making them members of the team.

Both the democratic administration that originated in educational settings and the human relations movement of the industrial era bear close resemblances. On the surface, both approaches react against autocratic administrative practices associated with scientific management. Most importantly, human relations research seems to confirm empirically what supporters of democratic administration have believed for some time, that organizational morale and productivity could be enhanced by humanistic leadership practices.

THE HUMAN RELATIONS MOVEMENT IN EDUCATION

The educational interest in applying human relations ideas to problems of school administration has been spurred by several developments taking place inside and outside schools. Outside the school, the growing urban character, as well as improvements in transportation, have narrowed the distance between home and school. More and more, schools are being located in suburban areas to accommodate the educational needs of the nation's middle class who are increasingly abandoning the cities (Link & Catton, 1967). This trend facilitates community involvement in educational affairs. Parent-teacher associations and interactions between school staff and the public have increased. The changing environment around the schools and the need for better public relations provide sound reasons for educators to adopt a view of management that promises to enhance their social and interpersonal skills. Conditions inside school organizations also cause administrators to look to human relations. Staffing difficulties, which began after 1941 when teachers left the classroom to join the armed forces or work in wartime industry, became an acute administration problem by the end of the war (Link & Catton, 1967). Teacher shortages and the general high rate of attrition within the profession were aggravated by economic factors that made teaching an unattractive occupation (Hill, 1947). To address such problems, school managers needed to gain public understanding and support and improve morale among school staff.

The changing character of school populations in the late 1940s and early 1950s was another factor that encouraged educators to develop human relations skills. More students from different backgrounds were enrolled in public schools than ever before (Moehlman, 1940). In addition, the increasing mobility of postwar society, the quickening pace of events, and the loosening of long-held values and traditions posed new and different problems, especially in the decades after the Supreme Court's landmark *Brown v. Board of Education* decision. Others condemned public schooling for its alleged anti-intellectual tone, its dominance by professional educa-

tors, and its undemocratic methods in preparing and selecting pupils for careers. In light of such criticisms, it is not surprising that professors of education recommended a form of management that suggested strategies for cooperation borrowed from industrial research.

Ralph Tyler was one of the first educators to appreciate the changing view of administration that human relations research espoused. Tyler (1941) noted the relevance of recent human relations research to school administrators and suggested that future research in educational management be guided by the Hawthorne studies. Wilbur Yauch's and Daniel Griffiths' studies were two other important milestones that applied concepts of human relations to education. Yauch (1949) provided one of the first complete educational studies that combined ethical generalizations from democratic administration with human relations research drawn from industry. He brought together the prescriptive approach to school management advanced by educators throughout the 1920s and 1930s with a more objective appreciation of administrative problems. He advocated teacher involvement in all areas of administration, including staff participation in decisions concerning supervision, budget allocation, curriculum, general policy making, and clerical duties associated with operating a school.

Griffiths' (1956) study synthesized more than a quarter century of educational and social science thought about administration. Griffiths believed that staff morale was related to the kind of leadership operating within schools. He saw the school leader as someone whose chief responsibility is to facilitate the actions of others: an initiator, a coordinator, a helper, and a resource person. The school leader is a social individual, sensitive to the human needs of all concerned. Griffiths' study was not intended as a handbook containing lists of human relations rules and techniques that can be applied to various situations, but rather, it sought to provide an intellectual basis for the study of schools drawn from research in other social sciences and from other fields of professional study. As such, it signalled the beginning of a shift in educational interest from a practical application of human relations research to a concern with theoretically grounded understanding of human behavior derived from the social sciences, a change later characterized as one in which educators begin to conceive administration as a domain of study rather than a domain of action (Getzels, 1977).

FROM DEMOCRATIC ADMINISTRATION TO HUMAN RELATIONS MANAGEMENT

Teacher performance in school affairs or democratic administration, as discussed by Dewey and others, represents a way of bringing organizational practices in schools in line with long-standing political and social values, thereby endowing teachers with rights of organizational citizenship. The most critical functions of schools may be their ability to serve as laboratories for democracy and agencies of national regeneration. Schools, therefore, must develop better human resource mechanisms to achieve these primary goals.

Human relations research stems from industrial experiments designed to improve worker performance and generally to assist the cause of management. Early scholars embraced human relations ideas because they promised to assist the cause of democratic leadership. Adoption of these early ideas, however, eventually helped in solving administrative problems and tasks more than in restructuring or democratizing schools.

By mid-century, students of educational administration cast aside the focus on democracy in schools and teacher participation in favor of other issues related to understanding the roles and responsibilities of school leaders. Human relations writers on school management generally were more concerned with

understanding how group dynamic skills could assist administrators in dealing with problems related to public relations and staff morale. Their writings, therefore, addressed issues related more to managing and administering schools than notions about what enlightened leadership should accomplish (Campbell, Fleming, Newell, & Bennion, 1987).

After mid-century, concepts of school leadership were no longer defended on philosophical worthiness but shifted to how well school executives understood human behavior and the dynamics of interpersonal relations. In human relations writings, development of skills in nondirective counseling and psychological testing were viewed as essentials for effective administrators (Campbell, Fleming, Newell, & Bennion, 1987).

EFFECTS OF THE HUMAN RELATIONS MOVEMENT ON EDUCATIONAL ADMINISTRATION

The human relations movement had relatively little impact on school district administrators, as compared to its substantial impact on supervisors (Owens, 1987). Superintendents today continue to emphasize such classical concepts as hierarchical control, authority, and formal organization, while supervisors emphasize such human relations concepts as morale, group cohesiveness, collaboration, and the dynamics of informal organizations.

Those who see their roles as educational administrators tend to emphasize budgets, politics, control, and asymmetrical exercise of power from the top down, while others concerned with instruction and curriculum place much more emphasis on participation and communication. Status-power relationships have been deemphasized. This difference in emphasis persisted into the 1980s. Additionally, motivation, the core concept of the human relations movement, was not implemented well in schools or the school environment. There was no good fit between teachers who tried to achieve excellence and at the same time demanded more entitlement.

A NEW FRAME OF LEADERSHIP

In ordinary times, people look to managers for predictable, smooth-running, and cost-effective operations. Managers help supply the clarity, certainty, and efficiency required to get the job done right. In times of crisis, however, good management is not enough. People facing uncertainty turn to leaders for direction, confidence, and hope. Leaders encourage long-range planning, spirit, and cohesion when doubts about the future of the organization occur. Leadership must consistently sense its history and, at the same time, look ahead to discover or rediscover why the new organization exists, what it stands for, and where it might be headed. As external circumstances shift and sway, organizations waver between their need for management and their need for leadership. The issue is not which is better, but rather what balance is best in view of contemporary challenges.

Several years ago, a national commission formally announced a nation at risk, a time of crisis in educational systems. Since that time there has been little success in reshaping schools. New structures, strengthened curriculum, less money, and greater diversity create formidable new administrative obstacles. Coupled with these issues is a strong belief that our nation's schools can never be as they once were. Moreover, this new call for leadership is not confined to education (Deal, 1992).

Volumes of literature have reinforced leadership as a crucial ingredient in all collective endeavors. But despite the attention, the essence of leadership remains mysteriously elusive. Modern concepts view leadership as a complex interaction among members of an organization, in which context rather than position usually determines who will take the lead. However, it is still possible to distill some essential attributes of leadership.

Bolman and Deal (1991) synthesized the organizational literature into four distinct frames, each emphasizing a different aspect of cooperative ventures. Each frame is explained by a corresponding arena of emphasis as shown in Table 9.1.

Recent studies of administrators in business, higher education, and schools suggest that most administrators operate primarily from either a structural or human resource orientation (Bolman & Deal, 1991). Both orientations are linked significantly to their administrator's effectiveness as a manager, and their effectiveness as perceived by subordinates. Today, however, symbolic and political orientations play much more dominant roles. Attention to symbols appears to be a very significant factor in effective leadership. Leaders operate more as negotiators and poets than as servants, catalysts, or social architects. In terms of crisis, effective leaders

Table 9.1
Frames of Leadership

Frames	Emphasis
Human Resources	Human needs and cares
Structural	Organizational goals and costs
Political	Power and competition
Symbolic	Symbols and cultures

barter and build coalitions and shape and reshape symbolic forms that influence organizational purpose and meaning.

A NEW PARADIGM FOR EDUCATIONAL LEADERSHIP

As predicted by national and international forces influencing the educational system, the leadership role in education is assuming new dimensions. The public expects educational leaders to improve the quality of schooling significantly. These expectations require leaders first to clarify educational outcomes and assessment strategies. They also require leaders to be proficient in staff development practices and experiments in labor relations. In another leadership role, school leaders are expected to develop new political, social, and business connections within the broader community (Wallace, 1992).

Student achievement in the United States compares unfavorably with achievement outcomes in Asia and Europe (Stevenson & Stigler, 1992). These results raise questions about the economic model and the human resources models used so pervasively in educational systems throughout the nation. Unless future generations are more effectively educated, serious deficiencies will continue to mount as achievement continues to wane further. For example, changing demographics suggest that schools must be more effective in educating an expanding population of poor and minority students. Reports today indicate that these pupils are underserved by the public schools. It is likely that in the future these students will form a major portion of the work force (Edmonds, 1979; Little, 1981). With these realizations, school leaders will be required to exhibit a higher level of educational, civic, and political leadership. Citizens must be better prepared to participate effectively in societies of the twenty-first century.

Perhaps the most significant recent change in educational administration is the demand for aggressive and effective leadership at the building and the district levels. More than ever, the general public expects school administrators to be active leaders of the instructional program. Educational leaders must envision strengthened schools and be able to bring about conditions that will ensure a high quality education. They also must be capable of conveying symbolic meaning to nourish aspirations and achieve these goals. They must articulate a coherent vision as well as define the components of quality education for students. More importantly, they must motivate professionals at the school and district levels to implement these new visions. In a word, schools need to become more collegial and less bureaucratic.

A MOTIVATIONAL MODEL FOR EDUCATIONAL LEADERSHIP

Motivation, as discussed earlier, is generally considered to be rooted in human needs. Individuals respond to their needs by attempting to fulfill them. Therefore, the basis for understanding motivation in organizations lies in understanding the needs that motivate the behavior of people in these organizations. These views of motivation, however, have not been implemented well in schools.

Research indicates that recognition, achievement, advancement, and responsibility are major forces in motivating educators to lift their performances to their maximum potentials (Savage, 1967; Schmidt, 1976; Wickstrom, 1971). Sergiovanni and Carver (1973) also found that routine housekeeping, such as taking attendance, paper work, lunch duty, insensitive or inappropriate supervision, irritating administrative policies, and poor relationships with colleagues and/or parents are major sources of job dissatisfaction among educators. Sergiovanni and Carver argued that teaching offers little opportunity for advancement. These general dissatisfactions cause teachers to consider other more satisfying professions in the educational realm.

In the past, there were two focal points in educational leadership. The first emphasized such things as planning, organizing, coordinating, commanding, and controlling. This approach long defined leadership as task structure and initiating structure. On the job, this means attending to scheduling, organizing, supervising, and monitoring, all of which are absolutely essential to running schools well. The second focal point of educational leadership is consideration based and develops concern for subordinates, morale, motivation, group process, conflict management, and decisionmaking, in essence a participative and human resource orientation.

However, there is more to educational leadership. For example, exemplary educational leaders have long been known to be skilled instructional leaders; that is, they are adept at diagnosing educational problems, counseling teachers, developing curriculum, developing staff, evaluating, and remediating the educational work of teachers. Sergiovanni (1984) defined the three types of leadership as technical, human, and educational. He maintained that these three types of leadership are essential for competent schools. However, in order to move from competence to excellence in schools, two other forms of leadership, symbolic leadership and culture-building leadership, are also necessary.

Symbolic leadership signals and demonstrates to others what is important, what is valued, what is wanted, and what goals override others. Symbolic leaders create and communicate a vision for followers; they describe a desired state of affairs to which followers commit themselves. They seek to make clear to subordinates the connections between, on the one hand, what they do, and what, on the other hand, they can do toward the achievement of excellence. In other words, symbolic leaders organize their personal time and

energies so as to provide a unified vision of the school to students and teachers alike.

However, research suggests that even symbolic leadership alone is incapable of achieving excellence in schools (Sergiovanni, 1984). Excellent schools are characterized by a distinctive organizational character that seems to set such schools apart from others. Equally important, excellent schools must be managed so that teachers feel that they belong to effective work groups, feel good about the work they do, and believe that their achievements are worthwhile. Leaders of excellent schools must take care, not only to preserve inherited traditions, but also to set about building new higher-order traditions.

Leadership and the development of an organizational culture means building behavioral norms that exemplify the best that a school stands for. It means building an institution in which people believe strongly, with which they identify personally, and to which they gladly render their loyalty. All of this gives meaning to the work that they do and additionally builds greater significance into the school environment. In total, the work environment becomes more motivating as commitment further develops.

Leaders who attempt to build strong organizational cultures in schools spend time articulating the purposes and the mission of the school. They bring others together to accept these values as the uniqueness of the school is constantly redefined. These schools are characterized by the bonding that occurs between people and organizations in which they have faith and toward which they have commitment. Under such leadership, students and teachers alike come to understand that they are part of an important and worthwhile larger mission.

Other profound effects upon the human relations movement stem from more recent studies of leadership in organizations. For example, Burns (1978) and Bass (1985) conceptualized leadership as transactional and transformational. Transactional leadership is an exchange process or problem intervention relationship and correlates with the traditional command and control styles of management. Transformational leadership is different. Leaders attribute their own power to better interpersonal skills, hard work, networking, and inspiration. In this view, leadership is individual consideration and intellectual stimulation, and inspires followers to raise their own levels of self-awareness.

Sergiovanni (1992) proposed that transformative leadership be capable of enhancing the ability of members in social organizations to realize their visions and achieve goals. Sergiovanni added a moral dimension to leadership that allows for the creation of a covenant of shared values, commitment, and vision that can move members to develop an effective, successful organization. However, he also asserted that transactional leadership has a role to fill within organizations. This can be seen in the expanded needs for instructional and interpersonal leadership. Burns (1978) and Greenfield (1987) also called for a moral aspect to leadership. Burns translated this as the ability to raise followers to higher levels of motivation and morality. Greenfield referred to the leader's ability to see things as they are and as they might be within a moral context.

Bass (1981) identified transactional leadership with first-order change based on expected performance. Transactional leaders provide rewards when merited, encourage individual self-interests, and attempt to align self-interests with organizational goals. He identified transformational leadership as second order changes in attitudes, beliefs, and values, based on performance beyond expectations. Both Bass and Sergiovanni asserted that the practice of transformational leadership can result in organizational members achieving beyond expectations because of the

intrinsic self-motivation. Organizational members become committed to a shared set of values and beliefs that become a professional covenant embodied in their thoughts and actions.

The New York State Department of Education's initiative for educational reform, *A New Compact for Learning* (1991), is transformational. In the new compact, the school superintendent is responsible for coordinating the creation of a shared vision for the school district, both symbolic and practical. Elements of this transformation include establishing means to achieve desired outcomes, nurturing community involvement, sharing planning and decisionmaking, and developing and sharing vision of the district with both schools and the community.

This type of leadership is not exercised solely at the district level, but rather, is diffused throughout the whole school environment to include the district, schools, and community. In the normally loose-structured district environment, development of a united subculture provides an opportunity for members to work collaboratively and collegially toward common goals. With the district, members of new coalitions share leadership as individual expertise and roles match with goals.

Sergiovanni's leadership concept is illustrated in Figure 9.6. Each circle is enveloped by a shared vision that drives all beliefs and actions within the district. This vision originates from the chief supervisor and is developed through meanings attached to that supervisors's actions, decisions, and behaviors. Congruent with this vision are the shared values, beliefs, and understandings that are developed by other organizational partners. The chief supervisor works with this constituency to develop means for shared planning and decisionmaking.

From these actions a compact forms that fuels the activities of each individual school or

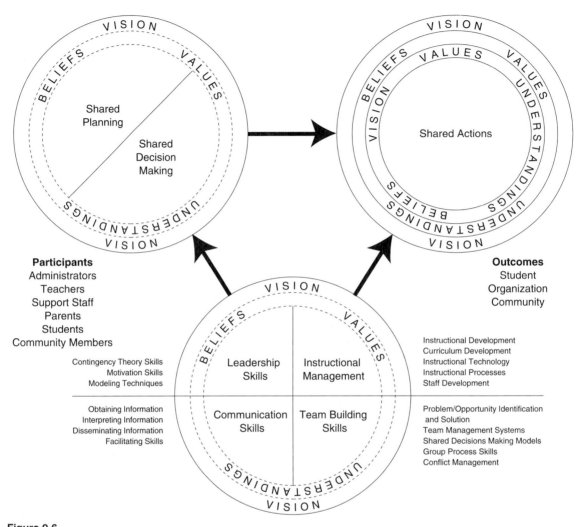

Figure 9.6
Sergiovanni's conceptualization of transformative leadership

department. Shared actions result in the school or departments as a culture forms to build shared commitment to action and enhance student success as outlined in the vision. In this budding environment, leaders in these settings must be adept at communication, team building, and instructional management. Equally important, a third arena represents the tactical leadership skills needed by the chief supervisor of the district. Newly formed teams will each need to learn

to rely on each others' expertise, develop collaboration mechanisms, become reflective, and, together, formulate plans, make decisions, and act. Supervisors must be adept at instituting an environment that builds the capabilities within all concerned.

More recently, Rosner (1990) studied this transactional-transformational continuum in relation to women's leadership roles and developed a style of leadership she termed *interactive.* Specifically, women encourage participation, share power and information, enhance other people's self-worth, and inspire excitement about work and the work environment. Rosner's views indicate that data supports a new view of the way women lead and contributes an added level of knowledge and understanding for human resource authors, theorists, and users. Other writers have given credence to other views of leadership. Leaders manage attention, meaning, trust, and self (Bennis & Nanus, 1985). Leaders are teachers, designers, and stewards (Senge, 1991). As further research continues to contribute to our understanding, leadership and human resource management will continue to evolve.

The study of human relations is concerned with human potential in organizations. In the future, supportive climates, more feedback, and increased investment in workers must somehow bring excellence to organizations. People work because they are motivated to do so. Studies of people in the work environment are extensive. Process models of motivation focus on how and why motivation works. Content models of motivation discuss what specifically motivates people. Expectancy models, behaviorist models, and social learning models are categorized as process models. Studies on content models fall into two areas: common human needs and motivation at work.

Although theorists have proposed a variety of needs components operating in human beings, they all assume that people are motivated in pursuit of the fulfillment of their own individual needs. The major tasks of leadership are to provide opportunities for workers to satisfy these needs. As Herzberg claims, people are motivated by factors he termed *motivators.* To motivate employees, leaders should consider building motivators into employees' jobs, giving them a sense of achievement and formal responsibility.

Morale reflects how members feel about their organizations. Morale is influenced by public perception of the organization, the employee's personal life, the nature of the work, interpersonal relationships, the employee's self-concept and needs, and leadership. Leaders need to observe the morale of the organization and develop a sensitivity to employees' needs. Leaders also need to improve the quality of employee worklife by using techniques like job rotation, job enlargement, job enrichment, and socio-technical systems.

Informal organizations emerge from individuals' social contacts within a formal organization. Informal organizations provide individuals with alternatives for achieving satisfaction not provided by the formal organization: social interactions, social control, informal communication, and alternatives for achieving satisfaction not provided by the formal organization. Informal organizations have four potential disadvantages. They tend to transmit false information, resist changes, cause excessive conformity to group norms, and even develop goals that conflict with formal organizational goals. However, informal organizations do provide some benefits for the formal organization. They satisfy employee social satisfactions, provide a useful employee communication network, and provide employees with an emotional escape valve. Faced with the inevitability of the existence of informal organizations, the job of leadership is to accept and understand them, to take into account the possible effects on informal organizations when taking actions, to integrate the interests of informal organizations into the formal organizational activities, and to avoid unnecessary threats to informal organizations.

Human relations is not a prescription to make people happy. Instead, the true essence of human relations management is an attempt to make people's contributions to organizational life more meaningful. The focus on provision of meaningful organizational life is evident in light of the theoretical works of

- Influence Expectancy Beliefs
- Timely and Sound Rewards
- Behavior Models
- Existence of Variable Needs
- Opportunities for Needs Satisfactions
- Job Enrichment
- Develop Collectivity Identity

- Supportive Climate
- More Feedback
- Training
  - Growth
  - Achievment
- Opportunities to Tackle Challenges

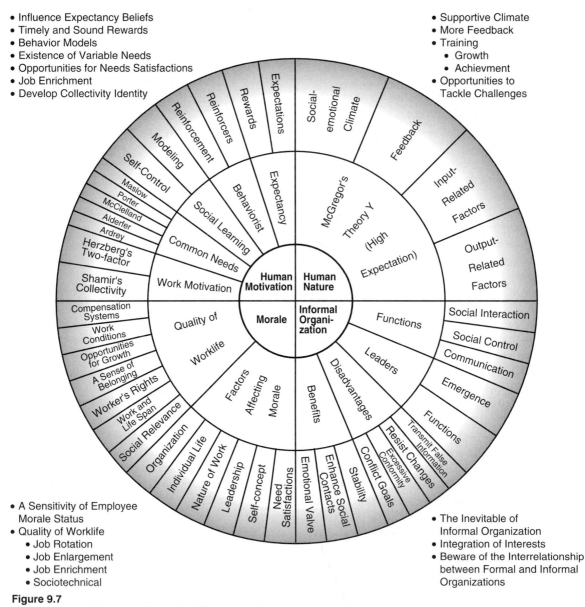

- A Sensitivity of Employee Morale Status
- Quality of Worklife
  - Job Rotation
  - Job Enlargement
  - Job Enrichment
  - Sociotechnical

- The Inevitable of Informal Organization
- Integration of Interests
- Beware of the Interrelationship between Formal and Informal Organizations

Figure 9.7
A taxonomy of theoretical works of human relations

human relations study as pictured in Figure 9.7.

In large part, human relations' thinkers have adopted McGregor's Theory Y viewpoint where human beings are viewed as full of potential. This potential can be tapped by holding and encouraging high expectations. To develop human potential in organizations, leaders need to provide workers with a supportive climate, more feedback, training programs for professional growth, and challenging opportunities.

CONTEMPORARY ISSUES IN HUMAN RELATIONS

Discrimination is a continuing problem in all organizational environments. It may be particularly critical in the educational environment as educators become more accountable for developmental responsibilities that once were largely family centered. Although much progress has been made in recent decades, considerable prejudicial and discriminatory practices remain. Too often this prejudice and discrimination is directed at ethnic minorities and other special employment groups. Prejudice stems from internal judgments based on insufficient evidence. A prejudiced person often tends to think in stereotypical terms without considering individual differences. Prejudice becomes a serious human relations problem when actions become discriminatory. Too often in our organizational activities, time constraints and prejudgments about others and situations create undue pressure to act. Our actions become inappropriate as we inadvertently fail to withhold judgment until issues are investigated fully.

In our attempts to build a just working environment, we must somehow learn to create a fair and equal working climate. Leaders and managers alike must balance objectivity and sensitivity. Kossen (1987) identifies some typical problems that further contribute to discrimination in the workplace. For example, some managers stereotype ethnic minorities and other special employment groups as less capable when compared to white males. As a result, managers tend to expect less from these groups and poor work results. In reality, these managers may be eliciting the exact poor behavior they expect. Their insensitivity to their own prejudices causes discrimination as they view these groups from an inappropriate perspective. In other cases, in attempts to avoid prejudice, managers may assign more difficult projects to these special groups in order to create an appearance of equal treatment. Managers' inabilities to understand their own prejudice contributes to further discrimination.

Racial discrimination is an emotional issue. A review of the research demonstrates that society is moving slowly to overcome racial discrimination (Wildstrom, 1986). Many of the events in the recent past have aroused greater public interest and protest. African-Americans were the first to recognize that protests and demonstrations play a significant part in forcing public recognition of racial injustice (Coulmad, 1992; Kossen, 1987). Their demands for new laws, better education, and government action have brought change. Strong self-pride has helped the African-American cause in the search for equal job opportunity and a better place in society. Equally important, discrimination against Hispanics, Native Americans, and Oriental Americans are as problematic for our society and educational institutions.

There has been great progress in women's rights in recent decades. One of the major concerns of women in the workplace has been equal pay for equal work. This issue asserts that women should be paid equally for performing tasks requiring the same skills, training, responsibility, and effort as men. Other issues are equally significant: calls for more and better quality child care, better promotion potential, better legal protection against sexual harassment, broader maternity benefits, and equal political power. While much action in these areas is evident today, more still needs to be accomplished.

Much still needs to be accomplished in the human resource realm as noted by the numerous commissions exploring reform and restructuring in the educational environment. Most problematic will be how to assure that educational leadership pinpoints action strategies that deal effectively with broad human resource activities. Most important, practitioners today must become adept at understanding human relations and devising visionary practices that elicit the best of human potential. As much literature has shown, the best outcomes generally occur in an environment where concern for the individual worker/administrator is responsible and accountable in a team atmosphere, where individual need achievement transcends entitlement, and where individuals strive for and have the opportunity to achieve excellence in their own terms.

■ CASE STUDY

Human Relations: The Case of the New Hires

Valerie Rizzo has just been appointed the new principal of the East Ruxton Middle School. East Ruxton is a city of approximately 20,000 persons serving as a marketing and light manufacturing center for the two adjacent rural counties. The city school district at one time had been one of the outstanding programs in the state for a community of its size. However, over the past decade, that reputation began to slip as changes in the economy caused reductions in the tax base and thus cutbacks in the schools' budgets and services. The superintendent and current administration have all held their positions for a number of years, with the junior administrator having seven years of service. The teaching staff also have tended to stay in place. In the Middle School, only two of the teaching faculty have less than five years' tenure.

When she was hired, Valerie was told by the superintendent that the most recent school board election had brought in three new persons, and that the balance of voting power on the new board lies with them. The new members ran on a platform of reform and upgrading for the schools, and they are looking to Valerie as the new administrator to spearhead change in her school. The new members are hoping that changes in the Mid-

dle School will provide an example that will influence the rest of the district.

■   ■   ■

Questions

1.   If you were Valerie Rizzo, what steps would you take in the first 30 days of your incumbency as the Middle School principal to introduce the change-related issues discussed above while simultaneously establishing effective human relations with your building staff?

2.   How will you approach the issues discussed above with your administrative peers across the district?

3.   What model(s) of human needs and leadership discussed in this chapter will you use to guide you in your new role? Why?

4.   Prepare an action plan for yourself for the first half-year that will allow you to begin the job, operate your school, and initiate appropriate changes. Be prepared to discuss the means by which you will motivate your staff to meet the challenges to come, and explain why you are selecting those particular means.

■ CASE STUDY

The Case of the Rumor Mill

Rumors are rampant at Schoolville. At recent school board meetings, the superintendent has been confronted on several occasions by irate parents and the local press. Somehow these groups have gained access to privileged state budget documents. The new budget has granted a sizeable pay increase to teachers. However, the community is not satisfied with recent student achievement scores. In addition, the student scores have been poor for several years running. In light of these circumstances, discuss the following:

1. How to deflect attention away from the apparent informal network that seems to have more information than the school board and the superintendent.

2. How to address the schools' fundamental problem, poor student achievement.

■ **CASE STUDY**

The Case of the Reality Check

The Schoolville superintendent has prided himself on the quality graduates his district has been able to recruit from excellent teachers colleges over the past several years. Recently, these graduates have raised complaints about the bureaucratic nature of the district and schools, and have additionally united an even larger group of dissatisfied tenured teachers. The new teachers bring with them high expectations. It seems the educational "excellence" movement has passed Schoolville by, and the "dissenters" are demanding more than the district can offer. Discuss this scenario in light of the following:

1. How to achieve more flexibility for teachers, but still maintain control.

2. How to maintain current levels of efficiency.

3. How to "fast forward" into the era of excellence.

■ **CASE STUDY**

The Case of Professionalizing

The Miller Middle School principal has kept up to date with recent educational literature.

But she is perplexed by some of the recent school-based management principles. Although she is an advocate of professionalization of the school environment, during discussions with teachers, she has become skeptical. For example, while she believes in the tenets of shared decisionmaking, she also realizes that this same approach has not been effective in other schools.

1. What steps can the principal take to bring school-based management to her school?

Annotated Bibliography

Argyris, C. (1957). *Integrating the individual and the organization*. New York: John Wiley & Sons.

Argyris contends that people are one of the many sources of energy in an organization. The energy of people increases with psychological success and decreases with its failure. Since the nature of organizations tends to require individuals to experience dependence and submissiveness, individuals are less likely to perform to their full potential. The integration of individual needs and organizational goals can help productivity.

Davis, K. (1977). *Human behavior at work* (5th ed.). New York: McGraw-Hill.

This is an excellent work that describes how people may be motivated to work together in harmony. The book's focus is on human needs and human motivation, leadership roles, worker environments, informal organizations, and communication networks in organizations.

Halloran, J. (1978). *Applied human relations: An organizational approach*. Englewood Cliffs, NJ: Prentice-Hall.

This book explores some of the human aspects of human relations as seen in action in organizations. Traditional theories and current reactions are blended into various categories for discussion. The traditional avenues of motivation and morale are investigated to see how they affect workers, as well as the more recent topics of employment, discrimination, creativity, and intercultural relations.

Kossen, S. (1987). *The human side of organizations* (4th ed.). New York: Harper and Row.

A comprehensive discussion of human factors in organizations: how to develop an improved understanding of people; how organizational leaders maintain and improve organizational climate; how to deal with forces that constrict leadership activities today and for the future; and challenges facing individuals in organizations. This text includes a variety of up-to-date and practical materials.

Maslow, A. (1954). *Motivation and personality*. New York: Harper & Brothers.

Maslow's seminal work on the theory of motivation. This book illuminates the hierarchy of needs and how these needs affect human behavior. The concept of need hierarchy underlies much of motivational study. It also launches the humanistic approach to the study of management in terms of providing opportunities for self-actualization within the workplace.

Mayo, E. (1933). *The human problems of an industrial organization*. New York: Macmillan.

This book reports the development and conclusions of the Hawthorne experiment. Initially, the experiment suggests that worker productivity is affected by management attention rather than by the worker's physical environment. Covering interviews over a five-year period, the experiment concludes that individual motivation is primarily determined by human factors.

Reitz, H. J. (1987). *Behavior in organizations* (3rd ed.). Homewood, IL: Irwin.

This book describes and explains human behavior in organizational settings. It relates what managers do and why understanding human behavior is vital. This section is followed by a discussion of three motivational models that explore the major determinants of behavior. A range of individual, group, and social behavior characteristics in organizations is also discussed.

References

Aldag, R. J., Barr, S. H., & Brief, A. P. (1981). Measurement of perceived task characteristics. *Psychological Bulletin, 90,* 415–431.

Aldag, R. J., & Brief, A. P. (1979). *Task design and employee motivation*. Glenview IL: Scott, Foresman.

Alderfer, C. P. (1969). An empirical test of a new theory of needs. *Organizational Behavior and Human Performance, 4,* 143–175.

Alderfer, C. (1972). *Existence, relatedness, and growth: Human needs in organizational settings*. New York: Free Press.

Ardrey, R. (1966). *The territorial imperative*. New York: Atheneum.

Argyris, C. (1957). *Personality and organization*. New York: Harper and Row.

Argyris, C. (1964). *Integrating the individual and the organization*. New York: John Wiley & Sons.

Argyris, C. (1985). *Action science*. San Francisco: Jossey-Bass.

Atkinson, J. W. (1964). *An introduction to motivation*. Princeton, NJ: Van Nostrand.

Bales, R. F. (1950). *Interaction-process analysis: A method for the study of small groups*. Reading, MA: Addison-Wesley.

Bales, R. F. (1953). The equilibrium problem in school groups. In T. Parsons, R. F. Bales, & E. A. Shils (Eds.), *Working papers in the theory of action*. Glencoe, IL: Free Press.

Bandura, A. (1968). A social learning of interpretation of psychological dysfunctions. In P. London & D. Rosenhan (Eds.), *Foundations of abnormal psychology* (pp. 293–344). New York: Holt, Rinehart & Winston.

Bandura, A. (1969). *Principles of behavior modification*. New York: Holt, Rinehart & Winston.

Bandura, A. (1976). Social learning theory. In J. T. Spence, R. C. Carson, & J. W. Thibait (Eds.), *Behavioral approaches to therapy* (pp. 1–46). Morristown, NJ: General Learning.

Bandura, A. (1977). *Social learning theory*. Englewood Cliffs, NJ: Prentice-Hall.

Bandura, A., & Walters, R. H. (1963). *Social learning and personality development*. New York: Holt, Rinehart & Winston.

Barnard, C. I. (1938). *The functions of the executive*. Cambridge, MA: Harvard University Press.

Bass, B. M. (1985). *Leadership and performance beyond expectation*. New York: Free Press.

Bass, B. M. (1981). *Stogdill's handbook of leadership: A survey of theory and research: Revised and expanded edition*. New York: Free Press.

Benge, E., & Hickley, J. (1984). *Morale and motivation: How to measure morale and increase productivity*. New York: Franklin Watts.

Bennis, W. G., & Nanus, B. (1985). *Leaders: The strategies for taking charge*. New York: Harper and Row.

Bensimon, E. M., Neumann, A., & Birnbaum, R. (1989). *Making sense of administrative leadership: The 'L' word in higher education*. Washington, DC: The George Washington University School of Education and Human Development.

Berlew, D. E., & Hall, D. T. (1966, September). The socialization of managers: Effects of expectations on performance. *Administrative Science Quarterly, 11*(11), 207–223.

Berney, M. F., & Ayers, J. B. (1990). *Evaluating preparation programs for school leaders and teachers in specialty areas*. Boston: Kluwer Academic.

Blake, R. R., & Mouton, J. S. (1964). *The managerial grid*. Houston, TX: Gulf.

Bolman, L. G., & Deal, T. E. (1991). *Reframing organizations: Artistry and choice in management*. San Francisco: Jossey-Bass.

Brophy, J. E. (1985). Teacher-student interaction. In J. B. Dusek, V. C. Hall, & W. J. Meyer (Eds.), *Teacher expectancies* (pp. 303–328). Hillsdale, NJ: Lawrence Erlbaum.

Burns, J. M. (1978). *Leadership*. New York: Harper and Row.

Campbell, J. D., & Pritchard, R. D. (1983). Motivation theory in industrial and organizational psychology. In M. D. Dunnette (Ed.), *Handbook of industrial and organizational psychology* (pp. 63–130). New York: John Wiley & Sons.

Campbell, R. F., Fleming, T., Newell, L. J., & Bennion, J. W. (1987). *A history of thought and practice in educational administration*. New York: Teachers College Publication, Columbia University.

Champagne, P. J., & McAfee, R. B. (1989). *Motivating strategies for performance and productivity: A guide to human resources development*. New York: Quorum Books.

Coulmad, F. (Ed.). (1992). *Attitudes and accommodation in multilingual societies*. New York: Mouton de Gruyter.

Dachler, H. P., & Mobley, W. (1973). Construct validation of an instrumentality-expectancy-task-goal model of work motivation: Some theoretical boundary conditions. *Journal of Applied Psychology, 58,* 397–418.

Davis, K. (1967). *Human relations at work* (3rd ed.). New York: McGraw-Hill.

Davis, K. D. (1977). *Human behavior at work: Organizational behavior,* (5th ed.). New York: McGraw-Hill.

Deal, T. E. (1992). *Leadership in a world of change*. In S. D. Thomson (Ed.), *School leadership: A blueprint for change,* (pp. 1–7). Newbury Park, CA: Corwin.

Dennison, H. (1931). *Organizational engineering*. New York: Macmillan.

Dewey, J. (1946). *Problems of men*. New York: Philosophical Library.

Dewey, J. (1966). *Democracy and education*. New York: Macmillan.

Duchon, D., Green, S. G., & Taber, T. D. (1986). Vertical dyad linkage: A longitudinal assessment of antecedents and gender label. *Journal of Personality and Social Psychology, 46,* 991–1004.

Duignan, D. A., & Macpherson, R. J. S. (1992). *Educative leadership: A practical theory for new administrators and managers*. Washington, DC: Falmer.

Eden, D. (1990a). Pygmalion without interpersonal contrast effect: Whole groups gain from raining manager expectations. *Journal of Applied Psychology, 75,* 394–398.

Eden, D. (1990b). *Pygmalion in management: Production as a self-fulfilling prophecy*. Lexington, MA: Lexington Books.

Edmonds, R. (1979). Effective schools for the urban poor. *Educational Leadership, 37,* 15–24.

Etzioni, A. (1961). *The moral dimension: Toward a new economics*. New York: Free Press.

Etzioni, A. (1988). *A comparative analysis of complex organizations*. New York: Free Press.

Feldman, J. M., Reitz, H. J., & Hiterman, R. J. (1976). Alternatives to optimization in expectancy theory. *Journal of Applied Psychology, 61,* 712–720.

Fiedler, F. E. (1967). *A theory of leadership effectiveness.* New York: McGraw-Hill.

Flanders, J. P. (1968). A review of research on imitative behavior. *Psychological Bulletin, 69,* 316–337.

Follett, M. P. (1930). *Creative experience.* London: Longman's, Green and Company.

Frankel, L. K., & Fleisher, A. (1920). *The human factor in industry.* New York: Macmillan.

Gantt, H. L. (1916). *Industrial leadership.* New Haven, CT: Yale University Press.

Getzels, J. W. (1977). Educational administration twenty years later, 1954–1974. In L. L. Cunningham, W. G. Weck, & R. O. Nystrand (Eds.), *Educational administration: The developing decades.* Berkeley, CA: McCutchan.

Greenberg, P. D., & Glaser, E. M. (1983). Viewpoints of labor leaders regarding quality of worklife improvement programs. In R. M. Steers & L. W. Porter (Eds.), *Motivation and work behavior* (3rd ed.) (pp. 547–561). New York: McGraw-Hill.

Greenfield, W. (1987). *Instructional leadership: Concepts, issues, and controversies.* Newton, MA: Allyn and Bacon.

Griffin, R. W. (1982). *Task design: An integrative approach.* Glenview, IL: Scott, Foresman & Company.

Griffiths, D. E. (1956). *Human relations in school administration.* Sixty-Third Yearbook of the National Society for the Study of Education, Part II, Chicago: University of Chicago Press.

Griffiths, D. E., Stout, R. T., & Forsyth, P. B. (Eds.). (1988). *Leaders for America's schools: The report and papers of the National Commission on Excellence in Educational Administration.* Berkeley, CA: McCutchan.

Guthrie, J. W., & Reed, R. J. (1991). *Educational administration and policy: Effective leadership for American education* (2nd ed.). Boston: Allyn and Bacon.

Hackman, J. R. (1983). Work design. In R. M. Steers & L. W. Porter (Eds.), *Motivation and work behavior* (3rd ed.) (pp. 490–516). New York: McGraw-Hill.

Hackman, J. R., & Oldham, G. R. (1980). *Work redesign.* Reading, MA: Addison-Wesley.

Hall, J. (1980). The managerial lens: What you see is what you get! In J. A. Shtogren (Ed.), *Models for management: The structure of competence* (pp. 4–10). The Woodlands, TX: Teleometrics International.

Halloran, J. (1978). *Applied human relations: An organizational approach.* Englewood Cliffs, NJ: Prentice-Hall.

Halpin, A. W., & Croft, D. B. (1962). *The organizational climate of schools.* Chicago: The University of Chicago, Midwest Administration Center.

Hammond, K. R. (1966). *The psychology of Egon Brunswick.* New York: Holt, Rinehart & Winston.

Hamner, W. C., & Hamner, E. P. (1976). Behavior modification on the bottom line. *Organizational Dynamics, 4*(4), 3–21.

Hellriegel, D., & Slocum, J. W., Jr. (1976). *Organizational behavior: Contingency views.* St. Paul: West.

Herzberg, F. (1966). *Working and the nature of man.* New York: Cro-Well.

Herzberg, F. (1968). One more time: How do you motivate employees? *Harvard Business Review, 46,* 56–57.

Herzberg, F. (1981). Motivating people. In P. Mali (Ed.), *Management handbook.* New York: John Wiley and Sons.

Herzberg, F., Mausner, B., & Snyderman, B. B. (1959). *The motivation to work.* New York: John Wiley and Sons.

Hill, H. (1947). Personal problems in American education. In *American Association of School Administrators official report,* 1946. Washington, DC: National Education Association.

House, R. J., & Mitchell, T. R. (1974). Path-goal theory of leadership. *Journal of Contemporary Business, 3,* 81–98.

Kanfer, F. H., & Karoly, P. (1974). Self-control: A behavioristic excursion into the lion's den. In M. J. Mahoney & C. E. Thoresa (Eds.), *Self-control: Power to the person* (pp. 200–217). Monterey, CA: Brooks/Cole.

Katz, R. (1980). Time and work: Toward a integrative perspective. In B. M. Staw & L. L. Cummings (Eds.), *Research in organizational behavior* (Vol. 2). Greenwich, CT: JAI.

Knezevich, S. (1984). *Administration of public education: A sourcebook for the leadership and management of educational institutions*. New York: Harper and Row.

Komaki, J. I. (1986). Toward effective supervision. *Journal of Applied Psychology, 71*, 270–279.

Kossen, S. (1987). *The human side of organization* (4th ed.). New York: Harper and Row.

Kouzes, J. M., & Posner, B. Z. (1987). *The leadership challenge: How to get extraordinary things done in organizations*. San Francisco: Jossey-Bass.

Lawler, E. E. III (1992). *Ultimate advantage: Creating the high involvement organization*. San Francisco: Jossey-Bass.

Lewin, K. (1938). The conceptual representation and the measurement of psychological forces. *Contributions to psychological theory* (Volume 1, No. 4). Durham, NC: Duke University Press.

Likert, R. (1961). *New patterns of management*. New York: McGraw-Hill.

Likert, R. (1967). *The human organization*. New York: McGraw-Hill.

Link, A. S., & Catton, W. B. (1967). *American epoch: A history of the United States since the 1890s*. New York: Alfred A. Knopf.

Little, J. W. (1981). *School success and staff development in desegregation schools*. Boulder, CO: Center for Action Research.

Luthans, F., & Otteman, R. (1977). Motivation vs. learning approaches to organizational behavior. In F. Luthans (Ed.), *Contemporary readings in organizational behavior* (2nd ed.). New York: McGraw-Hill.

Mahoney, M. J. (1974). *Cognition and behavior modification*. Cambridge, MA: Ballinger.

Mangieri, J. N. (1985). *Excellence in education*. Fort Worth, TX: Texas Christian University.

Maslow, A. H. (1954). *Motivation and personality*. New York: Harper and Row.

Maslow, A. H. (1962). *Toward a psychology of being*. New York: Van Nostrand.

Maxcy, S. J. (1991). *Educational leadership: A critical pragmatic perspective*. New York: Bregin & Garvey.

Mayo, E. (1933). *The human problems of an industrial civilization*. Cambridge, MA: Harvard University Press.

McClelland, C. D. (1955). *Power: The inner experience*. New York: Irvington.

McClelland, D. C. (1961). *The achieving society*. Princeton, NJ: Van Nostrand.

McClelland, D. C. (1975). *Power: The inner experience*. New York: Irvington.

McClelland, D. C. (1976). Power is the great motivation. *Harvard Business Review, 54*(2), 100–110.

McClelland, D. C. (1987). Characteristics of successful entrepreneurs. *Journal of Creative Behavior, 3*, 219–233.

McClelland, D. C., Atkinson, J. W., Clark, R. A., & Lowell, E. L. (1953). *The achievement motivation*. New York: Appleton-Century-Crofts.

McGregor, D. (1960). *The human side of enterprise*. New York: McGraw-Hill.

Merton, R. K. (1948). *The self-fulfilling prophecy*. Antioch Review, 8, 193–210.

Miles, R. E. (1975). *Theories of management*. New York: McGraw-Hill.

Mischell, W. (1973). Toward a cognitive reconceptualization of personality. *Psychological Review, 80*, 284–302.

Mitchell, V. F., & Moudgill, P. (1976). Measurement of Maslow's need hierarchy. *Organizational Behavior and Human Performance, 16*, 334–349.

Moehlman, A. B. (1940). *School administration*. Boston: Houghton Mifflin.

Moreno, J. L. (1947). Contributions of sociometry to research methodology in sociology. *American Sociological Review, 12*, 287–292.

Murray, H. A. (1938). *Exploration in personality*. New York: Oxford University Press.

New York State Education Department. (1991, March). *A new compact for learning: Improving public elementary, middle, and secondary education results in the 1990s*. Albany, NY: State University of New York.

O'Toole, J. (1981). *Making America work*. New York: Continuum.

Ouchi, W. G. (1981). *Theory Z: How American business can meet the Japanese challenge*. Reading, MA: Addison-Wesley.

Owens, R. G. (1987). *Organizational behavior in education* (3rd ed.). Englewood Cliffs, NJ: Prentice-Hall.

Pinder, C. C. (1984). *Work motivation: Theory, issues, and applications*. Glenview, IL: Scott, Foresman & Company.

Plous, F. K. (1987, March). Redesigning work. *Personnel Administrator, 99*.

Porter, L. W. (1961). A study of perceived need satisfaction in bottom and middle-management jobs. *Journal of Applied Psychology, 45,* 1–10.

Porter, L. W., & Lawler, E. E. (1968). *Managerial attitudes and performance*. Homewood, IL: Richard D. Irwin.

Reavis, C. A., & Griffith, H. (1992). *Restructuring schools: Theory and practice*. Lancaster, PA: Technomic.

Reitz, H. J. (1987). *Behavior in organizations* (3rd ed.). Homewood, IL: Richard D. Irwin.

Roethlisberger, F. J., & Dickson, W. J. (1939). *Management and the worker*. Cambridge, MA: Harvard University Press.

Rosenthal, R. (1974). *On the social psychology of the self-fulfilling prophecy*. New York: MSS Modular.

Rosenthal, R. (1981). Pavlov's mice, Pfungst's horse, and Pygmalion's PONS: Some models for the study of interpersonal expectancy effects. In T. A. Sebok & R. Rosenthal (Eds.), *The clever Hans phenomenon*. Annals of the New York Academy of Science, No. 364.

Rosenthal, R., & Jacobson, L. (1968). *Pygmalion in the classroom*. New York: Holt, Rinehart & Winston.

Rosner, M. (1990). *The second generation: Continuity and change in the kibbutz*. New York: Greenwood Press.

Ruben, B. D. (1988). *Communication and human behavior* (2nd ed.). New York: Macmillan.

Saltonstall, R. (1959). *Human relations in administration: Text and cases*. New York: McGraw-Hill.

Sanford, A. C. (1977). *Human relations: The theory and practice of organizational behavior* (2nd ed.). New York: Macmillan.

Savage, P. M. (1967). *A study of teacher satisfaction and attitudes: Causes and effects*. Unpublished doctoral dissertation, Auburn University.

Scandura, T. A., Graen, G. B., & Novak, M. A. (1986). When managers decide not to decide autocratically: An investigation of leader-member exchange and decision influence. *Journal of Applied Psychology, 71,* 579–584.

Schlechty, P. C. (1990). *Schools for the twenty-first century: Leadership imperatives for educational reform*. San Francisco: Jossey-Bass.

Schmidt, G. L. (1976). Job satisfaction and secondary school administrators. *Educational Administration Quarterly, 12,* 81.

Scott, W. G. (1962). *Human relations in management: A behavioral approach*. Englewood Cliffs, NJ: Prentice-Hall.

Scott, W. R. (1981). *Organizations: Rational, natural and open systems*. Englewood Cliffs, N. J.: Prentice-Hall.

Senge, P. (1991). *The fifth discipline: The art and practice of the learning organization*. New York: Doubleday.

Sergiovanni, T. J. (1984). Leadership and excellence in schooling. *Educational leadership, 41*(5), 4–13.

Sergiovanni, T. J. (1991). *The principalship: A reflective practice* (2nd ed.). Boston: Allyn and Bacon.

Sergiovanni, T. J. (1992). *Moral leadership: Getting to the heart of school improvement*. San Francisco: Jossey-Bass.

Sergiovanni, T. J., & Carver, F. D. (1973). *The new school executives: A theory of administration*. New York: Dodd, Mead & Company.

Sergiovanni, T. J., & Moore, J. H. (1989). *Schooling for tomorrow: Directing reforms to issues that count*. Boston: Allyn and Bacon.

Shamir, B. (1990). Calculations, values, and identities: The sources of collectivistic work motivation. *Human Relations, 43,* 313–332.

Silverman, D. (1971). *The theory of organizations: A sociological framework*. New York: Basic Books.

Silverman, D. (1989). The people of organizations. In D. Pugh & D. Hickson (Eds.), *Writers on organizations* (4th ed.) (p. 218). Newbury Park: Sage.

Skinner, B. F. (1953). *Science and human behavior*. New York: Macmillan.

Skinner, B. F. (1971). *Beyond freedom and dignity*. New York: Knopf.

Skinner, B. F. (1974). *About behaviorism*. New York: Knopf.

Staats, A. W. (1975). *Social behaviorism*. Homewood, IL: Dorey.

Steers, R. M., & Spencer, D. G. (1977). The role of achievement motivation in job design. *Journal of Applied Psychology, 4,* 472–479.

Stevenson, H. W., & Steigler, J. W. (1992). *The learning job.* New York: Summit Books.

Tannebaum, R., & Schmidt, W. H. (1958). How to choose a leadership pattern. *Harvard Business Review, 36,* 95–101.

Taylor, F. W. (1911). *The principles of scientific management.* New York: Harper & Brothers.

Tolman, E. C. (1932). *Purposive behavior in animals and men.* New York: Century.

Tosi, H. L., & Hamner, W. C. (1974). *Organizational behavior: A contingency approach.* Chicago: St. Clair.

Tyler, R. T. (1941). Educational adjustments necessitated by changing ideological concepts. In W. C. Reavis (Ed.), *Administrative adjustments required by socio-economic change: Proceedings of the tenth annual conference of administrative officers of public and private schools.* Chicago: University of Chicago Press.

Ure, A. (1835). *The philosophy of manufacturers.* London: Charles Knight.

Vroom, V. H. (1964). *Work and motivation.* New York: John Wiley & Sons.

Wallace, R. C., Jr. (1992). Leadership in school. In S. D. Thomson (Ed.), *School leadership: A blueprint for change* (pp. 8–9). Newbury Park, CA: Corwin.

Walton, R. E. (1975). Criteria for quality of working life. In L. E. Davis & A. B. Cherns (Eds.), *The quality of working life* (Vol. 1). New York: Free.

Watson, J. B. (1930). *Behaviorism.* Chicago: University of Chicago Press.

Wickstrom, R. A. (1971). *An investigation into job satisfaction among teachers.* Unpublished doctoral dissertation, University of Oregon.

Wildstrom, S. H. (1986, January 27). Affirmative action: A deal to patch up the Brock-Meese feud. *Business Week,* 51.

Wolman, B. (1956). Leadership and group dynamics. *Journal of Social Psychology, 43,* 11–25.

Yauch, W. (1949). *Improving human relations in school administration.* New York: Harper & Bros.

Chapter 10
Educational Environments

Education takes place not only within the social confines of the school, but also within the broader social and cultural contexts of the community it serves. In designing effective school environments, practices, and procedures, there must be an awareness of the impact on children of institutions beyond the control of the school. These include families, friends and peers, popular culture, social institutions of the community, other agencies of education, and general economic conditions.

School administration is a complex and pervasive human process in which the executive looks outward toward the community at large and inward toward the district and school. The essential administrative dilemma is that, on the one hand, the administrator must reconcile the nomothetic and ideographic conflicts within the organization (i.e., organizational values vs. personal values as discussed in Chapter 4), and, on the other hand, all school activity must be reconciled with the constraining, competing, and conflicting pressures of its environment (Hodgkinson, 1983).

Bennis (1984) pointed out that all organizations are surrounded by an increasingly active, incessant environment, one that is becoming more and more influential. Those responsible for governing enterprises will be spending more and more of their time managing external relations. Internally, administrators need to create appropriate social environments that can tap and harness the energies and abilities necessary to bring about desired results. School administrators are no exception.

From a systems perspective, the child/learner is a complex system of energy, human talent, potential, values, motivations and experience and the focus of schooling activities. The classroom is a system, surrounding the child for approximately six hours a day, intended to have an impact on the child that will produce desired learning results. The classroom is surrounded by the school, intended to be supportive of classroom activities, but not always successful in that regard. In total, school takes up only about 13 percent of the waking hours of a person's first 18 years of life (Walberg, 1984).

The rest of the time, the child is exposed to the very strong influences of his or her family and community which are related to the child's response to school stimuli. In this chapter, we will briefly examine the potential impact of each of these environments on children's ability to learn and upon those working within the school.

The Family

Research in the United States on the impact of a family's socioeconomic status on the achievement of its children has been clouded by the issue of racial and ethnic group membership. Despite the minority focus, low socioeconomic status has emerged as the dominating detracting factor from achievement with little, if any, effect being explained independently by minority group membership. This is not to deny that racial minority children experience discriminatory situations that have an additional negative impact on the development of self-concept and realistic aspirations and expectations. Some social scientists refer to the treatment of minorities in the United States as functioning more like a caste system than socioeconomic differentiation (Brown, 1990). As such, minorities quickly learn their caste-like status and adopt social habits in order to survive socially and psychologically in schools and elsewhere (Allport, 1958; Ogbu, 1978; Myrdal, 1962; Shade & Edwards, 1987).

Socioeconomic status is only a proxy for *interactions* within a family that *tend* to be related to socioeconomic status. Home environment predicts academic learning twice as well as socioeconomic status of families (Walberg, 1984), but it is much more difficult to measure for research purposes. The "curriculum of the home" includes informed parent/child conversations about everyday events, encouragement and discussion of leisure reading, monitoring and joint analysis

of television viewing, expressions of affection and interest in children's academic and personal growth, deferred gratification to accomplish long-range goals, time management, and discipline/reward patterns. In reality, the home environment varies markedly among families with similar financial backgrounds and many children from families of low socioeconomic status do succeed in school when the home environment is supportive (Clark, 1983; Datcher-Loury, 1989; Lee, 1984; Prom-Jackson et al., 1987; Scott-Jones, 1987; Taylor & Dorsey-Gaines, 1988). In a recent study of high achieving African-American children from low-income, single-parent families, Mark (1993) found that the parents who nurtured these children had high expectations for their children and good communication with them, high regard for reading, monitored television programs watched by the children, maintained structured households, and established a system of rewards and punishments for the children. The parents were fully aware of their precarious position in society, but possessed a sense of conviction in their own abilities and a determination to have their children mature into high achieving adults.

The W. T. Grant Foundation (1988) study of the *Forgotten Half* (those high school graduates not going on for further education) found that young people want and need adult support. According to their findings, teenagers constantly point to their parents as the most influential adults in their lives. A full 70 percent of high school seniors share their parent's views of what they should do with their lives; and the activity that young people most enjoy sharing with their parents is "just talking." Yet typical American adolescents spend only about five minutes per day alone with their fathers and 40 minutes alone with their mothers.

There are other environmental factors that have a direct relationship upon a child's potential success in school. For example, nearly half of all infants are born with one or more factors that potentially mark them for school failure later on (National Education Goals Panel, 1993). These include late or no prenatal care, a mother who smoked or drank alcohol during pregnancy, and low maternal weight gain. Nearly 37 percent of all two-year-olds have not been fully immunized for childhood diseases and only half of all preschoolers are read to daily by their parents. Further, each year more than one million children experience the divorce of their parents; and 60 percent of today's five-year-olds will live in a single-parent family before they reach the age of 18. Children from single-parent families are less likely to be high achievers; they are consistently more likely to be late to school, truant, and subject to disciplinary action; and they are more than twice as likely to drop out of school (Eitzen, 1992).

Even some privileged families can provide only uneven support for their children's school experiences. Real or perceived economic pressures force most parents to work long hours or at more than one job simply to keep the family's finances on track. Over 50 percent of mothers with children under the age of six work outside the home, and about 70 percent of mothers with children between the ages of six and 17 do so. As a result, more and more children are being raised in families in which the parents have less and less time for them. This also means that more and more school-age children are spending increasing amounts of time without adult supervision (latchkey children), and more and more preschoolers are being cared for by adults who are not their parents.

Large correlational and status studies are useful in pointing out the overall impact of socioeconomic status on pupil achievement, but they do little to advance our understanding of how the effect is transmitted or what educators can do to intervene. In this latter respect, the work of Basil Bernstein (1971) in England is particularly instructive. He attributed much of the disability of lower socioeconomic children to differences in language usage between lower- and middle-class people. Noting that the general problems involved in teaching children from lower classes are not necessarily derived from lack of innate capacity to learn, as indicated by intelligence tests, he suggested that the cause is the environment in which they grow up.

Bernstein labelled the communication code typically used by the lower class *restricted.* In the United States, it has been widely recognized that many lower-class African-Americans typically use a different communication code (sometimes referred to as "Black English" or "Ebonics" (Williams, 1975)) from the middle class white majority, but the similarities among this code and communication codes of other lower-class people are not generally recognized. An exception is Foster (1974, p. 118), who noted similarities in patterns of speech between Black English and immigrant groups, although the specific expressions and accents used may vary even from neighborhood to neighborhood within a city, and among cities and regions. Bernstein (1971, p. 143) suggested that "it is reasonable to argue that the genes of social class may be carried less through a genetic code but far more through a communication code that social class itself promotes."

The middle class also uses a restricted code in its more intimate relationships, but because of the breadth of contact and activities typical of the middle class, it has also developed an "elaborated" code that does not rely upon "non-verbal, closely shared, identifications" to serve as a backcloth for understanding (Bernstein, 1961). The elaborated code emphasizes the individual, the abstract, elaboration of process, exploration of motives and intentions, and personalized forms of social control. It is the language of instruction in the school.

Because the language code that typifies the schools is different from the code familiar to lower-class children, the lower-class child is at a severe disadvantage to benefit from school experiences. In commenting on Bernstein's findings, Deutsch (1965) noted that the resulting breakdown in communication between the school and the student is probably a major factor in explaining the generally poor performance of lower socioeconomic youth in school and their high drop-out rate for the student is no longer in communication with anything that is meaningful to him in the school.

Heath and McLaughlin (1987) have commented on this phenomenon more recently. They pointed out that children who come from families that are strongly oriented toward schooling learn numerous ways to use language in a variety of settings (e.g., dinner conversations, school, ballet classes, tennis and piano lessons, summer camp).

> *They [the children] have extensive experience in learning by listening to others tell how to do something, they themselves know how to talk about what they are doing as they do it, and they know how to lay out plans for the future in verbal form. On command, they know how to display in oral or written formats the bits and pieces of knowledge that the school assumes represent academic achievement. (p. 578; also see Heath, 1983)*

Children who come from families where the traditional orientation to learning has been through observing and assuming apprenticeship roles beside knowledgeable elders rather than through verbal communication come to school largely untutored in displaying knowledge in verbal form. Heath and McLaughlin have also observed that non–English–speaking parents, even with strong orientations to schooling, often stop speaking the mother tongue to their children in an effort to speed up the acquisition of English by their children. As a result, such children are denied exposure to sophisticated adult language models and to the wisdom and authority of their parents.

In an international review of research on social background and education, Husen (1972) stressed the importance of an action-rich environment in the classroom to assist in developing an elaborated code of language usage among those children who come to school without such a code. "The verbalistic feature of the school means a handicap for pupils from homes where the code of communication is 'restricted' rather than 'elaborated.' The more a verbally mediated docility is required, the greater the handicap" (p. 163).

Conversely, the more "action-rich" a school is, the greater its chances of bringing its linguistically impoverished pupils into the "mainstream." A three-way learning process must be established in the classroom among the pupil, the teacher, and the pupil's peers. The peer group should be as carefully structured as the instructional processes used by the teacher (Swanson, 1979); children skilled in using an elaborated code (normally middle class) need to be well represented. The mixing of children alone will not ensure that those not skilled in elaborated codes of communication will acquire such skills; mixing only supports deliberate instructional strategies of the teacher. Without appropriate leadership by the teacher, social class cohesion—and tension among classes—can easily develop within the classroom, reinforcing the pressures of class stratification in the larger society. To preclude this possibility, there needs to be a warm, open, accepting social climate in each classroom and throughout the school. Further, school officials must understand the codes of communication used by the children and deliberately help to develop communication skills using an elaborated code.

Studies of the relationships between home and school show that it is important for parents and educators to work together to develop high-achieving children (Bradley et al., 1987; Comer, 1980; Durkin, 1984; Reynolds, 1991; Walberg, 1984). Walberg endorsed the concept of home/school partnerships designed to improve the learning environment of the home in support of the efforts of the school. Programs that target parent/teacher cooperation and focus on specific achievement goals show the greatest learning effects. The principal plays a key role in establishing and maintaining such relationships.

Heath and McLaughlin (1987) admonished that responses to the generally low achievement of children coming from low socioeconomic families can be crafted only if we focus on the total functional requirements of a healthy, curious, productive, and motivated child. This compels us to view the child as an actor in a large social system and to identify the primary networks that make up a child's environment. They suggest that this moves the school from the role of "deliverer" of educational services to the role of "broker" of the multiple services that are available in support of the family and the child.

School

In this section, we look at four aspects of the school environment: school culture, peer groups, physical environment, and instructional technology.

CULTURE[1]

School culture is the physiological and psychological environment within which students, teachers, administrators, and support personnel work and live while school is in session. It is expressed through language, rituals, ceremonies, imagery, and symbols, all of which can serve to reinforce and maintain each other (Beare et al., 1989). School culture

is the pattern of beliefs and expectations of the members of the school community that shapes their predominant attitudes and behaviors. School culture affects everyone's ability to function cooperatively and productively. Differences in student achievement and behavior across schools have been shown to be a function of school culture (Rutter et al., 1979).

All schools have a "culture"; in some instances it is supportive of the societal intent for schooling and in some instances it is antithetical. As a group, suburban schools seem to have relatively few problems with respect to academic achievement, discipline, and teacher quality when compared with their urban and rural counterparts; thus, the spotlight of educational reform has focused most sharply on urban and rural schools as the weak links in the United States' educational system. Yet, even in suburban schools, the "unspecial" child may be neglected (Powell, Farrar, & Cohen, 1985).

Urban schools, in particular, are characterized as having unwholesome cultures. Many lack purpose and often have an unappealing physical appearance. They are characterized by a lack of coherent instructional programs and regular routines (Carnegie Foundation, 1988; Corcoran et al., 1988). Cusick (1983) among others has argued that the high level of ethnic diversity in the student populations of these typical urban schools works against the establishment of consensus on norms and standards within the school, contributing to their characteristic nondiscipline. Attitudes and comments by teachers who do not believe that inner-city children can learn cause discomfort, fear, and confusion among their students. All of these conditions combine to inspire little sense of community within schools (Lomotey & Swanson, 1989).

Addressing the issue of the unwholesome culture of many urban schools, the Carnegie Foundation (1988) observed:

---

[1] The discussion of organizational culture in Chapter 7 should be consulted to supplement that which is presented here.

Overcoming anonymity—creating a setting in which every student is known personally by an adult—is one of the most compelling obligations urban schools confront. Young people who have few constructive relationships with adults need a sense of belonging. They need positive encounters with older people who serve as mentors and role models for both educational and social growth. Building community must be a top priority if students in urban schools are to academically and socially succeed. (p. 24)

In those urban schools that have been found to be effective in boosting academic achievement, there is order and discipline, a positive physical appearance, a coherent structure to the instructional program, and preplanned routines (Venezsky & Winfield, 1980; Weber, 1971). Coherence is marked by agreement between school goals, classroom instruction, and test content, and principals and teachers consult regularly to discuss achievement. Instruction tends to be individualized (Jackson et al., 1983; Lomotey, 1989; Weber, 1971).

The culture of effective urban schools is characterized by a pervasive expectation of high academic achievement. Teachers are supportive and task-oriented, zeroing in on academic deficiencies of students. They set challenging, yet obtainable, goals and encourage all students to do their best. Student progress is carefully monitored through systematic evaluation (Brookover & Lezotte, 1979; Wellisch et al., 1978; Rist, 1970; Jackson et al., 1983).

Rural schools are generally characterized as having a strong sense of community within the school, as an extension of the family, and as an integral part of the larger community. These characteristics have been identified as overriding many of the admitted weaknesses of rural schools (Barker & Gump, 1964; Coleman, 1986; Newman, 1981). The fear of losing that sense of community and integration is largely responsible for rural opposition to schemes for school consolidation.

In suburban schools there is great emphasis placed on competitiveness to prepare students for survival in academic institutions and in the harsh economic climate. In rural areas, most organizations, not just schools, are small and tend to be quite personal; businesses are frequently family-owned. The warmth of these personal and familial relationships carries over into the schools where there is a climate of acceptance, cooperation, and mutual support (Skelly, 1988). Indeed, many of the innovations of the current educational reform movement have long been standard features of many rural schools, including individualized instruction, peer tutoring, cross-age grouping, school-based management, and community involvement (Barker, 1986).

Coleman (1986) hypothesized that "district ethos" of rural schools may account for the strong and unexpected negative relationship he found between student achievement and expenditure per pupil.

In particular, it [district ethos] seems capable of explaining the unexpectedly strong academic performance of small and rural districts, despite their traditional frugality with public funds. Secondly, it provides a useful linkage between classrooms, schools, and school districts, helping explain relationships known to exist between effective schools and central offices. (pp. 95–96)

Coleman and Hoffer (1987) used the term *social capital* to explain the higher levels of pupil achievement in Catholic schools compared with public schools. Social capital consists of the interrelationships between children and youth and the adults most proximate to them, first, and most prominently the family and second, a surrounding community of adults. Traditionally, the social capital of schools came from functional communities (serving residential, economic, commercial, cultural, and spiritual needs of its inhabitants) of which the schools were a part. Except for rural towns, villages, and small cities, schools are no longer related to functional communities, but, instead, to residential communities. The typical urban or suburban school does not provide for the intensive interaction with its surrounding community of adults as described for rural schools above.

In urban and suburban schools, there is little direct adult involvement with the formal educational process outside the professional and support staff of the school; thus, the school culture is dominated by student values and the gap in intergenerational values and understandings is exacerbated. According to Coleman and Hoffer (1987), a distinctive youth culture emerges. In rural areas, district employees are more likely to be supported in the education of the children entrusted to them by the families of the students and by the norms and sanctions growing out of the functional community. This external support (social capital) in Catholic schools is provided through the multigenerational religious community. Coleman and Hoffer suggest that in order to make social capital available to all schools (especially to urban and suburban schools) it will be necessary to abandon schools organized around residential areas and replace them with schools organized around value communities. To do this would require permitting parents freedom to choose the schools they want their children to attend regardless of school district boundaries.

While not using the term *social capital*, the W. T. Grant Commission (1988) identified the alienation between youth and adults as a major social problem and recommended social support structures that would provide young people with:

- more constructive contact with adults who can guide them into useful and satisfying paths;
- opportunities to participate in community activities that they and adults value, especially giving service to others;
- jobs (no matter how modest initially) that offer a path to accomplishment and to career opportunity;

- special help with particularly difficult problems, ranging from learning disabilities to substance addiction.

Powell, Farrar, and Cohen (1985) also recognized the poverty of the schools with respect to social capital (again, not using the term but implying the concept) and urged educating professionals to directly challenge the unwholesome aspects of the youth culture that has emerged. The accommodations of what they call "the shopping mall high school" serve many students poorly at the same time that they serve some students well. Especially disturbed over the passive and avoidance behavior of the middle- and lower-range of secondary school pupils, they charge that schools seem to welcome such behavior without guilt or embarrassment. They claim that most students who care about education can get it in most high schools; but most students are satisfied with exerting little effort and receiving a mediocre education. To correct this situation, they recommend that the school professionals aggressively follow a policy of purpose, push, and personalization. According to them, schools, and units within schools, should have a clear and unmistakable purpose of teaching students to develop their intellectual capacities to the fullest, i.e., high schools should push all students to hold high expectations. Finally, schools should replace anonymous individualization with personal attention. All students should be known by at least a few teachers, both as complex and distinctive people and learners.

PEER GROUPS

The concept of social capital also becomes manifest in schools through peer groups (Coleman & Hoffer, 1987). The norms and sanctions generated by fellow-students (i.e., youth culture) have a strong impact on how students respond to the instructional opportunities offered by a school; in designing those experiences, prevailing student attitudes need to be taken into account, especially at the secondary level.

A pupil's achievement is strongly related to the educational backgrounds and aspirations of the other pupils in the school; this is particularly true of "at-risk" children (Coleman, 1966; Mayeski & Beaton, 1975). Peer groups can provide incentives to high achievement or distractions and disincentives; they determine whether the associations and casual discussions outside the classroom support or undermine the educational mission of the school. Indeed, when parents and educators think of a "good" school, the criterion most frequently used is the nature of the student body, college bound and high achieving being the most preferred.

According to Coleman and Hoffer (1987), social capital varies among schools in two ways: in strength, and in content. With respect to strength in some schools nearly all of a student's social relationships beyond the family revolve around the community of youth in the school. With a high degree of closure, these social relations constitute extensive social capital for the formation of norms and sanctions that can positively shape behavior of students. In other schools, students develop most of their social relationships with others the same age outside the school in the neighborhood, in gangs, at work, or elsewhere. In these schools there is little social capital that school personnel can rely upon to support their educational mission.

> In the 1960s and 1970s, there was a general decline in the strength of the youth communities in schools, a decline manifested in the decreased interest in such school events as interscholastic sports, and an increase in the proportion of students holding part-time jobs and an increase in attention to phenomena that cut across schools, in particular popular music. The reduced focus of students on others within the school reduced the social capital in the youth community of the school, and thus reduced the potential of schools to change the students over this period. As a principal might put it, the principal "had less to work with." (Coleman & Hoffer, 1987, pp. 236–237)

With respect to the content of social capital in a school, the norms and sanctions of the peer group may reward athletic prowess, delinquent activities such as drug use and vandalism, social attractiveness, or academic achievement. The effect of the nature of peer values on achievement of educational goals is great when social capital is strong. If they support educational goals, then overall academic achievement is enhanced; but, if they demean academic achievement, the performance of all pupils is likely to be reduced below potential.

Coleman and Hoffer (1987) drew two implications for school personnel with respect to these possibilities: to develop a student body sufficiently integrated and cohesive that it constitutes social capital that can be a positive force in the lives of students and to direct that force toward educational objectives. The first goal can be best achieved through collective events in which the whole school is involved—events that compensate for the individualistic nature of the educational process. Interschool competitions are an effective way of doing this, usually taking the form of interscholastic sports. The school cohesion developed around athletics, however, needs to be deliberately and effectively broadened to include other educational objectives.

Pupil/teacher relationships can also be a powerful force in shaping peer values. As cited above, the W. T. Grant Foundation (1988) reported survey evidence that, despite popular belief to the contrary, young people want—and need—adult support. A nationwide study of outstanding middle schools reported that students who feel valued by teachers show respect for their schools (George & Oldaker, 1985). A study by Corcoran et al. (1988) found that many urban teachers want better relations with their students; but their efforts are hampered by disciplinary problems, large class size, lack of time for individual interaction, busing policies, and lack of student participation in extracurricular activities. Many of these inhibitors can be addressed through school policy and wise leadership.

FACILITIES

Ideally, the school plant is the spacial interpretation of the school curriculum (Earthman, 1992; Ortiz, 1994). The building should be designed to satisfy the pupils' instructional, physical and emotional needs. Physical needs are met by providing a safe structure, adequate sanitary facilities, a balanced visual environment, an appropriate thermal environment, a satisfactory acoustical environment, and sufficient space for work and play (Knezevich, 1984). Emotional and psychological needs are partially addressed through pleasant surroundings and an inspiring environment.

There isn't much research evidence linking the conditions and aesthetics of school facilities to student achievement, yet we all know that our moods and motivations are influenced by that which we see and feel. In Goodlad's (1984) massive study of "A Place Called School," he observed that only a few were architecturally pleasing—and then usually more in contrast to the ugliness of others than by virtue of their own merits. Describing schools as drab, dirty, and unadorned, he wondered about the impact on students who had to spend twelve consecutive years of their lives there. "Even the teachers sitting in their unattractive lounge appeared drab, as though chosen for their compatibility with the site" (p. 240). When he discovered a school in an aesthetic setting, Goodlad wondered if the handsome building and the terraced, landscaped, spacious grounds had any impact on those in attendance. He sensed that the students and educators were more spirited, but he worried that his own sense of pleasure might have distorted his perceptions. Regardless of the documented effect, Goodlad believes that schools provide unique opportunities to create pleasing places to live and work—for young and old alike, simultaneously sharing civic responsibility and developing aesthetic awareness.

Similarly, Cookson, Jr. and Persell (1985) tell of the positive impact on students created by the beautifully appointed and meticulously manicured school campuses of America's elite boarding schools. The aesthetics "speak to the soul of the child," addressing the student's importance and his or her specialness. According to Boyer (1989), the schools we build today reflect our priorities as a people. While schools in some communities speak to the importance that their citizens place upon education and those who attend them, others deliver a message of indifference. Should the benefits of aesthetically pleasing schools be reserved only for the children of the rich and the powerful?

The situation is especially critical in inner city areas (Kozol, 1991). There, facilities are characterized by shattered windows, leaky roofs, heating system failures, and corroded plumbing. While acknowledging that a good building does not necessarily make a good school, the Carnegie Foundation (1988) concluded that the widespread atmosphere of neglect in inner-city schools impairs the learning process. Crumbling, poorly maintained and uninviting inner-city schools distract teachers and students from the business of education. The need for healthful school surroundings is not just a physical need; it is absolutely and unequivocally an educational need as well (Piccigallo, 1989).

A study conducted by the Education Writers Association (Lewis, 1989) highlighted the severity of the current situation. It concluded that at least one-quarter of the nation's public school buildings are in poor physical condition and make shoddy places for learning. Only six percent of the nation's schools have been built since 1980. Over half were built during the 1950s and 1960s and many of those were erected quickly to accommodate the rapidly increasing population of "baby boomers." Cheap materials and fast construction techniques were used in many instances, reducing their reasonable life expectancy to only 30 years. According to the report, 43 percent of the nation's schools are obsolete; 42 percent have environmental hazards; 25 percent are overcrowded; and 13 percent are structurally unsound. It remains to be seen whether tomorrow's curricula can be accommodated within the confines of buildings built decades ago under different assumptions.

Aesthetics and safety are not the only considerations that affect the educational usefulness of school buildings. A major contributor to the obsolescence of schools is the rapid development in information and communication technologies. Kowalski (1989) points out that while the normal structural life span of a school building is 50 years, new computer generations are occurring about every five years. As a result, existing buildings must be renovated to accommodate these innovations and the new structures being built must be sufficiently flexible to adapt to a host of technological innovations that will become available over the next fifty years. Even more important, the whole organization of the school needs to be redesigned in such a fashion that emerging technologies can be integrated into the teaching/learning process.

TECHNOLOGY AND THE INDIVIDUALIZATION OF INSTRUCTION

Technology. Technology is the application of science to control the material environment for human benefit through the use of

tools and intellect. When used prudently, technologies allow society to produce more and better goods and services from a fixed amount of resources. Advances in technology have permitted mankind to live longer and more comfortably; but they have also led to undesirable results, including environmental exploitation, unemployment, and the capacity for total human annihilation.

Educational technology is the application of scientific knowledge, including learning theory, to the solution of problems in education. Education and technology interact in a cause and effect manner. Technological developments place continuing pressure on educators to keep curriculum and instructional methods up to date. At the same time, educational institutions are essential to the generation and assimilation of new technology. Changes in educational technologies strongly affect school culture and have important implications for the design of school facilities.

While society in general has tended toward enhanced technological sophistication and increased capital intensity, the education sector has retained a traditional, labor-intensive, craft-oriented technology. Vaizey et al. (1972, p. 228) referred to education as "the part of the economy where time has stood still." This "standing still" creates both sociological and economic problems. From an economic standpoint, labor-intensive education is unnecessarily expensive and it does not produce, in general, a work force with prerequisite attitudes and skills needed for the workplace. From a sociological standpoint, technologically unsophisticated schools are losing their credibility and thereby their effectiveness in teaching pupils because they are no longer congruent with the larger context of society. In other words, the prevailing technological environment of schools no longer reflects the prevailing technological environment of the larger society.

There is a tendency among educators to think of educational technology as being very expensive. But this is not necessarily the case. Even allowing for substantial increases in teacher salaries, Willett (1973) estimated the cost per pupil of an instructional system optimally integrating human and machine capabilities to be well below that of the existing system because:

- there would be fewer teachers, but with higher qualifications;
- technology would largely take over the information transfer function;
- extensive use would be made of relatively low cost paraprofessionals under the supervision of teachers;
- there would be extensive use of community resources.

Because the cost of instructional technology is even lower today relative to other costs, and the sophistication of the technology is much greater than when Willett made his analysis, it is likely that cost comparisons would be even more favorable.

The National Governors' Association's (1986) *1991 Report on Education: Time for Results* noted that " . . . despite extensive purchase and high expectations, most American schools have not become significantly more cost-effective or more efficient because of technology. The structure of most schools has not changed significantly because technology is available" (p. 123). A 1987 report by the National School Boards Association (Perelman, 1987) criticized the school reform movement because it failed to address the issue of increasing efficiency in education. This report anticipates an inevitable technological transformation of teaching and learning in the United States and elsewhere in the world.

Levin and Meister (1985) commented that educational technologies have been characterized by promise rather than realization of that promise. During this century, the educational potential of new inventions such as radio, motion pictures, television, video cassettes, compact disks, and computers, have been touted, only to be followed by disappointment as the invention remains ancillary to traditional instructional procedures. These authors diagnosed the generic failure of educational technologies as being due largely "to a misplaced obsession with the hardware and neglect of software, other resources, and instructional setting that are necessary to successful implementation" (p. 9). They point out that equipment purchase represents only about 10 percent of total costs of an innovation.

To improve the situation, Levin and Meister (1985, p. 38) proposed three initiatives: (1) more coordinated market information; (2) improved decision mechanisms in schools; and (3) large-scale institutional approaches to software development and funding. The decision mechanism they proposed provides for district-wide coordination of the purchase and installation of technology, integration of software in relation to district curricular objectives and materials, and training of professional and support staff in the use of hardware and software (p. 43).

In a similar vein, a 1982 report by the Office of Technology Assessment of the United States Congress pointed to the desirability of integrating technology into the instructional system. After presenting a series of case studies of the use of information technology in education, the report concluded that "information technologies can be most effectively applied to tasks when they are well integrated in their institutional environments" (p. 9).

This is not the way technology has been used in schools, however. The purpose of technology is to make labor go further by replacing it, to the extent possible, with mechanical devices and more efficient organization in order to produce a better product or service and/or to reduce the costs of production (Benson, 1961). Yet labor intensive strategies are the most common reforms being suggested today to improve public education. Schools have not neglected new technologies, but there is concern over the ways in which schools have chosen to accommodate these technologies. Technological devices have been used as "add-ons" to assist or supplement teachers rather than as integral parts of new instructional systems that combine the capabilities of people and machines to achieve results that people cannot achieve without machines. When technology is used as an add-on, or as enrichment, rather than reducing costs and increasing efficiency, costs are increased and efficiency is decreased unless there is evidence of greatly improved outcomes, which is not usually the case.

Becker (1982), in assessing the educational potential of the microcomputer, concluded that "disappointment and poorly utilized resources" will result without forethought about the integration of technology with traditional classroom instruction. The biggest problem he saw is overcoming the contrast between the computer's profitable interaction with a single student and the group-based organizational structure of schools.

Individualization of Instruction.   Since early in this century, industrial concepts of standardization and economies of scale have dominated thinking about the organization and administration of schools (Callahan, 1962). Increasingly larger schools have enabled a greater variety of course offerings and specialists. But this same trend has made the system so rigid that it cannot adequately respond to individual differences of students or changing conditions in the environment.

In our current school organization, too little recognition is given to the fact that learning is primarily a function of the interest, motivation and hard work of each student, individually. We frequently assume that learning takes place best in the physical presence

of a teacher to guide and supervise learning activities from moment to moment. The practical effect of this assumption has been to claim that, in order for a child to learn, a course has to be established. More critically, that course requires a certified teacher, and cost considerations require approximately 20 or more pupils per class. Under these assumptions, "individualization" requires many courses, many teachers, and many students.

Contemporary schooling has become "rigidified" and "standardized" in ways that actually thwart learning and fail to educate young people for productive lives in a society now facing accelerating change and diversity. Rather than create self-directed learners who can function independently and interpret change for themselves, the school has continued to create teacher-dependent role players. School organizations and instructional methods need to be made more flexible to provide students with programs and content that are individualized according to student learning abilities and personal interests. School curricula need to be interrelated across subject boundaries in order to permit the integration of ideas and to emphasize the interrelatedness of problems and solutions.

In an information-rich society, the teacher as a primary source of information is rapidly becoming obsolete. Libraries, textbooks, television, video disks and tapes, audio cassettes, CD-ROM data bases, computer software, information systems, and communication networks provide the means whereby any student, knowing how to read and to use these resources, can obtain most information needed in a manner of presentation which is at least as effective as today's typical teaching. This portends new roles for educational professionals. They need to become experts in managing information resources and in designing learning experiences for individual students relevant to their needs, growth and development; they need not be, for the most part, purveyors of information. Teachers should be involved primarily in diagnosis of learning needs, prescription of learning experiences (i.e., curriculum design), motivation of students, and evaluation of the results (Nelson, 1978). In carrying out these functions, the primary interactions with students are, of necessity, on a one-to-one basis, in essence eliminating the classroom as we know it.

The new focus of schools needs to be on learning rather than teaching. With the nearly unlimited accounting capabilities of mainframe and minicomputers, emphasis can be placed on *continuous* rather than discontinuous learning which is *individualized* to capitalize on student strengths and to remedy student weaknesses as these are diagnosed by education professionals. For two decades, it has been the law of the land that children with learning disabilities and other handicapping conditions receive individual diagnoses and education prescriptions; the time has come for all children to be so treated.

A multi-media approach to learning does not eliminate the need for traditional teaching, but traditional teaching becomes only *one* of many possible methods of instruction. Other media include: books, drills, computer–assisted instruction (CAI), video disk enhanced by computer, audio tape and audio disk, lecture (large group), discussion (small group), drama, chorus, band, athletic teams, tutors (teacher, aide, volunteer, or other student), laboratory, and field experiences. Learning is a function of all life experiences, not just those in a school; professional educators need to recognize this as they build curricula for individual students.

Combining teacher assessments of individual student needs with a multi-media approach to instruction makes possible the development of an individualized education plan for each student. But, simultaneously, the individualization of instruction increases the problems of scheduling and custodial functions of schools in society. Means need to

be devised to build into instructional management software a capability for handling far greater complexities of scheduling resulting from the use of a variety of media and information sources on an individual basis.

The difficulty of the task is not to be understated. It is of such magnitude that general systems and material need to be developed at the state and national levels with adaptations made at the district and school levels. While some good software packages do exist, they need to be adapted and networked into a comprehensive instructional system, and others need to be developed. Each media package needs extensive review, and objectives obtainable with each package need to be listed and cross-referenced in schools' information systems. The curriculum development effort required is substantial; but the existence of complex, computerized military defense systems, inventory and financial control systems in business, and on-line reservation systems for airlines, hotels, and entertainment events suggests that the problem is not insurmountable. Such systems are beyond the capacities of schools and most school districts to design, however.

In order to take full advantage of available technology, planned reliance needs to be placed on the machine for its complete range of capabilities, but subject to human direction, planning, and control. Teachers would still be absolutely essential, but their role would change from one of director and final authority, to one of diagnostician, prescriber, motivator, facilitator, and evaluator. Teachers, students, and aides should be seen as multidimensional human resources leading to specialization and division of labor, breaking the self-contained classroom mold of today's schools. Tasks requiring professional judgment need to be separated from those which are routine. High-cost, professionally trained persons should be assigned to the former and lower-cost paraprofessionals assigned to the latter. The pupil/teacher ratio is likely to increase under a system making maximum use of educational technology, but the pupil/adult ratio is likely to remain the same or even decline from current levels. Teachers would be perceived as managers—managers of instruction—supervising students and paraprofessionals with the aid of contemporary technological inventions.

Political-Economic Environment

American public schools are governed directly through democratic political control, another environment that shapes them. Democratic governance is built around the imposition of higher-order values through public authority, bringing public officials like school principals and superintendents under intense pressure from social groups of all political stripes. To ensure that public policy is faithfully implemented by a heterogeneous population of educators serving in the public schools, governmental authority relies on formal rules and regulations that tell the implementers what to do, how to do it, and hold them accountable for doing it. Thus, a bureaucracy is built and bureaucratic control is established making real school autonomy difficult in the public sector (Chubb & Moe, 1990). Private schools, on the other hand, are governed indirectly by market forces. In a market environment, the authority to make educational decisions is placed with those most immediately involved; schools compete for the patronage of parents and students, and parents and students are free to choose among schools.

Several proposals for restructuring educational systems by granting such schools greater autonomy draw upon market theory. Elmore (1988) identified two fundamental questions associated with these proposals. The first is whether or not parents and students should be empowered to choose

among schools or among programs within schools. He called this the "demand side" question. "It poses the question of whether the consumers of education should be given the central role in deciding what kind of education is appropriate for them" (p. 79). The second question is whether or not educators should be empowered to organize and manage schools, to design educational programs, and to receive public funds for providing education to students. He referred to this as the "supply side" question. "It poses the issue of whether the providers of education should be given the autonomy and flexibility to respond to differences in judgments of consumers about appropriate education" (p. 79).

THE SUPPLY SIDE QUESTION

School Autonomy. What difference does it make if schools are organized by democratic political control or by market forces? The analysis by Chubb and Moe (1985, 1990) of two large data bases drawn from national samples of public and private schools suggests that the differences are considerable. They concluded that school autonomy, of the more than 200 variables examined, has the strongest influence on the overall quality of school organization: "Bureaucracy is unambiguously bad for school organization" (1990, p. 183). Chubb and Moe believe that many public school systems have become so bureaucratized that their schools cannot develop the clear objectives and high academic expectations required for effective performance—an inevitable and logical consequence of direct democratic control. "Private schools therefore tend to be effectively organized because of the way their system naturally works. When public schools happen to be effectively organized, it is in spite of their system" (1990, p. 191).

Although the study done by Chubb and Moe has been widely criticized, they are by no means alone in their conclusions about the harmful effects of bureaucratic control on public schools. Sizer (1985) also pointed to hierarchical bureaucracy as paralyzing American education. "The structure is getting in the way of children's learning" (p. 206). Sizer's first imperative for better schools is to give room to teachers and students to work and learn in their own, appropriate ways. He sees decentralized authority as allowing teachers and principals to adapt their schools to the needs, learning styles, and learning rates of students individually. While not denying the need to upgrade the overall quality of the educating profession, Sizer believes that, if empowered, there are enough fine teachers and administrators to lead a renaissance of American schools.

Goodlad (1984) identified the school as *the* unit for improvement. The approach to educational reform that Goodlad viewed to be most promising was the one "that will seek to cultivate the capacity of schools to deal with their own problems, to become largely self-renewing" (p. 31). He did not see the schools as being "cut loose" from one another, but rather as being linked to the hub (district office) and to each other in a network. State officials should be responsible for developing "a common framework for schools within which there is room for some differences in interpretation at the district level and for some variations in schools resulting from differences in size, location, and perspective" (p. 275). According to Goodlad, the district should concern itself with the balance in curricula presented, the processes employed in planning, and the equitable distribution of funds. "What I am proposing is genuine decentralization of authority and responsibility to the local school within a framework designed to assure school-to-school equity and a measure of accountability" (p. 275).

Boyer (1983) also saw heavy doses of bureaucracy "stifling creativity in too many schools, and preventing principals and their staffs from exercising their best professional judgement on decisions that properly should be made at the local level" (p. 227). For Boyer, "Rebuilding excellence in education means reaffirming the importance of the local school and freeing leadership to lead" (p. 316). Among his recommendations for accomplishing this are that:

> *Principals and staff at the local school should have more control over their own budgets, operating within the guidelines set by the district office. Further, every principal should have a School Improvement Fund, discretionary money to provide time and materials for program development and for special seminars and staff retreats. Principals should also have more control over the selection and rewarding of teachers. Acting in consultation with their staffs, they should be given responsibility for the final choice of teachers for their schools. (p. 316)*

Cuban (1988) joined with others in arguing that the bureaucratic organization of schooling is responsible for the lack of professional leadership.

> *Autonomy is the necessary condition for leadership to arise. Without choice, there is no autonomy. Without autonomy, there is no leadership. . . . Schools as they are presently organized press teachers, principals, and superintendents toward managing rather than leading, toward maintaining what is rather than moving to what can be. The structures of schooling and the incentives buried within them produce a managerial imperative. (p. xx–xxi)*

Cuban also recognized the need for federal, state, and district regulations and their accompanying forms of accountability. He called for balanced procedures that permit sufficient discretion to those delivering a service while allowing prudent monitoring by higher levels of authority. Such procedures would focus "less on control through regulation and more on vesting individual schools and educators with the independence to alter basic organizational arrangements (if necessary) to reach explicit goals and standards" (p. 248).

The Supply Side Reform.   Reforms addressing the supply side question are known by many names, including: school-based management (SBM), self-managing schools, school site management, school site decisionmaking, shared governance, and decentralized management. These strategies are founded on the premise that the school is the fundamental decisionmaking unit within the educational system, and that its administrators, teachers, and other professional staff constitute a natural management team. Each school is considered a relatively autonomous unit with the principal in the role of chief executive officer.

One of the first proposals for SBM was made by New York State's Fleischmann Commission (1973). This proposal to decentralize state authority was made to balance another of its recommendations that would consolidate all decisions concerning the finance of public education with the state. Referring to studies by the Committee for Economic Development (1970) and The Urban Institute (1972), the Commission concluded that:

> *centralization and decentralization are not inconsistent concepts and that it is quite possible to have financing at one level and policymaking and other kinds of control at another, with the implication that state financing is not inconsistent with decentralized operating units.*
>
> *The Commission strongly urges greater powers of decision-making in the local school. . . . The effective point for expression of citizen and parent-citizen interest in education is the school, not the school district, for the school is the basic operating unit and cost center in the provision of educational services. (pp. 86–87)*

In order to facilitate citizen involvement in the educational process, the Commission called for a Parent Advisory Council (PAC) for every public school in the state. The PACs would participate in the selection of principals and would provide criteria for the employment of teaching staff; however, the final selection of staff would be the principal's responsibility (Fleischmann, 1972). These Commission recommendations were never implemented in New York State; however, they bear a striking similarity to the reforms recently implemented in Kentucky and Chicago described in Chapter 3.

Well before the advent of "effective schools" research, the Commission saw the principal as having the greatest potential for improving the quality of education. According to the Commission, the principal should be the major voice in setting the educational tone of the school. But principals were to work closely with local citizens, parents, faculty, and students, subject to strengthened measures of accountability and constraints imposed by higher levels of the educational hierarchy.

A decade later, the National Governors' Association (1986) renewed the call of the Fleischmann Commission for SBM. Their Task Force on Leadership and Management recommended that states provide districts with incentives and technical assistance to promote school site management and improvement. They proposed the identification and removal of legal and organizational barriers and the encouragement of local experimentation in school-based budgeting, school-based hiring of teachers, and provision of discretionary resources at the school level. Lamar Alexander, Governor of Tennessee and Chairman of the Association at the time the report was issued, commented that *if* schools and school districts were held accountable for results, "Then, we're ready to give up a lot of state regulatory control" (National Governor's Association, 1986, p. 4). A number of states have been moving toward implementing policies of SBM.

The findings of the Chubb and Moe (1985, 1990) studies are instructive as to the workings of the mechanisms by which SBM may permit the more effective use of human and physical resources in the educating process. They describe the very different environments in which public and private schools exist. The former is characterized by politics, hierarchy, and authority, and the latter by markets, competition, and volunteerism. Chubb and Moe hypothesize, however, that the differences these environments make for school organization may not be due entirely, or even primarily, to qualities that are inherently public or private. Rather, they suggest organizational differences may derive from environmental characteristics such as control, constraint, and complexity that differentiate among school environments regardless of sector. Thus, through organizational redesign, the strengths characteristic of schools in one sector may be incorporated into schools in the other.

As expected, Chubb and Moe found outside authority exerting much stronger influence on public schools than on private schools. Because of strong external influences, public schools have less freedom in choosing how to respond to their more difficult environments since they are more constrained by formal rules and regulations and informal norms. Unexpectedly, however, the external influence on Catholic schools was less than that experienced by other private schools even though, unlike other private schools, Catholic schools are part of a rather substantial hierarchy. This last finding supported their conclusion that bureaucracy need not, necessarily, be the stultifying force it often becomes.

Among their other findings was the fact that teachers in private schools rated their principals as better all-around leaders than did teachers in public schools. Private school principals were also rated by their teachers as being more helpful than their counterparts in the public sector. Further, private school teachers indicated that the goals of their schools were clearer and more clearly communicated by the principal than did public school teachers. Teachers in private schools were also more likely to rate their principals as encouraging, supportive, and reinforcing. "Private school principals are likely to be in a position to lead their organizations. They may not succeed, but they should have the tools and the flexibility to do what leaders need to do. Public school principals, on the other hand, are systematically denied much of what it takes to lead" (Chubb & Moe, 1990, p. 56).

Chubb and Moe found that private schools delegate significantly more discretion to their teachers and are more likely to involve them in school level policy decisions than are public schools. Private schools also seem to do a better job of relieving teachers of routine and paperwork. There is a higher level of collegiality among private school staffs; teachers are more likely to know what their colleagues are teaching and to coordinate content of their courses. Private school teachers spend more time meeting to discuss curriculum and students and observing each other's classes. Private school teachers feel that they have more influence over school policies governing student behavior, pupil assignment to classes, curriculum, and in-service programs. Within their classrooms, private school teachers feel that they have more control over text selection, course content, teaching techniques, and student discipline than do public school teachers. Private school teachers even feel that they have more influence over hiring and firing practices than do public school teachers.

Of all the potential barriers to hiring excellent teachers, Chubb and Moe found that not one barrier was rated higher by private school principals than by their public school counterparts. Public school principals regard "central office control" and "excessive transfers from other schools" as particularly onerous.

They also face substantially greater obstacles in dismissing teachers for poor performance than do private school principals. The complexity of formal dismissal procedures was the highest barrier to firing cited by public school principals. For private school principals, it was "a personal reluctance to fire."

Public school pupils were less likely to know what comprises school policy than were students in private schools. Public school students also regarded their school policies as less fair and less effective.

Parents appear to be much more involved and cooperative in private schools. In public schools, parents are more likely to be required to communicate with school officials through formal channels and school officials have less flexibility in addressing reasonable grievances of parents.

In contrast with private schools, Chubb and Moe (1985) concluded that the external environment places more complex and conflicting expectations on public school personnel which severely constrains their discretion in organizing and operating schools. In addition to the managerial role that public school principals share with their private school counterparts, public school principals serve in a political role due to their interactions with school boards, superintendents, state and national politicians, local pressure groups and parents. Like the middle managers they are, they emphasize efficiency as a safe way to please the hierarchy of which they are a part, consolidating whatever power is given to them and guarding the school's few prerogatives against the influence of a staff over which they have little control. As politicians, they campaign for the support of their schools from a host of sometimes hostile constituencies.

Is it possible that SBM in public schools can relieve the pressures of external authorities on the schools, permitting public schools to take on some of the desirable characteristics of private schools? Or might SBM create even greater conflict among principals, teach-

ers and community representatives—conflicts that they can currently ignore or push off to the school district for resolution?

There is no doubt but that the Chubb and Moe studies have given important insights into the process of policy formulation in public schools. It should be noted, however, that their work has been criticized for not taking sufficient account of certain societal concerns about an educated citizenry. Witte (1990), for example, challenged the perception that public schools are bureaucratically centralized, highly uniform, politically insulated public monopolies. Instead, he sees them as being decentralized, widely varied, fragmented and politically responsive to the point of being hyper-responsive. Witte acknowledged that there is much that is appealing in several of the decentralization proposals, but he cautioned that decentralization and choice should not be viewed as panaceas for solving the complex and serious problems confronting the most problematic public school districts with respect to resource equity and overall achievement. "For those districts where the problems are the most serious, undue expectations on singular adherence to these policies will have us in ten years looking backward on decentralization and choice as simply another set of failed reforms" (p. 43).

Cohen (1990) accepted Witte's decentralized view of public education in the United States and argued that public education's problems derive from its fragmentation rather than its centralization. As such, further decentralization and choice will exacerbate the problems rather than reduce them. Because of this fragmentation, he claimed that instructional guidance is weak and chaotic. He argued that for decentralization and choice to work, a coherent system of instructional guidance needs to be in place that implies a degree of greater decentralization with respect to this one aspect. Finally, Cohen is concerned that, under a choice system, those parents with the greatest need for improved education would have the greatest difficulty in taking advantage of their new freedoms.

Levin (1990) saw both costs and benefits in a market/choice approach to schooling and pointed out that there are important differences among proposed patterns. He projected some improvement in micro-efficiency in the provision of schooling; however, he fears that these would be over-shadowed by macro-efficiency considerations. Levin argued that proposals of decentralization and choice underplay the difficulties of monitoring and evaluating a highly diversified system. "The overall costs for sustaining the information, regulation, and other parts of the market system while providing, at least, minimum societal protection look high to prohibitive relative to a public choice approach" (p. 247). He concluded that it is not clear which system of choice is likely to be best without explicit comparisons of the versions being considered.

THE DEMAND QUESTION

The National Governors' Association (1986) also gave its endorsement to the concept of family choice of schooling in its *1991 Report on Education: Time for Results*.

> *We believe that we can remain dedicated to a system of public schools and still increase consumer sovereignty. . . .If we implement broader choice plans, true choice among public schools, then we unlock the values of competition in the educational marketplace. Schools that compete for students, teachers and dollars will, by virtue of their environment, make those changes that allow them to succeed. (p. 12)*

While the governors confine their support of choice to public schools, others argue that public funds should also be made available to private schools through vouchers or tax credits for parents' expenses, including tuition.

Chubb and Moe (1985) aptly described what the governors meant by "consumer sov-

ereignty" and "the values of competition in the educational market place":

> *Public schools have their resources allocated to them by authorities who do not directly consume their services while private schools receive their resources in a direct exchange for services rendered. The resources of public schools are therefore less closely connected to the school's performance. Effectiveness may be rewarded by the environment or it may not; the same is true of ineffectiveness. Public schools therefore operate under considerable uncertainty, never confident that their efforts will pay off. They must depend upon the beneficence of various political processes that include a host of participants other than parents, and on their own ability to bargain for funds from their local superiors. For private schools, resources are not necessarily easier to acquire. To the contrary, competition with other schools, coupled with parental demands for excellence, may make resources harder to acquire. But the resource problem is a simpler one, with a clear connection between school success in accomplishing goals and school rewards from the environment. "Perform or perish" brings considerable certitude to the relationship between private schools and their environments. (pp. 9–10)*

Family choice is proposed by theoreticians as a means of strengthening the linkages between resources allocated to schools by government, schooling outcomes, and client satisfaction (Sowell, 1993). This is accomplished by placing the authority over pupil assignment with parents rather than with school boards and by allowing publicly provided resources to "follow the child." The process increases consumer sovereignty while still vesting in public bodies authority to regulate societal concerns over schools.

In reality, however, most public school plans of choice have been initiated to facilitate school desegregation. In an alternative strategy to forced cross-district busing for controlling the racial/ethnic mix of school enrollments, some school boards designed magnet schools to *attract* children of different backgrounds who seek particular programs. Representing a compromise between consumer sovereignty and social justice, this procedure appears to have avoided creating fears on the part of parents for the safety and well-being of their children which are frequently engendered by "forced busing" plans. Thus, school choice is advocated to improve two quite different aspects of schools and school districts: their internal efficiency and social equity.

Noting that public schooling is the worst where parents have the fewest, or no, options, Friedman (1962) argued that equity and fraternal ends as well as libertarian and efficiency goals would be better served with governmentally financed vouchers than under the current scheme of government-run schools. An educational voucher is an entitlement extended to an individual by a government permitting that individual to receive educational services up to the maximum amount specified. The voucher can normally be redeemed according to the preference of the holder at any institution or enterprise approved by the granting agency. Vouchers would separate the existing nexus between public support of education, place of residence, and the public ownership of educational enterprises. The intent of vouchers is to enfranchise households as the basic decisionmaking unit in the selection of schooling. Vouchers do not eliminate government interest in education; rather, they retain the prospect of government responsibility for financing and maintain a marketplace of education providers that otherwise would require regulation.

Under the Friedman (1962) plan, parents sending their children to private schools would be paid a sum equal to the estimated cost of educating a child in a public school, providing that at least that amount was spent on education in an approved school. If the cost of the private school was greater, the parent would have to make up the difference.

Such a plan, Friedman argued, would greatly expand the educational options currently available to poor families.

> *One way to achieve a major improvement, to bring learning back into the classroom, especially for the currently most disadvantaged, is to give all parents greater control over their children's schooling, similar to that which those of us in the upper-income classes now have. Parents generally have both greater interest in their children's schooling and more intimate knowledge of their capacities and needs than anyone else. Social reformers, and educational reformers in particular, often self-righteously take for granted that parents, especially those who are poor and have little education themselves, have little interest in their children's education and no competence to choose for them. This is a gratuitous insult. (Friedman & Friedman, 1980, p. 150)*

Critics of the Friedman plan argue that unregulated vouchers would merely enable private schools to raise their tuition, still keeping them out of the reach of low-income families. At the same time, unregulated vouchers would make private schools more accessible to higher income families, encouraging them to abandon the public schools in even greater numbers than at present, making public schools havens for the poor. This, they claim, would further stratify society. Some critics do see merit in the general concept of vouchers, however, and propose modifications to the original plan which they believe would overcome perceived inequities while retaining what they consider to be its more attractive features (Center for the Study of Public Policy, 1970; Coons & Sugarman, 1978). Only a few experimental voucher schemes are operational at present, including those in Minnesota, Iowa, Arkansas, and Wisconsin.

Another approach to aiding persons attending private schools and strengthening market forces, rather than subsidizing the schools directly, is through tax credits and deductions. A tax credit reduces the amount of the tax owed (usually an income tax) up to a specified sum. Tuition payments (or a percentage of them, depending on how the law is written) can be subtracted from the computed tax amount owed. Tax deductions apply to income taxes exclusively and are not as favorable for qualifying taxpayers as tax credits. Tax deductions reduce the amount of taxable income upon which the tax is computed. Thus the reduction in tax liability is only a percentage (the marginal tax rate) of tuition payments. The credit and deduction proposals usually contain civil rights guarantees based on school eligibility requirements. Credits and deductions are only allowed for expenditures incurred in schools that received governmental approval.

Opponents of tax credits and deductions argue that the benefits flow disproportionally to high-income persons. To qualify for either a credit or a deduction, a person has to incur a tax liability and file a return. Thus, the very poorest would not benefit. Such parents could be brought into a tax credit scheme through refundability provisions, i.e., the government would reimburse to the individual the amount of the credit. This would still require the filing of a tax return and the up-front payment of the required tuition.

There are numerous opportunities for schooling choices under current arrangements; however, they tend to be highly constrained. For many years, students in Vermont school districts that do not operate high schools have been able to chose among public and non-sectarian private schools at public expense. More recent policy changes permit Minnesota parents to enroll their children in virtually any public school district they choose in the state (Nathan, 1989; Pearson, 1989). Iowa and Arkansas have similar plans and numerous other states are likely to follow suit. For over twenty years, Massachusetts has encouraged and financed interdistrict transfer

of pupils, which improves racial balance in the schools involved (Glenn, 1986). Similarly, St. Louis City and County school districts exchange students to improve racial balance as part of a court-ordered desegregation plan.

A number of large cities have developed open enrollment schemes within their districts. For generations, New York City has operated a variety of specialty schools, including the prestigious Bronx High School of Science, which draw their students from throughout the city. The Boston Latin School dates back to Colonial times. The Boston Public Schools have also recently embraced a school choice plan as an alternative to forced busing imposed by the courts to remedy racial imbalances in the district. The plan includes decentralized decisionmaking and school-based management. At least a dozen other large cities have used a variety of school choice plans to end racial segregation. One of the most successful has been the magnet school program in Buffalo, New York. Elmore (1988) estimated that about one third of big city school districts offer school choice in the form of magnet and/or specialty schools.

District 4 in New York City's East Harlem has received much attention in recent years for the academic success of its students and its open enrollment policies (Fliegel & MacGuire, 1993). The district serves a generally poor population. Ninety-five percent of the students are from minority populations with Hispanics constituting the majority of its enrollment. The average achievement gains of its students are impressive, although district critics attribute those gains to factors other than open enrollment such as the small size of its schools (about 300 pupils each) and favored treatment to academically stronger students (Snider, 1989).

Some public assistance is provided to students enrolled in private schools which, to a small degree, facilitates the possibility for family choice. Many states provide public support of transportation, health services, testing and remedial services, and textbooks to children enrolled in private schools. But the most common vehicle of school choice in the public sector is through the selection of a residence. Murnane (1986) pointed to compelling evidence that families pay premiums for housing in school districts with reputations for good schools. Kutner, Sherman and Williams (1986) reported on a survey of a national random sample of approximately 1200 households with school-age children. About half of the parents indicated that the public schools their children would attend influenced the choice of a place to live; 18 percent said that it was the most important factor in their choice of residence. Of course, to participate in this kind of choice, a family has to have access to sufficient resources to enable it to purchase (or rent) a residence in school districts perceived to be desirable.

In conclusion, after looking at several of the environments within which schools must function, it appears clear that the one that has the greatest and most direct impact upon pupil achievement is the home environment to which the child is exposed up to 87 percent of his or her waking hours. The home shapes the values, aspirations, and behaviors of the child as well as his or her mental processing through the development of language skills.

Since the school environment is another important influence on pupil development, the teacher-centered technology that dominates all schools today needs to be replaced with individualized instruction that integrates human resources with modern information and communication technologies.

Finally, it is from the political-economic environment that schools are given their structure, incentives and disincentives are set, and resources are allocated. Democratic control has its limitations. Professional educators need to be free to design appropriate environments for their clients through school-

based management and parents need to be free to choose among competing environments those judged to be most appropriate for their children.

Activities for Discussion

1. Describe possible systems for coordinating the delivery of social services (including educational services) to a child and his or her family. What are the advantages and disadvantages of each design?

2. Describe possible instructional systems for accommodating the diversity of backgrounds found in a school's pupil population. What are the advantages and disadvantages of each design?

3. Can the public interest be protected without the bureaucratization of schools? If so, how?

4. If parents have freedom to choose the schools their children attend, how might their interests best be represented in the process of designing educational programs (assuming school-based management)?

5. Discuss the advantages and disadvantages of alternative arrangements for expanding diversity in schooling options:

    a. the current arrangement of free publicly financed and operated schools with direct aid to private schools prohibited, but allowing supporting services that benefit children attending private schools;
    b. educational vouchers, with options among public and private schools;
    c. tax deductions for tuition and other expenses incurred in public and private education;
    d. tax credits that rebate the cost of tuition up to a specified amount;
    e. direct aid to private schools;

f. open enrollment among public schools without public aid for private schools.

Annotated Bibliography

Bernstein, B. (1971). *Class codes and control: Volume I, Theoretical studies towards a sociology of language*. London, England: Routledge & Kegan Paul.

This volume groups together a number of papers previously published showing the origin and development of Bernstein's theoretical studies into the relationships between social class, patterns of language use (restricted and elaborated codes), and the primary socialization of the child. They develop a social basis of knowledge made available in schools through the institutionalizing of elaborated codes of language that reflect social-class relationships. The theory has important implications for the organization and presentation of curriculum, especially for those working with children from lower socioeconomic class homes. The work remains relevant even though the papers were originally published twenty and thirty years ago.

Boyer, E. L. (1983). *High school: A report on secondary education in America*. New York: Harper and Row.

This book is a report of a study by the Carnegie Foundation for the Advancement of Teaching that examines the American high school and makes recommendations for the achievement of excellence in all schools. Concerned that most of the studies of educational reform focus on structure, this study goes inside the school and the classroom and provides a clear picture of how today's young people think and feel. The book addresses the following themes: goals, curriculum, teachers, teaching and learning, technology, structure, school leadership, connections beyond the school, and community support.

Chubb, J. E., & Moe, T. M. (1990). *Politics, markets and America's schools*. Washington, DC: The Brookings Institution.

This book explains how politics and markets affect the functioning of America's schools. The authors argue that the fundamental cause of poor academic achievement by pupils attending public schools is the structure of direct democratic control. This governance structure, they contend, burdens schools with excessive bureaucracy, inhibits effective organization, and stifles student achievement. They build a rationale for restructuring public education built around parent-student choice, school competition, and school autonomy. Their analysis is based upon High School and Beyond data sets that include responses from more than 20,000 students, teachers, and principals in a nationwide sample of some 500 public and private schools.

Coleman, J. S., & Hoffer, T. (1987). *Public and private high schools: The impact of communities*. New York: Basic Books.

The book develops a theory of the influence of "social capital" on schools. The authors provide a rich sociological account of the differences between public and Catholic high schools and the communities they serve which may explain why Catholic schools seem to have a stronger positive impact on students—especially from at-risk groups—than do public and other private schools. They point to two major changes in social context that have had a particularly debilitating effect on public schools: the destruction of functional communities based on residence, and the realignment of value communities around some dimension other than residence. The work of Catholic schools is buttressed by and with an active, supportive, multigenerational value community. Because of the heterogeneity of values held by those sending children to public schools, the social capital enjoyed by public schools of earlier times has been largely lost except in some rural communities. The authors make policy recommendations for the restructuring of public education based on their findings. Like the Chubb and Moe (1990) study cited above, this analysis is drawn from the High School and Beyond data bases that involved 1,015 high schools.

Cuban, L. (1988). *The managerial imperative and the practice of leadership in schools*. Albany, NY: State University of New York Press.

The author analyzes the dominant images (moral and technical), roles (instructional, managerial, and political), and contexts (classroom, school, and district) by which teachers, principals, and superintendents have defined their work over the last century. Cuban concludes that when these powerful images are combined with the structural conditions in which schooling occurs, managerial behavior results that reduces the potential for more thoughtful and effective leadership. He argues that teaching is central to administration and laments their current separation. Recommendations are made for structural reform in schooling which would free administrators and teachers from a managerial imperative, enabling them to provide society with the professional leadership so badly needed.

Goodlad, J. I. (1984). *A place called school: Prospects for the future*. New York: McGraw-Hill.

The book provides a detailed description of a place called school based upon data gathered from 38 schools, 1,350 teachers and classrooms, 17,63 students and 8,624 parents. Attention is given to teachers and teaching, to the curriculum and its impact, and to what we want the schools to do. The basic issue raised is whether or not we can have effective schools. He establishes priorities for reform and concludes with recommendations for the substance and process of improvement.

Kozol, J. (1991). *Savage inequalities: Children in America's schools*. New York: Harper Perennial.

In this book, the author has brought children's voices into the discussion of school reform. He thought that it was particularly unfortunate that their views had not been considered because of the pertinence of their perceptions to the day-to-day realities of life in schools. The author visited schools throughout the nation serving rich and poor children. He vividly describes the extremes of wealth and poverty in America's school system and the blighting effect of poverty on children. The book concludes with policy recommendations.

Powell, A. G., Farrar, E., & Cohen, D. K. (1985). *The shopping mall high school: Winners and losers in the educational marketplace*. Boston: Houghton Mifflin.

The authors look carefully inside fifteen public and private high schools and provide new insights into thinking about and improving schools. The authors have a special concern for the average student and the purposeless drifting that characterizes their experience in school. The book displays the complexity and subtlety of the American secondary school and the reasons why most of the public is satisfied with the status quo. The authors point out that through a series of "treaties and compromises" by students, teachers, and parents, strikingly different expectations and standards are played out, undermining any call for common standards and making any effort to improvement very difficult.

Sizer, T. R. (1985). *Horace's compromise: The dilemma of the American high school*. Boston: Houghton Mifflin.

This book is based on the same data set as Powell, Farrar, and Cohen's work cited above and is the first of a series. In this book, the author provides the reader with the essential "feel" of schools, giving a sense of the important, complicated life of a school and its people. Using a narrative format, and dealing with "adolescents' hearts as well as brains, with human idiosyncracies as well as their calculable commonalities," he is largely successful.

W. T. Grant Foundation Commission on Work, Family and Citizenship. (1988). *The forgotten half: Pathways to success for America's youth and young families*. Washington, DC: Author.

This report focuses on the 20 million 16- to 24-year-olds who are unlikely to attend college and will miss out on the special privileges our society accords to the college-educated. The report draws upon substantial research and practical knowledge about what works to improve the economic prospects of American youth. It sets out a series of recommendations to improve earning levels for the forgotten half including the chance of succeeding in school regardless of their learning styles. The recommendations reach beyond the boundaries of school and work into families and communities where young people learn the lessons of adulthood.

References

Allport, G. (1958). *The nature of prejudice*. Garden City, NY: Doubleday.

Barker, B. (1986). *The advantages of small schools*. Las Cruces, NM: New Mexico State University, ERIC Clearinghouse on Rural Education and Small Schools. (ERIC Document Reproduction Service No. ED 265988)

Barker, R. G., & Gump, P. V. (1964). *Big school, small school*. Stanford, CA: Stanford University Press.

Beare, H., Caldwell, B. J., & Millikan, R. H. (1989). *Creating an excellent school*. London: Routledge & Kegan Paul.

Becker, H. (1982). *Microcomputers in the classroom: Dreams and realities* (Report No. 319). Baltimore, MD: The Johns Hopkins University Center for the Social Organization of Schools.

Bennis, W. (1984). Transformative power and leadership. In T. J. Sergiovanni & J. E. Corbally (Eds.), *Leadership and organizational culture*. Urbana, IL: University of Illinois Press.

Benson, C. (1961). *The economics of public education*. Boston: Houghton Mifflin.

Bernstein, B. (1961). Social structure, language and learning. *Educational Research, 3,* 163–176.

Bernstein, B. (1971). *Class codes and control: Volume I, Theoretical studies towards a sociology of language*. London: Routledge & Kegan Paul.

Boyer, E. L. (1983). *High school: A report on secondary education in America*. New York: Harper and Row.

Boyer, E. (1989). Buildings reflect our priorities. *Educational Record, 70*(1), 24–27.

Bradley, R., Rock, S., Caldwell, B., Harris, P., & Hamreck, H. (1987). Home environment and school performance among black elementary school children. *The Journal of Negro Education, 56,* 499–509.

Brookover, W., & Lezotte, L. (1979). *Changes in school characteristics coincident with changes in student achievement*. East Lansing, MI: Michigan State University, College of Urban Development.

Brown, F. (1990). The language of politics, education and the disadvantaged. In S. L. Jacobson & J. A. Conway (Eds.), *Educational leadership in an age of reform* (pp. 83–100).

Callahan, R. (1962). *Education and the cult of efficiency: A study of the social forces that have shaped the administration of the public schools*. Chicago: The University of Chicago Press.

Carnegie Foundation for the Advancement of Teaching. (1988). *An imperiled generation: Saving urban schools*. Princeton, NJ: Princeton University Press.

Center for the Study of Public Policy. (1970). *Education vouchers: A report on financing education by grants to parents*. Cambridge, MA: The Center.

Chubb, J. E., & Moe, T. M. (1985). *Politics, markets, and the organization of schools*. Stanford, CA: Institute for Research on Educational Finance and Governance, School of Education, Stanford University.

Chubb, J. E., & Moe, T. M. (1990). *Politics, markets, and America's schools*. Washington, DC: The Brookings Institution.

Clark, R. (1983). *Family life and school achievement: Why poor black children succeed or fail*. Chicago: University of Chicago Press.

Cohen, D. K. (1990). Governance and instruction: The promise of decentralization and choice. In W. H. Clune & J. F. Witte (Eds.), *Choice and control in American education, Volume 1: The theory of choice and control in education* (pp. 337–386). London: Falmer.

Coleman, J. S., et al. (1966). *Equality of educational opportunity*. Washington, DC: Office of Education, U.S. Department of Health, Education, and Welfare.

Coleman, J. S., & Hoffer, T. (1987). *Public and private high schools: The impact of communities*. New York: Basic Books.

Coleman, P. (1986). The good school: A critical examination of the adequacy of student achievement and per pupil expenditures as measures of school district effectiveness. *Journal of Education Finance, 12,* 71–96.

Comer, J. (1980). *School power*. New York: The Free Press.

Committee for Economic Development. (1970). *Reshaping government in metropolitan areas*. New York: Author.

Cookson, Jr., P. W., & Persell, C. H. (1985). *Preparing for power: America's elite boarding schools*. New York: Basic Books.

Coons, J. E., & Sugarman, S. D. (1978). *Education by choice: The case for family control.* Berkeley, CA: University of California Press.

Corcoran, T. B., Walker, L. J., & White, J. L. (1988). *Working in urban schools.* Washington, DC: Institute for Educational Leadership.

Cuban, L. (1988). *The managerial imperative and the practice of leadership in schools.* Albany, NY: State University of New York Press.

Cusick, P. (1983). *The egalitarian ideal and the American high school: Studies of three schools.* New York: Longman.

Datcher-Loury, L. (1989). Family background and school achievement among low income blacks. *The Journal of Human Resources, 24,* 528–544.

Deutsch, M. (1965). The role of social class in language development and cognition. *American Journal of Orthopsychiatry, 35,* 78–88.

Durkin, D. (1984). Poor black children who are successful readers. *Urban Education, 18,* 53–76.

Earthman, G. I. (1992). *Planning educational facilities for the next century.* Reston, VA: Association of School Business Officials International.

Eitzen, D. S. (1992). Problem students: The sociocultural roots. *Phi Delta Kappan, 73,* 584–590.

Elmore, R. F. (1988). Choice in public schools. In W. L. Boyd & C. T. Kerchner (Eds.), *The politics of excellence and choice in education* (pp. 79–98). New York: Falmer Press.

Fleischmann, M., Chairman. (1972). *Report of the New York State Commission on the Quality, Cost and Financing of Elementary and Secondary Education* (Vol. 3). Albany, NY: Author.

Fleischmann, M., Chairman. (1973). *The Fleischmann report on the quality, cost and financing of elementary and secondary education in New York State* (Vol. I). New York: The Viking Press.

Fliegel, S., & MacGuire, J. (1993). *Miracle in East Harlem: The fight for choice in public education.* New York: Times Books, Random House.

Foster, H. L. (1974). *Ribbin', jivin', and playin' the dozens: The unrecognized dilemma of inner city schools.* Cambridge, MA: Balinger.

Friedman, M. (1962). *Capitalism and freedom.* Chicago: The University of Chicago Press.

Friedman, M., & Friedman, R. (1980). *Free to choose: A personal statement.* New York: Avon.

George, P. S., & Oldaker, L. L. (1985). A national survey of middle school effectiveness. *Educational Leadership, 42,* 81.

Glenn, C. L. (1986). The Massachusetts experience with public school choice. *Time for results: The governors' 1991 report on education.* Supporting works, Task Force on Parent Involvement and Choice. Washington, DC: National Governors Association.

Goodlad, J. I. (1984). *A place called school: Prospects for the future.* New York: McGraw-Hill.

Heath, S. B. (1983). *Ways with words: Language, life and work in communities and classrooms.* Cambridge, England: Cambridge University Press.

Heath, S. B., & McLaughlin, M. W. (1987). A child resource policy: Moving beyond dependence on school and family. *Phi Delta Kappan, 68,* 576–580.

Hodgkinson, C. (1983). *The philosophy of leadership.* Oxford, England: Basil Blackwell.

Husen, T. (1972). *Social background and educational career-research perspectives on equality of educational opportunity.* Paris, France: Organization for Economic Cooperation and Development.

Jackson, S., Logsdon, D. M., & Taylor, N. E. (1983). Instructional leadership behaviors: Differentiating effective from ineffective low-income urban schools. *Urban Education, 18,* 59–70.

Knezevich, S. J. (1984). *Administration of public education: A sourcebook for the leadership and management of educational institutions.* Cambridge, MA: Harper and Row.

Kowalski, T. J. (1989). *Planning and managing school facilities.* New York: Praeger.

Kozol, J. (1991). *Savage inequalities: Children in America's schools.* New York: Harper Perennial.

Kutner, M. A., Sherman, J. D., & Williams, M. F. (1986). Federal policies for public schools. In D. C. Levy (Ed.), *Private education: Studies in choice and public policy* (pp. 57–81). New York: Oxford University Press.

Lee, C. (1984). An investigation of psychosocial variables related to academic success for rural black adolescents. *Journal of Negro Education, 53,* 424–434.

Levin, H. M. (1990). The theory of choice applied to education. In W. H. Clune & J. F. Witte (Eds.), *Choice and control in American education,*

Volume 1: The theory of choice and control in education (pp. 247–284). London: Falmer.

Levin, H., & Meister, G. (1985). *Educational technology and computers: Promises, promises, always promises* (Project Report No. 85-A13). Stanford, CA: Stanford University, Stanford Education Policy Institute.

Lewis, A (1989). *Wolves at the schoolhouse door: An investigation of the condition of public school buildings*. Washington, DC: Education Writers Association.

Lomotey, K. (1989). *African-American principals' school leadership and success*. Westport, CT: Greenwood.

Lomotey, K. & Swanson, A. D. (1989). Urban and rural schools research: Implications for school governance. *Education and Urban Society, 21*(4), 436–454.

Mark, D. L. H. (1993). *High achieving African-American children in low income single parent families: The home learning environment*. Buffalo, NY: Unpublished Ph. D. dissertation completed at the State University of New York at Buffalo.

Mayeski, G. W., & Beaton, A. E. (1975). *Special studies of our nation's schools*. Washington, DC: Office of Education, Department of Health, Education, and Welfare.

Murnane, R. J. (1986). Comparisons of private and public schools: The critical role of regulations. In D. C. Levy (Ed.), *Private education: Studies in choice and public policy* (pp. 138–152). New York: Oxford University Press.

Myrdal, G. (1962). *The American dilemma: The Negro problem and modern democracy* (Vols. 1 and 2). New York: Harper and Row.

Nathan, J. (1989). Helping all children, empowering all educators: Another view of school choice. *Phi Delta Kappan, 71*, 304–307.

National Education Goals Panel. (1993). *National education goals report*. Washington, DC: Author.

National Governors' Association. (1986). *Time for results: the governors' 1991 report on education*. Washington, DC: Center for Policy Research and Analysis, National Governors' Association.

Nelson, E. (1978). *Occupational education in New York State: The transition from vocational to career education* (Occasional Paper No. 28). Albany, NY: Unpublished monograph, New York State Education Department, School Finance Law Study Project.

New York State Education Department. (1969). *Racial and social class isolation in the schools*. Albany, NY: Author.

Newman, F. M. (1981). Reducing student alienation in high schools: Implications of theory. *Harvard Education Review, 51*, 546–564.

Ogbu, J. (1978). *Minority education and caste*. New York: Academic Press.

Ortiz, F. I. (1994). *Schoolhousing: Planning and designing educational facilities*. Albany, NY: State University of New York Press.

Pearson, J. (1989). Myths of choice: The governor's new clothes? *Phi Delta Kappan, 70*, 821–823.

Perelman, L. (1987). *Technology and the transformation of schools*. Alexandria, VA: National School Boards Association.

Piccigallo, P. R. (1989). Renovating urban schools is fundamental to improving them. *Phi Delta Kappan, 70*, 402–406.

Powell, A. G., Farrar, E., & Cohen, D. K. (1985). *The shopping mall high school: Winners and losers in the educational marketplace*. Boston: Houghton Mifflin.

Prom-Jackson, S., Johnson, S., & Wallace, M. (1987). Home environment, talented minority youth and school achievement. *Journal of Negro Education, 56*, 111–121.

Reynolds, A. (1991). Early schooling of children at risk. *American Educational Research Journal, 28*, 392–422.

Rist, R. (1970). Student social class and teacher expectations: The self-fulfilling prophecy in ghetto education. *Harvard Education Review, 40*, 411–451.

Rutter, M., Maugham, B., Mortimore, P., Ouston, J., & Smith, A. (1979). *Fifteen thousand hours*. Cambridge, MA: Harvard University Press.

Scott-Jones, D. (1987). Mothers-as-teachers in the families of high- and low-achieving low-income black first-graders. *Journal of Negro Education, 56*, 21–34.

Shade, B. J., & Edwards, P. A. (1987). Ecological correlates of the educative style of Afro-American children. *Journal of Negro Education, 86*, 88–99.

Sizer, T. R. (1985). *Horace's compromise: The dilemma of the American high school*. Boston: Houghton Mifflin.

Skelly, M. E. (1988, August). Rural schools at the crossroads. *School and College*, 51–56.

Snider, W. (1989). Known for choice, New York's District 4 offers a complex tale for urban reformers. *Education Week, 9*(9), 1, 13.

Sowell, T. (1993). *Inside American education: The decline, the deception, the dogmas.* New York: The Free Press.

Swanson, A. D. (1979). An international perspective on social science research and school integration. *Journal of Negro Education, 48,* 57–66.

Taylor, D., & Dorsey-Gaines, C. (1988). *Growing up literate: Learning from inner-city families.* Portsmouth, NH: Heinemann Educational Books.

Urban Institute. (1972). *Public school finance: Present disparities and fiscal alternatives.* A report to the President's Commission on School Finance, Vol. I, Ch. 5. Washington, DC: U.S. Government Printing Office.

Vaizey, J., Norris, K., & Sheehan, J. (1972). *The political economy of education.* New York: John Wiley & Sons.

Venezsky, R., & Winfield, L. (1980). *Schools that succeed beyond expectations in teaching reading* (Technical Report #1). Newark, DE: University of Delaware, Studies on Education.

W. T. Grant Foundation Commission on Work, Family and Citizenship. (1988). *The forgotten half:*
Pathways to success for America's youth and young families. Washington, DC: Author.

Walberg, H. J. (1984). Families as partners in educational productivity. *Phi Delta Kappan, 65,* 397–400.

Weber, G. (1971). *Inner city children can be taught to read: Four successful schools.* Washington, DC: Council for Basic Education.

Wellisch, J. B., MacQueen, A. H., Carriere, R. A., & Duck, G. A. (1978). School management and organization in successful schools. *Sociology of Education, 51,* 211–226.

Willett, E. J. (1973). *Designs for structuring capital-intensive (rather than labor-intensive) education production functions for the promotion of individualized learning below college level.* Unpublished doctoral dissertation, State University of New York at Buffalo.

Williams, R. L. (Ed.). (1975). *The true language of black folks.* St. Louis, MO: Institute of Black Studies.

Witte, J. F. Choice and control: An analytical overview. In W. H. Clune & J. F. Witte (Eds.), *Choice and control in American education, Volume 1: The theory of choice and control in education* (pp. 11–46). London: Falmer.

Part IV

Analysis and Planning

I t is essential that members of an organization share a common understanding of the organization's purpose or mission; likewise, an essential function of leadership is to enable the organization to develop such an understanding, often called *vision,* and to articulate it. A shared vision provides direction to the organization, but the vision will never be realized without deliberate strategies for implementation.

Chapter 11 addresses the process of strategic planning, a process that moves from visioning to implementation, to evaluation, to adjusting. Strategic planning is one of the most common applications of systems theory at work in the schools today; but the concept, like many we have studied in this volume, is being transformed by paradigm shifts, discussed in Part II, Inquiry. Under the influence of the positivist paradigm, planning was conceptualized as a very logical, technical process performed by planning experts *for* an organization or government. Under interventionist paradigms, the concept of planning has been transformed with an emphasis on process in which planning is done by members of the organization. Planning is now considered, not only an activity, but also an attitude or way of life; it is a mental orientation (bias) toward the future that permeates all decisionmaking by all members of the organization. In the new view, planning needs to be an integral part of the behavior of all persons in the organization, especially of those formally responsible for providing leadership.

An essential part of planning and implementation is allocation of resources. Demands for resources always exceed their availability; therefore, it is incumbent upon an organization to use available resources to maximize productivity within the context of organizational priorities. Chapter 12 addresses issues concerning allocation of resources to the education sector and within educational enterprises. Studies relating to the efficiency of public schools indicate with great consistency that schools are not using the resources entrusted to them to full advantage. Other studies show that there are great inequities in the distribution of resources among schools and school districts. We conclude that the greatest allocation problems facing educational leadership today and for years to come is designing instructional systems that are educationally effective and economically efficient. The second most urgent problem is improving equity in the distribution of resources to schools so that all children may have access to good facilities, competent instruction, and state-of-the-art materials and equipment. Equity issues are placed second only because of the overwhelming evidence that more resources are unlikely to improve achievement of at-risk children as schools are currently organized.

Having committed an organization to a strategy of implementation, it is necessary to monitor the outcomes produced by the strategy against the established goals and objectives. This process is called evaluation and is the topic of concern in Chapter 13. Evaluation results in adjustments to the strategy when outcomes are not satisfactory, or in adjustments to goals when it seems appropriate to change organizational direction. Through evaluation, the overall educational enterprise is kept on target, made relevant, and improved.

Chapter 11
Strategic Planning

Strategic planning is one of the most common applications of systems theory at work in schools today, but the concept, like so many of the concepts we have discussed and will discuss in this book, is going through a transformation caused by the growing influence and disappointing results of postpositivist thinking in the social sciences. Initially, under the influence of positivist thinking (see discussion in Chapter 4), the focus was on the technology of planning; it was seen as a very logical and mechanistic process performed by "planning experts" *for* an organization or government. The outcome was a "plan" which was to be implemented by an organization or government. In large organizations and in national planning, "planners" were full-time employees, working out of a "planning office," usually reporting directly to the chief executive officer or head of government. The results were disappointing in that "the plan" was largely ignored by members of the organization or was unimplementable, leaving it to gather dust on the self (Weiler, 1980; Levin, 1980). Common sense told us

that, to be successful, an organization needed to have some conceptualization of its mission or purpose and to assess its environment for threats and opportunities that might interfere or facilitate realization of that mission. Indeed, successful organizations were doing just that, but not in the formally structured way described above (Peters & Waterman, 1982).

With insights generated by proponents of postpositivist philosophies, the human perceptual dimensions of planning were more clearly revealed. It became apparent that "the plan" was never implemented because it was based upon inaccurate assumptions about human behavior and there was no ownership of it by members of the organization; members of the organization envisioned multiple realities and "the plan" did not capture any of them because members had not contributed to the planning process. The actual steps in the planning process have not changed markedly, but the ways in which they are carried out have. The planning process is now intended to involve all members of the organization including those who are served by the organization—clients and customers—and, in the public sector, members of the community at large. Planning is now viewed as an integral function of management. Because of this pervasive view of planning, there is less likelihood of finding specific persons within an organization designated as "planners"; focus is on the process and not on the end product, the plan. Less emphasis is placed on the technology of planning.

Planning has always been considered a process designed to influence future events in a desired way through current actions. It is directed toward a future state that is desired, but which is not expected to happen unless some deliberate action is taken to facilitate its happening. Planning links useful knowledge with purposeful coordinated action. By means of planning, educational leaders are able to look ahead, formulate direction, anticipate events, map out activities, prepare for contingencies, and provide an orderly sequence for achieving desired goals (Cunningham, 1982, p. 4); it involves both leadership and management functions.

Russell Ackoff (1970, p. 1) defined wisdom as "the ability to see the long-run consequences of current actions, the willingness to sacrifice short-run gains for larger long-run benefits, and the ability to control what is controllable and not to fret over what is not." Planning helps to do this. While the essence of planning is concern with the future, the process is not satisfied with merely predicting the future—the objective is to *control* the future. Ackoff (1981) used the term *proactive futuring* to describe when an organization takes responsibility for its own future; rather than merely guessing as to what the future will bring, the organization balances the skills of anticipating the future and managing itself to attain its desired goals.

Planning is not only an activity, it is also an attitude or way of life; there is no natural conclusion or end point. Planning involves

processes, but more importantly, it is an orientation (bias) toward the future that permeates all decisionmaking. It is a dedication to acting in contemplation of the future; planning is anticipatory decisionmaking. In the new view, planning needs to be an integral part of the behavior of all persons in an organization, and especially of those formally responsible for providing leadership.

"Controlling" the Future

In actuality, we have less control over the present than we do the future. In the present, we can do little about our constraints, but over time, even constraints can be manipulated. With respect to school organization, there are limited opportunities to bring about immediate meaningful change. The staff is already hired and socialized into a specific mindset; the curriculum is in place; the books have been published, purchased, and are placed on the shelf or in the hands of students; the buildings are built and equipped. The children are born and, in too many instances, have been seriously harmed by the ravages of poverty, unwise parenting, and unwholesome social conditions. The future prospects of the unborn child, however, can be enhanced by acting now to improve the prenatal diet and behavior of the mother to reduce the effects of malnutrition and drug abuse on the fetus. We can provide counseling in wise parenting skills and develop support structures for new parents. We can make decent housing available in wholesome communities. We can reorient and reorganize existing school staffs to new and more effective educational approaches. We can change teacher and administrator preparation programs. We can design and implement new curricula. We can write new books and computer software. We can design new buildings incorporating information networks within them.

Planning is required when the future state we desire involves a set of independent decisions, i.e., a system of decisions. The principal complexity in planning derives from the interrelatedness of the decisions rather than the decisions themselves (Ackoff, 1970). Without systemic planning and implementation, however, our desired future is not likely to happen. Random incrementalism remains in control with school officials accepting their constraints as inevitable and functioning within those limitations; school officials work in isolation from social workers, community planners, and the health science industry as if they hold no relevance to the successful education of children. In the absence of systemic planning, we are likely to continue to experience our past failures.

We cannot continue to experience past failures if we desire to survive as a civilization. In Chapter 3 we identified many changes within our human environment that are forcing change in our schools and in our conceptualization of an educated person. Let's now relate the magnitude of that change with some "graphic" illustrations.

The twentieth century has been referred to as "the century of the J-curve" because rates of change in technology and in certain demographic attributes have been increasing exponentially (Anderson, undated). A typical J-curve is illustrated in Figure 11.1(a). Over much of the horizontal axis, change in the rate of increase is hardly perceptible; but then the rate rapidly accelerates until the graph becomes almost vertical. The curve prescribed resembles the letter "J": a line that is for a long time essentially horizontal suddenly bends and becomes almost vertical.

J-curves describe the rate of development of many aspects of the human condition and the twentieth century marks the point at which the rate of change suddenly accelerated. As we enter the twenty-first century, we are on the near vertical section of the curve. Several examples are given in Figure 11.1. Figure 11.1(b) traces the growth in world population. For most of human history, there were fewer than 500 million persons on the face of the earth. As we entered the twentieth century, there were a little over a billion people, and now, a century later, there are nearly six billion people and the population continues to grow. Part of this growth comes from increases in life expectancy, illustrated in Figure 11.1(c), due to improvements in medical technology and sanitary conditions. Few individuals reached the ripe old age of 40 for most of human history; now the average life expectancy is over age 70.

The "information explosion" is reflected in Figure 11.1(d) showing the total number of books published. The dramatic increase in knowledge is causing us to redefine what we mean by an educated person and to rethink how individuals are prepared to process knowledge. One of the factors contributing to the emerging "global village" is an increase in travel speed, illustrated in Figure 11.1f. Recall that throughout most of human history, mankind depended on self-locomotion; it wasn't until the nineteenth century that we began to turn to mechanical devices. Increases in the speed of transmission of information are even more dramatic. Figure 11.1(e), the increase in explosive power, illustrates the growing danger in which we all live.

When human events were developing along the horizontal portion of the curve, planning for the long term was not as critical as it is today because the tomorrows were very similar to the yesterdays. But now that many factors that strongly influence our lives are changing at accelerating rates along the vertical section of the curve, long-range (or strategic) planning has become essential. Our yesterdays are no longer accurate predictors of our tomorrows. The institutions that served us well yesterday are very likely to be inappropriate for meeting our emerging needs.

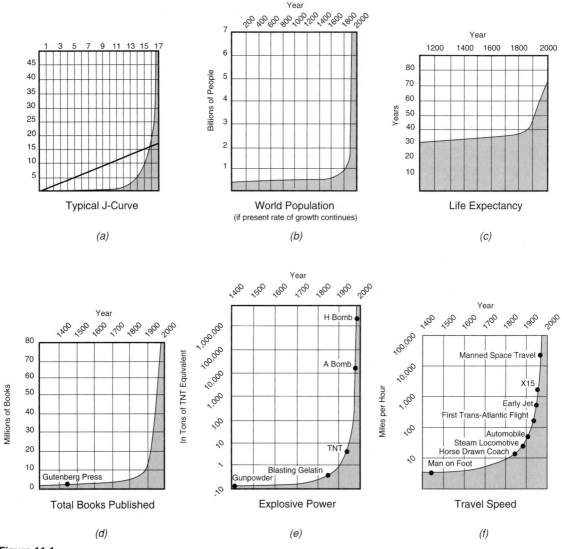

Figure 11.1
Human phenomena developing along a J-curve
SOURCE: L. Anderson. The Century of the J-Curve. Published in *Our World*, AFS Intercultural Programs, p. 13–14, undated.

Models of Planning

Adams (1991) categorized planning models into two general groups: rational and interactive. The rational group includes synoptic, resource allocation, manpower, rate-of-

return, and satisficing models. All emerged from a positivist philosophy and include the four classical elements of goal-setting, gap analysis, identification and evaluation of alternative means, and implementation of decisions. Interactive models grow out of post-positivist philosophies (e.g., critical theory and constructivism) and include political systems, incremental, organizational development, advocacy development, transactive, learning-adaptive, and mixed scanning models. Interactive models offer "a less precise and less quantifiable method for addressing ill-defined problems like those found in most social systems" (p. 9). The concept of planning varies from planning *for* people in the rational group to planning *with* people and *by* people in the interactive group.

Figure 11.2 was designed by Adams (1991) to illustrate where the planning model groups are located on a subjective/objective axis.

> *The objective paradigm incorporates the positivist assumptions of a value-free social and physical sciences, in which scientists are outside the orderly world being examined. In contrast, the subjective paradigm has, at its core, the notion that individuals create the world in which they live, and that any understanding of society, its institutions and its emergent social processes, depends on the vantage point of the participant. The distinc-*

> *tions implied by location along an objective/subjective dimension highlight the differences in rational and interactive models of planning. (pp. 12–13)*

The rational models, which assume the sufficiency and neutrality of expert knowledge and conceive of implementation as the execution of a plan, are limited in relevancy to such educational problems as enrollment projections, building construction, space allocation, pupil scheduling, transportation scheduling, and financial analysis. The interactive group includes both political and consensual models. In their purest form, political models reject the assumption of rational decision-making and view planning as a dynamic process of interaction and exchange involving bargaining, negotiations, and the exercise of power. Consensual models assume that legitimate action is based upon understanding and agreement among those involved. Communication is seen as fundamental to keeping the planning process moving—not political power, adversarial bargaining, or expert knowledge. The current interest in educa-

Figure 11.2
Models of educational planning
SOURCE: D. Adams. (1991). In Robert V. Carlson & Gary Awkerman (Eds.), *Educational Planning: Concepts, Strategies and Practices.* Fig. 1.1, p. 13. Copyright 1991.

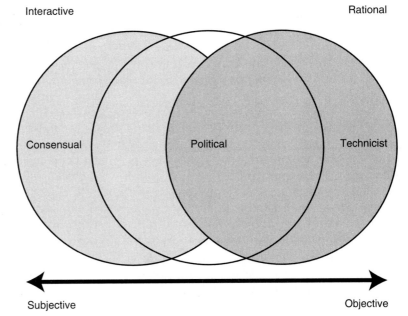

Interactive   Rational

Consensual   Political   Technicist

Subjective   Objective

tional reform provides a window of opportunity for developing new ways of viewing planning as an essential activity (Hamilton, 1991). The discussion of planning that follows assumes a central location on the subjective/objective axis in the area labeled "Political."

The Structure of the Planning Process

Planning, as conceptualized here, is a regular and continuous *social and political process*. It recognizes that individuals within the organization are constantly balancing their interests with those of the group (Lotto & Clark, 1986). Through negotiations, the preferences and activities of the organizational stakeholders are ordered and reordered, singularly and in groups. Underlying the process is a basic assumption that people who will be affected by a proposed plan will be extensively involved in its development because all members of the organization have relevant expertise, which will be translated into a better plan; also, the plan is more likely to be successfully implemented due to its enhanced pertinency and the sense of ownership on the part of stakeholders generated by involvement. The process produces a communal vision and understanding of the organization by its members.

Conceptually, planning is divided into two phases: its long-term aspects—*strategic* planning—and its short-term aspects—*tactical* planning. Strategic planning is that which is done to ensure that the organization is doing the right things. It involves visioning, mission setting, and goal development. Strategic planning is a function normally associated with leadership, providing an organization with direction; it is concerned with change and development. Tactical planning—also called *operational planning*—is a function normally associated with management, expressing the organizational concern over doing things right. It specifies the operations of the organization in the short term and monitors performance and results using criteria established in the strategic plan.

Figure 11.3 illustrates Steiner's (1979) conceptual model of the structure and process of systemic corporate planning and shows the division between strategic and tactical planning. Steiner is one of the seminal thinkers on corporate planning; his work is directed primarily to the private sector, but several adaptations of his model have been made to education, including those by Lewis (1983) and Cook (1990). In Steiner's model, strategic planning takes into account the expectations of major interests inside and outside the organization. It involves a database that describes past performance and the current situation and enables the forecasting of future conditions. Opportunities and threats posed by the environment are identified and the strengths and weaknesses of the organization in responding to those opportunities and threats are evaluated. Mission, purposes, and goals of the organization are established and master strategies are agreed upon. Tactical planning focuses on the design and evaluation of current operations within the context of strategic considerations. It includes the development of medium- and short-range planning and plans, implementation of plans, and review and assessment of the results against strategic goals.

In applying concepts developed in the private sector to the public sector, it is important to keep in mind the significant differences between the two sectors. The great majority of business decisions are dominated by economic factors, while decisions made by governments are hammered out on "the political anvil" (Steiner, 1979, p. 321). The singular focus of business simplifies the evaluation of alternative strategies. By its very nature, politics is pluralistic, resulting in numerous criteria that have to be satisfied by a given policy.

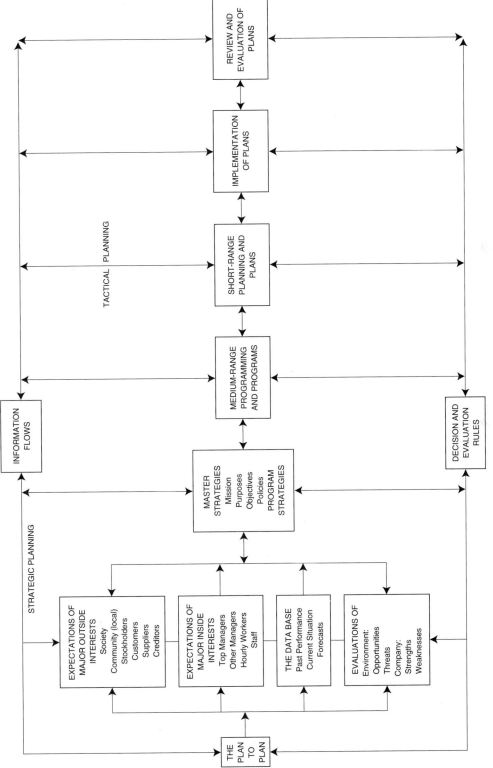

REVIEW AND EVALUATION OF PLANS

IMPLEMENTATION OF PLANS

SHORT-RANGE PLANNING AND PLANS

TACTICAL PLANNING

MEDIUM-RANGE PROGRAMMING AND PROGRAMS

INFORMATION FLOWS

DECISION AND EVALUATION RULES

MASTER STRATEGIES
Mission
Purposes
Objectives
Policies
PROGRAM STRATEGIES

STRATEGIC PLANNING

EXPECTATIONS OF MAJOR OUTSIDE INTERESTS
Society
Community (local)
Stockholders
Customers
Suppliers
Creditors

EXPECTATIONS OF MAJOR INSIDE INTERESTS
Top Managers
Other Managers
Hourly Workers
Staff

THE DATA BASE
Past Performance
Current Situation
Forecasts

EVALUATIONS OF
Environment:
Opportunities
Threats
Company:
Strengths
Weaknesses

THE PLAN TO PLAN

Figure 11.3
Structure and process of business companywide planning
SOURCE: G. A. Steiner. *Strategic Planning.* Exhibit 2-1, p. 17. Copyright 1979.

The "payoff" of a new program has to come before the next election for politicians, i.e., in two to four years; for business people it may take longer. Nevertheless, there are important similarities. Governments as well as businesses need to come to collective decisions; both are focused on survival and need to adjust to their respective environments. Both are managing scarce resources. Although the signals are not as clear in the public sector, there are pressures on government to be efficient, to maximize service, and to minimize taxes. We concur with Steiner's conclusion that management in the public and private sectors is more similar than dissimilar.

Cunningham's (1982) conception of strategic planning as applied to school districts is illustrated in Figure 11.4. He shows the planning process revolving around eight key questions:

1. *Where are we?*
2. *Where do we want to go?*
3. *What resources will we commit to get there?*
4. *How do we get there?*
5. *When will it be done?*
6. *Who will be responsible?*
7. *What will be the impact on human resources?*
8. *What data will be needed to measure progress? (p. 9)*

Determining "where we are" requires a self-assessment by the school district of the programs and services it offers, the strengths, weaknesses and adequacies of its staff and facilities, resources available in the community, and challenges being made to the status quo by internal weaknesses and trends, external community conditions, pressures exerted by external community interest groups, and by forces at the state and national levels. Within the documented social, political, and economic environments, district personnel realistically appraise the district's capabilities to meet the challenges before it, given the

resources available to it and the expectations of its citizens and staff. District personnel need to be proactive in looking for opportunities to serve its clients according to highest professional standards even when those standards are beyond the expectation or comprehension of its clients.

"Where we want to go" is expressed by the district's statements of missions, goals, and strategic objectives. The district's mission and goals express the nature of programs and services desired by the community, parents, students, and the profession. The strategic policy and objectives address in general terms the means for moving the district from where it is to where it desires to be.

The transition from strategic to operational (tactical) planning occurs in consideration of Cunningham's third question, commitment of resources. Annual operating budgets constitute an integral part of the operational plan, but they need to be developed under the umbrella of the district's strategic financial plan. The issues of where we are and where we want to be are also considered to be strategic in nature.

Entering into tactical (or operational) planning, the time frame shifts from several years to one year or less. Strategic policies and objectives are translated into operational objectives, programs, procedures, and projects for immediate implementation. Performance objectives are set and tasks are assigned in response to question 4, "how do we get there?" Deadlines are established (question 5, "when will it be done?") and responsibilities for meeting those deadlines in the manner specified are placed with specific individuals (question 6, "who will be responsible?").

New programs, projects and directions frequently require new skills and new organizational configurations. The members of the district must be well prepared to deal with such changes or serious morale problems may develop, damaging the ability of the dis-

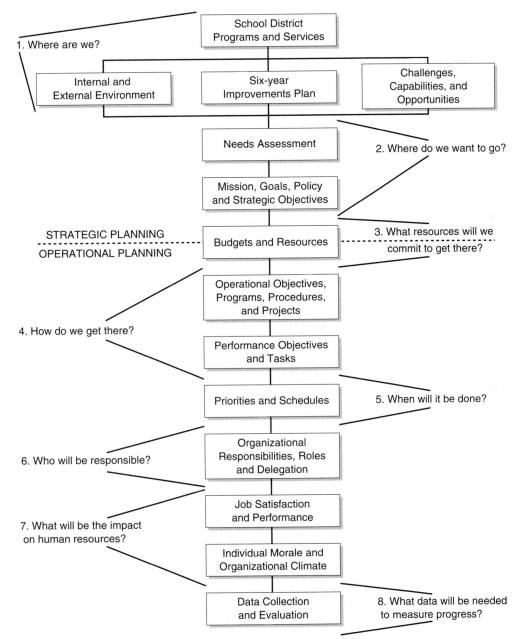

Figure 11.4
The planning process
SOURCE: William G. Cunningham. *Systematic Planning for Educational Change.* Fig. 1-2, p. 11. Copyright 1982.

trict to reach its goals. Providing those implementing the plan with the necessary knowledge and skills may require an extensive staff development program (responding to Cunningham's question 7, "what will be the impact on human resources?").

Evaluation of the success of the strategy comes at the end of a planning cycle, but deciding what data need to be collected to monitor success needs to be done before implementation begins. Measuring progress requires knowing the state of affairs before the plan was put into place; such information should have been part of the self assessment made at the beginning of the strategic planning process. By comparing the state of affairs periodically after implementation with the state of affairs prior to implementation, progress made toward district goals can be monitored. If progress is unsatisfactory, corrective measures need to be taken in future operational plans; and the strategic plan itself needs to be evaluated every few years to make sure that changing conditions have not rendered it obsolete.

Strategic Planning

The greatest strength of strategic planning is that it forces organizational decisionmakers to focus on current and future conditions in systemic ways. (See the related discussion of educational change in Chapter 16.) It considers the organization as a system with numerous quasi-independent subsystems. Strategic planning provides a mechanism for coordinating those subsystems in a manner that allows those subsystems maximum independence without sacrificing the welfare of the whole. The sum of solutions to individual parts of a problem is rarely equivalent to the best solution for the whole organization.

Systemic planning introduces new forces and tools into the decisionmaking process. For example, strategic planning can simulate

the future on paper. It encourages members of the organization to consider and evaluate alternative courses of action—even radical courses of action—that would not otherwise be considered because the cost of modeling them on paper is minimal while the cost of actual implementation is great.

The process asks and answers some key questions in a way that might otherwise be easily overlooked and establishes a scale of priority and urgency for dealing with the answers. What is our basic line of business? (Are we to offer children an *opportunity* to learn? Or, are we to *assume responsibility* for their learning?) What are our underlying values, philosophies and purposes? (Do we believe that every child can learn? Or do we believe that a child's ability to learn is largely conditioned by genetics and social circumstances? How committed are we to the principle of equity?) What are our long- and short-range objectives? What major changes are taking place in the environment that will affect us? (How relevant is our curriculum to contemporary society?) What resources will be available to us over the next several years? What opportunities or threats exist in the years ahead that we should exploit or avoid? (Adapted from Steiner, 1979, p. 36.)

Strategic planning provides guidance to members of the organization in making decisions that are consistent with the aims and strategies agreed upon for the organization. The members are thus better able to spend their time on activities that "pay off." Planning also provides an effective means of control. Resources can be allocated according to specified organizational priorities and accomplishments can be measured against carefully established criteria which are qualitative as well as quantitative in nature.

A well-organized planning system can provide an extremely useful communications network that links together all members of the organization. As plans approach completion, common understandings are generated about opportunities and problems that are important to individuals and to the organization.

> *The choices made in the planning process are discussed in a common language and the issues are understood (or should be) by all those participating in decision making. Once plans are completed and written there should be a permanent and clear record of decisions made, who is going to implement them, and how they should be carried out. Such a communication system is a valuable asset to any organization. (Steiner, 1979, p. 42)*

Improved employee motivation and morale and community support are potential by-products of strategic planning. Being involved in formulating organizational plans promotes a sense of satisfaction among participants gained from helping to shape—at least in part—their own destiny within the organization. Knowing what is expected of organizational members builds a sense of personal security and confidence. Taken together, these improved attitudes enable people to accept change more readily, a valuable attribute in any organization.

Figure 11.5 illustrates another way of representing strategic planning as it might be implemented in an educational organization. It is important to keep in mind that any general planning model—of which there are many—must be adapted to the specific circumstances under which it will be applied. A planning process for a school district must be different from that for a school. The process and format for a high school must be different from that for an elementary school; and the processes and formats will vary among elementary schools and high schools. The elements of the process illustrated by Figure 11.5 include a statement of beliefs and values, a statement of mission, strategic policies, an analysis of internal and external factors, a gap analysis, strategic objectives, and action plans. Figure 11.5 incorporates ideas about planning expressed by Steiner (1979), Cunning-

ham (1982), Lewis (1983), Cook (1990), and others.

Direction Setting. Direction setting involves establishing a vision for a school or district that includes an understanding of organizational beliefs, its mission, and the establishment of strategic policies. A vision is a mental image of a possible and desirable future state for the organization (Bennis & Nanus, 1985). It can be as vague as a dream or as precise as a goal or mission statement. The vision, however developed, must permeate the organization, being embedded in its structures and processes so that it shapes its operation and every decision made (Caldwell & Spinks, 1988). It creates a "consistency of purpose" throughout the organization (Deming, 1986).

Common beliefs held by members of the organization represent one of its primary bonding forces. The statement of beliefs is a formal expression of those fundamental principles that guide all district (or other unit, such as a school) decisions and activities. It describes the organization's moral character—its ethical code. The statement provides the value basis upon which subsequent portions of the planning process will develop and implementation will be evaluated; it is a public declaration of the moral essence of the district (Cook, 1990).

Articulating the beliefs of the organization is perhaps the most important part of the planning process. In their study of America's best-run companies, Peters and Waterman (1982) noted that, even though many of the companies did not follow a formal planning process, they all exhibited a values set that was shared by all members of the company. Peters (1988, p. 398) pointed out that "Effective leadership—at all levels—is marked by a core philosophy (values) and a vision of how the enterprise (or department) wishes to make its mark." Peters also stressed the importance of recruiting persons to the orga-

Figure 11.5
A schema of the strategic plan-
ning process as applied to
schools and school districts

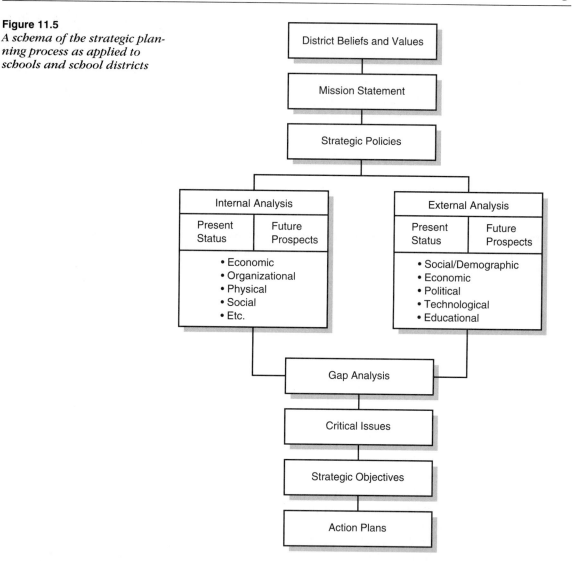

nization who share the organizational values. He acknowledged that to do so, an organization must know what its values are; but, unfortunately, most do not. The strategic planning process provides a natural opportunity for articulating organizational values, a step that can lead to desirable repercussions throughout the organization.

Developing a statement of beliefs begins with what Goodstein, Nolan, and Pfeiffer (1992) call a *value scan*. It examines the personal values of those assigned to do the scan, the current values of the organization, the organization's philosophy of operations, the assumptions that usually guide the organization's operations, the organization's preferred culture, and the values of the stakeholders in the organization's future. (See the related discussion of values analysis in Chapter 4.) In conducting the values scan, the planning team moves from an individual focus to a broader examination of the organization and how it works as a social system. It focuses attention on the frequently unacknowledged underpinnings that guide the behaviors and decisions of organization members and, thereby, the organizational culture. Figure 11.6 illustrates a set of belief statements as developed by the West Seneca, New York, Central School District.

The mission statement is a clear and concise expression of the district's purpose and function. It should be a bold declaration of what the organization aspires to be. The mission statement should address the specific, local situation and represent the uniqueness of the district (school). Mission statements don't have to be feasible, only desirable. Missions exist at the boundary between the organization and its environment; they represent expectations that constituents have for the organization (O'Brien, 1991). The mission is the focus toward which the planning process is directed. Every person in the organization should know and understand it; it frequently is the only formal statement of the organization's vision. Figure 11.7 presents the mission statement for the West Seneca, New York, Central School District. Figure 11.8 presents the mission statement for the Maple West Elementary School.

Defining a district's mission is closely akin to what Drucker (1974) referred to as "knowing your business." According to Drucker, management must decide, "What is our business and what should it be?" He argued that it is only upon the foundation of the basic purposes and missions of the company that more

Figure 11.6
Belief statements of the West Seneca, New York, Central School District

BELIEFS

We believe that . . .

Excellence in education cannot be compromised.

Each student can learn and is entitled to an equal opportunity to reach his/her potential.

All members of the community have life-long educational needs.

Education is student centered.

A safe environment is essential.

A fundamental responsibility of the school community is to create and maintain an environment to foster the dignity and self-esteem of students, parents, and staff.

Discipline is essential.

Education is broad-based, encompassing intellectual, emotional, physical, and social growth.

Education promotes behaviors, attitudes and values inherent in a democratic society.

Learning is challenging, exciting, and rewarding.

Our educational system is vital to the community.

Education requires the responsible commitment of students, staff, parents, and the community at large.

All members of the school community serve as role models.

Open communication with the community is essential.

Open communication within the educational system is essential.

Figure 11.7
Mission statement of the West Seneca, New York, Central School District

MISSION

The mission of the West Seneca Central School District is to provide, under the guidance of a competent and committed staff and a supportive community, a diversified educational program which will produce literate, caring, responsible, and productive citizens who demonstrate positive ethical beliefs, possess self-discipline, exhibit dignity of character, and are capable of adapting to change.

Figure 11.8
Mission statement of the Maple West Elementary School

MISSION STATEMENT
MAPLE WEST ELEMENTARY

Our mission at Maple West Elementary is to be responsible for the preparation of children for the future by providing an educational setting that has a nurturing environment where learning is valued, individual differences accepted, and potential maximized.

detailed objectives, strategies, and tactical plans can be worked out. School districts often labor under the mistaken assumptions that their missions are rigidly set by law. In actuality, they have considerable flexibility and defining its mission enables a district to become emancipated from common preconceptions and to focus on a common purpose.

Strategic policies establish the parameters within which the district will operate. They specify the postures that the district will either always take, or never take. Policies act to channel thinking and to serve as guides to action. They set constraints within which discretion can be exercised. By adding the modifier, "strategic," the bulk of district policy that deals with the routine of daily operations is eliminated from consideration. Cook (1990, p. 96) asserted that strategic policies "establish 'ground rules'; set in place protective mechanisms, ratios, formulas, and the like; dictate codes of behavior; define expectations; assert priorities; and define various boundaries." Policies focus the mission statement and prevent over-zealous pursuit of

them. Figure 11.9 illustrates strategic policies as developed by the West Seneca, New York, Central School District.

Internal and External Analyses. The internal analysis consists of a thorough and unbiased examination of the current and projected strengths and weaknesses of the district (school). Strengths are internal qualities, circumstances, or conditions that contribute to the district's ability to achieve its mission with respect to such attributes as financial, personnel, organizational, physical, and social characteristics. Strengths relative to similar organizations are not of particular interest here, but rather, strengths relative to the potential for accomplishing the district's (school's) mission. Strengths signal areas in which success may be most easily realized. Weaknesses, conversely, are internal qualities, circumstances, or conditions that impede the realization of the district's (school's) mission.

Data for the internal analysis are drawn from the district's information system. Lewis (1983) suggested that the information data

Figure 11.9
Strategic policy of the West Seneca, New York, Central School District

```
┌─────────────────────────────────────────────────────────┐
│                    STRATEGIC POLICIES                      │
│                                                            │
│   No student will be automatically promoted.               │
│                                                            │
│   No curriculum will be implemented or modified without    │
│   the input of the staff who will be required to teach it. │
│                                                            │
│   We will never add or eliminate programs without          │
│   careful analysis.                                        │
│                                                            │
│   We will always provide programs which will assist all    │
│   employees to perform more effectively.                   │
│                                                            │
│   Each employee will be evaluated and no employee will be  │
│   granted permanent status unless he/she achieves an       │
│   above-average rating.                                    │
│                                                            │
│   No student will participate in any extracurricular       │
│   activity who does not satisfy the eligibility            │
│   requirements for that activity.                          │
│                                                            │
│   We will not compromise health and safety laws.           │
│                                                            │
└─────────────────────────────────────────────────────────┘
```

base include data on: student characteristics, community characteristics, student learning and growth, faculty characteristics, programs and services, finance, school and district problems, and stakeholder characteristics. Information is needed, not only on the current situation, but also on the human and financial resources used in the past and the behaviors and accomplishments of students.

The external analysis looks beyond the district (school) into its environment and into its possible futures, predicting events and conditions likely to occur that will have a significant impact on the district. The purpose of the external analysis is to prevent surprises that may negatively affect the district's (school's) ability to accomplish its mission and to identify opportunities the district may wish to exploit. The analysis needs to deal with five categories of influence: social and demographic (e.g., family stability or instability, family structure, social structure, unemployment, general level of education, crime rate, size and composition of the population); economic (e.g., size of tax base, employment rate, salary levels); political (e.g., agendas of special interest groups); technological, scientific and environmental (e.g., new inventions

that may affect instruction or the life and employment of students, knowledge about human development and how people learn); and educational trends and influences (Cook, 1992, p. 105).

Gap Analysis. The gap analysis juxtaposes the internal and external analyses against the district's (school's) mission. Data, past, present, and future, are analyzed in a fashion that provides a rationale for the formulation of operating objectives and strategic commitment of resources. Organizations always represent states of inadequacy—the gap between the way things are and the way we want things to be at some future instance (Hodgkinson, 1991).

The gap analysis emphasizes the importance of systemic assessment of environmental impacts. Its major objective is to identify and analyze the key trends, forces, and phenomena having a potential impact on formulating and implementing strategies. It provides a forum for sharing and debating divergent views about relevant environmental changes enabling vague opinions about different parts of the analysis to be made more explicit (Steiner, 1979). According to Steiner,

Figure 11.10
Strategic objectives of the West Seneca, New York, School District, 1990–1995

STRATEGIC OBJECTIVES

By June 1992, increase by 50% the number of people who have a positive perception of the West Seneca Central School District.

By the year 1993, 90% of our students will participate in at least one human service project annually.

By June 1994, 100% of our students will perform at their expected achievement level.

To have 100% of our students, within six months after graduation, either gainfully employed or enrolled in an institution of higher learning.

---

such an analysis is not something that can or should be completed in the planning process solely on a formal basis. It should be done continuously in the personal surveillance of environments by individual managers and other personnel. This type of environmental scanning is performed in a variety of ways from reading journals systematically to conversing casually with fellow professionals.

Coming out of the gap analysis is an identification of critical issues that must be dealt with if the organization is to survive or re-create itself within the context of its own stated mission. Identifying critical issues focuses attention on paramount threats and opportunities, thereby providing a compelling rationale for the strategic deployment of resources (Cook, 1990).

Strategic Objectives. Objectives are statements that commit the organization to the achievement of specific, measurable end results. They spring from the mission statement and define it in measurable terms. The objectives are what the district must achieve if it is to accomplish its mission and be true to its beliefs. Cook (1990) observes that most school districts experience difficulty in writing suitable objectives because most educators seem to be more process-oriented than

results-oriented. True objectives create risks and impose accountability.

Awkerman (1991) warned that, in planning, we must clearly differentiate between means and ends. Too frequently we confuse the objectives of schools and school districts by expressing them in terms of means rather than ends. For example, we set goals for raising teachers' salaries or lowering class size when our true interest is in improving achievement or reducing dropout rates. Our assumption is that raising teachers' salaries will improve the caliber of teacher the district can hire which, in turn, will have a positive effect on student achievement and retention. The truth is that the linkage among teachers' salaries, class size, and retention is, at best, tenuous and there are other *means* that should be considered for reaching the desired *ends*. "The greater the clarity of a desired end, the greater the probability that any selected means will accomplish the same desired ends" (Awkerman, 1991, p. 206). Strategic objectives for the West Seneca, New York, Central School district are illustrated in Figure 11.10.

The strategic objectives list does not address all of the outcomes for which a district (school) is responsible. It only includes those that are to receive highest priority in the immediate future. The list will change over time as strategic objectives are realized or as they are replaced by more urgent concerns.

Integrated Action Plans. Integrated action plans are the means by which a district (school) will accomplish its objectives and thereby realize its mission. They specify the deployment of the district's resources in the quest of the district's (school's) mission. They indicate the district's basic operational emphasis, its priorities, and the standards by which it will measure its own performance. They need to be conceptually stated and allow for practical flexibility as they are translated into action.

The development of integrated action plans marks the transition from strategic to tactical planning and will be discussed more fully in the next section. Action plans provide detailed descriptions of specific actions required in the short term to achieve specific results necessary for the implementation of the strategic plan. They also address the ongoing business of the district (school) in keeping with the statements of beliefs, mission, and strategic policies, and giving special attention to strategic objectives. An effective action plan is conceived and written from an operations point of view. The content is predicated on progressive, direct cause and effect relationships and is immediately workable.

TACTICAL PLANNING AND BUDGETING

Strategic planning is clearly a function of leadership while tactical planning is a function of management. Tactical, or operational, planning is a process by which managers ensure that resources are obtained and used effectively and efficiently in the accomplishment of the organization's missions and goals (Cunningham, 1982, p. 12). Because of their focus

on operations, the instructional and service units initiate tactical planning. Figure 11.11 illustrates possible programmatic divisions for elementary and secondary schools. These include not only the expected instructional programs, but also support services such as administration, maintenance of building and grounds, food service, transportation, and new initiatives established in the strategic plan.

Perhaps the best way to describe tactical planning is to contrast it with strategic planning. Table 11.1, from Cunningham (1982, p. 15), summarizes the differences. While principals, teachers, students, and members of the community may be involved in strategic planning, the process is initiated and controlled by the policy makers of the district, the board of education, and the superintendent. It is top-down planning. Tactical planning, on the other hand, is a decentralized process that takes place within the framework established by the strategic planning process. Principals, supervisors, department heads, and teachers are the primary participants; it is bottom-up planning.

Tactical planning is bureaucratic in spirit; strategic planning is entrepreneurial. Tactical planning focuses on current operating problems and realities in order to improve present performance while strategic planning is directed toward long-term survival and development in order to ensure future school system success. Unlike strategic planning, tactical planning is constrained by present conditions and resources. Tactical planning seeks to maintain efficiency and stability in the organization while strategic planning seeks to change it in order to develop future potential and flexibility. Tactical planning is based on information concerning teacher, parent, and student conditions. Strategic planning uses such information as a base line for making projections of future conditions, desires and values.

Figure 11.11
Sample program structures for elementary and secondary schools

AN ELEMENTARY SCHOOL

Kindergarten   Early Intervention
Primary Grades, 1–3   Special Education
Intermediate Grades, 4–6   Computer Studies
Art   Administration
Music   Food Service
Physical Education   Operations and Maintenance
Library and Media Center   Co-curricular Activities

A SECONDARY SCHOOL

English   Computer Studies
Mathematics   Special Education
Social Studies   Co-curricular Activities
Science   Administration
Business Studies   Food Service
Foreign Languages   Operations and Maintenance
History   Technology
Physical Education   Art
Music   Inter-scholastic Sports

The leadership style that is most compatible with tactical planning is conservative, placing high priority on that which has succeeded in the past. The leadership style most compatible with strategic planning is visionary, inspiring change to meet future needs. Tactical planning is oriented to solving problems through standard operating procedures that have been successful in the past. Strategic planning is more prone to approach problem solving with new techniques and ideas. Tactical planning is designed to minimize risk. Because of the great uncertainty associated with possible future events, strategic planning involves high risks, but the risks can be managed through continual monitoring and adjustments.

Budgeting is an integral part of tactical planning; but, unfortunately, it is usually the only formal planning activity undertaken by most educational organizations. Typically,

financial constraints are emphasized to the exclusion of educational plans and mission.

The primary purpose of a budget is to translate a district's educational priorities and programs into financial terms within the context of available resources and legal constraints. The important decisions of who gets what, when and how are made through this process. Within the public sector, the budget is a legally adopted document that presents planned expenditures and anticipated revenues for a given fiscal year. It is this legal emphasis on financial aspects of the budget that largely explains the neglect of its programmatic aspects (Hartman, 1988).

Figure 11.12 portrays the budgeting process as an equilateral triangle with the sides representing the three equally important dimensions of budgeting: developing the educational plan, estimating expenditures needed to implement the plan, and estimat-

Table 11.1
Differences in Perspectives

	Operational Planning Principals, Supervisors, Department Heads	Strategic Planning Superintendent, School Board, and Central Office Staff
Focus	Operating problems and realities	Longer-term survival and development
Objective	Present performance	Future school system success
Constraints	Present resources/ school environment	Future resources/ desired system-wide environment
Rewards	Efficiency, stability	Development of future potential, flexibility
Information	Present teacher, parent, and student reaction/facts	Future community, state, and federal desires/values
Organization	Bureaucratic/stable	Entrepreneurial/flexible
Leadership	Conserve that which succeeded in the past	Inspire change for future needs
Problem solving	React, rely on past experience, standard operating procedures	Anticipate, find new approaches, creative ideas to meet future challenges
	Low risk	Higher risk

SOURCE: William G. Cunningham. *Systematic Planning for Educational Change.* Table 2-1, p. 15. Copyright 1982.

ing resources that can reasonably be anticipated to support the plan. Budgeting should begin with the development of the educational plan, which is shown in the figure as the base of the triangle—that upon which the rest of the budget is built. The educational plan specifies the means by which the district's or school's goals and objectives will be realized and is developed through the strategic and tactical processes described above, particularly those pertaining to the action plans. The second step is to determine what resources will be required to implement the plan. The information necessary to make such estimates will have been generated through the strategic planning process by the external analysis of the district's self study. Once these two steps have been completed, it is time to compare resource requirements with anticipated revenues which are usually less than needed to fully implement the educational plan. The fourth step in the budgetary

process is to reconcile the educational, expenditure, and revenue plans. It is at this point that the district's mission, goals, priorities, and beliefs established in the strategic planning process become critical.

Figure 11.12
The budgetary triangle

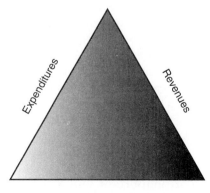

Educational Programs

Too frequently, budgets are developed, incrementally adding to the existing base without the guidance or direction provided by a strategic plan. This makes the resulting educational program more responsive to the pressures of special interest groups (e.g., teacher unions and taxpayer associations) than to professional judgment as to the educational experiences needed to be provided to children. Essentially, unstructured incrementalism results in a preservation of the status quo adjusted for price changes. Incrementalism within a strategic framework, however, over time, can lead to full implementation of the strategic plan.

In building the budget, and in reconciling it with available revenues, it is necessary to link the resources requested with strategic goals and objectives and the priorities given to them. Since the educational plan is usually built around specific instructional programs (i.e., reading, mathematics, science, music, physical education), it makes sense to build the budget around these same programs. District budgets are formed by aggregating the program budgets or the combined school budgets plus budgets of support programs that are district-wide such as instructional media and debt service.

Each program (i.e., instructional or service unit) should have at least one school or district policy that establishes it as a program and defines its purpose within the overall mission of the school or district. With the reality of constrained budgets, it is necessary to place these policies in some order of priority. Given that each school is likely to have 40 or 50 policies, and policies for the district may number 100 or more, it is unrealistic to expect that each policy can be ranked against every other priority. Caldwell and Spinks (1988) recommended that, instead, each policy be placed into one of three categories. All policies are important, but Priority 1 is of greater immediate urgency than Priority 2, and Priority 2 is of greater immediate urgency than Priority 3. Priorities are established each

year. A policy given a Priority 3 rating this year may be given a Priority 1 rating next year. Listing of the policy priorities is illustrated in Table 11.2 for the Rosebery District High School.

There are two schools of thought as to how to go about determining the resource needs for a school or district. One school says that the budget adopting authority (BAA) should provide each program with an approximate allocation amount in advance of the program beginning its budgeting process. The BAA has a fair idea of the total amount of resources that will become available from its external analysis; and it has good information on past resource requirements by programs from its internal analysis. It is argued that, not to give each program a tentative allocation amount will unrealistically inflate requests from programs beyond that which can be reasonably provided, make the reconciliation process more difficult, and lead to frustration because of dashed expectations on the part of programs.

The second school of thought would leave the programs free to design their operations in terms of the resources really required to obtain the goals and objectives expected of them. Proponents of the second school argue that the BAA will never truly know how much it will cost to reach school or district expectations if the programs are initially constrained in their planning with parameters unrelated to program objectives. Without such knowledge, the BAA lacks important evidence in lobbying for additional funds from local taxpayers, the state, and the federal government. The estimated cost of realizing expectations also provides those setting the expectations with some idea of how likely or unlikely it is that those expectations will be realized.

Either way, each program has to identify the resources it needs to conduct its operation in terms of teachers and other personnel, purchased services, equipment, supplies, space, etc. These are then converted into dollar amounts. According to the philosophy of

Table 11.2
Policy Priorities for the Rosebery District High School

Priority 1	Priority 2	Priority 3
Computer education	Arts and crafts	Art acquisition
Commercial education	Student assessment	Extra-curricular activities
Excursions	School certificate	Foreign language
Early intervention	Discipline	History
K–2 General studies	Drama festival	Home economics
3–6 General studies	Homework	House system
Language development	Handwriting	School assemblies
Learning to read	Journalism	Canteen
Technology	Kindergarten and preparatory education	Fund-raising
Mathematics	Music	
Physical education	Option subjects, 9–10	
Pastoral care	Preparing for school	
3–6 Regrouped language	Presentation Day	
Special education	Your Child's Report	
Sports	Social studies	
Technical subjects	Science	
Support services	Talented children	
Budget and planning	Transition education	
Teacher induction	Visual arts	
Communications	School magazine	
Decision-making	Buildings and grounds	
School council	Community bus	
	Curriculum resource	
	Staffing	
	Book sales	
	Administration	
	Formation of classes	
	School organization	
	Professional development	
	Public Relations	

SOURCE: B. J. Caldwell & J. M. Spinks. (1988). *The Self-Managing School.* p. 75.

the second school of thought, this is what would be submitted to the BAA. If allocation limits have been made according to the first school of thought, then the program will have to adjust its requests in such a fashion as to maximize its impact within those limits.

When faced with a prospective gap between revenues and expenditures, first thoughts usually turn toward decreasing expenditures through cutting programs or toward increasing revenue through raising taxes—neither of which is politically easy nor educationally desirable. The complexity of the situation, however, demands a more complete consideration of possible options.

As the budgeting process began with the educational plan, so should the reconciliation process. Numerous studies, to be reviewed in Chapter 12, indicate that schools are organized and run very inefficiently. Can the educational plan be implemented more efficiently permitting the district to realize its educational objectives with fewer resources? Can support services be organized more efficiently? While reexamining the educational plan, opportunities for special funding should also be identified. Aspects of the program may qualify for categorical aid from the state or federal governments or be of interest to foundations that have an educational mission. If the revenue/expenditure gap cannot be closed through more efficient operation or new funding, it is necessary to make program cuts or reductions within the parameters established by the strategic plan.

Once the BAA is satisfied that all program requests are reasonable given the objectives of the program, and total requests exceed available revenues, a strategy for reducing budgeted expenditures needs to be established. A simple strategy is to ask each program to take an across-the-board cut of, say, 3 percent. The problem with this approach is that, over a period of time, strong programs may be seriously weakened; or a weak but essential program is never provided with the resources necessary to overcome its weakness. A better strategy is to concentrate cuts in the Priority 3 category described above. This could mean the elimination of a nonessential program or the delay in implementing a new initiative. It could mean a larger cut of, say, 10 percent to all policies with a Priority 3 rating. When program funds are cut, persons implementing the program should be granted the authority to determine how the cuts should be distributed, e.g., personnel, equipment, supplies.

The budget is one of the primary management tools of educational administrators and the major one in the fiscal area. In addition to its importance to the planning process, for public schools, the budget serves as a vehicle for public review and approval. Once approved, the budget becomes the legal basis for spending funds. During the course of the year, the budget serves as a management control document, providing specific spending limits which are not to be exceeded without prior authorization. Through careful monitoring, overexpenditures can be avoided and compensation for possible revenue shortfall can be made at the earliest possible point allowing maximum flexibility for dealing with it (Hartman, 1988).

IMPLEMENTING PLANNING

It is generally agreed that for the planning process to function properly, strategic planning must precede tactical planning and it must originate with top management and policy makers, i.e., the board of education and central office administrators. The nature of the responsibilities of these officials is to focus their daily attention on political, economic, and social forces acting upon the school district. This orientation should make them well prepared to develop strategic objectives needed to provide direction to future operational activities. The strategic plan establishes the destination of the organization and sets the parameters within which tactical plans can be developed; tactical plans are the steps that eventually lead the district to that destination. Without a strategic plan, annual tactical plans will be without direction, leading nowhere and thereby reconfirming the status quo. Within the context of a strategic plan, even modest increments in tactical plans can result in revolutionary changes in time.

For strategic planning to succeed, the school board and the superintendent must give their wholehearted endorsement to the process and be significantly and visibly involved. As a matter of fact, initiating and monitoring the strategic planning process (i.e., providing vision and direction to the district) is probably the greatest single responsibility of the superintendent. Participation in the process is an effective means of exercising leadership in the district.

The responsibility for tactical planning is placed with line administrators, who have intimate understandings of the intricacies of day-to-day operations. In splitting the planning function, the basis for a two-way discourse is established. The discussion is initiated at the center that establishes the framework and sets the parameters in which tactical planning takes place. The detailed plans are developed by line administrators within the context provided by the center which are, in turn, reviewed by the center to make sure that they are truly consistent with the established guidelines.

Although there is still considerable debate, both research and experience suggest that the planning process works best when it flows from top to bottom. Strategic plans developed at the top more appropriately meet the long-term survival and development needs of the organization, while operational plans that are coordinated and focused by strategic plans better meet the operational realities that school administrators and teachers must face on a daily basis. (Cunningham, 1982, p. 17)

The top-down, bottom-up approach requires much less need to modify and change plans developed at the operational level. When operational plans are initiated at the bottom in the absence of a strategic plan, major modifications are usually required through the review by top administrators due to incongruous goals and lack of organizational perspective. Frequent and major modifications place in question the efficacy of the entire planning process and encourage an attitude of cynicism throughout the organization.

There is general agreement that the superintendent is the key player in strategic planning at the district level, but the role may be enacted in numerous ways. The superintendent must make sure that the climate for effective strategic planning is established and maintained and that the "plan to plan" is proper for the system. It is the superintendent's responsibility to determine if the coordination of the planning process should be assigned to another office. If the job is assigned, the planner should report directly to the superintendent and the superintendent should preside over the writing of the job description for the position. The superintendent is more likely to be directly involved in the planning process when it is first introduced into the system than in later cycles when the process has been perfected and integrated into the organizational culture. Even if the planning function is delegated, the superintendent must remain visibly involved to display interest, concern, and commitment.

The superintendent should meet face to face with middle managers (principals and service department directors) to discuss the tactical plans they have prepared. This is an effective means of conveying the superintendent's interest and commitment to the planning process and it keeps the superintendent better informed of the plans and provides a better basis for accepting, rejecting, or modifying them. Finally, it is the superintendent who should keep the board of education appraised of developments in the planning process and in implementation.

Strategic Planning at the School Level

The above discussion on strategic planning is focused primarily at the school district level; however, much is applicable to school-based planning. Within a district planning scheme, the school is likely to be viewed as a program—one of the quasi-independent units within the system. With the growing practice of school-based management, schools, themselves, are becoming the primary planning unit. This practice is relatively new in the United States, but is practiced extensively in England and Australia where a valuable experience base has developed. One of the school-based management models that has received wide attention in those countries, and to some degree in the United States and Canada, is Caldwell and Spink's (1992) Model for Self-Management. We feel that it offers an appropriate guide for American schools and will describe it in some detail.

The Model for Self-Management (MSM) is illustrated in Figure 11.13. It integrates the annual management functions of design, budgeting, implementing, and evaluating with the strategic governance functions of direction and priority setting and policy making. MSM focuses on the central function of schools—learning and teaching—and is designed to involve administrators, teachers, and other staff, students, parents, and other members of the community. The management of the school is organized around "programs" that correspond to the preferred patterns of work in the school.

MSM attempts to dispel the confusion created by the simultaneous shifts in authority toward centralization of some decisions (e.g., state curricular mandates, standards, and assessment) and decentralization of others (e.g., school-based management and school community empowerment). It acknowledges the influence of central authority, be it federal or state government or local school district,

through the "Central Framework" and the "Charter." "Policies" and "Development Plan" are the points where the laws and regulations within which each school must operate are integrated with the school's unique characteristics, philosophy, and mission.

A school charter is a document to which both government and school policy group assent (Caldwell & Spinks, 1992, p. 40). It summarizes the centrally determined framework of priorities and standards and outlines the means by which the school will address this framework. It provides an account of the school's mission, vision, priorities, needs, and programs, and it specifies the process by which decisions will be made and approaches to evaluation.

Caldwell and Spinks (1988) defined a policy as a statement of purpose accompanied by one or more guidelines as to how that purpose is to be achieved. A policy provides a framework for the operation of the school or a program, and it may allow discretion in its implementation. A policy's statement of purpose should be derived from the school's statement of philosophy as expressed in the school's charter or from a goal statement or statements. The guidelines should clearly state the intent of the policy and the desired pattern of action without becoming so specific as to prohibit professional judgment by those concerned with implementing the policy.

The development plan is adopted by the policy group as a strategic plan for improvement specifying in general terms priorities to be addressed in the next three to five years and the strategies to be employed. It includes a careful assessment of where the school is in relation to where it should be. A "need" exists when there is a significant gap between where the school is and where it desires to be. Schools typically have far more needs than their resources permit them to address, so priorities must be established as to which are the most pressing. Caldwell and Spinks

(1988) suggest that one consideration in setting priorities is the extent of identifiable harm caused by each gap or need.

The composition of the policy group varies according to the setting. In the Australian State of Victoria, it would be the legally established School Council. In England, it would be a school's Board of Governors. In the United States, where there is no universally established pattern of school governing boards, the nature of the policy group could be established by the state, as in the cases of Chicago and Kentucky, by the district, as in the case of Dade County, or left to the discretion of the school. The policy group could consist of the principal alone or supplemented with representatives of teachers, students, parents, the community, and/or the district office. The policy group is solely responsible for goal setting, need identification, and policy making, although it is likely to seek advice broadly in carrying out these responsibilities. It must approve budgets prepared by program teams, assuring that the proposals reflect established policy and are supportable by the resources allocated to the school. The policy group is responsible for summative evaluation of programs, making judgments on the effectiveness of each program and on the effectiveness of policy supporting program efforts.

A program is defined as an area of learning and teaching such as English, mathematics, art, and music, or a support service such as

Figure 11.13
Model for Self-Management (MSM)
SOURCE: B. J. Caldwell & J. M. Spinks. (1992). *Leading the Self-Managing School.* p. 33.

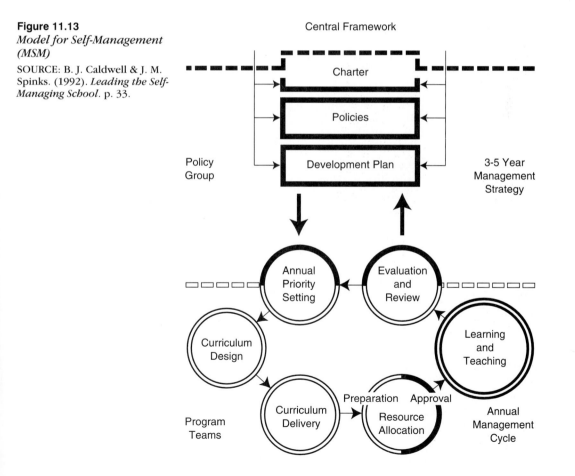

administration, audio-visual media, and main-tenance of buildings and grounds (see Figure 11.11). A program team is usually composed of everyone involved in the delivery of the program service. Each team should have a designated leader, usually a person with for-mal authority related to the program such as a subject coordinator or head of department. The teams prepare plans for their areas of responsibility within the parameters of the development plan and specify the resources needed to support those plans. The teams are responsible for the implementation of their plans as approved by the policy group. They are also responsible for formative evaluation of their respective programs and for submit-ting information to the policy group as required for their summative reviews. While the division of responsibility is clear, some individuals are likely to serve on both the pol-icy group and one or more program teams, thereby facilitating a high level of formal and informal communication.

On the surface, MSM resembles the largely discredited Planning, Programming, Budget-ing System (PPBS) model which was attempted in the United States during the 1960s and 1970s. While they are similar in concept, they are very different in design. The creators of MSM learned much from the fail-ures of PPBS and have largely succeeded in avoiding them. PPBS was very rigid, giving too much attention to the formal technology and minutia of planning and budgeting and requiring excessive paperwork.

> *To these shortcomings may be added an inap-propriate emphasis on the specification of performance requirements or criteria for evaluation. PPBS assumed a greater degree or capacity for rational or analytical planning than existed or was possible. In short, PPBS suffered from the "paralysis through analysis" which is to be avoided if effectiveness along the lines studied by Peters and Waterman (1982) is to be attained. (Caldwell & Spinks, 1988, p. 68)*

MSM keeps paperwork to a minimum. Each goal statement is limited to a single sen-tence; policies are limited to one page; pro-gram plans and budgets to two pages; and evaluation reports to one or two pages. Crite-ria for evaluation are kept simple and clearly related to learning and teaching. Priorities can be reordered quickly and simply as new needs emerge. All written material is to be free of technical jargon so that it can be easily read and understood by all members of the school community.

MSM recognizes three levels of planning: program, curricular, and instructional.

> *Program planning is determining in general terms how a program is to be implemented, specifying such things as the manner in which students will be grouped vertically (among grade or year levels) and horizontally (within a grade or year level); the number and nature of teachers and support staff associ-ated with the program; the supplies, equip-ment and services required and initiatives (additions or deletions) which are notewor-thy. Curriculum planning provides a rela-tively detailed specification of what will be taught, how it will be taught and when it will be taught. Instructional planning is consid-ered here to be planning undertaken by indi-vidual teachers when implementing a cur-riculum plan in their own classrooms. (Caldwell & Spinks, 1988, pp. 43–44)*

Cost of personnel allocated to specific tasks are made in program and school bud-gets even though the actual salaries may be paid by the district. The salary rate used is the average salary for the district (plus cost of fringe benefits) rather than the actual salaries paid to personnel assigned to a program. Caldwell and Spinks (1988) noted that "the inclusion of such [salary] estimates is an acknowledgement that the major resource in a school is the staff" (pp. 46–48).

A program budget is a comprehensive plan for a program. It contains a statement of the program's purpose, a listing of broad guidelines as to how the purpose is to be achieved, a plan for implementation with elements listed in order of priority, an estimate of resources required to support the plan, and a plan for evaluation. All must be reported in two pages or less.

The program budgets for all programs in the school are brought together in a single document for submission to the policy group for review, possible revision, and eventual approval. During the process of reconciliation, program expenditure requests will be adjusted, if necessary, so that combined approved expenditures will fall within the school's estimated income.

With the adoption of the program budget by the policy group, program teams are authorized to proceed with the implementation of their plans in the forthcoming year. There is no need for further reference to the policy group during the course of the year unless a program team desires to make a major change in its plan.

The final phase of the MSM cycle is evaluation and review, defined by Caldwell and Spinks (1988) as:

> . . . the gathering of information for the purpose of making a judgement and then making that judgement. Two kinds of evaluation should occur during or following the implementation of program plans. One is evaluation of learning, where information is gathered to form judgments about the progress or achievement of students. Another is evaluation of programs, when information is gathered to form judgments about the extent to which progress toward goals has been made, needs have been satisfied and policies have been implemented. (p. 49)

The policy group holds the major responsibility for program evaluation and may call in external authorities to assist them in the process. Planning teams have a similar, but more detailed, interest and gather much of the information needed for program evalua-tion for their own purposes and for use by the policy group. Minor evaluations are carried out annually and their reports to the policy group are limited to one page. Major evaluations are scheduled for a three- to five-year frequency and their reports are limited to two pages. "The emphasis is on a manageable and usable approach to program evaluation, in contrast to the frequently exhausting approach to school review and evaluation which has been encountered in many schools in recent years" (Caldwell & Spinks, 1988, p. 50).

The MSM cycle is completed when judgments in program evaluation result in the setting of new goals, the identification of new needs, the formulation of new policies or the introduction of new programs by the policy group. The model provides a comprehensive portrayal of all that eventually must be accomplished; but there seems to be no best point of entry to the model. A school may enter the cycle at any phase, completing the other phases in a manner appropriate for each setting.

Information Systems

Good plans are built upon good information and good information is required to monitor implementation. The strategic planning process and its implementation must be supported by a sophisticated information system. The district's information system is a critical element in making decisions and in maintaining organizational memory.

Good information is accurate, complete, reliable, and timely. Information should be relevant to a user's task; it should be tailored to his or her requirements, providing neither more nor less than what is needed to do the job. Information should be relatively inexpensive to produce and it should be verifiable.

School districts routinely collect all kinds of data—from birth dates and achievement test results to records of measles vaccinations. But, data are not information. Data consist of raw facts such as an employee's name, social security number, address, salary, and number of dependents. Such data must be retained by the employer as a routine business procedure in order to make payrolls and to comply with governmental regulations concerning withholding income and payroll taxes. When facts are organized in a meaningful manner, they become information. Information is a collection of facts organized in such a way that they have additional value beyond the value of the facts themselves (Stair, 1992).

For example, in collective negotiations, the superintendent and union negotiators need to know the total cost of salaries, their distribution, their average cost, and how all relate to salaries paid in similar districts. The raw data, except for the comparative information, are available in the payroll office, but organized for a different purpose. To serve the superintendent's purpose, it is not necessary to collect the data again, but only to organize the existing data differently.

Likewise, teachers need to know by name what students in their classes are illegally absent. The superintendent needs to know the aggregate amount of truancy in the district and the trend over time, but has little need to know who the individual truants are. Thus, the same data can be organized in numerous ways to meet the information needs of a variety of decisionmakers.

An information system is a set of interrelated elements or components that collect (input), manipulate and store (process), and disseminate to targeted persons data and information (output). An information system also typically has a feedback process whereby adjustments can be made to input and processing activities to enhance the efficiency of the system.

Input can take many forms from employee time cards to teacher grade sheets to a message taken by a telephone receptionist. An efficient information system will collect each data element only once for the entire district and eliminate the redundancy of having each department and office collecting similar data from the same people over and over again. Processing can be done mentally by a teacher or administrator or it can involve extensive computerized machinations. Information can be stored in a notebook, a traditional file cabinet, or electronically in a computer. Outputs are usually in the form of documents and reports, but can take a variety of forms including that of paychecks, report cards, tuition billing, letters, or computer display screens.

In the strategic planning process, the district's information system comes into play throughout the process. It is particularly important in providing information for the internal analysis of assessing strengths and weaknesses of the organization. It comes into play again in developing strategies, in designing action plans, and in building and administering the budget. It plays a critical role in contrasting actual accomplishments against expectations. Without good information, an organization is blind to its past achievements and failures and to its future potential.

The information system is also critical for monitoring and adjusting the implementation of action plans and programs. The proper use of statistics, for example, is central to Deming's (1986) philosophy of total quality management (TQM). According to him, management in any form is prediction. Statistical data are essential to improvement; facts, reasoning and evidence should drive decisions, not power or authority or personality.

We need to continually look to data in checking our progress. Research, experimentation, and data gathering are built into the daily routine of "learning organizations." Such organizations are able to anticipate and to accept new knowledge and to modify old organizational premises in order to optimize processes and achieve excellence in schooling (Schmoker & Wilson, 1993).

Deming (1986) identified the individual worker as key to program quality. The only proper use of data, according to him, is to help employees to perform better and to provide them with a basis for taking pride in their workmanship. The workers (e.g., principals, teachers, secretaries, bus drivers, cleaners) are the experts in what they do and are fully capable of improving their own performance when given feedback that enables them to monitor their own work. Deming placed much importance on the gathering of numerical data, but he emphasized that it must never be used to place blame on any employee or group of employees. Data are to be used to isolate problem areas, to design corrective action, and to identify staff training needs. Data do not have to be of the standard statistical variety, however; the most useful kinds of data are frequently those generated by the employees themselves.

Some Cautions from the Private Sector

Peters and Waterman (1982), in their study of America's best-run companies, drew some conclusions about planning and analysis in the private sector that are relevant to persons working in the public sector. They found that a lot of companies "overdo" planning. Managers find planning more interesting than getting the job done. It is a welcome respite from operating problems and intellectually more rewarding. This can easily lead to "wrong-headed" analysis—analysis that is too complex to be useful and analysis that strives to be precise about the inherently unknowable. A "paralysis through analysis" syndrome develops in which action stops while planning takes over.

Peters and Waterman warn against planning becoming an end in itself. Formal long-range planning almost always leads to overemphasis of technique. The plan too often becomes the reality, and data of the real world that don't fit the preconceived plan are blithely ignored. Emphasis on technique easily leads to the development of strategies that don't take into account "messy human stuff" such as persistent old habits of tenured staff, implementation barriers, and simple human inconsistencies. The messy human stuff can easily subvert the best laid plans—and often does.

Peters (1988) stressed the importance of maintaining flexibility in the strategic planning process by substantially modifying its format every year. He noted that most planning processes become bureaucratic within two years and lose their ability to be thought-provoking. A good strategic planning process:

(1) gets everyone involved, (2) is not constrained by overall corporate "assumptions," (3) is perceptually fresh, forcing the asking of new questions, (4) is not left to planners, and (5) requires lots of noodling time and vigorous debate. (Peters, 1988, p. 510)

Peters places much value on the process of developing the plan and virtually no value on the plan itself—as a matter of fact, he recommends that it be burned. The value of planning is as an assemblage of thoughts, not constraints. "Slavishly following the plan despite changing conditions (now the norm), because of time and political capital spent in assembling it, is counterproductive" (Peters, 1988, p. 511).

Activities for Discussion

Select a school district for the purpose of studying its planning, budgeting and information systems.

1. Is there a formal set of policies and procedures establishing a planning process for the district?

    a. If there is one, study it carefully and interview a number of key actors in the process to determine how closely the

policy is adhered to and find its perceived strengths and weaknesses.

b. If there is not one, interview a number
of persons whom you would expect to
be involved in the planning process at
all levels, including the board of education, the central office, principals,
teachers, parents, and students.
Describe the *de facto* process and its
perceived strengths and weaknesses.

2. Is there a formal set of policies and procedures establishing a budgeting process
for the district?

a. If there is a formal process, study it
carefully and interview a number of
key actors in the process to determine
how closely the policy is adhered to
and find its perceived strengths and
weaknesses.

b. If there is not one, interview a number
of persons whom you would expect to
be involved in the budgeting process at
all levels, including the board of education, the central office, principals, and
teachers. Describe the *de facto* process
and its perceived strengths and weaknesses.

c. Examine the complete budget, popularized versions of it, the budget calendar, and related forms.

3. Study the operating budget implementation process. How are purchases initiated,
made, and paid for? How is payroll handled? How are expenditures monitored?

4. What is the nature of the information system that supports the planning and budgeting processes?

Annotated Bibliography

Carlson, R. V., & Awkerman, G. (Eds.). *Educational
planning: Concepts, strategies, and practices.* New
York: Longman.

*This is an edited volume reporting the
thoughts, experiences, and criticisms of 25 scholars and practitioners about the theory and practice of planning. The traditional, rational, positivist approach to planning is challenged. In its
stead, the social and political aspects of planning
are emphasized. Planning is presented as a
process for mobilizing human intellect, energy,
and commitment, as well as setting organizational direction. The book is not a technical manual; but it presents many technical planning concepts through real-world examples. Part I presents
planning theory and concepts. Part II examines
the relationships between planning and policy.
The book distinguishes between strategic or long-
term planning (Part III) and operational or short-
term planning (Part IV), and shows how both are
essential and need to be coordinated. Part V presents case studies of school district planning.*

Caldwell, B. J., & Spinks, J. M. (1988). *The self-
managing school.* London: The Falmer Press.

*The book focuses on one of today's key educa-
tional issues: how schools can direct their own
destinies. The authors demonstrate this through
the presentation of the Collaborative School Management Cycle model. The model provides for
involvement of teachers, parents, and students as
well as administrators in an ongoing management process of goal setting, need identification,
policy making, planning, budgeting, implementing, and evaluating. The focus is on developing
high quality programs for students through the
efficient use of resources. The approach grew out
of a study of highly effective schools in Australia,
where it is widely used. It has also become popular in England as a means of supporting schools
in accommodating their newly granted powers
over budget and policy. The model is gaining in
recognition in the United States and Canada as
more and more school districts adopt policies of
school-based management. The book is divided
into three parts: a framework for self-management; the process of collaborative school management; and making the process work. An extensive
appendix provides illustrations of supporting
policies and documents.*

Cunningham, W. G. (1982). *Systematic planning
for educational change.* Palo Alto, CA: Mayfield.

The book is specifically designed to serve two major audiences: the student of planning and change in educational organizations, and the professional administrator. It is organized into three parts: the first discusses theory with appropriate citations and references; the second examines tools, techniques, and examples; and the third concludes with a discussion of future needs in education. The first part, "Process and Theory," places the process and context of planning and change into perspective and presents the theoretical background needed to evaluate the techniques described in the remainder of the book. The second part, "Tools and Techniques," develops the major component structures of the planning and change process. This part is the heart of an integrated system for planning and implementing change within educational organizations. The concluding chapter directs the reader's attention to the future as part of the planning process. The author succeeds in linking processes and technologies with the human dimension of the organization. The presentation is replete with numerous, careful descriptions of illustrative examples taken from educational settings. The result is a textbook that is well grounded in sound contemporary scholarship and provides a great deal of specific information that can be used by administrators confronting real problems in practice.

Hartman, W. T. (1988). *School district budgeting.* Englewood Cliffs, NJ: Prentice-Hall.

Budgeting is an important part of the planning process and this book is one of the few available dedicated solely to the school budgeting process. It provides administrators with systematic explanations of the underlying principles of school district budgeting, organizational arrangements, and practical procedures to be followed. The budgeting process is presented from its inception—the planning and organizing stages—through budget management. The in-between processes receive thorough treatment, including: development of budget estimates, techniques for evaluating and adjusting the budget, political strategies for obtaining approval, and financial control procedures. There is also extensive coverage of school accounting, the use of microcomputers in budgeting, budget analysis, budget elections, and handling budget reductions.

Lewis, J., Jr. (1983). *Long-range and short-range planning for educational administrators.* Boston: Allyn and Bacon.

This book adapts George Steiner's strategic planning model, originally developed for use in the private sector, to school districts. The book is written as an "operating manual" with clear step-by-step instructions of what to do and what not to do. Easy-to-use universal forms and illustrative policies are distributed throughout the book, enabling readers to adapt suggested planning procedures to varying local circumstances. The author places the planning function in a broad social context. Topics covered include: designing a planning system to meet a school's or school system's specific needs, establishing planning controls to enhance the obtainment of goals and objectives, forecasting the future of education with some degree of accuracy, and integrating human relation concepts into the total planning process.

Schmoker, M. J., & Wilson, R. B. (1993). *Total quality education: Profiles of schools that demonstrate the power of Deming's management principles.* Bloomington, IN: Phi Delta Kappa Educational Foundation.

This book is an exploration of actual applications to public schools of the management concepts formulated by W. Edwards Deming, known collectively as Total Quality Management or TQM. The authors believe that Deming's template provides an overarching body of principles that can promote intelligent action toward improving our schools. The authors' approach is not doctrinaire as they see Deming's philosophy being distinguished from other approaches to reforms in its adaptability—its capacity to embrace and refine much of what is already working. The book begins by presenting a capsule view of Deming's management philosophy. It then reports on the application of Deming's principles at the Toyota automobile plant in Georgetown, Kentucky, and draws implications for schools. The next several chapters present case studies of schools and school districts that have embraced Deming's philosophy. These include: the Johnson City, NY schools; San Francisco's Daniel Webster Elementary School; New York City's Central Park East schools; the Clovis, California, schools; and the Mt. Edgecumbe High

School in Sitka, Alaska. Based on their observations in these schools and at Toyota, the authors identify concepts they feel are useful for schools and school districts to follow in improving the quality of their service to children and youth.

Stair, R. M. (1992). *Principles of information systems: A managerial approach*. Boston, MA: Boyd and Fraser.

This is a basic text on information systems (IS), offering a broad survey of the entire IS discipline. It presents the components of information systems and how and why information systems should be used to meet organizational goals. The book is built around the concept that the right information, if it is delivered to the right person, in the right format, at the right time, can improve and ensure organizational effectiveness and efficiency. The book begins by providing a solid grounding in systems theory. It includes complete coverage of computer concepts, presented in relation to IS functionality. Other topics include: information technology concepts (hardware, software, telecommunications); business information systems (transaction processing, decision support systems, artificial intelligence); systems development; end-user computing; and management of business information systems including social and ethical considerations.

Steiner, G. A. (1979). *Strategic planning: What every manager must know*. New York: The Free Press.

This is one of the seminal books on strategic planning. It is written specifically for top- and middle-level executives in the private sector but it has stimulated a number of applications for educational administrators (e.g., Cook, 1990; Lewis, 1983). The author spells out practical, concrete measures for organizing the planning system, acquiring and using information, identifying opportunities, developing objectives, and translating strategic plans into decisions. Charts and checklists are presented which can be used as a workbook for actual planning, and a glossary of planning terms and techniques serves as a quick source of reference. The section entitled "Fifty Common Pitfalls" helps in avoiding typical mistakes. The book is brief, practical, and to the point, speaking directly to busy executives in need

of basic planning tools. One chapter is directed specifically to the translation of methods designed for the private sector to the not-for-profit sector.

References

Ackoff, R. L. (1970). *A concept of corporate planning*. New York: Wiley-Interscience.

Ackoff, R. (1981). *Creating the corporate future*. New York: John Wiley & Sons.

Adams, D. (1991). Planning models and paradigms. In R. V. Carlson & G. Awkerman (Eds.), *Educational planning: Concepts, strategies, and practices* (pp. 5–20). New York: Longman.

Anderson, L. (Undated). The century of the J-curve. *Our World*, AFS International/Intercultural Programs, 13–17.

Awkerman, G. (1991). Strategic ends planning: A commitment to focus. In R. V. Carlson & G. Awkerman (Eds.), *Educational planning: Concepts, strategies, and practices* (pp. 201–219). New York: Longman.

Bennis, W., & Nanus, B. (1985). *Leaders: The strategies for taking charge*. New York: Harper and Row.

Caldwell, B. J., & Spinks, J. M. (1988). *The self-managing school*. London: The Falmer Press.

Caldwell, B. J., & Spinks, J. M. (1992). *Leading the self-managing school*. London: The Falmer Press.

Cook, W. J., Jr. (1990). *Bill Cook's strategic planning for America's schools* (rev. ed.). Arlington, VA: American Association of School Administrators.

Cunningham, W. G. (1982). *Systematic planning for educational change*. Palo Alto, CA: Mayfield.

Deming, E. W. (1986). *Out of the crisis*. Cambridge, MA: MIT Press.

Drucker, P. (1974). *Management tasks, responsibilities, practices*. New York: Harper and Row.

Goodstein, L. D., Nolan, T. M., & Pfeiffer, J. (1992). *Applied strategic planning: A comprehensive guide*. San Diego, CA: Pfeiffer.

Hamilton, D. N. (1991). An alternative to rational planning models. In R. V. Carlson & G. Awkerman (Eds.), *Educational planning: Concepts, strategies, and practices* (pp. 21–47). New York: Longman.

Hartman, W. T. (1988). *School district budgeting*. Englewood Cliffs, NJ: Prentice-Hall.

Hodgkinson, C. *Educational leadership: The moral art*. Albany, NY: State University of New York Press.

Levin, H. M. (1980). The limits of educational planning. In H. N. Weiler (Ed.), *Educational planning and social change*. Paris: UNESCO, International Institute for Educational Planning.

Lewis, J., Jr. (1983). *Long-range and short-range planning for educational administrators*. Boston: Allyn and Bacon.

Lotto, L. S., & Clark, D. L. (1986). Understanding planning in educational organizations. *Planning and Changing, 17*(1), 9–18.

O'Brien, P. W. (1991). Strategic planning and management for organizations. In R. V. Carlson & G. Awkerman (Eds.), *Educational planning: Con-*

cepts, strategies, and practices (pp. 163–176). New York: Longman.

Peters, T. (1988). *Thriving on chaos: Handbook for a management revolution*. New York: Knopf.

Peters, T. J., & Waterman, R. H., Jr. (1982). *In search of excellence: Lessons from America's best-run companies*. New York: Warner.

Schmoker, M. J., & Wilson, R. B. (1993). *Total quality education: Profiles of schools that demonstrate the power of Deming's management principles*. Bloomington, IN: Phi Delta Kappa Educational Foundation.

Stair, R. M. (1992). *Principles of information systems: A managerial approach*. Boston, MA: Boyd and Fraser.

Steiner, G. A. (1979). *Strategic planning: What every manager must know*. New York: The Free Press.

Weiler, H. N. (1980). *Educational planning and social change*. Paris: UNESCO, International Institute for Educational Planning.

Chapter 12
Allocation of Resources in Education

Education is big business. Approximately $200 billion is spent annually on public elementary and secondary schools, making expenditures for education the largest single budgetary component of state and local governments (National Center for Education Statistics, 1989). These expenditures represent nearly 5 percent of our nation's gross national product. Forty-five million children attend these schools and they employ nearly seven million professional educators and support personnel (U.S. Department of Commerce, 1988). No matter how one looks at it, schooling involves a highly significant portion of the nation's human and economic resources.

But education is much more than "big business." Education deals with matters that relate to the heart and soul of the individual citizen and, at the same time, is critical to the political and economic welfare of the nation and its security. Making decisions about how much should be spent on schooling and how that spending should be distributed among

children, how such decisions should be made—and by whom—is the focus of this chapter.

Allocation of resources concerns the determination and distribution of human and material resources needed for the efficient realization of desired educational outcomes. Efficiency is defined as securing a given output with the least cost of scarce resources. Efficiency can be increased by improving outcomes without raising costs or by reducing the level of resources used for a given set of outcomes. Efficiency is frequently confused with "cheapness," but a less expensive procedure can actually be less efficient than a more expensive one if it is not successful in accomplishing the task at hand. In studying the efficiency of a procedure, the relationships among inputs, processes, and outputs must be understood. As stewards of the public purse, "efficiency" must be an ethical concern of those involved in educational leadership.

We begin this chapter by examining the basic arguments for financing education primarily through the public sector, i.e., government, and the social tension this creates in attempting to accommodate the personal preferences of individuals. Then we turn our attention to the political/economic process that determines how many and what kind of resources will be used for educational purposes, how those resources will be used, and who the beneficiaries will be. Next, we look at the equity implications of decisions concerning the distribution of financial resources among school districts. Finally, we review the evidence of relationships between inputs to the schooling process and desired outcomes. We look at these relationships at two levels: societal, where we are interested in the impact of resources used for education on desired social objectives such as economic growth, and the school or classroom, where we are interested in the impact of resources and their use on pupil behavior and pupil achievement. Such knowledge is necessary to improve the efficiency of educational institutions. The chapter concludes with a discussion of policy implications for improving the efficiency of schooling.

In making macro allocation decisions (committing resources to the "right" undertakings), educational leaders must fully appreciate the values of education to both society and to individuals. For society, schools are a means to overall improvement in the quality of life, political stability, social security, and economic growth. These are also important concerns for individuals, but the focus of the individual (or his or her family) is specific and not global, e.g., commitment to a specific value set, philosophy, curriculum, vocation and/or avocation. The educational manager (concerned about doing things "right") in contrast to the educational leader, has an enormous responsibility to see that the allocation decisions are executed legally, prudently, efficiently, and humanely. This chapter addresses primarily leadership (directional or strategic) issues.

Making Allocation Decisions for Educational Services

Education brings important benefits to both the individual and society. If public benefits were simply the sum of individual benefits, there would be no problem, but this is not the case. Frequently there are substantial differences between societal and individual interests. Full public interest would not be realized if provision of education were left solely to private vendors and to the ability of individuals to pay for education; and it is unlikely that the full private or individual interest would be satisfied if education were left solely to public provision. Thus, education is considered to be both a public and a private "good."

Private goods are divisible and their benefits are left primarily to their owners. If an individual desires a particular item or service, he or she can legally obtain the item by negotiating an agreed upon price with the current owner. The new owner can enjoy the item or service while those unable or unwilling to pay the price cannot. A good is "private" if someone who does not pay for it can be excluded from its use and enjoyment. This is known as the exclusion principle. Such goods are readily provided through the market system, i.e., the private sector.

The private (or individual) benefits of education, whether gained through public or private institutions, include the ability to earn more money and to enjoy a higher standard of living and a better quality of life. As part of this, educated persons are likely to be employed at more interesting jobs than are less educated persons. Schooling opens up the possibility of more schooling which in turn leads to even better employment possibilities; long-term unemployment is much less likely. Similarly, educated persons, through knowledge and understanding of the arts and other manifestations of culture, and with greater resources at their disposal, are likely to have more options for the use of leisure time and are likely to use such time in more interesting ways. As informed consumers, they are likely to get more mileage out of their resources. Finally, better educated persons are likely to enjoy a better diet and have better health practices. This results in less sickness and a longer productive life.

Educational opportunities can be excluded from those unwilling or unable to pay for them; thus schooling could be provided exclusively through the private sector as it was prior to the organization of public schools in the early nineteenth century. But there would be a number of socially undesirable external effects. The public (or societal) benefits of publicly and privately provided education include enlightened citizenship which is particularly important to a democratic form of government. In projecting a common set of values and knowledge, schools can foster a sense of community and national identity and loyalty among a diverse population. A public school system can provide an effective network for talent identification and development, spurring the creation of both cultural and technological innovations and providing the skilled work force required for the efficient functioning of society. This results in more rapid economic growth and in a generally more vital and pleasant quality of life for everyone. These benefits are considered to be of such social importance that public sponsorship now provides for the schooling of approximately 90 percent of the school-age population. At the same time, parents of at least 10 percent of the school-age population hold private preferences so strong that they are willing to pay tuition to private schools as well as taxes in support of the public schools.

Structuring the decisionmaking process for education is particularly complex because education provides both social and private benefits. Procuring educational services incurs costs and produces benefits that accrue to individuals independently and, at the same time, incurs social costs and produces benefits that accrue to society collectively. Levin (1987) concluded that there is a potential dilemma when schools are expected to provide both public and private benefits:

> *Public education stands at the intersection of two legitimate rights: the right of a democratic society to assure its reproduction and continuous democratic functioning through providing a common set of values and knowledge and the right of families to decide the ways in which their children will be molded and the types of influences to which their children will be exposed. To the degree that families have different political, social, and religious beliefs and values, there may be a basic incompatibility between their private concerns and the public functions of schooling (p. 629).*

To ensure that both individual and societal demands for schooling are met, decisions about the provision of education are made in both the public and private sectors. Decisions in the public sector are made through political processes by governments, whereas decisions in the private sector are made by individuals using market mechanisms. Easton (1965) described politics as the process by which *values* are allocated within society. Economics, on the other hand, is the study of the allocation of *scarce resources* within society. Economics is concerned with production, distribution and consumption of commodities. Efficiency in the use of resources is the objective of economics. Politics is powered by collective (societal) concerns while economics is powered by individual or private concerns. This chapter focuses primarily on economic considerations and Chapter 14 focuses primarily on political interactions in policy formulation. There is a good deal of overlap between the two perspectives; in studying one, you need to be conscious of the other.

Obviously, one's value priorities strongly influence one's judgment as to what is an efficient allocation of material resources. Thus, there is continuing interaction between economics and politics. Allocation of resources to education and within educational enterprises is a prime point of interaction. Decisions about public involvement in education are made in political arenas; but the decisions made in those arenas will have strong economic implications for individuals and for private businesses as well as for communities, states and the nation. Individuals and businesses will respond independently to political decisions by deciding whether or not to participate in government programs or to supplement or substitute for government programs by purchasing services provided through the private sector.

DECISIONMAKING IN A MIXED ECONOMY

Any society has to make certain fundamental economic decisions:

> *What shall be produced?*
> *How shall it be produced?*
> *For whom shall it be produced? (Samuelson, 1980, p. 16)*

In a capitalistic economy, the preference is to make such decisions for private-type goods through unrestrained or self-regulating markets. Figure 12.1 illustrates the circular flow of a monetary economy between two sets of actors, households and producers. It is assumed that households own all resources while producers have the capacity of converting resources into finished goods and services.

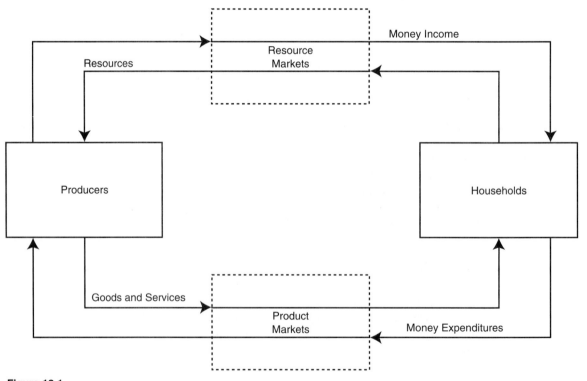

Figure 12.1
The circular flow of resources in a monetary economy

Resources are traditionally grouped into three categories called *factors of production*: land, labor, and physical capital. Land refers not only to the dry surface area of the earth, but also to its vegetation, wildlife, and mineral content. Labor represents the human resource that goes into production. Originally, economic analysts defined labor in quantitative terms as the number of workers and the time they worked. With the advent of human capital theory (Schultz, 1963), the quality of labor has been considered an important economic characteristic of labor. Formal education is, of course, an important means of improving the quality of the work force. Physical capital refers to the produced means of production, such as machinery, factory buildings, and computers. Households may own land and capital outright or as shareholders in a corporation, and they also control the availability of their individual labor. The education level of the work force correlates directly with the level of sophistication of capital that may be reasonably used in the production process.

The households (e.g., teachers and their families) and the producers (e.g., schools and school districts, colleges, and universities) each have something the other wants and needs. Producers need the resources controlled by households in order to produce finished goods and services. Households need the goods and services provided by the producers for survival in the case of food and shelter and for improved quality of life in the case of many other goods. To facilitate the exchange, markets provide a means of communication. Producers acquire the resources they need through resource markets by making money income available to households in the form of wages, rents, interest, and profits. Households in turn use the money acquired through the sale of resources to purchase finished goods and services in product markets. It is these sales that provide producers with

money to purchase resources from the households. And so the cycle continues.

Through markets, households and producers negotiate prices to be paid for resources and finished goods and services. The outcomes of these negotiations ultimately determine the answers to the three economic questions raised above. Resources are scarce and unevenly distributed among households, while household wants are unlimited. This means that each household must prioritize its wants and satisfy as many of them as possible within the constraints of the resources it controls and the value of those resources. The value, or price, of resources depends upon supply and demand. As illustrated in Figure 12.2, if the demand (Q_3) for labor (e.g., teachers) among producers (e.g., school districts), for example, exceeds the available supply (Q_1), the wage (P_1) producers are willing to pay increases to P_2. The higher wages entice more and more persons to make their labor available to producers (moving from Q_1 to Q_2). At the same time, higher costs dissuade some producers from employing as much labor, e.g., they may invest instead in more efficient technology. The process leads to

Figure 12.2
Supply and demand curves

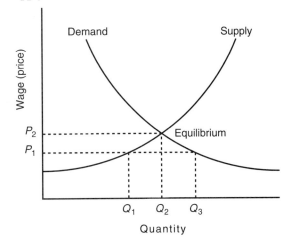

equilibrium, the point where supply matches demand.

Producers in the private sector will only produce that which will incur a reasonable profit. Profit depends on the amount of a good or a service that is sold, the price and the cost of production. If the demand for a product is not sufficient to sell all units produced at a price above the cost of production, no profit can be made. Under such circumstances, the producer has three options: reduce the cost of production by adopting more efficient means of production, shift production to another product that can be sold for a profit, or go out of business. When conditions permit an above-average profit for producing a given good, more producers are attracted into the field. The number of units produced increases to the point where supply equals demand. Competition forces prices down, returning the rate of profit to a normal range.

Each dollar controlled by each consuming household is a potential vote to be cast in favor of the production of one good or service over another or the product of one producer over the product of a competitor. The influence of a household over producers is approximately proportional to the value of the resources controlled by the household. This poses ethical dilemmas about the distribution of wealth. The rich make expenditures for improving the quality of life while the poor lack basic necessities. Or, new manufacturing technologies may be so efficient as to reduce the demand for labor causing a reduction in wages and/or widespread unemployment. The issue of equity with respect to allocation of resources for education will be discussed in a later section.

We do not rely solely on market mechanisms to make economic decisions, however, because society has many needs that cannot be met by the market. Approximately one-third of our gross national product (GNP) is distributed according to political decisions made by governments, e.g., municipalities and school districts. Important differences distinguish governmental units from households and producers in the ways they answer economic questions and the criteria they use. Downs (1957, p. 282) identified government as that agency in the division of labor which has as its *proper* function the maximization of social welfare. When results generated by free markets are ethically or economically unsatisfactory, government can be used as a tool of intervention to set things right (p. 292). Governments have the unique power to extract involuntary payments, called taxes, from households and producers alike, and the federal government controls the money supply upon which both public and private sectors depend. Governmental programs and agencies are not profit-oriented and they rarely "go out of business." When they do go out of business, it is the result of political decisions and not market forces, although conditions in the market may influence political decisions. Efficiency has not traditionally been an overriding objective of the public sector.

Figure 12.3 inserts government (the public sector) into the center of the circular flow of a monetary economy. As noted, government obtains money for its operations through taxes on producers and households. With this money, government acquires resources through resource markets and goods and services through product markets. There are no separate markets for the private and public sectors; government demands are factored into the resource and product markets in establishing prices. Thus, there is not a unique market for school personnel, for example; school districts compete with businesses, professions, and other governmental units for desired human services. When the federal government borrows heavily from the financial market, interest rates go up for everyone alike—the school district borrowing to build a building or an individual borrowing to buy an automobile.

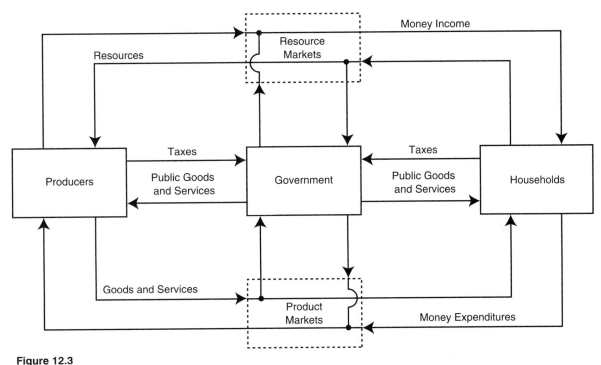

Figure 12.3
The circular flow of resources, including government (the public sector)

Governments produce some goods and services that are desired by households and producers. These include public schooling, national defense, fire and police protection, airports, harbor facilities, and roads. Governments also redistribute wealth through transfer payments and subsidies. These include social security and welfare payments, medicare, unemployment insurance, and subsidies to farmers and businesses.

Public sector decisions are political and, ideally, political power is distributed evenly among the electorate, i.e., one person, one vote. In the private sector, influence is distributed in proportion to the amount of resources controlled, i.e., the rich have much influence and the poor have little. Because of the difference in the distribution of influence over decisions made in the public and private sectors, there are marked differences between the sectors in the answers given to the three economic questions. The greater relative power of the poor in the public sector when compared with the private sector leads to an equalitarian bias in decisions made in the public sector. The private sector has a libertarian bias to permit the exercise of individual preferences.

Thus, in making decisions about education, natural tensions exist among households, members of the teaching profession, and society. To the extent that decisions are made in the private sector, individuals and families can maximize their personal aspirations within the limits of their economic resources and according to individual value preferences. Professionals are free to provide or to withhold services and to determine the nature of those services. But, when decisions are made through the political process, individuals and groups of varying value orientations must negotiate a single solution and their value preferences may be compromised in the process.

When Should Governments Intervene?

To this point, we have sketched the functioning of the economic and political systems separately and have indicated likely differences in decisions made in the two sectors. Each sector is capable of answering the three allocation questions posed; but we, as individuals and as a society, would probably be quite unhappy with the results if all decisions were made through one sector. Given the general preference of a capitalistic society for the private sector, we would like now to address the issues of when governments should intervene and how they should intervene.

Eckstein (1968) identified four situations where market mechanisms fail and where government intervention is necessary:

- collective goods,
- divergence between private and social costs or benefits (externalities),
- extraordinary risks,
- natural monopolies.

The case of collective goods has already been discussed along with markets and the circular flow of resources in a monetary economy. Education has some characteristics of a collective good, justifying governmental involvement in the provision of education. Other examples of collective goods are national defense and flood control.

Divergence between private and social costs or benefits may represent the strongest argument for public involvement in the provision of schooling. Persons who are able to provide for their schooling from private resources are likely to recapture their investment with an appropriate gain for themselves and substantial spillover benefits to others in society. The cost to society, however, of those who would remain uneducated in the absence of public provision would be sub-

stantial. School dropouts illustrate the point although public provision is available to them. When problem pupils drop out or are forced out of school, there is a high probability that they will become wards of society in one form or another. They are much less likely to be regularly employed than are persons completing their schooling and are more likely to receive governmental assistance in the form of unemployment insurance, welfare, and Medicaid. School dropouts are also more likely to turn to lives of crime and be incarcerated in penal institutions. The resources saved by society by not fully educating such persons may be lost many times over in providing social services to them later in life. Similarly, until intervention by the federal government, many persons with severe mental and physical disabilities were denied access to schooling because of the high cost of special education. This meant that they were institutionalized their entire lives. Now, having access to schooling, many are able to work and live independently or with minimal supervision. The increased expenditures for education are paying dividends in terms of lower costs for social services and a better quality of life for persons with disabilities.

Extraordinary risks refer to situations where risks are so large that private financing cannot be found or is impractical. The development of atomic energy, space exploration, and cancer research are examples. Investments in research on learning and curriculum may also fall into this category, although there has been relatively little government subsidization of research and development in these areas.

A natural monopoly is an enterprise enjoying a continually falling cost curve. In other words, the cost to produce a unit becomes less and less as the number of units produced or served increases. Thus, because of economies of scale, the largest firm has a distinct competitive advantage, eventually driving smaller firms out of business. Electricity, gas, and water utilities are examples. The technology governing most businesses and industries is such that economies of scale are realized only up to a point when diseconomies of scale set in, i.e., the cost per unit increases as the number of units produced or serviced increases. This produces a U-shaped cost curve, nullifying any advantage of large firms over small ones and preserving competition. While economies of scale are realized quite quickly in elementary and secondary schools (as discussed later in this chapter), schooling has been organized as a near public monopoly for noneconomic reasons.

Governmental intervention also takes place for other reasons. The federal government has assumed a responsibility for controlling business cycles and inflation, and, to a limited extent, the redistribution of wealth. All governments use the power of eminent domain where they can force the sale of private property for public use.

How Should Governments Intervene? Once the decision for intervention is made, there are numerous modes of intervention. Public schools are owned and operated by the government. So are police and fire departments and the United States armed forces. Ownership is not the typical type of governmental intervention, however. Governments may also oversee the public interest through regulation and licensure, taxation, subsidies, transfer payments, and contracts.

Most communication systems, utilities, and inter-city transportation enterprises in the United States are privately owned, yet they are carefully monitored and regulated. Restaurants are regularly inspected for health code violations. The licensing of professionals is done by governments although most professionals, an important exception being teachers, work in the private sector.

Governments can attempt to influence human behavior by changing the price paid for specific items through subsidies or taxation. Consumption of cigarettes, alcoholic beverages, and gasoline is discouraged through excise taxes, increasing the cost to consumers with the intent of reducing demand. On the other hand, the government may pay subsidies to farmers to encourage them to increase or decrease production or to businesses to enable them to remain in operation in the face of foreign competition or to relocate in areas of high unemployment. Similarly, subsidies and scholarships that reduce the cost of higher education encourage families and individuals to pursue education beyond high school.

Governments also contract for services from private companies. Federal, state, and local governments rely on contractors to build their buildings, highways, and parks. While the federal government coordinates space exploration, private vendors under contract conduct research and development and manufacture space vehicles. During periods of rapid enrollment increases, school districts may rent space from private vendors. Contracting for transportation, cleaning, and cafeteria services is a common practice among school districts.

Many governmental responsibilities are met through transfer payments to individuals. Social Security, Aid for Dependent Children, unemployment insurance, food stamps, and educational vouchers are examples. Through transfer payments, the government can equalize the distribution of resources while permitting the individual maximum discretion as to how the funds distributed are used. For example, prior to Social Security, elderly indigents were institutionalized in facilities owned and operated by local government ("poor farms" and "old folks' homes"). Now, with monthly payments from the Social Security System, recipients have many options open to them such as living in their own homes, smaller apartments, retirement communities, nursing homes, as well as living with relatives. The public policy of providing all citizens with at least a subsistence living standard is realized without prescribing their life styles. Educational vouchers have the potential of making schooling available to all without prescribing the specific nature of the schooling experience.

EQUITY AND THE ALLOCATION OF RESOURCES

Equality is defined as the state, ideal, or quality of being equal, as in enjoying equal social, political, and economic rights. The operational definition of equality within the sociopolitical context also includes factors of condition, placing emphasis on the *appropriateness* of treatment. As such, "equality" has taken on the broader connotations of "equity," defined in the *American Heritage Dictionary* (Morris, 1969) as "the state, ideal, or quality of being just, impartial and fair" (p. 443). In this chapter, the term *equity* is used instead of *equality* as more accurately reflecting modern usage in reference to public policy.

In analyzing the impact of a policy on equity concerns, one must be fully aware of the level of equity the policy is intended to address and should consider the horizontal and vertical dimensions of equity. Horizontal equity refers to the equal treatment of equals—the traditional meaning of *equality*. Vertical equity recognizes that equal treatment is not always fair and just for persons (or school districts) experiencing abnormal conditions such as poverty and physical, psychological, and mental disabilities (or high costs of living, dispersed populations, and municipal overburden). Thus, vertical equity refers to the appropriate unequal treatment of unequals. Some analysts add a third dimension, equal opportunity, defined in the negative as no differences in treatment according to characteristics (such as race or national origin) that are considered illegitimate (Berne &

Stiefel, 1984, p. 17). Other analysts treat equal opportunity as a condition of horizontal equity, the position taken here.

Virtually all studies of resource allocation equity deal only with the horizontal dimension (including equal opportunity). The lack of agreement on what "appropriate" treatment is for exceptional populations makes analysis of vertical equity very difficult if not impossible; nevertheless, recognition of the concept is very important in designing school finance policy.

Table 12.1 shows the ranking of states on a variety of measures of equity for 1984–85 as reported by Schwartz and Moskowitz (1988). The federal range ratio and the coefficient of variation measure the spread between the highest and lowest expenditure districts in each state. For both statistics, a smaller ratio indicates greater equity, i.e., less spread. These statistics are appropriate in evaluating policies in which the intent is to treat all districts in a state alike. But few state finance plans are intended to do this. More typically, states attempt to ensure a basic level of support above which districts are free to spend to the extent local resources permit. The McLoone index is designed to assess equity under these latter assumptions. With the McLoone index, perfect equity is represented by 1.00 and the greatest amount of inequity is represented by zero. The correlation coefficient reports the relationship between district per pupil valuation and per pupil district operating expenditures. The coefficient ranges in size from -1.00 to +1.00. A zero coefficient represents no relationship between the two variables—the desired state in analyses of equal opportunity. A coefficient of 1.00 (either positive or negative) indicates a perfect correspondence between the two variables. A positive coefficient indicates that the two variables increase or decrease in size together; a negative coefficient indicates that as one variable increases in size, the other variable decreases and vice versa.

There is a degree of inequity in the amounts spent on education by school districts in all states shown in Table 12.1 and in many states the inequity is substantial. It is reasonable to believe that the inequity among schools is even greater. The ranking among states corresponds quite closely with respect to the federal range ratio, the coefficient of variation, and the McLoone index. Each of these is unidimensional, i.e., involving only one variable, expenditure per pupil. According to these measures, Iowa, Nevada, and West Virginia are among the most equitable states, and Alaska, Montana, and Vermont are among the least equitable.

There is generally a lack of correspondence, however, between a state's ranking on the first three measures and the correlation coefficient, which is bivariate. Expenditures in New Hampshire, for example, are shown to be quite inequitable by the first three measures, but the state is judged to be quite equitable by the correlation coefficient. Apparently there is considerable variation in expenditure among school districts in New Hampshire, but state policy has succeeded in decoupling this variation from variation in property values—a major source of inequity in most states.

Interest in school finance equity peaked during the 1970s and has waned since then. Beginning in the 1960s with the civil rights movement and the related compensatory education programs of President Johnson's Great Society, concerns over equality of educational opportunities dominated the educational agenda. In the 1970s, attention focused on the equity of state school finance systems as litigation was brought in over half the states challenging their constitutionality. The 1970s was dubbed the decade of school finance reform as state after state restructured their finance systems to improve their equity—under court order in some instances and at their own initiative in others. Researchers from several disciplines joined with jurists, policy makers, interest groups, task forces and national foundations during this decade to sharpen the understanding of equity problems and to evaluate the effectiveness of remedies attempted.

In the 1980s, national attention shifted to excellence and efficiency; interest in equity declined, but did not disappear completely. In reviewing approximately 140 pieces of equity research since 1980, Barro (1987) referred to them as a "holding operation" (p. 3). He found no newly developed concepts or methods of analysis. The decline in research on school finance equity parallels a decline in the demand and funding for such studies over that which was available in the prior decade. In the late 1980s and continuing into the 1990s, there have been several new and significant court challenges to state school finance systems on the grounds of equity and efficiency, most notably in Kentucky, Texas and New Jersey.

One might suspect—or at least hope—that, with all the attention given to school finance equity during the 1970s, there would have been substantial gains; but this does not seem to be the case. Berne and Stiefel (1983) reviewed equity studies using data going back to 1940. They found that, prior to the school finance reform movement, from 1940 to 1960, horizontal equity improved in the overwhelming number of states. School district consolidation and increased state aid contributed indirectly to this goal. During the 1960s and 1970s, when concern over equity was an explicit issue, the trend was toward a worsening of equity.

Brown et al. (1978) also found that disparities in per pupil expenditures among districts in most states actually increased or remained constant between 1970 and 1975. The pattern was somewhat different among the 19 states that reformed their finance structures during that period. Ten of the 19 had reduced interdistrict disparities, although four remained among the ten states with the greatest expen-

Table 12.1
Measures of Equity for the States, 1984–1985

State	Federal Range Ratio		Coefficient of Variation		McLoone Index		Correlation Coefficient*	
	Ratio	Rank	Coefficient	Rank	Index	Rank	Coefficient	Rank
Alabama	.40	9	.11	7	.95	7	.21	6
Alaska	1.57	49	.52	48	.85	45	.39	15
Arizona	.58	22	.17	26	.91	28	.31	13
Arkansas	.48	14	.13	13	.92	18	−.07	2
California	.43	13	.13	12	.92	20	NA	NA
Colorado	.34	6	.12	9	.88	41	.63	36
Connecticut	.74	32	.21	36	.91	31	.31	13
Delaware	.41	11	.13	11	.84	48	.56	29
Florida	.37	7	.09	4	.91	12	.55	27
Georgia	.80	36	.18	31	.90	34	.31	13
Idaho	.56	21	.17	25	.91	22	.56	29
Illinois	1.21	46	.25	44	.85	46	.63	36
Indiana	.53	20	.15	16	.90	33	.16	3
Iowa	.25	3	.07	2	.96	3	.40	17
Kansas	.59	25	.16	21	.93	13	.70	41
Kentucky	.63	28	.17	24	.94	10	.75	43
Louisiana	.41	12	.13	10	.93	11	.52	26
Maine	.59	26	.18	30	.90	32	NA	NA
Maryland	.60	27	.15	17	.94	9	.80	45
Massachusetts	.91	43	.24	42	.90	35	.56	29
Michigan	.75	33	.20	35	.86	44	.39	15
Minnesota	.58	23	.16	20	.92	17	.58	34
Mississippi	.52	19	.17	23	.91	27	.44	20
Missouri	.96	44	.22	37	.90	38	.65	38
Montana	1.44	47	.74	49	.84	47	NA	NA

*District per pupil property valuation and district operating expenditures.

diture disparities. In 1970, reform states as a group had larger wealth-related disparities than nonreform states; by 1975, the situation was reversed.

Brown et al. take the most optimistic interpretation of their rather disappointing findings by pointing out that the reform states were "swimming against a tide of increasing disparity" (p. 212) and that inequities might have been even worse without reform. The lack of greater progress toward expenditure

equity was attributed by them, in part, to the desire to provide property tax relief. Considerable relief was provided and did lead to lower correlations between wealth-related measures and expenditures in reform states. It is also of interest that the six states with the least expenditure disparity operate relatively few school systems of comparatively large size.

A study by Carroll (1979) also provided little cause for optimism. He analyzed the

Table 12.1, continued
Measures of Equity for the States, 1984–1985

State	Federal Range Ratio		Coefficient of Variation		McLoone Index		Correlation Coefficient*	
	Ratio	Rank	Coefficient	Rank	Index	Rank	Coefficient	Rank
Nebraska	.90	41	.23	40	.86	43	.69	40
Nevada	.19	1	.10	6	1.00	1	.57	32
New Hampshire	.97	45	.27	45	.91	25	.21	6
New Jersey	.76	34	.18	29	.87	42	.30	11
New Mexico	.48	15	.16	18	.91	26	.17	4
New York	.89	39	.22	38	.96	2	.48	25
North Carolina	.33	5	.09	3	.94	8	.42	19
North Dakota	.80	35	.28	46	.91	29	.20	5
Ohio	.90	40	.24	41	.90	36	.47	23
Oklahoma	.59	24	.19	33	.92	21	.28	9
Oregon	.50	17	.13	14	.92	14	.26	8
Pennsylvania	.89	38	.19	34	.89	40	.45	21
Rhode Island	.32	4	.11	8	.91	24	.41	18
South Carolina	.40	8	.10	5	.96	5	−.09	1
South Dakota	.66	30	.18	32	.90	37	.47	23
Tennessee	.70	31	.18	27	.89	39	.71	42
Texas	.64	29	.18	28	.91	23	.60	35
Utah	.40	10	.16	22	.92	15	.57	32
Vermont	.47	48	.31	47	.82	49	NA	NA
Virginia	.90	42	.22	39	.91	30	.56	29
Washington	.51	18	.16	19	.95	6	.47	23
West Virginia	.22	2	.07	1	.96	4	.65	38
Wisconsin	.50	16	.14	15	.92	16	.29	10
Wyoming	.88	37	.24	43	.92	19	.75	43
Mean	.65	—	.19	—	.91	—	.45	—

*District per pupil property valuation and district operating expenditures.

SOURCE: Compiled from various tables reported in M. Schwartz and J. Moskowitz (1988). *Fiscal Equity in the United States, 1984–1985*. Washington, DC: Decision Resources Corporation.

impact of school finance reform in five states, California, Florida, Kansas, Michigan, and New Mexico, and concluded that the results were mixed: "Reform has brought about some advances; but judged in relation to the major goals that the proponents of reform have championed, the scattered victories of reform appear somewhat hollow" (p. v). Reform reduced the linkage between district wealth and expenditure per pupil and it increased statewide spending for education. Reform did not, however, change the distributions of revenues and instructional expenditures. In other words, taxpayer equity appears to have increased, but child equity did not.

Carroll offered two probable explanations for the ineffectiveness of the reforms in equalizing spending outcomes and opportunities. The first was that states simultaneously pursued diverse and conflicting objectives such as equalizing revenues, preserving some local control over spending, trying to avoid the political hazards of cutting back high-spending districts, providing tax relief, and avoiding excessive growth in state spending for schools. Carroll's second explanation is that each state made add-ons and adjustments to the basic plan; these policy changes had disequalizing effects. Kansas, for example, introduced income tax rebates and Florida introduced a cost-of-living adjustment. Both procedures provided more state aid to wealthy districts than to poor ones.

Of the states studied by Carroll, only New Mexico showed substantial equity among districts on both revenues and expenditures. New Mexico has assumed virtually full responsibility for school finance, while retaining the district as the operating unit. No local discretion is allowed to school districts in setting tax rates or determining revenues. In a subsequent study, King (1983) attributed New Mexico's wealth neutrality to property tax limitations, uniform tax rates, and a steady increase in state financial support. Commenting on King's conclusions, Hickrod and Goertz (1983) speculate that, "midwestern and northern state legislators will find these restrictions on local control too high a price to pay for greater education finance equity" (p. 3).

In a similar vein, Lake (1983), in a study of the public school systems in the four provinces of Atlantic Canada, found greatest equity in New Brunswick where schools are fully funded by the province.

> *If one focuses on Nova Scotia and New Brunswick, a policy implication of some importance arises. New Brunswick, the full provincial assumption case, made more progress toward equity than did Nova Scotia, the combined provincial/local funding case. However, in terms of sufficiency, Nova Scotia made more progress than did New Brunswick. This suggests, though it certainly*

> *does not rigorously prove, that the act of full provincial (state) assumption may help the educational community accomplish the equity goal at the expense of the sufficiency goal. (p. 460)*

Using the federal range ratio and coefficient of variation for all states except Montana, Berne (1988) analyzed changes in horizontal equity for the periods 1970 to 1977 and 1977 to 1985. For the first period, Berne found that horizontal equity improved by more than 5 percent on both measures in six states and worsened in eighteen states. For the 1977 to 1985 period, equity improved by more than 5 percent in fourteen states and became worse in sixteen states. For the two periods combined, 1970 to 1985, eleven states improved and eighteen became worse. He concluded that, even though it is a very crude indicator, there is some evidence that equity fared somewhat better during the more recent period.

Heinold (1983) studied the impact of federal aid on horizontal equity of revenues among states between 1960 and 1981. The coefficient of variation and the McLoone index showed movement toward greater equity among the states during the sixties and movement away from equity during the seventies. Federal aid enhanced equity for all years, but especially during the period from 1965 through 1976. In discussing the policy implications of his research, Heinold contrasted the situation in the United States with that in Canada.

> *During the period of years analyzed, the federal government portion of the funding of elementary and secondary public education ranged from three to nine per cent of the total revenues. In contrast, the level of funding by the federal government of Canada was 19 per cent of the total revenues in 1978, representing an effort greater than twice that of the United States government. This increased effort on the part of Canada has been*

rewarded by reductions in disparities among provinces to levels below the levels of disparities among states in the United States. While progress has been made in movement toward equity among the provinces in Canada, a reverse trend in the United States has been identified by this study. (p. 473)

Bezeau (1985) used public school systems of the United States and Canada to test relationships between equity and centralization of governance. Unlike Lake, Bezeau found that centralization had no effect on the magnitude of expenditures per pupil; but it did appear to be associated with greater equity, although the relationship was small.

The lack of progress in bringing about greater equity in expenditures per pupil have also been confirmed, with a few exceptions, by numerous single state studies: Illinois (Hickrod, Chaudhari, & Hubbard, 1983); Michigan (Berne & Stiefel, 1984; Kearney & Chen, 1989); New York (Berne & Stiefel, 1984); New Jersey (Goertz, 1983); and Minnesota (Krupey & Hopeman, 1983). Three states that seem to have resisted the general trend toward greater inequity are New Mexico (King, 1983), Texas (Verstegen, 1987) and South Carolina (Cohn & Smith, 1989).

On the whole, the evidence leaves little room for optimism about substantial improvements in school finance equity. Ironically, the greatest improvements in equity were made when equity was not an explicit issue. Jones (1985) pointed to the necessity of considering allocation and distribution patterns across time, covering periods of policy reform and periods of stability to monitor the sustained effects of efforts to change public policy.

The most likely explanation of the lack of predictability of policy initiatives on equity appears to be that equity is only one of many policy objectives of school finance reform. Equity collides with goals of improving adequacy and efficiency, meeting educational

needs, maintaining local control, providing property tax relief, and increasing public choice (Brown & Elmore, 1982). Hickrod and Goertz (1983) observed:

A legislative body is the appropriate forum to try to strike a balance between conflicting values such as equity and local control. It may have to be aided and abetted from time to time by the judicial branch, but it is the right place to make the decision. A compromise will be struck for these conflicting values for a given point in time with certain knowledge that that compromise is never final. The voice of the people speaks through a majority which is forever shifting through time. Each successive legislative body will change the balance point between egalitarian goals and libertarian goals and they will continue to do that so long as the democratic process is allowed to freely operate. (p. 418)

The 1980s saw a shift in favor of libertarian goals. Efficiency and standards moved center stage; "school finance reform" became "school reform," and there was little recognition that the two might in some way be connected. Existing fiscal and educational inequities among school districts may be exacerbated by allocations of state funds for educational reform that are not equalized for wealth variation among districts. Without equalized funds, wealthy, high-spending districts will be able to initiate program reforms in ways and in magnitudes that are denied to poor, low-spending districts.

There is little recognition in the "education reform" literature that school districts differ in their abilities and need for additional funding, to implement these reforms. These reports, for example, leave the impression that all districts are equally affected by the economic disincentives for persons to enter and stay in the teaching profession. They ignore that low salaries and poor working conditions for teachers tend to be greater problems for poor school districts than for those endowed with large tax bases and that these factors may produce teaching staffs of unequal quality. . . . Some children may actually be harmed by these reforms if equity issues are ignored. Higher educational standards, without more [resources], are likely to result in more educational failures, more retentions in grade, and more drop-outs. And the children most affected are minority and poor. (Long, 1986, pp. 341–342)

With constrained resources, equity objectives can only be realized through reallocation of resources. This is a very unpopular strategy—and politically dangerous. "Leveling up" poor districts, on the other hand, is very expensive and may be possible only with higher or new taxes—also unpopular and politically dangerous.

Efficiency, Adequacy, and Economic Growth

As noted above, equity is only one (although a very important one) of many criteria used to evaluate public policy. In this section, we turn our attention to consideration of efficiency, adequacy, and economic growth criteria. More specifically, we look at the role played by educational institutions in incorporating technological advances into the economy and the implications for economic growth. We also examine the efficiency of the operation of schools and the economies and diseconomies of scale experienced by them. In discussing school efficiency, we look at findings of studies from a variety of approaches as to the relationships between inputs to schooling, the organization of schooling, and per pupil behavior and experience.

A primary stimulus of the school reform movement launched in the 1980s was concern over the ability of the United States to compete in international markets. Fears stemming from economic competition replaced the threat of military conflict as a fundamental stimulant of social action. The technological revolution which had been gaining momentum since World War II emerged into a new social and economic order that substantially upgraded educational requirements for those who were to fully participate in it. Coupled with the demographics of fewer entrants into the labor market and longer working careers, business and industrial leaders recognized how critical it is for workers to have the basic mathematical and language skills needed to provide a foundation for learning other skills (McDonnell & Fuhrman, 1986). As a result, improving the efficiency of the educational system was seen as critical to any strategy for strengthening the nation's economic condition.

Hanushek (1986, p. 1166) defined economic efficiency as "the correct share of input mix given the prices of inputs and the production function." Production function is described as the causal relationship between inputs and outcomes. He cautioned against confusing economic efficiency and technical efficiency. The latter considers only the *process* of combining inputs to produce outcomes and does not take into account the *prices* of inputs. Both concepts are important considerations in designing educational systems; but the primary focus in this chapter is allocating resources to and within educational enterprises in order to achieve economic efficiency.

There are two aspects of economic efficiency, external and internal. External efficiency considers contributions to national economic growth made by the scarce resources allocated by society to various sectors of production such as education. With respect to education, we are interested in the returns on investments in education relative to returns from other investment opportunities. Internal efficiency relates to the allocation of resources *within* educational enterprises in order to maximize output (e.g., achievement, skill development, and behavioral and attitudinal changes among students) from the resources committed. Analyses of external efficiency assist in making decisions about the amount of resources to be committed to and among educational services and in determining the level of societal investment in population quality in order to promote economic growth. In other words, studying external efficiencies addresses the issues of how much to spend for educational services and of which kinds of services to provide in order to create the greatest amount of economic benefit. Internal efficiency relates to the means by which educational services are produced. The study of internal efficiency is directed toward gaining the maximum benefit from the resources committed to an institution. Whereas internal efficiency is studied through educational production functions and cost-benefit and cost-effectiveness analysis, external efficiency is studied through rate of return analysis.

EXTERNAL EFFICIENCY

Since approximately 90 percent of expenditures for elementary and secondary education are provided through the public sector, deciding how much to spend for educational services is largely a political process and the decisions made may not be efficient from an economic—or technical—perspective. "The market" has limited impact on setting the "price" or cost of public schooling. Economic analysis can estimate the efficiency by which we are using scarce resources for educational services; but economic efficiency is only one of many often conflicting objectives of social policy—equity, which we considered in the preceding section, being another. Other social concerns must be balanced against concerns for improving economic efficiency.

The rate of return on investments in education has been studied at two levels: the individual and society. The human capital

approach assumes that schooling endows an individual with knowledge and skills that enable him or her to be more productive and thereby receive higher earnings. This is, of course, beneficial to the individual. The accumulation of benefits derived by all individuals is beneficial to society as a whole through greater total production, higher tax yields, and possible spillover benefits which may contribute to a generally improved quality of life for all.

Causes of Economic Growth. In analyzing causes of economic growth, economists have traditionally considered only increases in the *quantity* of labor and physical capital and have largely ignored improvements in their *quality*. Schultz (1981, p. 11) condemned this assumption that capital is qualitatively homogeneous. Claiming that each form of capital has specific properties, he introduced the concept of variation in quality of both physical and human capital.

Schultz, who received the Nobel Prize in economics in 1979 for his work with developing countries, is generally credited with sparking a renewed interest in human capital theory. He turned attention to the economics of education, observing that the concepts commonly used to "measure capital and labor were close to being empty in explaining the increases in production that occur over time" (Schultz, 1963, p. viii). Schultz was referring to the fact that quantitative increases in labor and physical capital explained less than one-third of the rate of economic growth in the United States between 1929 and 1957 (Blaug, 1970).

In attempting to explain the cause of the remaining two-thirds of growth, called "the residual," Schultz drew an analogy between additions of stock to physical capital and increases in the amount of education available in the population at large. Schultz's (1963) thesis was that traditional measures of labor and capital understated the true investment. Schultz concluded that the unexplained economic growth "originates out of forms of capital that have not been measured and consists mainly of human capital. . . .[T]he economic capabilities of man are predominantly a produced means of production and . . . most of the differences in earnings are a consequence of differences in the amounts that have been invested in people" (pp. 64–65). Extending Schultz's analysis, Benson (1978, p. 72) estimated that the net "investment" through education accounted for approximately 21 percent of the growth in real national income of the United States between 1929 and 1957—or nearly half of the residual.

Denison (1962) took a different approach to measuring the contribution of education to economic growth. He examined earning differentials attributable to education as a measure of its economic value, rather than the costs of input factors as did Schultz. A subsequent analysis indicated that real national income grew at an average annual rate of 3.85 percent between 1948 and 1969 (Denison, 1974). Of that amount, Denison attributed .41 percent to the higher level of education of the work force, and 1.19 percent to advances in knowledge and technology. This latter factor is closely related to the mission of educational institutions—especially higher education—since advances in technology and growth in knowledge are among the products of colleges and universities, although not in their domain exclusively.

Rate of Return Approach. The Schultz and Denison studies showed that education contributed significantly to national economic growth. Those studies did not address the adequacy of investment in education, however. With respect to education, rate of return analysis is intended to inform policy makers about whether to spend on different kinds of programs (Benson, 1978, p. 91). Rate of return analysis compares the profit (increased

earnings) to the expense of acquiring knowledge and skills including earnings foregone in the process.

In a free market, when supply and demand for persons possessing a particular set of knowledge and skills are in equilibrium, the rate of return approximates that which is generally expected from other types of investments. If the rate is much higher, there is an apparent shortage of persons with these skills, permitting them to command higher wages. This encourages more people to acquire similar training and enter the work force until wages and the rate of return drop to the expected. If, on the other hand, the rate of return is much lower than that which can be obtained from other investments, there is a surplus of persons with similar skills—more than the market can absorb. Competition for employment drives wages down, discouraging people from acquiring such skills until supply again equals demand and the rate of return from earnings over expenditures equals the expected. (See the discussion of the interaction between supply and demand above and in Murphy and Welch [1989].) Market effects may be dampened by constraints placed on them through such vehicles as union contracts, which are quite common among public school districts.

Private rates of return are good guides for individual behavior, but rate of return analysis used in social policy development must be derived from total (public and private) cost and benefits. Since the price of an education in both public and private institutions is subsidized by public funds and/or private endowments, such costs must be included. To calculate the social rate of return, the amount of subsidization to individuals (e.g., the difference between tuition charged the student and actual cost, scholarships, and fellowships) is also included. Doing so reduces the rates of return. As a general rule, social rates of return to education are lower than private rates of return—an argument for having the cost of higher education paid in part by students' tuition and not totally subsidized by government.

Evaluating social policy by computing internal rates of return for investments in education was the focus of the pioneering work by Becker (1960, 1964). He estimated the social rate of return for white male college graduates to be between 10 percent and 13 percent. Assuming that rates for college dropouts and nonwhites would be lower, he estimated the rate for all college entrants to be between 8 percent and 11 percent. Becker (1964, p. 121) concluded, "The rates on business capital and college education seem, therefore, to fall within the same range." Rates of return for high school graduates were higher, and they were highest for elementary school graduates. Becker cautioned, however, that adjustments for differential ability would likely reduce or eliminate the differences in rates among levels of schooling. Estimates of rates of return from expenditures for secondary and higher education between 1939 and 1976 showed that the returns were falling over time, although not by a large amount (Woodhall, 1987). This trend appears to have reversed dramatically during the 1980s (Murphy & Welch, 1989), because of an increasing demand for highly trained workers and correspondingly higher wages relative to workers with less training.

Others have also discovered a lower rate of return for higher levels of education. Hanoch (1971, p. 205) found a rate of return in excess of 100 percent for Caucasians completing elementary school. The rate of return for a high school graduate fell to 16 percent and for a college graduate holding a baccalaureate degree to 12 percent. All are respectably above the 10 percent benchmark. In another study, Davis and Morrall (1974) estimated rates of return ranging from 5 percent to 11 percent for graduate education. They concluded: "The implications for policy makers are that relatively more funds should be devoted to the lower levels of schooling than are now being allocated" (p. 51).

Spending Levels for Education. When ten economically advanced countries were compared in terms of educational expenditures as a percentage of gross national product (GNP) in 1988, the United States ranked about in the middle, consuming 6.8 percent. Educational spending consumed more of the GNP in Sweden (9.1 percent), Canada (7.1 percent), the former Soviet Union (7.4 percent), and the Netherlands (6.9 percent). Countries that devoted proportionally less include Australia (6.8 percent), France (5.8 percent), Japan (5.6 percent), the United Kingdom (5.2 percent), and West Germany (4.6 percent) (U.S. Department of Commerce, 1983, 1988). Since then, the percentage for the United States has increased annually, reaching 7.8 percent in 1991 and 1992 (see Table 12.2).

Investment in education in the United States for the period 1959 through 1992 is reported in Table 12.2 along with the percentage of the total population enrolled in precollegiate and higher education. The percentage of GNP spent for all educational institutions rose steadily from 4.8 percent in 1959 to 7.5 percent in 1970. It then declined to 6.7 percent in 1980 and 1985, rising to 7.8 percent in 1991. The earlier peak allocation of GNP to education (1970) corresponds to the peak in the percentage of the population enrolled in educational institutions. The current peak allocation of GNP (7.8 percent) to education is for a smaller cohort than was the case in 1970.

For elementary and secondary school expenditures, the percentage of GNP rose from 3.4 percent in 1959 to 4.7 percent in 1970 and 1975. Although expenditure per pupil continued to increase in constant dollars, the percentage of GNP declined to 4.0 percent in 1985, but has since risen to 4.7 percent. The decline in the percentage of

Table 12.2
Percentage of Gross National Product (GNP) Spent on Education and Percentage of Total Population Enrolled in Educational Institutions, 1959–1992

Year	Elementary and Secondary Schools		Higher Education		Total	
	Percentage of GNP	Percentage Enrollment of Population	Percentage of GNP	Percentage Enrollment of Population	Percentage of GNP	Percentage Enrollment of Population
1959	3.4	23.0	1.4	2.0	4.8	25.0
1965	4.0	24.9	2.2	3.0	6.2	28.0
1970	4.8	25.0	2.7	4.2	7.5	29.2
1975	4.7	23.1	2.7	5.2	7.5	28.2
1980	4.1	20.3	2.6	5.3	6.8	25.6
1985	4.0	18.8	2.7	5.1	6.7	24.0
1990	4.5	18.4	3.0	5.4	7.5	24.0
1992	4.7	18.9	3.1	5.8	7.8	24.7

SOURCE: National Center for Education Statistics (Selected Years). *Digest of Education Statistics.* Washington, DC: U.S. Government Printing Office.

GNP spent for education can be attributed in part to the smaller proportion of the total population attending elementary and secondary schools. Enrollment peaked in 1970 at 25.0 percent of the total population, subsequently declining to 18.7 percent in 1988.

The percentage of GNP spent on colleges and universities rose from 1.4 percent in 1959 to 2.7 percent in 1970. Between 1970 and 1985, the statistic ranged between 2.6 percent and 2.7 percent and has risen since to a record high of 3.1 percent. Actual enrollments in postsecondary education rose from 3,640,000 in 1959 to 8,581,000 in 1970, and have continued to increase to over 12 million. The percentage of the population enrolled in higher education in 1959 was 2.0 percent. It rose to 5.3 percent in 1980 and has remained relatively stable (between 5.1 percent and 5.2 percent) since then.

As already noted, rate of return studies suggest that advanced countries, including the United States, are probably spending at or near the optimal rate for educational services given the existing state of employed educational technology. If the rate of investment in education were increased, it can probably be best justified at the elementary and preschool levels.

INTERNAL EFFICIENCY

We now turn to consideration of the efficiency with which resources allocated to schools are used in the education of children. The ability of such resources to improve individual and societal welfare will be enhanced or diminished according to the efficiency with which they are used. If the tentative policy conclusion of the previous section is correct that the United States (along with other advanced nations) is spending about the optimal amount on education given the technology currently in use, then improvements in the educational performance of American students will depend more on improving the internal efficiency of schools and school systems than on the addition of more resources.

Studies of the efficiency of schooling that relate outcomes to inputs are generally traced to the report by James Coleman (1966), *Equality of Educational Opportunity* (EEO). This type of study has been classified using the economic terms *educational production functions* and *input-output analysis*, even though the studies are not the exclusive domain of economists; indeed, Coleman is a sociologist. Such research has been pursued in an effort to improve educational productivity, i.e., improving the accomplishments of students relative to resources committed.

A production function may be conceptualized as a set of relations among possible inputs and a corresponding set of outputs for a firm or industry—in this case, schools and education (Burkhead, 1967, p. 18). According to Hanushek (1987):

> *A firm's production possibilities are assumed to be governed by certain technical relationships, and the production function describes the maximum feasible output that can be obtained from a set of inputs (p. 33).*

With respect to schooling, outputs include behavioral and attitudinal changes in pupils induced through school activities. Inputs studied have ranged from student background (e.g., socio-economic status of family, student IQ, previous achievement), to material provision (e.g., expenditures, teacher characteristics, characteristics of buildings), to process (e.g., time on task, teaching methods, and student-teacher interactions). Outputs are usually measured by standardized test scores, but occasionally include other measures such as high school graduation rate, attendance rate, rate of graduates continuing on to postsecondary education, etc. The existence of such relationships assumes that there is a common underlying technology in education, an assumption that may come as a surprise to many educators

because production technologies in education are inexact. Nevertheless, the sameness of American schools (and schools around the world for that matter) lend credence to an assumption of an implicit technology. School buildings are typically arranged with classrooms and certain ancillary spaces such as libraries, auditoriums, and gymnasiums. Each classroom is usually presided over by one teacher only, and there is a large degree of similarity in the ways teachers organize and manage classrooms.

Monk (1989) identified two traditions with respect to the study of the production of education services. The first attempts to estimate the parameters of the educational production function. The second is less developed, but uses "the production function as a gateway to broader economic theories and reasoning that can be used to guide inquiry" (p. 31). After discussing studies that illustrate the first tradition, we turn to the second tradition and address educational production in light of several related topics: effective schools research, psychological studies, comparisons with private schools, and economies and diseconomies of scale.

Estimating Education Production Functions. The EEO study (Coleman, 1966) was one of the first, and remains one of the largest, production function studies ever attempted. It involved over a half-million students in 4,000 schools and thousands of teachers. It is perhaps the best known and most controversial of all the input-output studies. The controversy extended not only to its conclusion that schooling had little potential for closing the achievement gap between white and minority students but also to the methodology used.

The most significant finding of studies of school effectiveness, beginning with the EEO study, is the very strong relationship between family background and pupil achievement. The relationship is so strong that findings of these studies have frequently been misinterpreted to mean that schools have relatively little impact on pupil achievement. It is well documented that schools have not been very effective in closing achievement gaps among racial and ethnic groups and among socio-economic classes; nevertheless, schools do have enormous impacts on the development of all children.

Even the most gifted children learn—or at least develop—their basic academic skills in schools. Children come into schools as non-readers and leave with varying levels of literacy skills. Similar statements could be made about mathematics, writing and other academic skills, as well as about knowledge and attitudinal development. Mayeske et al. (1972) stated it very well in a reanalysis of the EEO data, "Schools are indeed important. It is equally clear, however, that their influence is bound up with that of the student's background" (p. ix). Very little of the influence of schools can be separated from the social backgrounds of their students, and very little of the influence of social background on learning can be separated from the influence of the schools. According to Mayeske, schools, as presently constituted, produce the greatest amount of learning and foster the greatest amount of motivation among students from higher socio-economic strata and white and Oriental-American backgrounds; school's effect on achievement and attitudes grows for all groups with the length of time a student spends in school.

Hanushek (1987) identified in the literature some 144 separate studies of production relationships in education completed since the EEO study in 1966. Two recent reviews of such studies have been made by Hanushek (1986) and MacPhail-Wilcox and King (1986).

Per pupil expenditures generally correlate positively with student achievement and socio-economic status. But these two reviews agree that, when appropriate statistical control is made for socio-economic status, rela-

tionships for all students between per pupil expenditure levels and achievement are weak or nonexistent. Teacher's verbal ability appears to provide the strongest relationship between any school characteristic and student achievement. Schools with higher achieving students, when socio-economic factors are taken into account, quite consistently pay their teachers more than lower achieving schools. The evidence is mixed, however, concerning any relationships between teacher experience and advanced degree status and pupil achievement. This lack of relationship is particularly important given that the structure of most teacher salary schedules is based on longevity in teaching and degrees and/or graduate credit hours earned.

Hanushek (1986) and MacPhail-Wilcox and King (1986) differ sharply in their interpretations of findings with respect to relationships between class size indices and achievement. Hanushek unequivocally states that there is no consistent evidence of a relationship. According to Hanushek, of 112 studies investigating teacher-student ratios, only nine found positive statistically significant relationships with achievement. Fourteen found significant negative relationships; in the remaining 89 studies, there were no significant relationships. MacPhail-Wilcox and King, on the other hand, found "overwhelmingly" significant relationships between small classes and higher achievement. They observe that relationships are stronger, however, where opportunities for direct student-teacher instructional interaction are measured more precisely, i.e., size of specific class, specific staff to pupil ratios vs. average class size, and overall pupil-teacher ratios. They also note that the presence of paraprofessionals appears to enhance opportunities for pupil-adult interactions and improved achievement.

A meta-analysis of class size research by Glass and Smith (1979) may provide an explanation for the conflicting conclusions of Hanushek (1986) and MacPhail-Wilcox and

King (1986). Glass and Smith found little relationship between class size and achievement over the normal range of classes. In classes smaller than the normal range, better achievement was found. Unless the mode of teaching in small classes is individualized, however, the potential of the small class is not realized.

Benefits of small class size and individualized instruction seem to be more critical to the good performance of at-risk children than for other children (MacPhail-Wilcox & King, 1986). The negative effect of ability grouping is also greatest for at-risk children. Ability grouping is associated with lower performance among low socio-economic and minority students, while heterogeneous grouping is associated with higher achievement among such students and does not harm the achievement of high socio-economic and majority students (Summers & Wolfe, 1975).

In light of their analysis of findings from production function studies, MacPhail-Wilcox and King (1986) are concerned that a primary focus of recent educational reform efforts is on improving the credentials of teachers and standardizing teacher approaches to the instruction of all students.

> *Focused largely on teacher quality, these educational reforms overlook the obviously important role which students play in learning. They fail to acknowledge that teacher effects vary by the type of student, instructional context, and organizational characteristics. Despite more than fifteen years of research confirming these propositions, current reforms proceed on unwarranted assumptions that uniform teacher qualities, standard pedagogical practices, and existing organizational arrangements will eradicate the purported ills of public education. (p. 191)*

Effective Schools Research. Effective schools research is a variation of the production function approach. Education production functions research takes a normative approach in studying school efficiency. Effective schools research focuses on exceptions and usually ignores cost considerations; thus, its findings relate more to technical efficiency than to economic efficiency. It consists largely of case studies of schools and classrooms that have unusually positive effects on pupil achievement in order to identify practices that might cause or contribute to that effectiveness (Brookover & Lezotte, 1979; Edmonds, 1979; Jackson, Logsdon, & Taylor, 1983; Reed, 1985; Venezsky & Winfield, 1980; Weber, 1971).

Effective schools are characterized by effective classroom teaching practices including high teacher expectations, good classroom management techniques, and greater time spent on tasks than one would find in most schools. These schools are also characterized by strong leadership, usually in the person of the principal, which provides for the coordination of the instructional program at the building level in a manner that is tightly coupled, but not bureaucratic. The principal appears to be a key factor in establishing a common school culture and sense of community, consisting of: "shared goals; high expectations for student performance; mechanisms to sustain motivation and commitment; collegiality among teachers, students, and the principal; and a school-wide focus on continuous improvement" (Odden & Webb, 1983, p. xiv). Given current assumptions about schooling, effective schools research is identifying some ways for schools to make more efficient use of the resources they already have.

Psychological Studies. Psychological studies of schooling also have important implications for technical efficiency of schools. For the most part, like effective schools research, psychological studies do not take into account the price of inputs. Psychological studies have produced results that provide ground for greater optimism about the impact of schools on pupil achievement than those conducted by economists and sociologists.

Walberg (1984) analyzed nearly 3,000 investigations of the productive factors in learning conducted during the 1970s. Table 12.3 summarizes his synthesis of effects of various approaches to improve teaching and learning. Relationships between achievement and socio-economic status (.25 standard deviation) and peer groups (.24) are relatively small when compared with many of the instructional interventions reported in Table 12.3.

Reinforcement (1.17) and instructional cues and feedback (.97), both of which are psychological components of mastery learning, rank first and fourth in effect. Acceleration programs (1.00), which provide advanced activities to high achieving students, ranked second. Ranking third was reading training (.97), which involves skimming, comprehension, finding answers to questions,

Table 12.3

Walberg's Syntheses of Effects on Learning

SOURCE: H. J. Walberg. (1984). "Improving the Productivity of America's Schools." *Educational Leadership, 41*(8), Figures 3–4, p. 24. Reprinted with permission of the Association for Supervision and Cur-

Method	Effect	Size
Reinforcement	1.17	XXXXXXXXXXXX
Acceleration	1.00	XXXXXXXXXX
Reading Training	.97	XXXXXXXXXX
Cues and Feedback	.97	XXXXXXXXXX
Science Mastery Learning	.81	XXXXXXXX
Graded Homework	.79	XXXXXXXX
Cooperative Learning	.76	XXXXXXXX
Class Morale	.60	XXXXXX
Reading Experiments	.60	XXXXXX
Personalized Instruction	.57	XXXXXX
Home Interventions	.50	XXXXX
Adaptive Instruction	.45	XXXXX
Tutoring	.40	XXXX
Instructional Time	.38	XXXX
Individualized Science	.35	XXXX
Higher-Order Questions	.34	XXX
Diagnostic Prescriptive Methods	.33	XXX
Individualized Instruction	.32	XXX
Individualized Mathematics	.32	XXX
New Science Curricula	.31	XXX
Teacher Expectations	.28	XXX
Computer Assisted Instruction	.24	XX
Sequenced Lessons	.24	XX
Advance Organizers	.23	XX
New Mathematics Curricula	.18	XX
Inquiry Biology	.16	XX
Homogeneous Groups	.10	X
Class Size	.09	X
Programmed Instruction	−.03	−.
Mainstreaming	−.12	−x.

Note: The x symbols represent the sizes of effects in tenths of standard deviations.

and adjusting reading speeds. Other highly effective techniques include cooperative learning (.76), graded homework (.79), and various approaches to individualized instruction. High teacher expectations (.28) have a moderate impact, as do time spent on tasks, advanced organizing techniques, morale or climate of the classroom, and home interventions. Reduced class size has little impact at all. Although costs were not studied, it should be noted that most of the more successful interventions do not involve the commitment of significantly more resources, if any more; the interventions use already committed resources differently. Walberg (1984) concluded:

> *Synthesis of educational and psychological research in ordinary schools shows that improving the amount and quality of instruction can result in vastly more effective and efficient academic learning. Educators can do even more by also enlisting families as partners and engaging them directly and indirectly in their efforts. (p. 26)*

Comparisons with Private Schools.   Coleman returned to center-stage of school policy controversy with his comparison of public and private high schools (Coleman, Hoffer, & Kilgore, 1981). His methodology involved multiple regressions similar to his EEO study and other production function studies. Data for this study were from High School and Beyond, an ongoing national study of achievement and other high school outcomes sponsored by the National Center for Educational Statistics and carried out by the National Opinion Research Center. More than 50,000 students in over 1,000 schools participated in the initial data collection in 1980. The schools included approximately 80 Catholic and 25 other private high schools. Because of the small number of "other" private high schools, few conclusions were drawn concerning them. Longitudinal data became available in 1984.

The researchers found greater achievement growth in verbal skills and in mathematics between the sophomore and senior years among students in Catholic high schools than in public high schools when statistical controls were made for differences in student background characteristics (Coleman & Hoffer, 1987). The magnitude of the difference was equivalent to one grade on average, and it was greater for minority, low socioeconomic status, and other at-risk students than for other students. No differences were found in science knowledge and civics. Coleman's conclusions have been challenged but not refuted by others (Alexander, 1987; Alexander & Pallas, 1987; Willms, 1987). The challenges reinforce our understanding of the subjectivity of even quantitative research. In reviewing Coleman's work and the challenges to it, Haertel (1987) concluded:

> *Given our present state of knowledge, all of the authors' different choices are defensible. They are dictated by different conceptions of school policy, of the sources of individual differences in learning, of what is taught during the last two years of high school, and of appropriate public policy. (p. 16, emphasis added)*

Haertel also pointed out that none of the analysts found public school achievement to be superior to that in Catholic schools; the argument was over the size of the Catholic school advantage and whether or not it was significant from a policy perspective. The Coleman et al. analysis suggests that Catholic high schools tend to operate with greater technical efficiency than do most public high schools. The fact that Catholic schools can do this at *lower cost* suggests that they also operate with greater economic efficiency.

Hoffer, Greeley, and Coleman (1987) attribute the greater success of the Catholic schools to their higher demands on students. These schools place larger proportions of their students in the academic track including many who would be relegated to general or vocational tracks in public high schools. Catholic high schools also demand more course work, more advanced course work, and better discipline. The researchers found that at-risk pupils did especially well in Catholic schools and that the productive characteristics of this school climate could be successfully replicated in public schools.

> *Catholic schools are especially beneficial to the least advantaged students: minorities, poor, and those whose initial achievement is low. For these students, the lack of structure, demands, and expectations found in many public schools is especially harmful.* Our analyses show that those public schools which make the same demands as found in the average Catholic school produce comparable achievement. *(p. 87, emphasis added)*

The description of the average Catholic high school culture sounds very much like that characterized by "effective" public schools. The Hoffer, Greeley, and Coleman study was described more extensively in Chapter 10.

Chubb and Moe (1985, 1990) expanded the data base used by Coleman et al. to include organizational and environmental information. They attribute the poor performance of American public schools to the institutions of direct democratic control by which schools have been traditionally governed. Like Coleman, they recommend that public schools be built around parent-student choice and school autonomy, which would induce market-like competition among schools. The Chubb and Moe studies were described in some detail in Chapter 10.

Economies and Diseconomies of Scale.

Assuming a universal educational production function, economies of scale are realized when average production costs decline as more units are produced or serviced. Conversely, there are diseconomies of scale when average production costs increase as more units are produced or serviced.

These are important concepts in the efficient organization of educational enterprises.

Policies concerning school district consolidation are directed toward realizing economies of scale, whereas policies decentralizing large city school districts are directed toward avoiding diseconomies of scale. Likewise, during periods of declining enrollments, closing under-utilized buildings is a strategy for minimizing operating costs. Reorganizing very large schools into "houses" or "schools within schools," is a strategy for realizing the benefits of both large and small size units while minimizing their disadvantages. Interest in scale economies derive from concern over economic efficiency.

Policy implications drawn from studies on relationships between school and district size, pupil achievement, and cost have taken a dramatic turn in recent years. From the beginning of this century through the 1960s, the overwhelming evidence seemed to support large schools and school districts in terms of economies and the higher number, diversity, and caliber of professional and administrative personnel they could attract. These early studies were concerned primarily with inputs (costs) and gave little, if any, attention to outputs and ratios of outputs to inputs. As researchers began to take into account total cost and socioeconomic status of pupils, and to include measures of output such as achievement, pupil self-image, and success in college, economies of scale evaporated at relatively low numbers of pupils. The disadvantages of large size became readily apparent.

The new emphasis in research on the relationships between size and quality of schooling may have been a byproduct of the disenchantment with large city schools in recent years. City educational systems had served through the 1950s as the standard for measuring the quality of educational opportunities. But in the 1960s and up to the present, evidence of low cognitive pupil achievement, low attendance rates, and high dropout rates has surfaced in urban school systems. This, coupled with their inability to use substantial federal and state funds to raise significantly the achievement levels of most disadvantaged children, severely marred the images of urban schools. It now appears that, given present assumptions about how schools (and school districts) should organize, the relationships between size and quality of schooling are curvilinear. The benefits brought by larger enrollments increase to an optimal point and then decline following an inverted U-shaped curve (Riew, 1981, 1986; Fox, 1981).

Current research clearly suggests that small schools have the edge over large schools. Berlin and Cienkus (1989), after coediting an issue of *Education and Urban Society* devoted to the subject of size of school districts, schools, and classrooms, concluded that "smaller seems to be better."

Why does smaller seem to work better? . . . The literature on educational change repeats the answer. That is, people seem to learn, to change, and to grow in situations in which they feel that they have some control, some personal influence, some efficacy. Those situations in which parents, teachers and students are bonded together in pursuit of learning are likely to be the most productive. Small size by itself can only aid the complex process. (p. 231)

Economist Ronald Coase (1988), who received the Nobel Prize in economics in 1991, developed a theory of "transaction costs" to explain such phenomena in organizations in general. Transaction costs are costs of communication, coordination, and deciding. Eventually, expansion of an organization (e.g., school or district) can lead to diseconomies and higher unit costs because of managerial problems that are characteristic of large operations. Building on Coase's thesis, Williamson (1975) argued that conventional estimates of economies of scale have vastly underestimated "transactional costs." Peters

and Waterman (1982), in their study of "America's best-run companies," found that divisions, plants, and branches were smaller than any cost analysis would suggest they should be. Decentralization of function was practiced where classic economics would ordain otherwise. "The excellent companies understand that beyond a certain surprisingly small size, *diseconomies* of scale seem to set in with a vengeance" (p. 112).

Optimum school and district size is a function of desired standards, available technology, and governing structures. The criteria defining these change over time. In the past, providing diversity in curriculum and support services at an affordable cost were the primary justifications for large urban schools and suburban and rural school consolidation. Now, the disadvantages of bigness and the virtues of smallness have been well documented. Additionally, technological advances characteristic of the "Information Age" have made it possible for any individual in almost any place to access curricular diversity easily. These developments combine to impel a reassessment of the large school policies of central cities and state school consolidation policies for rural areas. Fowler (1989) concluded:

It is apparent that public school size and district size both influence schooling outcomes, and although other evidence of this relationship has accumulated, policy makers seem to ignore the finding and its significance. Much litigation has been undertaken to equalize expenditures per pupil, or to assure equivalent staff characteristics in an effort to increase learning; however, it appears that keeping schools relatively small might be more efficacious. (p. 21)

In summary, relationships between size and effectiveness and economy appear to be curvilinear as with nearly all cost curves. While there are disadvantages in being very small, there are also disadvantages in being very large. There is little agreement on an optimal size and optimal size appears to be a function of circumstances. The challenge before us is to provide stimulating learning environments with broad educational programs characteristic of large schools along with the supportive social structure characteristic of small schools.

After looking at how decisions are made about the allocation of resources to education in a mixed economy and examining equity in the distribution of resources among schools and school districts, we conclude that the United States devotes about the optimal proportion of its resources (GNP) to education given the current state of educational technology. If there are to be improvements in educational outcomes, those improvements will be primarily as a result of improvements in internal efficiency—not through the application of additional resources.

Studies relating to the efficiency of public schools indicate with great consistency that schools are not using the resources entrusted to them to full advantage. Given current organization and practice, the problem is not so much the lack of resources, but rather the nature of available resources and the ways in which they are being used. While there is inequity in the distribution of resources among schools and school districts, improving the equity of the flow of funds to schools is not likely to improve the educational experiences of children unless the application of those resources *within* schools is radically changed.

The greatest resource allocation problem facing policy makers during the 1990s and beyond is designing instructional systems that are educationally effective and economically efficient. The second most important problem is improving equity of distribution of resources to schools so that all children have access to good facilities, competent instruction, and state-of-the-art learning materials.

Equity issues are placed second only because of the extreme harm being done currently to at-risk children as a result of the inefficiencies of existing schooling arrangements.

■ CASE STUDY[1]

Setting Budget Priorities at Harmony Central School

Harmony Central School is located in a tiny rural village. Its lone school building was built in 1955 and houses 350 K–12 students. The District employs 31 full-time teachers and two full-time administrators.

Since June of 1984, when the superintendent of 18 years retired, there have been four changes. The fall of 1987 saw Harmony's first full-time K–12 principal.

After several unsuccessful attempts in earlier years, the district has had two renovation projects since 1985. The first was primarily for energy conservation, consisting of new windows and boilers. The second was an extensive project consisting of classroom ceilings and lights, hall lockers, a $40,000 science lab, a new roof, bleachers, and black topping of the parking lot. The district also constructed its own garage.

The Board of Education is studying a third project to address a shortage of classroom space. Presently, there is need for a pre-kindergarten room, two elementary classrooms, a resource room, art and music rooms, as well as a new gym. A new creative playground and extensive work on the athletic fields are also being studied.

Community support and involvement within the school is strong as the school is the activity center of the area. Though very traditional in their thinking, community residents

[1]Prepared by Joseph Backer, Lynda Cessario, and Melanie Vlosky.

are beginning to understand the importance of a strong educational system. The district has been slow in developing its use of technology though computer-based instruction and long-distance learning programs are starting to be discussed.

The present computer curriculum is weak; each elementary classroom has only two Apple computers and a lab of sixteen units is located in the high school. Business courses are taught on typewriters but are conducted by an excellent instructor.

The strengths of the district are its elementary program and science at the 7–12 level. Areas of concern include computer instruc-

tion, 7–12 math and social studies, and the absence of any advanced placement courses.

The extracurricular program has been successful, especially boys' soccer. Baseball has been weak though is still considered a priority by the community. The major concern in this area is the lack of outdoor fields, the field conditions, and the tremendous amount of use the fields get through little league teams, community teams, and school teams.

Problem

The district has $90,000 in unexpended funds to cover all or part of the expenditures listed below. You may spend up to $90,000 but may

---

1. The district has a Social Studies teacher opening; two finalists have been selected.

   a. Elizabeth is a 10-year veteran with excellent credentials wishing to relocate in the area.

      (With benefits) $38,500 _____

      or

   b. Bill is a recent college graduate who was awarded "Student Teacher of the Year" by his university. Bill also played four years of college baseball and is anxious to coach.

      (With benefits) $25,500 _____

RANK

____ 2. An IBM computer network with 12 stations. This system will be useable for all business courses and computer courses, and has expansion capabilities.

   $29,000 _____

____ 3. Carpeting for two classrooms. $ 3,000 _____

____ 4. Aerator for playing fields. $ 4,500 _____

____ 5. Fertilizer and seed for fields $ 2,000 _____

____ 6. Driveway and parking lot sealed. $ 5,000 _____

____ 7. Replacement of the 1985 school car (47,000 miles). $11,000 _____

____ 8. Replacement of the old copier with a new high quality, faster copier. $10,800 _____

not exceed that figure. You must choose 1A or 1B, but are then free to make selections from the remaining lists. Please rank your decisions starting with 1 as your highest priority. Be prepared to justify your rankings.

Activities for Discussion

1. Interview your superintendent of schools and/or members of your board of education about how resource allocation decisions are made in your school district.

2. In this chapter the authors conclude that the United States is already devoting an adequate proportion of its resources to formal education and that any improvements in education will have to come from using those resources more wisely (more efficiently). Do you agree with this position? List and discuss arguments supporting it and those which do not.

3. Using the information provided in the "Internal Efficiency" section of this chapter, devise a configuration or configurations for using public school resources that are likely to be more efficient than configurations typically employed at the present time.

4. Visit a large school and a small school serving the same grade levels and seek answers to the questions that follow. Alternatively, form a study group made up of persons with experience in different size schools and compare experiences as you discuss the questions below.

   a. Do you find any differences between schools that can be attributed to their variances in size?
   b. What are the advantages and disadvantages of large schools? Of small schools?

   c. What strategies might best neutralize the negative effects of school size?

Annotated Bibliography

Cohn, E., & Geske, T. G. (1990). *The economics of education* (3rd ed.). Oxford, England: Pergamon.

The principal aim of this book is to present a comprehensive and critical analysis of the economics of education. It addresses such topics as: the concept of human capital, the role of government in education, the benefits and costs of education, benefit-cost analysis in education, education and national economic growth, production and cost functions in education, educational planning, teachers' salaries, taxation, and financing education at all levels. There is considerable material on countries other than the United States, though the book is primarily focused on American institutions and data. Knowledge of economics and advanced mathematics is not a prerequisite for comprehension of its contents. Each chapter concludes with a list of Selected Literature as a guide for further study of the concepts presented in the chapter.

Odden, A. R., & Picus, L. O. (1992). *School finance: A policy perspective*. New York: McGraw-Hill.

The book has a clear policy focus that places school finance within its broader context of public finance. The emphasis is on setting education and fiscal goals, and on designing school finance structures to implement those goals. Drawing on the work of Berne and Stiefel (1984), the book uses an explicit framework to analyze school finance equity. The latter chapters address the issues of where education dollars go and how to improve school productivity. Strategies considered for improving productivity include site-based performance incentives and site-based management and budgeting. The most distinguishing feature of this book is the school finance computer simulation that accompanies it. The 100-district sample of the simulation allows the reader to develop and analyze the impact of alternative financial structures on desired goals of public policy. Other topics considered include the structure of inter-governmental grants for educational purposes, taxation, and the politics and impacts of changes in school finance structures.

Psacharopoulos, G. (Ed.). (1987). *Economics of education: Research and studies*. Oxford, England: Pergamon.

The economics of education is a field that only formally appeared as such in the literature in the early 1960s although its central thesis, human capital development, can be found in the work of Adam Smith, first published in 1776. The readings in this volume present reviews of key topics in the field as it has rapidly evolved since the 1960s. The handbook is organized on a thematic basis which enables the reader to find his or her way easily around the field. The sections include: the formation of human capital, educational production, the benefits of education, education and employment, the analysis of earnings, the distribution of educational outcomes, ability and screening, education and manpower planning, planning models, longitudinal analysis in education, educational costs, and the financing of education. An alphabetical list of entries is included for further guidance and each entry throughout the book contains extensive bibliographic references to help the reader pursue a particular topic further.

Swanson, A. D., & King, R. A. (1991). *School finance: Its economics and politics*. New York: Longman.

The strategy of the book is to respect the importance of economic theory in analyzing the impact of existing and alternative policies, while recognizing that such theories do little to help understand the forces shaping school finance legislation and the processes through which financial policy is developed. To understand fully what has happened in school finance legislation, and what is likely to happen, the authors contend that the field must also be studied drawing on concepts from political science. The book is distinguished in its use of both economic political models in analyzing school finance issues and its frequent use of international data and comparative perspectives. The authors examine the relevance of traditional theories and practice in school finance and evaluate potential alternatives in light of the ferment and changes that character-

ized education in the 1980s and continue into the 1990s. Part I addresses the context of school finance by laying out relevant economic, political, and structural information. Considerable attention is given to the importance of values in the development of public policy and how changes in priorities given to values require corresponding changes in policy. Part II looks at the tax structure that supports public education. Part III focuses on intergovernmental fund transfers, i.e., state and federal aid. Part IV addresses the issues of improving school finance structures and the use of resources. Particular attention is given to issues of equity and efficiency, teacher remuneration, educational technology, school-based decisionmaking, and family choice of schooling.

Thompson, D. C., Wood, R. C., & Honeyman, D. S. (1994). *Fiscal leadership for schools: Concepts and practices*. New York: Longman.

The book is intended to bridge the conceptual division between school finance and school business management by taking a principles-to-policy-to-practice approach. Each chapter begins with a discussion of theory and ends with observations and applications to practice. The text is arranged in two parts. Part I covers the social and economic context of public school finance: its origin, how public schools are funded, and the role played by the courts in shaping the nature of modern education finance. In Part II, the actual tasks performed by fiscal administrators in schools is developed around the broad theme of fiscal planning. Specific topics considered include: budgeting; accounting, auditing and reporting; fiscal aspects of personnel administration; purchasing, inventory, distribution, and control; risk management; transportation and food management; capital outlay, maintenance, and operations; and use of technology in support of educational decisionmaking.

References

Alexander, K. L. (1987). Cross-sectional comparisons of public and private school effectiveness: A review of the evidence and issues. In E. H.

Haertel, T. James, & H. M. Levin (Eds.), *Comparing public and private schools: Volume 2, School achievement* (pp. 33–66). New York: The Falmer Press.

Alexander, K. L., & Pallas, A. M. (1987). School sector and cognitive performance: When is a little a little? In E. H. Haertel, T. James, & H. M. Levin (Eds.), *Comparing public and private schools: Volume 2, School achievement* (pp. 89–112). New York: The Falmer Press.

Barro, S. M. (1987). *School finance equity: Research in the 1980s and the current state of the art.* Washington, DC: Decision Resources Corporation.

Becker, G. S. (1960). Underinvestment in college education? *American Economic Review* (Papers and proceedings), *50,* 345–354.

Becker, G. S. (1964). *Human capital: A theoretical and empirical analysis, with special reference to education.* New York: National Bureau of Economic Research.

Benson, C. S. (1978). *The economics of public education* (3rd ed.). Boston: Houghton Mifflin.

Berlin, B., & Cienkus, R. (1989). Size: The ultimate educational issue? *Education and Urban Society, 21,* 228–231.

Berne, R. (1988). Equity issues in school finance. *Journal of Education Finance, 14,* 159–180.

Berne, R., & Stiefel, L. (1983). Changes in school finance equity: A national perspective. *Journal of Education Finance, 8,* 419–435.

Berne, R., & Stiefel, L. (1984). *The measurement of equity in school finance: Conceptual, methodological, and empirical dimensions.* Baltimore, MD: The Johns Hopkins University Press.

Bezeau, L. M. (1985). *Level and inequality of per pupil expenditure as a function of finance centralization.* Paper presented at the Annual Meeting of the Canadian Society for the Study of Education, Montreal, Quebec, Canada.

Blaug, M. (1970). *An introduction to the economics of education.* Harmondsworth, England: Penguin Books.

Brookover, W., & Lezotte, L. (1979). *Changes in school characteristics coincident with changes in student achievement.* East Lansing, MI: State University, College of Urban Development.

Brown, L. L., Ginsburg, A. L., Killalea, J. N., Rosthal, R. A., & Tron, E. O. (1978). School finance reform in the seventies: Achievements and fail-ures. *Journal of Education Finance, 4,* 195–212.

Brown, P. R., & Elmore, R. F. (1982). Analyzing the impact of school finance reform. In N. H. Cambron-McCabe & A. Odden (Eds.), *The changing politics of school finance* (pp. 107–138). Cambridge, MA: Ballinger.

Burkhead, J. (1967). *Input and output in large-city high schools.* Syracuse, NY: Syracuse University Press.

Carroll, S. J. (1979). *The search for equity in school finance: Summary and conclusions.* Santa Monica, CA: Rand.

Chubb, J. E., & Moe, T. M. (1985). *Politics, markets, and the organization of schools.* Stanford, CA: Institute for Research on Educational Finance and Governance, School of Education, Stanford University.

Chubb, J. E., & Moe, T. M. (1990). *Politics, markets and America's schools.* Washington, DC: The Brookings Institution.

Coase, R. H. (1988). *The firm, the market, and the law.* Chicago: University of Chicago Press.

Cohn, E., & Smith, M. S. (1989). A decade of improvement in wealth neutrality: A study of school finance equity in South Carolina, 1977–1986. *Journal of Education Finance, 14,* 380–389.

Coleman, J. S. (1966). *Equality of educational opportunity.* Washington, DC: U.S. Government Printing Office.

Coleman, J. S., & Hoffer, T. (1987). *Public and private high schools: The impact of communities.* New York: Basic Books.

Coleman, J. S., Hoffer, T., & Kilgore, S. (1981). *Public and private high schools.* Washington, DC: National Center for Education Statistics.

Davis, J. R., & Morrall III, J. F. (1974). *Evaluating educational investment.* Lexington, MA: Lexington Books.

Denison, E. F. (1962). *The sources of economic growth in the United States.* New York: Committee for Economic Development.

Denison, E. F. (1974). *Accounting for United States economic growth, 1929–1969.* Washington, DC: The Brookings Institution.

Downs, A. (1957). *An economic theory of democracy.* New York: Harper and Row.

Easton, D. A. (1965). *A framework for political analysis.* Englewood Cliffs, NJ: Prentice-Hall.

Eckstein, O. (1967). *Public finance* (2nd ed.). Englewood Cliffs, NJ: Prentice-Hall.

Edmonds, R. (1979). Effective schools for the urban poor. *Educational Leadership, 37,* 15–24.

Fowler, Jr., W. J. (1989). *School size, school characteristics, and school outcomes.* Paper presented at the annual meeting of the American Educational Research Association, San Francisco, CA.

Fox, W. F. (1981). Reviewing economies of size in education. *Journal of Education Finance, 6,* 273–296.

Glass, G. V., & Smith, M. L. (1979). Meta-analysis of research on the relationship of class-size and achievement. *Educational Evaluation and Policy Analysis, 1,* 2–16.

Goertz, M. E. (1983). School finance in New Jersey: A decade after *Robinson v. Cahill. Journal of Education Finance, 8,* 475–489.

Haertel, E. H. (1987). Comparing public and private schools using longitudinal data from the HSB study. In E. H. Haertel, T. James, & H. M. Levin (Eds.), *Comparing public and private schools: Volume 2, School achievement* (pp. 9–32). New York: The Falmer Press.

Hanoch, G. (1971). An economic analysis of earnings and schooling. In B. F. Kiker (Ed.), *Investment in human capital.* Columbia, SC: University of South Carolina Press.

Hanushek, E. A. (1986). The economics of schooling: Production and efficiency in public schools. *Journal of Economic Literature, 24,* 1141–1177.

Hanushek, E. A. (1987). Education production functions. In G. Psacharopoulos (Ed.), *Economics of education: Research and studies* (pp. 33–42). Oxford, England: Pergamon Press.

Heinold, D. (1983). Impact of federal monies on equity among states in K–12 public school finance. *Journal of Education Finance, 8,* 461–474.

Hickrod, G. A., Chaudhari, R. B., & Hubbard, B. C. (1983). The decline and fall of school finance reform in Illinois. *Journal of Education Finance, 8,* 415–418.

Hickrod, G. A., & Goertz, M. E. (1983). Introduction: Evaluating the school finance reforms of the 1970s and early 1980s. *Journal of Education Finance, 8,* 415–418.

Hoffer, T., Greeley, A. M., & Coleman, J. S. (1987). Catholic high school effects on achievement growth. In E. H. Haertel, T. James, & H. M. Levin (Eds.), *Comparing public and private schools: Volume 2, School achievement* (pp. 67–88). New York: The Falmer Press.

Jackson, S., Logsdon, D., & Taylor, N. (1983). Instructional leadership behaviors: Differentiating effective from ineffective low-income urban schools. *Urban Education, 18,* 59–70.

Jones, T. (1985). *State fiscal behavior: A study of resource allocation and distribution.* Paper presented at the Annual Meeting of the American Educational Research Association, Chicago.

Kearney, C. P., & Chen, L. (1989). Measuring equity in Michigan school finance: A further look. *Journal of Education Finance, 14,* 319–367.

King, R. A. (1983). Equalization in New Mexico school finance. *Journal of Education Finance, 9,* 63–78.

Krupey, J. E., & Hopeman, A. (1983). Minnesota school finance equity, 1973–1982. *Journal of Education Finance, 8,* 490–501.

Lake, P. (1983). Expenditure equity in the public schools of Atlantic Canada. *Journal of Education Finance, 8,* 449–460.

Levin, H. M. (1987). Education as a public and private good. *Journal of Policy Analysis and Management, 6,* 628–641.

Long, D. C. (1986). An equity perspective on educational reform. In V. D. Mueller & M. P. McKeown (Eds.), *The fiscal, legal, and political aspects of state reform of elementary and secondary education* (pp. 325–344). Cambridge, MA: Ballinger.

MacPhail-Wilcox, B., & King, R. A. (1986). Production functions revisited in the context of educational reform. *Journal of Education Finance, 12,* 191–223.

Mayeske, G. W., & others. (1972) *A study of our nation's schools.* Washington, DC: U.S. Government Printing Office.

McDonnell, L. M., & Fuhrman, S. (1986). The political context of school reform. In V. D. Mueller & M. P. McKeown (Eds.), *The fiscal, legal, and political aspects of state reform of elementary and secondary education* (pp. 43–64). Cambridge, MA: Ballinger.

Monk, D. H. (1989). The education production function: Its evolving role in policy analysis. *Educational Evaluation and Policy Analysis, 11,* 31–45.

Morris, W. (Ed.). (1969). *The American heritage dictionary of the English language*. Boston, MA: Houghton Mifflin.

Murphy, K., & Welch, F. (1989). Wage premiums for college graduates: Recent growth and possible explanations. *Educational Researcher, 18, 4,* 17–26.

National Center for Education Statistics. (1989). *Targeted forecast* (No. CS 89–639). Washington, DC: U.S. Department of Education.

Odden, A., & Webb, L. D. (1983). Introduction: The linkages between school finance and school improvement. In A. Odden & L. D. Webb (Eds.), *School finance and school improvement: Linkages for the 1980s* (pp. xiii–xxi). Cambridge, MA: Ballinger.

Peters, T. J., & Waterman, R. H., Jr. (1982). *In search of excellence: Lessons from America's best-run companies*. New York: Warner Books.

Reed, L. (1985). *An inquiry into the specific school-based practices involving principals that distinguish unusually effective elementary schools from effective elementary schools*. Unpublished doctoral dissertation, State University of New York at Buffalo.

Riew, J. (1981). Enrollment decline and school reorganization: A cost efficiency analysis. *Economics of Education Review, 1,* 53–73.

Riew, J. (1986). Scale economies, capacity utilization, and school costs: A comparative analysis of secondary and elementary schools. *Journal of Education Finance, 11,* 433–446.

Samuelson, P. A. (1980). *Economics* (11th ed.). New York: McGraw-Hill.

Schultz, T. W. (1963). *The economic value of education*. New York: Columbia University Press.

Schultz, T. W. (1981). *Investing in people: the economics of population quality*. Berkeley, CA: University of California Press.

Schwartz, M., & Moskowitz, J. (1988). *Fiscal equity in the United States, 1984–85*. Washington, DC: Decision Resources Corporation.

Summers, A. A., & Wolfe, B. L. (1975). *Equality of educational opportunity quantified: A production function approach*. Philadelphia, PA: Federal Reserve Bank of Philadelphia, Department of Research.

U.S. Department of Commerce, Bureau of the Census. (1983). *Statistical abstract of the United States, 1983*. Washington, DC: U.S. Government Printing Office.

U.S. Department of Commerce, Bureau of the Census. (1988). *Statistical abstract of the United States, 1988*. Washington, DC: U.S. Government Printing Office.

Venezsky, R., & Winfield, L. (1980). *Schools that exceed beyond expectations in the teaching of reading: Studies on education, technical report #1*. Newark, DE: University of Delaware.

Verstegen, D. A. (1987). Equity in state education finance: A response to Rodriguez. *Journal of Education Finance, 12,* 315–330.

Walberg, H. J. (1984). Improving the productivity of America's schools. *Educational Leadership, 41* (May), 19–27.

Weber, G. (1971). *Inner-city children can be taught to read: Four successful schools*. Washington, DC: Council for Basic Education.

Williamson, O. E. (1975). *Markets and hierarchies: Analysis and antitrust implications*. New York: Free Press.

Willms, J. D. (1987). Patterns of academic achievement in public and private schools: Implications for public policy and future research. In E. H. Haertel, T. James, & H. M. Levin (Eds.), *Comparing public and private schools: Volume 2, School achievement* (pp. 113–134). New York: The Falmer Press.

Woodhall, M. (1987). Human capital concepts. In G. Psacharopoulos (Ed.), *Economics of education: Research and studies* (pp. 21–24). Oxford, England: Pergamon.

Chapter 13
Evaluation in Education: Theories, Models, and Processes

Evaluation is a critical, necessary dimension of educational administration and leadership. In broad terms, educational evaluation can be thought of as a deliberate and desirable monitoring and adjustment process that educators engage in for the sake of assuring or improving educational quality. Evaluation reveals how well educational programs are working and provides insight into how they can be improved.

As a general rule, evaluation activities that are sensibly conceived and competently carried out can only add to the quality and viability of schools, curricula, personnel, facilities, and institutional support systems. Conversely, the inability or unwillingness to undertake evaluation or conduct evaluation exercises inevitably detracts from educational quality. Effective self-managing organizations engage in data collection and create feedback-rich environments.

To a large extent educational evaluation today has evolved into a distinct professional field, represented by a variety of specialists and experts. For example, it is common to find state and district education offices, par-

ticularly in large districts, as well as offices within education associations and funding agencies, that are specifically organized to conduct evaluation functions. Typically, these offices are staffed by people who do specialized work as evaluators, researchers, analysts, statisticians, planners, economists, or accreditation experts. Even with this trend towards professionalism, however, it should be noted that the field of educational evaluation is still growing and changing and that evaluation systems and methods are based more upon enlightened practice than upon theory. Currently a great deal of debate centers on methodology, values and uses of evaluation processes. The use of qualitative methods has become increasingly effective as a means of lending flesh and bones to the skeletal pictures presented by empirical data alone.

Much of the work that falls into the category of educational evaluation remains in the hands of educational administrators, teachers and other personnel who, for the most part, are nonspecialists. This is particularly true in smaller districts and institutions. This approach helps to keep evaluation grounded to educational realities at the practitioner's level where educational delivery occurs. However, the middle and upper echelons of education systems often escape evaluation entirely. This may contribute to stagnation. The limited amount of evaluation of administrators is reflected in educational administration literature. As an example, Boyan (1988) noted that in the most recent edition of the *Handbook of Research on Educational Administration* there is no discussion of evaluation of administrators. To the research community this may suggest that researchers and practitioners may still be attempting to define the effective school administrator in light of the complex tasks they perform in school organizations. Unless a process, role, or task is clearly defined, it is not possible to establish validity and/or reliability of the evaluation. Equally, as seen in other organizations, evaluation by a superior of a subordinate may be problematic. Other types of personnel evaluation mechanisms, for example, peer evaluation and self-evaluation may be more appropriate and advantageous. In total, all evaluation may need to become more systemic, as we will show in this chapter.

Educational evaluation can be creatively employed to focus on numerous practical problems and issues, both simple and complex, that crop up in educational settings. It can focus on different institutional functions, including instruction, curriculum change, testing, facilities improvement, program funding, planning, and community relations. Evaluation can occur formatively as an ongoing process, or it can be interposed summatively as a periodic or special event. In addition, it may involve almost any combination of subjects and participants, including students, teachers, administrators, parents, community groups, and government agencies.

While recognizing that educational evaluation is very individualistic and uniquely problem-solving oriented, it is also important to note within the field the existence of some basic divisions and conflicts. Educational evaluation is characterized by the coexistence of different philosophical and theoretical perspectives. There is an assortment of models and methodologies that guide evaluation practices. These different evaluation perspectives and approaches (quantitative vs. qualitative methods, behavioral vs. humanistic) tend to provide a basis for both renewal and greater sophistication. At the same time, the assortment of evaluation models available makes it difficult for the practitioner to absorb and effectively utilize competing models. There are differences related to professional and political issues: conflicts, for example, over who controls evaluation and over who decides the purposes and priorities for evaluation.

This chapter presents a general overview of educational evaluation. It considers the historical development and contemporary nature of evaluation in education, including a consideration of the most prevalent models. It discusses program, teacher, and administrative evaluations, and it points out a number of practical evaluation aspects that are of particular concern to educational administrators.

Educational Evaluation: A Brief History

EARLY BEGINNINGS

The concept and practice of evaluation is hardly new. As Popham (1975) stated: "Through the centuries, most capable scholars have recommended that human beings engage in evaluative operations; that is, the evaluation of their own actions, . . . of other people's acts . . . [and] of myriad aspects of their environment" (p. 1).

Equivalent terms for "evaluation" can be found in ancient languages and texts, and the use of evaluation for educational purposes, to assess learning, knowledge, and skill, also was known in early times. Teachers in ancient Greece, such as Socrates, engaged in verbally mediated evaluations as part of the dialogic learning process, and emperors in China, as early as 200 B.C., made use of regular exams and proficiency tests to evaluate candidates for government service positions (Worthen, 1973, p. 2; Tyler, 1970, p. 687).

Despite its ancient roots, however, educational evaluation did not begin to take shape as a distinct field of endeavor until the advent of the Industrial Revolution. Evaluation issues emerged with the development of modern education systems in Europe and North America. As a general pattern, many early developments in the evaluation field, between 1800 and 1930, revolved around early psychological measurement and testing. However, around 1900 the field gradually began to expand its scope to include the formal evaluation of teachers, programs, and institutions, in addition to students.

MODERN DEVELOPMENT STAGES

A helpful outline of the modern history of educational evaluation is provided by Madaus, Scriven, and Stufflebeam (1983). They trace the development of educational evaluation in the United States through six periods or "ages," from 1800 to the present time.

1. The Age of Reform (1800–1900) was characterized by the development of the first mental tests and the application of psychological and behavioral measurements to educational problems. This age also saw the rise of experimental pedagogy and the use of external school inspectors to evaluate and promote schooling standards.

2. The Age of Efficiency and Testing (1900–1930) saw evaluation efforts that were largely dedicated to the development and use of standardized achievement tests and test batteries. During this time, leaders in the educational evaluation movement, such as Robert Thorndike, sought to make testing more scientific and to make test scores a key factor in educational decisionmaking, in student placements and pass-fail standards, and in comparative evaluation of programs via analyses of subject achievement scores.

3. The Tylerian Age (1930–1945) is associated with the work and thinking of Ralph W. Tyler, who is often considered the father of educational evaluation. Tyler was initially concerned with educational measurement, but he also stressed the importance of considering the goals and objectives of educational programs when evaluating student learning and program outcomes. Tyler's emphasis on goal identification and goal achievement had the effect of widening the field of educational evaluation, both theoretically and practically. These goal orientations allowed learning evaluation measurements to be criterion-referenced (as opposed to being norm-referenced). Tyler's work gave evaluators an analytical framework for comparing a program's intended effects and its actual outcomes.

4. The Age of Innocence (1946–1957) saw the proliferation of Tylerian-style evaluation, especially its application in local school programs. Educational evaluation and measurement courses became commonplace at teachers colleges. Many refinements of tests and testing methodologies developed throughout this period. Leading educators praised evaluation as a major foundation element for building new systems of schooling, curriculum, and program delivery. Evaluation also became a major issue in teacher employment and in-school supervision.

5. The Age of Expansion (1958–1972) is most notable for an increased emphasis on

personnel evaluation and the development of improved, multi-factor evaluation models. During this period in the United States, numerous Title I programs were established that required the development of evaluation programs for continuation of funding (Berk, 1981). The implications of required evaluation drew researchers' attention to the limitations of rigorous experimental designs. Evaluators were charged with assessing new programs and intervening in practical situations. Also, goal-attainment evaluation models of the Tylerian type were expanded and refined to account adequately for adverse or unique program operating conditions. These requirements led to the acceptance and use of new qualitative evaluation models and systems models by expert practitioners. The new generation of evaluation models tacitly allowed evaluations of educational programs and systems to go far beyond the assessments of goal-attainment.

6.   During the current Age of Professionalism (from 1973 to the present), educational evaluation emerged as a distinct realm of professional specialization. This period is marked by a recognition that useful evaluation must draw upon a number of different models and methods, both quantitative and qualitative, and a more general acceptance of the fundamental philosophical positions that tend to divide the profession (Cronbach, 1982). Also, widespread calls for educational reform during the 1970s and 1980s tended to enhance the role of evaluation in planning and monitoring significant projects and programs intended to create educational change, including policy change.

From this chronological sketch, it is apparent that the field of educational evaluation has become progressively larger and more sophisticated, especially since the 1930s. Today, educational evaluation is a diversified

field, involving educational specialists and generalists alike. Evaluation fulfills an essential role in educational development and change.

The Basic Aspects of Educational Evaluation

DEFINITION OUT OF DIVERSITY

As suggested already, educational evaluation is individualistic, more an applied art than a science. Evaluation approaches and designs are influenced by a variety of theories and models; evaluation practices can vary to suit different purposes (Shadish, Cook, & Leviton, 1991). In this regard, educational evaluation may be seen as lacking any one overriding theory or "best" method. There is a growing consensus that the existence of multiple evaluation approaches and methods presents no great problem for evaluation specialists and professionals. Rather, most problems seem to arise only when evaluation models are used inconclusively or inappropriately for purposes that are inconsistent with their inherent properties (Glasman & Nevo, 1988; Wolf, 1984).

Furthermore, the apparent diversity within the field of educational evaluation need not prevent the recognition of several major principles and conceptual features that give shape to the field as a whole. Despite its essential diversity, educational evaluation does have certain patterns associated with its usual functions and purposes. This awareness of commonalities, in fact, has stimulated recent attempts to develop integrated theoretical frameworks for the field (Shadish, Cook, & Leviton, 1991, p. 31). In a similar vein, as we survey the wider field we will note that many of the better definitions of educational evaluation have been constructed around a few major viewpoints and common notions.

In keeping with the historical development of the field, formal definitions of *educational evaluation* tend to emphasize three prevalent viewpoints. Some definitions emphasize a mode of evaluation that is primarily concerned with the achievement of specified norms or goals (e.g., Tyler, 1970). Other definitions emphasize a type of evaluation that is qualitative, open-ended, or goal-free, and primarily dedicated to insightful descriptions and judgments of educational realities (e.g., Scriven, 1980; Patton, 1984; Guba & Lincoln, 1989). There are also definitions that emphasize the pragmatic aspects of the evaluation process: information gathering, followed by analysis and judgmental assessment, followed by decisionmaking. The pragmatic, process-based definitions of educational evaluation appear to be the most serviceable ones for administrators. These methods also reflect the current thinking in the field.

Examples of process-based definitions can be seen in the writings of Cronbach (1982), Stufflebeam (1990), and Beeby (cited in Wolf, 1984). Their definitions all highlight two process elements: *the collection and use of information* and *the purpose of making decisions and taking actions* related to educational matters.

For instance, Beeby's definition of evaluation (in Wolf, 1984, p. 3) states that evaluation is a "systematic collection and interpretation of evidence leading to a judgment of value with a view to action." This definition is particularly nonrestrictive as it does not limit the evaluation process to any prescribed target or methodological approach. Yet, it does serve to emphasize the essential, purposeful connections among information, evaluation (i.e., judgment), and action. Evaluation, in other words, forms the rational center of a wider educational management process.

Investigating definitions further we frequently find that evaluation becomes confused with two other terms, measurement and research. *Measurement* simply identifies the act of measuring that is essentially a value-free technical exercise for collecting and arraying data. *Research* is a process that attempts to generate new knowledge for the sake of theory-testing and theory-building. The results of research are often compared and generalized. But evaluation, by definition, is more valuative than measurement and more decision-oriented and action-oriented than research (Kowalski, 1988, p. 151).

Some definitions of evaluation tend to get bogged down in attempts to establish hard semantic distinctions between kindred terms, for example, "testing" vs. "measurement," or "appraisal" vs. "assessment" vs. "evaluation" (Berk, 1981; Mehrens, 1973). Such terms often carry overlapping meanings and people tend to use the terms almost interchangeably in common parlance. Even experts use the terms differently, depending on the evaluation situation and focus. Global definitions of evaluation that dwell on such semantic distinctions actually do very little in the way of promoting a better or more realistic understanding of evaluation. A student of educational administration, however, does need to understand the variety of philosophical definitions of evaluation. This allows the practitioner to use evaluation processes for the right reason at the right time.

EVALUATION MODES AND PURPOSES

Educational evaluation is generally understood to fall into two main categories: summative evaluation and formative evaluation. When most people contemplate evaluation, they typically are thinking about *summative evaluation,* evaluation that occurs at (or near) some identifiable end-point of a project, program, or course. For example, comprehensive final exams and course grades for students, annual performance and merit reviews for teachers, and program assessments all represent different forms of summative evaluation applied to education.

Summative evaluation, as the term implies, is usually conducted with the intent of making summary judgments about the overall worth of educational endeavors, activities, and programs. Data collection and analysis usually aims at measuring outcomes and achievement levels with reference to formally stated or well-understood goals and standards. The value judgments made via this process become the formal bases for making official decisions. Examples are decisions regarding the continuation or noncontinuation of programs, school activities, teacher assignments, student placement, and grade promotion. Decisions can also stem from comparative value judgments, replacing old curricula with new curricula based on the results of pilot trials and multi-faceted comparisons (Scriven, 1980a, 1980b).

The term *formative evaluation,* on the other hand, refers to evaluation that occurs while processes or products are being designed. Formative evaluation is principally used to foster improvement, and it can be thought of as ongoing evaluation that accompanies some larger development effort or change process.

Formative evaluation is highly desirable, for instance, when implementing new programs or instructional delivery systems. Through formative measures, teachers and administrators can monitor the progress of implementation efforts. These measures give practitioners the means to detect and solve problems before they become unwieldy. Formative evaluation methods are also very useful in conjunction with programs aimed at staff development and organizational change. For obvious reasons, formative evaluation techniques also nurture effective teaching and

educational testing, the normal concerns related to "student development."

In addition to summative and formative evaluation, Tuckman (1985) suggests a third mode of evaluation: *ex post facto evaluation.* These "after the fact" review processes study events and data in a longitudinal manner in order to determine the factors that contributed to educational success or failure. This evaluation usually is done to obtain information and review assessments needed for educational planning, to note outcomes, trends, and problem factors. However, summative and formative modes of evaluation still command the most attention among evaluation researchers and school practitioners.

Several authors have commented on some of the essential distinctions and relationships between the summative and formative evaluation functions. Glasman and Nevo (1988) reinforced the point that summative evaluation emphasizes accountability in education, whereas formative evaluation emphasizes improvement. Walberg and Haertel (1990) contended that summative evaluations are conducted with greater formality, mainly to serve the needs of external audiences. Formative evaluations tend to be informal, limited and primarily intended for internal use by participants. Additionally, Lewy (1990) noted that summative evaluation is perceived as having more methodological rigor than formative evaluation.

However, it is possible to have methodological integrity at both levels and, as often as not, summative and formative evaluation functions can be regarded as complementary. Often, the same evaluation study can be viewed by one client as summative and by another client as formative (Borich, 1974; Lewy, 1990; Scriven, 1980). Much depends on when and where the mechanisms are utilized and by whom. Indeed, many experts suggest that evaluation designs ought to include related plans for both summative and formative evaluation (e.g., Edwards, Guttentag, & Snapper, 1975; Mark & Cook, 1984; Lewy, 1990).

It is also possible to identify other end-functions or purposes of educational evaluation that occur as formative or summative activities are used. These parallel purposes for evaluation reveal, more or less, the basic reasons for conducting evaluations in the first place. For example, Glasman and Nevo (1988) mention that educational evaluation may be undertaken for sociopolitical and psychological purposes, such as gaining public support and professional commitments. Evaluation may also be carried out for authoritative and administrative purposes, such as demonstrating administrative control and authority over educational systems and processes.

From the viewpoint of educational administrators, it appears that evaluation, whether formative or summative in nature, can be carried out for *motivational purposes,* on the one hand, and for *corrective purposes* on the other hand. This general viewpoint and combination of purposes is illustrated by Table 13.1.

EVALUATION TARGETS AND PROCESSES

As suggested earlier, educational evaluation may focus on a variety of targets or objects of interest. In general, evaluation targets tend to fall into five main categories or areas of visible concern.

1.   *Evaluations of learning.* Measurements, assessments, and inquiries regarding student learning gains, learning rates, and performance.

2.   *Evaluations of instruction.* Measurements, assessments, and appraisals of instructional quality, competence, and success in relation to instructional standards, goals, and norms.

Table 13.1
Evaluation Modes, Functions, and Purposes

Modes	Functions and Purposes	
	Motivational	**Corrective**
Formative Functions	• Improve individual performance • Improve efficiency • Determine future goals	• Modify poor performance • Determine operative problems in a new program
Summative Functions	• Reward outstanding performance • Determine degree of goal achievement • Granting tenure	• Dismiss deficiencies in a program • Determine deficiencies in a program • Establish institutional needs and priorities

3. *Evaluations of courses.* Evaluations of course design and content, of instructional support, and testing and remediation systems.

4. *Evaluations of programs.* Evaluations of program curricula and course combinations; evaluation of program design, efficiency and effectiveness, including assessments of administration, institutional fit, social impact and cost benefits.

5. *Evaluations of institutions and wider education systems.* Evaluations of multiprogram or multisite education systems including institutional and sectoral evaluations of national (or even international) education systems.

These target categories are interlinked, and, when taken together, they represent an integrated continuum selection of specific evaluation targets. Evaluation of targets in any one category of primary concern can easily lead to consideration of targets in other categories. Evaluations of learning (Target Level 1), for example, are not simply restricted to a consideration of student behaviors or test scores; learning evaluations can also include related assessments of instruction and course content. Similarly, course evaluations (at Target Level 3) can include assessments of instructional methods and materials (Target Level 2) in one direction, and of program design and institutional support (at Target Levels 4 and 5) in the other direction.

In practice, educational evaluation may focus on as few or as many targets as the specific evaluation situation dictates and allows. In this regard, evaluation becomes *situational,* as targets of any given evaluation will depend on the immediate concerns of the evaluators, participants, and audiences involved in the process and the commitment of resources and time.

It is also true that evaluation processes permit great *flexibility* with regard to the choice of procedures, methods, and participants. However, as previously indicated, there do appear to be commonalities that help define the general evaluation process. Glasman and Nevo (1988, p. 45) explain that all evaluation processes are characterized by three essential activities: (1) focus on a particular evaluation problem; (2) collection and analysis of empirical data; and (3) communication of findings and recommendation to evaluation audiences. Also, in keeping with the administrative, process-based definitions of evaluation offered by Popham (1988) and Wolf (1984), two other activities should be added to the general process description: (4) interaction between evaluators and people being evaluated; and (5) decisions and actions resulting from evaluation. Finally, it is also important to conclude with an overall (6) assessment of the entire evaluation project and its results.

The following outline reflects the logical sequence of the core processes of educational evaluation from the viewpoint of educational administrators and leaders.

SEQUENCE OF EVALUATION PROCESSES

1. Problem Setting

   A. Determine the situation to be evaluated.

   B. Determine the objects and people involved in the situation of interest.

   C. Determine the purpose(s) of the evaluation.

2. Problem Specification

   A. Determine relevant elements for examination in the evaluation problem.

   B. Select appropriate evaluation mode and method(s) of inquiry.

   C. Select participants and sample groups; identify likely data sources, informants, etc.

3. Data Collection and Analysis

4. Communication of Findings and Recommendations

5. Decisionmaking

6. Action Derived from Decisionmaking

7. Assessment of the evaluation

    A. In relation to the initial purpose.

    B. In relation to the process used.

    C. In relation to the expected results.

Throughout these evaluation stages, interaction among participants, evaluators, evaluation subjects, and evaluation audiences is necessary and especially advantageous. Interaction can occur at any stage of the evaluation process, but it is especially beneficial in the problem setting, communication, and evaluation review stages (Holloway, 1988; Glasman & Nevo, 1988; Cronbach, 1982).

As a final point, the last stage of the prototype evaluation process, overall assessment, has an impact apart from the evaluation reviewed. Assessments of any given evaluation ought to serve a corrective function. Problems and inadequacies noticed in the evaluation process are addressed to improve *future* evaluation efforts. Unless problems encountered in evaluation projects are thoroughly aired and examined, improvements in the process probably will not occur. Without corrective mechanisms in place, participants may come to regard evaluations as frustrating exercises devoid of worth.

Evaluation Perspectives and Models

In addition to recognizing the practical flexibility and situational adaptability of typical evaluation processes, it is necessary to recognize that educational evaluation also encompasses a wide range of theoretical perspectives and approaches. There is a plethora of models that have emerged in the field of educational evaluation. The array of models includes both descriptive and prescriptive models in various categories: research models, quantitative vs. qualitative models, goal-attainment vs. goal-free models, specialized limited-purpose models (such as cost-effectiveness) vs. comprehensive systems models, and more.

Some models are highly theoretical, and other models are more pragmatic and oriented towards field use by nonspecialists. Nevo (1983) contends that the term "model" is used inappropriately in the realm of educational evaluation because a large number of so-called models lack completeness and complexity. Many models appear to be single-use designs, created on the spot to meet the particular or peculiar need in a specific evaluation project(s). Research synthesis of these models-in-use into more generalized models is lacking. Nevertheless, practitioners need to be aware of the different theoretical bases reflected in various evaluation models, to better enable rational choice among the differing approaches and methods (Davis, 1986, p. 10).

In this regard, there are a number of different classification schemes for the various models that have been developed for educational evaluation. One classification, presented by Popham (1988), grouped evaluation models into five basic categories (p. 23). Table 13.2 includes Popham's five categories: goal attainment, judgmental, decision-facilitation, naturalistic models, and self-evaluation models. The fifth category for self-evaluation models was added to make the table reflect other current methods, including approaches suggested by Wilson (1988), Clift, Nutall, and McCormick (1988), and Holt (1981).

Given the numerous models, some experts suggest that an eclectic approach is both possible and desirable in coming to grips with the multifaceted evaluation problems facing educators today (Popham, 1988; Wilson, 1988; Glasman & Nevo, 1988). Indeed, Brandt (1981) showed how different methods and techniques can be used by different professionals to address identical evaluation problems. However, if an eclectic blend of approaches and methods is recommended, the blend can only be effective to the degree that practitioners know about different approaches and feel confident about their worth. This, additionally, implies that educators must become more knowledgeable, competent, and experienced with respect to educational evaluation.

Table 13.2
Categories of Educational Evaluation Models

Category/Model Type	Method/Terms	Representatives
Goal-Attainment Models The degree to which pre-determined goals are reached are the sole criteria for evaluation.	• goal-sources and goal screens • five-step model • eight-step model	Tyler, Ralph W. Hammond, Robert L. Metfessel & Michael
Judgmental Models Major attention is given to the evaluator's professional judgment. The evaluator concentrates on inputs or outputs of the system that is being evaluated and determines their value.	• accreditation model • comparative evaluation • countenance model • payoff evaluation • goal-free evaluation	School Associations Cronbach, Lee J. Stake, Robert Scriven, Michael Scriven, Michael
Decision-Facilitation Models Evaluation is viewed as the recollection of data to service decision-makers. Models only center on obtaining relevant information.	• CIPP Model • "Evaluator as Teacher" • discrepancy model	Stufflebeam, Daniel Cronbach, Robert Provus, Malcolm
Naturalistic Models The main instrument for data collection is the human being, and constraints imposed on the evaluation situation and evaluation activities are held to a minimum.	• human instruments • responsive evaluation • connoisseurship model • ethnographic evaluation	Guba & Lincoln Stake, Robert Eisner, Elliot LeCompte & Goetz
Self-Evaluation Models The main source of data collection *and* analysis are the subjects being evaluated. The evaluator is more a facilitator that helps the group evaluate itself.	• LEA schemes • curriculum reviews • school-initiated and/or teacher initiated evaluation • GRIDS	Turner, Clift McCormick & James Elliot, John McMahon, Fullan

The Main Types of Educational Evaluation

Scriven (1980a, 1980b) introduced the term *evaluand* to refer to the entity or set of targets being evaluated; he noted that virtually anything can serve as an *evaluand*. However, several authors (Glasman & Nevo, 1988; Walberg & Haertel, 1990) suggest that outside the popular realm of assessing student learning, the most common foci of educational evaluations are program and teacher evaluations. As educational administrators reflect, these do seem to be the most prominent. Both of these, program and teacher evaluation, warrant further discussion.

Additionally, however, evaluation of educational administrators is also becoming an issue. Miller (1979) noted that in 1973 there was so little material available on this topic that he placed three announcements in *The Chronicle of Higher Education* hoping to get some leads, and even then he had limited success. More recently, however, literature on this topic has expanded.

PROGRAM EVALUATION

Cronbach (1982, p. 233) justified the need for eclectic methods in program evaluation. He explained that varied educational situations, epistemological perspectives, methodologies, and political concerns that characterize the field each demand unique consideration. Given this tendency towards diversity, no single model or methodology for educational program evaluation can hope to prevail. Thus, as a general prescription for program evaluation, eclecticism provides the most realistic and efficient approach. Cronbach's eclectic view also focuses the evaluation process distinctly in the political realm as it is considered natural for people involved in the program evaluation to structure the evaluation activities in ways that coincide with their own priorities, preferences, and abilities. In this way, program evaluation methods inevitably reflect the values and perspectives of participants who control the evaluation process, seemingly to the exclusion of others. In any case, it is evident that the content and dynamics of any program evaluation will be determined by evaluators and other participants according to their motivation, intellectual outlooks, and expectations with reference to the evaluation problems and situations.

PERSPECTIVES ON PROGRAM EVALUATION

Theoretical and philosophical assumptions obviously help to shape any program evaluation. Historically, the scientific method of inquiry, which is based on hypothetic and deductive principles, has had a strong influence over the social sciences and disciplines such as education. Not surprisingly, then, educational program evaluations in earlier eras demonstrated a distinctive slant towards hypothesis testing via the collection and analysis of "hard" or quantitative data, preferably obtained via experimental or quasi-experimental studies. However, with the proliferation of education programs during the 1960s and 1970s, it became obvious that rigorous study designs and strict insistence on quantitative methods was insufficient to meet the needs of educators, administrators, and policy makers. This led to an expanded use of qualitative methods and of less rigid, more interpretive evaluation models.

Ultimately, program evaluation involves a judgment of the value of a given program endeavor (Wolf, 1984). However, the values to be addressed by evaluation must be clarified prior to the determination of an appropriate strategy and methodology. Mitzel et al.

(1982, p. 595) cited five questions that help to clarify the values inherent in a given program evaluation:

1. Is this thing any good? (an intrinsic value question)

2. What is it good for? (an instrumental value question)

3. Is it better than something else? (a comparative value question)

4. Can I make it better? (an idealization value question)

5. Is this the right thing to do? (a decision question)

The manner in which value issues above affect program evaluation are instructive. For example, addressing an optimization value would be best served by both formative and summative methodologies and would usually require a comparison against a standard. However, a decision question such as developing a new program may not entail any existing standard. In that case, no comparative judgment could be made.

Value assumptions, seen as having worth by interested parties and stakeholders, are often determined by external perspectives used. In many cases, programs that have federal or private funding bases may require some form of stricter accountability to demonstrate effective utilization of funding. Along these lines, Mitzel et al. (1982) contended that the political-economic and cost-benefit perspectives are most commonly used to determine the worth of a given program.

The political-economic perspective focuses on the principle of utilitarianism, and implies that program value can be determined by the benefits, the greatest worth or utility (House, 1978). This principle has influenced the assessment of value in programs. However, social interventionists have questioned the utilitarian perspective by noting that occasionally concern should be focused on sub-

groups within the population. Subsequently, Shapiro (cited in Mitzel et al., 1982) expanded the principle of utility using five criteria that address the distribution of benefits. These include: *equity,* emphasis on the equalization of outcomes or the minimization of individual differences; *pareto-optimality,* achieving outcomes for all, regardless of individual gains; *majority,* majority distribution of gain, even if those gains are minimal; *minimax,* addressing those at the bottom or in the most need, regardless of the status of the majority; and *dominance,* comparisons across competing groups in terms of outcome measures and implying those evidencing better concluding measures experience better programs.

Another common method to determine the worth of a given program is with a cost-benefit approach. This approach transcends the outcomes for a given group, as evidenced in Shapiro's focus on the criteria of distribution, and explores the consequences of such distributions. The field of economics has derived a variety of methods that accommodate the conversion of values to costs and benefits. But given the diverse thinking of multiple parties typically involved in most programs, consensus as to the costs and benefits corresponding to a specific value can be problematic (House, 1978). Debates over the worth of a program occasionally result in an examination of intrinsic versus pragmatic values as shown through classical, organizational, or bureaucratic decisions (Mitzel et al., 1982).

PROGRAM EVALUATION APPROACHES AND MODELS

Mitzel et al. (1982) contended that the field of educational program evaluation is dominated by four major evaluation viewpoints: experimental, eclectic, descriptive, and cost-benefit. Table 13.3 compares the characteristics of these four orientations along ten dimensions

Table 13.3
Four Methodological Approaches to Program Evaluation

	Experimentalists	Eclectics	Describers	Benefit-Cost Analyzers
	Cook & Campbell (1979) Riecken & Borich (1974) Rivlin & Timpane (1975)	Bryk (1978) Cronbach & Associates (1980) R. S. Weiss & Rein (1972)	Parlett & Hamilton (1977) Patton (1980) Stake (1975)	Haller (1975) Levin (1975) Thompson (1980)
Philosophical base	Positivist	Modified positivist to pragmatic	Phenomenological	Logical/Analytic
Discrepancy base	Psychology	Psychology; sociology; political science	Sociology; anthropology	Economics; accounting
Focus of methodology	Identify causal links	Augment search for causal links with process and contextual data	Describe program holistically and from perspective of the participants	Judge worth of program in terms of costs and benefits
Methodology	Experimental and quasi-experimental designs	Quasi-experimental designs; case studies; descriptions	Ethnography; case studies; participant observation; triangulation	Benefit-cost analysis
Variables	Predetermined as input-output	Predetermined plus emerging	Emerging in course of evaluation	Predetermined
Control or comparison group	Yes	Where possible	Not necessary	Yes
Participants' role in carrying out evaluation	None	None to interactive	Varies (may react to field notes)	None
Evaluator's role	Independent of	Cooperative	Interactive	Independent of program
Political pressures (internal-external)	Controlled in design; or ignored	Accommodated	Describe	Ignore
Focus of evaluation report	Render "go/no go" decision	Interpret and recommend for program improvement	Present holistic portrayal of program in process	Render judgment

SOURCE: Adapted from Mitzel, H. E. (Ed.). *Encyclopedia of educational research* (5th ed.) (Vol. 2) (p. 600). New York: The Free Press.

noted in the left-hand column. Distinctive features of these four orientations may help us understand program evaluation more thoroughly.

An experimentalist attempts to discover causal links between a program and its outcomes. The eclectics draw upon experimental or quasi-experimental designs that accommodate intervening variables such as contextual constraints and search for multiple causality to generate probable explanations of reality. The describers reject experimental designs, contending that meaningful data can only be obtained through in-depth, contextual descriptions of the program and through personal testimony. The cost-benefit analyzer attempts to gauge a program's economic worth. However, rather than adopt any single generic approach and attempt to adapt it to the needs of specific applications, evaluators may want to utilize a mixed evaluation approach, one that is suitable for the program environment and its socio-political context (Berk, 1981).

There is no one generalizable model for conducting program evaluations (Mitzel et al., 1982), as already stated. Yet it is important to note that there is a basic typology of the numerous program evaluation models that are currently in use. Regardless of the debate over what can be classified as a model, House (1982) contended that a model gives direction to evaluation design and provides a mechanism for explicitly or implicitly conveying the evaluation assumptions and evaluand relationships. For this reason, model building for program evaluation is extensive, and most evaluations are planned with one model or another in mind.

Like educational evaluation models already discussed, models for program evaluation take various forms. The most comprehensive classification scheme for program evaluation models is provided by House (1978) in his "Taxonomy of Major Evaluation Models." This taxonomy appears in Table 13.4, and shows eight basic model types that are applicable to program assessment and evaluations.

The same limitations and complications discussed earlier about general evaluation exist for program evaluation models. Program evaluations must therefore be designed with reference to certain external factors and constraints in addition to the primary evaluands. In education, program evaluations also include instructional effectiveness information gained through teacher evaluation. As noted by Stufflebeam (1990, p. 104), it is "fundamentally impossible to remove personnel evaluation from sound program evaluation." In the educational environment, that directs attention to teacher evaluation.

EXAMPLES OF PROGRAM EVALUATION MODELS

Without attempting an expansive presentation of program evaluation models, it is at least possible to consider briefly a few of the more prominent "all purpose" models that educational administrators might find most useful.

One type of "total evaluation" model is the CIPP Model, developed a number of years ago by Daniel Stufflebeam and others (Worthen, 1973; Stufflebeam, 1990). The CIPP model for educational program evaluation is billed as a "total" model for several reasons. First, it compels evaluators to consider four integral areas of concern, indicated by the letters C-I-P-P: Context evaluation, focused on the program context and evaluation situation; input evaluation, focused on the resources and human energies pertaining to the evaluation problem(s); process evaluation, focused on the internal program dynamics and interactions related to the evaluation problem; and product evaluation, focused on program products and accomplishments. Figure 13.1 graphically illustrates the main conceptual aspects of the CIPP model, including the relationships among program decisions, program activities, and program evaluation influences.

Table 13.4
A Taxonomy of Major Program Evaluation Models

Model	Proponents	Major Audiences	Assumes Consensus on	Methodology	Outcome	Typical Questions
Systems analysis	Rivlin	Economists, managers	Goals: known cause and effect; quantified variables	PPBS: linear programming; planned variation; cost benefit analysis	Efficiency	Are the expected effects achieved? Can the effects be achieved more economically? What are the most efficient programs?
Behavioral Objectives	Tyler, Popnam	Managers, psychologists	Prespecified; objectives; quantified outcome variables	Behavioral objectives; achievement tests	Productivity; accountability	Are the students achieving the objectives? Is the teacher producing?
Decision Making	Stufflebeam, Alkin	Decision-makers, especially administrators	General goals: criteria	Surveys, question-naires, interviews; natural variation	Effectiveness; quality control.	Is the program effective? What parts are effective?
Goal Free	Scriven	Consumers	Consequences: criteria	Bias control; logical analysis; modus operandi	Consumer choice; social utility	What are all the effects?
Art Criticism	Eisner, Kelly	Connoisseurs, Consumers	Critics, standards	Critical review	Improved Standards	Would a critic approve this program?
Accreditation	North Central Association	Teachers, public	Criteria, panel, procedures	Review by panel; self study	Professional acceptance	How would professionals rate this program?
Adversary	Owens, Levine, Wolf	Jury	Procedures and judges	Quasi-legal procedures	Resolution	What are the arguments for and against the program?
Transaction	Stake, Smith, MacDonald, Parlett-Hamilton	Client, Practitioners	Negotiation: activities	Case studies, interviews, observations	Understanding, diversity	What does the program look like to different people?

SOURCE: Adapted from House, E. (1978). Assumption underlying evaluation models. *Educational Researcher, 7*(3), 12.

The CIPP model and its nearest cousins can be used for both formative and summative evaluations. It is best regarded as a decision-making model, strongest when used in a formative mode to plan and implement change.

A similar type of model, though more succinct, is the Provus Model represented in Figure 13.2. Like the CIPP Model, the Provus model can be regarded as a planning and decisionmaking model, useful for monitoring program innovations. Evaluation is both formative and summative in the Provus model, so that it can be viewed as an ongoing event that produces information needed for deci-

sionmaking from the beginning to the end of a project or change attempt.

Figures 13.3 and 13.4 illustrate the principles of another type of program evaluation model: Stake's Congruence-Contingency Model for evaluation. Like the two preceding models, Stake's model seeks to provide a rather complete understanding of program contexts and problems. It gathers information from as many sources as possible. As illustrated by Figure 13.3, multiple program features listed in the left column are examined in relation to a program's performance (i.e., with reference to data about intents, stan-

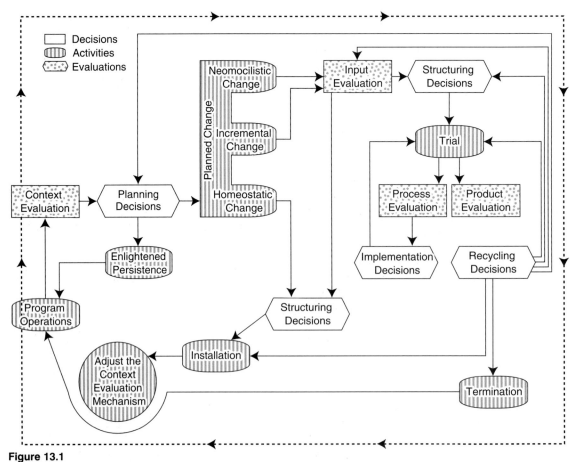

Figure 13.1
A total evaluation model: CIPP

SOURCE: Worthen, B. R. (1973). *Educational evaluation, theory, and practice* (p. 41). Worthington, OH: Chas. A. Jones Publishing.

Figure 13.2
The five stages of the Provus model and steps of evaluation associated with them

SOURCE: Saylor & Alexander. (1981). *Curriculum planning for better teaching and learning* (4th ed.). New York: Holt, Rinehart & Winston.

Stage	Content		
	Input	Process	Output
Design	Design Adequacy		
Installation	Installation Fidelity		
Process	Process Adjustments		
Product	Product Assessment		
Program Comparison	Cost–Benefit Analysis		

dards, and judgments) shown across the top of the figure. Data collection using the Stake model tends to be naturalistic because it relies on in-depth interviews and status reviews.

The analysis framework of Stake's model, represented in Figure 13.4, seeks to compare intended program conditions or logical contingencies to program conditions that are actually found to exist (empirical contingencies). If congruence is lacking between what is intended and what actually exists within a program, the "gap" or problem indicated can become the focus of corrective action.

The three program evaluation models discussed in this section may help educational administrators appreciate some of the theoretical and practical implications of model building that have taken place in the research field.

TEACHER EVALUATION

Teacher evaluation has received increasing attention. As evidenced by the 1979 Gallup Poll, emphasis on "improving teacher quality" was a high concern (Gallup, 1979). The quality emphasis has continued to this day, as shown in the 1991 Gallup Poll; nearly 70 per-

cent of respondents favored effective teaching (Elam, Rose, & Gallup, 1991). However, teacher evaluation, like program evaluation, is not characterized by any one best or universal method. For example, both the theory and practice of teacher evaluation reflect disagreements as to whether instructor evaluations should detect incompetencies, prevent incompetence, or correct deficiencies, all of which suggest different methodologies and approaches. Additionally, different characterizations of the act of "teaching" mandate a variety of ways for collecting information and making evaluative judgments about the worth of instructional abilities and quality. In this regard, even these "bare essentials" above are not holistic enough. As shown earlier with program evaluation, teacher evaluation may be accomplished for a variety of reasons, none of which are or can be explicitly measured in isolation. In this sense, teacher evaluation, in fact all evaluation, remains problematic.

PERSPECTIVES ON TEACHING AND TEACHER EVALUATION

Darling-Hammond, Wise, and Pease (1983) contended that the work of teaching is variously perceived as a labor, a craft, a profession, or an art. Each viewpoint suggests a theoretical framework for teacher evaluation. When teaching is viewed as labor, teaching activities are characterized by standard operating procedures, and evaluation involves direct inspection of the teacher's work (e.g., monitoring lesson plans and classroom performance). If teaching is conceptualized as a craft, it requires a repertoire of specialized techniques, and the corresponding evaluation is indirect in ascertaining whether a teacher

Program Rationale	DATA FOR THE EVALUATION OF AN EDUCATIONAL PROGRAM			
	Intents Sources	Observations Sources	Standards Sources	Judgment Sources
ANTECEDENTS Student Characteristics Teacher Characteristics Curricular Context Curricular Context Instructional Materials - - - - - - - - - - - - - [A] Physical Plant School Organization Community Context				
TRANSACTIONS Communication Flow Time Allocation Sequence of Events - [D] Reinforcement Schedules Social Climate				
OUTCOMES Student Achievement - - - - - - - - - - - - - - - - - [B] - - - - - - - - - - - - [C] Student Attitudes Student Motor Skills Effects on Teachers Institutional Effects				

Example A: Manufacturer Specifications of an Instructional Materials Kit

Example B: Teacher Description of Student Understanding

Example C: Expert Opinion of Cognitive Skill Needed for a Class Problem

Example D: Administrative Judgment of Feasibility of a Field Trip Arrangement

Figure 13.3
Elements of Stake's congruence-contingency model for educational evaluation

SOURCE: Stake, R. E., in W. H. Beatty (Ed.). (1969). *Improving educational assessment and an inventory of measures of affective behavior.* Washington, DC: Association of Curriculum Development.

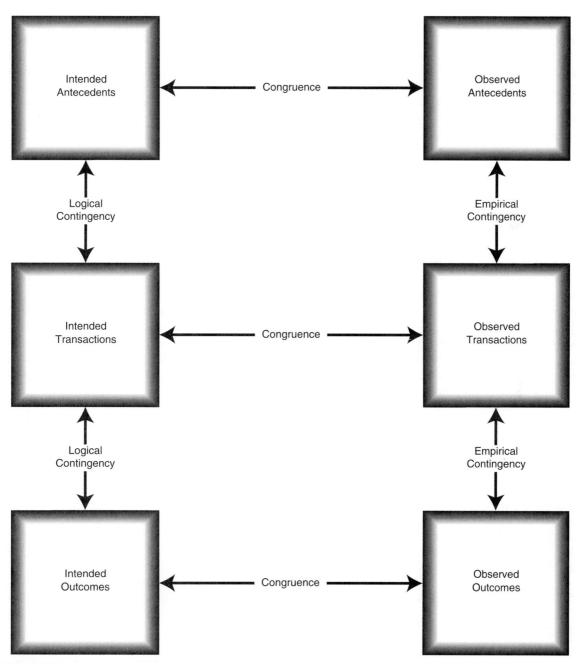

Figure 13.4
Analysis framework for Stake's congruence-contingency model for educational evaluation

SOURCE: Stake, R. E., in W. H. Beatty (Ed.). (1969). *Improving educational assessment and an inventory of measures of affective behavior.* Washington, DC: Association of Curriculum Development.

has the requisite skills to practice the craft. As a profession, teaching requires a repertoire of specialized techniques, similar to the craft perspective. But evaluation here calls for a judgment about when those techniques should be applied. Thus, some evaluation standards are developed by peers and evaluation focuses on the degree to which teachers are competent at professional problem solving. When teaching is perceived as an art, it primarily calls for intuition, creativity, and expressiveness. Corresponding evaluation methods that address holistic qualities and involve both self-assessment and critical assessment by others are applicable.

In practice, these four perspectives on teaching will not be found in their pure form. People will have mixed or overlapping opinions about what teaching entails or ought to emphasize. Such overlapping of teaching perspectives is natural given the fact that instructional behaviors that are effective in moderation can produce negative effects when they are overutilized or applied in inappropriate circumstances. The very nature and dynamics of teaching make it impossible to define a single perspective or set of behaviors that are globally successful (Coker, Medley, & Soar, 1980). Yet, as noted by numerous authors (e.g., Darling-Hammond et al., 1983; Millman, 1981; Shavelson & Stern, 1981), these perspectives on teaching undeniably determine varying definitions of success as well as corresponding values that are evident in different teacher evaluation systems.

PURPOSES OF TEACHER EVALUATION

Teacher evaluation generally addresses four purposes: (a) individual improvement, (b) school improvement, (c) individual accountability, and (d) organizational accountability (Darling-Hammond et al., 1983). Individual and organizational improvement needs are primarily addressed via formative evaluation. Accountability needs are typically satisfied by

summative evaluation, with evaluation results subsequently used for personnel decisions and school status decisions (Darling-Hammond et al., 1983). However, some purposes, such as teacher promotion or tenure, are most frequently served by focusing the assessment on teacher competence, performance, or effectiveness (Millman, 1981).

TEACHER EVALUATION METHODS

Teacher evaluations tend to utilize quantitative or qualitative methodologies, depending upon whether the evaluation is used to determine competence, performance, or effectiveness. Darling-Hammond et al. (1983) reported that eight evaluation methods are most commonly mentioned in current literature on teacher evaluation: teacher interviews, competency tests, indirect measures, classroom observation, student ratings, peer review, student achievement, and faculty self-evaluations.

Darling-Hammond et al. (1983) also noted that in the past teacher appraisal interviews and classroom observation constituted the instructor evaluation process. Currently the interview is used as just one element of the broader evaluation procedure. The two common uses of the teacher interview are to facilitate employment or promotion decisions and to communicate performance appraisals to practicing instructors. Moreover, the interview process has evolved from a primarily unstructured activity into a more formal one that employs standardized methodologies, such as Teacher-Perceiver Interviews (Haefele, 1981).

Teacher competency tests represent a growing trend in response to the public's demand for institutional and professional accountability. Although there are also numerous state and locally developed examinations, the most widely used professional test is the National Teacher Examination (NTE). Competency tests are most commonly used for initial certification and hiring. These instruments offer the advantages of eliminating interviewer bias and verifying minimum standards of knowledge. The tests are usually legally defensible as screening mechanisms (Darling-Hammond et al., 1983). However, critics contend that the tests cannot assess actual performance or higher levels of knowledge, and success on the tests does not necessarily guarantee effective teaching, which is reflected by data showing that only 11 percent of teachers believe that NTE scores are valid measures of effectiveness (Haefele, 1981). As noted here, teacher competency as measured by the NTE may be a minimal necessity and must be combined with other evaluation mechanisms.

Traditionally, indirect measures, such as work experience and educational level, have been linked to teacher promotion opportunities. However, "no single set of skills, attitudes, interests or abilities" have been identified as capable of distinguishing between ineffective and effective instructors, although some research suggests a correlation between flexibility and effectiveness (King, 1981, p. 174). Subsequently, less indirect measures connected to career and job performance, such as indications of professional advancement and commitment, seem appropriate as supplementary sources of evaluation data.

Classroom observation is a central aspect of most instructor evaluations and is typically used as a formative technique to address performance improvement (Mitzel, Best, & Rabinowitz, 1982). Classroom observations may include a preliminary interview. However, observation protocols reflect a range of structures and methodologies, from observations that entail standardized observation forms to those that address items agreed upon by both the instructor and the evaluator (Darling-Hammond et al., 1983). Observations are often conducted internally by an administrator, and this offers the advantage of including information as to the instructional

climate and performance that is not available to outsiders. However, the numerous limitations of this method include observer bias, insufficient sampling of performance to provide reliable data, and measurement instruments that frequently lack appropriate focus (Darling-Hammond et al., 1983; Mitzel et al., 1982).

Student ratings, in actuality, are simply another form of classroom observation. These ratings provide a different perspective from that of an independent evaluator or administrator. Although this form of evaluation is most typically utilized at the higher education level, several authors (e.g. Haefele, 1981; Peterson & Kauchak, 1982) contend that student ratings could be effectively applied at the secondary level or, in some cases, even at the elementary level. This method of evaluation has several inherent advantages: for example, the proven correlation between student ratings and student academic achievement (i.e., minimally 0.8). Even so, some authors have debated the validity and utility of this form of evaluation (Darling-Hammond et al., 1983).

Mitzel et al. (1982) noted that, despite the potential benefits of teachers evaluating their colleagues, peer review is rarely used and is not desired by teachers themselves. This form of evaluation usually entails peer examination of lesson plans, examinations, and other instructor-designed materials and documents, plus classroom observation. Peer review is based on the assumption that peers are in the best position to assess competence and performance because of their familiarity with classroom conditions and subject matter. In addition, peers are in a position to render specific and practical suggestions for improvement. However, many authors (Darling-Hammond et al., 1983; Haefele, 1980; Mitzel et al., 1982) concur that this form of evaluation should serve a formative function and not be used for personnel decisions or summative purposes.

Although evidence of student achievement should be included as part of the overall evaluation system, specifically for formative purposes, teacher evaluation based on student achievement has inherent limitations. For example, research has indicated that the connection between student test scores and teacher effectiveness is quite low, so the connection between appropriate teaching behaviors and resultant learning appears to be situational (Darling-Hammond et al., 1983). Also, the use of student test results to measure teacher effectiveness often leads to putting instructors' teaching to the test (Centra & Potter, 1980). However, when student scores are used as a formative evaluation methodology as part of a larger evaluation system, students' scores provide a mechanism of addressing the overall goal of the teaching endeavor, student outcomes (Darling-Hammond et al., 1983).

Faculty self-evaluations are an important source of information and evaluation in a broader evaluation program. Two of the most widely discussed teacher evaluation models, Manatt's "Mutual Benefit Evaluation" model and Redfern's "Management By Objectives Evaluation" model include faculty self-evaluation components. Typically, this methodology allows an instructor to use data derived from any technique (such as peer ratings, student ratings, or student achievement) to assess his or her own strengths and weaknesses. Although this methodology should not be considered an evaluation method in itself, self-evaluation is becoming a more popular technique in teacher evaluation systems. When combined with individual goal-setting, self-evaluation may lead to self-reflection and motivation promoting professional change and growth (Darling-Hammond et al., 1983).

Overall, the low levels of reliability, generalizability, and validity attributed to teacher evaluation methods suggest that the one-dimensional approaches for assessing effectiveness, competence, or performance are unlikely to capture adequate data about teaching attributes to completely satisfy any of the purposes of the evaluation process. Numerous authors (Millman, 1981; Peterson & Kauchak, 1982) note that additional research is needed in this area to determine and develop instructor evaluation systems that rise above the limitations already noted. Mitzel et al. (1982) suggested that, despite the questions raised regarding the efficacy of feedback, the most useful outcome of current teacher evaluation efforts is that it provides instructors with accurate information, whether developed from administrators or students.

TEACHER EVALUATION MODELS

The configurations of methodologies and processes used for teaching evaluation are often classified as models. Although Nevo (1983) noted that the term *model* is applied inappropriately to many of the evaluation methodologies, certain approaches appear consistently in the literature and warrant mention. Borich (1977) contended that teaching models, including teaching evaluation models, are a combination of iconic, analogue, and symbolic typologies, and generally can be divided into two major categories: planning models and quantitative models. One basic planning model that serves as a basis for many others is Knezevich's systems evaluation model. This model is formative in nature, addressing personnel and organizational improvement, and it includes four phases: (1) determination of the purpose and effectiveness of the system, (2) development of monitoring procedures, (3) data collection, and (4) decisionmaking and actions (Borich, 1977). Although Knezevich's model is not specific, precise, and verifiable, it does include all the steps necessary to develop an appraisal system.

The planning model by Coleman (cited in Borich, 1977) offers advantages over Knezevich's model in that it is more precise. Coleman's model specifies a number of teacher behaviors (i.e., warmth, indirectness, cognitive organization, and enthusiasm) and suggests corresponding measurement methods. This model is intended to address both formative and summative data. However, a limitation of this model is that research fails to support the assumption that Coleman's four teaching behaviors have wide application as effective instructional behaviors; rather the behaviors may only have relative, situational merit (Darling-Hammond et al., 1983).

Two common quantitative models that have served as the basis for other models of this genre are Klein and Aikin's model and Dyer's model. Klein and Aikin's model uses an objective-based approach that excludes all subjective judgments of teachers. This model uses a regression analysis to measure the performances of one teacher's pupils against those of all teachers being appraised, to weigh only those variables under a teacher's control, and to adjust for variables considered as contaminating influences, such as differing pretest score levels (Borich, 1977). Dyer's model is also quantitative in nature, addressing four groups of variables: input variables of the students, output of the students, educational process variables of the school, and surrounding conditions. However, Dyer's model has diagnostic advantages not inherent in Klein and Aikin's model. Using Dyer's model, it is possible to adjust pupil outcome measures and those variables beyond the teacher's control and to focus on teacher behaviors that are "easy to change" (Borich, 1977).

Whereas quantitative models tend to be underrepresented in teacher evaluation systems, the planning approach is strongly reflected in two of the most widely discussed evaluation models: Manatt's "Mutual Benefit Evaluation" model and Redfern's "Management By Objectives Evaluation" (Darling-Hammond et al., 1983). Both models have

been implemented in numerous schools and are characterized by centralized teaching standards and criteria and by goal-setting and teacher involvement in the evaluation process. Essentially, both models are designed to address teacher improvement by promoting professional growth and by integrating individual performance objectives with school policies. Both models straddle the competency-based and outcomes-based evaluation philosophies, and both models are results oriented while they accommodate the numerous perspectives of "results." Manatt's model includes four major steps:

1. the administrative establishment of minimum teaching standards,

2. diagnostic evaluation to determine instructors' status as compared to the standards via a multimethod approach,

3. cooperative establishment of measurable objectives for teacher improvement,

4. reevaluation leading to the establishment of new job targets.

The steps in this model are basically similar to those included in Redfern's model, that is, they are based upon the "Management By Objectives" (MBO) approach borrowed from the field of business. However, in Redfern's model the teacher is involved in the development of mutually established objectives and standards prior to any evaluation. In this model, self-evaluation is more integral to the process (Darling-Hammond et al., 1983). The models mentioned above for teacher evaluation are the seminal models upon which most other models are based (House, 1978; Mitzel, 1982). These key models assume that teacher effectiveness should be evaluated in an environment in which teaching occurs in order to address stable, consensual programmatic, and instructional goals. However, Knapp (1982) contended that, in actual practice, most teacher evaluation systems are based upon other multiple organizational demands. Evaluations must strive to be legally "defensible" while simultaneously addressing the needs to rate teachers, maintain staff morale and collegiality, and maintain organizational distance from environmental demands. Moreover, despite idealistic claims, most teacher evaluation schemes tend to call for improvements that require only modest, incremental change.

Evaluation of Administration

While the literature on formal evaluation of educational administrators has been limited until quite recently, as noted above by Miller (1979), this is an area of growing activity. As Farmer (1979) stated, there is no question that administrators are continuously evaluated informally. The real issue is to determine when and why formal evaluation should take place.

Farmer (1979) enumerated the arguments for and against formal evaluation of administrators. Arguments against include (a) diversity, including program diversity, role diversity, and evaluation participant diversity, all of which make it difficult to get a consistent evaluation system for persons with like titles; (b) lack of technique, which argues that no valid, reliable means of evaluating educational administrators has been devised; and (c) politics, which argues that evaluation is merely used to bolster subjective impressions and political agendas when dealing with educational administrators. Farmer countered these arguments by noting that (a) diversity may be a problem, but it is a fact of academic life and must be coped with by devising a flexible system and attending to the problem of inappropriate data; (b) the lack of technique argument is based more on perception than reality, and there are techniques that

have been tested and validated over time; and (c) while politics is a real issue, establishing clear criteria for evaluation and developing good descriptive data can minimize the impact.

The basis of effective administrative evaluation, according to several authors (including Hoyt, 1982; Dressel, 1976), is to clearly define the role of the person being evaluated. Then the procedure, including appropriate instruments, should be designed to match the circumstances.

In any event, in any educational setting there is a clear relationship between the effectiveness of instruction and programs and the effectiveness of those assigned responsibility for management of those activities. Evaluation of a system without evaluating the performance of an important leading part would not be rational behavior.

PURPOSES OF ADMINISTRATIVE EVALUATION

"Given the time-consuming and complex nature of administrator evaluation, the single most important step for any institution is to make sure that there are compelling reasons for starting a formal program of administrator evaluation." (Genova et al., 1976).

Arguing that the primary function of an administrative evaluation is to form a basis for establishing and attaining institutional goals, Genova et al. (1976) went on to enumerate the reasons for such an evaluation. These include (1) establishing and attaining institutional goals; (2) helping individual administrators to improve their performance; (3) making decisions on retention, salary, or promotion; (4) increasing the effectiveness and efficiency of the administration as a team; (5) keeping an inventory of personnel resources for reassignment or retraining; (6) informing the governing body of the degree of congruence between institutional policy and institutional action; (7) sharing governance; (8)

informing internal and external audiences on administrative effectiveness and worth; or (9) conducting research on factors related to administrator effectiveness.

Farmer (1979) used the Genova listing to establish three major functions of administrative evaluation: formative, summative, and institutional. Formative functions are to: (a) serve as a basis for administrative development; (b) help administrators compare their perceptions of performance with those of superiors, peers, and faculty; (c) provide a vehicle for team building; and (d) determine factors that influence effectiveness by analyzing evaluation date. Summative functions are to: (a) determine retention, promotion, and salary decisions and (b) formulate and measure an administrator's specific program objectives. Institutional functions are to: (a) explicitly define desired administrative roles and relationships; (b) assess strengths and weaknesses of administrative staff in order to assign them to appropriate tasks; (c) determine the congruence between instructional policy and administrative action; (d) extend participation in decisionmaking by permitting staff input in the personnel process; (e) serve as a model and inducement for other evaluative processes; and (f) increase awareness of administrative efforts and achievements with external audiences, such as legislators and funding agencies.

PRINCIPLES OF ADMINISTRATIVE EVALUATION

Based on a review of the literature of administrative evaluation, Hoyt (1982) discussed the basic principles of an effective evaluative program. Two basic principles underlie all effective evaluation, according to Hoyt. These are (a) uniqueness, in that there needs to be mutual understanding of the unique set of job expectations under which the administrator works, and (b) contextual interpretation,

in that evaluation should be done within the context of the resources available to work with, the personal and situational obstacles encountered, and other factors beyond the administrator's control.

Further criteria for effective evaluation, Hoyt (1979) noted, are the principles of credibility, validity, and fairness.

Credibility. Concerned parties must have confidence that the procedures are appropriate and will yield meaningful results. In order to be credible, an evaluation needs to be developed with input from all affected parties. Also, there needs to be a clear understanding that the evaluation has potential for producing positive results.

Validity. Validity of evaluations is based on their comprehensiveness and accuracy. In order to accomplish this, a description of relevant outcomes for each major activity of the evaluated person needs to be developed. Based on these criteria, the evaluation should measure meaningful change in persons or situations that resulted from the administrator's efforts. Further, any evidence used in the evaluation must have a direct relationship to the criteria identified. Face value of the evidence is vital. Finally, there should be a representative sampling of respondents to the evaluation, from as wide a variety of sources as is feasible.

Fairness. The evaluation must be open, even though it may create some problems in validity. Participants in the evaluation, both the evaluee and the respondents, should know what they are doing, why they are doing it, and how the results will be used. Further, the person being evaluated should not be held responsible for events or conditions beyond his or her control. If this person does not establish salary scales nor assign levels of pay, then that is not a reasonable area to include in the evaluation.

ADMINISTRATIVE EVALUATION MODELS

Evaluation of an administrator must be tied to the context of the person's work, as noted above. Lists of the tasks and responsibilities of an administrator abound in the literature. Goodwin and Smith (1981) provided a representative example: (a) accomplishment of goals and objectives, (b) implementation of policy, (c) organizing skills, (d) position knowledge, (e) quality of work, (f) quantity of work, (g) innovating or taking the initiative, (h) professional development, (i) judgment, (j) facilities management, (k) planning, (l) budgeting, (m) delegating, (n) staffing, (o) communications, (p) decisionmaking, (q) evaluating, (r) supervising, (s) professionalism/integrity, (t) reliability/dependability, (u) personal qualities, (v) attitude, (w) fairness, (x) human relations, (y) public/internal relations, (z) conflict management, (aa) recognition of performance, and (bb) producing reports. Not all of these items are of equal value, nor is their relative value fixed. It is the breadth of this list and its fluidity that makes definition of the role in the specific case such a vital initial step.

Once the role is defined and the areas to be evaluated selected, then the standards against which the person being evaluated is to be measured must be identified. Farmer (1979) cited the individual's own past performance, stated performance goals, and the performance expectations of others as workable standards. The performance of predecessors, the performance of others in similar positions, and an ideal standard are all unsatisfactory from his point of view, since conditions may have changed. Similarly named positions may be quite different, and no one has yet identified a valid theoretical standard for this work.

Participants in the evaluation process should include as broad a representation as possible of those directly affected by the administrator's performance. These might include faculty, peers, supervisors (both upper level administrators and boards), students, alumni, clerical staff, and members of the public, depending upon the situation.

With these elements determined, the means of evaluation must be determined. Farmer (1979) identified four general models: (1) rating scales, (2) growth contracting, (3) ad hoc committee, and (4) management by objectives.

Rating scales. Rating instruments include forms, scales, and questionnaires. They may be closed-form with a limited number of preset answers, or open-form. While seemingly the least complicated of the models to use, they are considered the most abused because of the skill needed for valid construction and proper interpretation of results. Rating scales allow the user to classify information from various sources rapidly and efficiently. They are relatively easy to make confidential, allow for classification of responses, and also allow for longitudinal study when the same questions are used from year to year. However, professionally produced rating scales do not generally include institutional expectations for specific administrators nor do they match the administrator's performance to institutional goals. Rating scales are often low in validity, subject to the biases of the respondents, and may seek the simplest and most quantifiable aspects of the evaluee's performance. Because they tend to fragment responses, they do not generally give an effective overall picture of the person being evaluated.

To be effective, rating scales need to be developed for each individual in his or her specific situation, with the attendant difficulty in producing a valid and reliable instrument.

Growth contracting. Growth contracts are evaluation plans that allow the evaluee to think through and write out goals and objectives for the future. These goals and objectives are generally job related, but often will include personal as well as professional development issues. Growth contracts are generally considered an acceptable means of demonstrating professional competence. They can lead to improved satisfaction with personal and professional growth. They have the advantage of specificity in setting goals when they are properly done.

Growth contracts generally contain four elements: (1) self-evaluation, including a statement of past performance and a perception of strengths and weaknesses; (2) areas for improvement, selected from those areas of difficulty discussed in the self-evaluation; (3) plan for improvement, based on the areas selected for improvement and phrased as clearly defined objectives; and (4) long-range goals, which allow the individual to place the improvement plan into a larger context.

Ad hoc committee. The ad hoc committee is an extension of the screening committee concept, according to Farmer (1979). Ad hoc committees are appointed for a specific evaluation. They should be broadly representative of the constituency served by the administrator, but should not be so large as to be ungainly. They should operate within stated rules and guidelines that are recorded in writing and open to all. Parameters for effective ad hoc committee evaluations, according to Farmer, include: (a) assurance of confidentiality and dignity; (b) understanding that criticism as well as recognition is inherent in evaluation; (c) open disclosure of the evaluative processes and criteria; (d) understanding of the complexity of a valid evaluation; and (e) understanding of the specifics of time and place, expectations at the time of appointment, and issues at the time the administrator was hired as they impinge on the administrator's work and evaluation.

Management by objective. Management by objective (MBO) is a systems planning and management process that includes evaluation as a component. Evaluation (as performance review) follows naturally upon the process steps of goal clarification, establishment of measurable objectives, unit and individual

self-analysis, action planning, and implementation. Following implementation, evaluation, feedback, and renewed planning and implementation complete the system.

The premise for MBO, according to Farmer (1979), is that no individual can direct all of the activities of a complex organization. Under the MBO model various individual administrators assume responsibility for a defined set of institutional outcomes for a defined period of time. At the end of that period the results are matched to previously stated measurable objectives, and performance evaluation results.

MBO has been discussed at length elsewhere in the literature. For the purposes of this discussion, we will simply note that its strengths and its weaknesses stem from the same source: the individuals involved. If the participants are committed, clearly definable and measurable progress can be made toward specific individual and organizational goals. If the participants are not committed, then MBO deteriorates to ineffectiveness.

Standards and Requirements for Educational Evaluation

During the past 30 years, there have been substantial efforts in the United States to control and ensure the quality of evaluation endeavors, a trend that has accompanied the emergence and growth of educational evaluation as a distinct discipline. One result of these efforts was the document produced by the Joint Committee on Standards for Educational Evaluation entitled "Standards for Evaluations of Educational Programs, Projects and Materials" issued in 1981. The document sets forth program evaluation standards in four major areas: (1) utility standards; (2) feasibility standards; (3) propriety standards; and (4) accuracy standards. Moreover, the document promotes the view that evaluation itself should be subject to quality assurance efforts (Stufflebeam, 1990, p. 104).

The *utility standards* are intended to guide the evaluation process so that it will be timely, informative and influential, and address the needs of the audiences to be served by the process. Essentially, the utility standards focus on eight areas: (1) audience identification, or specifying the group to be served so that their needs can be addressed; (2) assuring evaluator credibility, which requires that the person conducting the evaluation be both competent and ethical; (3) adequate information scope and selection, which suggests that the evaluation information gathered should sufficiently address pertinent questions about the person or activities being evaluated and be responsive to the needs of the audiences served; (4) evaluation interpretation, which requires adequate description of the perspectives, procedures and rationale used for data interpretation so that the reasons for corresponding judgments are clear; (5) report clarity, which specifies that the evaluation report should explicitly describe the evaluand and its context, the evaluation process, procedures and rationale, and any resultant conclusions and recommendations; (6) report dissemination to appropriate audiences; (7) report timeliness, which is important to the usefulness of the data; and (8) evaluation impact, which suggests that evaluations should be planned and conducted in a manner that fosters appropriate follow-through by the audiences served by the process (Stufflebeam, 1990). These utility standards require that evaluators give priority to the interests of clients and stakeholders and that evaluators satisfy the intended purposes of evaluations, even if it means they must supersede their own interests or methodologies.

The *feasibility standards* are designed to ensure that program evaluations are cost-effective and practical, particularly since such assessment efforts occur in a political environment in that constituent interests are inherent. Basically, the feasibility standards advocate: (a) practical procedures, to ensure the evaluation process is not overly disruptive and can be managed in a real-world setting; (b) political viability, to ensure the process is planned and conducted in a manner that promotes cooperation among the various constituencies while inhibiting the misuse of the results; and (c) cost effectiveness, to ensure that resource expenditures are justified, given the value and adequacy of the information generated by the process (Stufflebeam, 1990).

Propriety standards reflect the American value system. They address the areas of formal obligations (e.g., contracting); conflict of interest issues; full and frank disclosure; the public's right to know, balanced against the limits and statutes dealing with the right to privacy and public safety; human subjects considerations; human interactions, or assuring participants' dignity; balanced reporting that includes notation of an evaluation's strengths and limitations (such as the limits of certain methods or the generalizability of results); and fiscal responsibility, which addresses ethics, accountability and prudence (Stufflebeam, 1990). Some of these areas are guided by regulations, such as those standards promulgated for the protection of human subjects. In addition, Worthen and Sanders (1987) suggest that one of the most viable means of addressing evaluation propriety is by an evaluation contract, which can protect the evaluator against arbitrary or unethical actions by the client while it also protects the client from an unscrupulous evaluator.

Accuracy standards address whether an evaluation has produced sound information. In fact, Stufflebeam (1990) contends that the rating of an evaluation against these standards provides a good indication of the evaluation's overall "truth value." Basically, the accuracy standards address eleven issues: object identification; context evaluation;

description of purposes and procedures so they can be assessed; defensible information sources; valid measurement; reliable measurement; systematic data control; analysis of qualitative information; justified conclusions; and objective reporting. These accuracy standards are of great importance; without accurate results, the usefulness of the whole educational evaluation process is suspect.

In 1981, when "Standards for Evaluations of Educational Programs, Projects and Materials" was released, the Joint Committee on Standards for Educational Evaluation knew that standards for personnel evaluation were also needed, as these could not be logically separated from other forms of evaluation (Stufflebeam, 1990, p. 104). However, because of concerns over support from teachers' organizations, the "Personnel Evaluation Standards" document was not released until 1990. The personnel evaluation standards are classified into similar categories used for presentation of the program evaluation standards (i.e., utility, feasibility, propriety, and accuracy); but some of the topics, out of necessity, differ between the two sets of standards. For example, the program evaluation propriety standard of "full and frank disclosure" is not included in the personnel standards because of confidentiality requirements; likewise, service orientation (i.e. requiring that evaluators show concern for the rights of students to be taught well), a key entry in personnel evaluation standards, is not included in the program standards.

It is also noteworthy that neither of the two reports on evaluation standards promote or endorse any one approach to evaluation. However, they do encourage the sound use of a variety of methods and approaches to meet the needs of the evaluation project and client. Overall, the pervasive message in both of these important documents on standards is that all evaluators should strive to make their evaluations useful, feasible, ethical, and accurate, regardless of the evaluation situation or

targets. In essence, these standards may be most beneficial when examined a priori and used as guidelines for designing evaluations.

Requirements for Conducting Evaluations

Administrators of education systems must exert a leading role if the program and teacher evaluation standards mentioned above are to be attained in actual evaluation situations. Whether evaluation is summative or formative, motivational or corrective, primarily external or internal, administrators are bound to play a leading role in organizing and implementing the evaluation process. Therefore, it is incumbent upon educational administrators to be knowledgeable and competent with respect to evaluation functions and to have a through understanding of evaluation requirements.

As suggested earlier, the evaluation requirement can be regarded as "an evaluation problem with an evaluation context" (Glasman & Nevo, 1988, p. 63). The administrator needs to understand the evaluation problem as it exists within the particular educational situation, with the aim of determining efficient evaluation methods that will result in better analyses to aid decisionmaking. However, in addition to the need to understand key aspects of the evaluation problem, it is necessary for the administrator involved in any evaluation to understand the operational context in which the evaluation will occur. In this regard, the administrator must consider time and resource factors and must also take into account the values, routines, and perceptions of others who are directly or indirectly involved in the evaluation process.

Once the evaluation problem and evaluation context are examined and weighed together, an administrator can get a fair understanding of the overall evaluation requirement. This, in turn, will allow the administrator to organize and support the evaluation at hand more effectively, so that evaluation activities can proceed with efficiency and produce the information and judgments needed. A conceptual illustration of "Understanding the Evaluation Requirement" is presented in Figure 13.5.

The Future

Predicting the future of educational evaluation is as risky as predicting the future of the educational effort in general. However, some things seem reasonably clear.

As long as education remains a human process, it will remain imperfect and open to improvement. As long as education remains a broad public concern, it will continue to be subject to scrutiny from multiple constituencies. As long as education remains a complex system, it will need to consider evaluation and feedback as legitimate components of that system.

There has been an increasing move toward assessment of the performance of educational institutions for the past two decades. This has taken clear form in the student outcomes assessment movement in colleges and universities (see Gray [1989], *Achieving Assessment*

Figure 13.5
Understanding the evaluation requirement

SOURCE: Glasman, N., & Nevo, D. (1988). *Evaluation in decision making: The case of school administration.* Boston: Kluwer Academic Publishers.

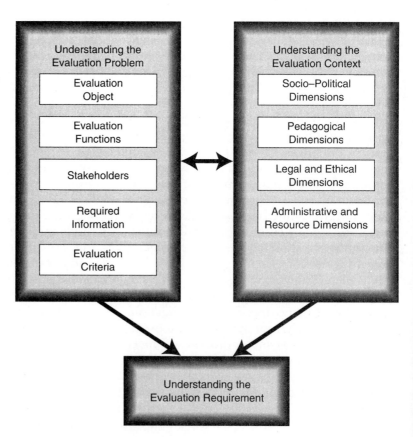

Goals Using Evaluation Techniques, and Banta [1988], *Implementing Outcomes Assessment: Promises and Perils,* as examples of discussion of the movement). Developed in part as an extension of management by objectives, outcomes assessment has drawn widespread public and professional attention. In one form or another, its emphasis on defining prospective outcomes and then looking closely at the results can be expected to figure strongly in the future design of the overall educational enterprise. Equally importantly, if we use previous chapter discussions as a reference point, we must realize that evaluation mechanisms to date are highly systematic. They lack the critical systemic emphasis and action orientation that ties evaluation to its other subsystems. Evaluation systems will need to be rethought, for example, as the era of the knowledge worker ensues (Drucker, 1993), or as society becomes more global and as we recognize the interdependence of seemingly disconnected systems and subsystems. The era of postpositivistic thought may be dying or dead. That points to the necessity for more usable evaluation orientations for the future. To date, evaluation hasn't yet approached this crossroad.

Evaluation is, and will continue to be, pervasive in the field of education. At its best, evaluation serves to aid in the improvement of the overall enterprise (i.e., personnel performance, student and program outcomes, and school and systemwide success). Even so, the benefits of evaluation must be considered in light of the corresponding limitations. As a general rule, evaluations do not yield generalizable results; they are time dependent in that most objects of the evaluation are not static; and, although they may be useful in the diagnosis of problems, they may not be helpful in elucidating appropriate solutions (Wolf, 1984). Additionally, both evaluators and their clients must be sensitive to relevant ethical issues (e.g., informed participation) and be able to weigh and make use of evaluation results in arriving at educational judgments and decisions.

Problems are inherent in both program and personnel evaluation applications. For example, program evaluations often do not involve curricula appraisal; there is little empirical evidence regarding the efficacy of alternate evaluation plans, techniques, or components common in most models; evaluators rarely call in outside expertise, even when warranted; and discipline-prone evaluators sometimes tend to cluster around their respective evaluation banners like "vassals in a form of provincial bondage" (Worthen, 1990, p. 47). Many of these same faults apply to teacher and administrative evaluations, but major problems in these areas occur for other reasons, too. There is no definitive agreement about effective teaching competencies, behaviors, and skills. There is a wide diversity of administrative tasks and responsibilities, even under the same job titles. Also, most personnel evaluations are conducted by administrators or supervisors who have little or no training in evaluation, and they may lack the knowledge needed to make informed, eclectic decisions in planning and carrying out the evaluation process (Walberg & Haertel, 1990).

In view of the problems that exist in the realm of applied evaluation, there is a significant need for empirical research, particularly with regard to instructor applications. This need is supported by an observation by Worthen, Worthen, and Sanders (1987) that the literature regarding educational systems shows large deficits on topics concerning effective educational evaluation.

Models of evaluation used in reviewing programs, teachers, and administrators have been discussed, with a review of their respective strengths and weaknesses. Means of establishing validity and reliability have been considered in each case.

In the future, evaluation of the educational system and its various components can be expected to continue to be a significant issue for all, professional educators and public alike.

■ **CASE STUDY**

Assessment Problem

Background. You have just completed your second year as Assistant Principal at Washington High School. As a teacher in this building for five years prior to your current assignment, you noticed a number of problem areas: teachers appeared to be growing more complacent, student achievement and progress had steadily declined, coursework often had little to do with job skills needed for the community work force, school administrators seemed to lack the know-how to effect change, and the school seemed to lack the resources to combat even the simplest of these problems. This morning you were called in to meet with the building principal, who was appointed three months ago. During the discussion it was clear that the principal shared your view of the school. The principal is developing a long-range plan to attack the problems as described above. The principal expects to present the plan to the faculty and staff and to the superintendent of schools in 60 days. As part of that plan, you have been asked to develop an evaluation model for the school.

Your Task. Design an evaluation model for Washington High School. Draw on the information provided in this text; on your own experience as a student, teacher, administrator, parent, and/or taxpayer; and on other relevant reading and experience. Your overall model should include subsystems that evaluate programs, teaching, and administration.

Be sure to consider issues of responsibility for follow-up and continued assessment of results. When you have completed designing the model, be prepared to discuss the implications of putting this plan into effect in a real school in the real world.

Annotated Bibliography

Baugher, D. (Ed.). (1981). *Measuring effectiveness* (Volume 11). San Francisco, CA: Jossey-Bass.

This volume focuses on the difficulties inherent in measuring effectiveness and offers some potential solutions to these problems for a diverse set of measurement situations. Content focus is on the assessment of effectiveness for organizational activities, psychopharmacological research, and education.

DeRoche, E. F. (1987). *An administrator's guide for evaluating programs and personnel: An effective schools approach* (2nd ed.). Boston, MA: Allyn and Bacon.

Determining the effectiveness of a school's programs and personnel is one of the major tasks faced by principals. The author of this text studies the issue of evaluation strategies of effective schools. The content includes methods of improving relations between the community and school, effectiveness of the student activities program, teacher evaluation, effectiveness of personnel services, and research on instructional improvement.

Erwin, T. D. (1991). *Assessing student learning and development: A guide to the principles, goals, and methods of determining college outcomes.* San Francisco, CA: Jossey-Bass.

This book is a primer intended for those who collect, review, use, and submit evidence about the strengths and weaknesses of their educational programs—that is, the success or lack of it in nurturing student learning and development. Specifically, it is designed for higher education faculty, student affairs professionals, and administrators who are starting or continuing an assessment pro-

gram. A series of assessment steps that are common to any assessment program are also presented.

Glasman, N. S., & Nevo, D. (1988). *Evaluation in decision making: The case of school administration.* Boston, MA: Kluwer Academic Publishers.

This book describes the practice of decision-making by school principals and ways to improve this practice by capitalizing on evaluation dimensions. The authors conceived this text with the idea of combining thoughts about educational administration with thoughts about educational evaluation. Implications or new generalizations about what principals can do and their evaluation techniques are presented.

Kells, H. R. (1992). Purposes and means in higher education evaluation. *Higher Education Management, 4*(1), 91–10.

This is a discussion on institutional and program evaluation in higher education that focuses on the need for congruence between the purposes of the assessment and the procedures used to accomplish it. The factors relating to success in evaluation are examined, with special attention given to those that promote improvement.

Tavernier, K. (1991). Strategic evaluation in university management. *Higher Education Management, 3*(3), 257–264.

This article urges improved evaluation of higher education teaching and research, strategic capacity to adapt to external demands and closer links between evaluation and institutional goals. Industry's strategic management methods and difficulties of evaluation in different organizations are assessed.

References

Allen, M. C., & Ellett, F. S. (1990). Development of evaluation models. In H. J. Walberg & D. Haertel (Eds.), *The international encyclopedia of educational evaluation* (pp. 15–21). New York: Pergamon Press.

Anderson, S. B., Ball, S., Murphy, R. T., and Associates. (1975). "Hard" and "Soft"—Shibboleths in evaluation. In *Encyclopedia of educational evaluation* (pp. 191–195). San Francisco: Jossey-Bass.

Banta, R. W. (Ed.). (1988, Fall). Implementing outcomes assessment: Promises and perils. *New Directions for Higher Education,* No. 59. San Francisco: Jossey-Bass.

Berk, R. A. (Ed.). (1981). *Educational evaluation methodology: The state of the art.* Baltimore: The Johns Hopkins University Press.

Borich, G. D. (Ed.). (1974). *Evaluating educational programs and products.* Englewood Cliffs, NJ: Educational Technology Publications.

Borich, G. D. (1977). *The appraisal of teaching: Concepts and process.* Reading, MA: Addison-Wesley.

Brandt, R. S. (Ed.). (1981). *Applied strategies for curriculum evaluation.* Washington, DC: ASCD.

Bratton, B. A. (1988). Ten psychometric reasons why similar tests produce dissimilar results. *Journal of School Psychology, 26,* 155–166.

Centra, J. A., & Potter, D. A. (1980). School and teacher effects: An interrelational model. *Review of Educational Research, 50*(2), 273–291.

Choppin, B. H. (1990). Evaluation as a field of inquiry: Evaluation, assessment, and measurement. In H. J. Walberg & G. D. Haertel (Eds.), *The international encyclopedia of educational evaluation* (pp. 7–8). New York: Pergamon Press.

Clift, P., Nutall, D., & McCormick, R. (Eds.). (1988). *Studies in school self-evaluation.* London & New York: Falmer Press.

Coker, H., Medley, D., & Soar, R. (1980). How valid are expert opinions about effective teaching? *Phi Delta Kappan, 62*(2), 141–144, 149.

Cronbach, L. J. (1982). *Designing evaluations of educational and social programs.* San Francisco: Jossey-Bass.

Darling-Hammond, L., Wise, A. E., & Pease, S. R. (1983, Fall). Teacher evaluation in the organizational context: A review of the literature. *Review of Educational Research, 53*(3), 285–328.

Davis, B. G. (Ed.). (1986). *Teaching of evaluation across the disciplines.* San Francisco: Jossey-Bass.

Dressel, P. L. (1976). *Handbook of academic evaluation.* San Francisco: Jossey-Bass.

Drucker, P. (1993). *Post capitalist society*. New York: Harper Business.

Edwards, W., Guttentag, M., & Snapper, K. (1975). A decision- theoretic approach to evaluation research. In E. L. Strevening & M. Guttentag (Eds.), *Handbook of evaluation research* (Vol. 1) (pp. 139–181). Beverly Hills: Sage Publications.

Elam, S. M., Rose, L. C., & Gallup, A. M. (1991, September). The 23rd annual Gallup poll of the public's attitude toward public schools. *Phi Delta Kappan*, 41–56.

Farmer, C. H. (1979). In R. C. Nordvall (Ed.), *Evaluation and development of administrators*, AAHE-ERIC/Higher Education Research Report No. 6. Washington, DC: American Association for Higher Education.

Firestone, W. A. (1987, October). Meaning in method: The rhetoric of quantitative and qualitative research. *Educational Researchers*, 6(7), 16–21.

Gallup, G. H. (1979). The eleventh annual Gallup poll of the public's attitudes toward the public schools. *Phi Delta Kappan*, 60, 33–45.

Genova, W. J., Madoff, M. K., Chin, R., & Thomas, G. B. (1976). *Mutual benefit evaluation of faculty and administrators in higher education*. Cambridge, MA: Ballinger Publishing Co.

Glasman, N. S., & Nevo, D. (1988). Evaluation in education. In *Evaluation in decision making: The case of school administration* (pp. 31–45). Boston: Kluwer Academic Publishers.

Goodwin, H. I., & Smith, E. R. (1981). *Faculty and administrator evaluation: Constructing the instruments*. Morgantown, WV: West Virginia University.

Gray, P. (Ed.). (1989, Fall). Achieving assessment goals using evaluation techniques. *New Directions for Higher Education, No. 67*. San Francisco: Jossey-Bass.

Guba, E. G., & Lincoln, Y. S. (1989). *Fourth generation evaluation*. Newbury Park, CA: Sage Publications.

Haefele, D. L. (1981). Teacher interviews. In J. Millman (Ed.), *Handbook of teacher evaluations*. Beverly Hills, CA: Sage Publications.

Holloway, M. L. (1988). Performance appraisal. In R. Middler & E. Holzapel Jr. (Eds.), *Issues in personnel management*. San Francisco: Jossey-Bass.

Holt, M. (1981). *Evaluating the evaluators*. London: Hodder & Stoughton.

House, E. R. (1978, March). Assumptions underlying evaluation models. *Educational Researcher*, 7(3), 4–12.

Hoyt, D. P. (1982, March). Evaluating administrators. In R. F. Wilson (Ed.), Designing academic program reviews. *New Directions for Higher Education, No. 37*. San Francisco: Jossey-Bass.

King, J. A. (1981). Beyond classroom walls: Indirect measures of teacher competence. In J. Millman (Ed.), *Handbook of teacher evaluation*. Beverly Hills, CA: Sage Publications.

Knapp, M. S. (1982). *Toward the study of teacher evaluation as an organizational process: A review of current research and practice*. Menlo Park, CA: SRI International.

Kowalski, T. T. (1988). Program evaluation. In *The organization and planning of adult education* (Ch. 11). Albany, NY: State University of New York Press.

Lewy, A. (1990). Formative and summative evaluation. In H. J. Walberg & G. D. Haertel (Eds.), *The international encyclopedia of educational evaluation* (pp. 26–27). New York: Pergamon Press.

Madaus, G. F., Scriven, M. S., & Stufflebeam, D. L. (1983). *Evaluation models: Viewpoints on educational and human services evaluation*. Boston: Kluwer-Nijhoff.

Mark, M. M., & Cook, T. D. (1984). Design of randomized experiments and quasi-experiments. In L. Rutman, *Evaluation research methods: A basic guide* (2nd ed.) (pp. 65–120). Beverly Hills, CA: Sage Publications.

Mehrens, W. A. (1973). *Measurement and evaluation in education and psychology*. New York: Holt, Rinehart & Winston.

Meyers, W. R. (1981). Making sense of quantitative and qualitative methods. In *The evaluation enterprise* (pp. 151–170). San Francisco: Jossey-Bass.

Miller, R. I. (1979). *The assessment of college performance*. San Francisco: Jossey-Bass.

Millman, J. (Ed.). (1981). *Handbook of teacher evaluation*. Beverly Hills, CA: Sage Publications.

Mitzel, H. E., Best, J. H., & Rabinowitz, W. (1982). *Encyclopedia of educational research* (5th ed.) (Vol. 2). New York: The Free Press.

Nevo, D. (1990). Normative dimensions of evaluation practice: Role of the evaluator. In H. J. Walberg & G. D. Haertel (Eds.), *The international encyclopedia of educational evaluation* (pp. 89–91). New York: Pergamon Press.

Nevo, D. (1983, Spring). The conceptualization of educational evaluation: An analytical review of the literature. *Review of Educational Research, 53*(1), 117–128.

Patton, M. Q. (1984). Data collection: Options, strategies, and cautions. In L. Rutman (Ed.), *Evaluation research methods: A basic guide* (2nd ed.) (pp. 39–63). Beverly Hills, CA: Sage Publications.

Peterson, K., & Kauchak, D. (1982). *Teacher evaluation: Perspectives, practices and promises.* Salt Lake City, UT: Center for Educational Practice, University of Utah.

Popham, J. W. (1975). *Evaluation in education.* Englewood Cliffs, NJ: Prentice-Hall.

Popham, J. W. (1988). *Educational evaluation.* (2nd ed). Englewood Cliffs, NJ: Prentice-Hall.

Provus, M. (1971). *Discrepancy evaluation.* Berkeley, CA: McCutchan Publishing.

Saylor, J., Alexander, W., & Lewis, A. (1981). *Curriculum planning for better teaching and learning* (4th ed.). New York: Holt, Rinehart & Winston.

Scriven, M. (1980a). *Evaluation thesaurus* (2nd ed.). Inverness, CA: Edgepress.

Scriven, M. (1980b). *The logic of evaluation.* Inverness, CA: Edgepress.

Seller, M. S. (1988). *To seek America: A history of ethnic life in the United States.* Englewood Cliffs, NJ: Jerome S. Ozer.

Shadish, W. R., Cook, T. D., & Leviton, L. C. (1991). *Foundations of program evaluation: Theories of practice.* Newbury Park, CA: Sage Publications.

Shavelson, R., & Stern, P. (1981). Research on teachers' pedagogical thoughts, judgments, decisions and behavior. *Review of Educational Research, 51*(4), 455–498.

Stake, R. (1969). Language rationality and assessment. In W. Beatty (Ed.), *Improving educational assessment and an inventory of measures of affective behavior.* Washington, DC: Association for Supervision of Curriculum Development.

Stufflebeam, D. L. (1990). Professional standards for educational evaluation. In H. J. Walberg & G. D. Haertel (Eds.), *The international encyclopedia of educational evaluation* (pp. 94–105). New York: Pergamon Press.

Talbott, M. J., & Church, K. (1988). *Evaluation and assessment: A literature review.* (Report No. HE 022 459). Phoenix, AZ: Arizona Board of Regents. (ERIC Document Reproduction Service No. ED 306 798).

Tuckman, B. (1985). *Evaluating instructional programs.* (2nd ed.). Boston: Allyn and Bacon.

Tyler, R. W. (1970). *Educational evaluation: New roles, new means.* Chicago: University of Chicago Press.

Walberg, J. J., & Haertel, G. D. (Eds.). (1990). *The international encyclopedia of educational evaluation.* New York: Pergamon Press.

Walker, R. (1986). Three good reasons for not doing case studies in curriculum research. In E. House (Ed.), *New directions in educational evaluation* (pp. 103–116). London: The Falmer Press.

Wilson, J. D. (1988). *Appraising teacher quality.* London: Hodder & Stoughton.

Wolf, R. M. (1984). *Evaluation in education* (2nd ed.). New York: Praeger.

Worthen, B. R. (1973). *Educational evaluation, theory and practice.* Worthington, OH: Chas. A. Jones Publishing.

Worthen, B. R. (1990). Program evaluation. In H. J. Walberg & G. D. Haertel (Eds.), *The international encyclopedia of educational evaluation* (pp. 42–47). New York: Pergamon Press.

Worthen, B., Worthen, B. R., & Sanders, J. R. (1987). *Educational evaluation: Alternative approaches and practical guidelines.* New York: Longman.

Part V

Decisionmaking and Change

All that has gone before—understanding education as a complex network of systems; grasping the nature of leadership; developing the skills of observation, inquiry, human relations, and communication; and mastering the practicalities of planning, resource allocation, and evaluation—is a prelude to the ultimate task of the educational leader: decisionmaking. Without decisionmaking, all other activities are academic exercises; it is only when translated into action that their potential for good becomes a reality.

Educational decisionmaking assumes many forms. Formally, it is practiced in the political context of educational policy development at the school, district, regional, state, and national levels. The resulting policies directly affect the daily operation of all educational enterprises including public and private schools, colleges and universities, and vocational/technical training programs. Policies are sets of rules for guiding the operation of an organization that have been formally adopted through a prescribed process. Chapter 14 focuses on policy formulation that is collective decisionmaking. A number of public policy models are described and critiqued. Special attention is given to assessing the impact of current proposals for decentralizing decisionmaking in education, placing more authority at the school level and involving teachers, parents, and students.

Decisions are also made by individuals; this is the focus of Chapter 15. Decisionmaking is the process of choosing among alternatives, and is one of the most crucial skills needed by an effective educational leader. We criticize the common practice of viewing decisionmaking as a linear process (identifying a problem, defining the problem, weighing alternative solutions, and making a choice). Instead, we propose a circular process that is more compatible with the inherent dynamics of the educational environment.

The ultimate objective of educational organizations—or any organization, for that matter—is to maintain internal stability. To maintain stability while existing within turbulent environments, however, requires constant change—the focus of Chapter 16. Change is not a product to be pursued in and of itself; it is a process by which other ends may be reached. Those organizations that are able to maintain flexibility and react appropriately to new environmental conditions survive and prosper; those that do not become less and less able to serve society.

It is one of the great paradoxes of educational systems that they are simultaneously conservators of knowledge and social values *and* direct instruments of change, both for the individuals with whom they interact and for society at large. For the educational leader, this means that he or she must be attuned to the complexities of selecting courses of action in a changing environment for a system that values stability while in a state of flux and serving individuals who are in the process of changing themselves.

Educational leaders of the twenty-first century must be prepared to develop, to articulate, and to bring to fruition a new conceptualization of educational systems, and to do it in such a way that the new systems, themselves, meet societal demands for flexibility and quality. It is that great challenge that is discussed in Part V of this volume.

Chapter 14
Policy Formulation

Any functioning group, whether it is the United States Government, a state government, a business or industry, a voluntary or charitable association, a local school district or a school, needs to agree on a set of rules under which it will operate. These rules are called policies—or laws in the case of government when formally adopted through a prescribed legislative process. Rules and regulations generated by a government bureau or agency under authorization of a law are also considered policy.

Policies establish the parameters within which the organization will function. They specify the activities that the organization will or will not do. Policies act to guide coherent action by channelling the thinking of employees and other members of the organization. They set constraints within which discretion can be exercised. They are necessary so that all partners in an endeavor have the same "marching orders," visions, and intentions (Kaufman & Herman, 1991).

The state and federal constitutions specify the formal procedures to be followed in adopting laws. But laws are usually written in quite broad terms and must be interpreted in order to be implemented. The interpretation begins with the bureau within the executive branch of government given the responsibility for administering the law, e.g., state education departments and the U.S. Education Department. Decisions made by bureaucrats to guide actions at lower levels of authority, and written in the form of regulations, are as much policy as the laws themselves. State law specifies general procedures to be followed by local school districts in formulating policy although variation is permitted in specific practices. School districts may specify procedures to be followed by schools in setting policy or they may let the schools establish their own procedures subject to district review and approval. Private organizations may go through formal incorporation that specifies a corporate procedure to be followed in making decisions—or they may informally agree upon a constitution or a set of bylaws to guide corporate decisionmaking. In the public sector, policies are usually (and preferably) written. Policies may, however, be informal, unwritten, and unstated agreements by which members of an organization bind their actions.

While constitutions, laws, charters, bylaws, etc. spell out the formal steps to be followed in arriving at group decisions (i.e., policy), the human interactions in carrying out those steps are not specified. Often these interactions involve elaborate strategies, power plays and intrigue employed by individuals and subgroups of individuals bonded by common interests to shape an organization's (or government's) decisions. These interactions, whether simple or elaborate, can be referred to as *politics.* Indeed, Hodgkinson (1983) has referred to politics as "administration by another name." The nature of both the structure of the policymaking process and the politics employed within the structure are believed to influence policy outcomes (Dye, 1987).

This chapter focuses on educational policy formulation and begins with a discussion of some basic educational policy issues and the nature of the individuals and groups having a stake in the decisions made. Attention is given to the tension between centralization and decentralization forces over the placement of authority to make public policy. This discussion is followed by a discussion of the way governments, including school boards, manage input from interested parties and make decisions, i.e., laws and policies. Special attention is given to the role of the courts in policy formulation. Unlike most countries, courts play an especially important role in policymaking in the United States because the powers of state and federal governments are constrained by their constitutions and the rights of individuals are protected against violation by democratic majority rule through bills of rights.

The concluding section of this chapter addresses school-based decisionmaking, which tends to be less formal than decisionmaking at the district level and higher. There is considerable overlap between school-based decisionmaking and decisionmaking as dis-

cussed in Chapter 15, which focuses on procedures followed by individuals and small groups. With respect to decisionmaking at the school level, this chapter focuses on structural considerations and the next chapter focuses on processes. An understanding of school-based decisionmaking is becoming increasingly important as decisions formerly made at the district level are being devolved to schools.

Allocation of Policymaking Authority within the Education Sector

In Chapter 12, Allocation of Resources in Education, we noted that structuring the decisionmaking process for education is particularly complex because education is both a public and a private good. If public benefits were simply the sum of individual benefits, this would not constitute a problem, but such is not the case. Differences between societal and individual interests are quite common. (See the discussion of metavalues in Chapter 4.) Full public interest would not be realized if the provision of education were left solely to supply and demand forces of the market (ultimate decentralization); and it is equally improbable that all individual interests would be fully satisfied if education were left solely to public provision (ultimate centralization).

The allocation of authority for making decisions about education among interested parties appears to shape the nature of the decisions made and the effectiveness with which they are implemented. Determining a satisfactory pattern of allocation of authority is a continuing problem changing along with priorities placed on fundamental social values and new technologies. Thus, many of the reforms described in Chapter 3, The Context for Leadership, would reallocate policymaking authority from what it is at present. Examples include school-based decisionmaking, parental choice of schools, state and national curricula and standards, and national certification of teachers.

POLICY ISSUES AND POTENTIAL DECISIONMAKERS

In studying the merits of alternative decision-making structures for education within the context of specific policy objectives, it is useful to examine the type of issues that need to be addressed according to the interests and expertise of the potential decisionmakers, i.e., individuals (or families), the teaching profession, and society. Regardless of who makes the decisions, there are five broad areas in which educational policy must be formulated (Benson, 1978). These are:

1. setting goals and objectives for the educational enterprise,

2. determining for whom educational services are to be provided,

3. determining the level of investment in population quality (e.g., education) to promote economic growth and the general welfare,

4. allocating resources to and among educational services,

5. determining the means by which educational services are to be provided.

These five policy areas represent an elaboration of the three fundamental economic decisions presented in Chapter 12. The five policy areas and the three categories of decision makers, society, the teaching profession, and families, are represented as a matrix in Figure 14.1.

The potential concern of each group of decisionmakers extends to each of the issues although the actual level of interest and expertise of a given group will vary from issue to issue. Societal concerns are expressed by individuals and interest groups and moderated through the political process of government including school boards, and through

Type of Issues	Decision Makers		
	Society	Profession	Family
Set Goals and Objectives			
Allocate Resources			
Produce Services			
Distribute Services			
Make Investments			

Figure 14.1
Educational decision matrix showing general policy areas and potential decisionmakers

the formation of coalitions such as those now negotiating a national curriculum and standards and procedures for national certification of teachers. Societal concerns take precedence over family and professional concerns for those issues in education where there is significant spillover of benefits (i.e., "collective" or "public" goods) and where there are redistributive considerations (shifting of wealth and benefits from one group to another).

The teaching profession holds the technical expertise about schooling, and, with its members employees of the education system(s), it has a vested interest in the conditions of employment. Teachers, along with other members of the polity, participate in general elections and referenda and the related political activities accompanying them. Professional educators also have a very strong impact on public policy through the lobbying activities of their unions and professional associations. Lobbyists for the National Education Association (NEA) and the American Federation of Teachers (AFT) are particularly effective at the state and national levels. At the local level, in addition to serving on advisory committees, etc., teachers and administrators have had great impact on educational policy through the collective bargaining process (Bacharach & Shedd, 1989; Mitchell, 1989).

Parents are the guardians of interests and needs of individual children. In most instances, the family holds the most intimate knowledge about and caring concern for the child. It is through the family that the child's voice is heard (Bridge, 1976; Coons & Sugarman, 1978). In addition to participating in school board elections and referenda, individual parents may approach school board members or school administrators directly to express their concerns. They may also align themselves with other parents holding similar concerns forming such associations as the National Congress of Parents and Teachers (PTA) and the Council for Basic Education (CBE), which direct their activities largely at influencing state and federal policy. Other parent groups focus on the needs of special children, such as the emotionally disturbed, physically disabled, or intellectually gifted.

Organizations such as the League of Women Voters and the American Association of University Women embrace educational issues as a continuing secondary concern. Other organizations attempt to influence educational policy as a means of accomplishing ends that transcend the school. These might include taxpayers groups or groups with a specific political agenda such as civil rights, affirmative action, pro-choice and anti-abortion, environmental protection, the promotion of patriotism, religious fundamentalism, etc.

CENTRALIZATION AND DECENTRALIZATION OF POLICYMAKING

Within any given context, significantly different patterns of allocation of authority among levels of government and potential decisionmakers can be structured depending upon the relative priorities given to policy objectives (Kirst, 1988). Extreme centralization of authority is characterized by making all decisions collectively and by administering them through public institutions. Extreme decentralization of authority is characterized by having no public schools and no subsidies, leaving the production and distribution of educational services to be determined solely by market forces. This position enhances the potential for realizing values of efficiency and personal freedom, but it has severe negative implications for the realization of other societal values such as equity.

Increasing centralization of authority has been used in the post-World War II years as a vehicle for promoting equity considerations; but, judging from the flood of national criticism over the past decade, the efficiency of the education system may have suffered. To promote values of efficiency and liberty while retaining considerable control over equity, some school districts have taken modest steps in decentralizing decisionmaking by adopting policies that create magnet schools and/or permit open enrollment among schools (Raywid, 1985). Other districts have devolved substantial policymaking authority to schools and teachers, i.e., school-based decisionmaking and teacher empowerment. Recent centralizing policy proposals aimed at improving efficiency in the educational system include setting state standards for student academic performance and raising state standards for entering the teaching profession.

Wirt and Kirst (1982) diagnosed centralization/decentralization tensions as a function of the inherent conflict between "individualism and majoritarianism." They saw the political stress in today's society stemming from the emphasis that we, as a society, place on translating private preference and need into public policy. In acknowledging that all persons are regarded as important, government, if it is to survive, must mediate conflicts arising out of diverse individual desires so that the conflicts remain at tolerable levels. Majority rule is an integral part of democratic governance. Individualism, on the other hand, is reflected in our economic system and in the bills of rights in our national and state constitutions designed to protect individuals from the "tyranny of the majority."

McGinn and Street (1986) characterized centralization and decentralization as a dyad.

Decentralization is not primarily an issue of control by government of individual citizens. Instead it is a question of the distribution of power among various groups in society. A highly participatory society—one in which all citizens actually do participate—is likely to require a competent and powerful state that actively and continuously seeks to redistribute power among groups and individuals in the society. The location of authority in local government does not protect the local citizen from tyranny, and the redistribution of power through the market mechanism in a society that currently is highly inequitable is a guarantee that inequities will persist and worsen. On the other hand, competition and markets can contribute to social justice in circumstances where there is a relatively equitable balance of powers among the participants in the competition or market. . . . A strong state must first achieve some minimal degree of social equity so that decentralization can lead to genuine participation. (pp. 489–490)

Friedman (1962) analyzed the situation as follows:

The widespread use of the market reduces the strain on the social fabric by rendering conformity unnecessary with respect to any activities it encompasses. The wider the range of activities covered by the market, the fewer are the issues on which explicit political decisions are required and hence on which it is necessary to achieve agreement. In turn, the fewer issues on which agreement is necessary, the greater the likelihood of getting agreement while maintaining a free society (p. 24).

With respect to education, driven by a priority concern for equity, the trend during the 1960s and 1970s was toward centralizing decisions at the state and federal levels. In seeking higher educational standards, the first wave of reform in the early 1980s produced further centralization; the second wave, however, was directed toward greater decentralization. These may appear to be contradictory developments, but they are happening throughout the western world and in the private as well as the public sector (Beare, Caldwell, & Millikan, 1989; Iannaccone, 1988; Lawton, 1992; Whitty, 1992). Peters and Waterman (1982) referred to the phenomenon in the private sector as "loose/tight structures." In the organizational literature it has been referred to as "loose coupling" (see Chapters 7 and 15).

It appears that some decisions about education may best be made by central authorities, particularly those involving equity and fraternity, but others are best left to those with professional expertise at the school level or to those having a personal stake in the happiness and welfare of a specific child, the family (Coleman & Hoffer, 1987; Coons & Sugarman, 1978; Cremin, 1976; McNeil, 1986; Wise, 1979, 1988). Determining the optimal allocation of authority in education is a complex and unending process.

Thus, centralization and decentralization of authority should be viewed as means toward desired ends, not ends in themselves (Hanson, 1986). The same is true of state power, teacher power, and people power. There are legitimate concerns about education at all levels of the socio-political hierarchy; the critical issue is achieving the best balance among legitimate interests. The best balance will vary from society to society and over time within a society as contexts, value definitions, and priorities change (Wirt, 1986).

In Chapter 3, The Context for Leadership, we described current formal structures for making decisions about education and operating schools and the reforms being proposed for the system. In this section of Chapter 14, we have seen how changes in the formal structure of educational decisionmaking might affect the nature of decisions being made. In the next section, we look at several theories of how individuals and groups work within the system to obtain policies favorable to their respective causes.

Political Decisionmaking

There is no overarching general theory of political decisionmaking, but there is a "grab bag" of heuristic theories and contrasting methods (Wirt & Kirst, 1982). Heuristic theory is a method of analytically separating and categorizing items in experience. Among the most useful for understanding policy relating to schools are: (1) institutionalism, (2) incrementalism, (3) group theory, (4) elite theory, (5) rationalism, and (6) systems theory. These theories and models complement one another. Each emphasizes a particular aspect of the policymaking process. Taken together, they provide a rather complete picture of the total process. While these theories were developed primarily to describe policy formulation at the national level, they are fully applicable at the state level and can provide much insight to understanding the policymaking process at the school district and school levels as well.

INSTITUTIONALISM

Institutionalism focuses on the structure of the policymaking process (Grodzins, 1966; Elazar, 1972; Walker, 1981) and is highly relevant to the discussion in the previous section of the allocation of authority within that process. Unlike most of the rest of the world where education is a function of the national government, educational governance in the United States is characterized by the primacy

of state governments with delegated power to school districts. On the positive side, this arrangement has produced educational systems that are quite diverse, dynamic, and responsive to local conditions. On the negative side, the structure has resulted in gross financial and curricular inequities. Some school districts spend several times as much per pupil as do other districts. Some districts operate schools that are unequaled in quality throughout the world, while others operate schools that are an embarrassment to the profession and to the nation. The devolved nature of school governance impeded state and federal efforts during the 1960s, 1970s, and 1980s to equalize educational opportunities in terms of finance, curricular provision, and the integration of students and staff with respect to race, ethnicity, and national origin.

But the structure of educational governance has changed over the years and it continues to change. The change was reflected in Figure 3.3 of Chapter 3, which showed the trends in school revenue provided by each level of government in the United States since 1890. During the early part of the twentieth century, state governments on average paid less than 20 percent of the cost of elementary and secondary education; the rest was provided by school districts and/or local governments. The state share has been growing steadily since 1930. In 1986 total aggregate state aid of the 50 states exceeded 50 percent of school revenues for the first time; school districts provided 44 percent. Federal participation grew from virtually nothing at the beginning of the century to nearly 10 percent in 1980. Federal aid has since declined to 6 percent of all revenues for public schools (National Center for Education Statistics, 1993, p. 34).

The growing participation by state and federal governments in the financing of schools parallels their growing interest in and influence over educational policy in general. State governments have become particularly active in the prescription of basic curricula, monitoring student progress through mandatory testing programs, and the certification of teachers (Darling-Hammond & Barry, 1988; Elmore & McLaughlin, 1988). State education departments and the U.S. Education Department have increased in size and influence (Moore, Goertz, & Hartle, 1983; Murphy, 1982).

According to Wirt and Kirst, (1982, p. v), "The 1970s will be remembered as an era when the previous hallmark of American education—local control—became fully a myth." The local superintendent has lost his or her once preeminent position in setting the school district agenda and controlling decision outcomes. The discretionary range of superintendents and school boards has been narrowed at the top by federal and state action and at the bottom through collective bargaining with employee unions. The more recent trend toward school-based management is narrowing the range even further. Nevertheless, local school districts continue to exert a considerable, though declining, amount of influence on educational policy (Odden & Marsh, 1989).

Other structural changes of political institutions are taking place that will have an impact on the decisionmaking process and the ultimate nature of decisions made. Small districts have consolidated and large districts have decentralized. Progress is being made toward the professionalization of teaching and parental choice of schools. Adoption of policies such as educational vouchers and tax credits would further change the face of educational governance, increasing the role of private providers.

SYSTEMS THEORY

The most comprehensive of the models is systems theory. As explained in Chapter 1, Systems Theory and Educational Administration, a system is made up of a number of interrelated elements. An open system, which is characteristic of political systems, draws resources from its environment, processes them in some fashion, and returns the processed resources to the environment. All systems tend toward entropy or disorganization and they must consciously combat this tendency in order to maintain equilibrium. A key function for combating entropy is feedback, i.e., continual monitoring of a system's internal operations and its relationship with its environment. Accurate feedback is particularly critical to a system's health in that the system depends upon the environment for resources without which the system would shrink or die. Equilibrium is maintained by modifying or adapting system structures and processes based on analysis of feedback. Maintaining equilibrium is a dynamic process leading to growth and evolution of the system in harmony with its environment.

Easton (1965) adapted general systems theory to political systems. His model, illustrated in Figure 14.2, conceptualizes public

Figure 14.2

A simplified model of a political system

SOURCE: Easton, D. (1965). *A systems analysis of political life.* Chicago: University of Chicago Press, p. 32. (Copyright 1965 by University of Chicago Press. Reprinted by permission.)

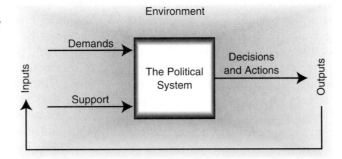

policy as a response by a political system to forces from the environment. Environmental pressures or inputs come in the forms of (1) demands for public action through interest groups and (2) support of government by individuals and groups through obeying laws, paying taxes and accepting outcomes of elections. The inputs are processed through the political system and transformed into policy outputs. Political systems consist of sets of identifiable and interrelated institutions and activities at all levels such as those associated with the U.S. Congress, state and county legislatures, common councils, town councils, village boards, school boards, commissions, authorities, and courts. Feedback in a political system is both formal and informal. Formal feedback is provided through elections, referenda, hearings, and policy analysis. Informal feedback occurs through personal interactions with constituents and others.

The decision matrix presented in Figure 14.1 of this chapter, depicting five types of educational policy that have to be made and by the primary groups of decisionmakers, represents one way of characterizing the political system. As a vehicle for synthesizing the concepts and issues discussed in the previous section with this section, we now take that matrix and place it within Easton's (1965) simplified model of a political system. The result is Figure 14.3. The decision matrix, in its new context, is called "The Political-Economic System." Social values and goals (of multiple interest groups) are treated as "Demand" inputs to the policymaking process in the new model. Other demand inputs include existing knowledge (e.g., the professional expertise of teachers and administrators) and requirements for a qualified workforce. The latter requirement is, at the same time, a "Support" input in that trained personnel (teachers and administrators) are required to implement any educational policies that are made and, indeed, the qualifications of available labor will strongly influence

which educational policy alternatives are feasible and which are not. Other support inputs are the economic base from which resources must be drawn to finance implementation and the behavior of citizens in general that sustain the political-economic system. The outcomes of the process are educational policies, categorized in the figure according to the five types of issues addressed through the socio-political process. The policies are a composite of decisions made by society, the profession, and the family.

INCREMENTALISM

Lindblom (1959) described the public policy process in the United States as a continuation of past government activities with only incremental modifications. He insightfully labeled the process as "muddling through." While some deplore his exaltation of the process, one of his most ardent critics credits him with presenting "a well considered theory fully geared to the actual experience of practicing administrators" (Dror, 1964, p. 153). Lindblom (1968, p. 32) took issue with the popular view that politics is a process of conflict resolution. He argued that "governments are instruments for vast tasks of social cooperation" and that "conflicts are largely those that spring from the opportunities for cooperation that have evolved once political life becomes orderly." Within this context, he described the play of power as a process of cooperation among specialists. It is gamelike, normally proceeding according to implicitly accepted rules. "Policy analysis is incorporated as an instrument or weapon into the play of power, changing the character of analysis as a result" (Lindblom, 1968, p. 30).

The focus of the play of power is on means (policy) not ends (goals or objectives). This, according to Lindblom, is what permits the political system to work. Because of the overlap in value systems among interested groups, and the uncertainty of the outcomes of any course of action, partisans across the value spectrum are able to come to agreement on means where agreement on ends would be impossible.

Since agreement on goal priorities is impossible in a pluralistic society according to Lindblom (1968, p. 33), the type of analysis appropriate to the political process is termed *partisan analysis.* It is analysis conducted by advocates (organized interest groups) of a relatively limited set of values and/or ends such as teacher associations, taxpayer groups, and religious and patriotic organizations. Comprehensiveness is provided by the variety of partisans participating in the political process. The responsibility for promoting specific val-

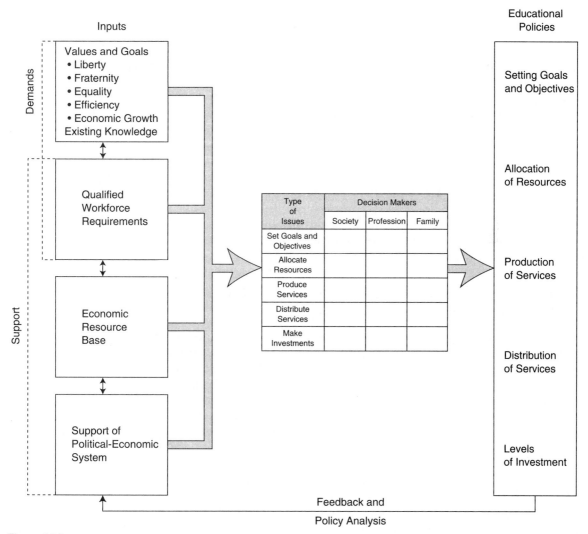

Figure 14.3
A model of the political-economic system of educational policy development
SOURCE: Swanson, A. D., & King, R. A. (1991). *School finance: Its economics and politics.* Copyright 1991 by Longman Publishers USA. Reprinted with permission.

Figure 14.4
Group theory model
SOURCE: Dye, T. R. (1987). *Understanding public policy* (6th ed.). Englewood Cliffs, NJ: Prentice-Hall, p. 27.

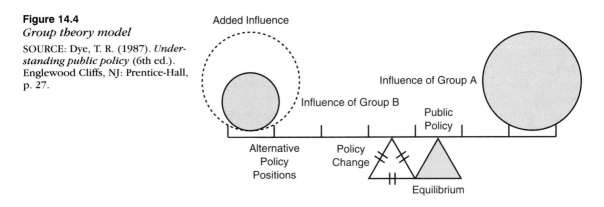

ues thus lies in the hands of advocates of those values (pressure groups and lobbyists) and not in the hands of some "impartial" analyst (as would be the case with rationalism, to be discussed later).

The net result of this advocacy process is incremental rather than revolutionary changes in policy. In light of our grand state of ignorance about the relationships between public policy and human behavior, Lindblom viewed incremental policy decisions as being well justified. Incrementalism permits the expansion of policies that prove successful while limiting the harm caused by unsuccessful policies. Within the context of strategic planning, incrementalism can assure that each increment leads toward desired goals while minimizing organizational disruption. Incrementalism preserves the system while changing it.

In the next two sections we discuss group theory and elite theory. Both provide explanations of how incrementalism works in practice.

GROUP THEORY

Truman (1951), a leading proponent of group theory, saw politics as the interaction among groups (as opposed to individuals) in the formulation of public policy. Individuals band together into formal or informal groups, similar to Lindblom's partisans, to confront gov-

ernment with their demands. The group is the vehicle through which individuals can influence government action. Even political parties are viewed as coalitions of interest groups. Elected and appointed officials are seen as being continually involved in bargaining and negotiating with relevant groups to work out compromises that balance interests.

Group theory, as portrayed by Dye (1987), is illustrated in Figure 14.4. Public policy at any point in time represents the equilibrium of the balance of power among groups. Because the power alignment is continually shifting (e.g., toward Group B, in Figure 14.4, as it gains supporters or partners in coalition on a particular issue), the fulcrum of equilibrium also shifts, leading to incremental changes in policy (in the direction desired by Group B as illustrated).

Stability in the system is attributed to a number of factors. First, most members of the electorate are latent supporters of the political system and share in its inherent values. This latent group is generally inactive, but can be aroused to defend the system against any group that attacks it. Second, there is a great deal of overlap in the membership of groups; a given individual is likely to be a member of several. This tends to have a dampening effect with respect to any group taking extreme positions because, while the group may be focused on a single issue, its membership is much more broadly oriented. The third factor promoting system stability results from group competition. No single group constitutes a majority in American society. Coalitions are easily formed to counter the influence of any group appearing to gain undue influence. As a result the political process is characterized by evolution as in incrementalism rather than revolution.

ELITE THEORY

Elite theory focuses on actions by a select group of influential elite citizens. Elite theory (Dye & Zeigler, 1981) characterizes the general public as apathetic, ill-informed and uninterested where public policy is concerned—not unlike the characterization of the latent group in group theory. This leaves a power vacuum that is happily filled by an elite. The elites do more to shape the opinion of the masses on public issues than the general public does to shape the opinions of the elite, although influence is reciprocal (e.g., civil rights legislation [Dye, 1987, Chapter 3]). According to this theory, policy is developed by the elites among the trappings of democratic government.

Elites tend to be drawn from upper socioeconomic levels. They are not necessarily against the general welfare of the masses, as in the case of civil rights legislation, but approach their welfare through a sense of *noblesse oblige*. While not agreeing on all issues, the elite share a consensus on basic social values and on the importance of preserving the system. The masses give superficial support to this consensus that provides a basis for elite rule. When events occur that threaten the system, elites move to take corrective action. According to elite theory, changes in public policy come about as the result of elites redefining their own positions, although this redefinition may be a function of external pressures. Because of the elite's conservative posture with respect to preserving the system, policy changes tend to be incremental.

RATIONALISM

Adherents of rationalism seek to shape the policymaking process in such a fashion as to assure the enactment of policies that maximize social gain. According to Dror (1968, p. 132), the assumptions of pure rationality are deeply rooted in modern civilization and culture and are the basis of certain economic theories of the free market and political theories of democracy. Rationalism is derived from the postpositivist philosophy described in Chapter 4. Dror characterized the pure rationality model as having six phases:

1. Establishing a complete set of operational goals, with relative weights allocated to the different degrees to which each may be achieved.

2. Establishing a complete inventory of other values and of resources, with relative weights.

3. Preparing a complete set of alternative policies open to the policy maker.

4. Preparing a complete set of valid predictions of the costs and benefits of each alternative including the extent to which each will achieve the various operational goals, consume resources, and realize or impair other values.

5. Calculating the net expectation of each alternative by multiplying the probability of each benefit and cost for each alternative by the utility of each, and calculating the net benefit (or cost) in utility units.

6. Comparing the net expectations and identifying the alternative (or alternatives, if two or more are equally good) with the highest net expectation. (p. 132)

These phases are organized sequentially in Figure 14.5.

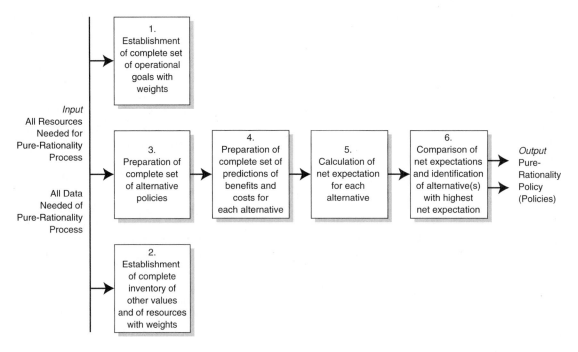

Figure 14.5
The phases of pure-rationality policy making

In theory, rationalism involves all individual, social, political, and economic values, not just those that can be converted to dollars and cents. In reality, the measurement difficulties make inclusion of other than economic values unlikely. Thus, this model elevates economic efficiency above other potential societal objectives such as equity and liberty.

To "know" all that would be required to select a policy "rationally," i.e., all of society's value preferences and relative weights, all available policy alternatives and the consequences of each alternative, is what Lindblom (1959, p. 88) termed *superhuman comprehensiveness*. In essence, rationalism attempts the impossible by quantifying all elements of the political process and human behavior and expressing the decisionmaking function in mathematical terms (Lavoie, 1985). While imperfect, the representative legislature (e.g., school boards and Congress)

is a political mechanism for approximating "all of society's value preferences and relative weights."

Rational techniques that are based on economic principles and procedures should be an important factor in budget development. However, Cibulka (1987) acknowledged that even budgetary decisions are not actually made on the basis of rationality. Wildavsky (1964) also argued that pure rationality is an illusion. He emphasized the political nature of the budgetary process:

> *If one looks at politics as a process by which the government mobilizes resources to meet pressing problems, then the budget is the focus of these efforts. . . . In the most integral sense, the budget lies at the heart of the political process. (pp. 4–5)*

Political realists argue that decisions in the public sector, including public education, are made on the basis of political rationality rather than economic rationality. To them, "rationalism" is at best irrelevant and can be downright dysfunctional to the political process (Schultz, 1968).

Rationalism was a key principle behind the comprehensive centralized planning schemes of socialist and communist countries. With the collapse of many of the latter, and with the routine failure of five-year plans in social-ist—mostly developing—countries, rational-ism has lost much of its credibility (Agarawala, 1984; Weiler, 1980).

Nevertheless, rationalistic philosophy has had an important impact on policy analysis and an indirect effect on policy decisionmak-ing. Its bias of economic efficiency is a value that is all too frequently neglected in the tra-ditional political process. The spirit of ratio-nalism has fostered such management devices as Planning Programming Budgeting Systems (PPBS), Zero Based Budgeting (ZBB), Man-agement by Objectives (MBO) and Operations Research (OR) as well as cost-benefit and cost-effectiveness analysis. The terms "accountability" and "assessment" are now a part of the schooling vernacular and teacher, pupil and program evaluations are accepted procedures. Local school boards and state and federal governments are adding to their long-standing concerns over the quantity and quality of school inputs a similar concern over school outputs through mandatory eval-uation and testing programs, i.e., "outcomes based education."

While tools of rational analysis have had some effect on the educational decisionmak-ing process, rationalistic approaches have fallen short of the expectations of their sup-porters and have met with strong opposition from some segments of the traditional educa-tional decisionmaking process. A major source of resistance to the use of analysis in schools is the teaching profession, itself. In addition to their vested interests as employ-ees, teachers are acutely aware of the almost impossible task of quantitatively measuring

the complex variables associated with educa-tional inputs and outputs and with the learn-ing process.

The most ardent supporters of rational analysis are economic purists who seek eco-nomic efficiency in the public sector. Within the private sector powerful mechanisms exist to weed out inefficiencies. Indeed, one of the roles of government is to police the market place, keeping in check those forces that would impede the functioning of these mech-anisms. Few, if any, similar mechanisms oper-ate in the public sector, making efficiency advocates very uncomfortable with current processes for allocating resources. When gov-ernment was small, inefficiency could be tol-erated; however, with one-third of the U.S. economy being allocated through political processes, 4 percent by school districts alone, inefficient use of resources can be extremely harmful to the general welfare.

Unlike incrementalism, which focuses on means, rationalism requires agreement on outcomes, which is unlikely in pluralistic organizations (e.g., state and federal govern-ments and large urban school districts). Because of the reduced number of conflicting interest groups at the school level (which may also be the case with small, homogeneous school districts), such agreement is frequently obtained and rationalism can become func-tional at that level.

In the next section we look at the implica-tions for educational policy formulation when much of the authority for decisionmaking is devolved to school buildings.

Policy Formulation under a System of School-Based Management

Moving to a system of school-based manage-ment (SBM) reflects a faith in the theory of institutionalism, described above, that the governance structure by which public policy is formulated affects the nature and quality of the policy produced. Increasing numbers of school districts (and states) are devolving significant amounts of educational policymaking authority to the school level (e.g., the state of Kentucky; Dade County, Florida; Chicago; Edmondton, Alberta, Canada). Under SBM, school personnel make many of the decisions formerly made at the school district level. They may develop the budget, select staff, and refine the school's curriculum to meet the specific needs of its pupils within legal constraints set by the school district or higher levels of government (Cawelti, 1989). Such decisions may be made by the principal alone or the responsibility may be shared with teachers, parents, and upper-grade students (Lindelow, 1981). The school district usually continues to set general priorities within which all schools must function, develop overarching educational objectives and the curriculum to meet those objectives, allocate lump sums of money to schools based on student needs, negotiate labor contracts, and provide facilities and other support services such as transportation, payroll, and accounting. The experiences of selected states and school districts with SBM and the effect on policy formulation are described in the following subsections.

KENTUCKY

In 1990, the State of Kentucky enacted sweeping legislation transforming its entire educational governance structure. This action was precipitated by a ruling of the Kentucky Supreme Court that the total school governance and finance system was in violation of the state's constitutional requirement of an "efficient system of common schools." The Kentucky reforms are considered by some to be a blueprint for change nationally (Danzberger, Kirst, & Usdan, 1992). The reforms involve both centralizing and decentralizing features.

Student achievement is the centerpiece of the new system in Kentucky, which focuses on outcomes, not inputs. The expectation is that every child will learn and that the education system will become performance-driven and results-oriented. A state Council on School Performance Standards was established to set learning goals and definitions of expected student learning outcomes. Each school is to be governed by a school council made up of three teachers, two parents, and the principal. Councils are empowered to adopt curriculum, select instructional materials, set policies for discipline and classroom management, oversee extracurricular activities, and assign students and staff. A council can select staff, including the principal, from a list of candidates recommended by its district's superintendent of schools.

DADE COUNTY, FLORIDA

Dade County, Florida, which includes the City of Miami, began implementing its school governance experiment, School Based Management/Shared Decision-Making (SBM/SDM) during the 1987–88 school year. Dade County is the fourth largest school district in the United States with over a quarter of a million students.

SBM/SDM is a pilot program designed to give teachers and administrators the opportunity to voice and implement their ideas on how students should be taught. Thirty-three schools participated the first year; additional schools were added in subsequent years. To participate in the program, a school or group of schools must submit a proposal to the district office. The proposal must carry the approval of the principal, union steward, and two-thirds of the faculty. Technical assistance in developing proposals is available from the district office. Proposal assessment criteria include: educational impact/accountability; collegial process; shared decisionmaking model; targeted changes; feasibility for implementation; rationale; community involvement; school climate; and replication.

Schools selected for participation have significantly increased flexibility in both budgeting and staffing. The decisions on how to allocate funds, as well as how to organize instructional plans, are left to SBM/SDM schools. Parents and other community representatives may participate in the school's decisionmaking process as advisors and as supportive and helpful partners. These schools report directly to the central office, bypassing midlevel management. Dade County School Board rules, teacher labor contract provisions, and State Department of Education regulations may be waived. The school board has suspended requirements regarding maximum class size, length of school day, number of minutes per subject, and distribution of report cards. The union has allowed teachers to give up planning periods, working longer hours for no additional pay, and participation in peer evaluation programs (Mojkowski & Fleming, 1988).

Under district guidelines, the participating schools receive the same level of funds as non-SBM/SDM schools based on a lump-sum allocation. Average district salaries plus fringe benefits are used for purchase of additional units of staff or return of dollar equivalent of staff relinquished for reallocation to other purposes. Equivalent dollars for the special services that once were provided at the area or district level are distributed to participating schools. Such funds may be used to purchase services from the district or private vendors as determined by the school.

Alternative arrangements proposed by schools vary considerably. Some schools have opened on Saturdays; others have added programs before and after school. Several are modifying staffing patterns by hiring aides in place of assistant principals, employing teachers by the hour, and creating new positions (Mojkowski & Fleming, 1988).

Initial evaluations have been generally positive. Teachers indicate some increased involvement in decisionmaking activities usually considered management prerogatives. Teachers also indicated a shift in their attitudes in favor of a collegial approach to school operation. Principals felt that SBM/SDM has had a favorable impact on the school environment. SBM/SDM was seen as facilitating the generation of instructional ideas, design of specific interventions, and provision for feedback. Principals acknowledged that SBM/SDM was more time-consuming than previously employed management methods and that it made their jobs more complex (Collins, 1988).

Timar (1989) linked the Dade County experience with state actions dating back to 1971 when Governor Ruben Askew appointed the Citizens' Committee on Education. Among other things, the committee recommended that decisionmaking be placed at the level of instruction. Enabling legislation was subsequently adopted. Within the Dade County School District, the school board, administration and teachers union have cooperated fully in the development and implementation of SBM/SDM. According to Timar, "Restructuring was not something that one side wanted and the other resisted; hence, it could not be held hostage and used as a bargaining chip" (p. 272).

According to Timar, the Dade County experience showed that genuine restructuring is possible. For successful implementation, he underscored the importance of a policy climate that fosters an integrated and organizationally coherent response to restructuring—one that redefines the roles and responsibilities of just about every party connected with schools: teachers, administrators, professional organizations, policymakers, parents, students, and colleges and universities. Timar concluded that an integrated response to restructuring at the school level is not likely to occur in politically balkanized and programmatically fragmented districts and states.

CHICAGO

While it is too early to evaluate its effectiveness, one of the most ambitious attempts at school-based management is being made by the city of Chicago. The plan was adopted by the Illinois Legislature in December of 1988 in a desperate attempt to reform a school system that was alleged to contain the worst schools in the country by realigning its incentives and power structure (Hess, 1991). The plan was phased in over a five-year period. Ten goals of the reform were identified in the act, but the primary goals were to raise student achievement, attendance rates, and graduation rates to national norms for *all* schools.

The key for achieving the goals of the act are Local School Councils (LSCs) composed of six parents, two community representatives, two teachers, and the principal. For high schools, they also include one nonvoting student. Except for teacher representatives and the principal, employees of the system may not serve as members of LSCs. District employees are also barred from voting in elections of parent and community representatives. This configuration was designed to give parents a major voice in the education decisions affecting their children and to avoid the problems encountered in New York City where employees have been able to dominate elections to the 32 community Boards of Education that govern elementary schools in that city (Hess, 1991).

The councils are responsible for adopting a School Improvement Plan, a budget to implement that plan based upon a lump-sum allocation from the City Board of Education, and for selecting a new principal or retaining the incumbent. The amount of discretionary funds available to each school annually averages about $500,000.

Unlike most other school-based management plans, the Chicago plan places greater

responsibility with parents and community representatives than with teachers. The importance of participatory decisionmaking was recognized, however, in relationships mandated between the LSCs and the professional staff. A Professional Personnel Advisory Committee (PPAC) is to be created in each school to advise the principal and the LSC on the educational program. The PPAC is composed of teachers and other professional personnel in the school.

Although never stated explicitly, the Chicago School Reform Act is built on the assumption that the principal is the chief instructional leader in each school (Hess, 1991). Principals are given the right to select teachers, aides, counselors, clerks, hall guards, and any other instructional program staff for vacant or newly created positions. Principals are responsible for initiating a needs assessment and a School Improvement Plan in consultation with the LSC and the PPAC. They are also responsible for drafting a budget for amendment and/or adoption by the LSC. Principals hold no tenure rights in their positions other than those they hold as teachers.

Subdistrict councils were established for each administrative division in the city. They are composed of one parent or community representative from each school. The subdistrict councils serve in a coordinating capacity for schools within the division. They also have the power to retain, terminate, or select a subdistrict superintendent. Each subdistrict council elects one representative to a system-wide Board Nominating Commission. The Commission is charged with providing the mayor with a slate of three persons for each vacancy on the City's Board of Education. The mayor must appoint from among the slate or reject the entire slate and ask for another.

The job description for the subdistrict superintendent (DS) was changed from that of a line officer with authority over principals and school employees into a staff officer who monitors and facilitates school improvement

(Hess, 1991). The DS is charged with providing training to the LSCs, mediating disputes at local schools, and monitoring the development and implementation of a School Improvement Plan at each school.

The City Board of Education consists of 15 members serving four-year staggered terms. The new board was given most of the powers of the previous board with the exception of powers granted to the LSCs. To recognize the existence of these new semiautonomous LSCs, the powers of the Board were redefined from *"management of"* to *"jurisdiction over"* the public education and the public school system of the city (Hess, 1991). Among other responsibilities, the Board is charged with establishing system-wide curriculum objectives and standards that reflect the multicultural diversity of the city.

A MULTIDISTRICT ANALYSIS OF SBM

Brown (1990) analyzed the implementation of SBM in five districts including Edmonton and Cleveland. The other districts were Langley (a suburb of Vancouver) and two rural districts in British Columbia. He identified two main processes as part of the structure of SBM: the mechanism by which resources are allocated to schools and the budgeting process within the school. Schools in his study received the bulk of their financial allocations by multiplying their enrollments by a district established amount such that "[t]he money follows the child." Adjustments were made for special programs and for school attributes. Districts in his study provided schools with system-wide goals and objectives, and schools responded with their own curricular plans and budgets for implementation that were mostly absorbed by personnel costs. Teachers were usually purchased from the district at a uniform rate, and those not located in a particular school were placed within the district pool for selection.

Brown's analysis found that the SBM school boards became more concerned with policy matters than with the administration of schools. Under SBM, the district hierarchy was sharpened whereby each person had only one supervisor; nonline central office staff assumed a strictly advisory, on-call relationship with school level personnel (as in Dade County and Chicago). "Most importantly, authority and responsibility are largely brought together, particularly for the school principal, but also for others in the administrative structure" (Brown, 1990, p. 2).

Still, many things remained the same in the districts studied. Brown detected little change in the accountability model employed under SBM; ultimate authority came from the electorate and was directed through school boards and administrators. Thus, the district school boards still retained responsibility for establishing general direction for the districts through the setting of goals and the reservoir of funds whether they come from local sources such as the property tax or from the state or federal governments. Collective bargaining continued to be a district prerogative and the districts continued to provide financial and other support services. The districts retained responsibility for monitoring and evaluating school performance.

Under SBM, Brown (1990) found that specific budgetary and personnel decisions are made at the school level, but the school district board sets the general parameters by which schools' lump-sum allocations are determined. District school boards must answer such questions as: What should the size of the pupil allocation be? Should it vary according to type of program, e.g., elementary, secondary, vocational? Should the allocation vary according to characteristics of children served, e.g., socio-economic status, learning disabled, gifted, handicapped? Should the allocation vary according to characteristics of the school, e.g., size and complexity of services offered? In many respects, Brown found that decisions made by school district boards under SBM are similar to those currently made by state governments.

By the same token, Brown found that many of the decisions made at the school level under SBM are similar to those made by most school boards today in non-SBM arrangements. School level authority under SBM approaches that of a single building rural district; the primary differences are that the school does not control the size of its budget (it has no authority to levy taxes or to charge tuition) and it cannot set wage scales. The role of principal takes on aspects of a superintendent of a small district (Jacobson, 1988; David, 1989). While SBM introduces substantial procedural changes at the district level, Brown found the changes at the school level to be revolutionary. Schools were freed to make "Production of Service" type decisions in the political-economic system of the educational policy development model shown in Figure 14.3. These decisions included the setting of goals and objectives and the allocation of resources when specifically related to the teaching/learning process.

As a result, Brown (1990, 1991) found that, under SBM, schools are considered to be much more able to adapt resources and procedures to student needs as perceived by school personnel. He reported that SBM may be a viable avenue for school improvement because of the flexibility it accords schools, but it does not appear to be a key stimulus for innovation. In the five districts studied, Brown observed tradeoffs between personnel and material. Examples of personnel-related decisions included more dollars for professional development, teacher choice of school, swaps of personnel, and increases in personnel allocations for specific learning tasks.

The experiences of SBM districts clearly show that SBM is no trivial change from traditional centralized decisionmaking. It involves new relationships between the district and the school and among people within the school itself. Principals strongly favored SBM in the five districts Brown (1990) studied;

they felt that it enhanced their ability to be educational leaders. Teachers were less positive in their endorsement. Teachers and principals agreed that the primary strength of SBM is greater flexibility at the school level, and that the greatest weakness is the additional time required in implementing it.

In placing greater policy-making authority at the school level, decisionmaking at that level becomes more political, but not necessarily in a partisan sense. Some school personnel, especially the principal, must be comfortable functioning in a parliamentary mode (Beare, Caldwell, & Millikan, 1989). This mode requires the principal to serve as the school's executive officer and as chief advisor to policy boards and committees attached to the school. The principal, and perhaps others, will find it necessary to work with power coalitions and lobby groups, dealing with the reality of group theory and elite theory described in a previous section. One of the primary purposes of moving to an SBM mode is to reduce the necessity for an incremental approach to policy formulation created by the diverse forces impacting on policy at national, state, and sometimes local, levels (incrementalism). At the school level, the number of interest groups having an impact on educational policy is greatly reduced, enabling a more rational approach to organizing and operating schools (rationalism). SBM is an attempt to affect policy outcomes through restructuring the policymaking framework (institutionalism).

Judicial Influence on Educational Policy Formulation

Federal and state courts are having an increasing influence on the formulation of school policy. This section examines that influence and how judicial procedures and influence differ from those of the legislative branch of government.

Judicial and legislative branches of government perform different functions in the formation of policy. State and federal education programs can only be enacted through the legislative process, but the judiciary may be asked to test whether or not these policies satisfy societal expectations as expressed in federal and state constitutions. This external review provides a check on legislative actions, and judicial reviews often stimulate (even force) legislatures to alter legislated policies. The courts do not, however, initiate the subjects of judicial review; they react to conflicts and problems posed to them by members of society, i.e., plaintiffs.

In our discussion of metavalues in Chapter 4, the ideological conflict between equality and liberty or freedom was described. The value of equality was identified as one that could only be championed effectively at the societal level (by state or federal governments). The value of liberty, on the other hand, is best realized through an unregulated market that is anathema to equality. Adherents of each value battle incessantly in both courts and legislatures. Federal courts made equality a national concern through numerous decisions affecting education starting with the Supreme Court's decision in *Brown v. Board of Education* (1954). Congress responded in the mid-1960s with such legislation as Title VI of the Civil Rights Act to ease inequities in children's educational opportunities.

Despite strong national pressures from a variety of sources to improve educational opportunities for poor and minority students, state legislatures were slow to respond. The nature of the state legislative process, characterized by "give-and-take, negotiation, and compromise" (Fuhrman, 1978, p. 160), inhibited reform by the states. Even when states responded to pressure brought by impending

and actual court reviews, the equality thrust raised at the national level and by both state and federal courts deferred to consensus-building processes that shape the actual content of reforms adopted through state legislatures.

Unlike judicial decisionmaking, which is narrowly focused on constitutional principles, policy development in legislatures is broadly influenced by their representative nature, the distributive nature of education policy, and the ongoing nature of the decisionmaking process (Brown & Elmore, 1982). First, legislators, as representatives of school districts to be affected by proposed reforms, are frequently more concerned with protecting their school districts' interests (subdivisions of state government) than with equalizing opportunities for poor children. Second, the distributive nature of educational policy requires at least a majority of the population to perceive that the reforms benefit them. In the process of finding solutions, equity goals are frequently bargained away. Major consideration in the bargaining and compromise process is given to which districts gain and which lose. Finally, the resolution of issues is not isolated from other concerns placed before legislators. Rather than concentrating solely upon the specific merits of the proposal at hand, lining up votes on an education issue may depend upon positions taken by legislators on prior and subsequent policy issues that are likely to have no relation to education whatsoever.

Unlike the legislative process that gives attention to school districts' interests and to consensus building, challenges to states' educational policies heard in the courts are more likely to consider inequities in the treatment of pupils. The plan that results from negotiations through the legislative process may or may not reflect the equity concerns of the courts or the original proponents of reform. "The closer one gets to the process of reform in specific states, the more elusive equity seems and the more complex are the values and objectives operating on reform proposals" (Brown & Elmore, 1982, p. 113).

On the whole, the evidence leaves little room for optimism about substantial and long-term improvements in educational equity through either the legislative or judicial process (Swanson & King, 1991). The conflict among the values of equality, efficiency, and liberty is ongoing.

Activities for Discussion

1. How will leadership styles need to change in order to accommodate school systems and other educational institutions as they shift from a hierarchical structure to a decentralized one? Select a position (principal, superintendent, school board member, curriculum supervisor, school business manager, teacher union president, university president, dean) and describe how the characteristics of the new situation will differ from traditional, more bureaucratic systems and how follower needs and the resultant leadership styles will differ.

2. Political decisionmaking:

    a. Interview your superintendent of schools or college president and/or members of your board of trustees about how educational policy is developed in your school district.
    b. On the basis of the information gathered from these interviews, describe situations that illustrate each policymaking model listed on page 454.

3. Restructuring education: Numerous proposals have been put forth for reforming education. Discuss each proposal listed below in reference to Figure 14.3. For each, describe the change from the status quo in the allocation of decisionmaking authority and in the relative priorities given to the three values: equity, efficiency, and liberty.

    a. family choice of public schools
    b. unregulated educational vouchers
    c. tax credits for private school tuition
    d. professional control over admission to the teaching profession
    e. career ladders for teachers
    f. school-based decisionmaking
    g. full state financing of public schools
    h. state achievement testing to determine successful completion of high school.

4. School governing boards: Imagine a policy board for each public school made up of the principal, serving as the chief executive officer, and representatives of teachers, parents, and students.

    a. What are the advantages and disadvantages of such an arrangement?
    b. Would you add representation from any other group?
    c. Would you eliminate representation of any group?
    d. Assuming each representative has one vote, how many representatives should there be from each group?
    e. What constraints, if any, would you place on the decisionmaking powers of the board?
    f. Provide the rationale for each of your answers.

5. Allocation of decisionmaking authority: Within the context of the decisionmaking matrix presented in Figure 14.1, what educational decisions are best placed at the school level? What safeguards need to be implemented to protect family and societal interests? Give the rationales for your responses.

Annotated Bibliography

Boyd, W. L., & Kerchner, C. T. (Eds.). (1988). *The politics of excellence and choice in education*. New York: Falmer.

This edited volume is presented in two parts: understanding the politics of choice and implementation of excellence and choice. Its contents range broadly from discussions of civic virtue and a national curriculum to the shift from equity to excellence concerns. Together these essays illuminate facets of the complex developments characteristic of today's excellence movement in the United States. The book emphasizes the problems and inconsistencies of the excellence movement rather than its accomplishments. Part I is concerned with the philosophical and policy issues and the political and economic dynamics associated with the current reform movement. Topics addressed include: an analysis of market and bureaucratic failure in schooling; economic choice and the dissolution of community; conflict between the values of equity and excellence; exploring the political economy of educational reform; and the connection between the excellence movement, academic standards, a core curriculum and choice. Part II of the book focuses on the problems encountered in implementing plans designed to foster excellence and choice in education. Topics addressed include: politics, markets, and education; political and organizational perspectives on why reform doesn't change schools; and the future of national education policy. Case studies of school districts in Tennessee, Texas, and Minnesota illustrate the applied politics of reform.

Brown, D. J. (1991). *Decentralization: The administrator's guidebook to school district change*. Newbury Park, CA: Corwin.

The purpose of this book is to help readers decide whether decentralization (or its closely related term, school-based management) is a logical choice for their districts. The author presents the pros and cons of school-based management in a nontechnical way and shows that it is no longer an ivory tower theory, but a reality taking place—or under serious consideration—in many school districts. The book provides a reliable explanation of the entire process of decentralization. It is organized around three phases that a district will follow in implementing decentralized decisionmaking and management: exploration, trial, and commitment. Each phase is examined in terms of the real-life experiences of administrators and others who have participated in the process. The author explains what happens when authority shifts to the local school, and shows how to avoid the pitfalls awaiting the unprepared.

Brown, D. J. (1990). *Decentralization and school-based management*. London: Falmer Press.

The general aim of this book is to provide a focused and scholarly discussion on decentralization and school-based management (SBM). It presents the background ideas to decentralization and the theoretical principles on which they can be based. The perspective taken is one largely of organizational theory. It is grounded in research undertaken by the author in leading school districts in North America that have adopted SBM. The author does not take a position on SBM, but instead shows how it works and what its effects are. The book presents both theoretically interpreted and research-based views of decentralization and SBM, exploring their implications for theory and policy. Simply, the book discusses decentralization, how it is conceived, how it works, what its outcomes are, and how it is attained.

Cibulka, J. G., Reed, R. J., & Wong, K. K. (1992). *The politics of urban education in the United States*. Washington, DC: Falmer.

This edited volume affords scholars and policymakers an opportunity to examine trends and developments affecting urban school systems in the United States and to consider how their problems might be addressed effectively. It is divided into three parts: the study of the politics of education, the political condition of urban schools, and the political implications of urban school renewal. Part I addresses the issues of urban education as a field of study and public choice perspectives on urban schools. In Part II, political perspectives on urban schools are considered with respect to finance, leadership turnover, business mobilization, and urban schools as organizations. The focus of Part III is on implementation strategies leading to school renewal. Specific issues addressed include desegregation, decentralization, empowerment, federal aid, and judicial intervention. The epilogue brings together the various emphases and themes of the book.

Danzberger, J. P., Kirst, M. W., & Usdan, M. D. (1992). *Governing public schools: New times, new requirements*. Washington, DC: The Institute for Educational Leadership.

This book reports on a reanalysis of a study of 400 school board chairs in nine major metropolitan areas in 1986 by The Institute for Educational Leadership. Noting the shift in educational reform strategies toward systemic and structural change, the authors seek to provide a set of expectations and principles for drastic change in the role and operations of school boards. Initially the book analyzes external changes affecting the functioning of school boards including the striking increase in children living in poverty, family disorganization, and youth violence. New demands placed on schools and school boards by business and other leadership sectors are identified. The book explores the interrelationships between education and other children's services that are essential if children are to succeed in school. Finally, the authors present their views about some appropriate expectations and principles for improving school board performance.

Dye, T. R. (1987). *Understanding public policy* (6th ed.). Englewood Cliffs, NJ: Prentice-Hall.

This volume is an introduction to the study of public policy and to the models political scientists use to describe and explain political life. The book begins with a brief description of eight analytical models in political science and the potential contribution of each to the study of public policy. They are: institutionalism, a process model, group theory, elite theory, rationalism, incrementalism, game theory, and systems theory. The author then uses each model singly and in combination to describe and explain a public policy issue and its development. The policy areas studied are: civil rights, criminal justice, poverty and welfare, health, education, budgeting and spending, taxation, national defense, and state and local spending and services.

Fuhrman, S. H., & Malen, B. (Eds.). (1991). *The politics of curriculum and testing*. London: Falmer.

During the past two decades, nearly all states have enacted policies to inspire or require more rigor in the academic component of school programs and nearly all states adopted policies to generate more detailed assessments of student performance. This book is an anthology of papers that address aspects of a broad, complex, and evolving field of study that seeks to understand such core concerns as: the development, implementation, and assessment of policies that affect what should be taught in schools and to whom, how instruction should be carried out, and who should decide these matters; the forms and effects of governmental action, i.e., the nature of instruments and symbols government selects or combines to influence individuals and institutions, the manner in which various governmental interventions penetrate practice and operate to promote (or impede) particular policy objectives; the ways in which policy processes, designs, and effects interact; and the impact of these interactions on broad dimensions of interest such as the content of schooling, the quality and equity of educational opportunities, and the distribution of power and authority in social systems. The book serves as a catalyst for identifying prominent patterns that both policy researchers and policymakers may wish to consider.

Hannaway, J., & Crowson, R. (Eds.). (1989). *The politics of reforming school administration*. New York: Falmer.

The chapters of this edited volume were selected to examine the politics of reforming school administration from both top-down and bottom-up perspectives. The book is divided into three parts. In Part I, state-level reform initiatives are examined, with legislation-into-practice questions about the impact of reform on local schools and local administrators. Part II explores the micro-politics of reform within schools, for it is the editors' view that it is ultimately within the context of the school that basic changes in educational administration will have to occur. Finally, as a central issue, Part III addresses the politics of reforming the profession itself. This section explores the actors, the interests, and the incentives involved in a heated debate regarding the training of the nation's cadre of school adminis-trators.

Hess, G. A., Jr. (1991). *School restructuring, Chicago style*. Newbury Park, CA: Corwin Press.

This book is a case study of the third largest urban school system in the United States and the reform movement that was mobilized to address its problems. The book grew out of the author's experiences as one of the participants of that reform movement. The book is intended for students of the management of public schools, and policymakers who are contemplating ways to improve their own public schools. After a brief introduction that focuses on the policy problem of improving urban schools, the necessity for school reform in Chicago is documented. The second part of the book describes what is involved in restructuring a major urban school district. The final two chapters address the significance of the restructuring experiment in Chicago and placing it within a national context.

Marshall, C. (1993). *The new politics of race and gender*. Washington, DC: Falmer.

The purpose of this edited volume is to demonstrate that liberal policy, alone, cannot adequately address deep-seated assumptions and traditional practices that undermine minorities and women in schools. It is the editor's contention that, with today's shifting demographics, disillusionment with conventional liberal policies, and new political conditions, the politics of race and gender require new analyses. The chapters in this book demonstrate how the politics of race and gender enter into proposals for parental choice, business involvement in schools, definitions of good leadership, special schools for young African-American boys, curriculum debates, and debates about testing and accountability. The chapters are written by scholars and policy analysts focusing on policy and its implementation at all levels of school politics in the United States, Australia, and Israel. The book ends with a critical policy analysis that raises deep theoretical questions and pulls out the chronic race and gender issues in educational politics.

Mitchell, D. E., & Goertz, M. E. (1990). *Education politics for the new century*. London: Falmer.

This edited volume concentrates on the changing social, economic, technological, and political forces that will shape educational politics and policy in the twenty-first century. It focuses on the roles to be played by education professionals, local citizen groups, government agencies, and business leaders in formulating education policy, responses to racial and ethnic segregation, school restructuring, technology utilization, and the development of education policy and politics. The book ends with a historical review of the foundations of the politics of education and seven critical issues are identified that are likely to shape school politics and policymaking in the years ahead.

Wise, A. E. (1979). *Legislated learning: The bureaucratization of the American classroom*. Berkeley, CA: University of California Press.

The author challenges the widely held belief that the community determines what and how children should be taught in public schools through local school boards, administrators, and teachers. He contends that the legislative, judicial, and executive branches of federal and state governments have intruded into the management and control of public education to the point where nothing less is at stake than individual freedom in a democratic society. In addition, the author charges that the cumulative impact of these and other forms of well-intentioned state and federal interventions is causing unforeseen and momentous changes in schools and colleges in the form of centralization of educational decisions that were formerly made locally, excessive rationalization of educational policy (i.e., rules, regulations, and red tape), and narrowing of the goals of education to those that can be measured and counted. He concludes that legislative learning and bureaucratization of the classroom will lead to a decline in the quality of education for all children as well as a general loss of freedom.

References

Agarawala, R. (1984). *Planning in developing countries: Lessons of experience*, World Bank staff working papers, No. 576. Washington, DC: The World Bank.

Bacharach, S. B., & Shedd, J. B. (1989). Power and empowerment: The constraining myths and emerging structures of teacher unionism. In J. Hannaway & R. Crowson (Eds.), *The politics of reforming school administration* (pp. 139–160). New York: Falmer.

Beare, H., Caldwell, B. J., & Millikan, R. H. (1989). *Creating an excellent school: Some new management techniques*. London: Routledge.

Benson, C. S. (1978). *The economics of public education* (3rd ed.). Boston: Houghton Mifflin.

Bridge, R. G. (1976). Parent participation in school innovations. *Teachers College Record, 77,* 366–384.

Brown, D. J. (1991). *Decentralization: The administrator's guidebook to school district change*. Newbury Park, CA: Corwin.

Brown, D. J. (1990). *Decentralization and school-based management*. London: Falmer Press.

Brown, P. R., & Elmore, R. F. (1982). Analyzing the impact of school finance reform. In N. H. Cambron-McCabe & A. Odden (Eds.), *The changing politics of school finance* (pp. 107–138). Cambridge, MA: Ballinger.

Brown v. Board of Education, 347 U.S. 483 (1954).

Cawelti, G. (1989). Key elements of site-based management. *Educational Leadership, 46,* 46.

Cibulka, J. G. (1987). Theories of education budgeting: Lessons from the management of decline. *Educational Administration Quarterly, 23,* 7–40.

Coleman, J. S., & Hoffer, T. (1987). *Public and private high schools: The impact of communities*. New York: Basic Books.

Collins, R. A. (1988). *Interim evaluation report, school-based management/shared decision making project, 1987-88, project-wide findings*. Miami, FL: Dade County Public Schools, Office of Educational Accountability.

Coons, J. E., & Sugarman, S. D. (1978). *Education by choice: The case for family control*. Berkeley, CA: University of California Press.

Cremin, L. A. (1976). *Public education*. New York: Basic Books.

Danzberger, J. P., Kirst, M. W., & Usdan, M. D. (1992). *Governing public schools: New times,*

new requirements. Washington, DC: The Institute for Educational Leadership.

Darling-Hammond, L., & Barry, B. (1988). *The evolution of teacher policy* (Report No. JRE-01). Santa Monica, CA: The RAND Corporation.

David, J. L. (1989). Synthesis of research on school-based management. *Educational Leadership, 46,* 45–53.

Dror, Y. (1964). Muddling through—"science" or inertia? *Public Administration Review, 24,* 153–157.

Dye, T. R. (1987). *Understanding public policy* (6th ed.). Englewood Cliffs, NJ: Prentice-Hall.

Dye, T. R., & Zeigler, H. (1981). *The irony of democracy*. Monterey, CA: Brooks Cole.

Easton, D. A. (1965). *A systems analysis of political life*. New York: John Wiley & Sons.

Elazar, D. J. (1972). *American federalism*. New York: Harper and Row.

Elmore, R. F., & McLaughlin, M. W. (1988). *Steady work: Policy, practice, and the reform of American education* (Report No. R-3574-NIE/RC). Santa Monica, CA: The RAND Corporation.

Friedman, M. (1962). *Capitalism and freedom*. Chicago: University of Chicago Press.

Fuhrman, S. (1978). The politics and process of school finance reform. *Journal of Education Finance, 4,* 158–178.

Grodzins, M. (1966). *The American system*. Chicago: Rand McNally.

Hanson, E. M. (1986). *Educational reform and administrative development: The cases of Colombia and Venezuela*. Stanford, CA: Hoover Institution Press.

Hess, G. A., Jr. (1991). *School restructuring, Chicago style*. Newbury Park, CA: Corwin Press.

Hodgkinson, C. (1983). *The philosophy of leadership*. Oxford, England: Basil Blackwell.

Iannaccone, L. (1988). From equity to excellence: Political context and dynamics. In W. L. Boyd & C. T. Kerchner (Eds.), *The politics of excellence and choice in education* (pp. 49–65). New York: Falmer.

Jacobson, S. L. (1988). The rural superintendency: Reconsidering the administrative farm system. *Research in Rural Education, 5*(2), 37–42.

Kaufman, R., & Herman, J. (1991). *Strategic planning in education: Rethinking, restructuring, revitalizing*. Lancaster, PA: Technomic.

Kirst, M. W. (1988). Recent educational reform in the United States: Looking backward and forward. *Educational Administration Quarterly, 24.* 319–328.

Lavoie, D. (1985). *National economic planning: What is left?* Cambridge, MA: Ballinger.

Lawton, D. (1992). *Education and politics in the 1990s: Conflict or consensus?* London: Falmer.

Lindblom, C. E. (1959). The science of muddling through. *Public Administration Review, 19,* 79–88.

Lindblom, C. E. (1968). *The policy-making process.* Englewood Cliffs, NJ: Prentice-Hall.

Lindelow, J. (1981). School-based management. In S. C. Smith, J. A. Mazzarella, & P. K. Piele (Eds.), *School leadership: Handbook for survival* (pp. 94–129). Eugene OR: Clearinghouse on Educational Management, University of Oregon.

McGinn, N., & Street, S. (1986). Educational decentralization: Weak state or strong state? *Comparative Education Review, 30,* 471–490.

McNeil, L. M. (1986). *Contradictions of control: School structure and school knowledge.* New York: Routledge, Chapman and Hall.

Mitchell, D. E. (1989). Alternative approaches to labor-management relations for public school teachers and administrators. In J. Hannaway & R. Crowson (Eds.), *The politics of reforming school administration* (pp. 161–181). New York: Falmer.

Mojkowski, C., & Fleming, D. (1988). *School-site management: Concepts and approaches.* Andover, MA: The Regional Laboratory for Educational Improvement of the Northeast and Islands.

Moore, M. K., Goertz, M., & Hartle, T. (1983). Interaction of federal and state programs. *Education and Urban Society, 4,* 452–478.

Murphy, J. (1982). The paradox of state government reform. In A. Lieberman & M. McLaughlin (Eds.), *Educational policy-making.* The 81st Yearbook of the National Society for the Study of Education. Chicago: University of Chicago Press.

Odden, A., & Marsh, D. (1989). State education reform implementation: A framework for analysis. In J. Hannaway & R. Crowson (Eds.), *The politics of reforming school administration* (pp. 41–59). New York: Falmer.

Peters, T. J., & Waterman, R. H. (1982). *In search of excellence: Lessons from America's best-run companies.* New York: Warner Books.

Ravitch, D. (1985). *The schools we deserve: Reflections on the educational crises of our times.* New York: Basic Books.

Raywid, M. A. (1985). Family choice arrangements in public schools: A review of the literature. *Review of Educational Research, 55,* 435–467.

Schultz, C. L. (1968). *The politics and economics of public spending.* Washington, DC: The Brookings Institute.

Swanson, A. D., & King, R. A. (1991). *School finance: Its economics and politics.* New York: Longman.

Timar, T. (1989). The politics of school restructuring. *Phi Delta Kappan, 71*(4), 265–275.

Truman, D. B. (1951). *The governmental process.* New York: Knopf.

Walker, D. B. (1981). *Toward a functioning federalism.* Cambridge, MA: Winthrop Press.

Whitty, G. (1992). Urban education in England and Wales. In D. Cowlby, C. Jones, & D. Harris (Eds.), *World yearbook of education: Urban education* (pp. 39–53). London: Kogan Page.

Weiler, H. N. (1980). *Educational planning and social change.* Paris: UNESCO.

Wildavsky, A. (1964). *The politics of the budgetary process.* Boston: Little, Brown and Company.

Wirt, F. M. (1986). *Multiple paths for understanding the role of values in state policy.* Paper presented at the Annual Meeting of the American Education Research Association, San Francisco, CA. (ERIC Document Reproduction Service No. ED-278086)

Wirt, F. M., & Kirst, M. W. (1982). *School in conflict: The politics of education.* Berkeley, CA: McCutchan.

Wise, A. E. (1979). *Legislated learning: The bureaucratization of the American classroom.* Berkeley, CA: University of California Press.

Wise, A. E. (1988). Two conflicting trends in school reform: Legislated learning revisited. *Phi Delta Kappan, 69,* 328–332.

Chapter 15
Decisionmaking

In the traditional view of educational organizations, power was thought to reside solely in a top-to-bottom structure. As a consequence, principals, deans, and directors possessed wide latitudes, while those lower in the hierarchy shared limited power. Decisionmaking in this tradition was thought to be the domain of those in charge. Today, these traditional views of educational organization are changing. Power, decisionmaking, and other organizational elements and responsibilities are shared among principals, teachers, students, and parents alike. While we can all relate instances of highly productive teachers who have always shared their decisionmaking in the classroom with students or even parents, and of principals who also share substantial responsibility, these instances are not the norm.

Weick (1976) was undoubtedly correct in stating that our theories of how organizations function are rarely generalizable and that we would be hard pressed to find instances of rational practice or outcome realization existing in reality. Textbook decisionmaking would be hard to find. "No example of a general the-

ory of decision proper exists that is even modestly developed, although dimensions have been developed quite far" (Hooker, Leach, & McClennen, 1978, p. viii). In truth, practitioners may construct for us a fully different view of organizational decisionmaking. It is the purpose of this chapter to explore the realm of organizational decisionmaking from theory to practice and beyond.

Decisionmaking is the process of choosing among alternatives (Baron, 1985; Conway, 1984; White, 1969). Numerous authors (Cornell, 1980; Hoy & Miskel, 1978; Krepel, 1987; Steers, 1977) concur that decisionmaking is among the most crucial skills for an effective educational administrator. Furthermore, Baird (1989) contends that the "primary output of all administration is decisions" (p. 4) and that "most executives are evaluated by superiors, peers, and subordinates in terms of their last few decisions" (p. 5), regardless of their prior decisionmaking performance. This is a general perception of those studying the field. The decision process is at the core of administration and all administrative action is dependent on making a decision. Decisionmaking may be seen as the process whereby organizations adapt. Despite the importance of skills in this area, research suggests, however, that individuals tends to make decisions that do not reflect optimal or "rational" choices (Bazerman, 1991; McNeil, Pauker, & Tversky, 1988; Tversky & Kahneman, 1988).

Approaches to Decisionmaking

There are two basic approaches to decisionmaking: the normative approach and the descriptive approach. The rational/idealized normative approach explores how the process should occur, while the descriptive approach considers how the process actually occurs, accommodating cognitive constraints, idiographic traits and other factors that impose limitations on idealized, rational decisionmaking (Baird, 1989; MacPhail-Wilcox & Bryant, 1988; Reitz, 1987). Normative literature explores how decisions should be made to achieve a particular standard or outcome. These standards or outcomes are typically explicit or objective. Descriptive literature relates how decisionmaking occurs in empirical terms. Decision styles, decision process maps, and devising mathematical models are often used in descriptive typologies. Some authors (Baron, 1985; Keeny & Raiffa, 1976) use a trichotomy that includes a "prescriptive" category. This prescriptive approach essentially extends the normative approach to describe how individuals' decisionmaking skills can be improved. Authors who use the "prescriptive" classification as an extension of the normative approach concede that it "may not be necessary . . . if we were to clarify further the normative category" (Bell, Raiffa, & Tversky, 1988, p. 2).

The literature on decisionmaking ranges from these highly quantitative descriptions of

how decisions should be made and can be analyzed, to elaborate discussions of the cognitive implications of information processing relative to choice strategies, all encompassing models of the process that defy empirical testing.

Historically, normative decisionmaking has been associated with decision theory and quantitative methods such as Bayesian statistics, probability, and inference. Normative decisionmaking was first expressed formally in the theoretical works of social economists of the Industrial Revolution. These economists, most notably John Stuart Mill and Jeremy Bentham, explained that choices are made on the basis of utility. Mill claimed that individuals choose alternatives according to the maximum return that the alternative will produce. This is the original economic theory used by entrepreneurs and industrial planners who were fascinated with the possibility of creating a great deal of capital through mechanized labor in the nineteenth century. As the division of labor in organizations became more complex in the twentieth century, theorists in economics and behavioral science attempted to construct models of decisionmaking. These early theorists were, by and large, dealing with rational decisionmaking and conditions of certainty.

Decisionmaking involving risk and uncertainty were still considered problematic. Descriptive decisionmaking theorists investigated this arena. One of the seminal contributions to descriptive decisionmaking was provided by Simon (1955, 1956), who proposed a behavioral model of rational choice. This model is founded on the premise that because of psychological constraints and other limiting factors, such as time, a decisionmaker's behavior could be described in terms of "bounded rationality." Individuals tend to operate from a simplified or approximate model of an actual decision situation and "satisfice," or make decisions that are satisfactory rather than optimal. Simon's work is credited with directing researchers to "examine the psychological processes by which decision problems are represented and information is used in action selection" (Slovic et al., 1988, p. 674). These areas have remained the dominant focus of empirical work on decisionmaking since the mid-1950s. As a result of this focus, empirical evidence on the psychological factors that influence decisionmaking has raised serious issues regarding the feasibility of existing theories and "poses a challenge to the decision-aiding technologies that have been derived from these theories" (Slovic et al., 1988, p. 674).

The administrative or management training components of some professions have traditionally addressed decisionmaking skills as a distinct component of their training programs. Some research suggests that certain types of training, such as formal statistical training, can facilitate the avoidance of common reasoning errors (Fong, Krantz, & Nisbett, 1989). Other studies suggest that training in statistics and decisionmaking does not necessarily reduce the incidence of basic decisionmaking errors (Eddy, 1982; Elstein & Bordage, 1979; McNeil et al., 1988) and may be domain specific (McGuire, 1985). Carroll and Johnson (1990) noted that "studies of expert decision makers suggest that they sometimes do little (if any) better than novices, and that people sometimes learn the wrong things from expertise" (pp. 27–28).

Decisionmaking and Problem Solving

Decisionmaking, which includes the "mental activities that recognize and structure decision situations and then evaluate preferences to produce judgments and choices" (Carroll & Johnson, 1990, p. 21), must also be distinguished from the broader process of problem solving. Problem solving is considered a series of related decisions (Tallman & Gray, 1990). Huber (1980) noted the importance of making this distinction because the terms, along with associated theories and research and their respective applications, are differentiated in the literature of various fields, including education, management, and psychology (Atkinson, Herrnstein, Lindzey, & Luce, 1988; Dejnozka & Kapel, 1991; Bittel & Bittel, 1978). However, Alkin (1991) does not specifically attend to the distinctions between these two processes and uses problem-solving terminology (ill-structured and well-structured problems) in discussions of decisionmaking. Others include theories under decisionmaking when another classification may be more appropriate. For example, Janis and Mann's Conflict Decision Theory "comes closer to approximating problem solving" (Tallman & Gray, 1990, p. 424).

Group Decisionmaking

Decisionmaking as discussed to this point has been confined to individual choice behavior. The decisionmaking stages employed by individuals and groups may essentially be the same. However, in decisionmaking tasks involving several people, the process used to reach consensus is influenced by other factors such as leadership, group pressures, status differentials, intergroup competition, and group size (Reitz, 1987). Some authors (MacPhail-Wilcox & Bryant, 1988) suggest that participative decisionmaking may balance out the idiographic traits inherent in an individual, and, in this respect, yield better decisions.

Reitz (1987) claimed that group decisionmaking may not be more effective than individual choice when the "situation requires a sequence of multiple stages, when the problem is not easily divisible into separate parts, and when the correctness of the solution is not easily demonstrated" (p. 346). Group decisions (a) can be more accurate, particularly when a member or members of a group have experience with the problem being addressed, (b) tend to be compatible with widely held beliefs, and (c) can result in greater member understanding and commitment. However, Conway (1984) suggested that participative decisionmaking does not necessarily yield heightened support or other benefits commonly associated with the process, and labels several of these claims "myths."

Although group judgment and problem-solving skills tend to exceed those of the average group member, they are frequently inferior to those of the best group member who is influenced toward mediocrity in a group forum (Reitz, 1987). There is no group technique capable of enabling groups to yield more numerous or creative ideas than the same numbers of individuals working alone (Hill, 1982). Furthermore, group decisionmaking promotes the likelihood of problems specific to a collective process, such as "groupthink," which results in premature consensus and failure to examine realistic decision options (Janis, 1989). Decisions involving risk and uncertainty can polarize a group toward prevailing cautions or a risk-taking stance. Group polarization hampers examination of decision options (Myers & Lamm, 1976).

In reviewing the literature on decisionmaking, Carroll and Johnson (1990) found that many authors failed to extend the elements of individual decision concepts to groups by noting a lack of ease in applying the same concepts to inherently more complex groups. However, "studies that have directly compared groups and individuals on the same problems find that groups fall prey to the same errors and biases as do individuals" (Carroll & Johnson, 1990, p. 28). Further-

more, individual decisionmaking reflects the choice processes at an elemental level.

Types of Decisions

Decision situations are commonly classified by the amount of prior information known about the consequence of the choices; specifically, whether outcomes associated with the decision options involve certainty, risk, or uncertainty (Baird, 1989; Roberts, 1979). Krepel (1987) and Reitz (1987) add other decision situations such as those involving competition or novelty. However, these classifications meet the criteria of, and can be subsumed under, the standard classifications of decision problems (i.e., certainty, uncertainty, and risk).

Certainty is used to describe a situation in which the outcome is known if a particular decision option is selected (Baird, 1989; Roberts, 1979). Although this decisionmaking situation appears straightforward, as the number of options increases so does the complexity of the decision. The optimal choice among options involving certainty can be determined quickly by computers, which can compensate for human cognitive limitations. The ability to easily employ a computer to determine the "optimal" choice under the condition of certainty may account for the focus on decisionmaking under conditions of risk or uncertainty. Decisions under certainty do not warrant inclusion in discussions of the complexity of decisionmaking.

Risk is used to describe situations in which "for each act there is a set of possible consequences, none of which occurs with certainty, but each of which occurs with a known probability (Roberts, 1979, p. 6). Uncertainty applies to situations "if the probabilities that consequences will occur are unknown" (p. 6). While some accept risk and uncertainty as dimensions of the same continuum, others attempt to clarify the term *uncertainty,* which is imprecise. For example, Curley, Eraker, and Yates (1984) differentiate between the partial uncertainty associated with (a) risk, in which the outcomes are unknown but have known probabilities associated with their occurrence, and (b) ambiguity, in which there is uncertainty as to both the outcomes as well as their associated probabilities of occurrence.

In the educational environment, it is apparent that decision situations vary dramatically. While conditions involving certainty are identifiable, for example, budgeting and scheduling, it is also apparent that situations involving risk and uncertainty are much more prevalent. Today this realization has become more pronounced as the availability of information explodes. The simple availability of extensive information and new knowledge has compounded decisionmaking to the point that most models of decisionmaking must deal with complex situations involving risk and uncertainty. Simply understanding the apparent cause and effect of illiteracy or dropping out cannot and has not produced decisions which then solve the illiteracy or dropout problems. Equally evident, the typologies of certainty, risk, and uncertainty do not deal effectively with the interpretivistic or critical theorists' perspective. For example, if situations are indeed constructed and interpreted in real time, no amount of optimalizing, maximizing, or any other decision format can be devised that will accommodate these extremes of changeability. Decision theorists and practitioners will be naturally prone in this environment to explore heuristics and biases that explain the limitations of decisionmaking models and explicitly demonstrate relevance.

At best, decision situations under conditions of risk and uncertainty, particularly those with multiple attributes, can be facilitated by the aid of decisionmaking tools and techniques, even when they yield only probable optimal choices.

Decisionmaking Tools and Techniques

The tools and techniques that can facilitate decisionmaking are numerous, often quantitatively oriented, and require that the user can meet many associated assumptions such as the ability to quantify the usefulness or probability associated with a particular choice. Tools and techniques frequently preferred for use in normative decisionmaking include: evaluation methodologies, such as break-even or payback analysis; decision trees; the delphi technique; game theory; linear programming methods; marginal analyses models that include verbal, computer, mathematical, and conceptual topologies; networks, including Program Evaluation and Review Techniques (PERT) and Critical Path Method; probability techniques that include Bayesian decision theory and the Bernoulli process; sampling; simulation techniques; statistical forecasting methods such as linear regression and correlation analyses; time series analyses; and various other quantitative techniques, including a fortiori analysis, systems analysis, operations research, and utility theory (Baird, 1989; Cornell, 1980; Watson & Buede, 1987). Selection of a particular technique requires that the decisionmaker understand the characteristics of each tool or technique being considered.

The tools and techniques employed by a decisionmaker are often influenced by the number of attributes associated with a decision such as single- versus multiple-attribute decisions, as well as the corresponding level of risk or uncertainty. For example, Reitz (1987) claimed that individuals facing higher levels of risk tend to prefer tools and techniques that provide substantial quantitative data to indicate the optimal alternative, regardless of the fact that effective decisions are more than information quantity (Zeleny, 1981). Although many tools and techniques are routinely employed quite effectively, in practice those actually used by decisionmakers may not yield optimal choices, as evidenced by the polarization of decisionmaking models between the normative (ideally rational) models and those that describe actual choices.

Problem Areas

Bell, Raiffa, and Tversky (1988) contended that the lack of "cohesion" in the area of decisionmaking is partially attributable to the differing approaches to the process: normative, or quantitative and ideally rational, versus descriptive, or how the process actually occurs. Assumptions that an individual's decisionmaking can be idealized, rational, and maximized are strongly reflected in early normative approaches to the decisionmaking process. However, within the past several decades the feasibility of these assumptions has been questioned. Empirical evidence that decisionmakers do not necessarily make choices in an ideally rational or maximizing fashion (Einhorn & Hogarth, 1978; Fischhoff, 1982; Kahneman, Slovic, & Tversky, 1982; McNeil et al., 1988) has served as a catalyst for the development of descriptive decisionmaking with an emphasis in two areas: explaining behaviors that violate the tenets of rationality and determining ways to improve individuals' choice behavior.

A number of authors (Baron, 1985; Cornell, 1980) have suggested that decisions should be evaluated by the strategy used rather than the outcome because ideally rational decisionmaking occasionally yields unfavorable or undesirable outcomes. This contention suggests that the strategy employed should be consistent with the normative approach, although numerous researchers (Chapman & Chapman, 1967; Kahneman et al. 1982; Tversky & Kahneman, 1988) have identified several commonly used heuristics and biases that, although economical and often effective, also lead to serious decisionmaking errors in violation of normative principles. For example, a bias associated with the representativeness heuristic, the failure to recognize base-rates, may lead to serious outcome errors (Tversky & Kahneman, 1982a). In other instances, biases associated with decisionmaking heuristics may be compounded in that choice behavior can be externally influenced by the ways in which decision options are presented or framed (Bazerman, 1991; Tversky & Kahneman, 1974). The phenomenon has been observed in individuals with training in the domain in which the decision task is posed (McNeil et al., 1988).

Normative, descriptive, and prescriptive decisionmaking research has too often treated the elements of decisionmaking as discrete when, in fact, much evidence suggests that more complex and interactive models aid understanding and description of decision processes and outcomes. Differences of opinion are numerous about the exact stages or subroutines within stages. Even proper ordering of stages may not be clear (Hogarth, 1980; Mintzberg, 1979; Simon, 1957). MacPhail-Wilcox and Bryant (1988) suggested at least three stages that appear with frequency in the literature: perception and information gathering, information manipulation and processing, and choice strategies.

Fragmentation in the decisionmaking literature transpires frequently due to the evolution of the area. Decisionmaking had its roots in game theory, probability, and inference, and was developed under the premise that the process should be ideally rational. Decisionmaking in this context was amenable to quantification via axioms that could define the appropriate approach to choice behavior. However, within the past several decades, empirical research has demonstrated that people do not always make choices in a manner consistent with the traditional tenets of rationality. This has fostered a reexamination of existing theories and considerable development both normatively and descriptively (Slovic et al., 1988). Although this fragmentation has led to useful efforts to unify work from the various disciplines (Bell et al., 1988; Hooker et al., 1978), decisionmaking remains a fertile area for empirical work, particularly for those interested in advancing applied decisionmaking.

An understanding of the current fragmentation in the area of decisionmaking can be gained by examining several fundamental components of choice behaviors. The remainder of this chapter will explore decision theory, normative and descriptive processes, system theory applications, idiographic factors, and decisionmaking heuristics and biases. Lastly, the chapter will close with a look at implications for educational administration.

Historical Underpinnings of Decision Theory

Decision theory is a methodology for structuring and analyzing risky or uncertain situations. The origins of decision theory lie in both statistical decision theory and game theory. Game theory provided the basis for probability theory that was initially applied to games in the middle of the sixteenth century (Tallman & Gray, 1990). Probability theory provided the mathematical basis for classical statistical inference that was developed at the onset of the nineteenth century (Baird, 1989). In the mid-twentieth century, in deference to classical and Bayesian inference, radical new approaches to decision theory were devel-

oped as decisionmakers' judgements were allowed into analysis (Baird, 1989).

As currently practiced, decision theory is a discipline for dealing with alternative courses of action by a critical analysis of all possible alternative courses and their outcomes. Although there is some variation in the specific methodology, all decision-theoretic analyses share a common structure and the some basic elements (Holloway, 1979). The basic components of decision theory include: the "acts," or strategies, available as decision choices; the "states of the nature," or outcomes, to which probability of occurrence may be assigned; the payoff, or consequences, of a given decision; and the criteria for selecting the optimal alternative (Cornell, 1980). Some expand this framework, others reduce it.

Although the term *decision theory* is used to describe choices when probabilities are unknown and unpredictable, as currently used it assumes that the decisionmaker enters a situation with judgments about relative probabilities for uncertain events and with preferences for decision outcomes or consequences (Baird, 1989). Thus, theory combines these preferences and judgments along with objective data in a systematic, structured, and quantitative analysis of the problem that permits the decisionmaker to evaluate potential outcomes and, subsequently, identify the best decision (Baird, 1989). Traditional decision theory is primarily normative in that it is most useful in describing how decisions should be reached in a given situation rather than explaining how a decisionmaker actually behaves although it has been used for both purposes (Bell, et al., 1988).

Original economic theories tied to utilitarian ideals were not focused on explaining how decisions are made in conditions of uncertainty. According to Hicks (1939), these theories could not account for the predicted utility of decisions made in situations where risks could not be calculated. In economics this gap in theory was addressed in 1947 by von Neumann and Morgenstern in *The Theory of Games and Economic Behavior*. They asserted that all decisionmaking assumes that there are hidden costs in any choice and theorize that decisionmaking is not purely linear and a process-product event. As precursors of cost-accounting theorists, economic theorists suggest that the decisionmaking models must include scales for assessing the utility and the total costs of any decision. Von Neumann and Morgenstern (1947) proposed denser models for economic decisionmaking. They acknowledged the effects of uncertainty or rational, utilitarian decisionmaking processes, but explained that all risks and utility can be measured. Thus, their model, rooted in mathematical game theory, is normative. The fact that von Neumann and Morgenstern appealed for the application of less linear decision models in economics, however, later served to inform the construction of descriptive models for decisionmaking in the behavioral sciences.

Influenced by the work of von Neumann and Morgenstern, economists developed game theories as normative models for decisionmaking. While these theories may have limited application in the social sciences, they have been used as reservoirs from which single ideas have been extrapolated for the construction of descriptive theories. The use of the term *game* in no way connotes that these theories are constructed for recreation. Instead, they have been defined as theories that represent decisionmaking situations, wherein the decisionmaker has some type of opponent and a strategy must be employed to overcome that opponent (Taylor, 1965). Game theory deals with those situations where there is a definite risk factor since there is uncertainty. The uncertainty is generated when the decisionmaker is not able to estimate exactly the impact of his decision on other player(s) in the situation. The degree of uncertainty is limited in game theory because each player knows the objectives of the other.

Over time, game theorists expanded the work of von Neumann and Morgenstern in several ways. McKinsey (1952) commented that mathematicians might find the theory faulty when applied to situations with more than two players because coalition-building could result in greater, incalculable uncertainty. Coalition-building is called *regret payoffs* in game theory. In a field of several players with several decisions to be made, the decisionmaker may select from a range of choices that will maximize utility or minimize regret (loss/risk). In another theory, the concept of weighed choice was proposed. Using a mathematical matrix, this concept inferred that choices could be weighted, almost commonsensically, to offer some rendition of an equation.

Overall, others have concluded, as did von Neumann and Morgenstern (1947), that game theory can only be used for determining optimal strategies and decisions when there are two players in a given situation. Game theory may not be flexible enough to use as a predictor of behavior when a mixed strategy emerges as the result of the varied interests of several players. The development of coalitions confuses the clarity of game theory when more than two players confront the decisionmaking situation.

Luce and Raiffa (1967) explained that game theory might form the conceptual construction of decisionmaking theories in the social sciences. They advised caution, however, in using the theory and its five key assumptions/behaviors in the decisionmaking situation. The assumptions are: (1) all the possible outcomes of a specific decision must be clearly specified; (2) each player has a constant pattern of preferential behavior in reference to the outcomes; (3) each player will make his decisions in order to maximize the utility of the choice; (4) each player knows fully the utility that is preferred by the other players in the situation; and (5) all the variables in the situation that effect the outcomes are clearly specified in numerical or value statements. Clearly game theory and its rigid assumptions were becoming troublesome.

Shubick (1964) saw the criteria above as essential in the purely normative models of game theory. However, he warned that these key characteristics do not account for the wide range of conflict-of-interest situations that many decisionmakers in complex social organizations are forced to confront. Shubick suggested that decisionmakers usually have some control over the game. They may simply be able to see more alternatives. This may help the decisionmakers understand the influence of situational variables. Shubick modified game theory to include more flexible concepts reflecting what he considered to be the nature of human behavior in organizations. He addressed the issues of conflict and cooperation in his model and outlined four conditions that must be present in a decisionmaking setting if his model is to be used: (1) each decisionmaker must be autonomous and in control of resources, (2) the rules of game theory must specify how the resources will be utilized, (3) the outcomes will depend on the strategies selected by the players, and (4) for every outcome of the game each player will have an evaluation. In Shubick's model, the game theory is applied to situations with certainty. In other words, the model may be more aptly applied to situations that do not occur in dense social organizations.

Game theory can also be expanded to include the concept of bargaining as an essential component of the decisionmaking process. In social organizations, decisionmakers are part of an interactive process where: (1) there is no interpersonal comparison of utilities; (2) the solution condition requires that neither party will accept, as a resolution to their negotiations, any outcome for which

another alternative outcome is better for both; (3) the solution is independent of irrelevant alternatives; and (4) symmetric bargaining will give both players the same payoff. This view simultaneously acknowledges the interactive nature of the decisionmaking process and chooses to ignore the effects of the interdependence of decisionmakers within an organization.

Negotiation as a concept of game theory was introduced by Schelling in *The Strategy of Conflict* (1970). Schelling used the language of game theory to explain the variables of conflict and cooperation in the decisionmaking process. He saw conflict as a bargaining opportunity where one participant's ability to achieve a specific end is dependent on the decisions that another participant makes. Schelling recognized that this theory does not offer a decisionmaking model that may be applied to complex social organizations where there may be more than two decision centers. He acknowledged that normative models must provide some flexibility to include the factors of bargaining among players, coalitions, or constituencies.

Other theories featured negotiation and bargaining as key concepts. Game theory was viewed as too simple to explain human behavior. Layers of concepts needed to be added to the theory in order to explain the factors that stabilize conditions in a decisionmaking process. In these theories, continual oscillation in the bargaining process occurs as initial decisions and preferences are aligned and realigned by decisionmakers.

Bargaining is a prerequisite condition related to resource allocation in a given decisionmaking situation. Game theory could only inform normative models in the utility of decisions that could be articulated in definite negotiable utility.

Few of the economic-normative models, however, have been applied as normative models in the behavioral sciences. In economics and mathematics the models have been questioned because of the exhaustive number of conditions under which they would have to be tested for validity. As Taylor (1965) concluded, "no normative model for decision making under uncertainty has been found."

Decisionmaking Models

As described above, there are two major classifications of decisionmaking models within conventional dogma: normative and descriptive models (Grandori, 1984; Bell, Raiffa, & Tversky, 1988). Normative models are primarily quantitative and suggest how decisionmaking should be conducted to be consistent with rational behavior. While descriptive models address how the process actually occurs, accommodating cognitive limitations and idiographic influences inherent in the decisionmaker, normative models are based upon the assumption that the decisionmaker recognizes all possible alternatives and their corresponding congruences, can evaluate the consequences against some value system, and can rank and ultimately select the best alternative. In the normative realm, the economic model reflects the essence of this approach. The expected utility model is also fundamental to the traditional tenets of rational decisionmaking. Taylor (1965) reported that the use of highly complex social organizations as test examples has been difficult for researchers who hope to use the pure, normative models as a means of offering fruitful descriptions of how decisionmaking may occur. Nevertheless, these normative models have fueled the debate.

Conversely, descriptive models accommodate the psychological constraints that make the probability of an individual's operating in a consistent and highly rational manner unlikely (Reitz, 1987; Watson & Buede, 1987).

Although the distinction between the two classes of decisionmaking models appears unambiguous, debate over the differences between these two classifications and their appropriate definitions continues. Models that are constructed as descriptive by one group occasionally are perceived as normative by another (Baird, 1989; Grandori, 1984). The confusion is further compounded when a model, such as subjective expected utility, is treated descriptively but used to characterize normative applications (Bell et al., 1988).

Descriptive methods of the decisionmaking process continue to emerge as social scientists attempt to apply theoretical constructs as a lens to understand or predict individual human or organizational behavior. The models are built on the assumption that decisions in organizations are made via complex processes.

The most prominent developer of these theories was Herbert Simon, who in his work *Administrative Behavior* (1976) defined the decisionmaker in an organization as a "rational administrative man" (p. 9). Borrowing from the earlier work of C. I. Barnard (1938), Simon suggested that decisions are actually a composite of rational choices and refuted the theory of the purely economic man as a theory that can legitimately describe the behavior of decisionmakers in real-life organizations. He called for the construction of new models that attend to the rational processes involved in human choices. In contrast, he rejected the economic rational models that assume that a decisionmaker can be completely informed when making a decision and able to maximize something through a decision.

NORMATIVE MODELS

Elemental to normative decisionmaking models are the concepts of maximization and rationality (Einhorn & Hogarth, 1988). Traditionally, these models have reflected the assumptions that every possible outcome may be assigned a "utility" or subjective value as well as a subjective "probability" or expectation and that such a decision should reflect the outcome with the greatest utility and probability (Neel, 1977). According to Neel, five principles serve as the bases for rational, normative decisions: transitivity, comparability, dominance, irrelevance, and independence. Transitivity refers to a phenomenon in which an individual prefers A to B and B to C, when in reality he or she could also prefer A to C. Comparability implies a willingness to compare options and determine a preferred outcome or a lack of preference, such as indifference. Dominance, or the sure-thing principle, suggests that the alternative that is not worse than the others on any attribute and is better on at least one should always be selected (Montgomery, 1983). Irrelevance refers to a situation in which two choices may yield the same outcome. Under these circumstances the selection should not matter. Independence suggests that an individual's wishes for a particular outcome should not influence his or her "expectation about the outcome" (Neel, 1977, p. 547).

Although the essence of the normative principles of decisionmaking are reflected in the axioms of the benchmark expected utility model, various other models, particularly some of the newer ones, omit some of these axioms to accommodate empirical evidence demonstrating that individuals often violate them (e.g., people occasionally display intransitive preferences or violate stochastic dominance). The model that is often used to exemplify the normative approach to decisionmaking is the economic model.

ECONOMIC MODEL OF DECISIONMAKING

The economic person is assumed to be a maximizer, that is, he or she will make decisions that will provide the highest return. In keeping with this notion, the economic model assumes that the decisionmaker recognizes all possible decision alternatives, is aware of all consequences of each alternative, evaluates the consequences against some value system, ranks the alternatives by the order in which they are likely to meet the decision objective, and makes a choice that maximizes the objectives (Reitz, 1987; Watson & Buede, 1987).

Although this model represents idealized, rational decisionmaking, its application is questionable given its limited ability to indicate the best choice in some situations. Bell et al. (1988) provided the example of an individual in a gambling scenario who bluffs more than is profitable to maximize his or her personal monetary gain and suggests that psychological baggage may make the notion of maximization subject to loose interpretation. In applying the model to financial decisions Moore contended, "one could do as well and with less ambiguity by tossing a coin" (cited in Reitz, 1987, p. 133). As the economic model exhibits limitations in actual application due to its inability to accommodate violations because of psychological factors, so too does the fundamental normative model. The expected utility model, a normative model, is the "most extensively applied and most often maligned" (Bell et al., 1988, p. 20).

EXPECTED UTILITY MODEL

Bell et al. (1988) stated that, although expected utility has been used as a descriptive model of economic behavior, it serves primarily as one form of idealized rational behavior and addresses normative applications. With the evaluation of probability theory came the concept that the best choice was the one that maximizes the expected value of the decision, a major premise of this model. In 1738, Bernoulli (cited in Fishburn, 1988) proposed the concept of expected utility, rather than expected value, to explain the decisionmaker's violation of expected profit maximization (e.g., the more money an individual possesses the less he or she values additional increments of the same amount of money). This concept was discussed further in Atkinson, Herrnstein, Lindzey, and Luce (1988), who developed axioms to accommodate the "simultaneous measurement of utility and subjective probability" (p. 692).

The current assumptions underlying expected utility assume that a decisionmaker is capable of (a) assessing probability for the state of the world, (b) designating a utility value for each consequence, (c) determining the expected utility value associated with each "lottery" corresponding to each alternative, and (d) comparing the alternatives based upon their utilities (Bell et al., 1988, p. 21). Baron (1985) provided a useful explanation of the quantitative substance of expected utility stating: " . . . the relative attractiveness of behavioral choices should be determined by the expected utility of each of the (objective) probabilities of each outcome times its (subjective) utility, given the decision maker's goals" (p. 9).

Four axioms that serve as the foundation of expected utility include: (a) cancellation, or the elimination of any state of the world that regardless of choice yields the same outcome, a property encompassed in other formal properties such as von Neumann and Morgenstern's substitution; (b) transitivity, the assignment of an option value that does not depend upon the value assigned to other options; (c) dominance, which suggests that an option should be selected if it is better in one state of the world and at least as good in all other states; and (d) invariance, which suggests that differing representations of the same option should yield the same choice (Tversky & Kahneman, 1988). However, empirical studies (e.g., McNeil et al., 1988; Tversky & Kahneman, 1988) have demonstrated that many of the axioms of expected utility theory are "systematically and consciously violated" (Slovic et al., 1988, p. 697), leading to the development of models and

theories that weaken or eliminate axioms. For example, the cancellation axiom has been eliminated by many authors to address the violations noted in the Alias paradox (cited in Slovic & Lichtenstein, 1983). Others have maintained invariance and dominance but relinquished transitivity. Some have eliminated invariance and dominance (Tversky & Kahneman, 1988).

Violations of expected utility theory have led to modifications and new development in both normative and descriptive theories of decisionmaking (Fishburn, 1988). The limitations of utility theory do not suggest that the model is not valid in some situations, as it "still forms the basis for the analysis of many applied decision problems . . . and provides an excellent approximation to many judgments and decisions" (Slovic et al., 1988, p. 674). One reason for continuing to use this theory is that it provides good approximations, even though it may be wrong in principle, and so it is going to be used until a more useful theory comes along. (Slovic et al., 1988, p. 704). Although noted violations of expected utility theory have led to questions regarding previously held tenets of rationality, the controversy has facilitated useful developments in descriptive decisionmaking.

Descriptive Models

Unlike normative models, descriptive models recognize that individuals do not always make ideally rational decisions; their preferences for consequences "are often ill-formed, labile, shifting and endogenous to the problem" (Bell et al., 1988, p. 20). Like normative models, descriptive models also run the continuum as to the level of complexity of decisions they address from single attribute to multiattribute choice. "Even the most elaborate descriptive theories . . . are viewed by their creators as useful approximations, but incomplete and not fully adequate" (Slovic et al., 1988, p. 710). Furthermore, some descriptive models are modifications of the expected utility model although not all are necessarily intended as such (Neel, 1977). As the economic model is frequently used to embody the normative approach, the administrative model is frequently employed as the model that embodies the vistas of the descriptive approach.

Administrative Decisionmaking Model

The administrative model holds that the decisionmaking process is guided by the principle of "bounded rationality." Due to computational limitations, decisionmakers use simplified decision procedures or "satisfice," accepting the first simplified decision procedure rather than pursuing an optimal or perfectly rational solution (Bell et al., 1988; Simon, 1955, 1956; Watson & Buede, 1987). In developing the model, Simon (1955) conceded that although perfectly rational decisions are ideal, they are unlikely because of the time and cost involved in attempting to undertake the normative model. There are several subsets of the administrative model.

Affiliative Decision Rules.
Janis (1989) noted that, in a crisis, decisionmakers seek solutions that will not endanger their relationships with those to whom they are accountable and will not be opposed by subordinates expected to implement the decision. To cope with the demands of such affiliative constraints, decisionmakers use a corresponding set of rules. Tetlock (1985) referred to the "acceptability heuristic" whose central theme is to avoid blame. It is applied by finding out whether other powerful persons in the organization already favor a particular action, then supporting that action without consideration of alternative choices. Janis

called attention to the subtle effects of *groupthink*, an affiliative rule whose underlying motivation is the strong desire to avoid spoiling the harmonious atmosphere of a group from which members are dependent for maintaining self-esteem and for coping with the stress of decisionmaking. The rule calls for preserving group harmony by going along with whatever consensus seems to be emerging (Janis, 1989, p. 57).

Emotive Rules (Conflict Theory).
Simon (1976) noted that emotions interfere with cognitive processes in decisionmaking. He postulated that anxiety and stress are aroused when decisionmakers realize that whichever course of action they choose could turn out badly and that they will be held accountable. Mann and Janis (1977) specified conditions that determine whether the stress of decisional conflict facilitates or interferes with decisionmaking. According to their "conflict theory," extremely low and extremely intense stress produce defective coping patterns, whereas intermediate levels are associated with analytic decisionmaking. Whenever decisionmakers deal with unconflicted adherence or unconflicted change, they are so unaroused by the risks that they resort to "lazy" or routine ways of making judgments because of lack of motivation to engage in the analytic process.

The Vigilant or Reflective Approach.
When the stakes are high, Janis (1989) observed that many executives do not stick to the seat-of-the-pants approach they ordinarily use in daily decisionmaking. They adopt what he refers to as a *vigilant decision-making approach,* in which they do not ignore the various constraints but take full account of them and go out of their way to obtain more information about them. The state of vigilant, or reflective, problem solving requires the decisionmaker to ask and answer a variety of questions that can be conceptualized as a

complex set of decision rules that put heavy emphasis on eliciting and critically evaluating information feedback. In contrast to giving one of the constraints top priority and resorting to one or two simple decision rules to cope with it, decisionmakers treat the constraints they are aware of as requirements to be met in their search for a solution.

PROSPECT THEORY

In developing the administrative model, Simon (1955) conceded that although perfectly rational decisions are ideal, they are unlikely because of the psychological constraints of the decisionmaker as well as the time and cost involved in attempting to undertake the idealized version of the decisionmaking process. The premise forwarded by Simon has served as a catalyst for the development of other descriptive models that accommodate noted violations of normative theory. For example, regret theory holds that choices are influenced by the potential regret and/or rejoicing associated with option selection (Loomes & Sugden, 1982). Prospect theory (Kahneman & Tversky, 1979) holds that individuals are averse to risk in the positive or gains domain and risk-seeking in the area of losses. Staw and Ross (1991) contended that this phenomenon explains behavior in escalation situations where people appear to continue commitment to a losing course of action. Prospect theory has been used as the basis of numerous other efforts in the area (Fiegenbaum & Thomas, 1988; Fischhoff, 1983; Schurr, 1987) with many researchers attending to a particular aspect of this model. For example, framing refers to the way a decision option is presented or framed, such as a loss or a gain, and has been shown to influence choice selection (Kahneman & Tversky, 1979).

Kahneman and Tversky's (1979) prospect theory, an algebraic model, addressed the tendency of individuals to violate the implications of utility theory, specifically the axioms of dominance and invariance. The development of this theory demonstrated three pervasive phenomena: (a) the certainty effect, which is the tendency to overweigh outcomes considered certain and conversely underweigh those considered as merely probable; (b) the reflection effect, which addresses the tendency of individuals to demonstrate risk aversion in the positive domain as compared to losses and gains determined by the reference point adopted by the decisionmaker; and (c) the isolation effect, which reflects a tendency to discount characteristics common to alternatives and focus on those that differentiate them and lead to inconsistent preferences if the same option is presented in another form (Slovic et al., 1988).

Prospect theory includes two distinct steps in the choice process, a framing and editing phase and an evaluation phase (Kahneman & Tversky, 1979). One of the major contributions of this model is the notion of "framing," a phenomenon by which the choice process is influenced by the manner in which the choice problem is viewed relative to an adopted negative or positive reference point. This poses an interesting dilemma since many decisions can be viewed as either gains or losses.

Numerous authors (Kahneman & Tversky, 1979; McNeil et al., 1989; Slovic, Fischhoff, & Lichtenstein, 1982a) noted that manipulation of the decision frames presented to a decisionmaker can influence his or her preferences for options and that these effects are sizable. The effects sometimes include preference reversals and violate the tenets of rationality. Concern for framing effects has been noted in the medical and legal literature with respect to their influence on patients' preferences in informed consent (Eraker & Sox, 1981; Meisel & Roth, 1983) as well as in discussions of the presentation of information to the users of computer decision support systems (Holtzman, 1989).

Other studies have noted differences in framing effects by gender, although gender differences in response consistency may be an artifact of other underlying characteristics, such as quantitative skills. Slovic et al. (1988) discussed the example of an insurance policy that actually provides only partial coverage. For example, one that provides insurance protection against fire and theft but not flood appears more attractive if framed as offering unconditional protection against a set of risks. This provides an illusionary sense of certainty.

Decisionmakers, when given decision tasks, appear to utilize only displayed information in problem formulation, which places significant responsibility on those charged with presenting decisionmakers with information (Slovic et al., 1982a). Ewell (1989) suggested that institutional researchers should know those for whom they provide data and either organize information to address their preferences or explain why various formats are used. He failed to elaborate on the associated framing effects if this approach is adopted. Some authors (McNeil et al., 1988; Bell et al., 1988) suggested that the potential to influence a decisionmaker by intentionally or unintentionally framing decision options warrants further exploration as an ethical issue, in cases such as framing information presented on informed consent forms. However, framing is also influenced by the decisionmaker's inherent characteristics (Tversky & Kahneman, 1988). To some extent that leaves an individual to his or her own devices in problem formulation. Framing and editing requirements place significant responsibility on those charged with information presentation and use.

PARTICIPATIVE DECISIONMAKING

In the recent past, decisionmaking has moved beyond individual choice discussions to include the analysis of participation in the decisionmaking process. The data on participative decisionmaking did not appear to support a participative decisionmaking model. But with the advent of productivity increases readily apparent in Japanese education and management, renewed interest has stirred.

Participative decisionmaking has widespread applications. Inherent in participation are questions about how subordinates respond to shared decisionmaking. Subordinates may have been motivated to participate for various reasons: to meet needs of achievement, for financial incentives, and to bring meaning to work. Management may see other advantages: an improved quality, increased worker commitment, increased productivity, and peer pressure. But studies to replicate these beliefs have not demonstrated accurate understanding about participation and decisionmaking. It is possible to point to ambiguities. Participation may be a result of stronger training or differences within groups, better goal setting may be a more effective rationale, and distribution of control may advance participative effects more readily than needs, incentives, or other issues.

Conway (1984) provided a summary of the literature on participation. According to him, participation does not demonstrate a higher level of quality decisions, although it does increase feelings of self-worth. Participation may influence decisionmaking more due to stronger goal setting among participants, and while this does seem to increase satisfaction, the satisfaction varies largely by type of organization. Much surrounding participative decisionmaking is still not clear.

Idiographic Factors That Influence Decisionmaking

Various idiographic factors, personality (e.g., confidence and dogmatism), and status (e.g., age and gender) influence decisionmaking (Johnson, 1990; MacPhail-Wilcox & Bryant, 1989). Hogarth (1980) identified thirteen idiographic factors, including ego strength, autonomy and tolerance for cognitive ambiguity, that he contended affect decisionmaking and are associated with productive scientists. However, the generalizations that can be made from Hogarth's work, as well as other studies of idiographic factors that influence decisionmaking, are limited.

Many studies explore single variables (Johnson, 1990) or a limited combination of idiographic factors (e.g., Hogarth, 1980). Others compare a study variable to only one aspect of the decisionmaking process, such as information search, thus limiting the generalizations that can be made from the research. For example, in her study of age as a factor in decisionmaking, Johnson (1990) found differences in the information search and use techniques but not in the time spent to reach a decision. In her study, younger subjects used more information but spent less time examining the information than did older subjects addressing the same decision tasks. Although Johnson's study demonstrated that the older subjects used noncompensatory decision rules that have lower cognitive processing demands, the quality of the decision outcome was not evaluated. The study did not indicate whether a particular strategy was detrimental to the decision outcome. Johnson (1990) conceded that other factors, such as vocabulary skills, which were higher in the older subjects, and intelligence, may have affected the information search and use patterns. However, other research suggests that it is difficult to generalize about age-related differences in intellectual functioning, particularly in older subjects (Bloom & Lazerson, 1989). However important the factors, generalizations are still limited.

In another interesting observation, Reitz (1987) noted that "there is little clear-cut evi-

dence to directly relate intelligence and decisionmaking ability" (p. 137). He suggested that if intelligence does affect decisionmaking success, it is not a major factor. Tversky and Kahneman (1974) contended that intelligence is not associated with any particular heuristic processing or information search pattern; even individuals with training in statistics and medicine make the same decisionmaking errors as others. Reitz (1987) stated that the apparent lack of correlation between intelligence and decisionmaking may be attributed to the complexities of intelligence, as well as the fact that decisionmaking requires various types of skills, a contention supported by McGuire (1985). He noted that a physician's problem solving and decisionmaking skills in the professional domain do not necessarily carry over into other areas.

While single and dualistic approaches to decisionmaking research have not fully and significantly enlightened the study of choice behavior, four quadrant combinations have proven somewhat more thorough despite concerns about the validity of formats. Myers' Briggs Type Indicator (Myers & Lamm, 1976) attempts to classify individuals by preferred modes of information gathering and processing. On one continuum, information gathering ranges from sensation to intuition. In another continuum, information processing is classified from feeling to thinking. The four measures combine to yield four decision styles: interpersonal, pragmatic, verbal expressive, and occupational. Decisionmakers may be classified as convergers, divergers, assimilators, and accommodators. The most current and popular four quadrant typology is based on hemispheric specialization. In this view, qualitative and quantitative differences are seen between the functions of the right and left hemispheres of the brain. The left side of the brain maintains responsibility for verbal expression and linear, analytical, and deductive processing. The right side of the brain functions as a synthesizer, processing information more holistically, creatively, intuitively, and inductively. Similarities have been found between hemispheric specialization and classes of decision behavior, right- and left-hemispheric and logical and nonlogical decisions, right- and left-hemispheric and rational and intuitive decisions, and so forth. Tacit and explicit knowledge produce a type of knowing critical to management performance. Numerous other inferences have been drawn from hemispheric studies: women function more integratively than men, planners are more left-hemispheric, managers more right, analysts left, and executives right. In combination, these studies propose important ways of understanding choice behavior more completely, particularly in information-processing functions. While decision styles and dispositional variables influence decisionmaking processes and outcomes as developed from two- and four-quadrant research, more research needs to be accomplished from a unifying perspective. A fully systemic approach exploration of decision style and dispositional variables as they interact in decision processes and result in outcomes is needed (MacPhail-Wilcox & Bryant, 1988).

Without knowing how one or several variables interact with other factors that influence the decisionmaking process (e.g., one factor may negate another or several others), the usefulness of information about discrete or several idiographic factors is limited at best. Even MacPhail-Wilcox and Bryant (1988), who developed a descriptive decisionmaking model in which decision styles (e.g., hemispheric dominance and intelligence) and dispositional variables (e.g., age, race, and gender) affect choice behavior, conceded that the relations between the variables have not been adequately studied. Existing research does not specify whether idiographic and other personal factors affect "decision outcome directly or indirectly" (p. 18).

Current research on idiographic factors that affect decisionmaking is still limited in its ability to explain or improve individual choice behavior. Other useful insights and improved individual choice behavior have been noted in decisionmaking literature, resulting from the study of heuristics and biases.

Decisionmaking Heuristics and Biases

Individuals often use heuristics to simplify the decisionmaking process. Although heuristics processes can be economical, by reducing cognitive load, as well as effective, they occasionally result in serious decisionmaking errors. Tversky and Kahneman (1982a) claim that individuals "rely on a limited number of heuristic principles which reduce complex tasks of assessing probabilities and predicting values to simpler judgmental operations" (p. 3). Some authors have identified errors specific to applications, such as those that Nisbett, Krantz, Jepson, and Kunda (1983) refer to as *statistical heuristics* (i.e., intuitive, abbreviated, and abstract versions of statistical principles). However, a broader perspective on heuristics may be obtained by examining the major biases associated with the commonly used heuristics noted by Tversky and Kahneman (1974): the availability heuristic, the representativeness heuristic, and anchoring and adjustment.

AVAILABILITY

Occasionally, individuals assess the probability or frequency of an event by other instances of the same event that can be recalled or are available in memory. Tversky and Kahneman (1973) refer to this heuristic as *availability,* and note that it can be very useful in addressing complex tasks that involve assessing probability or frequency "because instances of large classes are usually reached better and faster than instances of less frequent classes" (Tversky & Kahneman, 1982a, p. 11).

Bazerman (1991) noted three biases commonly associated with the availability heuristic: the ease of recall, retrievability, and illusionary correlation. The ease of recall bias is evidenced when individuals assign higher probabilities to events than are warranted. Based upon their ability to recall easily more recent or vivid occurrences, use of these probabilities often overestimates unlikely events. This assumption is erroneous. For example, because plane crashes are spectacular, some people assume that they should be associated with a higher mortality rate than car accidents, which are often less spectacular.

As decisionmakers recall information, retrievability may influence their perceptions. Essentially, instances that are readily available in memory will seem more numerous than those that are less retrievable, even if they occur with equal or lower frequency (Tversky & Kahneman, 1982b). Tversky and Kahneman (1973) illustrated this bias by asking subjects which was more prevalent, words that began with the letter "r" or those that had an "r" in the third position, hypothesizing that people tend to alphabetize words by the letter in the first position. Most subjects erroneously answered that there were more words beginning with an "r" and could readily list examples for their reasoning.

Presumed associations, or illusory connections, refer to a bias in which individuals assume higher probabilities of phenomena co-occurrence than actually exist. These paired associations take precedence, whether or not the pairing is warranted (Bazerman, 1991). Paired associations are commonly evidenced in stereotypes, such as the "smart kid with glasses," or folklore. For example, Chapman and Chapman (1967) demonstrated the phenomena in clinical psychologists, who overestimated the correlation between patients' diagnoses and features in their drawings. Social lore dictated that certain types of eyes on patients' drawings implied suspiciousness, for instance.

Tversky and Kahneman (1974) noted another bias associated with the availability heuristic: the bias of imaginability. They pointed out that this bias may be exemplified by the risks imagined to be associated with a trip, even though the imaginable risks may exaggerate or underestimate the actual situations that could be encountered.

Although the availability heuristic may be useful in assessing probabilities, it can lead to biases that are predictable and cause decisionmakers to overestimate the probability of event occurrence because of their experiences and learned associations (Tversky & Kahneman, 1974). When decisionmakers are provided with contradictory information that demonstrates their erroneous and inaccurate assumptions, they tend to resist changing their conclusions (Chapman & Chapman, 1967).

REPRESENTATIVENESS

People often assess the probability of a relationship by evaluating the extent to which one item or phenomenon is representative of, or similar to, another. The representativeness heuristic (Kahneman & Tversky, 1982) is often used in making intuitive predictions regarding outcomes. However, "this approach to the judgment of probability leads to serious errors, because similarity, or representativeness, is not influenced by several factors that should affect judgments of probability" (Tversky & Kahneman, 1982b). Use of this heuristic leads to decisionmaking errors when individuals attend to "normatively irrelevant" characteristics or ignore those that are "normatively important" (Slovic et al., 1988). Studies have shown that this heuristic is used by both naive and sophisticated subjects (Kahneman & Tversky, 1973).

Biases associated with the representativeness heuristic include a failure to recognize base-rates, insensitivity to sample size, misconceptions of chance, insensitivity to predictability, the illusion of validity, and misconceptions of regression (Bazerman, 1991; Tversky & Kahneman, 1974). Although individuals can use base-rates correctly, they tend to overlook them in assessing probabilities when descriptive information is provided, even if it is irrelevant (Kahneman & Tversky, 1972, 1973). An example of how base-rate information is ignored can be elicited by asking subjects about a description that suggests a stereotype, such as whether a male Asian-American student is likely to be an engineering or education major. More often than not, responses are based upon the provided physical characteristics rather than the base-rate of people actually engaged in the occupation (Tversky & Kahneman, 1982a).

Individuals frequently demonstrate an insensitivity to sample size, a fundamental issue in statistical generalizability, by assigning probabilities based upon a sample of limited representativeness. As noted by Tversky and Kahneman (1974), "intuitive judgments are dominated by the sample proportion and are essentially unaffected by the size of the sample, which plays a crucial role in the determination of the actual posterior odds" (p. 1125). This bias is evidenced by a study of theirs in which subjects, provided with information that approximately 50 percent of all babies are boys, projected that an instance in which the birth of male babies exceeded 60 percent was likely to be the same for two different-sized hospitals, one with 15 births per day and another with 45. This phenomenon is more likely in the smaller hospital, the one with 15 births per day, because a larger sample is less likely to deviate from the mean, they noted. Frequently, this bias unknowingly influences an individual's decisions regarding the probability of events. However, it is occasionally intentionally used, as seen in Bazer-

man's (1991) example of the advertising slogan: "Four out of five dentists surveyed recommended sugarless gum for their patients who chew gum" (p. 461). Who would question this claim? The advertiser benefits from the fact that most consumers will not question whether the data cited in this claim is representative of all dentists.

The misconceptions of chance bias occur with the gambler's fallacy. For example, after observing a long streak of black on a roulette wheel, an individual may unwittingly assume that red would be the next occurrence, even though events do not necessarily occur in a manner likened to "equilibrium." This "equilibrium" dilutes the distribution as more observations are made (Kahneman et al., 1982; Tversky & Kahneman, 1974). Citing assumptions regarding hitting streaks in baseball is another area in which this bias occurs. McKean (1988) reported that people often overlook the idea that streaks are sometimes contained in random sequence simply due to probability, and repeated exposure to chance incidents does not necessarily lead people to "recognize them as such" (p. 29). Bazerman (1991) summarized this bias by noting that individuals expect a series of random events to look "random," even when a series of observations is too limited to be "statistically valid." Tversky and Kahneman (1971) demonstrated that succumbing to this bias extends beyond the lay public to research psychologists and is frequently evidenced in research communities where decisions are based upon the assumption that results can be replicated. For example, drug trials conducted prior to the use of some new medication for human therapeutic purposes often use limited samples. Too often these studies include only young to middle-aged male subjects to determine drug efficacy and safety for the general population.

Tversky and Kahneman (1974) noted two biases emanating from the representativeness heuristic not included in Bazerman's (1991) corresponding listing: insensitivity to predictability and the illusion of validity. Insensitivity to predictability reflects a tendency to violate normative statistical theory by making predictions based upon "representativeness" regardless of the reliability or accuracy of the observation on which the conjecture is made. The illusion of validity refers to the over-confidence often placed in the correlation between an input observation or data used to predict a corresponding outcome (Tversky & Kahneman, 1974). This bias has been documented in experts and nonexperts and may be particularly problematic when used by individuals entrusted as expert decisionmakers. Einhorn and Hogarth (1978) claimed that research suggests that "neither the extent of professional training and experience nor the amount of information available to clinicians necessarily increases accuracy" (p. 395). People may persist in their overconfidence because they fail to learn from experience and selectively forget their incorrect judgment. Overconfidence and conjecture increase. Operating in conjunction, these biases can lead to an erroneous prediction based upon the representativeness of evidence and an overconfidence in the accuracy of the conjecture.

Individuals tend to be cognizant that observations regress toward the mean in extreme cases, but are less likely to acknowledge its occurrence in unusual circumstances and may develop spurious explanations for the phenomenon when it is noted. For example, McKean (1985) reported that flight instructors claimed that pilots' performances diminished after positive feedback and improved after reprimand. This change in performance was spuriously attributed to the feedback, even though "by regression alone, behavior is most likely to improve after punishment and to deteriorate after reward" (p. 25). This bias has implications for the usefulness of reward and punishment in promoting changes in performance. However, the evalua-

tor's judgment of a performance level may be affected by another heuristic: anchoring and adjustment.

ANCHORING AND ADJUSTMENT

Anchoring refers to a process in which people develop estimates. In the process, people with a specific value or reference point adjust the point up or down to yield a final value. However, adjustments are typically insufficient to negate the influence of the initial anchor as final answers tend to be biased toward the anchor, even when it is irrelevant (Slovic & Lichtenstein, 1971). The biases emanating from anchoring and adjustment include insufficient anchor adjustment, biases in the evaluation of conjunctive and disjunctive events, and overconfidence in judgments (Bazerman, 1991; Kahneman et al., 1982; Tversky & Kahneman, 1974).

Insufficient anchor adjustments are reflected in individuals' failure to adequately alter their initial values in establishing a final or estimated value. Anchoring occurs when individuals are given or have a starting value or when they have their final value estimate on incomplete computation (Tversky & Kahneman, 1974). This bias includes assessments of clinical pathology, risk assessments, projections as to the probability of nuclear war, and conjunctive and disjunctive events (Carlson, 1990). Bazerman (1991) cited a study in which real estate brokers and undergraduates who were provided with various listing prices for a house were asked to estimate the true value of the house. The study demonstrated that even experts are prone to the anchoring bias, although they "are less likely to realize their use of this bias" in decisionmaking (p. 467). Anchoring biases occurred in both groups. Furthermore, this bias may be detrimental to efforts to improve individuals' decisionmaking skills. Nisbett and Ross (1980) contended that the anchoring bias impedes efforts to improve individuals' decision strategies because existing heuristics and biases serve as cognitive anchors and are inherent in the corresponding judgment process.

Bias in evaluating conjunctive and disjunctive events is reflected in individuals' tendency to overestimate the probability of chain-like conjunctive events and underestimate the probability of chain-like disjunctive events. Tversky and Kahneman (1974) contended that occasionally the anchoring bias direction can be inferred from the event structure. They noted that overestimating " . . . the probability of conjunctive events leads to unwarranted optimism in the evaluation of the likelihood that a plan will proceed or that a project will be completed on time and underestimating the probability of disjunctive events can lead to an underestimation of the probability of failure in complex systems, composed of multiple components, each with its own associated error or probable failure rate" (p. 112).

Bazerman (1991) stated that most individuals tend to demonstrate overconfidence in their estimation abilities, fail to acknowledge the appropriate level of uncertainty associated with their assessments, and are likely to evidence a confidence level inversely correlated to their knowledge level in a given subject area. This bias affects not only layman in their everyday decisionmaking, but researchers have demonstrated that this bias is also evidenced by "experts" in decisionmaking tasks within their own specialty area. This bias was shown in clinical psychologists (Oskamp, 1982), physicians (Elstein & Bordage, 1979), and the United States Nuclear Regulatory Commission (cited in Slovic, Fischhoff, & Lichtenstein, 1982a). Tversky illustrated the implications of this bias: " . . . to think that, by and large, the world is run by people who have faith that they know exactly what's going on" (p. 26). However, some of the overconfidence people place in their judgments may be due to the confirmation bias.

CONFIRMATION BIAS

Confirmation bias occurs in the process individuals adapt to seek confirmatory data in their information searching, recollection, and assimilation, and exclude or overlook disconfirming evidence in this process (Bazerman, 1991; Einhorn & Hogarth, 1978). As a consequence of the confirmation trap, evidence tends to bolster an initial hypothesis or belief and sustain it. This is true even in the face of empirical rejection or attacks on the original evidence, a phenomenon evidenced by numerous researchers (Ross, Lepper, Strack, & Steinmetz, 1977). In educational forums this bias is demonstrated through the "Pygmalion" studies (Ross & Anderson, 1982, p. 150). Although this bias may help circumvent cognitive dissonance, Einhorn and Hogarth (1978) suggested that it may impede individuals' abilities to learn from experience as the failure to attempt to disconfirm initially held beliefs precludes gathering new insight. Another bias that has been associated with impeding learning is the hindsight bias.

HINDSIGHT BIAS

The common axiom that "hindsight is 20-20" inadvertently reflects a decisionmaking bias. The hindsight bias refers to the tendency of individuals, once given the results of a decision, to overestimate the degree of accuracy to which they would have predicted the correct outcome (Bazerman, 1991). Once individuals are given information about an occurrence, this information is integrated into their existing knowledge about the subject and reinterpreted to seem logical. The result is a "tendency to view reported outcomes as having been relatively inevitable," an inclination that has also been called *creeping determinism* (Fischhoff, 1982, p. 342). Staw and Ross

(1991) noted that other authors such as Tversky and Kahneman and Slovic and Fischhoff suggested that the hindsight effect may be influenced by other heuristics, such as anchoring, representativeness, or availability. They also suggest the major effect of this bias may be an impairment of ability to judge past events adequately and learn from them.

The Implications of Systems Theory and Decisionmaking

While the literature explored in this chapter investigated the two primary decisionmaking approaches, normative and descriptive, further attention needs to be given to the implications of decisionmaking and the systems movement. Decisionmaking theorists have, by and large, viewed decisionmaking from within their own reductionist paradigms. An all-analytical approach or an all-conceptual or descriptive approach cannot extend to the dynamic relationship that exists in systems. Oversimplification in decisionmaking implies submitting to a cause and effect relation that cannot account for the existing variety present in educational systems or their interrelations. However, a multitude of new points of view are available from systems theorists. This has only recently become useful to decision theorists and decisionmakers. A systems view of decisionmaking recognizes the complexity of the decisionmaking process. Decisionmaking, like inquiry, requires complex science.

Decisionmaking models may also deteriorate from the same systematic tendencies of the more traditional systems approach, the input-throughput-output model. Decisionmaking can never simply be an aggregate phenomenon. Simply creating another decisionmaking model to explain a particular new phenomenon only creates another snapshot. The decisionmaker cannot just add variety or

another combination of inputs, as complexity can still overwhelm the process and the decisionmaker. In this sense, decisionmaking must begin to incorporate a thinking or reflective component (Argyris, 1985). This thinking or reflective component allows a decisionmaking model to become dynamic, to enable its own continuing relevance and growth. To be effective, this "living" quality can be enabled repeatedly through leveraging mechanisms, thus allowing the decisionmaker or the decision process to constantly remain generative (Senge, 1990).

Decisionmaking could also benefit from a more interdisciplinary focus. Decisionmaking and inquiry may be isomorphic. While many developers of models of inquiry stumble as a result of their positivistic tendencies, other inquiry researchers have proposed models that are systemic. Argyris (1985), for example, proposed an interpretive inquiry model that at the same time demonstrates generative capabilities. In his inquiry model significant research questions must be explored in their totality and exposed to the whole of its system: problem definition, problem study, problem identification, intervention, and redefinition. Only when inquiry "reinvents" itself or recycles itself can it be useful from a systems perspective. Similarly, decisionmaking can be renewed from this viewpoint. In devising and using any decision process one must thoroughly explore alternatives and invent a variety of action strategies which then create the next need for a new decision. As decisionmakers become accustomed to using new systemic approaches, perhaps decisionmaking will then become truly iterative. Decisionmaking as a process with a beginning and end breeds decisionmakers who are ineffective in a constantly changing and evolving environment.

Feedback is also critical. The dynamic nature of systems requires mechanisms be available for renewal. As the inquiry process and the decisionmaking process are utilized, additional internal and external inputs open the processes. This "openness" allows the existing variety of the system to emerge and is a requisite need for the system. Closing the process to input typically assures less than complete action and future action. Feedback is a primary ingredient.

This connection between systems thinking and decisionmaking is by no means complete. Decisionmaking theory has long been viewed from the narrow confines of the normative and descriptive approaches of the past. Decisionmaking must be explored from a more informed and enlightened arena, systems thinking. Prospect theory and the descriptive agenda discussed earlier and proposed by MacPhail-Wilcox and Bryant (1988) are steps in this direction.

Decisionmaking Implications in Educational Practice

As stated earlier in this chapter, decisionmaking is a central responsibility for many educational administrators. Knowledge about decisionmaking idiographic factors, decision processes, and choice outcomes are requisite skills necessary to arrive at successful accomplishment of educational objectives. But how does all this theory convert to practical use? In other words, how does a general theory of educational administration and decision theory unite in organizational principles that ensure effective action?

While the classical model of decisionmaking is an ideal, a more realistic approach to decisionmaking has evolved from satisficing strategies (Simon, 1957). In practical use, satisficing strategies have evolved to be viewed as a dynamic process or cycles of decision events that include development, initiation, and appraisal sequences. It is the administrator's responsibility to assure that the organi-

zation perpetuates itself and survives, maintains stability, and progresses and grows. In this context, the administrator becomes a maximizer acting on behalf of the organization to maintain internal and external integrity and preserve and enhance all educational practice. While these ideals are admirable, educational administrators most often operate in arenas filled with incomplete information. Administrators may never maximize as they lack the knowledge to do so. In situations in which specific goals drive action, maximizing may only be partially accommodated. As complexity continues to increase, options expand beyond what can feasibly be utilized, and prediction becomes less likely due to expanding consequences contained within alternatives. Individuals are not capable of making completely rational decisions when dealing with complex matters. As a result, satisficing strategies or good enough solutions replace optimizing strategies. To accomplish this, administrators limit the scope of decisions to approach rationality as closely as possible. Limits are, in turn, confined to comfortable functional areas: policy, resources, and execution. Policy is derived from goals that guide action across the school organization, and execution occurs as integration and synthesizing of resources unite to create a purpose-bound organization. Administrators seek choices that serve to "quantify" curriculum and instruction, physical facilities, finance and business, evaluation, recruitment and selection, public relations, and more (Hoy & Miskel, 1978).

In situations where administrators find undefinable alternatives and greater unpredictability, Hoy and Miskel (1978) propose substituting satisficing strategy with an incremental model, a process of successive limited comparisons (Lindbloom, 1965). In this decisionmaking process, goal setting and generation of alternatives become intertwined. Feasible actions are identified as limited consequences and their alternatives are explored in turn. In this sense, incremental steps are achieved and progress observed in comparison to a previous stage.

Within these implications, deficiencies can be noted in educational decisionmaking. In the classical sense, decisionmaking is a means-ends analysis, an optimizing strategy. It engages all alternatives and relies heavily on theoretical constructs. From the satisficing point of view, a means-ends analysis is typical, but ends are changeable as a result of analysis. Satisficing achieves results that fall within established boundaries, alternatives result from a problemistic search, and theory and experience guide the total process. Incremental strategies investigate goals and alternatives concomitantly. Choice is a matter of agreement between successive comparisons made by the various decisionmakers, and practical application replaces the need for theory.

Decisionmaking has been considered in a systems-like context by various educational authors. In these models decisionmaking is still a linear process (identify problem, define problem, weigh alternatives, and make choice), but, in addition, these models come replete with feedback loops, environmental factors, subsystems, and boundaries. As discussed in Chapter 1, systems thinking is more than additive thinking. To truly move beyond the limiting boundaries of aggregate thinking, school leadership must learn to address decisionmaking scenarios from a more dynamic viewpoint. Senge (1990) suggests that organizational management, including school administration, must learn to deal with circles of influence, those patterning actions that display and describe the inherent dynamics of the educational environment. Administrators who continually remain committed to linear, satisficing or incremental decisionmaking methodologies may arrive at choices that seem fitting (symptomatic), but eventually suffer again from inadequate understanding of the dynamic nature of the school and its environment (fundamental). A constant struggle ensues as principals, deans, and directors exchange snapshots.

Decisionmaking, like any other thinking system in the educational environment, must continue to observe those traditions that have molded educational thought to date. Various instances of satisficing and incremental decisionmaking strategies can produce worthy results. But future administrators must also become cognizant of the power of thinking and acting in a dynamic fashion. Only then will leadership truly occur in our educational institutions.

■ MINI CASE STUDIES

Teaching Versus Research

For half a century your college has been known for its teaching excellence. However, over the last decade a number of faculty have successfully begun important technological research. Others have proposed and obtained funding through government and industry grant programs. During the last three years enrollment and retention has declined modestly. Apply decisionmaking techniques and strategies to arrive at one of the options listed below.

1. Increase technological research.
2. Recapture status of an excellent teaching college.
3. A combination of the two spheres of interests described in (1) and (2) above.

Budget Reductions and More

As superintendent of schools, you have reduced the budget to your schools this year by 20 percent each. One principal, in order to "live within budget," proposed that the following changes will need to be considered: (a) increased class size, (b) a 5-percent reduction in teaching staff, (c) a 2-percent reduction in support staff, and (d) more efficient control of heating and air conditioning. Consider these in light of the additional constraints listed below. Apply decisionmaking techniques and strategies to arrive at a workable solution.

1. A large citizens group opposes all options.

2. The state board is considering school choice.

3. You can expect litigation from the teachers union if class size increases.

Math and Science and Dropouts

The school dropout rate reached 22 percent last year, an all-time high. A combination of reasons exist for the high rate. Additionally, the math chairman advised that the state has mandated a number of new requirements in the math curriculum. The math faculty agrees with the changes. However, you know math and science are significant factors in the dropout problem. Apply decisionmaking techniques and strategies to arrive at workable solutions for the problems listed below.

1. Implement the new math requirements from the state.

2. Decrease the dropout problem.

3. Staff the math department.

Do More with Less

As a classroom teacher, you have arrived at a difficult crossroad in your own lesson planning. Year after year, district requirements seem to keep adding "essential" new knowledge components with little regard to how they fit into the total schema of an individual teacher's plans. You realize some of your most effective learning devices will not be practical when more "essentials" are added. Devise decisionmaking strategies to arrive at optimal use of instructional time, use of existing instructional materials and delivery systems, and integration of newly identified, producible instructional materials.

Who's to Blame?

Illiteracy exists in segments of the population in which your school district is located. As superintendent of schools, you have heard community and business leaders constantly lay the blame upon the education process. In contrast, administrators and teachers indicate illiteracy rates have increased because of dropout rates, increased state requirements, and lack of adequate resources. Devise a holistic problem-solving strategy to address the problem of illiteracy in your school district.

Annotated Bibliography

Bell, D. E., Raiffa, H., & Tversky, A. (Eds.). (1988). *Decision making: Descriptive, normative and prescriptive interactions.* Cambridge: Cambridge University Press.

This book represents a collection of papers presented at a conference held at the Harvard Business School in June 1983 in an attempt to bring cohesion to the broad field of decisionmaking. It includes contributions from the disciplinary bases of the normative, descriptive, and prescriptive branches of decisionmaking. The collected works include contributions from the major researchers and authors in the field of decisionmaking (e.g., Simon; Tversky and Kahneman; Fishburn; Einhorn and Hogarth; Slovic, Fischhoff, and Lichtenstein; etc.). The book is essential introductory reading for those wishing to pursue a basic understanding of the field of decisionmaking. The merit of this collection is that it provides a balanced overview of decisionmaking by addressing the normative, descriptive, and prescriptive approaches, a feature that publications from specific disciplines fail to note.

Conway, J. A. (1984). The myth, mystery, and master of participative decision making in education. *Educational Administration Quarterly, 20*(3), 11-40.

This article provides an overview of participative decision making (PDM), with specific application to the field of education. It covers a broad spectrum of relevant research and serves as an excellent source of information on the topic. The author summarizes the major reviewers of the topic as well as the relevant research specific to the field of education, and suggests implications of these findings for school leaders. Conclusions drawn from the numerous reviews and extensive research works reviewed in this article suggest that PDM does not necessarily yield higher quality decisions or greater support from those involved in the process, though it does enhance participants' feelings of worth and confidence and may promote more positive attitudes about school among involved students. The author notes the need for further research on PDM in the school environment as many questions remain unanswered.

Heyel, C. (Ed.). (1982). *The encyclopedia of management* (3rd ed.) (pp. 198–207). New York: Van Nostrand Reinhold.

Two sections in this encyclopedia are specifically devoted to decisionmaking: (a) decisionmaking and organizational effectiveness—the systems approach, and (b) decision theory. The merit of using this reference is that information is provided concisely. For example, in three pages, basic information on the origins, elements, and strengths and limitations of decision theory are discussed, and example decision trees are presented. These sections of the encyclopedia provide a basic overview of the topics from the perspective of one the disciplines credited with theory development in this area. Though this reference will not provide a reader with insight into the relevant research and applications of this information, it does serve as a basic informational resource.

Kahneman, D., Slovic, P., & Tversky, A. (Eds.). (1982). *Judgement under uncertainty: Heuristic and biases.* Cambridge, England: Cambridge University Press.

This book includes a collection of works by numerous scholars in the field that address the heuristic and biases that frequently lead to decisionmaking errors and can impede learning. Major areas covered in this book include representativeness, causality and attribution, availability, covariation and control, overconfidence, multistage evaluation, corrective procedures, and risk perception. Some of the findings presented by the various contributing authors have served as the catalyst for development in the area of descriptive decisionmaking as they evidence the human limitations to idealized super-rational choice behaviors, characteristic of the normative approach.

MacPhail-Wilcox, B., & Bryant, H. D. (1988, Fall). A descriptive model of decision making: Review of idiographic influences. *Journal of Research and Development in Education, 22*(1), 7-22.

These authors present a descriptive model of the idiographic factors that influence the decisionmaking process and the resultant outcomes based upon an extensive review of the relevant literature. This article addresses the foundations of decisionmaking, corresponding individual and organizational processes, idiographic factors influencing this process, as well as the model proposed by these authors. Of particular use to the beginner in the field of descriptive decisionmaking are the relevant research articles on idiographic variables that influence the choice process reviewed in this article.

Reitz, H. J. (1987). Individual decision making. In *Behavior in organizations* (3rd ed.) (pp. 128–162). Homewood, IL: Irwin.

This chapter addresses a basic overview of the major components of individual decisionmaking. Topics addressed in this section include (a) the elements of decisionmaking, major models, and individual differences in choice behaviors; (b) decision problem characteristics; (c) the decisionmaking process; (d) the decisionmaking environment and how it influences the decisionmaking process; and (e) implications for managing behavior in organizations. Though this chapter provides a cursory review of the area, the author covers a broad range of literature on the subject and provides an excellent overview of the basics of individual decisionmaking. (Note: This reference also includes a chapter on group decisionmaking (GDM) that provides a broader overview of the area than that included in the book by Staw, referenced below.)

Staw, B. M. (Ed.). (1991). *Psychological dimension of organizational behavior.* New York: Macmillan.

One section in this book, titled "Dimension V," is entirely devoted to decisionmaking and addresses several areas via contributions by a variety of authors (e.g., Bazerman; Janis and Mann; and Staw and Ross). This section of the book includes articles on (a) the foundations of decision processes, which specifically address decisionmaking heuristic and biases; (b) limitations on individuals' decisionmaking in an organization (e.g., the time and cost needed to search for alternatives) and strategies used in this setting, such as satisficing and mixed scanning; (c) decisionmaking behavior in escalation situations; (d) group processes and decisionmaking; and (e) groupthink.

References

Alkin, M. C. (Ed.). (1991). *Encyclopedia of educational research* (6th ed.), (Vol. 3). New York: Macmillan.

Archer, E. R. (1980, February). How to make a business decision: An analysis of theory and practice. *Management Review, 69,* 54–61.

Argyris, C. (1985). *Action science.* New York: Jossey-Bass.

Atkinson, R. C., Herrnstein, R. J., Lindzey, G., & Luce, R. D. (Eds.). (1988). *Steven's handbook of experimental psychology* (Vol. 2). New York: John Wiley & Sons.

Baird, B. F. (1989). *Managerial decisions under uncertainty.* New York: John Wiley & Sons.

Barnard, C. I. (1938). *The functions of the executive.* Cambridge, MA: Harvard University Press.

Baron, J. (1985). *Rationality and intelligence.* Cambridge, England: Cambridge University Press.

Bazerman, M. H. (1991). Foundations of decision processes. In B. M. Staw (Ed.), *Psychological dimensions of organizational behavior* (pp. 451–478). New York: Macmillan.

Bell, D. E., Raiffa, H., & Tversky, A. (Eds.). (1988). *Decision making: Descriptive, normative and prescriptive interactions.* Cambridge, England: Cambridge University Press.

Bittel, L. R., & Bittel, M. A. (1978). *Encyclopedia of professional management.* New York: McGraw-Hill.

Bloom, F. E., & Lazerson, A. (1988). *Brain, mind, and behavior* (2nd ed.). New York: W. H. Freeman and Company.

Carlson, B. W. (1990). Anchoring and adjustment in judgments under risk. *Journal of Experimental Psychology: Learning, Memory and Cognition, 16*(4), 665–676.

Carroll, J. S., & Johnson, E. J. (1990). *Decision research: A field guide.* Newbury Park, CA: Sage.

Chapman, L. J., & Chapman, J. P. (1967). Genesis of popular but erroneous diagnostic observations. *Journal of Abnormal Psychology, 72,* 193–204.

Cohen, I. (1990). Discriminatory labelling and the five-finger discount. *Journal of Crime and Delinquency, 16,* 37–49.

Conway, J. A. (1984). The myth, mystery, and mastery of participative decision making in education. *Educational Administration Quarterly, 20*(3), 11–40.

Cornell, A. H. (1980). *The decision-makers handbook.* Englewood Cliffs, NJ: Prentice-Hall.

Curley, S. P., Eraker, S. A., & Yates, J. F. (1984). An investigation of patients' reactions to therapeutic uncertainty. *Medical Decision Making, 4*(4), 501–511.

Dejnozka, E. L., & Kapel, D. E. (1991). *American educators' encyclopedia.* New York: Greenwood Press.

Dempster, A. P. (1988). Probability, evidence, and judgment. In D. E. Bell, H. Raiffa, & A. Tversky (Eds.), *Decision making* (pp. 284–292). Cambridge, England: Cambridge University Press.

Deutsch, M., & Krauss, R. M. (1963). *Theories in social psychology.* New York: Basic Books.

Eddy, D. M. (1982). Probabilistic reasoning in clinical medicine: Problems and opportunities. In D. Kahneman, P. Slovic, and A. Tversky (Eds.), *Judgment under uncertainty: Heuristics and biases* (pp. 249–267). Cambridge, England: Cambridge University Press.

Einhorn, H. J., & Hogarth, R. M. (1978). Confidence in judgment: Persistence of the illusion of validity. *Psychological Review, 85*(5), 395–416.

Einhorn, H. J., & Hogarth, R. M. (1988). Behavioral decision theory: Processes of judgment and choice. In D. Bell, H. Raiffa, & A. Tversky (Eds.). *Decision making: Descriptive, normative, and prescriptive interactions* (pp. 113–151). Cambridge, England: Cambridge University Press.

Elstein, A. S., & Bordage, G. (1979). Psychology of clinical reasoning. In G. Stone, F. Cohen, & N. Alder (Eds.), *Health psychology* (pp. 333–368). San Francisco: Jossey-Bass.

Eraker, S. A., & Sox, H. C. (1981). Assessment of patients' preferences for therapeutic outcomes. *Medical decision making, 1*(1), 29–39.

Ewell, P. T. (1989). *Enhancing information use in decision making*. San Francisco: Jossey-Bass.

Fiegenbaum, A., & Thomas, H. (1988). Attitudes toward risk and the risk-return paradox: Prospect theory explanations. *Academy of Management Journal, 31*(1), 288–299.

Fischhoff, B. (1982). For those condemned to study the past: Heuristics and biases in hindsight. In D. Kahneman, P. Slovic, & A. Tversky (Eds.), *Judgment under uncertainty: Heuristics and biases* (pp. 335–351). Cambridge, England: Cambridge University Press.

Fischhoff, B. (1983). Predicting frames. *Journal of Experimental Psychology: Learning, Memory and Cognition, 9*(1), 103–116.

Fishburn, P. C. (1988). Normative theories of decision making under risk and under uncertainty. In D. Bell, H. Raiffa, & A. Tversky (Eds.), *Decision making: Descriptive, normative, and prescriptive interactions* (pp. 78–98). Cambridge, England: Cambridge University Press.

Fong, G. T., Krantz, D. H., & Nisbett, R. E. (1989). The effects of statistical training on thinking about everyday problems. In D. Bell, H. Raiffa, & A. Tversky (Eds.), *Decision making: Descriptive, normative, and prescriptive interactions* (pp. 299–340). Cambridge, England: Cambridge University Press.

Grandori, A. (1984). A prescriptive contingency view of organizational decision making. *Administrative Science Quarterly, 29*, 192–209.

Gross, I. D. (1953). *Design for decision*. New York: Macmillan.

Hicks, J. R. (1939). *Value and capital: An inquiry into some fundamental principles of economic theory*. Oxford, England: Clarendon Press.

Hill, G. W. (1982). Group versus individual performance: Are N + 1 heads better than one? *Psychological Bulletin, 91*, 517–539.

Hogarth, R. (1980). *Judgment and choice: The psychology of decision*. New York: John Wiley & Sons.

Holloway, C. A. (1979). *Decision making under uncertainty: Models and choices*. Englewood Cliffs, NJ: Prentice-Hall.

Holtzman, S. (1989). *Intelligent decision systems*. Reading, MA: Addison-Wesley.

Hooker, C. A., Leach, J. J., & McClennen, E. F. (Eds.). (1978). *Foundations and applications of decision theory* (Vol. 1). Boston: D. Reidel Publishing.

Hoy, W. K., & Miskel, C. G. (1978). *Educational administration: Theory, research. and practice*. New York: Random House.

Huber, G. P. (1980). *Managerial decision making*. Glenview, IL: Scott, Foresman.

Janis, I. L. (1989). *Crucial decisions: Leadership in policymaking and crisis management*. New York: The Free Press.

Johnson, M. S. (1990). Age differences in decision making: A process methodology for examining strategic information processing. *Journal of Gerontology, 45*(2), 75–78.

Kahneman, D., Slovic, P., & Tversky, A. (Eds.). (1982). *Judgment under uncertainty: Heuristics and biases*. Cambridge, England: Cambridge University Press.

Kahneman, D., & Tversky, A. (1972). Subjective probability: A judgment of representativeness. *Cognitive Psychology, 3*, 430–454.

Kahneman, D., & Tversky, A. (1973). On the psychology of prediction. *Psychological Review, 80*, 237–251.

Kahneman, D., & Tversky, A. (1979). Prospect theory: An analysis of decision under risk. *Econometrica, 4*(2), 263–291.

Kahneman, D., & Tversky, A. (1984). Choices, values and frames. *American Psychologist, 39*(4), 341–350.

Katz, D., & Kahn, R. (1978). *The social psychology of organizations* (2nd ed.). New York: John Wiley & Sons.

Keeny, R. L., & Raiffa, H. (1976). *Decisions with multiple objectives: Preferences and value tradeoffs.* New York: John Wiley & Sons.

Kissinger, H. (1979). *White house years.* Boston: Little, Brown.

Krepel, T. L. (1987). Contemporary decision theory and educational leadership. *Educational Research Quarterly, 11*(4), 37–44.

Lindbloom, C. E. (1965). *The intelligence of democracy decision making through mutual adjustments.* New York: The Free Press.

Loomes, G., & Sugden, R. (1982). Regret theory: An alternative theory of rational choice under uncertainty. *The Economic Journal, 92*(368), 805–824.

Luce, R. D., & Raiffa, H. (1967). *Games and decision, introduction and critical survey: A study of the behavioral models project, Bureau of Applied Social Research, Columbia University.* New York: John Wiley & Sons.

MacPhail-Wilcox, B., & Bryant, H. D. (1988, Fall). A descriptive model of decision making: Review of idiographic influences. *Journal of Research and Development in Education, 22*(1), 7–22.

Magjuka, R. (1988). Garbage can theory of organizational decision making. *Research on Social Organizations, 6,* 225–259.

Mann, L., & Janis, I. (1977). *Decision making: A psychological analysis of conflict, choice, and commitment.* New York: The Free Press.

March, J. G. (1988). Bounded rationality, ambiguity and the engineering of choice. In D. Bell, H. Raiffa, & A. Tversky (Eds.), *Decision making: Descriptive, normative, and prescriptive interactions* (pp. 33–57). Cambridge, England: Cambridge University Press.

March, J. G., & Olsen, J. P. (1976). *Ambiguity and choices in organizations.* Bergen, Norway: Universitetsforlaget.

March, J. G., & Simon, H. A. (Eds.). (1958). *Organizations.* New York: John Wiley & Sons.

McGuire, C. H. (1985). Medical problem solving: A critique of the literature. *Journal of Medical Education, 60*(8), 587–595.

McKean, K. (1985, June). Decisions, decisions. *Discover,* 22–31.

McKinsey, J. C. (1952). *An introduction to the theory of games.* New York: McGraw-Hill.

McNeil, B., Pauker, S., & Tversky, A. (1988). On the framing of medical decisions. In D. Bell, H. Raiffa, & A. Tversky (Eds.), *Decision making: Descriptive, normative, and prescriptive interactions* (pp. 562–568). Cambridge, England: Cambridge University Press.

Meisel, A., & Roth, L. H. (1983). Toward an informed discussion of informed consent: A review and critique of the empirical studies. *Arizona Law Review, 25,* 265–346.

Mintzberg, H. (1979). *The structuring of organizations.* Englewood Cliffs, NJ: Prentice-Hall.

Montgomery, H. (1983). Decision rules and the search for a dominance structure: Towards a process model of decision making. In P. Humphreys, O. Svenson, & A. Vari (Eds.), *Analyzing and aiding decision making processes* (pp. 343–369).

Myers, D. G., & Lamm, H. (1976). The group polarization phenomenon. *Psychological Bulletin, 83,* 602–627.

Neel, A. (1977). *Theories of psychology: A handbook.* New York: Schenkman.

Nisbett, R. E., Krantz, D. H., Jepson, C., & Kunda, Z. (1983). The use of statistical heuristics in everyday inductive reasoning. *Psychological Review, 90,* 339–363.

Nisbett, R., & Ross, L. (1980). *Human inherence: Strategies and shortcoming of social judgment.* Englewood Cliffs, NJ: Prentice-Hall.

Oskamp, S. (1982). Overconfidence in case-study judgments. In D. Kahneman, P. Slovic, & Tversky, A. (Eds.), *Judgment under uncertainty: Heuristics and biases* (pp. 287–293). Cambridge, England: Cambridge University Press.

Reitz, H. J. (1987). *Behavior in organizations* (3rd ed.). Homewood, IL: Irwin.

Roberts, F. S. (1979). *Measurement theory with applications to decision making, utility and the social sciences.* Reading, MA: Addison-Wesley.

Ross, L., & Anderson, C. A. (1982). Shortcomings in the attribution process: On the origins and maintenance of erroneous social assessments. In D. Kahneman, P. Slovic, & A. Tversky (Eds.), *Judgment under uncertainty: Heuristics and biases* (pp. 129–152). Cambridge, England: Cambridge University Press.

Ross, L., Lepper, M. R., Strack, F., & Steinmetz, J. L. (1977). Social explanation and social expectation: The effects of real and hypothetical explanations upon subjective likelihood. *Journal of Personality and Social Psychology, 35,* 817–829.

Schelling, T. C. (1988). The mind as a consuming organ. In D. Bell, H. Raiffa, & A. Tversky (Eds.), *Decision making: Descriptive, normative, and prescriptive interactions* (pp. 343–357). Cambridge, England: Cambridge University Press.

Schön, D. (1983). *The reflective practitioner.* New York: Basic Books.

Schurr, P. H. (1987). Effects of gain and loss decision frames on risky purchase negotiations. *Journal of Applied Psychology, 72*(3), 351–358.

Senge, P. (1990). *The fifth discipline: The art and practice of the learning organization.* New York: Doubleday-Currency.

Shubick, M. (Ed.). (1964). *Game theory and related approaches to social behavior.* New York: John Wiley & Sons.

Simon, H. A. (1955). A behavioral model of rational choice. *Quarterly Journal of Economics, 69,* 99–118.

Simon, H. A. (1956). Rational choice and the structure of the environment. *Psychological Review, 63,* 129–138.

Simon, H. A. (1957). *The new science of management decisions.* New York: Harper.

Simon, H. A. (1976). *Administrative behavior: A study of decision making processes in administrative organizations* (3rd ed.). New York: The Free Press.

Slovic, P., Fischhoff, B., & Lichtenstein, S. (1982a). Response mode framing and information-processing effects in risk assessment. In R. Hogarth (Ed.), *New directions for methodology of social and behavioral science: Question framing and response consistency* (pp. 21–36). San Francisco: Jossey-Bass.

Slovic, P., Fischhoff, B., & Lichtenstein, S. (1982b). Facts versus fears: Understanding perceived risks. In D. Kahneman, P. Slovic, & A. Tversky (Eds.), *Judgment under uncertainty: Heuristics and biases* (pp. 463–489). Cambridge, England: Cambridge University Press.

Slovic, P., & Lichtenstein, S. (1971). Comparison of Bayesian and regression approaches in the study of information processing and judgment. *Organizational Behavior and Human Performance, 6,* 649–744.

Slovic, P., & Lichtenstein, S. (1983). Preference reversals: A broader perspective. *American Economic Review, 73,* 596–605.

Slovic, P., Lichtenstein, S., & Fischhoff, B. (1988). Decision making. In R. Atkinson, R. Herrnstein, G. Lindzey, & R. D. Luce (Eds.), *Stevens' handbook of experimental psychology* (Vol. 2) (pp. 673–738). New York: John Wiley & Sons.

Smith, C. (1974). *Voluntary associations.* Cambridge, MA: Harvard University Press.

Staw, B. M., & Ross, J. (1991). Understanding behavior in escalation situations. In B. Staw (Ed.), *Psychological dimensions of organizational behavior.* New York: Macmillan.

Steers, R. M. (1977). *Organizational effectiveness: A behavioral view.* Santa Monica, CA: Goodyear.

Tallman, I., & Gray, L. N. (1990). Choices, decisions and problem-solving. In W. R. Schoo & J. Blake (Eds.), *Annual Review of Sociology* (Vol. 16) (pp. 405–433). Palo Alto, CA: Annual reviews.

Taylor, D. W. (1965). Decision making and problem solving. In J. G. March (Ed.), *Handbook of organizations.* Chicago: Rand McNally.

Tetlock, P. (1985). *Accountability: The neglected social context* of judgment and choice. In B. M. Staw & L. Cummings (Eds.), *Research in organizational behavior* (Vol. 1). New York: Oxford University Press.

Tversky, A., & Kahneman, D. (1971). The belief in the "law of small numbers." *Psychological Bulletin, 76,* 105–110.

Tversky, A., & Kahneman, D. (1973). Availability: A heuristic for judging frequency and probability. *Cognitive Psychology, 4,* 207–232.

Tversky, A., & Kahneman, D. (1974). Judgment under uncertainty: Heuristics and biases. *Science, 185,* 1124–1131.

Tversky, A., & Kahneman, D. (1982). Evidential impact of base rates. In D. Kahneman, P. Slovic, & A. Tversky (Eds.), *Judgment under uncertainty: Heuristics and biases* (pp. 153–160). Cambridge, England: Cambridge University Press.

Tversky, A., & Kahneman, D. (1982). Judgment under uncertainty: Heuristics and biases. In D. Kahneman, P. Slovic, & A. Tversky (Eds.), *Judgment under uncertainty: Heuristics and biases* (pp. 3–20). Cambridge, England: Cambridge University Press.

Tversky, A., & Kahneman, D. (1988). Rational choice and the framing of decisions. In D. Bell, H. Raiffa, & A. Tversky (Eds.), *Decision making: Descriptive, normative, and prescriptive interactions* (pp. 167–192). Cambridge, England: Cambridge University Press.

Von Neumann, J., & Morgenstern, O. (1947). *Theory of games and economic behavior*. Princeton, NJ: Princeton University Press.

Watson, S. R., & Buede, D. M. (1987). *Decision synthesis: The principles and practice of decision analysis*. Cambridge, England: Cambridge University Press.

Weick, C. (1976). *Applied electronics*. New York: McGraw-Hill.

Weiss, C. H., & Bucuvalas, M. J. (1980). *Social science research and decision-making*. New York: Columbia University Press.

White, D. J. (1969). *Decision theory*. Chicago: Aldine.

Wolfinger, R. E. (Ed.). (1970). *Readings in American political behavior*. Englewood Cliffs, NJ: Prentice-Hall.

Zeleny, M. (1981). Descriptive decision making and its applications. *Applications of Management Science, 1*, 327–388.

Chapter 16
Change

Basic Issues

In the popular imagination of educational leaders over the past few years, images of themselves as changemasters, pathfinders, gamesmen, entrepreneurs, visionaries, and transformational leaders have been widely evident. The spirit of the educational leader has been founded in novelty, chaos, innovation, and change. Educational administrators everywhere have been called on to envision alternatives, to inflame the collective human spirit in renewal, to capture the turbulent environment, and to break the barriers of conventional practice. Change may be about to take on a value of its own (Bell, 1976). For organizations, it may be a foregone conclusion that change is ubiquitous; it is and will remain the norm. Winners will be managed by those who love change and battle bureaucracy. While change resides as a cure-all, numerous examples of change programs fail as a result of their disruptiveness and from the confusion and threats they pose to participants who must change (Beer, Eisenstat, &

Spector, 1990). Tried and true practices, already established personal investments, and already aligned commitments are devalued in favor of innovations that lack continuity (Srivastva, Fry, & Associates, 1992).

Schooling today is confronted with numerous pressures. The ideological, political, and economic environment, as viewed by the American public, is vastly different today than it was in the past. The public demands a more significant connection between effective schooling and national development in the light of dramatic changes in demographics and economic circumstances. A more learning-oriented literate work force will be in high demand. Continuous improvement will be in high demand while changes in schooling that have been judged as fundamentally inadequate during the 1980s will fade (Cetron & Gayle, 1991). Change, as the never-ending task, will necessitate an understanding of what change is, what change scenarios are available or can be developed, and how and why change is necessary. In the early stages of professional development, educators and administrators must become familiar with the interactive and interdependent nature of these contexts. With all this understood, change will remain a difficult process to handle as leaders of change must learn to resolve several basic conflicts: change versus tradition, self-fulfillment versus participation, and decentralization versus integration (Hahn, 1991). The tasks will seem overwhelming.

What Is Change?

Change in organizations is defined by Hanson (1985) as the altering of " . . . behavior, structures, procedures, purposes, or outputs of some unit within an organization" (p. 286). Some describe change as innovation, others adaptability, even novelty. Thompson (1965) viewed innovation as "the generation, acceptance, and implementation of new ideas, processes, products, or services" (pp. 1–20). Mort (1962) preferred adaptability and simply labeled change as the capacity to respond to various roles in society.

Change is not a product to be pursued in and of itself for its own value. It is a process by which other ends may be reached. It is the primary means by which any organization or system remains fit, healthy, and able to cope with new and differing demands. The adaptations produced by change in an organization constitute an evolution of the organization. Those organizations that are able to maintain flexibility and react appropriately to new environmental conditions survive and prosper. Those organizations that cannot become less and less able to serve society.

Change is important to schools. Whether change occurs as a result of self-renewal or continuous improvement programs, or as a result of adjustment to new and different environmental conditions, change must be viewed as an extension of administration and

normative action. The primary function of a school system is service, in the broadest sense, to its students, its community, and its political state. It is the responsibility of the school system to prepare our youth to function in an adult world. To do this, the school system must remain constantly aware of the nature and requirements of that environment. As the environment changes and as new technology, new social structures, and new values develop, schools must be aware of those changes and be prepared to adjust curriculum, instruction, and organization to remain viable.

While it is necessary for schools to remain sensitive to changes in the nature and expectations of their environments, there are also countervailing expectations that schools be conservators of culture, transmitting values and an understanding of the cultural history from one generation to the next. With these new cultural "tools" they can become the initiators of their own self-renewal and continuous improvement. School systems must remain constantly aware of the nature and lessons of the past, must constantly work to fit them into the current world, and must seek to create their own new futures. The task is formidable, but any less may be insufficient.

These expectations, that schools continuously monitor the environment, initiate self-renewal, and adjust to change while simultaneously remaining conservators of the past, mean that change in school systems will be fraught with complexity. Educational systems are in a constant state of dynamic tension, drawn between the natural responsiveness to change necessary in a dynamic system and the natural stability of a conservator. This tension generates resistance to change within the system and is a hallmark characteristic of educational systems in general. Schools, therefore, have in the past changed incrementally with too little consideration given to self-renewal or continuous improvement.

In any system, including educational systems, there is a built-in inertia that tends to maintain the stability of the organization. Kowalski and Reitzug (1993) noted that educational systems, as all social systems, develop a character that moves them toward resistance to change. A function of all such organizations is to provide a framework for values, beliefs, and practices that allow individuals to function effectively. In schools, policy, regulation, and curricula provide a meaningful environment for the work of teachers, students, and staff. Change may threaten this framework of meaning and produce anxiety and resistance.

Kowalski and Reitzug (1993) summarized the extensive discussion of the nature of change by noting that change occurs along a variety of continua. This continuum includes the source of change, the type of change, and the time orientation. "One change may be externally generated, unplanned, and spontaneous, whereas another may be internal, evolutionary, and planned" (Kowalski & Reitzug, 1993, p. 306). Internal variances by source might include curriculum committee actions and administrative initiatives. Pressure groups and court decisions would be considered external sources. Types of change include planned and unplanned. For example, an unexpected drop in funding that calls for budget cutbacks would be considered unplanned change while the use of long-range goals and objectives would be considered planned change. The time duration can vary from spontaneous to evolutionary, with changes occurring quickly versus changes occurring over a longer time frame.

Types of Change

Lipham, Rankin, and Hoeh (1985) conceptualized change as enforced, expedient, or essential. Enforced change is the result of needs identified from external forces. It would not have taken place if it were not for the external influence(s) involved. The task of leadership or management is to devise methods to cope with change, to act as a change-master. But, in this sense, the organization functions at the whims of others with more authority, influence, or political clout. Examples in the school environment could include state or federal mandates or the impact of community pressure groups. Expedient change generally involves meeting immediate concerns of external sources and is generally short-term or reactionary. Although it can also be internally driven, it is more likely that expedient change in the organization will result from meeting external demands. In each case the school system adjusts to the disequilibrium present and seeks to reestablish a status quo. Examples in the school environment could include last-minute changes in the school budget or storm damage to a school building.

Essential change is derived from internal rather than external sources. It is driven by the ability of the system to monitor itself and work toward improved performance. It requires that persons within the system work cooperatively to transform behavior or system components. In any system the ability to change is vital to the survival of the organism. Change may also be seen as planned or unplanned. Planned change, as defined by Owens (1987), is a deliberate attempt to direct change within a set of predetermined goals and values. Unplanned change is often enforced change, unanticipated, and often forced on a school system or an organization. It generally meets the needs of an external agent rather than the needs of the organization being changed. An example would be a merger of two small but functional school districts that resulted from the budgetary needs of the state rather than any dysfunction in the local districts. Expedient change is generally also unplanned, meeting operational needs as they arise but not causing deep adjustments in the nature or overall activities of the organization. Planned change, on the other hand, is foreseen and managed. It is brought about by persons directly connected within the system that is changing. Strategic planning in the school district would be an example of planned change.

Resistance to Change

Change efforts may be long awaited by some and strike fear in others. Change should be viewed as not only an intellectual process, but a psychological process as well. Psychologically, change may be resisted because of interference with self-esteem needs, social status, and relationship fulfillment. The most obvious sources of personal resistance to change originate in the individual's fear of the unknown. Organizational and individual routines have a high degree of certainty and are not easily altered without some opposition. People will resist change if they fear it will reduce their power and influence or make their knowledge and skills obsolete. Resistance arises from an individual's or a group's concerns about the innovation's applicability, perceptions of their own abilities, concerns about other changes taking place at the same time, and the support that they are provided in change situations.

Resistance to change is an emotional/ behavioral response to real or imagined threats to one's equilibrium or routine (Kreitner & Kinicki, 1989; Stanislao & Stanislao, 1983). Resistance can be manifest in overt or covert behaviors. Stanislao and Stanislao (1983) outlined eight reasons for employee resistance:

1. *Surprise and fear of the unknown.* This emerges when radically innova-

tive changes are introduced without warning or official announcement. The rumor mill creates its own informal sources of information.

2. *Climate of mistrust.* Mistrust can come from prechange organizational climates as well as from climates arising from the change process. The best conceived changes can be doomed by mutual mistrust—mistrust perpetuates mistrust. Leaders and followers both suffer as the motivation necessary to change is absent.

3. *Fear of failure.* Self-doubt and lack of confidence drain growth and development when change participants are not allowed to prepare for change by participating in decisionmaking or retraining.

4. *Loss of status and/or job security.* Resistance can quickly be triggered by real or perceived changes in power bases, loss of jobs, and loss of status due to administrative and technological changes.

5. *Peer pressure.* Resistance can arise in those not directly affected by the proposed change but also in those who anticipate negative effects on peers, colleagues, or friends.

6. *Disruption of cultural traditions and/or group relationships.* If it is believed that the human element is the backbone of the organization, any modifications in work or personal relationships caused by transfers, promotions, or reassignments alter group dynamics and create disequilibrium.

7. *Personality conflicts.* The personality of the change agent can breed resistance if adversarial relationships develop between the change agent, the change-inducing system, and the target system.

8. *Lack of tact or poor planning.* The system's readiness is a key ingredient in successful change. A good idea may fall flat, not

on its own merits, but due to poor timing or a poor manner of introduction.

The overall climate of the educational system will also have a major impact on the ability to create lasting change. Miskel and Ogawa (1988) defined climate as perceptions of expected work behavior. These perceptions are based on existing patterns of behavior and existing organizational characteristics, such as schedules, curricula, and so forth. Organizational culture, according to Rossman, Corbett, and Firestone (1988), is knowledge of how things are and how things ought to be. This knowledge includes basic assumptions and beliefs shared by members of the organization. The shared assumptions and beliefs have often been developed over time as the organization produces resolutions to the problems of response to external demands and to the need for internal integration.

Climate and culture combine to provide a powerful matrix in which individuals function within the educational system. Because climate and culture are in one sense the organizational memory and an action context, they are also a powerfully conservative force within the organization. Therefore, during organizational change, attempts that do not address culture and climate are at great risk of failure.

Change is resisted if it does not adhere to preestablished norms and values. Norms are products of culture in organizations and, according to Watson (1969), correspond to habits in individuals, making it possible for the members of the organization to work together. Norms, as representations of an invisible framework of standard beliefs and values, are valuable to the organization if they have worked well in the past, helped participants interpret daily occurrences, and minimized confusion. Strong norms that project integrity and sensibility in the organization, and are shared by the participants across organizational roles, are especially difficult to change.

Additional obstacles that may impede change include resource limitations or the inability to increase production, augment services, purchase new equipment, or hire staff. In contemporary school districts, an additional barrier to change may be collective bargaining agreements that commonly stipulate that specific changes in job descriptions may be subject to negotiation, thus placing added constraints on an administrator's ability to implement a desired change. Additionally, it is often the case that management and administrative responsibilities carry more importance than do leadership or change-agent roles. This barrier denigrates leadership and the ability of real change agents to act outside the normative/administrative functions of budgeting, scheduling, or even disciplinarian. Kowalski and Reitzug (1993) concurred and identified the structure of public schools as a quasi-monopoly, where bureaucratic structures with their division of responsibility and concentration of power create a sense of disenchantment and alienation on the part of many staff.

Connor and Lake (1988) grouped barriers to change into three general categories: (1) barriers to understanding, not fully understanding what is proposed; (2) barriers to acceptance, those affected will not accept the change; and (3) barriers to acting, factors inhibiting implementation. Basom and Crandall (1991) identified seven common barriers that were specific to change in schools: (1) discontinuity of leadership, (2) managers' fears that change was unmanageable, (3) lack of training in management regarding change, (4) following a top-down model of decision-making, (5) socialization and conditioning of school staff that leads to the belief that the system is not the problem, (6) unresolved competing visions of what schools should be, and (7) inadequate time and resources.

Research on barriers to change indicates that resistance can be reduced significantly when planning is cognizant of the barriers as described above. Broad support from the change agent is also valuable. Additionally, Fullan (1982) found that four other characteristics enhance the potential for success with regard to change: necessity, the need for change; clarity of purpose, clear and consistent procedures and objectives; complexity, whether change is worth the expanded effort; and practicality, the capability of putting the change into practice. In each of the preceding lists about how to accomplish change, the primacy of integrative elements is critical as they seek to define the complexity of change and, at the same time, demonstrate common action strategies.

Theoretical Implications of Change

Social thinking about change takes two different approaches. The first emphasizes a historical-deterministic thread that often reduces change to inexorable laws. In a second venue the human component is given center stage. Recognizing that greater knowledge and greater self-awareness leads to progressive improvement, the latter approach appears to have spearheaded the "widespread acceptance of change as a natural process and the equally widespread desire to mold that change in one direction or another—to imbue social change with human purpose." (Warren, 1977, p. 3)

Three major theoretical themes related to social change have emerged. In one view, change is seen on a grand scale, as a grand change theory. In this context, change explores a macro environment—total societies or total civilizations. The second theme looks for the general laws that account for these changes—laws that have energized

change in the past and would operate to shape the future as well. The third theme raises the question of whether deliberate intervention into social change processes is feasible or desirable. William Graham Sumner, an American sociologist and adherent of Herbert Spenser, saw direct intervention as undesirable and not feasible. Sumner wrote that change will occur as "the great stream of time and earthly things will sweep on just the same in spite of us" (Sumner, 1914, p. 209). While humans could attempt to modify and control, our efforts to create change would take a long time. The impact would at the most be slight. Another American sociologist, Lester F. Ward, took the active approach to social change and saw the whole development of knowledge and science serving to improve the human condition as its end, or development of a better human society (Warren, 1977).

Another sociologist more often cited by those interested in broad social planning and social intervention is Mannheim (1940). He cited three stages in the development of human society. The first is change by chance, discovery, trial, and error. The second is that of intervention, where intermediate processes and tools devised by humans enable them to pursue systematic social adjustment rather than merely accept society as it is. The third stage encompasses democratic planning. In this stage, most often observed in western society, various individual efforts are coordinated toward democratically agreed-upon ends. Both Mannheim and Ward, according to Warren (1977), were more interested in knowledge creation than in action or intervention strategies surrounding change.

Much of the action, intervention, and strategizing in social change literature focuses on three levels of social structure: across organizations, communities, and society. Organizational change literature falls into two camps. One focuses on the gradual change that formal organizations make over time and studies the complex processes that occur. The second focuses on planned or deliberate change and its outcomes. The intent is to learn how best to implement change objectives in organizations. Study of the formal organization, according to Warren, then forms the basis for understanding change at other levels of social structure, in communities and society. The second level of change literature is community development. Much of this literature evolves from the social action climate of the 1960s. Community organization and development projects emerged from attempts to bring about greater coordination among social service agencies. But this social action climate later broadened to include change in other parts of the community. Community change drives organizational change. The social macrocosm, national society, was the third level for planned social change. Societal change has a long history and is more closely related to the "grand theory" of social change (Warren, 1977). According to Warren, "Most major social change goals, whether or not this is recognized by their proponents, include or pre-suppose major changes in organizations, often in large numbers and types of them" (1977, p. 6).

The contexts of change in organizations are viewed through several different frameworks. The first and most prominent practice is through management. Change is seen through the eyes of the change agent since it is the change agents, most often leaders and managers, that dominate decisionmaking in most organizations. In another view, organizational change is assumed to occur from impetuses within the organization. Forces within the organization, scanning and responding to the environment, set the change process into motion. In this examination, change may be merely an adaptation to environmental changes, or it may be a comprehensive and more innovative approach intended to capitalize on opportunities presented from the environment.

Literature related to informal organizational structures centers about two schools of thought. Summarizing that literature, Warren (1977) noted that the work of such people as Bernard, Simon, Cyert, and March challenge the bureaucratic/rational model first proposed by Weber. He stated that Bernard saw organizations as not always functioning as rational decisionmaking units, but as organizational subsystems vying for different outcomes and making highly political decisions. More recently, he said, Argyris and Bennis emphasized the human relations aspects of change among people at and between all levels of the organization.

Investigations of organizational change over the years reveal that change does not necessarily occur solely as a result of management manipulation of the formal structure. Organizational change can also be supported or resisted by the informal structure created by networks of people who may seek quite diverse ends. The study of organizational change should consider both formal and informal structures.

To minimize the importance of informal structures on change efforts would create an inaccurate model for change. The significance of informal organizational structures was brought to light by the Hawthorne experiments of the 1930s. Informal structures came to be seen as fulfilling the function of making life more bearable while at the same time meeting the demands of the formal organization. The importance of informal structure in organizational change is now widely recognized in the abstract, if not always in actual practice (Warren, 1977).

Strategies of Change

Change strategies developed by various authors emphasize a variety of aspects of the process. Some attempt to encompass the entire process, while others are restricted to a particular focus. Most tend to be very general or descriptive rather than prescriptive (Warren, 1977, p. 33).

Chin and Benne (1969, 1976) trace change strategies to three basic roots: rational-empirical, normative-reeducative, and power-coercive. The rational-empirical model that underlies liberal education, scientific approaches to management, and expert or authoritarian views of what is right is clearly deterministic in nature. Normative-reeducative strategies are patterned after Kurt Lewin's (1951) work and emphasize intervention in a client system. Intervention strategies are devised based on the system's perception of its own problems and need for change. These strategies involve a change agent in collaboration with a client system working together to discover elements that may impede change. In essence, the change agent and the client search for a pathology and its remedy. The third strategy, the power coercive, applies political, economic, and moral power in order to manipulate or reconstitute power elites. This model underlies many of the community development and sociopolitical change strategies. Many consider them overly disruptive. Several strategies and models are outlined for comparison.

Change strategy can be seen as normative-reeducative. These models have been explored across a wide range of client systems: individual, small group, organizations, and large communities. In these models, a client voluntarily engages a consultant as a change agent. In partnership, the client and consultant use a five-stage change model to invoke change. The steps of the model include definition of the need for change, establishment of the change-client relationship, implementation of change strategies, generalization and stabilization of change, and achievement of a terminal relationship. The model is premised, however, on the importance of information flow. Information must be freely and openly shared between the target system and the change agent. This information is only useful if it can be translated into action.

Others have developed models that closely parallel the above. Ross (1967) demonstrated a four-stage model very similar to most problem-solving models. Bennis (1966) also devised a parallel model that demonstrates added consideration to a broader set of variables and results in a more lengthy topology. He outlined, as a result, eight different types of change: planned change, indoctrination, coercive change, technocratic change, interactional change, socialization change, emulative change, and natural change.

Kreitner and Kinicki (1989) profiled a three-way topology of change. They believed their strategy applies to all types of change scenarios, including administrative and technical. Furthermore, radically innovative change involving high degrees of complexity, cost, and uncertainty also breed great difficulty in implementation and, additionally, pose the greatest threat to participants.

Nutt (1986) contributed a five-stage model of change he called the Transactional Model. In this strategy, management and a development team occupy a central role. The manager represents formal authority and maintains ultimate responsibility for the proposed change. Change development and implementation occur through the combined efforts of management and development committees or project teams. The manager and teams interact in each stage of the process: defining needs, clarifying premises and assumptions, weighing alternatives, and installing the change. Management ensures that needed structures and mechanisms are in place for the teams. The constituents of the developmental teams assist in problem identification, suggest objectives, recommend options and tentative plans, consider costs and benefits, and gather feedback information once the change has been installed (Kreitner & Kinicki, 1989).

Walton (1965) proposed two strategies related to social change: a power strategy and attitude change strategy. The underlying assumption of the power strategy is that attainment of change is built on a power base involving the strategic manipulation of this power. Attitude change can best be achieved by developing mechanisms that promote trust and good will. The change objective involves both a desired concession and a reduction of intergroup hostility. While both strategies are useful, they may also demonstrate incompatibility. For example, hostile participants must learn to deal with power and trust, ambiguity and evasiveness, and bargaining through threat, and conversely deal with openness and frankness, and conciliatory gestures at the same time (Walton, 1965, cited in Warren 1977, p. 29).

Meyerson and Banfield's (1964) experience with the Chicago Housing Authority demonstrates a deterministic model. Their model involves: analysis of the situation, end reduction and elaboration, designing courses of action, and comparative evaluation of consequences. During analysis, attention is devoted to identifying opportunities and limiting conditions such that differentiation is possible between incidental ends and principal ends. As elaboration of principal ends occurs, developmental action can ensue to more specific levels. Consequences are then evaluated for effectiveness across cost/benefits criteria.

Lauer's process (1973) incorporates targets of change, agents of change, and methods of change. Targets of change may be individuals, groups, or societies, or some combination. Differing strategies are undertaken depending on the chosen target of change. For example, if the change target is a group, then change may be sought through recomposition of the group itself. Two forms of change agents may emerge, authoritative or participative. Lauer, like Walton, also found a distinction between power and attitude strategies. Lauer asserted that attitude strategies are best directed at changing individuals and gaining mass support for developmental programs, while power strategies are applied more within social movements and organizational and interorganizational change.

Kostler's process (1972, in Lauer, 1973) is one of social action rather than social change. This strategy addresses three causes of social change: helping, protest, and revolution. These self-explanatory causes are the objectives or goals that those undertaking the change believe will remedy an identified problem. This discussion also addressed the concept of change agency, identifying two types: leaders and supporters. Kostler's strategies for change include: power, persuasion, and reeducative strategies. Targets of change can be classified as ultimate targets and intermediate targets. These targets are acted upon through response or influence channels.

Lewin (1951) provided one of the earliest models of planned change. His model focuses on identifying and using sets of forces to bring about change. According to Lewin, states of equilibrium are maintained by two sets of forces, those maintaining the status quo and those that push for change. Both sets of forces must be present at relatively equal levels of tension for equilibrium to exist. To bring about change it is necessary to shift tension toward change forces and away from state-maintaining forces. Various combinations can be seen; for example, by pushing for change and decreasing maintenance forces, change should occur more rapidly. Lewin felt that tension and resistance related to change could be minimized if the chosen approach involved modifying state-maintaining forces. This modification of state-maintaining forces can be encouraged by instituting three steps: unfreezing, changing, and refreezing. Lewin's model provides a general framework for understanding organizational change.

Lastly, the Action Research Model of Huse and Cummings (1985) holds broad applicability and is adaptable to fit many differing situations. This model focuses on planned change as a cyclic process involving collaboration between organization members and organizational development practitioners. It places strong emphasis on data collection and diagnosis, as well as careful evaluation of action results. The model involves seven steps, including:

1. *Problem identification.* Key organizational members who influence and hold power identify problems that might need attention.

2. *Consultation.* The change agent and the client begin developing a relationship wherein the change agent, mindful of the assumptions and values of both systems, shares his or her frame of reference with the client. This sharing establishes a beginning, essential atmosphere of openness and collaboration.

3. *Data gathering and preliminary diagnosis.* This stage takes place in collaboration with the change agent and members of the organization. Four basic data collection tools may be used: interviews, questionnaires, process observations, and organizational performance. Using different data collection tools assures a more holistic set of data.

4. *Feedback.* Data gathered must be fed back to the client, usually in a group or work team meeting. The change agent provides the client with all relevant and useful data, which in turn helps these groups to determine the strengths and weaknesses of the system or subsystem under study.

5. *Joint diagnosis of the problem.* A diagnosis and recommendation, to be useful, must be understood and accepted. This occurs through an ongoing collaborative process where data and diagnosis are shared with the group for validation and further diagnosis. Schein (1969) noted that the failure to establish a common frame of reference in the client-consultant relationship may lead to faulty diagnosis or a communication gap, whereby the client is sometimes unwilling to accept the diagnosis and recommendations (p. 98).

6. *Action.* A joint agreement is reached with regard to the chosen action. This is the beginning of the unfreezing process, as the organization moves toward a different state-maintaining equilibrium.

7. *Data gathering after action.* The cyclic process begins with the recollection of data as it relates to the actions taken. The action is monitored and measured to determine the effects of the action taken. Feedback of the results are communicated to the organization. This, in turn, leads to redefinition of the diagnosis and new action.

Models for Planned Change and Their Use

Beckhard and Harris (1977) presented a general model of change that encompasses a number of aspects of the planned change process. The general model had six facets: (1) diagnosing the present condition, including the need for change; (2) setting goals and defining the new state or condition after the change; (3) defining the transition state between the present and the future; (4) developing strategies and action plans for managing the transition; (5) evaluating the change effort; and (6) stabilizing the new conditions and establishing a balance between stability and flexibility.

Most models of change have steps similar to the Beckhard and Harris general model above. There are a variety of other strategies for initiating and managing models of planned change. Lipham, Rankin, and Hoeh (1985) identified four models: problem solving, research-development-diffusion-utilization, social interaction, and linkage.

PROBLEM-SOLVING MODELS

Any organizational change, according to Lippett, Langseth, and Mossop (1985) is directed toward one specific end. "They are all initiated in order to achieve some organizational objective and to solve problems" (p. 27). Hersey and Blanchard (1988) noted that a problem exists " . . . when there is a discrepancy between what is actually happening (the real) and what you or someone who hired you . . . would like to be happening (the ideal)" (p. 334). A problem situation in a school setting might involve a high level of absenteeism by students, a significant dropout rate, or poor achievement test scores.

Most problem solving models involve the following elements: (1) *Diagnosis*. The problem is noticed, identified, and defined; (2) *Alternative solutions*. A variety of possible solutions are developed, and the actions necessary to accomplish them are outlined; (3) *Selection and implementation*. One possible solution is selected, based on its appropriateness and feasibility, and the solution is applied; (4) *Evaluation*. The results of the actions taken are monitored. If the problem has been resolved, action ceases except to consider how to avoid the problem in the future. If the problem is not resolved, further alternative solutions are considered and the model is recycled as appropriate.

The most appropriate applications of the problem-solving model, according to Lipham et al. (1985), occur when problem solving is a norm within the system, when there is effective leadership to sustain the model, when problem solving is an agreed upon vehicle for accomplishing change, and when time, space, and finances allow solution of the problem.

RESEARCH-DEVELOPMENT-DIFFUSION-UTILIZATION MODELS (RDDU)

Research-development-diffusion-utilization, like the problem solving models, is also a rational-empirical approach to managing planned change. It provides a systematic framework for change. The RDDU model involves the following elements: (1) *Research*. Research leads to the discovery or invention of new knowledge, products, or techniques; (2) *Development*. The new knowledge, product, or technique is validated through pilot testing and experimentation, and then modified as appropriate for practical use; (3) *Diffusion*. The new knowledge, product, or technique is packaged appropriately and marketed; (4) *Utilization*. If it is supported, encouraged, and accepted, the new knowledge, product, or technique becomes a new element in the overall system. This model is most applicable when there are cooperative arrangements among developers, users, and distributors, when research products are perceived as legitimate solutions to real-world problems, and when there is political support and leadership that encourages the use of research.

RDDU models, according to Havelock (1973), are based on a series of assumptions. First, there should be a rational sequence in the evolution and application of the change. Second, because the innovations under consideration are usually major, planning may take a long period of time. Third, the recipients of the changes are assumed to be passive but willing beneficiaries of the change.

SOCIAL INTERACTION MODELS

Social interaction models are also a rational approach to change. These models assess the need for change based on communication and information from outside the system, and involve members of the change system in planning and implementation. Active participation in the process by the members of the system is the norm unlike the passive role members played in the RDDU models.

There are typically four stages in social interaction models: (1) *Knowledge*. Leaders and/or members of the system have information about a proposed innovation; (2) *Persuasion*. Members of the system are provided with information leading to positive (or negative) attitudes about the proposed innovation; (3) *Decision*. Members of the system can accept or reject the proposed innovation; (4) *Confirmation*. There is confirmation from peers that the decision to adopt or reject was appropriate.

The most effective use of the social interaction models occurs when there is support to establish external contacts, when opportunities to gather external information, such as journals and conferences, are available, when there are funds to purchase products, and when there is a desire to gain status or recognition. The social interaction model is widely used in educational systems.

LINKAGE MODELS

Linkage models encompass elements of the problem solving, RDDU, and social interaction models. An agent within the system has an interest both within and outside of the system, thereby serving as a link.

Stages involved in linkage models include the following: (1) *Identification*—a problem is identified and defined; (2) *Communication*—communication channels linking the system to outside resources are established; (3) *Research*—external information and/or skills bearing on the defined problem

are sought out and acquired; (4) *Solution*—with the assistance of the external resource, a solution to the problem is identified or designed; (5) *Implementation*—the solution is applied; (6) *Evaluation*—the applied solution is monitored, often in collaboration with the external resource, and appropriate action follows if necessary. Linkage models offer the best of all worlds in that they encompass many of the parameters of other models.

Leadership and Change

Throughout this book leadership and management have been defined and contrasted to management. Leadership is a process whereby leaders and followers intend mutually agreed upon changes, while management involves an authority relationship that is intended to meet a specific goal, between a manager and at least one subordinate. Leadership may be a requisite factor to create and spearhead change, while management is necessary in order to maintain the stability of the educational system.

London (1988) suggested that change agents are leaders and managers who see a need for change, visualize what can be, and seek those strategies that will produce the required effect. The classical rational vista of leadership focuses on two groups: those who are in charge and those who are not. The classical theorists define roles and delineate hierarchical structures and patterns of interaction. The classical rational view is impersonal, formal, and task-centered. It focuses on optimizing organizational performance by optimizing organizational structure. It suggests a structural approach to change where emphasis is on unilateral decisionmaking, where people are assumed to be highly rational, and where authoritative directions are considered the best motivator of results (Grenier, 1989). It is assumed that compliance will lead to more effective results. The classical approach often uses leadership and management interchangeably. Likewise, change strategies in this arena are also rational.

Participative leadership models, in contrast, view the organization as a democratic network having as its goal establishment of an environment that addresses the needs of its members and those functionally related to it (Lorsch & Trooboff, 1989). Supportive leadership, group decisionmaking, and open channels of communication and information flow contribute to the maintenance of a healthy organization. This model suggests that key people be made a part of the change process. "According to participative designers, change should start by altering the most influential causal variables affecting what needs to be changed. Then there should be systematic plans prepared to modify all other affected parts of the organization in carefully coordinated steps" (Lorsch & Trooboff, 1989, p. 74). Authority may be present, but there is a sharing of power. Group decisionmaking and group problem solving both reflect the participative approach to change.

Organizations, particularly educational organizations, are essentially bureaucratic in design and highly rational. However, leadership within the bureaucratic structure is a decidedly social concept "for it automatically presumes an interactive condition between leaders and followers" (Monahan & Hengst, 1982, p. 220). Leaders do not exist in a vacuum; leadership is a group phenomenon. Much of the literature on leadership focuses on how the leader views himself or herself in relation to followers or subordinates. The leader may assume an autocratic or democratic stance, or employ an interactional or situational approach to leadership and change.

Contingency and situational approaches recognize that position is not enough to ensure commitment or compliance. However, compliance may be enhanced through interpersonal interactions. The situational approach suggests that leadership in organi-

zations is more dependent on its members and the nature of the circumstances that confront the organization. "The leadership task within this context is to relate specific behaviors to effective group performance and satisfaction" (Monahan & Hengst, 1982, p. 248). Change in this environment tends toward a rational and reeducative stance.

WHAT IS A CHANGE AGENT OR CHANGE SYSTEM?

A change agent is a person, group, or organization seeking to produce change in a system. The change agent may be external to the target system or may be an element in the target system. The change agent may initiate the change in question or may join a change process already under way and facilitate the activity. The change agent may be a chief executive officer, foreman, school superintendent, or principal.

Change agents, initiators of change, also may or may not hold formal leadership roles within the target system. In these instances, it is vital to the success of the effort that significant elements of the formal leadership be incorporated into the change system. When that is not possible or when the leadership is in active opposition to the change effort, it may be necessary to supplement the existing leadership, change it, or force it into compliance with the effort.

A change system, according to Warren (1977), is the set of connections established between the change agent and the target system in which change is desired. This may be a system separate from the target system, or, in the case of self-change, the change system may be a subset of the target system.

CHARACTERISTICS OF EFFECTIVE CHANGE AGENTS

Effective change agents know about the task at hand, understand the cultural context in which the task must be performed, know their followers, and know themselves, according to Hodgkinson (1991). They are generally leaders who see a need for change, visualize what can be done, and move toward the strategies necessary to accomplish their ends. Effective leaders (change agents) possess high intellect, high initiative, strong orientation to both people and goal accomplishment, and a clear vision of what the organization can be. (Mazarella & Grundy, 1988; Stogdill, 1974; Yukl, 1981).

FUNCTIONS OF EFFECTIVE CHANGE AGENTS

Change agents perform three functions in establishing an effective change-inducing system. These are recruitment, development, and control. Since the change agent working alone is unlikely to be successful in seeking change, one necessary function is recruitment of like-minded persons or subsystems. Warren (1977) pointed out that the larger and more complex the system, the more likely it is that there will be others either actively seeking change or predisposed toward it.

Development of a change-inducing system may involve creating a coalition or mobilizing already existing change-minded individuals or groups to take control of assets they did not previously control. In either case, as the process develops, three issues arise. One is to balance inclusion with coherence. That is, the more individuals or subgroups who are involved in the change effort the better, as long as the original purposes remain clear and coherent. The second is to balance the original goals with the interests and positions of new members of the change group, and not to be diverted toward other and sometimes private ends. Third, the change-inducing system should not exist for its own sake but in order to accomplish a clearly defined end. If resources are diverted to maintain the change-inducing system for its own sake rather than meeting the original goals, that perverts the process.

The change agent's ability to balance control of the change process and share control when appropriate is the third function to consider. Once the change system is established, the change agent will begin to lose sole control of the process. Sharing of control is necessary in order to broaden the base of the effort. Ideally, shared values among the members of the change system will lead to shared understandings and effective decisions made by consensus.

Another concern for the change agent is the appropriate degree of change to be undertaken. This issue leads to incremental change, planning for change in stages with careful checks at intermediate points. This may lead to reducing the difficulty of the change objective, while at the same time increasing the likelihood of success. Given these concerns, the change agent needs to be sensitive to what is possible as well as what is desirable. Viewing the task in this way will lead the successful change agent to the development of allies, access to additional resources and sources of power when appropriate, and development of long-range multilevel plans that have an improved chance of success. Even in the best of situations, the change agent may well run into either passive or active resistance. There is a variety of tactics that the change agent may use to reduce that resistance.

Lunenberg and Ornstein (1991) stated that change agents use six methods to reduce resistance to change. (1) *Participation*—involvement of those who will be affected by the change to participate in the planning, design, and implementation. Participation establishes ownership, builds commitment, and reduces anxiety; (2) *Communication*—employees need to know the purpose of the change and how it will affect them; (3) *Support*—high-level support generates commitment; (4) *Rewards*—resistance will be less if some benefit, tangible or intangible, is seen; (5) *Planning*—well thought-out infusion processes should be designed; and (6) Coercion—though coercion may ensure that change occurs, it may also produce anger and resentment.

Kanter (1983) contended that "change brings pain when it comes as a jolt, when it is seemingly abrupt and shocking. The threat of change arouses anxiety when it is still just a threat and not an actuality, while too many possibilities are still open and before people can experience themselves in a new state" (p. 63). Feelings, thoughts, and actions that affect the lives of those who populate the system will influence how they react to change.

Huse (1975) cited several factors that aid in reducing resistance to change. (1) Any change process needs to take into account the needs, attitudes, and beliefs of the individuals involved, as well as the forces of organization. The individual must perceive some personal benefit to be gained from the change before willingness to participate in the change process will be forthcoming. (2) The greater the prestige of the supervisor, the greater the influence he or she can exert for change. (3) Strong pressure for changes in behavior can be established by providing specific information desired by the group about itself and its behavior. The more central, relevant, and meaningful the information, the greater the possibility for change. (4) Facts developed by the individual or the group, or the involvement and participation by the individual or the group in the planning, gathering, analysis, and interpretation of data, highly influence the change process. (5) Change that originates from within is much less threatening and creates less opposition than change that is proposed from the outside. (6) Information relating to the need for change, plans for change, and consequences of change must be shared by all relevant people in the group.

London (1988) also identified several factors that can aid in minimizing resistance to change. (1) Evaluate the characteristics of the change. Consider complexity, psychological and financial cost, the extent to which the purpose and intended outcome are clear, and the amount of mutual agreement. (2) Consider who and what is affected by the change. Try to determine how the change affects the work that is done and the working and personal relationships of those affected. (3) Envision how the change will be implemented. Reduce uncertainty to a minimum. (4) Be prepared for multiple interventions. As an example, training staff for new tasks will not necessarily be effective unless the social system and the reward structure reinforce the desirability of implementing the new behavior.

The key point is that planned change is most effective when human systems are an integral part of the change process. Whether it focuses on the introduction of new personnel or new technologies, planned change must be based on knowledge and must incorporate strategies derived from such knowledge (Chin & Benne, 1969).

Effective change agents are systems thinkers prepared for and planning for the complexities of multisystem interactions and long-term ripple effects once a change is implemented. Indeed, they should be prepared for such complexities once a change is suggested, since the anticipation of change will often produce an impact of its own.

Implementing this multisystem interactions perspective by the change agent involves development of clear answers to questions related to the situation, not only for the change agent but for all involved in the process. Essential questions for condition are: (1) What is to be changed? (2) Why is it to be changed? (3) How is it to be changed? (4) When is it to be changed? (5) Who will be involved in the change? (6) What barriers to the change will need to be overcome? (7) What impact can reasonably be expected on individuals, on subsystems, on the overall system, on the external environment? (8) What support for the change can be expected? (9) What will be the costs of the change? (10) What will be the benefits of the change?

Managing Planned Change

Beckhard and Harris (1977) present a general model that outlines six aspects of management of the change process. (1) Diagnose the present condition, including the need for change. (2) Set goals and define the new state or condition after the change. (3) Define the transition state between the present and the future. (4) Develop strategies and action plans for managing this transition. (5) Evaluate the change effort. (6) Stabilize the new conditions and establish a balance between stability and flexibility.

Beckhard and Harris emphasize that there are two essential conditions for any change effort to be effectively managed. First, the organization leadership must be aware of the need for change and the consequences of their actions. Second, the desired end state must be relatively explicit. A clear differentiation between causes and symptoms is an essential component of the first aspect of the change process. What often occurs is poor system diagnosis that provides an inaccurate statement of the change problem. Change strategies can be effective if the symptom statement describes the fundamental condition needing change. Diagnosis must include probable causes of the problems as well as a goal statement. Such questions as "What would be different or better?" and "How much does it matter?" would provide clarity for the problem and goal statement. Problem definition and goal setting are interlinked and both must be explicit. It is important to recognize that, although the concern for change is often triggered by the existence of some need or set of problem symptoms, it is the goal set by the leadership that should be the

determining factor in defining both the strategy and direction for change (Beckhard & Harris, 1977, p. 20).

Detailed attention is required to define the present system and develop a description of what the system will appear to be when the desired change is achieved. In defining the present system, many organizations embark on a change process with erroneous assumptions about the current state of the organization. If action plans are developed on an inaccurate set of assumptions and then implemented, resistance, confusion, frustration, and general failure to achieve desired goals will result. Analyzing the present scenario involves analyzing what subsystems of the system are most significantly involved in the change process and what changes in their present attitudes or behavior or ways of work would have to occur if the desired goal is to be reached.

This requires a total organization perspective, since change in one part of the system will affect the total system. It is best to anticipate the degree and direction of anticipated change within the total system. This allows a proactive stance rather than a reactive stance to changes in subsystems that were not direct targets of the change process.

An additional focus is on the processes that would need to be changed in order for the overall innovation to be effective. These could include required changes in attitude, practices, policy, and structure including rewards. Once a diagnosis is complete, priorities need to be set, keeping in mind the potential domino effect inherent in the change process.

Continuing the assessment process, there must be a clear understanding of each subsystem's readiness and capacity for change. Motivation to change is directly related to readiness and capability. The state of readiness to change is closely connected to attitudes of the system. Attitudes of the subsystem toward anticipated change will be influenced by assumptions, reality based or perceived, about the effect of the change as it relates directly to this subsystem. The success of change efforts is influenced as much by the processes of change as it is by the actual tasks involved. Capacity for change is related to readiness and encompasses analysis of available resources to support the change and offset negative consequences. Resources include not only personnel and equipment, but also technology, time, and funds.

Will the expected ends derived from the change offset the costs involved? This question can only be answered accurately if a whole system analysis is done. What may appear to have positive benefits for one part of the system may have immediate or long-term negative effects on other crucial elements.

The quality of input information in any decisionmaking process will directly affect the appropriateness of the decision. The input information, according to Beckhard and Harris (1977, p. 28), includes determining (1) the degree of choice whether to change, (2) what needs changing, (3) where to intervene and (4) intervention technologies.

Forces for change may be internal or external. Often forces outside the system call for change. Under these circumstances the leadership may have limited control over events. This control may only extend to the means of making the change or coping with the results.

Decisionmaking

Change in any part of a system will create change requirements in other parts of the system. Given that, the question becomes, which change is the best approach for solving a particular problem? This is a particularly important concept in considering change in an educational system that operates with multiple layers of subsystems, each with its own goals and objectives that must be taken into consid-

eration if the effort to change is not to be self-defeating.

Decisionmaking has been described elsewhere in this book as a matter of choosing among alternatives. These choices involve assessment of the level of risk involved, the amount of information available, some level of rationality (although most recent students of decisionmaking note that rationality is not the only base for making individual choices), evaluation of preferences, identification of probable consequences, and communication of the decision.

Training of educational leaders and managers has traditionally included efforts to improve decisionmaking skills. This is seen as particularly important since the educational decisionmaker functioning in a public arena makes decisions and communicates them in a highly politicized environment. Decisionmaking in this situation often calls for the ability to bargain and negotiate in the manner described by Lindbloom (1965), as well as for significant communications skills.

Decisionmaking in education has a heightened level of risk because full information is rarely available. Therefore, the educational decisionmaker generally operates on the basis of Simon's "bounded rationality": considering the real world situation as he or she sees it, reviewing the choices, and then constructing a simplified model through which a decision can be made. While the behavior is rational within the frame of reference of the model, the rationality is bounded in the sense that the effective decisionmaker understands the model to be limited by such factors as time and available information, and, therefore, is incomplete.

Once a choice has been made to initiate change, it remains to determine what needs changing and increase the system's readiness and capacity for the change. Here the need for unfreezing and freezing techniques may be considered as a means of increasing readiness and capability. This is particularly true if a system's norms, attitudes, and ways of work are entrenched. Goal setting exercises may be helpful if the system's goals are not shared. Structural change would be called for if the organizational chart does not reflect the new tasks to be done. New information or technical knowledge or skills may be required to achieve the change conditions.

Following the decision to initiate change and identification of change targets, there must be a determination of where to begin. Potential targets could include the top of the system, subsystems known to be ready for and capable of change, the "hurting system," or new teams or systems that may be more open to change because of a lack of history and experience in the old ways.

Change needs to be initiated and moved forward. This is accomplished by selecting the appropriate intervention techniques and technologies. Beckhard and Harris (1977) made several points about these choices. One is to identify and think through the most likely possible early activities and their consequences. They also warned against falling into the "quick fix" trap or the assumption that "we only need . . . [a Management by Objectives system, a planning exercise, new training programs]. . . ." What may be needed to initiate and move the change process forward is creation of a temporary system that can raise the possibility of novel solutions involving new approaches. It can be very difficult for a stable system to change itself.

Much can be accomplished through the use of planned change models, but there is no guarantee that these models will be appropriate. Problems may arise with the process: consultants can become wedded to one technique to the exclusion of others, organizations may not be willing to do what is necessary for success, or management may only want to buy into certain steps or may focus on validating their own or earlier positions. These and other problems may arise not from the change model but from its implementation.

Effecting Educational Change

Change is ever present in schools, as it is in any organization. Given the variety of challenges that educational systems face today, the ability to cope with change becomes even more of a necessity. (Cetron & Gayle, 1991; Mauriel, 1989; Millard, 1991). The shift of school ownership, advent of the information age, demographic shifts in funding, growing poverty among underclass children, demands of new market segments, and the quality of output of schools all have focused attention on reexamination of the efficiency and effectiveness of school systems.

Planned change in schools, however, is affected by the particular nature of educational systems. Schools tend to be loosely coupled with vague system boundaries, diffuse goals, relatively low technical capacity, a constrained decentralized structure, and a noncompetitive environment. These characteristics make effecting change in schools somewhat different from effecting change in other social organizations.

In the past, change in American education was viewed as an evolutionary process, a process of natural diffusion. As a result, the systems changed quite slowly. Mort and Ross (1957) reported that the average American school lagged a quarter-century behind the best practice of the time. However, as the pace of change has increased in society, natural diffusion of educational change has given way to planned, managed diffusion (Owens, 1987). This shift has led to identification of a number of models for change that fit educational systems.

MODELS FOR EDUCATIONAL CHANGE

Educational change can be considered in terms of the problem solving, social interaction, research-development-diffusion-utilization, and linkage models discussed in this chapter. In recent years, these models have been refined to fit the specific nature of educational systems.

The problem solving model is based on a rational approach to change. It is user-centered, featuring user diagnosis of problems with emphasis on building the problem solving capacity of users. There are four basic stages: diagnosis of the problem, development of a number of alternatives, implementation of selected alternative(s), and evaluation of the outcomes. This model is useful when there is sufficient time and funding, there is little controversy, and the staff has an open mind. School systems have used this approach to change frequently in the past. But as complexity has grown, so too has the ineffectiveness of these simplistic models.

The social interaction model emphasizes communication channels and messages for diffusing innovations, interpersonal influence, and the impact of external stimuli for adoption of changes. Four stages are involved: knowledge of the innovation, persuasion leading to the formation of attitudes about the innovation, a decision to adopt or reject the innovation, and confirmation by peers of the decision. This model can be effective when the organization provides sufficient information, when the information is accessible, and when sound organizational communication networks exist. As society continues to change rapidly, schools will need to use these models more frequently as constituents will demand greater and greater say.

The research-development-diffusion-utilization model identifies four stages in the change process: research on a given topic, frameworks formed from the research findings, diffusion of the new knowledge, product, or techniques, and implementation of the change. This model can be effective when planning on a massive scale is desirable, when rational division of labor and coordination of tasks is essential, when a cooperative arrangement exists among developers, distributors, and users, and when there is sufficient time to discover and implement new products or processes. The model can be particularly useful considering the overwhelming magnitude of change needed in education today.

The linkage model involves reciprocal change. This model emphasizes establishing communications networks among the sources and users of an innovation. The user establishes a reciprocal relationship with outside sources who are experiencing events that correspond with the events experienced by the user. There are three basic elements to this model: identifying potential need for change, establishing effective communication channels, and transmitting new knowledge from researchers to potential users. This model is useful when the school administrator who must effect the change is able to connect with the larger educational community and serve as a change agent through all stages of the change process.

PHASES OF EDUCATIONAL CHANGE

Effective educational change may come in a variety of sizes and shapes, depending upon the system involved and the circumstances. However, the four models discussed above suggest a general model comprised of a combination of several stages: awareness, initiation, implementation, routinization, renewal, and evaluation (Lipham, Rankin, & Hoeh, 1985).

The awareness stage of this general model involves the discovery of problems that indicate anomalies in the present goals or programs. Participation of staff is helpful in clarifying goals, identifying discrepancies, defining problems, and identifying tentative alternatives for improving existing conditions. The initiation stage involves evaluation of current conditions and practices in terms of existing goals and exploring both expanded and ultimate goals, along with various means for achieving them. At this point, decisions are made for further action. Implementation is the next stage of this general model. Activities to assist the full staff in understanding and initiating change are begun. Approval, commitment, and cooperation of others are important. The basic problems, goals, and roles of change are identified at this stage. Once the change is implemented, routinization is the next stage. Change agents assist implementers in their efforts. A facilitative, supportive environment must be established. Decisionmaking moves from the group to the individual level. In the renewal stage, implementers develop their ability to maintain the change and continue appropriate use without external help. A supportive climate will encourage high morale. Continuous feedback on the ongoing change continues the change moving toward the desired goal. Evaluation is the feedback loop that reveals ways to improve the change. With utilization of this model, the change process and outcomes are continually monitored and evaluated. Both formative and summative approaches to evaluation are employed. Criteria for evaluation are developed very early in the change process and are used to guide the evaluation efforts. Positive results open the way to routinization and renewal. Negative results point in the direction of other alternatives for change.

EFFECTIVE CHANGE AGENTS IN SCHOOLS

Moving an educational system through a desired change requires the efforts of a leader who functions as a change agent. In most cases, the person will either be a formal organizational leader or will be brought in from the external environment. External consultants have proven useful in developing and guiding educational change, particularly when the educational administrators involved have limited experience in implementing change.

A change agent must be able to identify and analyze complex organizational problems, must have insight into the effects of culture and climate on employees, must be able to conceptualize and implement broad plans for change, must be able to share power and develop consensus for collaborative decisions, must be able to maintain the openness of the educational system while monitoring the quality of input, output, and change, and must be able to maintain the positive aspects of the system while working toward improvement through change. Ultimately, since a leader (either system administrator or consultant) by definition does not work in isolation, the change agent must be able to assist others to develop appropriate goals, motivations, and behaviors that will lead to the desired ends. Effective change agents recognize that implementing major change takes time. Enough time must be allowed for modifying existing roles or creating new roles and then internalizing the changes.

As change agent, an educational administrator serves as catalyst, resources linker, solution giver, and process helper (Havelock, 1973; Lippett & Lippett, 1985). A change agent serves as a catalyst because of the built-in inertia of systems leading to reluctance to change. The change agent can become a source of pressure helping staff to see the need for change. As a resource linker, the change agent can bring human and nonhuman resources together, either external or internal to the system, and help to make the most effective use of those resources. During the process of change, the change agent can help set objectives, acquire resources, select solutions, adapt solutions, and evaluate the process and results.

Steeples (1990) elaborated on these tasks of the change agent in discussing management of change in higher education. He noted that the issue for leaders in higher education (and, by extension, in educational systems generally) is not whether or not to change, but which changes will be required. A first consideration is to understand the necessity of identifying goals and means to accomplish change. Even when it is clear that external or internal developments dictate a change, it is not always obvious what changes are appropriate. Therefore, decisions about change must be based on a strategic concept. The educational leader must create a strategic vision that must precede and help structure plans for innovation, so that the change meets more than short-term needs. "Properly undertaken, strategic planning can provide the vision which will show the way for meaning, purposeful institutional change" (Steeples, 1990, p. 103).

Planning for a Changing Future in Education

Cunningham (1982) proposed that school administrators or managers of educational systems must work to anticipate the future. As decisionmakers today, their roles as change agents are critical. "Those who cannot project themselves into the future can only respond to the immediacy of the present, unable to envision and assess possible futures," he warned (p. 246). "The administrator cannot just decide whether or not to make decisions with futurity in mind; he or she must make them by the definition of the role" (p. 247) He argued for the skill of anticipation as a key element in the success of any administrator or manager. Anticipation is the ability to foresee and evaluate the medium and long-range future consequences of current decisions. It is a key to effective planning, and so to effective management of long-range change.

The Fate of Educational Changes

Even with the best intent in the world, no change can be considered permanent. Some take hold, flourish, meet long-term needs, and become an integral part of the original system. Some meet relatively short-term needs and disappear when the need is gone. Some flash brightly, but briefly, and are just as quickly gone.

Goodlad, reviewing the school reforms of the 1960s, commented that, while much good could be found in many new practices, many suffered from unrealistic expectations on the part of practitioners, members of the school systems, and members of the general community. He called the period " . . . an extraordinarily innovation period in American education . . . [that] ended in considerable disillusionment regarding the potency of schools, in large part (because) of unreasonable expectations." (Goodlad, in Knezevich, 1984, p. 112).

Problematic Features of Change

As may be assimilated from the brief comment by Goodlad, change may be problematic. As with all theorizing and praxis, models of change may be too rational, too constrained, and too systematic. Some have concluded that our understanding of change may be ill-founded (Pettigrew, 1985; Alderfer, 1977). A brief review of problematic features follows (Srivastva, Fry, & Associates, 1992).

Models of change frequently require practitioners to use a process that only provides brief glimpses of reality. Models are often too linear and forego the dynamics of organizational life. Change may not be the phenomenon that begins, happens, and ends. It may be drastically more disorderly than theorized. Change agents need to be more cognizant of the daily complexity found in organizational life and adapt action methodologies that observe what choices are framed with why choices are made.

Equally critical are change scenarios that lack sufficient time horizons. Seldom are change intervention strategies concerned with lengths of time sufficient to display alternate rationale for the events observed. In most studies of organizational culture, the broad history of basic assumptions is equally important to the constrained views most models presume. Change must be immersed in the totality of organizational life, its old practices and its new ones. Both are necessary if cohesion is to be satisfied.

Srivastva, Fry, and Associates (1992) also concluded that the study of change in organizations may lack true systemic understanding. More often than not, the study of change excludes interrelationships, interdependencies, environmental contingencies, and relationship factors. The context of change may be equally as important as identifying common characteristics or factors. As is often the case, the best change programs may be employed without understanding their context and, more inappropriately, with purposeful disregard for important contextual parameters. Organizational change must be linked to its total environment, along with assurance of continuity with social, technical, and ecological consequences of organizational action. Understanding the systemic context of change is paramount to thorough change modeling.

Concomitantly, change often is paralyzed in the existing, often limited, paradigms. As is often the case in organizational change study, frames are bipolar. There is Theory X or Theory Y. There are democratic or authoritarian styles. In reality, multiplicity is evident as change strategies often encompass situational or contingency approaches. Even multiplicity can be a trap. It is possible to comprehend what applications are available, but not why. A thorough understanding of change can seemingly only be formative if it is interpretive and interactive in its utilization of knowledge and conversion to praxis.

Lastly, Srivastva, Fry, and Associates (1992) challenged the deterministic/outcome orientations of change strategies. This may also result from a highly systematic approach to change. While we view organizations as open systems, we also tend to worry more about the effects of remaining a closed system. In this regard, we rarely mobilize energy to change, but more often draw attention to resistance factors. As a result, our models may be focused on reduction of barriers at the expense of equi-final methodologies.

In the above display of problematic features, a distinctive summons can be noted for a more systemic understanding of change. The organizational world is full of examples that demonstrate the systemic nature of organizational functioning. Schools often exhibit their systemic proclivities in spite of their traditional bureaucratic form. For example, teachers ignore the mandates of curriculum with results equal to or better than prescribed by mandates, alternate organizational structures increase teacher and administrator latitudes and work equally well, and new basics (critical thinking and creativity development) create more well-rounded graduates. Our attention needs to focus on why these work and where they work, as much as on what they are and the processes involved. Just as important, our search for whys must include thinking about new methodologies. As Srivastva, Fry, and Associates (1992) believe, "Our cup is partly full (with useful models, guidelines, and experiences), it is also partly empty" (p. 9).

■ CASE STUDY I

The Total Quality School

Numerous change programs have been instituted within education to curb the seemingly unlimited attacks about poor quality in schooling today in America. The precepts of Total Quality Management (TQM) have been adjusted to the educational environment and adopted in varying degrees at educational institutions. These new quality schools may be the "ticket" for the future. As the educational environment settles into TQM, the business community begins to sound alarms. Some are labeling TQM efforts in industry as dead, another quick fix that has all but failed. The following vignette relates the story of a fictitious school system that adopted TQM and sensed some problems. Read the case attached. When you have finished reading, continue the discussion of the group. What options do you see? Why are we so willing to do away with recent change? How does change affect us? How do we better cope with change from an administrative point of view? Can you articulate any change prescriptions that could benefit this group? What effects will be felt throughout the district by teachers? Students? Parents? The community?

TQM at the Falling Rock School District

Bill Shaller and Susan Asad, both principals in the Falling Rock School District, were carpooling together to a special meeting called by Superintendent Jean Kessler. Rumor had it that the superintendent was about to shut down the Total Quality Management program in the district. "I sure hope we don't go the way quality circles has gone in industry," said Susan. "I hear even industry is beginning to believe that TQM isn't all that it's touted to be. My neighbor was just caught in a restructuring at Xerox. Things were going great for them, but as the bottom fell out of the copier market, corporate management returned to their old habits and cut costs drastically. Their TQM effort wasn't the first to go, but the restructuring wasn't effectively planned and many well functioning teams were broken up. Management couldn't resolve how to mend the team structures, so they put TQM on hold."

"I heard the same thing," said Bill. "They waited too long and TQM may never be reinstituted there."

Bill found a parking spot near the district administration building and honked at Mike

Rafferty. Mike, another principal, was the spirited designer of the TQM effort the district had launched just over three years ago. "Good afternoon you two," commented Mike. "Wonder what Jean has up her sleeve today?"

"Rumors are rampant, I guess," said Susan. "We heard the complete gamut. Funding is down again, poorer than expected results came in from the spring testing, and the union is raising its hackles again. We even heard she may be considering shutting down TQM and entering another series of downsizing discussions with the school board, unions, and the parents. I sure don't envy what she has to do."

"I sure hope we can convince her to deal with this differently than she did last time," Mike said, as he opened the door to the superintendent's conference room. Seated in the room were the other eight principals from the district. They had all just finished greeting each other when Jean Kessler entered the room and sat down.

"Good morning," said Jean, "I'm glad you could make it on such short notice. I didn't expect to call this meeting so suddenly, but the school board wanted me to discuss all this with you before any final considerations were proposed. Funding is down drastically from the state this year, and we are not going to be able to continue operations without some pretty heavy downsizing. The form that this will take hasn't been decided yet, but I think you all should assume you'll each feel the effects."

"I've asked some of our educational administrators from the university to stop by this morning, so we could hear from them," continued Jean. "I saw them entering the building as I came in the room. Ah, here they are now." Greetings were again exchanged and the discussion renewed. Jean filled in the two university colleagues on the discussion to this point.

"We are really at a loss," said Jean, "as to how to handle these continued problems that surface. Our TQM efforts have had profound effects at nearly all the schools. I think we'd all agree that the program was making good progress. But with an impending downsizing, I can't see how we're going to be able to justify the additional time we spend on extras like our TQM program."

Miles Bromberg, a professor in Educational Administration, was the first to speak. "I can really relate to what you're saying, Jean. We went through a similar exercise just last year when our enrollment figures declined. Administration and faculty alike voted with their pocketbooks. They couldn't justify the additional work loads they'd agreed to, while at the same time our administration wasn't keeping its end of the bargain. Rumors were rampant there too. No pay raises, combining departments, even dropping some programs were considered."

Nell Spires chimed in, "We didn't have anywhere near the investment you've had with TQM in our quality program, so most weren't overly concerned about the program dying. Your investment is much greater. I don't see how you can downsize to meet state goals and at the same time maintain the costly TQM program."

Mike Rafferty interrupted, as he couldn't listen to much more. "Nell, you and Miles were the real influences behind our adopting the quality focus here in our school district. Your guidance and counsel has been significant, and I, for one, am not ready to abandon those strengths we've achieved simply because the state cannot keep its house in order. I think I can speak for most of us when I say that TQM is well liked across the board and most importantly has really served to breathe new spirit into many of our teachers and students alike. They like their new latitudes. While some of the cost of quality figures haven't been achieved and testing hasn't fully reversed itself, the trends are very positive. I, for one, wouldn't be in favor of drop-

ping TQM. Let's find some other methods of cutting costs!"

Bill Shaller broke in. "I don't know where you're getting your figures from, Mike, but TQM hasn't been a bed of roses. At our end of town, we're still having some significant problems. Having to measure all those new factors is time consuming. Some of the teachers are pretty upset, too. They've been saying for some time that TQM is just another way to get more from them for less."

Susan Asad chided Bill, "We all know that's because of that military command style you haven't been able to shed, Bill. You ought to lighten up some on those poor folks."

Bill, usually able to roll with jabs like this, wasn't as agreeable today. "You all may still be reading my style poorly, but I'm really concerned here. We cannot continue to ask more and more from our people and then turn around and yank the carrot away again. They're really wise to those old tricks we've played for years. They see it differently today, and they expect us to get it right as often as they do, if not more often."

"Nell and Miles, do either of you have any suggestions about how we can view this differently?" asked Jean Kessler as she regained control of the group.

"There are so many variables here," said Nell. "I think you may just need to take it on the chin with this one. We can't see many options. Even industry is smarting with the recent recession and all. Many have scrapped their TQM programs, returned to more centralization, taken away from much of the latitudes they'd passed out, and worse, some are into their second and third downsizing attempts. Times are just tough!"

Jean was hoping for encouragement from her university friends, but didn't get it. "I'd like to see some discussion about this," she said. "I've got to meet with a couple of the school board members here shortly. Could you all begin some deliberation? I'll join in when I return. We've got to find some answers soon!"

Directions

Assume you are the principal participants at this meeting and, as the superintendent has asked, discuss the situation further.

■ CASE STUDY II

The New Dean

When Dr. Jack Prince accepted the new post as Dean of the Business School at State College he knew the tasks ahead of him were formidable. While he had had experience as a dean, all his experience had been at community colleges. State colleges were different institutions. Jack knew he would be replacing a dean who had stepped down after a vote of no confidence. It was rumored that the old dean would be staying on for the time being, since she was tenured. It was also a well-known fact that the faculty of the Business School were a large part of the problems Jack would face.

Jack's new staff consisted of his secretary, the Associate Dean, three department chairpersons, and five other staff members who accomplished routine administrative tasks. Two of the three department chairs had risen recently from within the faculty ranks, and the third chair, Dr. Bob Neuman, had held his position for over ten years. The school had forty-five faculty members, with the largest percentage in Bob Neuman's department. Jack could feel instinctively that Neuman's Management Studies Department would be a large headache for him.

After the announcement had been made concerning Jack's acceptance as dean, he had met with State College's Provost and his long time mentor, Dr. Amy Kim. Dr. Kim was an old friend and colleague, and had herself moved to the state colleges from the community college environment. She knew that environment well. At their first meeting, Dr. Kim provided stern warnings about some issues Jack would have to work through during the term. She said that the faculty in the Business School were, for the most part, very aggressive educators, were liked by the student body, and were considered highly competent, as indicated by consulting evaluations of industry. These faculty would be a pleasure to work with. But Bob Neuman led a small group of faculty who had become complacent. Their material was outdated, their participation as consultants was minimal, their classes were avoided by students except when required, and their instructional techniques were obsolete. Bob Neuman himself was probably the worst of them all. However, Neuman was influential with his own faculty and exerted methods to control much of the younger faculty. For the past several years, he was also the Faculty Governance Chairman.

Several days into the new fall semester, Jack contemplated how he would cope with his new challenge. It was too early to make any judgments, but he was beginning to observe indications of exactly what Amy Kim had spoken about. Later that same day, after much thinking, Jack decided he would, in his words, "stir up the pot." During the first faculty meeting of the semester he would announce his intention to create quality teams. His intention was to give more power to all faculty and, at the same time, the student body. He had been a strong advocate of the quality movement in the community college environment, and he would begin developing exactly that in the State College.

Directions

This case poses some typical problems faced by a new administrator. Use the following questions to begin your discussion.

1.   What do you think about the "pot stirring" the new dean decided upon?

2.   How would you proceed in this situation? What would you have done differently?

3.   Identify the following in the case: the change agent, supporters, dissenters, and other actors you see.

4.   Devise further questions as you see fit to include processes used, and so forth.

■ **CASE STUDY III**

Discussion Case

A study in 1979 by the education section of the World Future Society and Old Dominion University developed a taxonomy of issues that were believed central to the future of education (Allen & Dede, 1979). These issues were grouped under six headings: responsibilities of different agents, content, process, improvement of the profession, interaction with the individual, and interface with society. Within these six headings there were 23 issues that can be examined when considering potential future educational changes. Address the questions posed.

I. *Responsibilities of Different Agents*

A. *Schooling.* Rapid technological innovations and unstable financial and social conditions will require great sophistication and flexibility in education. Do schools, as now defined and operated, provide the best delivery system for educating children and adults?

B. *Families.* In recent history, both the extended and the nuclear family structure have come under considerable strain because of changes in social values, and many educational tasks once

the responsibility of the family are now seen as the function of the school system. Regardless of the allocation of responsibility, how can the schooling system work toward a position of educational partnership with the family?

C. *Communities.* Should communities assume major educational responsibilities? If so, which ones?

D. *Media.* Drastic changes in existing media delivery seem probable. To what extent will schools increase reliance on media and shape its concepts, programming, and delivery?

E. *Industries/Professions.* How can training be best structured to foresee and address short- and long-term variations in career goals? How should counseling best be done to maximize fit between individual abilities and interests and the types of work society needs? How should society coordinate training agents so as to minimize total cost?

II. *Content*

A. *Social responsibility.* What are the values and attitudes vital to successful cultural evolution into the twenty-first century, and by which educational agent is each best conveyed? How can and should instruction be individualized to respond to the diverse array of attitudes and values held by learners?

B. *Basic cognitive skills.* What cognitive skills are needed by all citizens, and by which educational agent is each best conveyed? How can the expression of creativity be encouraged?

C. *Basic affective skills.* Recent rapid and unexpected changes have caused many people to feel stressed, overwhelmed, and unable to control their futures. How can affective skills build self-awareness, personal esteem, and ability to resist diversity? How should the affective domain be interfaced with social responsibility?

D. *Values*. Should the educational system deliberately communicate values and attitudes beyond those needed for socialization? By what means? Is this desirable if at all possible? How should values education be integrated with instruction for social responsibility?

E. *Future thinking*. World support systems have become interdependent before world cultural systems have recognized this shift. How can education best convey an understanding of ecological, cultural, and social interdependence? In what ways should education build toward a "global consciousness?" To what extent can education prepare citizens for issues that may first become important in five years? a decade? a generation?

III. *Process*

A. *Diversity of learning*. Each learner has different needs, expectations, capacities, life experiences, and readiness— and all these attributes vary with time. To what extent and in which areas of instruction should individualized learning packages be developed? What needs to be done toward furthering understanding of the development and cultural basis of learning styles?

B. *Educational technology*. What major role can technology legitimately play in the educative process? What effect will large-scale uniform instructional programming have, and to what extent is the specialization and individualization of technological instruction possible, given high software production costs? What new types of training for educators will be required?

C. *Evaluation*. Evaluation in education is concerned with providing feedback on performance. For each type of educational agent, which evaluation techniques are most accurate and in which manner should these be incorporated? How can evaluation validity be maximized? What are the best strategies for communicating results? By what methods can evaluation results of "work in progress" be incorporated into decision structures?

IV. *Improvement of the Profession*

A. *Professionalism*. How can the scope of education be more clearly delineated so that a more detailed analysis of the nature of the profession can be made? By what means can the most effective practitioner techniques be identified? What role differentiations are appropriate within the field, and what standards of technical and ethical training should each role meet? How can recognition of the importance and difficulty of education be increased?

B. *Staff development*. How can the image of the profession be improved? Given unionization, how can procedures be developed for removal of practitioners who have ceased to be effective? How can "burnout" be prevented? For each educational agent, how might professional development take place?

C. *Professional governance*. Leadership and cooperation are needed to meet the tremendous responsibilities and financial challenges society will place on education (in the foreseeable future). How can different educational agents (schooling system, family, community, media, industry) develop a framework for collaboration on common issues? What types of authority and power distribution systems will function most effectively?

V. *Interaction with the Individual*

A. *Lifelong learning.* What types of educational experiences are important during infancy and early childhood, and by which educational agents would these best be delivered? What instructional systems can most effectively serve the needs of people and society for retraining, more sophisticated citizenship, and social interaction? How can instruction facilitate the fusion of work and leisure styles? By what means can this expansion in traditional instructional services be best staffed and financed?

B. *Credentialing.* Credentialing is a means of certifying future performance. How can educational credentialing systems be made a more effective means of determining quality, without eliminating the diversity and individual uniqueness valued in a free society?

C. *Special needs.* Education is primarily provided for the middle-range-of-talent, physically and emotionally healthy individual in the majority culture. In as diverse a society as ours, this assumption means that many people are ill-served by educational institutions. How can instructional settings be structured to incorporate the maximum range of learner needs, so that through direct experience our culture will lose its fear of physical, sexual, intellectual, behavioral, emotional, linguistic, racial, cultural, and chronological differences? How can learners with special needs best be given a sense of personal worth? At what point does the responsibility of educational systems cease for learners for whom no instructional strategy seems to function?

D. *Equity.* What biases in each type of educational agent need to be removed, and how can these agents act to promote equity of access, outcome, staffing? What are the limits (if any) to the pluralism for which education is responsible? How can equality of outcome be best interpreted so as to allow for maximization of individual potential?

VI. *Interface with Society*

A. *Relation to other human services.* The field of human services is split into numerous specialties that encourage viewing a person only from certain perspectives, rather than as a total human being. How can educational and other social services best be coordinated and under what overall authority? How can administrative governance systems be evolved that will transcend the problems of hierarchical authority and allow human services to view the individual holistically?

B. *Funding.* What is the best mixture of educational funding sources: individual, local, state, national, international? Can new sources of funding be generated? How should resources be allocated among the educational agents? What should be the relationship between funding and policy control? How can the costs/benefits of education be delineated to society so that informed expenditure decisions can be made? What economies of scale in education are significant? What is the most likely means for improving educational productivity?

C. *External controls.* How can a coherent picture of the accomplishments and limits of the educational system, and the tradeoffs between its duties and costs, be communicated to the public? What mix of governmental, community, family, and individual input should shape educational policy? Can these different groups be organized to coordinate demands and evaluation procedures, and what types of assessment can best be made from outside the profession? (The above excerpted from Allen and Dede [1979].)

Directions

This case provides an opportunity to develop a team approach to change. Utilize the case to formulate and create a plan for change for a specified school in a specified community, or for a school district.

Annotated Bibliography

Bennis, W. G., Benne, K. D., Chin, R., & Corey, K. E. (1976). *The planning of change*. New York: Holt, Rinehart & Winston.

This third edition publication emphasizes the new theory building models, research and practical experimentation in the area of organizational change. The authors are interested in developing people who can function as effective agents of planned change. Topics covered include: the history of planned change; general strategies for effecting changes in human system; diagnosis of planned change via a variety of models for practitioners; resistance to change; interventions for planned change; social change; and ethical dilemmas for change agents.

Conner, D. R. (1993). *Managing at the speed of change*. New York: Villard Books.

The author believes there is a healthy tension associated with knowing that his mortgage will not be paid unless someone finds immediate, practical value in the observations and lessons he offers. Being an entrepreneurial-based researcher means he must place at least as much effort into making sure that his findings can be widely

understood and used as he does into determining the meaning of the data and observations. The premise of the book is not the introduction of a newly formulated "theory" of organizational change, but, instead, a discussion of what actually works through the author's observation of people successfully implementing major transformations in organizations.

Fombrun, C. J. (1992). *Turning points creating strategic change in corporations*. New York: McGraw-Hill.

The author breaks the text into three different sections based on three phases of the unfolding process of change: (1) How to recognize and agree on the need for strategic change; (2) How to revise our firms' competitive postures; (3) How to energize the process of re-creation. Based on these premises, the author emphasizes that strategic change is a subjective process, as well as a collective enterprise. A discussion of the whys and hows of strategic change follows.

Havelock, R. G. (1973). *The change agent's guide to innovation in educations*. Englewood Cliffs, NJ: Educational Technology Publications.

This book is a guide for change agents within the school. The author outlines a six-step process for educational change and gives concrete suggestions for implementation at each stage. This guide also reviews and assesses how agents' roles differ. The book also includes an excellent resource guide that gives a wide variety of reference that may assist a change agent in initiating and implementing an educational change.

Huse, E. F., & Cummings, T. G. (1985). *Organization development and change* (3rd ed.). St. Paul, MN: West Publishing.

The purpose of this book is to place the current theory and practice of organization development into a broad systems perspective and to describe the concepts, approaches, and techniques of OD. The book can serve as a basic text for undergraduate and graduate level content in organizational development. The book is organized to provide the reader with a comprehensive understanding of OD, starting with how it is applied to organizations, then major interventions used in OD, and the evaluation and practice of OD.

Naisbitt, J. (1982). *Megatrends*. New York: Warner Books.

This book outlines ten new directions transforming American lives. Determination of those trends comes from a unique content analysis methodology employed by the Naisbitt Group. Through daily monitoring of newspaper stories, this futuristic consulting group is able to discern major trends in our society. In Megatrends, *Naisbitt restructures and illustrates what the new information society would be like. The critical restructuring referenced include: the move from an industrial society to an information society; the trend toward high tech/high touch; the interdependence of countries and the world's time frames rather than short-term ones; the rediscovery of humankind's ability to act innovatively and achieve results from the bottom up; the shift from institutional help to more self-reliance; the era of instantaneously shared information; giving up dependence upon hierarchical structures in favor of informal networks; the fact that more Americans are living in the South and West, leaving behind old industrial cities in the North; and the exploding of our culture into a free-wheeling, multiple option society.*

Orlich, D. C. (1989). Education reforms: Mistakes, misconceptions, misuses. *Phi Delta Kappan, 70*(7), 512–517.

The author articulates his belief that for true sustained school reform local system analysis is needed. He describes efforts such as A Nation at Risk, A Nation Prepared . . . , Tomorrow's Teachers . . . , *the Comprehensive School Improvement Program and Elementary and Secondary Educational Act of 1965 have not accomplished significant changes or reforms. He suggests that reformers must first find out what really needs improving by studying schools and determining what specifically makes them effective. Orlich contends that a National Moratorium on reforms be declared and that each local school district be allowed to systematically study its own culture and then implement a carefully researched, well-coordinated, and well-funded plan for specific improvement.*

Owens, R. G., & Steinhoff, C. R. (1976). *Administering change in schools*. Englewood Cliffs, NJ: Prentice-Hall.

This book provides a thorough description of schools as organizations. It is meant to serve as an instructional tool for administrators concerned with changing schools. The authors claim that the message in this publication should be of interest to a wide audience, including parents, teachers, and school board members. Throughout the dialogue, Owens and Steinhoff argue for what schools ought to become and assert that the administrative role is pivotal to change.

Pondy, L. R., Boland, R. J., Jr., & Thomas, H. (Eds.). (1988). *Managing ambiguity and change*. New York: John Wiley & Sons.

This book is divided into two parts. Part 1 presents a number of maps and models for bringing order and guiding action in the face of ambiguity and change. An overview of the problems and prospects of managing ambiguity and change is presented, with lessons from companies that succeeded or failed in meeting the challenge as reference. The need for creative problem solving and appropriate mental maps are highlighted. Part 2 explores the special importance of the metaphors that frame our fundamental conceptions of what organizations are and what the process of decisionmaking is.

Timar, T. B., & Kirp, D. L. (1989). Education reform in the 1980s: Lessons from the states. *Phi Delta Kappan, 79*(7), 505.

In this article the authors take a look at school reform movements, particularly over the past five years. They discuss the three dimensions of school reform: authorized movement, regional movement, and conversation. They also expound upon strategies for promoting the implementation of reform citing the three case studies of Texas, California, and South Carolina. In conclusion, the authors note that policymakers and practitioners should focus on what excellent schools do and how they go about doing it. The concept of local school control must be developed and strengthened.

Waugh, R. F., & Punch, K. F. (1987). Teacher receptivity to system-wide change in the implementation stage. *Review of Educational Research, 57*(3), 237–254.

This article summarizes the research findings on teacher attitudes toward the implementation of planned change. It provides a brief historical summary of change over the past forty years and analyzes the fundamental characteristics common to all change processes. The authors conclude that there are a number of variables that must be considered before implementing any change. These include: practicality of the new educational system in the classroom, alleviation of fears and uncertainties associated with the change, articulation of perceived expectations associated with the change, and support of teachers' role changes in reference to the change.

Weiss, J. W. (1986). *The management of change: Administrative logics and actions.* New York: Praeger.

The intended contribution of this study is aimed at reviving classical and contemporary theoretical action perspectives that have paved the way for studying executive strategy-making and implementation activities. This study is an exploratory attempt to describe and examine the observed relationships among three individual administrators' strategies and changing environmental conditions characterized as growth, critical turbulence, and cutback.

References

Alderfer, C. (1977). Organizational development. *Annual Review of Psychology, 28,* 197–223.

Allen, D., & Dede, C. (1979). *An invitation to participate in creating better futures for education.* Norfolk, VA: Old Dominion University Press.

Basom, R. E., & Crandall, D. P. (1991). Implementing a redesign strategy: Lessons from educational change. *Educational Horizons, 69*(2), 73–77.

Beckhard, R., & Harris, R. T. (1977). *Organizational transitions: Managing complex change.* Reading, MA: Addison-Wesley.

Beer, M., Eisenstat, R., & Spector, B. (1990, November–December). Why change programs don't produce change. *Harvard Business Review, 90*(6), 158–166.

Bell, D. (1976). *The coming of the post-industrial society.* New York: Basic Books.

Bennis, W. (1966). *Changing organizations: Essays on the development and evolution of human organization.* New York: McGraw-Hill.

Bennis, W. (1977). *Organizational transitions: Managing complex change.* Reading, MA: Addison-Wesley.

Cetron, M., & Gayle, M. (1991). *Educational resistance: Our schools at the turn of the century.* New York: St. Martin's Press.

Chin, R., & Benne, K. S. (1969). General strategies for effecting change in human systems. In W. G. Bennis, K. D. Benne, & R. Chin (Eds.), *The planning of change* (2nd ed.) (pp. 297–312). New York: Holt, Rinehart & Winston.

Chin, R., & Benne, K. S. (1976). General strategies for effecting changes in human systems. In W. Bennis, K. Benne, & R. Chin (Eds.), *The planning of change.* New York: Holt, Rinehart & Winston.

Connor, P. E., & Lake, K. L. (1988). *Managing organizational change.* New York: Praeger.

Cunningham, W. G. (1982). *Systematic planning for educational change.* Mountain View, CA: Mayfield Publishing Co.

Fullan, M. (1982). *The meaning of educational change.* New York: Teachers College Press, Columbia University.

Goodlad, J. I. (1984). The dynamics of educational change: Toward responsive schools. In S. J. Knezevich (Ed.), *Administration of public education* (4th ed.). New York: Harper and Row.

Grenier, L. E. (1989). Common approaches to change. In R. McLennan (Ed.), *Managing organizational change* (pp. 138–140). Englewood Cliffs, NJ: Prentice-Hall.

Hahn, D. (1991). Strategic management: Tasks and challenges of the 1990's. *Long Range Planning, 24*(1), 26–39.

Hanson, E. M. (1985). *Educational administration and organizational behavior* (2nd ed.). Boston: Allyn and Bacon.

Havelock, R. G. (1973). *The change agent's guide to innovation in education.* Englewood Cliffs, NJ: Educational Technology Publications.

Hersey, P., & Blanchard, K. H. (1988). *Management of organizational behavior utilizing human resources* (5th ed.). Englewood Cliffs, NJ: Prentice-Hall.

Hodgkinson, C. (1991). *Educational leadership: The moral art*. New York: State University of New York Press.

Huse, E. F. (1975). *Organizational development and change*. St. Paul, MN: West Publishing Co.

Huse, E. F., & Cummings, T. G. (1985). *Organizational development and change* (3rd ed.). St. Paul, MN: West Publishing Co.

Kanter, R. M. (1983). *The change masters: Innovation and entrepreneurship in the American corporation*. New York: Simon & Schuster.

Katz, D., & Kahn, R. (1978). *The social psychology of organizing* (2nd ed.). New York: John Wiley & Sons.

Kostler, P. (1973). The elements of social action. In R. H. Lauer (Ed.), *Perspective on social change*. Boston: Allyn and Bacon.

Kowalski, T. J., & Reitzug, U. C. (1993). *Contemporary school administration: An introduction*. New York: Longman.

Kreitner, R., & Kinicki, A. (1989). *Organizational behavior*. Boston: BPI/IRWIN.

Lauer, R. H. (1973). *Perspective on social change*. Boston: Allyn and Bacon.

Lewin, K. (1951) *Field theory in social sciences*. New York: Harper and Row.

Lindbloom, C. E. (1965). *The intelligence of democracy decision making through mutual adjustments*. New York: Free Press.

Lipham, J. M., Rankin, R., & Hoeh, J. (1985). *The principalship: Concepts, competencies, and cases*. New York: Longman.

Lippett, G. L., Langseth, P., & Mossop, J. (1985). *Implementing organizational change: A practical guide to managing change efforts*. San Francisco, CA: Jossey-Bass.

Lippett, G. L., & Lippett, R. (1985). The consulting function of the human resource development professional. In L. Nadler (Ed.), *The handbook of human resource development* (pp. 5.1–5.27). New York: John Wiley & Sons.

Lippett, R., Watson, J., & Westley, B. (1958). *The dynamics of planned change*. New York: Harcourt, Brace and World.

London, M. (1988). *New roles and innovation strategies for human resource professionals*. San Francisco, CA: Jossey-Bass.

Lorsch, J. W., & Trooboff, S. (1989). Two universal models. In R. McLennan (Ed.), *Managing organizational change* (pp. 68–75). Englewood Cliffs, NJ: Prentice-Hall.

Lunenberg, F. C., & Ornstein, A. C. (1991). *Educational administration: Concepts and practices*. Belmont, CA: Wadsworth Publishing Co.

Mannheim, K. (1940). *Man and society in an age of reconstruction: Studies in modern social structure*. New York: Harcourt & Brace.

Mauriel, J. J. (1989). *Strategic leadership for schools: Creating and sustaining productive change*. San Francisco, CA: Jossey-Bass.

Mazarella, J., & Grundy, T. (1988). Portrait of a leader. In S. C. Smith & P. K Piele (Eds.), *School leaders' handbook for excellence* (2nd ed.). Eugene, OR: ERIC Clearinghouse on Educational Management, College of Education, University of Oregon.

Millard, R. M. (1991). *Today's myths and tomorrow's realities: Overcoming obstacles to academic leadership in the 21st century*. San Francisco, CA: Jossey-Bass.

Miskel, C., & Ogawa, R. (1988). Work motivation, job satisfaction, and climate. In N. J. Boyan (Ed.), *Handbook of research on educational administration*. New York: Longman.

Monahan, W. G., & Hengst, H. R. (1982). *Contemporary educational administration*. New York: Macmillan.

Mort, P. R., (1962, October). Studies in educational administration from the Institute of Administrative Research. *IRA Research Bulletin, 3*(1), 1–8.

Mort, P. R., & Ross, D. H. (1957). *Principles of school administration*. New York: McGraw-Hill.

Meyerson, M., & Banfield, E. C. (1964). *Politics, planning, and the public interest: The case of public housing in Chicago*. New York: The Free Press of Glencoe.

Nutt, P. (1986, June) Tactics of implementation. *Academy of Management Journal*.

Owens, R. G. (1987). *Organizational behavior in education* (3rd ed.). Englewood Cliffs, NJ: Prentice-Hall.

Pettigrew, A. (1985). *The awakening giant: Continuity and change in imperial chemical industries*. Oxford, England: Blackwell.

Ross, M. G. (1967). *Community organization: Theory and principles*. New York: Harper and Row.

Rossman, G. B., Corbett, H. D., & Firestone, W. A. (1988). *Change and effectiveness in schools: A cultural perspective*. New York: State University of New York Press.

Schein, E. (1969). *Process consultations: Its role in organization development*. Reading, MA: Addison-Wesley.

Simon, H. A. (1957). *The new science of management decisions*. New York: Harper.

Srivastva, S., Fry, R. E., & Associates. (1992). *Executive and organizational continuity: managing the paradoxes of stability and change*. San Francisco, CA: Jossey-Bass.

Stanislao, J., & Stanislao, B. C. (1983, July–August). Dealing with resistance to change. *Business Horizons*, 74–78.

Steeples, D. W. (Ed.). (1990). *Managing change in higher education*. San Francisco, CA: Jossey-Bass.

Stogdill, R. (1974). *Handbook of leadership*. New York: The Free Press.

Sumner, W. G. (1914). *War and other essays*. New Haven, CT: Yale University Press.

Thompson, V. A. (1965). Bureaucracy and innovation. *Administrative Science Quarterly, 10*(1), 1–20.

Walton, R. E. (Ed.). (1965). *A behavioral theory of labor negotiations: An analysis of a social interaction system*. New York: McGraw-Hill.

Warren, R. L. (1977). *Social change and human purpose: Toward understanding and action*. Chicago: Rand McNally College Publishing Co.

Watson, G. (1969). Resistance to change. In W. G. Bennis, K. D. Benne, & R. Chin (Eds.), *The planning of change* (2nd ed.) (pp. 488–498). New York: Holt, Rinehart & Winston.

Yukl, G. A. (1981). *Leadership in organizations*. New York: Prentice-Hall.

Part VI

Conclusion

Chapter 17
Educational Leadership

We are nearing the end of our treatise on the fundamental concepts of educational leadership and administration. We have addressed the general principles underlying the knowledge base of leadership and management as specifically applied to educational institutions. The review of current scholarship in a wide range of areas was intended to compel the reader to consider critically the theoretical underpinnings of the subject within the context of current issues, problems and proposed solutions.

Our approach has been an analytical one—thinking between paradigms—and mapping the theoretical and practical worlds of leadership and management. Four dimensions of leadership were examined (Inquiry, Communication and Human Interaction, Analysis and Planning, and Decisionmaking and Change) from several perspectives (human inquiry, observation, philosophy, human relations, communication, organization, environmental interaction, planning, allocation of resources, evaluation, decisionmaking, policy formulation, and change). In this concluding chapter, we will look back on that which has preceded

and reflect on its significance for leadership in contemporary educational institutions.

Interlinking Concepts

In Chapter 1, we turned to an expanded version of systems theory to serve as a vehicle for integrating the many faces of leadership. It was observed that the levels of traditional systems discourse had hit a glass ceiling imposed between biological based systems and human social systems. As things stood, nothing learned or seen above that ceiling could be valued by systems scientists unless it yielded both positivistic and predictive systems knowledge. Flood's (1990) arguments for a complementarist theoretical position which is open and conciliatory overcomes the theoretical fortress mentality of traditional systems thinking and encompasses the emancipatory forces of critical self-reflection. Critical reflection views all theories and methodologies as complementary. Intellectual tension among competing theories and methodologies can lead to new understandings while universality and convergence lead to complacency with what is known.

This pioneering approach allows researchers and practitioners to deal with issues like employee empowerment, work place diversity, cultural abnormalities, coercion, ideologies, and ownership of values in a deliberative normative way. Subjectivity is openly acknowledged, not as antithetical to system science, but as part of its legitimate discourse. Postulating a role for critical systems theory immediately removes most of the "two-value" (either-or) constraints that have plagued systems literature on educational administration. "Machine" images as metaphors for social systems can be complemented by contextual analysis. In this spirit, the aspects of leadership discussed in separate chapters in Parts II through V can be viewed as subsystems with the concept of leadership serving as the system.

Each aspect of organizational leadership is related to every other aspect to some degree. The philosophy, values and ethics of the leader guides what is observed, his or her approach to inquiry, and the way the leader deals with other people (human relations). Leadership philosophy also has a strong influence on what decisions and policies are made and how resources are allocated.

Inquiry, the process of finding and knowing, was discussed as a key component of leadership. It was viewed as a philosophic issue, beginning with a discussion in Chapter 4 of the various philosophical points of view that shape the individual's interpretation of experience. In Chapter 5 the process of inquiry was considered directly, and the impact of the traditional scientific paradigm was balanced against the possibility of new ways of gathering and interpreting data. There was discussion of the possibility of taking an eclectic approach and drawing upon several paradigms when working in the fields of education. This was considered further in

Chapter 6 in the discussion of observation, which is a fundamental element in the ability of the school leader to detect and recognize relevant events and information.

Communication was referred to as the breath of the organization. The means and networks of communication reflect the value placed on human interactions and the extent to which leadership is open or closed to inputs from members of the organization and the community (environmental interactions) was considered. The function of communication as a significant element of school systems was explored in Chapter 7, and communication was considered as the binding agent in human interaction on the personal and group levels in Chapters 9 and 10.

Analysis and planning as the prerequisites for rational decisionmaking and management of change were considered in Chapter 11. Strategic planning, a process that moves from development of a vision to sharing the vision to implementation of the vision, was considered from the perspective of the educational leader who will have to implement that process. The relation of a variety of paradigms held by the leader and/or by the members of the organization was explored, and the effects of these paradigms and the related planning models on the allocation of resources was discussed in Chapter 12. Planning grows out of the values held collectively by members of the organization and from the evaluation of the successes and failures of current efforts. Allocation of resources is a product of rational planning and political policy formulation. The problem of effective resource allocation (Chapter 12) and the concomitant need to monitor results (in Chapter 13, Evaluation) was identified as a major concern for leaders at all levels of the educational enterprise.

Educational decisionmaking—the raison d'etre for all that has gone before—was considered in Chapter 14 with respect to collective policy formulation and in Chapter 15 with respect to individuals and groups. A variety of approaches to decisionmaking which are applicable in a public setting were considered and evaluated. Decisionmaking as the process of choosing among alternatives was identified as one of the most crucial skills needed by an effective educational leader. A circular model appropriate to the view of education as an open general system was proposed. Each activity of the organization requires innumerable decisions made informally by individuals with varying degrees of discretion and formally by the bureaucratic hierarchy. The impact of constant change within and outside of educational systems on decisionmaking and on the systems themselves was discussed in Chapter 16. For the organization to adapt to ever-shifting environments (internally and externally), organizational change must take place. The success or failure of the change process depends to a large extent on the collective philosophy of the organization and the nature of its human relations and communication networks.

Chapter 2, Leadership, reviewed the scholarship on leadership in general terms. In Chapter 17, we focused more specifically on leadership in educational institutions. We found in Chapter 2 that there was little agreement on how leadership should be defined or how it works. For our purposes, we have defined leadership quite broadly as influencing others' actions in achieving mutually desired ends. Leadership provides direction to an organization, concentrating on doing the right things. Leadership involves philosophy, values, and ethics. Leaders are people who shape the goals, motivations, and actions of others. Frequently, they initiate change to reach existing and new goals. Occasionally, they lead in order to preserve what is valuable, such as to protect core organizational functions. We have not viewed leadership as being role specific since the roles of leader and follower are interchangeable. Both roles are critical to an organization's success. Some roles, however, offer greater opportunities for

exercising leadership such as the role of principal or superintendent.

We do differentiate between leadership and management/ administration. Management is concerned with doing things right; it focuses on the technology of administration. Leadership provides purpose and direction, i.e., doing the right things. While leadership and management/administration are different, both are important. The success of modern organizations requires the objective perspective of the manager *and* the vision and commitment that wise leadership provides (Boleman & Deal, 1991). It may be possible to be an effective manager without strong leadership skills, but it is not possible to be an effective leader without good management skills. Superficial managerial tasks can be transformed by skilled leaders into opportunities for communicating organizational meaning and purpose in the context of the routine and the mundane (Sergiovanni, 1992).

Traditional Role of Principal

Foster (1989) identified two foci for leadership research—the political-historical model and the bureaucratic-managerial model. The bureaucratic-managerial model is based on business practices and assumes that (a) leadership is a function of position; (b) leadership is goal centered with goals driven by organizational, not social or follower, needs; and (c) the leader's role is to motivate workers to perform and thus achieve organizational goals. The leader's focus in this model becomes one of assuring employee conformance to managerial desires. Leadership resides not in an individual but in a hierarchical power position where manipulation is used to control tasks, people, and structures. It was once believed that tasks, people, and structures could be strictly controlled to safeguard goal achievement. Leadership, however, can no longer be equated with organizational management.

Today, according to Foster (1989), the concept of leadership seems to focus narrowly on such a bureaucratic definition. Vision and follower empowerment is translated into profit, growth, and illusory power for followers through extrinsic rewards. In today's society, teachers act as therapists adjusting students to social conditions *and* as managers controlling situations for personal and organizational gain. Loose coupling of educational organizations makes rational and goal-oriented control of schools illusory. Leadership in schools cannot be achieved neatly through managerial techniques that are unable to control and predict human action. Instead, Foster argued that leadership should be critical, focused on social vision and change, not organizational goals.

The political-historical model is a study of power, politics, and historical facts. Individuals possessing qualities, values and vision are capable of achieving new and different social orders through transactional or transformative leadership. Transactional leadership, employing exchange relationships between followers and leaders, uses concessions, negotiations, and accommodations to manipulate and integrate social variables. Transformational leadership deals with the leader's ability to create a new social situation, communicate that vision to followers, and engage followers in the pursuit and accomplishment of that vision. Infusing leader and follower with goals and aspirations leads to a higher level of social reality, a new social morality. Leadership becomes a moral and value-driven elevation of the social group with transformational leadership rather than a technocratic, managerial tool for goal achievement.

Foster (1989) criticized today's emphasis on instrumentality that portrays people as "instruments for the achievement of organizational goals" (p. 59). Instrumentality is evi-

denced in education by practices that judge students by SAT scores, basic skills scores, and employability measures and judge schools by comprehensive assessment reports. Instead, school districts should identify what they want students to achieve at the end of their schooling experience as whole people and members of a community.

Over three decades ago, Parsons (1959) contended that a functionalist perspective has dominated thinking about public education that views the primary role of schools as socializing students to adapt to and share basic norms and values, thus assuring the continuance and survival of society and maintenance of the social power and economic status quo. More recently, Smyth (1989) and Angus (1989) have taken positions similar to that of Parsons.

A functionalist perspective that maintains the status quo assures that power remains in the hands of those who already possess it. Compulsory education is valued by functionalists for it provides a system that ensures that youth will be educated to assume the existing and emerging adult work roles of a technological society and develop values to assure societal solidarity. This sociological perspective is reflected in educational leaders who practice a top-down, hierarchical, authoritarian, Weberian leadership style. These educational leaders may rely on incremental changes, certification through testing, and increased requirements to foster educational improvement by fixing the participants (teachers and students) while still maintaining the management system's structure and status quo.

Similarly, Codd (1989) asserted that a socialization process dominates elementary and secondary education. Students are led to conform to accepted, preset standards; traditional common beliefs and values are imparted in both the formal and informal curriculum; and willing acceptance of their role in school and society is ingrained in students. At the tertiary level, students are called upon to examine critically, reflect upon, and challenge accepted values, theories, and practices in society. Codd warned that this dichotomy of socialization and education must not be allowed to persist.

The socialization function of schools is reflected in the typical roles performed by the titular school leader, the principal. Throughout the past 30 years, the principal's central role has been interpreted as "building manager, administrator, politician, change agent, boundary spanner, and instructional leader" (Smith & Andrew, 1989, p. 1). Depending upon school district policy, building principals' authority can range from empowered site management and leadership to rote implementation and maintenance of district policies and programs (Guthrie & Reed, 1991, p. 87). Building administrators spend most of their time on noninstructional activities: supervising students between classes in the hallways, at lunch, at various extracurricular events, before and after school, during bus loading and unloading; responding to parental and community concerns; preparing reports and responding to central office requests; resolving conflicts between students, between students and teachers; handling student discipline; requiring and distributing teacher resources; scheduling classes and other school activities; supervising staff; meeting with individual and small groups of students, teachers, and parents; and responding to any number of unexpected school emergencies that may arise during the day (Guthrie & Reed, 1991, p. 230). Instructional leadership activities (teacher supervision, classroom observation, curriculum development, staff development, and technical support) are not the predominant focus of the building principal's routine, for principals are faced with unpredictable, varied situations each day. Although principals regret their inability to spend more time on instructional matters, research has shown that teachers prefer the absence of principals from the teachers' private, quasi-autonomous classrooms (Smith & Andrew, 1989).

These tasks cast the principal as an administrator-manager rather than as an instructional leader (Cuban, 1988). Subordinates value administrative behavior that conducts these tasks efficiently while giving attention to human relations and school politics (Bredeserl, 1989). Firestone and Wilson (1989), however, among many others, have criticized principals for leaving instruction wholly to teachers and not trying to shape thinking about what should be taught and how.

Effective Schools and Reform Literature

The publication in 1965 of the Coleman Report, *Equality of Educational Opportunity,* dominated thinking about elementary and secondary education for over a decade. In many respects, it was a very pessimistic report. It documented the gap in academic achievement between minorities and the majority population and concluded that the primary means of social intervention, the schools, was ineffective in closing the gap. Low achievement was attributed chiefly to family background and peer group associations (see the discussion in Chapter 10). Many interpreted the findings as saying that "schools don't make a difference." In 1979, Brookover and Lezotte published the results of a study they had made of inner-city schools with relatively high-achieving pupils. While acknowledging that achievement levels of such schools were, in general, unacceptably low, they identified several intervention strategies that appeared to narrow the achievement gap. This approach of studying urban schools that differed positively from the norm was conceptualized into the "effective schools movement" by other researchers such as Edmonds (1979).

Cunningham (1990) observed that since the educational reform era began in the 1980s, "principals and superintendents have been cited in the spate of national reports over and over again as both [the] Achilles heel of American education and the Adonis for improved performance of the nation's schools" (p. 2). The literature clearly identifies the principal as essential to school improvement and reform. In effective school programs, as discovered by Edmonds (1979) and Brookover and Lezotte (1979), staff and students formulate mission and vision statements that develop consensus and ownership about the school's goals and purposes. As the key educational actor, the "effective school" principal is seen as the one who is primarily responsible for school improvement and who ensures: an atmosphere of order, discipline, and purpose; a climate of high expectations for staff and students; collegial and collaborative staff relationships; commitment among staff and students to school goals; adequate time for instruction; and adequate staff development.

After examination of varied definitions of instructional leadership, Weber (1989) surmised a general goal to improve or maintain conditions that encourage student learning. Achievement of this goal, according to Weber, requires instructional leadership that involves "long-term dedication to instructional excellence, not a one-time resolution to 'get more involved instruction'" (p. 192). He further concluded that leading the instructional program requires both an understanding of educational techniques and a personal vision of academic excellence that can be translated into effective classroom strategies.

Principals perform numerous activities that have varied impact on the instructional program; but Weber (1989) identified several that seem to be particularly critical for directly influencing the instructional program. According to Weber, principals must define the school's mission and develop common goals and a vision to establish a shared sense of direction for employees; visions and missions are made a reality by articulating and demonstrating a commitment to these ideals. In managing curriculum and instruction, the principal must have knowledge of trends in content areas, media, instructional processes/programs, and instructional strategies/approaches. A positive learning climate is promoted by raising teacher expectations of students' achievement abilities, establishing a link between daily activities and student achievement, and rewarding and recognizing academic achievement. Time devoted to instruction must be protected while ensuring that the quality of this time is maintained or improved. Principals need to manage instruction through observation and evaluation of teachers' instructional strategies. The instructional program needs to be assessed regularly through formative and summative evaluation, matching the intended curricula to the actual curricula and classroom practices; teachers' perceptions of the program's effectiveness should be solicited and program revisions should be made as needed.

Also, Weber (1989) found three leadership traits common to principals successfully carrying out the above tasks. They exercised style flexibility in varied situations involving student needs. They displayed a willingness to attempt various innovative strategies while consistently trying to achieve the goal of improved student achievement. Finally, successful principals imbued their vision, mission, and goals for their schools in the performance of daily school activities, thus connecting and reinforcing their instructional program with the entire school program.

Similar findings have resulted from other research including Peterson (1987), Smith and Piele (1989), and Smith and Andrew

(1989). In addition, Smith and Piele asserted that teachers are not influenced by a principal's status or position or ability to reward and punish, but by the teachers' perception that the principal is expert, competent, and able to empower and inspire others. An examination of principals' daily activities by Smith and Andrew found that, in most cases, effective principals are strong instructional leaders as well as strong building managers. Principals who are effective instructional leaders are capable of managing their time so that instructional matters are the focus of their discretionary time.

Criticism of Effective Schools Research

Criticism of the effective schools research and literature takes two forms: criticism of its conceptualization, and criticisms of its research designs. Beginning with the research design issues, Deal (1987) contended that the effective schools literature's emphasis on the principal as the key and crucial ingredient for school and curriculum improvement has created a mythological representation of the principal as the instructional leader. Although education reformists identify building-level leadership focused on instruction as a key indicator of school effectiveness, research has been unable to establish a clear relationship between leadership and school effectiveness (Anderson, 1989; Angus, 1989; Burlingame, 1987; Codd, 1989; Deal, 1987; Hallinger & Murphy, 1987). Burlingame further charged that the research has been hasty to make generalizations and has tended to ignore contextual issues. By ignoring context, researchers disregard the influence of the community on school goals, leadership, and teaching. In a similar vein, Hallinger and Murphy (1987) stressed that leadership is situational and that selecting the appropriate style of instructional leadership will be influenced by organiza-

tional and environmental factors. However, most effective schools research focuses upon poor, urban elementary schools and advocates strong instructional leadership as necessary for school improvement.

Hallinger and Murphy (1987) identified other limitations in the effective schools research. Most studies have been conducted at a single point in time; case studies are usually limited to one year. Researchers focus on identifiable characteristics of effective schools and neglect investigation of the processes used by principals to effect these improvements. Most studies focus on poor, urban elementary schools and use student achievement as the sole criterion for assessing effectiveness. There is no validity that this research can be generalized to high schools, to schools of differing socioeconomic conditions, or to educational goals other than student achievement. Finally, lack of a uniform operational definition of instructional leadership restricts researchers' abilities to make comparisons among various research studies.

Moving into conceptual considerations, many researchers contend that educational leadership must be defined more broadly than effective schools researchers have tended to do; definitions of leadership should include rational, reflective, and deliberate action and should not be confined narrowly to management strategies.

Burlingame (1987) saw three incompatible images of leadership projected by effective schools research. In the first image, the principal is the key figure, possessing traits of supreme rationality (intellectually able to develop appropriate goals, review alternatives, weigh consequences, choose appropriate solutions) and supreme pragmatism (when solutions are ineffective, evaluates the situation and develops an alternative plan). Leadership is top-down; goals are aimed at raising basic skills test results; and scores are improved by providing a stable, orderly environment and raising teachers' expectations of student academic achievement. This image portrays the leader as dominant and the follower as passive.

In the second image, cultural context is emphasized as leaders model and set goals that align with the community's goals, mores, and norms. Leaders act rationally and pragmatically, to be certain that their leadership behavior and goals conform to community expectations. Thus, leadership is constrained by cultural context. Reproduction of the status quo prohibits any inferences of the school's leadership and schooling practices to education in general. Both leaders and followers are portrayed as conformists in this image.

In the third image, the leadership style focuses on faculty consensus in decisionmaking and planning and uses a bottom-up leadership approach. This image portrays leaders as followers and followers as leaders.

These incompatible images of leadership produce several problems for the effective schools literature. One set of problems is that influence flows from the principal to teachers, and a benign relationship exists between school and classrooms. The principal is not influenced by the environment, and he or she isolates the school from negative community influences just as teachers control external influences within the classroom (Burlingame, 1987; Angus, 1989). Another set of problems involves search for the one best system of schooling; educators have overestimated the power of prescribed strategies (Madeline Hunter, Lezotte) and ignored the abilities of external groups to define education and schooling (parents, business). These strategies are used by some to control teaching and make it "foolproof" by insisting on one best and accepted way. Such strategies limit and constrict teacher autonomy in the classroom.

Blind acceptance of the first leadership image may have two major consequences. Principals are encouraged to believe that they

must define school goals, create a stable environment, raise teacher expectations, and maintain a dominant leadership role. However, teachers view these strategies as an encroachment upon their professional roles. Parents and students protest these changes in routine community actions and activities and cultural constraints of the school act to limit principal-initiated change strategies.

With any of the images, there is a real danger of blind acceptance of coined slogans that are meant to represent the philosophy of education within a school. These slogans are likely to be ambiguous and vague. The word "effective," for example, can imply a description of a condition or a prescription for a condition. Slogans reduce complex educational concerns to simplistic terms that gloss over ambiguities, turn complex situations into simple, misleading models, highlight commonalities, and deemphasize differences (Burlingame, 1987). Slogans restrict the uses of power and authority to promote uniform, universal educational practices.

Angus (1989) charged that the effective schools research has shifted the focus of education from providing educational equality for all students to achieving excellence in education. Attention is focused on analysis of educational factors and variables while ignoring the political and social context of education—the people. He criticized the common view of leadership that ignores the complexity of administrator and teacher roles and the social, cultural, and political contexts within which they operate. It assumes a functionalist approach to education, described earlier, in which the society's power structures and social systems are maintained and perpetuated through the prescribed socialization of students in the schooling process. Angus argued that the leadership of the principal is not unilaterally controlled and determined by the principal but that it is influenced by teachers, the reputation and history of the school, and institutionalized expectations of the school and community. Leadership is influenced by interactions of organizational subsystems, situational factors, and intervening variables.

Monk (1989) made a similar criticism of the effective schools research. He charged that the research has focused our attention on institutions using an outdated technology directed toward outmoded goals in a highly efficient manner. Instead, he believed we should be designing radically new schools directed toward meeting contemporary conditions and needs that make full use of our new communications technology.

The simplistic interpretation of the school as a stable, consensually shared goal-oriented organization holds teachers and administrators responsible for school outcomes while ignoring the influence of other subsystems in the internal and external environment. This is evidenced by the shift in educational focus from curriculum improvement to the matching of students' skills, attitudes, and beliefs to the work ethic required by business's agenda to achieve economic superiority.

A limited, traditional view of school effectiveness, corroborated by statistical data—basic skills tests results—ignores the skills, habits, and attitudes that are a part of education but cannot be captured and measured by traditional, quantitative testing methods. Thus, instructional leadership, as defined by the effective schools movement, addresses the lower levels of Bloom's taxonomy. This numerical representation of education, basic skills test results, focuses upon maintenance of the status quo, where minimum competency is interpreted as excellence in educational endeavors. This type of leadership values control, predictability, and efficiency in the educational process (Angus, 1989).

According to Angus, the effective schools literature conceptualizes schools as an educational contest wherein the principal is encouraged to manipulate teachers and situations to ensure that they share the same visions. Leadership creates and reinforces beliefs, values, and norms within the organization as a subtle form of control in a loosely coupled organization in which direct, authoritarian control is ineffective. Control is achieved through perception modifications, monitoring and reinforcing actions and statements, and appropriate behavior modeling. The literature assumes the passive, docile acceptance of this form of control by the members of the educational organization. It also assumes that the person whose authority is legitimated by position is the only leader in the school organization.

In summary, effective schools research has focused on instructional leadership as a technical, rational function related to supervising, evaluating, and improving the instructional delivery within the school building. This results in a perspective of leadership that engages the instructional leader in roles that emphasize a human resource view (focused upon people, organizational effectiveness, and morale) or structural view (focused upon productivity, role specialization, goals, and instructional technology) of the school organization (Deal, 1987, p. 235). However, if instructional leadership is defined to include the culture, politics, and power relationships within schools perceived as social organizations, the instructional leader, through negotiation, conflict resolution, and culture building (values, symbols, ceremonies, rituals), performs a role that is complex, directly and indirectly influencing school performance. We broaden the views of educational leadership considered in the next section to include these aspects. Much has been learned from the effective schools research, and it helped to remove the blinders of pessimism that dominated the thinking of policymakers during the 1970s about the potential positive influence of schools, but it is not sufficient to inform the type of leadership required to meet the challenges facing schools today.

Emerging Views of Leadership for Schools

EDUCATIONAL LEADERSHIP AS TRANSFORMATIVE LEADERSHIP

Sergiovanni (1989) defined leadership as "the process of persuasion by which a leader or leadership group . . . induces followers to act in a manner that enhances the leader's purposes or shared purposes" (p. 213). For some policymakers and administrators, leadership is expressed in ideas and symbols that inspire and create meaning in followers. Leadership also is conveyed in the leader's ability to analyze situations and people, psychologically affect followers, and control the environment.

Sergiovanni (1989) viewed effective schools as organizations that are culturally tight (controlled by norms, group mores, patterns of beliefs, values, socialization, and socially constructed reality) and structurally loose (less emphasis on bureaucratic rules, management rules, contingency tradeoffs, and rational reality). Teachers respond better to informal traditions and norms than to management systems. Schools that are loosely structured and culturally tight respond better to transformative leadership for school improvement where order and direction help coordinate efforts and develop shared values. On the other hand, school improvement programs that attempt to prescribe teacher actions and behaviors are based on transactional leadership premises that respond well to tightly structured, culturally loose environments. Transactional leaders attempt to affect improvement by tightly managing and controlling objectives, curriculum, teaching strategies, and evaluation. By contrast, trans-

formational leaders realize that autonomy in classrooms and schools is a prerequisite to fundamental change. In schools, transformative leadership is able to coordinate and order followers through shared beliefs, culture, and imitation—not management—to achieve shared goals.

Sergiovanni (1989) stated that "authentic accountability can be achieved only when teachers and principals are provided with authority to match their responsibility" (p. 223). The over management and under leading of schools impede the goal of quality schooling. Emphasis on leadership is evidenced in long-range planning, attention to and manipulation of the external environment to achieve goals, attention to vision and values, ability to cope with conflict and complexity, and desire to initiate change. Transformative leadership produces a broad value perspective that includes "justice, community, excellence, democracy, and equality" (Sergiovanni, 1989, p. 224) and enables schools to achieve excellence.

Transformative leadership develops shared meanings and significance that leads to increased motivation and commitment. Bennis (in Sergiovanni, 1989) identified vision, which is creation and communication of a desired state of affairs that explains the present and assures future commitment as a requirement of purposive leadership because it reflects the needs, desires, values, and beliefs of the group.

Attaining the empowerment of transformative leadership requires the leader to delegate and surrender power over people and events in order to achieve power over accomplishments and goal achievement. Empowerment coupled with purposing leads to increased motivation and commitment in teachers and administrators.

Leadership density, the extent of leadership role sharing and leadership exercise, relates to the school principal as the leader of a collegial team of administrators and teachers. Principals maintain their hierarchical position of accountability. Because of the loosely coupled nature of subsystems in schools, dispersed individuals within schools may perform leadership functions. Understanding the gap between those who have the ability and those who have the authority to make decisions that is present in schools, if it is acknowledged by school leaders, will help to develop situations where leaders lend their authority to teachers in order to borrow teachers' ability.

Transformative leadership views as mandatory a commitment to a shared core of beliefs about the school by administrators, teachers, and students but allows discretion in implementing these values in teaching, supervision, and administration. Transformative leaders shape school culture and protect school values, thus validating the importance and meaning of these cultural imperatives.

Developing attributes such as community, established patterns of living based on mutual need, affection, development, and protection, requires transformational leaders capable of changing community structures, forms, and order (Foster, 1989). To succeed, leaders must be able to evaluate critically present social conditions and envision and forge an emancipatory community free of social, economic, and discriminatory constraints. Because leadership occurs within the community (such as a school), it resides in the community and is developed through communal relationships. Leadership is shared and exchanged among leaders and followers, and does not permanently reside in a power position.

MORAL LEADERSHIP

Sergiovanni (1992) proposed that the present "effective schools" emphasis on instructional leadership in education which requires strong, forceful, direct leadership from principals may not be the type of leadership that can effectively improve schools. Although instructional leadership is capable of initiating large scale, school-wide instructional programs that involve teachers in curriculum redesign, instructional leadership alone is not capable of sustaining these initiatives over an extended period of time. Sergiovanni, instead, espoused moral leadership that relies upon the development of substitutes for leadership that are capable of initiating and sustaining changes in the school through the actions of and values held by the workers, i.e., the teachers.

Sergiovanni (1992) argued that in addition to the traditional bases of authority that rely on bureaucracy, psychological knowledge, and technical rationality that emerges from theory and research, professional and moral authority need to be added. Acting as a school community, the members of the school need to form a covenant based upon their shared values that unite the members to act in a morally responsive way to satisfy the needs of the school. He maintains that there remains a place for command leadership, instructional leadership, and interpersonal leadership, but the heart of one's leadership practice is to become the embodiment of one's ministerial role.

Sergiovanni asserted that authority based upon bureaucratic, psychological, or technical-rational authority requires an external force to induce people to comply. However, professional authority (craft knowledge and personal expertise) and moral authority (obligations and duties resulting from shared values and ideas) derive from an inner responsibility, shared commitment, and communal interdependence. Thus, emphasis is placed on the teacher as being superordinate to the knowledge base. Teachers who are skilled and able to reflect and understand knowledge and experiences exercise professional authority by integrating these diverse inputs and applying this newly derived knowledge to practice.

Sergiovanni (1992) identified four substitutes for leadership that can provide those who work in the school community with an inner motivation or meaning to respond to and achieve the shared goals of the school. These include (a) school norms—a connectedness that binds school members around a shared set of values and beliefs; (b) the professional ideal—responsibility for one's professional development and serving one's students; (c) rewarding work—teachers perceive their work as meaningful, are accountable for results, and able to evaluate the results of their efforts; and (d) collegiality—connects teachers together with shared support and aid while developing self-management and self-leadership skills. The substitutes make principal leadership less necessary. By implementing these substitutes for leadership, teachers are empowered and administrators become facilitators as schools develop the capacity to improve from within. However, when schools rely predominantly upon command and instructional leadership, teachers become dependent subordinates who do what is required of them and little more.

Servant leadership is evidenced when professional competence and community values are the basis for defining the leader's actions rather than personal interests and commitments (Greenleaf, 1977). Moral leadership, Sergiovanni (1992) asserted, necessitates the replacement of the traditional hierarchical structure of schools where those in positions of authority reside at the apex with a structure in which leaders and followers have equal status and the apex is reserved for the values, commitments, vision, and covenants that guide community actions.

MORAL IMAGINATION OR VISIONING

According to Greenfield (1987), most researchers agree that successful principals have a vision of what they want to accomplish and that the vision guides them in managing and leading activities. Situations and dilemmas addressed by principals require them to assign values to facts, evaluate alternative actions, and reach decisions. "The ability to see the discrepancy between how things are and how they might be—not in terms of the ideal, but in terms of what is possible" (p. 16) is called *moral imagination* by Greenfield. The term *moral* refers to the application of an accepted standard of goodness.

Once the principal has been able to analyze the school situation and formulate a moral vision, the principal must be able to convey this vision and enlist the supportive actions of the school community members. Through situational identity, the principal is able to influence others to a desired response. To achieve this, the principal must help develop a consensus among teachers in defining the situation and prescribing actions. To be successful in this endeavor, it is critical that principals be able to view and understand situations from other participants' perspectives. Interpersonal competency thus requires sensitivity to others' views and work situations to elicit desired actions.

Qualities of interpersonal competence and moral imagination are developed through formal socialization processes (administrative preparation programs, staff development programs, and in-service education) and informal socialization processes (norms, values, and orientations of groups). Moral outcomes of socialization are the sentiments, beliefs, standards, and values of the reference group to which one belongs or aspires (Greenfield, 1987). Technical outcomes of socialization are knowledge and skills necessary for satisfactory role performance. Moral and technical outcomes are influenced by both formal and informal socialization processes. "Moral imagination requires technical skills in observation and analysis as well as formal knowledge about standards of good practice" (p. 68). Greenfield believed that interpersonal competence requires interpersonal communication skills and knowledge about teachers, tasks, and teacher perspectives.

SCHOOL CULTURE AND PARTICIPATORY DEMOCRACY

Participatory democracy in education requires (a) an administration that deals with self-criticism, ethics, transformation, and education; (b) appropriate use of participative and leader decisionmaking strategies where participants are educated to their democratic responsibilities; and (c) an attitude of respecting the past while challenging the future. In their research, Smith and Andrew (1989) found that many principals perceive an imbalance of authority and responsibility between district level and building level administrators that prohibits the implementation of broad participatory practices. Building principals claim that their authority is inadequate to operate their buildings as effective instructional organizations in the sense being discussed, while being held accountable for operating efficient, well-managed schools at the district level.

School-based management is one technique that may facilitate a participatory, or transformative, style of leadership. School-based management is a strategy of school governance that allows each school to act as a relatively autonomous unit, being responsible for budget, curricula, and personnel decisions. These decisions are made at the building level by building personnel and may include participation by parents, students, and community representatives. When school-based management is employed, the school board's role remains that of providing general goals and policies to guide decisions made throughout the district. "By establishing the principal as the 'total educational leader,' one person becomes truly accountable for what takes place in each building" (Lindelow & Heynderick, 1989, p. 127). Through school-based management, principals gain the authority and control necessary to lead and manage their buildings and the opportunities for involving others in the decisionmaking process are greatly enhanced.

Rallis (1990) contended that the dichotomy that exists between principals and teachers will erode as administrators and teachers collaboratively identify and meet the needs of diverse ethnic groups and student populations. Eliminating the isolation and hierarchical structuring of schools will require administrators who can deftly build an organizational culture that connects the varied members into a cohesive, collaborative network where expertise and leadership are shared willingly. The principal is often the only person who has access to all the varied systems operating more or less independently in the loosely coupled school.

In Foster's (1989) interpretation of leadership as a consensual task, i.e., a sharing of ideas and a sharing of responsibilities, a "leader" is a leader for the moment only. Leadership lies in the struggles of a school community to find meaning for itself; it must be validated by the consent of followers. Rallis (1990) described the reconceptualized view of leadership as being more context-oriented than person- or role-specific. Leadership is a process of bringing people together, helping them to belong, so that they may do the work of the organization. They belong by accepting and sharing the norms, values, and beliefs of the organizational culture, however large or small the organization may be.

Emphasizing that schools are simultaneously tightly and loosely coupled organizations, Sergiovanni (1984) contended that excellent schools need to have a clear sense of purpose while providing staff members with the freedom to determine how they will achieve that purpose. Firestone and Wilson (1989) acknowledged the loose coupling of schools but argued that principals can provide a tighter structure by using cultural linkages to influence the delivery of the instructional program in their schools. Cultural linkages can be used to influence task definition and task commitment through principals' manipulation of symbols, icons, and rituals. Icons and rituals provide opportunities for principals to demonstrate and communicate school culture. Through stories, events and symbols, principals can emphasize values, portray school members as heroes, and monitor the information that flows through the school.

In most cases, instructional leaders start with a preexisting program. They must be able to recognize the existing norms, culture, and resources of a school and apply strategies of persuasion and change to maintain and/or enhance the school culture and norms, thus having a positive impact upon the instructional program. Principals can become a cultural expression of their schools through demonstrated modeling, daily routines, and commitment. For culture manipulation to be effective, principals must be able to weave both bureaucratic and cultural linkages to create an impact on curriculum and its delivery. Limits may be placed upon the principal's authority, however, by external policies (district policies, judicial decisions, legislated mandates) and superordinate and subordinate members' inclusion in the decisionmaking process. To ameliorate these influences, principals can capitalize upon the ambiguity that exists in school organizations. Principals may interpret policies to influence favorably their instructional program and intercede on behalf of teachers to improve and/or protect the instructional climate (Firestone & Wilson, 1989).

SITUATIONAL VARIATIONS

The technology of schools, the curricula and instructional strategies employed, vary in clarity and complexity and thus influence the amount of coordination and control over teacher tasks exerted by principals (Hallinger & Murphy, 1987). Clarity, the extent to which the instructional process is understood and can be specified, has been traditionally unclear as teachers determined the best instructional strategies and curricular content for each situation. Complexity, the degree to which the instructional processes of the school require interdependence and coordination among the teaching staff, is exhibited in the way schools organize, such as departmentalized curricula, elementary, funded programs, and team teaching.

Three staff characteristics that influence the way principals exercise and adapt leadership have been identified by Hallinger and Murphy (1987). Structural factors, such as age of staff, educational level, experience, and staff stability, affect principals' ability to coordinate the work of teachers. Leadership styles change from formal, directive styles to informal, indirective styles as faculties mature and stabilize. When considering faculty intellectual ability, teachers with greater abstract thinking skills require a less directive leadership style than those with lower abstract thinking skills. Directive leadership styles are appropriate when staff commitment to organizational goals is low and more directive styles are appropriate when staff commitment is low. Weak commitment requires more control; high commitment requires more collaborative behavior.

Differences between elementary and secondary school organization also influence the way instructional leadership is practiced. Research has not addressed this concern sufficiently. Because of the complexity of structure and operation at the secondary level, secondary principals cannot exercise the same leadership style used by elementary principals. This complexity and the size of the school limit principals' ability to be involved directly in all instructional management activities. This necessitates delegation of some of these responsibilities.

In schools serving communities of low socio-economic status (SES), principals tend to assume a directive role closely supervising classroom instruction and establishing expectations and standards (Hallinger & Murphy, 1987). In high SES schools, principals tend to exercise less control, providing teachers with more autonomy over instructional decision-making and monitoring student outcomes. In low SES schools, time is allocated to basic skills instruction. The staffs in both high and low SES effective schools need to hold high academic expectations for their students. However, in low SES schools, the principal may be the key figure in setting, developing, and accepting responsibility for these expectations.

CRITICAL THEORY

Angus (1989) proposed an alternative concept of leadership that addresses education's complexity, critically scrutinizes school issues, and relates school to society. The "new" leadership rhetoric that is based upon business administration theory and research emphasizes organizational change to overcome mediocre levels of performance. Business asserts that improved productivity can be achieved by organizational members if they work within the boundaries of the leader's vision. Educational leadership thus becomes the ability to transform an educational organization into a successful, excellent "enterprise." Principals become the main actors in developing effective schools, affirming a productive organizational culture, and assuring teacher and student performance. Angus believes that an interventionist leadership is needed in today's schools rather than the autocratic, hierarchical, formal position power that the effective schools literature assumes.

Like Angus (1989) and Sergiovanni (1992), Codd (1989) asserted that educational leadership is a form of moral action. An educational leader's philosophical perspective, influenced by a sociological premise, will determine how the individual defines the purpose and goals of education. This may lead to a functionalist's orientation in which socialization and competency in basic skills becomes the major thrust in education, and thus society is preserved and reproduced. Or, it may lead to a critical theorist's orientation in which education in critical skills, problem solving, and open inquiry becomes the major thrust; society may, thereby, be challenged, improved, and redefined through rational, reflective thought and action.

Codd (1989) predicted that, as educational leaders relinquish reliance on the managerial orientation to leadership and develop a critical, philosophical approach, they will be capable of reforming both the structure and functions of schools. Managerial approaches to educational leadership, which place little importance on the values inherent in education, result in teacher compliance to achieving minimal performance levels that demonstrate efficiency without necessarily achieving excellence. Codd urges that educational leaders not only facilitate learning and socialization, but that they also embody and impart educational values. In Codd's view, educational leaders need to develop a commitment to a defined set of values, not merely to a specific organization.

Codd (1989) identified three ways by which administrators evolve theories that influence and determine their practices: (a) developing a body of theories formulated through the scientific study of educational administration; (b) acting upon personal experience and common sense through habit, convention, and intuition; and (c) critiquing practices philosophically through empirical and interpretive modes of inquiry. The third alternative—and Codd's preference—calls for the integration of theory and practice.

Analytical philosophy attempts to clarify the way people think about human activity by identifying concepts, influences, and choices that are made and by questioning premises, consequences, and alternatives (Codd, 1989). Common sense is defined as those beliefs that people share unquestionably and that shape the way they view reality, relations, and ideals. Common sense is formed to a large extent through social institutions such as schools, mass media, religion, and culture, yielding enormous influence to those who control them. Philosophy challenges common sense's complacency and tradition through the exercise of skepticism and reason. Ultimately, philosophy and common sense are two different ways of thinking. Actions can be derived from philosophical thought, commonsense thought, or a combination of both.

The critical theorist uses philosophy to criticize and reformulate common sense. Thus, philosophy becomes a method of reflecting upon societal conditions and practices, and rationally addressing issues through creative and critical inquiry and theoretical perspective. Codd (1989) argued that educational leadership is distinguished from management because of its commitment to educational values and principles for practice rather than skill competency. He also contended that educational leadership must serve to preserve democratic administrative values by practicing within schools moral principles of justice, freedom, and respect. According to Codd and other critical theorists, education should not support social conformity but, rather, be an active informed social critic.

Administrators following the model of philosophical conjecture are able to reflect upon the organizational actions and structures of schools to initiate reforms that change both the structure and functions of school. Managerial perspectives that focus on preserving present social structures will be replaced by reflection in action that challenges the status quo and leads to excellence in education and society. Critical theorists strive for an educational system that will influence society rather than permit society to dominate and control educational and other social institutions.

Leadership at the District Level

Current population increases, continued school district consolidation, intensified public expectations for schools, growth of suburban school districts, and a general trend toward societal bureaucratization have contributed to the contemporary widespread use of school administrators at many organizational levels—superintendent, central office, school site, county, state, and federal agencies. For educational leaders to be successful today and in the future, these leaders must be able to blend their visions, actions, and analyses in order to evaluate their organizations' missions and effectiveness and to determine whether instituting change or maintaining the status quo is appropriate and effective for their organizations (Guthrie & Reed, 1991). Because schools are affected continually by changes and pressures from their internal and external environments, educational leaders must be able to anticipate change, develop a broad knowledge base, and be cognizant of external and internal dynamics throughout the world, not just those of their local communities. Although state and federal government agencies have assumed a more active role in the regulation and policy formulation of schools since 1950, the local school board is still considered the major and predominant unit for forming policy and making decisions.

The superintendent of schools, the school board's chief operating officer, possesses a position of high visibility within the community which is both practical and symbolic. However, only 20 to 25 percent of the superintendent's time actually is devoted to instructional or student matters; budgetary, financial, personnel, facilities, and public relations activities consume most of the superintendent's time (Guthrie & Reed, 1991).

DeYoung (1989) argued that school superintendents play a critical role in formulating district policy and programs to achieve educational excellence. Superintendents must be able to balance external political forces that call for change with the needs of pupils in district schools and with organizational needs. Although the superintendent maintains the role of chief administrator and is still responsible to the board for all administrative decisions, other central administrators assume roles of developing standards concerning student and staff performance, providing technical assistance to building personnel, and monitoring and evaluating instructional effectiveness through standardized testing.

History has demonstrated the ineffectiveness of top-down, mandated reform efforts imposed upon local educational agencies by state and federal edict that threaten local control. Yet local control provides a dilemma. On the one hand, it provides a vitality and a sense of school district ownership that is lost in a monolithic organization; on the other hand, great inequalities are created. Because of the Balkanization of our school governance, some districts, the ready and the able, are well in advance of state and federal leadership; other districts are neither ready nor able, however, and fall far behind state and national aspirations. If governance is decentralized further, the possibility of even greater inequalities and disparities looms large. Issues of equality and coordination can still best be handled at the district, state, and federal levels under a system of school-based management. However, the last 30 years have witnessed the erosion of superintendents' ability to influence public school policy by public interest groups, state and federal man-

dates, teacher unions, and mass media criticism of the American educational system.

Peterson (1987) addressed the issue of administrative control exercised by district-level leaders; he noted that it can shape, constrain, or support the activities, goals, and beliefs of building-level principals. Recent research indicates that control is zoned and can be loosely or tightly linked to constrain and shape principal behavior. These controls are designed to ensure principals' coordination, cooperation, goal achievement, and motivation. Six mechanisms of control are commonly used to influence decisions, behaviors, and norms of principals (Peterson, 1987). *Supervision,* the direct observation of subordinates' work, is followed by positive or corrective feedback. *Input control,* control over the amount, use, and flow of money and human resources, influences managerial autonomy at the building level. *Behavior (bureaucratic) control,* standardization of work through rules, directives, and task specifications, has limited use as a control. *Output control,* monitoring and evaluating outputs or outcomes and providing feedback, are more difficult to apply because of ambiguous, difficult-to-measure outcomes of principals' and schools' work. *Selection-socialization control,* nonhierarchical and derived from internal norms and values, ensures that the subordinates are socialized to the norms and values held by district-level leaders. *Environmental control,* nonhierarchical and originating from agents outside the school, is exercised when superiors allow outside agents to bring school-related information to the district administration.

Application of these six controls comprise the districts' control system over principals. Administrative tasks are more tightly controlled than instructional leadership tasks. A balance of control and autonomy is achieved when principals' administrative tasks or outcomes are strictly controlled while allowing autonomy in selecting methods to achieve ends. For example, research supports the prevalent use of input control over teacher transfers but not over teacher hiring. Behavior controls are used predominantly over reports, meetings, evaluations, and curriculum objectives; normally, these controls are employed on tasks that are specific and standard (Peterson, 1987).

Although the six mechanisms of control can individually apply to directive, restrictive, or formative control, these mechanisms can be modified to address more than one form of control; for example, supervisory mechanisms that are directive can also be used in a formative control context to shape values and goals. In effective districts, these controls are used to: provide a coordinated, directive style for setting goals; develop specific models of instruction and curricular objectives on which to base training, supervision, and evaluation of subordinates; and model proactive leadership and address district level mission statements. In effective districts, emphasis is placed on supervisory, behavioral, and output controls (Peterson, 1987). District superiors need to increase formative control in order to enhance instructional leadership in principals. Socialization to district expectations and norms and provision of technical expertise will result in attention to instructional leadership behaviors.

Wimpelberg (1987) contended that for significant instructional leadership and school improvement, there must be a collaboration between intermediate central office administrators and the individual school units. He felt that there is a paucity of successful schools in the nation and that number will not increase significantly if school-by-school reform continues.

The typical principal, lacking adequate training to assume instructional leadership roles, spends little time on curricular or instructional matters, concentrating, rather, on managerial functions (Cuban, 1988).

There is scant research about the influence exerted by central office administrators on successful schools (Hallinger and Murphy, 1987; Wimpelberg, 1987). Nevertheless, as the principal has become the key agent for change according to effective schools research and teachers have increased their pedagogical knowledge and skills, central office administrators have to assume an integrator role. As the superintendency has shifted to a more political, statesmanship role, little direct attention is focused on instruction by that office.

Because of the loose coupling in school organizations, coordination of activities can be lost without district level intervention. This can best be accomplished by mid-level central office administrators. They can provide linkages that facilitate change and promote improvement strategies among all schools. Hierarchical, top-down decisionmaking can be replaced by an interactive top-down and bottom-up process.

Wimpelberg (1987) outlined five roles that the central office can assume in support of school improvement through school-based management and shared decisionmaking. (1) District-level leadership develops linkages between central office, schools, among schools, and among building teachers; cooperative learning among the different units is cultivated, coordinated, and networked by district administrators. (2) To effect positive linkages, central office administrators and principals collaboratively determine how improvement will be defined and achieved. (3) Intermediary central office administrators supervise and evaluate principals and supplement the expert knowledge and expertise (referent authority) available to principals in support of their actions. (4) Intermediary district administrators assist principals in developing technical management expertise required by school-based management and shared decisionmaking. (5) District instructional leadership encourages a shared relationship between district and school personnel; the central administrator must be knowledgeable about positive and negative school conditions, provide communication networks among schools for professional information exchanges, and devote time of sufficient frequency and duration for consultations with the schools.

The development of a mission and goals statement for a school can help to achieve a school culture conducive to academic achievement; development of a districtwide mission and goals statement is equally important. Such statements can be used to select administrators, to define administrative team composition, and to socialize administrators to share district goals. In addition, supervision, output, and environment control mechanisms are used to disseminate district goals among subordinates. Some of these control mechanisms, such as output control, foster rapid goal orientation while others, such as selection-socialization control, may require more time to achieve results.

Without strong, internal motivation, principals will not become effective instructional leaders. Motivation increases commitment and persistence to achieve instructional goals and improve instructional programs. Limited motivation results in leaders who focus primarily on maintenance and stability behaviors. Directive controls used with management by objectives can lower principals' expectations of their effectiveness and lower their motivation. To ensure effective instructional leadership, superiors should initially exercise supervisory control to help shape values, provide feedback, and communicate high expectations. With increased subordinate experience, superiors should adopt less directive, more formative controls to reinforce values and provide supportive feedback. As district administrators develop an optional mix of controls for their districts, a balance between control and autonomy will result that enables principals to be effective instruc-

tional leaders working toward a shared vision and goals and focused upon instructional program and improvement of student performance.

Reforming Leadership Preparation Programs

Recognizing the principal as the key player in achieving excellence in schools, Anderson (1989) critically examined present training and selecting practices. He found that university programs do not address adequately the complexity of this position nor do school districts invest sufficient resources to identify, select, orient and train principals.

Research, through behavioral and situational approaches, affirms that leadership can be learned. However, practicing administrators are critical of the adequacy of their preparation. Many find that university programs place emphasis on theory and knowledge but do not bridge effectively the transition from theoretical perspectives to practical applications. Anderson (1989) contended that, although present research emphasis on the principal as a critical ingredient for school improvement cannot be empirically proven, it has led to demands for universities, school districts, and training institutes to collaboratively address and bridge the gap between theoretical and technical education and the practical requirements of the job. He advocated activities that will emphasize improvement of the ability of administrators to develop critical analytical skills for application in reflective activities. He called for a partnership between universities, school districts, and training institutes to ensure that principals have adequate technical and theoretical bases, meaningful and relevant training experiences, and smooth transition and continued assistance in developing skills while performing their jobs.

Greenfield (1987) reiterated the theme concerning the role that professional development programs and school districts play in training and preparing potential educational leaders. Identification of the personal qualities and technical skills needed for successful leadership can influence what and how skills and knowledge are transmitted and developed in administrative students. It also guides in selecting, orienting, and promoting growth of leadership capabilities in school administrators.

Murphy (1993) made an extensive survey for the University Council Educational Administration (UCEA) of the restructuring taking place in university programs providing preservice preparation for school administrators. Programs undergoing restructuring were redefining curricular content to include recommendations by the National Policy Board for Educational Administration (NPBEA) (1989): societal and cultural influences on schooling; teaching and learning processes and school improvement; organizational theory; methodologies of organizational studies and policy analysis; leadership and managerial processes and functions; policy studies and politics of education; and the moral and ethical dimensions of schooling.

Reforming programs based their changes on a set of normative assumptions that constituted a programmatic ideology. A new concern for ethics is prevalent, acknowledging the fact that administrators are representatives of values and that the responsibility for the education of children and adolescents is a moral one. There is a greater emphasis than in the past on social and cultural trends that affect various understandings and expectations about schooling. In many of the reformed programs, there is a commitment to critical inquiry and evaluation of educational practice. There is greater correspondence between the work of students and administrators and there is a reconnection between the practice and academic arms of the profession; these endeavors are of two types: stronger field-based components and stronger connections with district- and school-based educators.

Murphy (1993) concluded:

The preparation programs that we currently have simply are not good enough. They need to be made better. The task ahead of us is an important one, both at the individual department level and across the profession as a whole. (p. 252)

Persons preparing for roles of educational leadership are faced with the reality of pervasive social change. While these changes affect persons in all walks of life, there is bound to be greater impact upon those in positions of greater social visibility and concern. Thus, the spotlight of social responsibility rests upon those persons holding responsibility for educational systems. Society has the right to expect competent performance in those positions; preparatory programs and the state have an obligation to assure it as far as humanly possible. Under these circumstances, competent leadership behavior cannot be a matter of copying conventional behavior. To advance education, there is a clear need for its leadership to have the ability to comprehend the dynamics of human affairs as a basis for relevant action under novel conditions, the need for better understanding of issues and processes in educational institutions, and the need for greater originality in designing instructional and administrative strategies.

It is no longer enough to be aware of educational issues and problems and their theoretical remedies. In these times of sophisticated technological development and change there is increased need for systematic understanding in all content areas with particular emphasis on methods of analysis and synthesis, and flexibility in adapting to the variety of individual interests and social needs. Educational leaders also need to have an understanding of shifting social issues and developments that form the context in which educational institutions function. Finally, educational leaders need on-the-job skills to act effectively.

In sum, educational leadership includes the ability (1) to have a vision of the future, (2) to see into the intentions of others, and (3) to take effective action. Clearly, there is much to discover about the dynamics of human leadership; the approach needs to remain hypothetical and open-ended so that more may be learned by what is done.

Annotated Bibliography

Firestone, I. J., & Wilson, B. L. (1989). Using bureaucratic and cultural linkages to improve instruction: The principal's contribution. In J. L. Burdin (Ed.), *School leadership: A contemporary reader* (pp. 275–296). Newbury Park: Sage Publications.

Because schools are not self-correcting, lack consensus on goals, and have unpredictable problems and solutions, principals should rely on management of symbols to unite loosely coupled organizations. Firestone and Wilson state that cultural linkages are needed to provide a tighter structure and influence task definition and commitment through manipulation of symbols, icons, and rituals. Principals control information flow through the school and develop school culture through the creation and manipulation of events and symbols.

Greenfield, W. (1987). Moral imagination and interpersonal competence: Antecedents to instructional leadership. In W. Greenfield (Ed.), *Leadership, concepts, issues and controversies* (pp. 56–73). Boston: Allyn and Bacon.

Greenfield defines instructional leadership as actions undertaken to develop productive and satisfying work environments. Leadership is seen through a behavioral framework where technical skills and moral imagination are developed through socialization processes. Moral imagination produces the norms, beliefs, and values of the organization and technical skills develop the

interpersonal skills and formal knowledge. Moral and technical outcomes are influenced by both formal and informal socialization processes.

Hallinger, P., & Murphy, J. (1987). Instructional leadership in the school context. In W. Greenfield (Ed.), *Instructional leadership: Concepts, issues and controversies* (pp. 179–207). Boston: Allyn and Bacon.

Leadership is situational and is influenced by organizational and environmental factors. Three staff characteristics that influence leadership style are structural factors, faculty intellectual ability, and goal commitment. Other situational factors include the complexity of the school setting and social contexts.

Peterson, K. D. (1987). Administrative control and instructional leadership. In W. Greenfield (Ed.), *Instructional leadership, concepts, issues and controversies* (pp. 139–152). Boston: Allyn and Bacon.

Administrative control exercised by district-level leaders can shape, constrain, or support the activities, goals, and beliefs of building-level principals. Controls can be used to ensure principals' coordination, cooperation, goal achievement, and motivation. Six mechanisms of control include supervision, input control, behavior control, output control, selection-socialization control, and environmental control. Administrative tasks are seen as more tightly controlled than instructional leadership tasks. A balance of control and autonomy is achieved when administrative tasks and outcomes are strictly controlled and autonomy is allowed in choosing methods for goal attainment. Districts control principals directly and by restrictive and formative means. The proper mix of district controls will provide the local principal with the balance of control and autonomy that will allow effective instructional leadership. Supervisors initially exercise supervisory control to shape values, provide feedback, and communicate high expectations. With increased experience superiors adopt less directive modes, reinforcing values and providing supportive feedback. This introduces a power-based framework into the leader-follower relationship.

Rallis, S. (1990). Professional teachers and restructured schools: Leadership challenges. In B. Mitchell & L. L. Cunningham (Eds.), *Educational leadership and changing contexts of families, communities and schools* (pp. 184–209). Chicago: The National Society for the Study of Education.

The principal is critical to school improvement. To develop an organizational culture that connects varied members into a cohesive, collaborative network in which leadership and expertise are shared requires elimination of isolation and hierarchy. The dichotomy of principal-teacher needs will be eliminated as the principal and teachers work together to meet the organization's needs. Leadership is context-oriented rather than person- or role-specific. Principals develop a culture with shared beliefs, norms, and values.

Sergiovanni, T. J., & Corbally, J. E. (Eds.). (1986). *Leadership and organizational culture.* Urbana, IL: University of Illinois Press.

Because of the cultural tightness (shared norms, beliefs, and values) and structural looseness (less emphasis on bureaucratic rules, contingency tradeoffs) of schools, teachers respond to informal norms rather than management systems. Transactional and transformative leadership are both needed in schools, depending upon the situation. Although transactional leadership is able to initiate school-wide instructional programs and reforms, it is not capable of sustaining these initiatives over time. Moral leadership that develops substitutes for formal leadership within the school community can initiate and sustain change through actions and values of teachers. Substitutes for formal leadership include community norms, professional ideals, rewarding work, and collegiality. These substitutes empower followers and develop the capacity to improve from within the culture. Schools that rely on command and instructional leadership develop teachers who are dependent subordinates who do what is required. Moral leadership replaces positions of authority with values, commitments, vision, and covenants that guide community actions.

References

Anderson, M. E. (1989). Training and selecting school leaders. In S. C. Smith & P. K. Piele (Eds.), *Leadership: Handbook for excellence* (2nd ed.) (pp. 53–86). Eugene, OR: University of Oregon, ERIC Clearinghouse on Educational Management.

Angus, L. (1989). "New" leadership and the possibility of educational reform. In J. Smyth (Ed.), *Critical perspectives on educational leadership* (pp. 63–92). Philadelphia, PA: The Falmer Press.

Bolman, L. G., & Deal, T. E. (1991). *Reframing organizations: Artistry, choice, and leadership.* San Francisco: Jossey-Bass.

Bredeserl, P. V. (1989). An analysis of the metaphorical perspectives of school principals. In J. L. Burdin (Ed.), *Leadership: A contemporary reader* (pp. 297–317). Newbury Park, CA: Sage.

Brookover, W., & Lezotte, L. (1979). *Changes in school characteristics coincident with changes in student achievement.* East Lansing MI: Michigan State University, College of Urban Development.

Burlingame, M. (1987). Images of leadership in effective schools literature. In H. Greenfield (Ed.), *Instructional leadership: concepts, issues, and controversies* (pp. 3–16). Boston: Allyn and Bacon.

Codd, J. (1989) Educational leadership as reflective action. In J. Smyth (Ed.), *Critical perspectives on educational leadership* (pp. 157–178). Philadelphia, PA: The Falmer Press.

Coleman, J. S., et al. (1966). *Equality of educational opportunity.* Washington, DC: Office of Education, U.S. Department of Health, Education, and Welfare.

Cuban, L. (1988). *The managerial imperative and the practice of leadership in schools.* Albany, NY: State University of New York Press.

Cunningham, L. L. (1990). Education leadership and administration: Retrospective and prospective views. In B. Mitchell & L. L. Cunningham (Eds.), *Educational leadership and changing of families, communities and schools* (pp. 1–17). Chicago: The National Society for the Study of Education.

Deal, T. (1987). Effective school principals: Counselors, engineers, pawnbrokers, poets . . . or instructional leaders. In W. Greenfield (Ed.), *Instructional leadership: Concepts, issues, and controversies* (pp. 230–246). Boston: Allyn and Bacon.

DeYoung, A. J. (1989). Excellence in education: The opportunity for school superintendents to become ambitious. In J. L. Burdin (Ed.), *School leadership: A contemporary reader* (pp. 34–55). Newbury Park, CA: Sage Publications.

Edmonds, R. (1979). Effective schools for the urban poor. *Educational Leadership, 37,* 15–24.

Firestone, I. J., & Wilson, B. L. (1989). Using bureaucratic and cultural linkages to improve instruction: The principal's contribution. In J. L. Burdin (Ed.), *School leadership: A contemporary reader* (pp. 275–296). Newbury Park: Sage Publications.

Flood, R. L. (1990). *Liberating systems theory.* New York: Blenum.

Foster, W. (1989). Toward a critical practice of leadership. In J. Smyth (Ed.), *Critical perspectives on educational leadership* (pp. 39–62). Philadelphia, PA: The Falmer Press.

Greenfield, W. (1987). Moral imagination and interpersonal competence: Antecedents to instructional leadership. In W. Greenfield (Ed.), *Leadership, concepts, issues and controversies* (pp. 56–73). Boston: Allyn and Bacon.

Greenleaf, R. K. (1977). *Servant leadership: A journey into the nature of legitimate power and greatness.* New York: Paulist.

Guthrie, J. W., & Reed, R. J. (1991). *Educational administration and policy: Effective for American education* (2nd ed.). Boston: Allyn and Bacon.

Hallinger, P., & Murphy, J. (1987). Instructional leadership in the school context. In W. Greenfield (Ed.), *Instructional leadership: Concepts, issues and controversies* (pp. 179–207). Boston: Allyn and Bacon.

Lindelow, J., & Heynderick, J. (1989) School-based management. In E. C. Smith & P. K. Piele (Eds.), *School leadership for excellence* (2nd ed.) (pp. 109–134). Eugene OR: University of Oregon: ERIC Clearing House on Educational Management.

Monk, D. (1989). The education production function: Its evolving role in policy analysis. *Educational Evaluation and Policy Analysis, 11,* 31–45.

Murphy, J. (Ed.). (1993). *Preparing tomorrow's school leaders: alternative designs.* University Park, PA: The University Council for Educational Administration.

National Policy Board for Educational Administration. (1989). *Improving the preparation of school administrators: The reform agenda.* Charlottesville, VA: Author.

Parsons, T. (1959). The school class as a social system: Some of its functions in American society. *Harvard Educational Review, 2,* 297–318.

Peterson, K. D. (1987). Administrative control and instructional leadership. In W. Greenfield (Ed.), *Instructional leadership, concepts, issues and controversies* (pp. 139–152). Boston: Allyn and Bacon.

Rallis, S. (1990). Professional teachers and restructured schools: Leadership challenges. In B. Mitchell & L. L. Cunningham (Eds.), *Educational leadership and changing contexts of families, communities and schools* (pp. 184–209). Chicago: The National Society for the Study of Education.

Sergiovanni, T. J. (1984). Leadership and excellence in schooling. *Phi Delta Kappan, 41,* 4–13.

Sergiovanni, T. J. (1989). The leadership needed for quality schooling. In T. J. Sergiovanni & J. H. Moore (Eds.), *Schooling for tomorrow, directing reforms to issues that count* (pp. 213–226). Boston: Allyn and Bacon.

Sergiovanni, T. J. (1992). *Moral leadership: Getting to the heart of school improvement.* San Francisco: Jossey-Bass.

Sergiovanni, T. J., & Corbally, J. E. (Eds.). (1986). *Leadership and organizational culture.* Urbana, IL: University of Illinois Press.

Smith, E. C., & Piele, P. K. (Eds.). (1989). *School leadership: handbook for excellence* (2nd ed.). Eugene, OR: ERIC Clearing House on Educational Management, University of Oregon.

Smith, W. F., & Andrew, R. L. (1989). *Instructional leadership: How principals make a difference.* Alexandria, VA: Association for Supervision and Curriculum Development.

Smyth, J. (Ed.). (1989). *Critical perspectives on educational leadership.* Philadelphia: The Falmer Press.

Weber, J. R. (1989). Leading the instructional program. In E. C. Smith & P. K. Piele (Eds.), *School leadership: Handbook for excellence* (2nd ed.) (pp. 191–224). Eugene, OR: ERIC Clearinghouse on Educational Management, University of Oregon.

Wimpelberg, R. K. (1987). The dilemma of instructional leadership and a central role for central office. In W. Greenfield (Ed.), *Instructional leadership, concepts, issues, and controversies* (pp. 100–117). Boston: Allyn and Bacon.

Name Index

Subject Index

ISBN 0-02-398732-4